Macmillan Law masters

Contract Law

Ewan McKendrick QC (Hon)

Professor of English Private Law in the University of Oxford

Fellow of Lady Margaret Hall

Professor of Anglo-American Private Law in the University of Leiden

Fourteenth edition

 macmillan international
HIGHER EDUCATION

 RED GLOBE PRESS

This edition published 2021 by
RED GLOBE PRESS

Previous editions published under the imprint PALGRAVE

Red Globe Press in the UK is an imprint of Macmillan Education Limited, registered in England, company number 01755588, of 4 Crinan Street, London, N1 9XW.

Red Globe Press® is a registered trademark in the United States, the United Kingdom, Europe and other countries.

ISBN 978-1-352-01206-4 paperback
ISBN 978-1-352-01207-1 ebook

This book is printed on paper suitable for recycling and made from fully managed and sustained forest sources. Logging, pulping and manufacturing processes are expected to conform to the environmental regulations of the country of origin.

A catalogue record for this book is available from the British Library.

A catalog record for this book is available from the Library of Congress.

Publisher: Ursula Gavin

Cover Designer: Laura De Grasse

Production Editor: Elizabeth Holmes

Marketing Manager: Amy Suratia

Contents

Part II   The content of a contract

Part III   Policing the contract

Part IV   Performance, discharge and remedies for breach of contract

Preface

My aim in writing the fourteenth edition of this book has not changed from the stated aim of previous editions: namely, to provide a clear and straightforward account of the basic rules of English contract law. I have also sought to introduce the reader to some of the debates about the nature, the scope and the functions of the law of contract and to discuss some of the wider controversies which surround certain basic doctrines of English contract law, such as consideration. In discussing these issues I have attempted to build a bridge between this introductory work and some of the more advanced and detailed writings on the law of contract by making frequent reference throughout the book to both the periodical literature and the standard textbooks on the law of contract (full citations are contained in the Bibliography located at the end of the book). My hope is that these references will encourage the reader to pursue the issues raised in this book in greater detail in the writings to which I have made reference.

The text has been fully revised and updated to take account of the various developments in the law which have taken place since the publication of the previous edition. The principal changes in this edition take account of recent Supreme Court and Privy Council decisions dealing with the relationship between the interpretation and the implication of terms, certainty of terms, remoteness of damage and the scope of the restraint of trade doctrine. Other cases of note deal with the extent to which English law recognises an implied term of good faith in the performance of a contract and whether Brexit had the effect of frustrating a long-term contract for the lease of premises.

Finally, I must acknowledge the debts which I have incurred in writing this edition. I must acknowledge the assistance which I have derived from colleagues and students who have helped to clarify my thoughts and offered a number of constructive criticisms and suggestions. But my greatest debt continues to be to my wife, Rose, and our children, Jenny, Sarah, Rachel and Katie, who are now joined by AJ, Richard and Sam, and grandchildren Emma, Alfie, Daniel, Rosalie, James and Edward. I am grateful to them for their encouragement and support.

The book is dedicated to the memory of my grandparents and our granddaughter Alice.

I have endeavoured to state the law on the basis of the materials available to me on 1 October 2020.

Ewan McKendrick
Lady Margaret Hall,
Oxford,
1 October 2020

Table of cases

Table of legislation

Chapter 1

Introduction

1.1 Introduction

> If the 'law of contract' were not already entrenched in the traditions of legal education, would anyone organise a course around it, let alone produce books expounding it? (Wightman, 1989)

The fact that a lawyer can ask such a question would, no doubt, confound laymen. Yet, it is true that the scope, the basis, the function and even the very existence of the law of contract are the subject of debate and controversy among academic lawyers.

But such questioning seems absurd. After all, we enter into contracts as a regular part of life, and generally we experience no difficulty in so doing. Simple cases include the purchase of a morning newspaper or the purchase of a bus or train ticket when travelling to work. What doubt can there possibly be about the existence of such contracts or their basis? However, behind the apparent simplicity of these transactions, there lurks a fierce controversy. In an introductory work of this nature, we cannot give full consideration to these great issues of debate. The function of this chapter is simply to identify some of these issues so that the reader can bear them in mind when reading the ensuing chapters and to enable the reader to explore them further in the readings to which I shall make reference.

1.2 The scope of the law of contract

A good starting point is the scope of the law of contract. Contracts come in different shapes and sizes. Some involve large sums of money, others trivial sums. Some are of long duration, while others are of short duration. The content of contracts varies enormously and may include contracts of sale, hire-purchase, employment and marriage. Nevertheless, we shall not be concerned with all such contracts in this book. Contracts of employment, marriage contracts, hire-purchase contracts, consumer credit contracts, contracts for the sale of goods, contracts for the sale of land, mortgages and leasehold agreements all lie largely outside the scope of this book. Such contracts have all been the subject of distinct regulation and are dealt with in books on employment law, family law, consumer law, commercial law, land law and landlord and tenant law, respectively. At this stage, you might be forgiven if you were to ask the question: if this book is not about these contracts, what is it about, and what is its value?

The answer to the first part of such a question is that this book is concerned with what are called the 'general principles' of the law of contract, and these general principles are usually derived from the common law (or judge-made law). Treatises on the general principles of the law of contract are of respectable antiquity in England, and can be traced back to Pollock (1875) and Anson (1879). This tradition has been maintained today in works such as Treitel (2020), Anson (2020) and Cheshire, Fifoot and Furmston (2017). One might have expected that these treatises would gradually disappear in the light of the publication of books on, for example, the contract of employment or the contract of hire-purchase, which subject the rules relating to such contracts to close examination. Yet, textbooks on the 'general principles' of the law of contract have survived and might even be said to have flourished.

The existence of such general principles has, however, been challenged by Professor Atiyah (1986b), who maintains that these 'general' principles 'remain general only by default, only because they are being superseded by detailed *ad hoc* rules lacking any principle, or by new principles of narrow scope and application'. Atiyah argues that 'there is no such thing as a typical contract at all'. He maintains (1986a) that it is 'incorrect today to think of contract law as having one central core with clusters of differences around the edges'. He identifies the classical model of contract as being a discrete, two-party, commercial, executory exchange but notes that contracts can be found which depart from each feature of this classical model. Thus, some contracts are not discrete but continuing (landlord and tenant relationships), some are not two-party but multiparty (the contract of membership in a club), some are not commercial but domestic (marriage), some are not executory (unperformed) but executed (fully performed) and finally some do not depend upon exchange, as in the case of an enforceable unilateral gratuitous promise. Atiyah concludes by asserting that we must 'extricate ourselves from the tendency to see contract as a monolithic phenomenon'.

Atiyah uses this argument in support of a wider proposition that contract law is 'increasingly merging with tort law into a general law of obligations'. But one does not have to agree with Atiyah's wider proposition to accept the point that the resemblance between different types of contract may be very remote indeed. A contract of employment is, in many respects, radically different from a contract to purchase a chocolate bar. The considerations applicable to a contract between commercial parties of equal bargaining power may be very different from those applicable to a contract between a consumer and a multinational supplier (see Chapters 17 and 18). This fragmentation of the legal regulation of contracts has reached a critical stage in the development of English contract law. The crucial question which remains to be answered is: do we have a law of contract or a law of contracts? My own view is that we are moving slowly in the direction of a law of contracts as the 'general principles' decline in importance.

Given this fragmentation, what is the value of another book on the general principles of contract law? The principal value is that many of the detailed rules relating to specific contracts have been built upon the foundation of the common law principles. So it remains important to have an understanding of the general principles before progressing to study the detailed rules which have been applied to particular contracts. The general principles of formation, content, misrepresentation, mistake, illegality, capacity, duress and discharge apply to all contracts, subject to statutory qualification. These principles therefore remain 'general', but only 'by default'.

1.3   The basis of the law of contract

The basis of the law of contract is also a matter of considerable controversy. Atiyah has written (1986e) that 'modern contract law probably works well enough in the great mass of circumstances but its theory is in a mess'. There are many competing theories which seek to explain the basis of the law of contract (on which see generally Smith, 2004).

The classical theory is the will theory. Closely associated with *laissez-faire* philosophy, this theory attributes contractual obligations to the will of the parties. The law of contract is perceived as a set of power-conferring rules which enable individuals to enter into agreements of their own choice on their own terms. Freedom of contract and sanctity of contract are the dominant ideologies. Parties should be as free as possible to make agreements on their own terms without the interference of the courts or Parliament, and their agreements should be respected, upheld and enforced by the courts. As Lord Toulson observed in *Prime Sight Ltd v Lavarello* [2013] UKPC 22; [2014] AC 436, [47], 'parties are ordinarily free to contract on whatever terms they choose and the court's role is to enforce them'. However, the will theory cannot explain all of the rules that make up the law of contract. Thus it is not possible to attribute many of the doctrines of contract law to the will of the parties. Doctrines such as consideration, illegality, frustration and duress cannot be ascribed to the will of the parties, nor can statutes such as the Unfair Contract Terms Act 1977 or the Consumer Rights Act 2015.

The will theory has, however, been revived and subjected to elegant refinement by Professor Fried (2015). Fried maintains that the law of contract is based upon the 'promise-principle', by which 'persons may impose on themselves obligations where none existed before'. The source of the contractual obligation is the promise itself. But, at the same time, Fried concedes that doctrines such as mistake and frustration (Chapter 14) cannot be explained on the basis of his promise-principle. Other non-promissory principles must be invoked, such as the 'consideration of fairness' or 'the encouragement of due care'.

But Fried's theory remains closely linked to *laissez-faire* ideology. Fried maintains that contract law respects individual autonomy and that the will theory is 'a fair implication of liberal individualism'. He rejects the proposition that the law of contract is an appropriate vehicle for engaging in the redistribution of wealth. But his theory is open to attack on two principal grounds.

The first is that it is difficult to explain many modern contractual doctrines in terms of liberal individualism or *laissez-faire* philosophy. The growth of standard form contracts and the aggregation of capital within fewer hands has enabled powerful contracting parties to impose contractual terms upon consumers and other weaker parties. The response of the courts and Parliament has been to place greater limits upon the exercise of contractual power. Legislation has been introduced to regulate employment contracts and consumer credit contracts in an effort to provide a measure of protection for employees and consumers. Such legislation cannot be explained in terms of *laissez-faire* ideology, nor can the expansion of the doctrines of duress and undue influence, or the extensive regulation of exclusion clauses which Parliament has introduced (see Chapter 11 and, more generally, see Chapter 18, which examines the law relating to unfair terms in consumer contracts). Conceptions of fairness seem to underpin many of the rules of contract law (see Chapter 17). Such departures from the principles of liberal individualism have led some commentators to argue that altruism should be recognised as the basis of contract law (Kennedy, 1976), while others have argued that the law of contract should have as an aim the redistribution of wealth (Kronman, 1980). We shall return to this issue in Chapters 17 and 18.

A second attack on the promise-principle has been launched on the ground that, in many cases, the courts do not uphold the promise-principle because they do not actually order the promisor to carry out his promise. The promisee must generally content himself with an action for damages. But, as we shall see (in Chapter 21), the expectations engendered by a promise are not fully protected in a damages action. One of the principal reasons for this is the existence of the doctrine of mitigation (see Section 21.10). Suppose I enter into a contract to sell you ten apples for £2. I then refuse to perform my side of the bargain. I am in breach of contract. But you must mitigate your loss. So you buy ten apples for £2 at a nearby market. If you sue me for damages, what is your loss? You have not suffered any, and you cannot enforce my promise. So how can it be said that my promise is binding if you cannot enforce it? Your expectation of profit may be protected but, where that profit can be obtained elsewhere at no loss to you, then you have no effective contractual claim against me. Your expectations have been fulfilled, albeit from another source.

Although you cannot enforce my promise, it is very important to note that in our example you suffered no loss, and I gained no benefit. Let us vary the example slightly. Suppose that you had paid me in advance. The additional ingredients here are that you have acted to your detriment in reliance upon my promise, and I have gained a benefit. Greater justification now appears for judicial intervention on your behalf. Can it therefore be argued that the source of my obligation to you is not my promise, but your detrimental reliance upon my promise or your conferment of a benefit upon me in reliance upon my promise? Atiyah has written (1986b) that 'wherever benefits are obtained, wherever acts of reasonable reliance take place, obligations may arise, both morally and in law'. This argument is one of enormous significance. It is used by Atiyah (1979) in an effort to establish a law of obligations based upon the 'three basic pillars of the law of obligations, the idea of recompense for benefit, of protection of reasonable reliance, and of the voluntary creation and extinction of rights and liabilities'. The adoption of such an approach would lead to the creation of a law of obligations and, in consequence, contract law would cease to have a distinct identity based upon the promise-principle or the will theory (see further Section 1.4). This is why this school of thought has been called 'the death of contract' school (see Gilmore, 1974). We shall return to these arguments at various points in this book, especially in Chapters 21 and 22.

My own view is that Fried correctly identifies a strong current of individualism which runs through the law of contract. A promise does engender an expectation in the promisee and, unless a good reason to the contrary appears, the courts will call upon a defaulting promisor to fulfil the expectation so created. But the critics of Fried are also correct in their argument that the commitment to individual auton-omy is tempered in its application by considerations of fairness, consumerism and altruism. These conflicting ideologies run through the entire law of contract (for a fuller examination of these ideologies under the titles of 'Market-Individualism' and 'Consumer-Welfarism', see Adams and Brownsword, 1987). The law of contract is not based upon one ideology; both ideologies are present in the case law and the legislation. Indeed, the tension between the two is a feature of the law of contract. Sometimes 'market-individualism' prevails over 'consumer-welfarism'; at other times 'consumer-welfarism' triumphs over 'market-individualism'. At various points in this book, we shall have occasion to note these conflicting ideologies and the tensions which they produce within the law.

1.4   Contract, tort and unjust enrichment

A further difficulty lies in locating the law of contract within the spectrum of the law of civil obligations. Burrows (1983) has helpfully pointed out that the law of obligations largely rests upon three cardinal principles. The first principle is that expectations engendered by a binding promise should be fulfilled. Upon this principle is founded the law of contract. The second principle is that compensation must be granted for the wrongful infliction of harm. This principle is reflected in the law of tort. A tort is a civil wrong, such as negligence or defamation. Let us take an example to illustrate the operation of the law of tort. You drive your car negligently and knock me down. You have committed the tort of negligence. Harm has wrongfully been inflicted upon me, and you must compensate me. The aim of the award of compensation is not to fulfil my expectations. The aim is to restore me to the position which I was in before the accident occurred, to restore the 'status quo' or to protect my 'reliance interest'.

The third principle is that unjust enrichments must be reversed. This principle is implemented by the law of restitution or, to use the terminology which is gradually gaining acceptance, the law of unjust enrichment. There are four principal stages to an unjust enrichment claim. First, the defendant must be enriched by the receipt of a benefit; second, that enrichment must be at the expense of the claimant; third, it must be unjust for the defendant to retain the benefit without recompensing the claimant and, finally, the defendant does not have a defence to the claim to the reversal of the enrichment. The third stage does not depend upon the unfettered discretion of the judge; there are principles to guide a court in deciding whether, in a particular case, it is unjust that the defendant retain the benefit without recompensing the claimant (see Burrows, 2010). The classic unjust enrichment claim arises where I pay you money under a mistake of fact. I have no contractual claim against you because there is no contract between us. Nor have you committed a tort. But I do have an unjust enrichment claim against you. You are enriched by the receipt of the money, that enrichment is at my expense, and the ground on which I assert that it is unjust that you retain the money is that the money was paid under a mistake of fact.

Contract, tort and unjust enrichment therefore divide up most of the law based upon these three principles, and they provide a satisfactory division for the exposition of the law of obligations. This analysis separates contract from tort and unjust enrichment on the ground that contractual obligations are voluntarily assumed, whereas obligations created by the law of tort and the law of unjust enrichment are *imposed* upon the parties by the operation of rules of law. Occasionally, however, these three principles overlap, especially in the context of remedies (Chapter 22). Overlaps will also be discussed in the context of misrepresentation (Chapter 13) and third-party rights (Chapter 7).

Finally, it must be noted that these divisions are not accepted by writers such as Professor Atiyah. His recognition of reliance-based and benefit-based liabilities cuts right across the three divisions. The writings of Atiyah deserve careful consideration, but they do not represent the current state of English law. Although we shall make frequent reference to the writings of Atiyah, we shall not adopt his analysis of the law of obligations. Instead, it will be argued that the foundation of the law of contract lies in the mutual promises of the parties and, being founded upon such voluntary agreement, the law of contract can, in the vast majority of cases, be separated from the law of tort and the law of unjust enrichment.

1.5 Contract and empirical work

Relatively little empirical work has been done on the relationship between the rules that make up the law of contract and the practices of the community which these rules seek to serve. The work that has been done (see, for example, Beale and Dugdale, 1975; Lewis, 1982) suggests that the law of contract may be relied upon in at least two ways. The first is at the planning stage. The rules which we shall discuss in this book may be very important when drawing up the contract and in planning for the future. For example, care must be taken when drafting an exclusion clause to ensure, as far as possible, that it is not invalidated by the courts (see Chapter 11). Secondly, the law of contract may be used by the parties when their relationship has broken down. Here the rules of contract law generally have a less significant role to play than at the planning stage. The rules of contract law are often but one factor to be taken into account in the resolution of contractual disputes. Parties may value their good relationship and refuse to soil it by resort to the law. Litigation is also time-consuming and extremely expensive, and so the parties will frequently resort to cheaper and more informal methods of dispute resolution. In the remainder of this book, we shall discuss the rules that make up the law of contract, but it must not be forgotten that in the 'real world' the rules of contract law may be only one of many factors taken into account by the parties on the breakdown of a contractual relationship. This is not to suggest that there is no connection between the formal rules of the law of contract and the 'real world' of the parties' relationship. In many cases, the relationship between the parties is governed both by informal understandings (or 'relational norms') and by the formal contract document and the rules of contract law, with the influence of these different factors depending upon the circumstances of the individual case (Mitchell, 2009).

1.6 A European contract law?

The subject-matter of this book is the English law of contract, and so the focus is upon the rules that make up the English law of contract. But it should not be forgotten that we live in a world which is becoming more interdependent and where markets are no longer local or even national but are, increasingly, international. The creation of global markets may, in turn, encourage the development of an international contract and commercial law. There are two dimensions here. The first relates to the impact of our membership of the European Union prior to our departure from the EU on 31 January 2020; the second is the wider move towards the creation of a truly international contract law.

In terms of the UK's membership of the EU, the major impact which EU law has had on English contract law can be seen in areas such as the law relating to public procurement, the regulation of anti-competitive practices and in a number of areas of consumer law, that is to say contracts concluded between a trader and a consumer. In terms of this book, the major development has been the implementation of the European Directive on Unfair Terms in Consumer Contracts (93/13/113). It is now to be found in Part 2 of the Consumer Rights Act 2015 (on which see Chapter 18). The UK's departure from the EU will not result in the repeal of, or amendments to, the Consumer Rights Act. But it will have an impact on the Act. First, the decision whether to amend or repeal Part 2 of the Act in the future will be a matter for the UK Parliament and the EU will not have any say in, or influence over, any proposals to amend or repeal the Act. Second, in the interpretation of Part 2 of the Act, it will no longer be possible for the courts of the UK to make a reference to the Court of Justice of the European Union ('CJEU') for a ruling on the meaning of any disputed provision of Part 2 which has been derived from the Directive. Third, decisions of the CJEU made after the end of the transition period will no longer be binding on the courts of the UK, although judges may have regard to such decisions in so far as they are relevant to the matter before them. In relation to decisions of the CJEU prior to the end of the transition period, the Supreme Court can depart from existing EU law but must when doing so apply the test which it would apply when deciding whether or not to depart from its own case law. More controversially, Ministers have been given an additional power to provide by regulation that other courts and tribunals will not be bound by retained EU law. The latter power, which thus far has not been exercised, seems to owe its origins to considerations of a symbolic nature (particularly in political spheres) and could be a recipe for damaging uncertainty in relation to the outcome of cases.

It cannot be said that the departure of the UK from the EU will immediately and inevitably bring an end to the influence of EU law over aspects of English contract law. The principal reason for this is that the European Union (Withdrawal) Act 2018, as amended, incorporates a great deal of EU law into domestic law as it exists at the end of the transition period. Thus, as far as the future is concerned, developments in EU law will not take effect within the UK. But, to the extent that existing EU law has been retained as part of domestic law, it will continue to be applicable, unless and until repealed or amended by the UK Parliament. Matters may prove to be more difficult in relation to the status of decisions of the CJEU. While there is clearly political antagonism in many quarters to the role of the CJEU, judicial comity is likely to result in the courts in the UK continuing to consider decisions of the CJEU respectfully. While the courts will no longer be bound to follow future decisions of the CJEU, it does not follow that they will ignore them entirely, particularly where the decision of the CJEU is one that is concerned with the interpretation of a provision in a Directive, such as a provision of the Unfair Terms in Consumer Contracts Directive which has also been incorporated into the drafting of Part 2 of the Consumer Rights Act 2015. The influence of the EU will not therefore disappear entirely, but it will reduce considerably and that influence is likely to diminish still further over time.

It is, however, important to draw attention to one document which may continue to exert influence over the development of English contract law even after we have left the EU and that is the Principles of European Contract law, a set of non-binding principles drawn up by the Commission on European Contract Law (a non--governmental body of lawyers drawn from the various Member States). The Principles are divided into 17 chapters: general provisions, formation, authority of agents, validity, interpretation, contents and effects, performance, nonperformance and remedies in general, particular remedies for non-performance, plurality of parties, assignment of claims, substitution of new debtor, transfer of contract, set-off, prescription, illegality, conditions and capitalisation of interest. Reference will be made to the Principles at various points in this book.

1.7   An international contract law?

A broader vision of the future is concerned with the internationalisation of contract law. There are, essentially, two different ways of proceeding. The first is the production of non-binding statements of principle or model contracts; the second is the attempt to impose mandatory uniform rules on the international community.

The first category consists of non-binding statements of principle and model contracts or standard contract terms. We shall give one example from each category. The most important example of a non-binding statement of principles is to be found in the UNIDROIT Principles of International Commercial Contracts. The Principles were first published in 1994 and are now in their fourth edition. The fourth edition, agreed in 2016, consists of 211 Articles, and each Article is accompanied by a brief commentary setting out the reasons for its adoption and its likely practical application. These Articles are not intended to be imposed upon the commercial community in the form of mandatory rules of law. They are non-binding principles which, it is hoped, parties to international commercial contracts will incorporate into their contracts either as a set of contract terms or as the law applicable to the contract. While national courts are presently either unwilling or unable to recognise the Principles as a valid choice of law and thus the law applicable to the contract, the same cannot be said of arbitrators. The UNIDROIT Principles now have a significant role to play in international commercial arbitration. They are particularly useful where parties from different parts of the world are unable to agree on the law applicable to their contract: the UNIDROIT Principles offer a neutral set of Principles which may be acceptable to both parties to the contract.

Standard contract terms also have an important role to play in international commerce. Two prominent examples are the INCOTERMS (a set of standard trade terms sponsored by the International Chamber of Commerce) and the FIDIC (Fédération Internationale des Ingénieurs-Conseils) Conditions of Contract for Works of Civil Engineers, which have achieved widespread acceptance in international sales and international construction contracts respectively. There can be little to object to in such developments because they seek to bring about harmonisation through persuasion rather than imposition. Their alleged weakness is, however, the fact that they are not mandatory. They can therefore be ignored or amended by contracting parties and thus are a rather uncertain method of seeking to achieve uniformity.

In an effort to ensure a greater degree of uniformity, it has been argued that there is greater scope for mandatory rules of law. But the attempt to impose uniform terms on the commercial community has given rise to considerable controversy. The most notable example of an international convention in this category is provided by the United Nations Convention on Contracts for the International Sale of Goods, commonly known as the Vienna Convention or CISG. Unlike earlier conventions, the Vienna Convention does not enable states to ratify the Convention on terms that it is only to be applicable if the parties choose to incorporate it into their contract. It provides that, once it has been ratified by a state, the Convention is applicable to all contracts which fall within its scope (broadly speaking, it covers contracts for the international sale of goods) unless the contracting parties choose to contract out of the Convention or of parts thereof. The Convention has been in force since 1988 and, although the United Kingdom has not yet ratified it, it has been ratified by many major trading nations, such as the United States, France, Germany and China. Supporters of such Conventions argue that they promote the development of international trade by ensuring common standards in different nations. Contracting parties can then have greater confidence when dealing with a party from a different nation, and such uniformity should result in lower costs because there will be no need to spend time arguing about which law should govern the transaction, nor will there be any necessity to spend time and money seeking to discover the relevant rules which prevail in another jurisdiction.

But such Conventions have also been the subject of considerable criticism. It is argued that they do not achieve uniformity because national courts are likely to adopt divergent approaches to their interpretation (some courts adopting a literal approach, others a purposive approach). In this way, the aim of achieving uniformity will be undermined. The Vienna Convention took many years to negotiate and, even now, over 30 years after agreement was reached, it has not been adopted by all the major trading nations of the world. Furthermore, it is not at all clear how the Convention will be amended. The commercial world is constantly on the move, and the law must adapt to the changing needs of the market if it is to facilitate trade. An international code which is difficult to amend is unlikely to meet the demands of traders. It is also argued that such Conventions tend to lack clarity because they are drafted in the form of multicultural compromises in an effort to secure agreement and thus lack the certainty which the commercial community requires. Lord Hobhouse (1990), writing extra-judicially, summed up these arguments when he wrote that:

> international commerce is best served not by imposing deficient legal schemes upon it but by encouraging the development of the best schemes in a climate of free competition and choice ... What should no longer be tolerated is the unthinking acceptance of a goal of uniformity and its doctrinaire imposition on the commercial community.

While these arguments have a great deal of force, they are not universally shared (for a reply, see Steyn, 1994) and it should be noted that they do not deny the value of internationally agreed standards. But it is suggested that they do show that we should proceed by way of persuasion rather than imposition. Attempts to draft international standard form contracts and non-binding statements of the general principles of contract law should be encouraged as they are most likely to produce uniform standards which will meet the needs of contracting parties and, in so doing, lower the cost of concluding international contracts.

1.8 The role of national contract law in a global economy

What is the likely role of national contract law in a global economy? This is not an easy question to answer. Much is likely to depend on the various projects currently in existence which aim to produce either a European or an international law of contract. If they are successful, the role for national contract law is likely to diminish considerably. On the other hand, if they are unsuccessful, the national laws of contract will continue to regulate the vast majority of contracts that are made. But it should not be thought that trade across national boundaries is a new thing. It is not. While the volume of such trade has increased significantly in recent years, international trade is not a new phenomenon. Indeed, many of the cases to be discussed in this book were litigated between parties who had no connection with England other than the fact that their contract was governed by English law (usually by virtue of a 'choice of law clause' in their contract). The explanation for the choice of English law as the governing law is undoubtedly to be found in England's great trading history, which has been of great profit to the City of London and English law, if not to other parts of the United Kingdom. The commodities markets have had their centres in England for many years, and many contracts for the sale of commodities are governed by English law. London has also been an important arbitration centre, and a number of our great contract cases started life as arbitration cases which were then appealed to the courts via the stated case procedure, before the latter procedure fell into disrepute and was abolished in the Arbitration Act 1979. The fact that English contract law has had this 'global' influence in the past may make English lawyers reluctant to accede to attempts to create a European or an international law of contract: they may have too much to lose if English law diminishes in importance. Of course, much depends on the reasons why contracting parties choose English law as the governing law or choose to litigate or arbitrate in London. If the reason is to be found in the way in which English lawyers handle disputes or in procedural factors, then there is little for English lawyers to fear from the creation of a European or an international law of contract. But if parties choose English law because of the quality of the substantive law, then the City may well lose out if English contract law is to be abandoned at some future time in favour of some uniform law. The threat to national contract law in the short to medium term is relatively low, but in the longer term it is much harder to quantify, and the arguments for and against the adoption of a uniform law may be governed as much by economics and practical politics as the quality of the uniform law which is ultimately produced.

1.9 Contract law and human rights

One of the most significant events in recent legal history is the enactment of the Human Rights Act 1998, which incorporates the European Convention on Human Rights into English law by creating 'Convention rights' which are enforceable in domestic law (Human Rights Act 1998, s 1). The impact which the rights contained in the Convention will have on the law of contract remains somewhat uncertain.

In this introductory chapter, there are two issues which are worthy of brief note. The first is that the Act makes it 'unlawful for a public authority to act in a way which is incompatible with a Convention right' (Human Rights Act 1998, s 6(1)). It therefore clearly applies as between a public authority and a natural or a legal person. But does the Act also have 'horizontal effect', that is to ask, does it apply between two private citizens or between an individual and a business?

The answer to this question has been the subject of an extensive debate. It is clear that the Act does have some horizontal effect, in the sense that Convention rights can be invoked in litigation between private parties when seeking to interpret domestic legislation. It is more difficult to ascertain whether, and if so to what extent, the Act has greater horizontal effect. Support for the proposition that it does may be found in the fact that section 6 includes 'a court or tribunal' within the definition of public authority. Given that it is unlawful for the courts, as a public authority, to act in a way which is incompatible with a Convention right, the courts may conclude that they must give effect to the Act even in litigation between two private individuals (where the issue between the parties is not one that relates to the interpretation of domestic legislation). On the other hand, it can be argued that, while the court must not act in a way which is incompatible with a Convention right, given that the Convention does not apply against a private individual, a court cannot act incompatibly with a Convention right if it refuses to apply the Convention in a claim against a private individual. While there remains some uncertainty in relation to the extent to which the Act is applicable in litigation between private individuals, there can be no doubt that, at the very least, the Act will apply to contracts entered into by public authorities.

The second question relates to the scope of the 'Convention rights' and the extent to which they may be violated by contracts or by the rules of contract law. Some examples are obvious. A contract of slavery would be a violation of Article 4 of the Convention, but English law already refuses to recognise the validity of such a contract. The difficult cases are going to be those rules of contract law which are currently valid but, in fact, can amount to a violation of a Convention right. At the moment, it is only possible to speculate as to which Convention rights may suddenly surface in contract litigation. The most obvious are perhaps Article 6 (which states that 'in the determination of his civil rights and obligations … everyone is entitled to a fair and public hearing within a reasonable time by an independent and impartial tribunal established by law'), Article 14 (which states that 'the enjoyment of the rights and freedoms set forth in this Convention shall be secured without discrimination on any ground such as sex, race, colour, language, religion, political or other opinion, national or social origin, association with a national minority, property, birth or other status') and Article 1 of the First Protocol (which states that 'every natural or legal person is entitled to the peaceful enjoyment of his possessions. No one shall be deprived of his possessions except in the public interest and subject to the conditions provided for by law and by the general principles of international law'). So, attempts to expropriate contract rights or to deny to claimants the right to have their disputes resolved by a court of law may involve a violation of a Convention right.

Here it will suffice to give an example of the potential impact of Convention rights on the law of contract. The case is the decision of the House of Lords in *Wilson v First County Trust Ltd (No 2)* [2003] UKHL 40; [2004] 1 AC 816, in which their Lordships allowed an appeal from the decision of the Court of Appeal ([2001] EWCA Civ 633; [2002] QB 74). The Court of Appeal had made a declaration that section 127(3) of the

Consumer Credit Act 1974 was incompatible with the rights guaranteed by Article 6(1) of the Convention and by Article 1 of the First Protocol. Section 127(3) renders an improperly executed consumer credit agreement unenforceable by the creditor where the debtor does not sign a document which contains all the prescribed terms of the agreement. The Court of Appeal held that this absolute ban on the enforceability of the agreement was incompatible with the defendant pawnbroker's human rights. The problem identified by the Court of Appeal was that section 127(3) imposes an absolute ban on enforcement, and this was held to be a disproportionate response to the problems created by consumer credit agreements which are not in the prescribed form. In this respect, section 127(3) was contrasted with sections 127(1) and (2) of the 1974 Act, which give to the court a discretion to enforce a consumer credit agreement notwithstanding the failure to comply with formal requirements. The Court of Appeal stated that the contrast between sections 127(1) and 127(3) was 'striking', and they concluded that no reason had been advanced which could justify an 'inflexible prohibition' on the enforcement of such agreements when it was possible to regulate the issue by giving the court the power 'to do what is just in the circumstances of the particular case'.

The House of Lords held that the Court of Appeal had erred in concluding that section 127(3) was incompatible with Article 6(1) of the Convention. In so deciding, their Lordships emphasised that Article 6(1) cannot be used in order to create a substantive civil right of action which otherwise has no basis in national law. The target of Article 6(1) is procedural bars on bringing claims to court. As Lord Nicholls recognised (at [35]): 'the distinction between the substantive content of a right and an unacceptable procedural bar to its enforcement by a court can give rise to difficulty in distinguishing the one from the other in a particular case'. But on the present facts, no such difficulty arose. Section 127(3) was a restriction on the scope of the right which the creditor acquired, and it did not bar access to the court in order to decide whether the case was caught by the restriction.

In relation to the claim that there had been a violation of Article 1 of the First Protocol, their Lordships concluded that Article 1 was applicable on the facts of the case but that it had not been breached. Importantly, the House of Lords concluded that the word 'possessions' includes contractual rights so that the deprivation of a contractual right may raise human rights issues in an appropriate case (see, for example, *Pennycook v Shaws (EAL) Ltd* [2004] EWCA Civ 100; [2004] Ch 296). On the facts, the majority concluded that section 127(3) did operate to deprive the creditor of his contractual rights in such a way as to trigger the operation of Article 1 but that on the facts there had been no breach. Section 127(3) was held to be a 'legitimate exercise in consumer protection'. Borrowers who fall within the scope of the Consumer Credit Act are often 'vulnerable' and do not bargain on an 'equal footing' with lenders. Parliament was entitled to conclude that the protection of such borrowers required the automatic invalidation of contracts which did not satisfy the requirements of the subsection in order to give lenders the strongest incentive to comply with its clear and transparent requirements. The fact that the aim could possibly have been achieved by conferring a discretion on the court to invalidate the contract could not be dispositive. The response of Parliament could not be said to be disproportionate to the policy which underpinned the legislation, and it did not amount to a breach of the Article.

Hot topic 1...

What impact will the departure of the UK from the EU have on the English law of contract? At this point it is difficult to tell. It is clear that the UK will not be bound by subsequent developments in EU law and thus one might reasonably expect there to be greater differences in future between EU law and English law. Whether these differences will act as a barrier to trade between the UK and the EU will likely depend on the outcome of the negotiations on the conclusion of a trade deal between the UK and the EU. In other words, the quality of the future relationship between the UK and the EU will be determined by the existence or not of a trade deal rather than by any differences between the laws of contract in England and the Member States of the EU.

In terms of retained EU law that has been incorporated into UK law, it will be interesting to see how the English courts develop that law and the extent to which they will continue to follow the jurisprudence of the CJEU. The courts may come under political pressure to chart their own course, but considerations of judicial comity and respect for the European origin of the legislation that is being interpreted may incline many courts to follow an approach which is very similar to, if not identical with, the jurisprudence of the CJEU.

The final question in this context relates to the standing of English law in the wider world. Contracting parties who have no other connection with the UK have frequently chosen English law as the law that is to govern their contract. One of the reasons they have done so is because of the certainty which English law is said to provide. The experience of the journey from the referendum to exit from the EU has put at risk the view that English law provides security and certainty for contracting parties. It may be that contracting parties will in future respond by choosing the law of another jurisdiction as the law that is to govern their contract, to the detriment of English law and the economy of the UK. This is not to say that we will inevitably see a move away from reliance on English law. But it is a risk that cannot be ignored.

Part I

The formation and scope of a contract

Chapter 2

Agreement: clearing the ground

To say that contract is based upon the agreement of the parties may be a trite statement but it is also a statement which begs a number of questions. Two of these questions will be dealt with in this chapter. The first is: who decides whether or not the parties have indeed reached agreement? Is it the parties or is it the courts? The second question is: how is it decided whether or not the parties have actually reached agreement?

2.1 Who decides that an agreement has been reached?

When discussing the standard which is adopted in deciding whether or not a contract has been concluded, a useful starting point, which is quoted in most of the reference works on the law of contract, is the judgment of Blackburn J in *Smith v Hughes* (1871) LR 6 QB 597. He said:

> If, whatever a man's real intention may be, he so conducts himself that a reasonable man would believe that he was assenting to the terms proposed by the other party, and that other party upon that belief enters into the contract with him, the man thus conducting himself would be equally bound as if he had intended to agree to the other party's terms.

More recently, the same point was made by Lord Clarke in giving the judgment of the Supreme Court in *RTS Flexible Systems Ltd v Molkerei Alois Müller GmbH & Co (UK Production)* [2010] UKSC 14; [2010] 1 WLR 753, [45] when he stated:

> Whether there is a binding contract between the parties and, if so, upon what terms depends upon what they have agreed. It depends not upon their subjective state of mind, but upon a consideration of what was communicated between them by words or conduct, and whether that leads objectively to a conclusion that they intended to create legal relations and had agreed upon all the terms which they regarded or the law requires as essential for the formation of legally binding relations.

These statements establish the important point that the test for the existence and the scope of an agreement is objective rather than subjective. A subjective test attempts to ascertain the actual intention of the contracting parties, whereas an objective test examines what the parties said and did and not what they actually intended to say or do (see Section 2.3). The commercial justification for the adoption of an objective test is that great uncertainty would be caused if a person who appeared to have agreed to certain terms could escape liability by claiming that he had no 'real' intention to agree to them.

A good example of the application of the objective test is provided by *Centrovincial Estates plc v Merchant Investors Assurance Co Ltd* [1983] Com LR 158. The claimants let premises to the defendants at a yearly rent of £68,320, subject to review from 25 December 1982. The parties were obliged by their contract to endeavour to reach agreement before 25 December 1982 on the then current market rental value of the property and to certify the amount of the current market rental value. In June 1982 the claimants wrote to the defendants inviting them to agree that the current market rental value should be £65,000. The defendants accepted. When the claimants received the defendants' written acceptance they immediately contacted the defendants to inform them that they had meant to propose £126,000 and not £65,000. The defendants refused to agree to this new figure and insisted that a contract had been concluded at a rental value of £65,000. So the claimants sought a declaration that no legally binding agreement had been entered into between the parties. They sought summary judgment against the defendants but the Court of Appeal gave the defendants unconditional leave to defend the action on the basis that the claimants had failed to demonstrate that the defendants had no defence to the claim. It was held that the claimants had failed to 'negative the existence of the apparent agreement of the parties to treat £65,000 as the current market rental value for the purpose of the Lease and to deprive the defendants of the right to defend this action on the basis of such agreement'. Slade LJ said that:

> it is contrary to the well-established principles of contract law to suggest that the offeror under a bilateral contract can withdraw an unambiguous offer, after it has been accepted in the manner contemplated by the offer, merely because he has made a mistake which the offeree neither knew nor could reasonably have known when he accepted it.

An alternative argument which was relied upon by the claimants in *Centrovincial* was that the objective test of intention was founded upon the principle of estoppel. Estoppel is based upon the proposition that a representor will be prevented from going back on his representation when the representation was intended to be acted upon and is acted upon to his detriment by the representee (see Sections 5.25–5.27). The claimants argued that the defendants had not relied upon the claimants' offer to their detriment because the proposed rent of £65,000 was lower than the original rent of £68,320. This argument was rejected by the court on the ground that 'the mutual promises alone will suffice to conclude the contract'.

Professor Atiyah (1986f) has attacked the decision in *Centrovincial* on the ground that he can see no reason why an offeree should be entitled 'to create legal rights for himself by the bare act of acceptance when he has in no way relied upon the offer before being informed it was made as a result of a mistake and did not in reality reflect the intention of the offeror'. He has further argued that the decision of the House of Lords in *The Hannah Blumenthal* [1983] 1 AC 834 lends support to his argument that *Centrovincial* was wrongly decided.

The Hannah Blumenthal concerned an agreement between two parties to settle a dispute by reference to arbitration. There was then a delay of some six years, during which time nothing happened in relation to the arbitration. When the buyers attempted to fix a date for the arbitration, the sellers sought an order that the buyers were not entitled to proceed with the arbitration because of the delay which had occurred. One of the grounds relied upon by the sellers was that the parties had, by their silence and inactivity, agreed to abandon the reference to arbitration; the offer being made by the buyers and the acceptance by the sellers (see Section 3.11). Lord Brandon held that there were two ways in which the parties could agree to abandon a contract to arbitrate. The first was where they actually agreed to do so. The second was where one party created a situation in which he was estopped from asserting that he had not abandoned the contract. In the latter context it was held that the sellers must have 'significantly altered [their] position in reliance' upon their belief that the contract had been abandoned. Lord Diplock also placed emphasis upon the need for detrimental reliance, saying that this was 'an example of a general principle of English law that injurious reliance on what another person did may be a source of legal rights against him'. However it must be remembered that *The Hannah Blumenthal* is a rather unusual case in that it was alleged that the parties had entered into a contract to abandon an arbitration by mere inactivity on both sides. In the absence of express communication between the buyers and the sellers, the only way of showing that the sellers had accepted the buyers' offer to abandon the arbitration was to show that they had acted in reliance on the fact that the contract had been abandoned. The function of reliance was therefore to provide *evidence* of the fact that the sellers had accepted the buyers' offer to abandon the agreement to arbitrate; it is not the case that the House of Lords was laying down a rule that such reliance was a prerequisite to the formation of any contract. Thus interpreted, *The Hannah Blumenthal* does not cast doubt upon the correctness of *Centrovincial* because in *Centrovincial* the defendants' acceptance was evidenced by the fact that they wrote and accepted the claimants' offer. In such a case, the acceptance concludes the contract without the need for any further act in reliance upon the offer.

2.2 A residual role for a subjective approach?

It should not, however, be assumed that the subjective intentions of the parties are irrelevant to the law of contract. In many cases the subjective intentions of the parties will coincide with the interpretation put upon their intentions by the objective test, and to that extent their subjective intentions are protected. Further, as was made clear by Slade LJ in *Centrovincial Estates plc v Merchant Investors Assurance Co Ltd*, there are two situations in which the objective test is either displaced or modified by a test which at least on the face of it appears to place greater emphasis upon the subjective intentions of the parties.

The first arises where the offeree knows that the offeror is suffering from a mistake as to the terms of the offer. In such a case the offeree cannot create a contract between the parties by purporting to accept the offer. Matters are otherwise where the mistake relates, not to the terms of the contract, but to the facts on which the offeror based his decision to enter into the agreement. In the latter case, the contract remains binding on the offeror, even in the case where the offeree was aware of the mistake made by the offeror (*Statoil ASA v Louis Dreyfus Energy Services LP* [2008] EWHC 2257 (Comm); [2008] 2 Lloyd's Rep 685). But where the offeror's mistake relates to the terms of the offer or to the terms of the contract, and the offeree knows that the offeror is so mistaken, then there is no contract between the parties. In such a case the courts, on one view, have regard to the subjective understanding of the offeree (see *Statoil* at [87]). But it is not necessary to adopt this view in order to explain the result in such cases. The result can be explained by adopting the approach of a reasonable person in the position of the offeree. An example is provided by the facts of *Hartog v Colin and Shields* [1939] 3 All ER 566. The defendants entered into a contract to sell 3,000 Argentinian hare skins to the claimants. However by mistake they offered them for sale at 10d per pound instead of 10d per piece. When they discovered their mistake, the defendants refused to deliver the skins. The claimants brought an action in respect of the defendants' non-delivery of the skins. It was held that they were not entitled to succeed because the negotiations had proceeded upon the basis that the skins were to be sold at a price per piece and that, as there were three pieces to the pound, the claimants could not reasonably have thought that the defendants' offer matched their true intention. The claimants were thereby prevented from snatching a bargain which they knew was not intended by the defendants. However, it is not necessary to have resort to a purely subjective test in order to explain the outcome of the case. It can be accommodated within an objective test on the basis that the reasonable person in the position of the claimants would have known that the offer made by the defendants did not reflect their true intention. Had the test been a subjective one it would have been necessary for the defendants to show that the claimants actually knew that the defendants were mistaken; instead it sufficed that the reasonable person in the claimants' position would have known of the defendants' mistake.

The second situation in which it has been argued that the subjective intentions of the parties are relevant is where the offeree is at fault in failing to note that the offeror has made a mistake. Such was the case in *Scriven Bros v Hindley* [1913] 3 KB 564. An auctioneer acting for the claimants put up for sale lots of hemp and tow. The auction catalogue was misleading because it implied that the lots were the same when, in fact, the second lot only contained tow. Tow was considerably cheaper than hemp. The defendants bid for the lot, thinking that it was hemp when in fact it was tow. The auctioneer did not realise that the defendants had misunderstood what was being auctioned; he merely thought that they had overvalued the tow. When the defendants discovered their mistake, they refused to pay the price and so the claimants sued them for the price. It was held that no contract for the sale of the tow had been concluded when the tow was knocked down to the defendants, because the auctioneer intended to sell tow and the defendants intended to purchase hemp, and the defendants' mistake had been induced by the carelessness of the claimants in preparing the auction catalogue. The importance of the misleading nature of the auction catalogue can be seen in the fact that, had it not been misleading, a contract would have been concluded on the claimants' terms because, in the usual case, an auctioneer is entitled to assume that a bidder knows what he is bidding for. Thus, in the ordinary case, a contract would have been concluded for the sale of tow. But, once again, it is not necessary to have regard to the subjective understandings of the parties in order to explain the outcome of the case. The case simply stands for the proposition that the carelessness of the claimants prevented them from enforcing their understanding of the contract. The result can be explained in terms of 'defendant' objectivity (see Section 2.3) on the basis that the court was concerned to scrutinise the understanding of the reasonable person in the position of the defendants. Given that the reasonable person in the position of the defendants would have been misled by the auction catalogue, the claimants were not entitled to enforce their version of the contract against the defendants.

A further situation in which it has been argued (see Spencer, 1974) that the subjective intentions of the parties are relevant arises where the parties are subjectively agreed but that subjective agreement is at variance with the result achieved by applying the objective test. Spencer gives the admittedly rather far-fetched example of two immigrants who have little command of the English language and who enter into a contract under which one is to sell to the other a 'bull'. Both parties intend to use the word 'bull' but they both think that the word 'bull' means cow. The application of the objective test, Spencer argues, leads to the conclusion that a contract has been concluded for the sale of a bull. But, as Spencer points out, this is absurd as the seller does not have a bull to sell and the buyer does not want one. He argues that while:

> it may be acceptable for the law occasionally to force upon *one* of the parties an agreement he did not want ... surely there is something wrong with a theory which forces upon *both* of the parties an agreement which neither of them wants.

Thus Spencer concludes that the subjective intentions of the parties must prevail. But if both parties in fact wished to contract to sell a cow and a cow was delivered and accepted then the law of contract would not force upon the parties an agreement which neither of them wanted because, in such a case, the objective approach would lead to the conclusion that a contract had been made for the sale of a cow. The actions of the parties, in delivering and accepting delivery of the cow, would displace the inference which had been raised by the words which they had used. So, in this example, there is no question of the law forcing upon the parties an agreement which neither of them wants and no need to invoke any reference to the subjective understandings of the parties.

It is, however, important to understand that the subjective understandings of the parties will not generally prevail over their intention, objectively ascertained. As Lord Normand stated in *Mathieson Gee (Ayrshire) Ltd v Quigley* 1952 SC (HL) 38:

> when the parties to a litigation put forward what they say is a concluded contract and ask the Court to construe it, it is competent for the Court to find that there was in fact no contract and nothing to be construed.

Conversely, it has been stated that 'if the parties' correspondence and conduct shows [objectively that they intend to make a contract] it will not, or may not, matter that neither privately intended to make a contract' (*The Amazonia* [1990] 1 Lloyd's Rep 236, 243). The existence or non-existence of a contract is ultimately a question for the court which will generally be decided by the application of an objective test.

2.3   The objective test

So the general rule is that the intention of the parties is to be assessed objectively. Thus far, it has been assumed that there is only one objective test which can be applied by the courts, but it has been argued (Howarth, 1984) that there are, in fact, three different interpretations of the objective test which can be applied by the courts. The first is the standard of detached objectivity. This approach takes as its standpoint the perspective of the detached observer or the 'fly on the wall'. In other words, it asks what interpretation would a person watching the behaviour of the contracting parties place upon their words and actions. The second possible interpretation suggested by Howarth is to interpret the words as they were reasonably understood by the promisee (called 'promisee objectivity' by Howarth). This is the standard which finds the greatest support in the case law (see *Smith v Hughes* (1871) LR 6 QB 597 (above)). The third and final interpretation is the standard of the reasonable person in the shoes of the person making the offer (called 'promisor objectivity' by Howarth). The approach which is preferred by Howarth is 'detached objectivity' but there is little judicial support for such a test (Vorster, 1987).

However, the distinction which Howarth draws between 'promisor' and 'promisee' objectivity has been criticised on the ground that it is misleading because, in a bilateral contract, each party is both a promisor and a promisee (Vorster, 1987, especially 276–78). Thus, for example, in *Scriven Bros v Hindley* [1913] 3 KB 564 (above) the defendant purchaser was a promisor in relation to his promise to pay for the lot and a promisee concerning the auctioneer's promise to sell him the tow. On the other hand, the auctioneer was a promisor in relation to the promise to sell the lot and a promisee concerning the defendant's promise to purchase the lot. It is true that the nomenclature which Howarth employs is rather misleading but it should not blind us to his essential point, which is that there are two parties to a contract and that a court could elect to apply the perspective of one or the other contracting party. One could meet the criticism by restyling the classification as 'claimant' and 'defendant' objectivity to underline the point that one is simply looking at the contract from the position of one or the other contracting party. Although it is true that, in our terminology, 'defendant' objectivity has the greatest support in the case law this may be a product of the way in which the cases have come before the courts rather than distinct judicial preference. The case of *Scriven Bros v Hindley* (above) provides a good example of this point. In that case the court considered whether the claimants were entitled to recover the price of the lot which they alleged that the defendants had contracted to buy. The emphasis of the court was upon the defendants' understanding of the offer made by the auctioneer. This was because the defence to the claim was based on the defendants' understanding of the offer and therefore the court was forced to examine that understanding. It is crucial to note that the defendants simply denied liability; they did not take the further step of asking the court to enforce their version of the 'contract'. This had the consequence that the court did not consider whether the defendants would have been able to sue the claimants for breach of a contract to sell hemp. Had the defendants counterclaimed for breach of their version of the 'contract', the roles would have been reversed and the court would have been compelled to consider the claimants' understanding of the bid made by the defendants. The infrequency of such counterclaims by defendants means that 'defendant' objectivity is most commonly considered by the courts, but it does not follow that the courts are averse to applying 'claimant' objectivity; it is simply the case that they are not often asked by defendants to apply such a standard.

2.4   Has agreement been reached?

An instructive example of the approach which the courts adopt in deciding whether or not the parties have reached agreement is provided by the case of *Butler v Ex-Cell-O Corp (England) Ltd* [1979] 1 WLR 401. The sellers, Butler, offered to sell a machine tool to the buyers, the offer being made on Butler's standard terms of business, which included, *inter alia*, a price variation clause. The buyers sent an order for the machine tool which, in turn, was on their own standard terms of business, which made no provision for a price variation clause and stated that the price of the machine tool was to be fixed. The buyers' order form contained a tear-off acknowledgement slip, which stated that 'we [the sellers] accept your order on the terms and conditions stated thereon'. The sellers signed and returned this slip to the buyers, together with a letter stating that they were carrying out the order on the terms of their original offer. After constructing the machine tool, but before delivering it, the sellers sought to invoke the price variation clause contained in their original offer and claimed the additional sum of £2,892. The buyers refused to pay this increase in price, claiming that they were not contractually bound to do so. The sellers accordingly sued the buyers for £2,892 in damages. The Court of Appeal held that they were not entitled to recover the sum claimed because a contract had been concluded on the buyers' terms which did not include the price variation clause. Although the Court of Appeal was unanimous in holding that a contract had been concluded on the buyers' terms, the court was divided in its reasoning.

2.4.1   The reasoning of the majority

The reasoning of the majority, Lawton and Bridge LJJ, proceeded by applying the traditional 'mirror image' rule of contractual formation. According to this rule, the court must be able to find in the documents which passed between the parties a clear and unequivocal offer which is matched or 'mirrored' by an equally clear and unequivocal acceptance. A purported acceptance which seeks to introduce new terms is not in fact a true acceptance at all but is a counter-offer which 'kills off' the original offer and amounts to a new offer which can in turn be accepted by the other party. Applying this, they held that the buyers' order could not be construed as an acceptance of the sellers' offer because it did not mirror exactly the terms of the sellers' offer and therefore amounted to a counter-offer. They held that this counter-offer was accepted by the sellers when they signed the tear-off acknowledgement on the buyers' order form. The letter accompanying the acknowledgement slip was held not to be an attempt to reintroduce the terms of the sellers' original offer and so was not a counter-offer, but was simply a means of identifying the order for the machine tool.

This traditional approach has a number of advantages. The first is that it provides some degree of certainty because legal advisers at least know the principles which the courts will apply in deciding whether or not a contract has been concluded (a point recognised by the Court of Appeal when applying the traditional approach in *Tekdata Interconnections Ltd v Amphenol Ltd* [2009] EWCA Civ 1209; [2010] 1 Lloyd's Rep 357, [25]). Further, there is no separation between the formation of the contract and the ascertainment of the terms of the contract because the offer and acceptance must mirror each other exactly before a contract is concluded. Thus this approach gives the parties a clear standard against which to measure their conduct and sends out a message that a failure to reach agreement on all points may lead a court to hold that a contract has not been concluded. The second advantage of this approach is that it provides a standard which is of general application.

However, the traditional approach has also been subjected to considerable criticism. One such criticism is that it is excessively rigid. It produces an 'all or nothing' result, in the sense that it is either the terms of the buyer or the terms of the seller which govern the relationship of the parties; the court cannot pick and choose between the respective sets of terms and conditions or seek to find an acceptable compromise.

This is unfortunate in cases involving the 'battle of the forms' (as cases such as *Butler* are commonly called), where both parties may reasonably believe that their terms are the ones which govern their relationship and where a compromise may produce the fairest result on the facts of the case. The traditional approach has also been criticised in its application to battle of the forms cases on the ground that it encourages business people to continue to exchange their standard terms of business in the hope of getting the 'last shot' in and it places the party in receipt of the last communication in a very difficult position. If he refuses to accept the goods, it is likely that it will be held that no contract has come into existence, but if he accepts the goods it is possible that he will be held to have accepted them on the sellers' terms (as happened in *Tekdata Interconnections Ltd v Amphenol Ltd* (above)). This suggests that the onus will generally be upon the buyer and that a seller which insists that its terms prevail and refuses to sign the buyer's tear-off acknowledgement slip will be in a strong position. As Leggatt LJ observed in *Hitchins (Hatfield) Ltd v H Butterworth Ltd*, Unreported (CA, 25 February 1995): 'if express terms are to govern a contract of sale, a buyer would expect to buy goods upon the seller's terms, unless supplanted by the buyer's own'.

2.4.2 The approach of Lord Denning

The strains on the traditional approach have led some judges to reject it in favour of a new approach. In *Butler*, Lord Denning, who was in the minority (in terms of reasoning, but not result), rejected the traditional mirror image approach to contractual formation, holding it to be 'out-of-date' (see too his judgment in the case of *Gibson v Manchester City Council* [1978] 1 WLR 520, 523, where he said that 'to my mind it is a mistake to think that all contracts can be analysed into the form of offer and acceptance'). He stated that the:

> better way is to look at all the documents passing between the parties and glean from them, or from the conduct of the parties, whether they have reached agreement on all material points, even though there may be differences between the forms and conditions printed on the back of them.

He also held that, even where the terms used by the parties were mutually contradictory, it was possible for a court to 'scrap' the terms and replace them by a 'reasonable implication'. Applying this reasoning, he held that the signing of the tear-off acknowledgement by the sellers was the 'decisive document', which made it clear that the contract was concluded on the buyers' terms. A case which demonstrates that a court may, in an appropriate case, find that a contract has been concluded on terms other than those to be found in the parties' respective standard terms is *GHSP Inc v AB Electronic Ltd* [2010] EWHC 1828 (Comm); [2011] 1 Lloyd's Rep 432. In this case Burton J concluded that there was a conflict between the parties' standard terms of business and that neither party had accepted the other's terms. But, rather than find that there was no contract between the parties, he held that the terms of the contract were to be found in the terms to be implied into the contract by the Sale of Goods Act 1979. But in this case it is important to note that counsel for both parties agreed that 'there was plainly a contract' between the parties. Had it not been for this concession, Burton J might not have been so willing to find the existence of a contract given the parties' failure to reach agreement on the terms that were to apply to their relationship. However, these doubts may be misplaced. In *Transformers & Rectifiers Ltd v Needs Ltd* [2015] EWHC 269 (TCC), [2015] BLR 336 Edwards-Stuart J was content to find that, notwithstanding the fact that neither party had succeeded in incorporating its own standard terms and conditions into the agreement, the parties had nevertheless entered into a binding contract. It is not entirely clear what the terms of this contract were but the case serves to demonstrate the strength of the judicial impulse to find the existence of a contract where substantial performance has taken place even in the case where the paperwork, in the sense of the written terms of the deal, has not all been put in place.

The approach adopted by Lord Denning clearly conflicts with the mirror image approach to contractual formation because it adopts a two-stage approach. At the first stage, it must be decided whether a contract has been concluded and, at the second stage, it must be decided what the terms of the contract are. At the latter stage, the court has considerable discretion in filling the gaps. The approach adopted by Lord Denning seeks to construct a more flexible framework for the law of contract which can accommodate inconsistent terms and an apparent lack of consensus within the law of contract.

This approach has in turn been criticised on the ground that it produces uncertainty because it gives too little guidance to the courts, or to legal advisers, in determining whether or not an agreement has been reached. Certainty is a particularly important commodity in the law of contract because business people will often want to know the standard which the law applies so that they can plan their affairs accordingly.

2.4.3   Evaluation of the two approaches

Despite the attempt by Lord Denning to introduce this new general approach to the issue of agreement, English law remains wedded to the traditional approach. This was confirmed by Lord Diplock in *Gibson v Manchester City Council* [1979] 1 WLR 294, 297 when he said that, although there may be certain 'exceptional' cases which do not 'fit easily into the normal analysis of a contract as being constituted by offer and acceptance', these cases were very much the exception and they have not displaced the traditional rule. The survival of the traditional approach was more recently affirmed by the Court of Appeal in *Tekdata Interconnections Ltd v Amphenol Ltd* (above), where Dyson LJ stated (at [25]) that 'the general rule should be that the traditional offer and acceptance analysis is to be applied in battle of the forms cases'. It should be noted that this is a 'general' rule and, as such, it admits of exceptions. But a court is likely to be slow to recognise such exceptions, at least in cases involving the battle of the forms. As Longmore LJ observed in *Tekdata Interconnections Ltd v Amphenol Ltd* (at [21]), 'it will always be difficult to displace the traditional analysis, in a battle of the forms case, unless it can be said that there was a clear course of dealing between the parties'. So in the case where the parties have an established course of dealing and that course of dealing is governed by certain terms, the courts may give effect to these terms without the need to apply the traditional analysis. But these cases are the exception. In the vast majority of cases, the traditional analysis will be applied.

It would be a mistake, however, to think that the traditional rule is always rigidly applied by the judiciary. For example, in the case where the parties both sign a written agreement containing the terms of their contract, there is no need to look for an offer and a matching acceptance. The fact that the parties have signed an agreed text will in general suffice to establish the existence of an agreement. Thus, it has been stated that 'where there is agreement, it is unnecessary to identify the precise mechanics of offer and acceptance' (*Premier Paper Group Ltd v Buchanan McPherson Ltd* [2018] EWCA Civ 15, [29]). Further, in *The Eurymedon* [1975] AC 154, 167 Lord Wilberforce stated that 'English law, having committed itself to a rather technical and schematic doctrine of contract, in application takes a practical approach, often at the cost of forcing the facts to fit uneasily into the marked slots of offer, acceptance and consideration'. We shall see, when discussing issues such as the application of the rules of offer and acceptance to transactions in the supermarket (see Section 3.2), that the courts do have some room for manoeuvre in identifying the offer and the acceptance and so have some flexibility in applying the rules in a particular factual context.

In the next chapter we shall give consideration to the schematic approach to agreement by examining in greater detail the constituent elements of offer and acceptance. Then, in Chapter 4, we shall give further consideration to the application of the objective test.

Hot topic 2...

Contracting parties very often develop their own standard terms and conditions of contract. A problem which these standard terms generate is that they frequently conflict with each other so that it can be difficult to ascertain whether or not the parties have reached agreement. In such cases the courts can face a difficult choice. If they focus exclusively on the paperwork, they are likely to reach the conclusion that the parties have not entered into a binding contract as a result of their failure to reach agreement on material points. On the other hand, if the courts focus attention on the conduct of the parties, they are more likely to decide that a contract has been entered into. If one party has been providing services and the other party has been making payment for these services, the most likely explanation for this course of conduct is that the parties have entered into a contract. The conclusion that they were each conferring gifts on one another is commercially improbable. The reality is that the courts have regard both to the paperwork and to the conduct of the parties when seeking to decide whether the parties have entered into a contract. The more work that is done on both sides, the more likely it is that the court will find the existence of a contract, at least in the absence of active disagreement between the parties (as opposed to mere gaps in their agreement). In the case where the parties are in active disagreement but work has nevertheless been done on both sides, the court will examine the evidence carefully and balance the competing considerations in deciding whether or not the parties have entered into a binding contract (see, for example, *Transformers & Rectifiers Ltd v Needs Ltd* [2015] EWHC 269 (TCC), [2015] BLR 336).

Summary

▶ The test for the existence of an agreement is objective rather than subjective. The principal justification for the adoption of this test is the need to promote certainty.

▶ Where the offeree knows that the offeror is suffering from a mistake as to the terms of his offer and where the offeree is at fault in failing to note that the offeror has made a mistake, the offeree will not be entitled to enforce the contract according to his version of its terms.

▶ There are three potential forms of the objective test: detached objectivity, claimant (or promisor) objectivity and defendant (or promisee) objectivity. The latter form has the greatest support in the case law but this may be a product of the way in which the cases have come before the courts rather than distinct judicial preference.

▶ The courts apply the 'mirror image' rule in deciding whether or not a contract has been concluded. The acceptance must mirror the offer exactly. The general approach to contract formation advocated by Lord Denning has been rejected.

Exercises

2.1 Do you think that *Centrovincial Estates plc v Merchant Investors Assurance Co Ltd* [1983] Com LR 158 was correctly decided?

2.2 Andrew, an old man aged 80, agreed to sell his house to David for £16,800. Andrew in fact meant to sell it for £168,000. David is now seeking to enforce the agreement. Advise Andrew.

2.3 Compare and contrast the reasoning of the majority and the minority in *Butler v Ex-Cell-O Corp (England) Ltd* [1979] 1 WLR 401. Which approach do you prefer and why?

Chapter 3

Offer and acceptance

We noted in Chapter 2 that the courts adopt the 'mirror image' rule of contractual formation; that is to say they must find a clear and unequivocal offer which is matched by an equally clear and unequivocal acceptance. In this chapter we shall give more detailed consideration to the constituent elements of an offer and an acceptance. However, three points should be noted at the outset of our discussion.

The first point is that most of the cases which we shall discuss in this chapter are cases which came to court because one party was alleging that the other had broken the contract between them. This can be seen in *Butler v Ex-Cell-O Corp (England) Ltd* [1979] 1 WLR 401 (see Section 2.4), where the discussion of the rules of offer and acceptance was crucial because the court had to find the existence of a contract and ascertain its terms before it could decide whether the buyers were in breach of contract or not. Thus, the context of most of these cases is an allegation of *breach* of contract.

The second point which should be borne in mind relates to the way in which the courts use the requirements of offer and acceptance in deciding cases. Professor Atiyah has argued (2006, 41) that the courts could either 'reason forwards' or they could 'reason backwards'. By 'reasoning forwards', Professor Atiyah means that the courts reason from the legal concepts of offer and acceptance towards the solution to the dispute. This is the traditional approach which has been adopted by the courts; they 'find' the existence of an offer and an acceptance, and only then do they reason towards their conclusion. On the other hand, the courts could 'reason backwards'; that is to say they could reason from the appropriate solution back to the legal concepts of offer and acceptance. On such a model, the court can decide which solution it wishes to adopt and then fit the negotiations within the offer and acceptance framework in order to *justify* the decision which they have already reached. The distinction which Professor Atiyah is seeking to draw is a difficult one to grasp in the abstract but it is one to which we shall return when discussing some of the cases.

The third point is that, on a number of occasions, we shall note that great difficulty is experienced in accommodating many everyday transactions within the offer and acceptance framework. This point will lead us to conclude by discussing the utility of the offer and acceptance model. With these preliminary points in mind, let us examine the detailed rules of law relating to offer and acceptance.

3.1 Offer and invitation to treat

An offer is a statement by one party of a willingness to enter into a contract on stated terms, provided that these terms are, in turn, accepted by the party or parties to whom the offer is addressed. There is generally no requirement that the offer be made in any particular form; it may be made orally, in writing or by conduct.

Care must be taken, however, in distinguishing between an offer and an invitation to treat. An invitation to treat is simply an expression of willingness to enter into negotiations which, it is hoped, will lead to the conclusion of a contract at a later date. The distinction between the two is said to be primarily one of intention; that is, did the maker of the statement intend to be bound by an acceptance of his terms without further negotiation, or did he only intend his statement to be part of the continuing negotiation process? Although the dichotomy is easy to state at the level of theory, it is not so easy to apply in practice, as can be seen from the case of *Gibson v Manchester City Council* [1978] 1 WLR 520 (CA); [1979] 1 WLR 294 (HL).

In 1970 the defendant council prepared a brochure explaining how a council tenant could purchase his council house, and sent a copy to those tenants who had previously expressed an interest in purchasing their council house. Mr Gibson completed the form contained in the brochure and sent it to the council, together with a request that he be told the purchase price of the house. The treasurer of the council wrote to inform him that the 'council may be prepared to sell the house' to him at a stated price and that if he wished to make a 'formal application' to purchase the house he should complete a further form. Mr Gibson completed the form, but he left the purchase price blank because he wished to know whether the council would repair the path to his house or whether he could deduct the cost from the purchase price. The council replied that the price had been fixed according to the condition of the property, and so allowance had been made in the price for the condition of the path. Mr Gibson accepted this and asked the council to continue with his application. The council took the house off the list of houses for which they were responsible for maintenance, and Mr Gibson carried out maintenance to the house. At this point, the Labour Party gained control of the council after the local elections and promptly discontinued the policy of selling off council houses, unless a legally binding contract had already been concluded. The council refused to sell the house to Mr Gibson because they claimed that no contract had been concluded for the sale of the house.

The trial judge and the Court of Appeal held that a contract had been concluded between the parties. Lord Denning, in a broad and sweeping judgment, held that a contract had been concluded because there was agreement between the parties on all material points, even though the precise formalities had not been gone through. The House of Lords took a different view and held that no contract had been concluded. It was held that the letter written by the treasurer, which stated that the council *may* be prepared to sell, was not an offer as it did not finally commit the council to selling the house. It was simply an expression of their willingness to enter into negotiations for the sale of the house and was not an offer which was capable of being accepted. This was further evidenced by the fact that Mr Gibson was invited to make a 'formal application' to purchase the house and not to signify his agreement to the stated terms.

The difficulty in a case such as *Gibson* arises from the fact that it is not easy to ascertain when the preliminary negotiations end and a definite offer is made. The court must examine carefully the correspondence which has passed between the parties and seek to identify from the language used and from the actions of the parties whether, in its opinion, either party objectively intended to make an offer which was capable of acceptance. *Gibson* shows that judges can and do differ in the results which they reach in this interpretative exercise and that each decision must ultimately rest on its own facts (contrast the decision of the Court of Appeal in *Storer v Manchester City Council* [1974] 1 WLR 1403, where the court held that a contract had been concluded where the negotiations had advanced beyond the stage reached in *Gibson* but had not resulted in an exchange of contracts).

In a case such as *Gibson* the court is clearly engaged in trying to ascertain the intention of the parties from the documents which have passed between them (although it should be noted that, even in *Gibson*, the case was seen as a test case for 350 other similarly placed prospective purchasers, and these purchasers would be presumed to have the same intention as Mr Gibson). There is, however, another group of cases, which concern certain standard transactions, such as advertisements and shop-window displays, where the courts are less concerned with the intention of the parties and are more concerned to establish clear rules of law to govern the particular transaction. Treitel has stated (2020, para 2-007) that:

> it may be possible to displace these rules by evidence of contrary intention, but in the absence of such evidence [these rules of law] will determine the distinction between offer and invitation to treat, and they will do so without reference to the intention (actual or even objectively ascertained) of the maker of the statement.

These situations are discussed in Sections 3.2 to 3.6.

3.2 Display of goods for sale

As a matter of principle, there are at least three different approaches which could be adopted to the display of goods for sale in a shop or supermarket. The first is to hold that the display of goods is an offer which is accepted when the goods are picked up by the prospective purchaser and put into his shopping basket. However, such a conclusion would have the undesirable consequence that a purchaser would be bound as soon as he picked up the goods and he could not change his mind and return them to the shelves without being in breach of contract. The second approach is to hold that the display of goods is an offer which is accepted when the purchaser takes the goods to the cash desk. This solution avoids the weakness of the first approach, but it has been argued that it too is undesirable. Three criticisms have been levelled against this solution. The first is that it has been argued that a shop is a place for bargaining and not for compulsory sales, and that to hold that the display of goods is an offer will take away the shopkeeper's freedom to bargain (Winfield, 1939). This argument can be countered by pointing out that, apart from second-hand shops, bargaining is not a reality in the shops of today. Goods are displayed on a 'take it or leave it' basis. If the customer is not prepared to comply with the stated terms, he can go elsewhere. Secondly, it has been argued that this conclusion is undesirable because it takes away the freedom of the shopkeeper to decide whether or not to deal with a particular customer. It would compel the shopkeeper to trade with his worst enemy. However, it is submitted that, in an era when shopping in vast superstores has become commonplace, such an argument can no longer be regarded as conclusive. Thirdly, it has been argued that to treat a display of goods as an offer might result in the vendor being bound to a series of contracts which he would be unable to fulfil (see *Partridge v Crittenden* [1968] 1 WLR 1204, discussed in Section 3.3). This objection can be countered by holding that the shopkeeper's offer is subject to the limitation that it is only capable of acceptance 'while stocks last'.

The third possible conclusion is that the display of goods constitutes an invitation to treat and that the offer is made by the customer when he presents the goods at the cash desk, where the offer may be accepted by the shopkeeper. This conclusion preserves the freedom of the shopkeeper to decide whether or not to deal with a particular customer, but it can fail adequately to protect the interests of the customer. For example, a customer who takes the goods to the cash desk may be told that the goods are in fact on sale at a higher price than the display price. In such a case the shopkeeper may be subject to criminal sanctions under the Consumer Protection from Unfair Trading Regulations 2008 (SI 2008/1277) if it has provided the consumer with misleading information as to the price or the manner in which the price is calculated. The consumer may also have a right of redress under Part 4A of the 2008 Regulations (in the form of an action for damages) but he or she is not given the right to insist that the shopkeeper sell the goods at the advertised price.

In this simple everyday situation, the rules of offer and acceptance simply do not demand that a particular conclusion be reached. Nor can the intention of the parties provide a useful guideline because, in truth, the parties often have no discernible intention one way or the other. The general rule which the courts have, in fact, adopted is that the display of goods in a shop window is an invitation to treat rather than an offer (*Fisher v Bell* [1961] 1 QB 394). The application of this rule can be seen in the case of *Pharmaceutical Society of GB v Boots Cash Chemists* [1953] 1 QB 401 (see Montrose, 1954). The defendants organised their shop on a self-service basis. They were charged with a breach of section 18(1) of the Pharmacy and Poisons Act 1933, which required that a sale of drugs take place under the supervision of a registered pharmacist. There was no pharmacist present close to the shelves, but a pharmacist supervised the transaction at the cash desk and was authorised to prevent a customer from purchasing any drug if he thought fit to do so. It was held that the sale took place at the cash desk and not when the goods were taken from the shelves; the display of the goods was simply an invitation to treat and therefore there had been no breach of the Act.

However, a rigid application of the rule established in *Boots* could lead to injustice in certain cases. An instructive example of a factual situation in which the application of the *Boots* rule may lead to injustice is provided by the American case of *Lefkowitz v Great Minneapolis Surplus Stores* 86 NW 2d 689 (1957). On two occasions the defendants placed an advertisement in a newspaper. The first advertisement stated 'Saturday 9 am sharp; 3 Brand new fur coats, worth $100; First come first served, $1 each', and the second stated 'Saturday 9 am … 1 Black Lapin Stole … worth $139.50 … $1.00; First Come, First Served'. On each of the Saturdays following publication of the advertisement the claimant was the first person in the store at 9 am, but on both occasions the defendants refused to sell the goods to him. On the first occasion the reason given was a 'house rule' that the offer was intended for women only, and on the second occasion he was informed that he knew the 'house rules'. The claimant brought a claim for damages for breach of contract. His claim in relation to the first advertisement was dismissed on the ground that the value of the fur coats was too speculative and uncertain to found a claim. But his claim for damages succeeded in relation to the second advertisement, and he was awarded damages of $138.50. The Supreme Court of Minnesota held that the advertisement was an offer and not an invitation to treat and that the defendants were not entitled to confine their offer to women only because no such restriction was explicit in the offer itself. But would an English court conclude that these advertisements constituted an offer? Some authority can be adduced for treating a display of goods as an offer; in *Chapleton v Barry UDC* [1940] 1 KB 532, it was held that the display of deck chairs for hire on a beach was an offer which was accepted by a customer taking a chair from the stack (see too *Carlill v Carbolic Smoke Ball Co* [1893] 1 QB 256, discussed in Section 3.3). But if a court were to rely on the authority of *Chapleton* would it not be because the court thought that it was unfair to leave the claimant without a remedy? Would this not be an example of what Professor Atiyah calls 'reasoning backwards'; that the court feels that the claimant ought to have a remedy and it justifies that conclusion by treating the advertisement as an offer rather than an invitation to treat?

3.3 Advertisements

The general rule is that a newspaper advertisement is an invitation to treat rather than an offer. In *Partridge v Crittenden* [1968] 1 WLR 1204, the appellant advertised Bramblefinch cocks and hens for sale at a stated price. He was charged with the offence of 'offering for sale' wild live birds contrary to the Protection of Birds Act 1954. It was held that the advertisement was an invitation to treat and not an offer, and so the appellant was acquitted. Lord Parker CJ stated that there was 'business sense' in treating such advertisements as invitations to treat because if they were treated as offers the advertiser might find himself contractually obliged to sell more goods than he in fact owned. However, as we have seen, this argument is not conclusive because it could be implied that the offer is only capable of acceptance 'while stocks last'.

Nevertheless, there are certain cases where an advertisement may be interpreted as an offer rather than an invitation to treat. The classic example is the case of *Carlill v Carbolic Smoke Ball Co* [1893] 1 QB 256. The defendants, who were the manufacturers of the carbolic smoke ball, issued an advertisement in which they offered to pay £100 to any person who caught influenza after having used one of their smoke balls in the specified manner, and they deposited £1,000 in the bank to show their good faith. The claimant caught influenza after using the smoke ball in the specified manner. She sued for the £100. It was held that the advertisement was not an invitation to treat but was an offer to the whole world and that a contract was made with those persons who performed the condition 'on the faith of the advertisement'. The claimant was therefore entitled to recover £100 (for a more modern application of the rule see *Bowerman v Association of British Travel Agents Ltd* [1996] CLC 451).

3.4 Auction sales

The general rule is that an auctioneer, by inviting bids to be made, makes an invitation to treat. The offer is made by the bidder which, in turn, is accepted when the auctioneer strikes the table with his hammer (*British Car Auctions Ltd v Wright* [1972] 1 WLR 1519). The advertisement of an auction sale is generally only an invitation to treat (*Harris v Nickerson* (1873) LR 8 QB 286). For many years, there was some uncertainty as to the effect of the addition of the words 'without reserve', that is that the auction is to take place without a reserve price. In *Warlow v Harrison* (1859) 1 E & E 309, Martin B stated *obiter* that in such a case the auctioneer makes an offer that the sale will be without reserve and that that offer is accepted by the highest bidder at the auction. It should be noted that the offer is made by the *auctioneer* and not the owner of the goods, so that there is no concluded contract of sale with the owner of the goods (unless, perhaps, the auctioneer is the agent of the vendor). This analysis was affirmed by the Court of Appeal in *Barry v Davies (Trading as Heathcote Ball & Co)* [2000] 1 WLR 1962.

The contract that comes into existence between the auctioneer and the highest bidder is a collateral contract; that is to say, it is collateral to, or separate from, the contract for the sale of the auctioned goods. The judge at first instance in *Barry*, whose decision was upheld by the Court of Appeal, analysed the nature of the relationship between the parties as follows: 'there was a collateral contract between the auctioneer and the highest bidder constituted by an offer by the auctioneer to sell to the highest bidder which was accepted when the bid was made.'

While the essential nature of the contractual relationship between the auctioneer and the highest bidder has been established, a number of issues of detail remain to be resolved. First, at what point in time is the offer made by the auctioneer? Is it when the advertisement of the auction without a reserve price is issued, or is it when the goods are actually put up for sale? This point has not been resolved by authority, and academic opinion is divided (see Gower, 1952; Slade, 1952, 1953; Scott, 2001), albeit that the balance of opinion appears to support the proposition that the offer is made when the advertisement is issued. Second, on what basis is the highest bidder to be identified if the auctioneer never brings down his hammer? The courts are likely to take a pragmatic approach to this issue and conclude that the highest bidder is the person who made the last bid before the lot was withdrawn from the sale. Third, it has been argued (Scott, 2001) that a similar analysis to that adopted in *Barry* should be employed in the case where an auction is held with a reserve price and that price is exceeded during the bidding process. In other words, once the reserve price has been reached, the auctioneer cannot withdraw the lot from the sale without incurring a liability for breach of a collateral contract to the highest bidder at the point in time at which the lot was withdrawn. This point remains to be resolved, but there is much to be said for this view.

Barry and *Warlow* may be examples of the courts reasoning backwards in that they decide that in such a case the bidder ought to have a remedy, and they then accommodate that conclusion within the offer and acceptance framework, even though the fit is somewhat uneasy.

3.5 Tenders

Where a person invites tenders for a particular project, the general rule is that the invitation to tender is simply an invitation to treat. The offer is made by the person who submits the tender, and the acceptance is made when the person inviting the tenders accepts one of them. However, in an appropriate case a court may hold that the invitation to tender was, in fact, an offer. Two cases are relevant here.

The first is *Harvela Investments Ltd v Royal Trust Co of Canada* [1986] AC 207. The first defendants decided to sell their shares by sealed competitive tender. They invited the two parties most likely to be interested in the shares each to submit a single sealed offer for their shares and stated that they would accept the highest 'offer' received by them which complied with the terms of their invitation. The claimants tendered a fixed bid of $2,175,000. The second defendant tendered a 'referential' bid of '$2,100,000 or ... $101,000 in excess of any other offer ... whichever is the higher'. The first defendants accepted the second defendant's bid, treating it as a bid of $2,276,000. But the House of Lords held that the first defendants were bound to accept the claimants' bid. It was held that the invitation to tender was an offer of a unilateral contract to sell the shares to the highest bidder, despite the fact that the invitation asked the claimants and the second defendant to submit an 'offer'. The bid submitted by the second defendant was held to be invalid because the object of the vendors' invitation was to ascertain the highest amount which each party was prepared to pay, and this purpose would be frustrated by a referential bid.

The second case is *Blackpool and Fylde Aero Club Ltd v Blackpool BC* [1990] 1 WLR 1195 and it provides us with a very good example of the flexibility which the courts have in applying the rules relating to offer and acceptance. In 1983 the defendant local authority invited tenders for a concession to operate pleasure flights from Blackpool airport. The form of tender stated that: 'the council do not bind themselves to accept all or any part of the tender. No tender which is received after the last date and time specified shall be admitted for consideration.' Tenders had to be received by the Town Clerk 'not later than 12 o'clock noon on Thursday 17 March 1983'. The claimants posted their bid in the Town Hall letter box at about 11 am on 17 March. A notice on the letter box stated that it was emptied each day at 12 o'clock noon. Unfortunately, on this particular day, the letter box was not emptied at 12 o'clock and so the claimants' bid remained in the letter box until the morning of 18 March. The claimants' bid was not considered by the council because they considered it to be a late submission, and the concession was awarded to another party. The claimants brought an action for damages for, *inter alia*, breach of contract. The obvious difficulty which they faced was that they did not appear to be in a contractual relationship with the defendants because an invitation to tender is only an invitation to treat. The claimants had therefore simply submitted an offer which the defendants had not accepted. But the Court of Appeal took a different approach. They held that the defendants were contractually obliged to consider the claimants' tender and, for breach of that obligation, they were liable in damages. The court appeared to adopt a two-contract analysis. A contract was concluded with the party whose tender was accepted, but the invitation to tender also constituted a unilateral offer to 'consider' any conforming tender which was submitted, and that offer was accepted by any party who submitted such a tender. It is suggested that there are two problems with this approach.

The first lies in ascertaining the circumstances in which a court will see fit to imply an offer to consider all tenders submitted. The council did not expressly accept an obligation to consider conforming tenders, yet the court saw fit to imply such a duty. Indeed, the court had to imply both a contract and its terms because the parties were not otherwise in a contractual relationship. The Court of Appeal relied upon a number of factors, none of which appear to be conclusive. The first was that the invitation to tender was directed to a small number of interested parties; the second was that the duty to consider was alleged to be consistent with the intention of the parties; finally, the court stated that the tender procedure was 'clear, orderly and familiar' and, the greater the precision, the easier it is for a court to spell out an offer which is capable of acceptance. But were there other factors of importance? Was there any significance in the fact that the defendants were a local authority (and so owed a fiduciary duty to ratepayers to act with reasonable prudence in their financial affairs) or in the fact that the claimants were the existing holders of the concession and so may be said to have had a legitimate expectation of being considered? The answer to these questions remains unclear. In each case, the court must decide whether the parties intended to initiate contractual relations by the submission of a bid in response to the invitation to tender. There is no automatic rule that an invitation to tender triggers a contractual obligation to consider bids submitted, although the courts may be relatively willing to imply such an obligation where there is a formal tendering process involving complex documentation and terms which must be complied with by the tenderers (see *MJB Enterprises Ltd v Defence Construction (1951) Ltd* (1999) 170 DLR (4th) 577). In *Pratt Contractors Ltd v Transit NZ* [2003] UKPC 33 the preliminary contract imposed on the party inviting the tenders an implied duty to act fairly and in good faith. The latter duty required the party inviting the tenders to express views honestly and to treat all parties who submit a tender equally, but it did not require that party to act judicially by, for example, giving a hearing to parties who submitted a tender. A party issuing an invitation to tender who does not want to be subject to an obligation to consider bids made or to act fairly and in good faith would be well advised to say so expressly in the invitation to tender.

The second difficulty lies in determining the scope of this 'duty to consider'. Bingham LJ stated that the duty would have been breached had the defendants 'opened and thereupon accepted the first tender received, even though the deadline had not expired and other invitees had not yet responded' or if they 'had considered and accepted a tender admittedly received well after the deadline'. Could the defendants have rejected all the tenders? It would appear so. Stocker LJ stated that the obligation to consider 'would not preclude or inhibit the council from deciding not to accept any tender or to award the concession, provided the decision was *bona fide* and honest, to any tenderer'. So the obligation to consider tenders submitted does not preclude a local authority from removing a contractor from the tendering process when it discovers that there is a conflict of interest between a senior council employee and one of the tenderers (see *Fairclough Building Ltd v Port Talbot BC* (1993) 62 Build LR 82).

Finally, this two-contract analysis may have implications for those who submit tenders, as can be seen from the Canadian case of *R in Right of Ontario v Ron Engineering & Construction Eastern Ltd* (1981) 119 DLR (3d) 267. The defendants invited tenders on the basis that tenders had to be accompanied by a deposit which was to be forfeited if the tender was withdrawn or if the tenderer otherwise refused to proceed. The claimants discovered, shortly after the tenders were opened, that they had made a mistake in the submission of their tender and they refused to proceed with the execution of the contract documents. They sued to recover their deposit of $150,000. It was held that they were not entitled to recover because the invitation to tender followed by the submission of a tender created a contract, the terms of which were that the claimants were not entitled to recover their deposit if they refused to proceed with the contract. There is, as yet, no English case on this point, but it is suggested that, in the light of the *Blackpool* case, an English court might reach the same conclusion.

3.6   Time-tables and vending machines

It is remarkable how difficult it is to distinguish between an offer and an invitation to treat in many everyday transactions. One simple example is boarding a bus. One could say that the bus time-table and the running of the bus are an offer by the bus company which is accepted by boarding the bus (although it should be noted that most time-tables contain express disclaimers of any obligation to provide the services contained in the time-table). Such was the view of Lord Greene in *Wilkie v London Transport Board* [1947] 1 All ER 258, when he stated that the offer was made by the bus company and that it was accepted when a passenger 'puts himself either on the platform or inside the bus'. Alternatively, it could be said that the acceptance takes place when the passenger asks for a ticket and pays the fare. A further possibility is to say that the bus time-table is an invitation to treat, the offer is made by the passenger in boarding the bus, and the acceptance takes place when the bus conductor accepts the money and issues a ticket. Finally, it could be said that the bus conductor makes the offer when he issues the ticket, and this offer is accepted by paying the fare and retaining the ticket.

In many ways the issue may seem to be an academic one, devoid of any practical consequence. But this is not the case. It has serious consequences if, for example, there is an exclusion clause contained on the back of the ticket (see further Chapter 11). If the first analysis is adopted, then the exclusion clause is not part of the contract because the contract is concluded before the ticket is handed over. On the other hand, if the final alternative is adopted, then the exclusion clause is part of the contract because it is contained in the offer made by the conductor. A court might adopt the first of these alternatives in our exclusion clause example in order to protect the passenger, but would it also apply where the same passenger boards the bus by mistake and wishes to get off the bus before it moves from the stop without paying for his fare? As Treitel has stated (2020, para 2-012), the cases 'yield no single rule' and all that can be said is that 'the exact time of contracting depends in each case on the wording of the relevant document and on the circumstances in which it was issued'.

Other everyday examples could be provided which defy simple classification. What is the status of a menu outside a restaurant? What about a vending machine selling tea and coffee? The former is probably an invitation to treat but, in *Thornton v Shoe Lane Parking Ltd* [1971] 2 QB 163, Lord Denning stated that an automatic machine which issued tickets outside a car park made a standing offer which was accepted by a motorist driving so far into the car park that the machine issued him with a ticket.

3.7   Acceptance

An acceptance is an unqualified expression of assent to the terms proposed by the offeror. There is no rule that acceptance must be made by words; it can be made by conduct, as was the case in *Carlill v Carbolic Smoke Ball Co* [1893] 1 QB 256 (see Section 3.3). While it is clear that conduct can, in an appropriate case, amount to acceptance, it may be difficult to pinpoint the precise point in time at which the conduct is sufficient to evidence the existence of a contract. This difficulty tends not to arise where the contract is formed by an exchange of promises (in which case the point of entry into the contract can usually be identified with some precision). But, in the case where acceptance is said to take the form of conduct, some steps may be said to be preparatory to the conclusion of the contract rather than evidence of its existence. In all cases the courts must examine the evidence with care to determine whether the conduct relied upon does amount to an acceptance such as to create a contract between the parties (*Reveille Independent LLC v Anotech International (UK) Ltd* [2016] EWCA Civ 443; 116 Con LR 79, [46]). Conduct will only amount to an acceptance if it is clear that the offeree did the act in question with the intention, objectively assessed, of accepting the offer (*Day Morris Associates v Voyce* [2003] EWCA Civ 189; [2003] All ER (D) 368 (Feb)). The word 'clear' is important in this context given that conduct must be 'unequivocal' if it is to amount to an acceptance (*Aroca Seiquer & Asociados v Adams* [2018] EWCA Civ 1589; [2018] PNLR 32, [33]). What the courts are looking for is 'final and unqualified' assent to the terms of the offer. This is most straightforwardly evidenced by use of the word 'accept' or 'acceptance'. However, there is no formal need for the use of such words provided that the court can discern from the evidence a final and unqualified expression of assent to the terms of the offer. Nor does the law require that expression of assent to refer to each and every term of the offer. Once the court is satisfied on the evidence that there has been acceptance by conduct that acceptance will extend to all of the terms of the offer (*Arcadis Consulting (UK) Ltd v AMEC (BCS) Ltd* [2018] EWCA Civ 2222; [2019] BLR 27, [91] – [93]). This being the case, a party who does not wish to accept a particular term of the offer should say so in express terms because otherwise there is a risk that the court will infer that it has accepted all of the terms of the offer.

A purported acceptance which does not accept all the terms and conditions proposed by the offeror but which in fact introduces new terms is not an acceptance but a counter-offer, which is then treated as a new offer which is capable of acceptance or rejection. The effect of a counter-offer is to 'kill off' the original offer so that it cannot subsequently be accepted by the offeree. This rule can be seen in operation in the case of *Hyde v Wrench* (1840) 3 Beav 334. The defendant offered to sell some land to the claimant for £1,000 and the claimant replied by offering to purchase the land for £950. The defendant refused to sell for £950. So the claimant then wrote to the defendant agreeing to pay the £1,000 but the defendant still refused to sell. It was held that there was no contract between the parties. The claimant's offer of £950 was a counter-offer which killed off the defendant's original offer so as to render it incapable of subsequent acceptance. It is this rule that acceptance must be unqualified which has given rise to difficulties in the battle of the forms cases, such as *Butler v Ex-Cell-O Corp (England) Ltd* [1979] 1 WLR 401 (see Section 2.4).

3.8   Communication of the acceptance

The general rule is that an acceptance must be communicated to the offeror. The acceptance is generally only validly communicated when it is actually brought to the attention of the offeror. The operation of this rule was illustrated by Denning

LJ in *Entores v Miles Far East Corp* [1955] 2 QB 327. He said that if an oral acceptance is drowned out by an overflying aircraft, such that the offeror cannot hear the acceptance, then there is no contract unless the acceptor repeats his acceptance once the aircraft has passed over. Similarly, where two people make a contract by telephone, and the line goes 'dead' so that the acceptance is incomplete, then the acceptor must telephone the offeror to make sure that he has heard the acceptance. Where, however, the acceptance is made clearly and audibly, but the offeror does not hear what is said, a contract is nevertheless concluded unless the offeror makes clear to the acceptor that he has not heard what was said. In the case of instantaneous communication, such as telephone and telex, the acceptance takes place at the moment the acceptance is received by the offeror and at the place at which the offeror happens to be (see *Brinkibon Ltd v Stahag Stahl* [1983] 2 AC 34). The rule, as it applies to instantaneous communications, is easy to state but it can give rise to difficulties in practice when seeking to decide when or where a contract was concluded. As Lord Sumption observed in *Brownlie v Four Seasons Holdings Inc* [2017] UKSC 80; [2018] 1 WLR 192, [16] 'serious practical difficulties' can arise because the 'analysis of an informal conversation in terms of invitation to treat, offer and acceptance will often be impossible without a recording or a total recall of the sequence of exchanges and the exact words used at each stage, in order to establish points which are unlikely to have been of any importance to either party at the time.' Notwithstanding such occasional practical difficulties, English law continues to adhere to the rules as set out by Denning LJ in *Entores*.

3.9 Acceptance in ignorance of the offer

An offer is effective when it is communicated to the offeree. This requirement generally does not give rise to problems, but difficulty does arise in the following type of case. X offers £100 for the safe return of his missing dog. Y returns the dog but is unaware of X's offer. Is Y entitled to the money? A good argument can be made out to the effect that Y should be entitled to the money. X has got what he wanted, and there seems no reason in justice why he should not be required to pay what he has publicly promised to pay. At the same time Y has performed a socially useful act in returning the dog, and he should be rewarded for so doing. On the other hand, in the case of a bilateral contract which imposes mutual obligations upon the parties, the effect of such a rule would be to subject the 'accepting' party to obligations of which he was unaware. For example, if X offered to sell the dog for £50 to the first person who returned it to him, Y, who returns the dog, unaware of the offer, should not thereby be held to have accepted an offer to purchase the dog for £50. In the light of these considerations it has been argued that the best approach to adopt is to hold that knowledge of the offer is not necessary in the reward type of case but that knowledge should be required in the case of bilateral contracts (Hudson, 1968).

However, the rule which has been adopted in England is that a person who, in ignorance of the offer, performs the act or acts requested by the offeror is not entitled to sue as on a contract. The case of *Gibbons v Proctor* (1891) 64 LT 594, which was thought to stand for the contrary proposition, appears on closer examination of the facts to be a case where the person claiming the reward knew of the offer at the time when the information was given to the police (Treitel, 2020, para 2-049). It is here that we see the importance of the schematic approach to agreement. It is not suffi-cient to show that the parties were, at some moment in time, in agreement. There must be a definite offer which is mirrored by a definite acceptance. For the same reason, cross-offers which are identical do not create a contract unless or until they are accepted (*Tinn v Hoffman & Co* (1873) 29 LT 271). These cases reinforce the point made in Chapter 2 that contract law adopts an objective rather than a subjective approach to agreement and therefore the fact that the parties are subjectively agreed is not conclusive evidence that the parties have entered into a contract (contrast the view of Spencer discussed at Section 2.2).

Once it is shown that the offer has been communicated to the other party, a person who knows of the offer may do the act required for acceptance with some motive other than that of accepting the offer (*Williams v Carwardine* (1833) 4 B & Ad 621, on which see Mitchell and Phillips, 2002). But the offer must have been present to his mind when he did the act which is said to constitute the acceptance. Thus, in *R v Clarke* (1927) 40 CLR 227, where the party claiming the reward had forgotten about the offer of a reward at the time he gave the information, it was held that he was not entitled to the reward.

3.10 Prescribed method of acceptance

Where the offeror prescribes a specific method of acceptance, the general rule is that the offeror is not bound unless the terms of his offer are complied with. However, the offeror who wishes to state that he will be bound *only* if the offer is accepted in a particular way must use clear words to achieve this purpose. Where the offeror has not used sufficiently clear words, a court will hold the offeror bound by an acceptance which is made in a form which is no less advantageous to him than the form which he prescribed. This can be seen in the case of *Manchester Diocesan Council for Education v Commercial and General Investments Ltd* [1969] 3 All ER 1593. The claimant decided to sell some property by tender and inserted a clause in the form of tender stating that the person whose bid was accepted would be informed by means of a letter sent to the address given in the tender. The defendant completed the form of tender and sent it to the claimant. The claimant decided to accept the defendant's tender and sent a letter of acceptance to the defendant's surveyor but not to the address on the tender. It was held that communication to the address in the tender was not the sole permitted means of communication of acceptance and that therefore a valid contract had been concluded. The defendant was not disad-vantaged in any way by notification being given to its surveyor and, in any case, the stipulation had been inserted by the claimant, not the defendant, and so it was open to the claimant to waive strict compliance with the term, provided that the defend-ant was not adversely affected thereby.

3.11 Acceptance by silence

The general rule is that acceptance of an offer will not be implied from mere silence on the part of the offeree and that an offeror cannot impose a contractual obligation upon the offeree by stating that, unless the latter expressly rejects the offer, he will be held to have accepted it. The rationale behind this rule is that it is thought to be unfair to put an offeree to time and expense to avoid the imposition of unwanted contractual arrangements. The principal English authority on this point is *Felthouse v Bindley* (1862) 11 CB (NS) 869. The claimant and his nephew entered into negotiations for the sale of the nephew's horse. The claimant stated that if he heard nothing further from his nephew then he considered that the horse was his at a price of £30 15s. The nephew did not respond to this offer but he decided to accept it and told the defendant auctioneer not to sell the horse because it had already been sold. Nevertheless, the auctioneer mistakenly sold the horse, and so the claimant sued the auctioneer in conversion (a tort claim in which it is alleged that the defendant has dealt with goods in a manner inconsistent with the rights of the true owner). The auctioneer argued that the claimant had no title to sue because he was not the owner of the horse as his offer to buy the horse had not been accepted by his nephew. This argument was upheld by the court on the ground that the nephew's silence did not amount to an acceptance of the offer. The application of the general rule to the facts of *Felthouse v Bindley* has been the subject of criticism on the ground that the uncle had waived the need for communication of the acceptance, and the nephew had manifested his acceptance by informing the auctioneer that the horse had been sold (see Miller, 1972).

But the rule that acceptance of an offer will not be implied from mere silence has not emerged unscathed from a line of cases represented by *The Hannah Blumenthal* (see Section 2.1), where the House of Lords held that a contract to abandon a reference to arbitration could be concluded by the silence of both parties.

As Bingham J noted in *Cie Française d'Importation et de Distribution SA v Deutsche Continental Handelsgesellschaft* [1985] 2 Lloyd's Rep 592, 599, this line of authority does:

> some violence ... to familiar rules of contract such as the requirement that acceptance of an offer should be communicated to the offeror unless the requirement of communication is expressly or impliedly waived.

But no case actually sought to overrule or to question explicitly the correctness of *Felthouse v Bindley*, and the reasoning in the arbitration cases was distorted by the fact that neither arbitrators nor courts had, at common law, the power to dismiss an arbitration for want of prosecution and so the courts were asked to employ any common law doctrine which appeared even remotely suitable to enable them to reach a commercially just solution, namely that the agreement to arbitrate had been abandoned. Now that Parliament has intervened in the form of section 41(3) of the Arbitration Act 1996 and given to arbitrators the power to dismiss a claim for want of prosecution, the courts no longer need to engage in such subterfuge, nor to distort the rules relating to offer and acceptance (see *The Amazonia* [1990] 1 Lloyd's Rep 236, 243).

Instead, it is submitted that these arbitration cases remind us that the rule that silence does not amount to an acceptance is not an absolute one: 'our law does in exceptional cases recognise acceptance of an offer by silence' (*Vitol SA v Norelf Ltd* [1996] AC 800, 810, per Lord Steyn citing the case of *Rust v Abbey Life Assurance Co Ltd* [1979] 2 Lloyd's Rep 334). For example, a course of dealing between the parties may give rise to the inference that silence amounts to acceptance. It is also unclear whether the general rule will apply where the offeree assumes that his silence has been effective to conclude a contract and then acts in reliance upon that belief. It is suggested that, in such a case, the general rule should give way and a court should hold that a contract has been concluded between the parties (see Miller, 1972, although it is very difficult to reconcile this proposition with *Felthouse v Bindley*). As we have noted, the purpose behind the general rule is to protect the offeree and therefore it should not apply where its application would cause hardship to the offeree. However, where the offeree only mentally assents to the offer but does not act in reliance upon it, it is suggested that the general rule should apply, because otherwise the offeree would be able to speculate against the offeror, by stating that he had accepted the offer when the contract was a good one for him and by stating that he had not accepted it when the contract turned out to be a bad one. Therefore it is submitted that some positive action is required on the part of the offeree to provide evidence that he has in fact accepted the offer.

3.12 Exceptions to the rule requiring communication of acceptance

The rule that acceptance must be communicated to the offeror is not absolute. For example, the terms of the offer may demonstrate that the offeror does not insist that the acceptance be communicated to him (*Carlill v Carbolic Smoke Ball Co* [1893] 1 QB 256, see Section 3.3). The offeror may be prevented by his conduct from arguing that the acceptance was communicated to him (*Entores v Miles Far East Corp* [1955] 2 QB 327, see Section 3.8). But the major and most controversial exception relates to acceptances sent through the post.

As a matter of theory, any of a number of possible solutions could be used to ascertain when an acceptance sent by post takes effect. It could be when the letter is posted, when it reaches the address of the offeror, when it is read by the offeror or when, in the ordinary course of the post, it would reach the offeror. The general rule which English law has adopted can be traced back to *Adams v Lindsell* (1818) 1 B & Ald 681, which is now understood to stand for the proposition that acceptance takes place when the letter of acceptance is posted by the offeree.

3.12.1 What are the justifications cited in support of the postal rule?

However, the justifications put forward in support of this rule are, to say the least, rather tenuous (see Gardner, 1992). The first justification is that the Post Office is the agent of the offeror, and so receipt of the letter by the agent is equivalent to receipt by the offeror. This justification is open to the criticism that it cannot be said in any meaningful sense that the Post Office is the agent of the offeror because the Post Office has no power to contract on behalf of the offeror. The second justification is that the offeror has chosen to start negotiations through the post, and so the risk of delay or loss in the post should be imposed upon him. However, it is not necessarily the case that the offeror must have started the negotiations through the post. It could be the case that the offeree initiated negotiations through the post by asking the offeror for the terms on which he was prepared to do business. Nevertheless, it must be conceded that this justification has some element of validity because, in *Henthorn v Fraser* [1892] 2 Ch 27, it was held that the postal rule only applies where it is reasonable to use the post. However, it is reasonable to use the post where the parties

live at a distance from each other; it is not necessary for the offeror to have commenced the negotiations by post. So it is not entirely true to say that the offeror has
accepted the risk of delay in the post. A more promising justification is that the
offeree should not be prejudiced once he has dispatched his acceptance and he
should be able to rely on the efficacy of his acceptance. This argument is a strong
one, but it could be met by providing that, once the acceptance has been posted, the
offeror can no longer revoke his offer; it does not demand that the acceptance be
treated as taking effect when it is dispatched. In fact, the explanation for the initial
adoption of the rule may lie in the public perception of the postal service in the middle of the nineteenth century (Gardner, 1992). The uniform penny post was introduced in 1837. At around the same time postage began to be prepaid rather than
paid for on receipt, and the cutting of letter boxes in doors meant that a letter need
no longer be handed to the addressee individually. These factors, Gardner argues,
meant that the public perception of the time was that a letter, once posted, would
reach its destination 'without further subvention from outside the system' and that
this led to the 'notional equation of the posting of a letter with its delivery'. In the
modern world, this perception seems ridiculous: with the advent of truly instantaneous means of communication, the idea that posting is equivalent to delivery is not
credible. This may help explain why it was that the judiciary in the late nineteenth
century (in cases such as *Byrne v Van Tienhoven* (1880) 5 CPD 344, see Section 3.14)
began to confine the postal rule within narrow limits. As quicker methods of communication, such as the telephone, were developed, so the equation of posting with
delivery began to look increasingly anomalous. Indeed, on this basis it can be said
that the postal rule is now 'something of a museum piece', continuing to exist in a
world which bears no relationship to the world in which the rule was introduced
and therefore serving a purpose which is entirely different from the one intended by
those who initially adopted and developed the rule.

Not only are the justifications for the general rule weak, but the operation of the
rule can give rise to manifest injustice. Take the following example. X makes an offer
to Y and states that it will be open for acceptance until 5 pm on Friday. Applying the
general rule, Y may validly 'accept' that offer by posting his acceptance at 4.45 pm on
Friday afternoon, even though it will not reach X until Monday or Tuesday of the following week. It is true that X could avoid such hardship by stating in his offer that the
acceptance must *reach* him by 5 pm on Friday (see below) but the fact that the parties
can contract out of the general rule is no justification for the general rule itself.

3.12.2   Practical difficulties created by the current rule

In addition to creating injustice, the general rule gives rise to practical difficulties.
Two such difficulties will be dealt with here. The first arises where the letter of
acceptance is lost in the post. A logical application of the general rule leads to the
result that a contract has been concluded because the acceptance takes effect when
it is posted and not when it reaches the offeror. This was held to be the case in
England in *Household Fire Insurance v Grant* (1879) 4 Ex D 217. But in Scotland, this
view was rejected by Lord Shand in *Mason v Benhar Coal Co* (1882) 9 R 883. He stated
that, in his opinion, no contract came into existence when the acceptance was posted
but never reached the offeror. It is suggested that the latter rule is the preferable one

because it is the offeree who has sent the acceptance, and so he is in the best position to know when his acceptance is likely to reach the offeror and to take steps to check that it does so reach the offeror. Nevertheless, English law is presently committed to the view that a contract is concluded on the posting of the letter of acceptance even where it gets lost in the post. However, where the reason for the loss of the letter is that it has been incorrectly addressed by the offeree, acceptance will not take place on posting because, while the offeror may take the risk of delay or loss in the post, he does not take the further risk of carelessness by the offeree (*Korbetis v Transgrain Shipping BV* [2005] EWHC 1345 (QB) at [15]).

The second practical difficulty arises where the offeree posts his acceptance and then sends a rejection by a quicker method so that the rejection reaches the offeror before the acceptance. Once again, a logical application of the general rule leads to the result that the contract was concluded when the letter of acceptance was posted, and so the subsequent communication is not a revocation of the offer but a breach of contract, which may be accepted or rejected by the offeror. But it can be argued that it would be absurd to hold that a contract has been concluded when both parties have relied on the fact that there was no contract (although in such a case it could be argued that both parties have entered into a second contract under which they agreed to abandon their rights and obligations under the first contract). On the other hand, it can be argued that to hold that the contract was not concluded when the letter of acceptance was posted allows the offeree to speculate at the offeror's expense by sending a rejection by a faster means where the contract turns out to be a bad one for him. It is unclear which of these approaches will be adopted in English law (for contrasting views, see the Scottish case *Countess of Dunmore v Alexander* (1830) 9 S 190 and the South African case *A to Z Bazaars (Pty) Ltd v Minister of Agriculture* (1974) 4 SA 392).

3.12.3 The limits of the postal rule, its exceptions and some comparative reflections

Given these practical difficulties to which the general rule gives rise, it is no surprise to find that the postal rule is subject to some limitations. In the first place, as we have seen, it must have been reasonable for the offeree to use the post (see *Henthorn v Fraser* (above)). Secondly, the offeror can avoid the operation of the rule by stating that the acceptance will only be effective when it actually reaches him. Thirdly, it is interesting to note that the rule has not been adopted in many other cases where the parties are not dealing face-to-face. Thus, in *Entores v Miles Far East Corp* (above) it was held that the postal rule did not apply to telexes and that it was confined to non-instantaneous forms of communication. Therefore, a distinction is drawn between instantaneous and non-instantaneous forms of communication; only the latter being caught by the postal rule. Many forms of communication in the modern world, such as email, will qualify as instantaneous and so will not be governed by the postal rule (see, for example, *Thomas v BPE Solicitors (a firm)* [2010] EWHC 306 (Ch); [2010] All ER (D) 306 (Feb), *Greenclose Ltd v National Westminster Bank plc* [2014] EWHC 1156 (Ch); [2014] 2 Lloyd's Rep 169, [138] and, more generally, Nolan, 2010). The widest exception to the general rule was recognised in *Holwell Securities Ltd v Hughes* [1974] 1 WLR 155, where it was suggested that the postal rule ought not to apply 'where it would lead to manifest inconvenience and absurdity'.

The width of the latter exception illustrates the weakness of the arguments which have been put forward to support the general rule but, rather than recognise that it is the general rule which is the source of the problem, the English courts have chosen to widen the scope of the exceptions to the general rule. It is submitted that the better approach would be to abolish the general rule and replace it with the normal rule that acceptance takes place when the acceptance is received by the offeror, subject to the qualification that the offeror cannot revoke the offer once the acceptance has been posted (see, for example, Articles 16(1) and 18(2) of the United Nations Convention on Contracts for the International Sale of Goods, more commonly known as the Vienna Convention, and Articles 2:202(1) and 2:205(1) of the Principles of European Contract Law).

3.13   Acceptance in unilateral contracts

A unilateral contract is a contract whereby one party promises to pay to the other a sum of money or to do some act if that other party will do or refrain from doing something without making a promise to that effect. Classic examples are the reward cases or *Carlill v Carbolic Smoke Ball Co* [1893] 1 QB 256 (see Section 3.3). The effect of classifying a contract as unilateral rather than bilateral is that acceptance can be made by fully performing the requested act; there is no need to give advance notification of acceptance. The principal difficulty lies in determining when the offer can be withdrawn, which, in turn, depends upon when the offer has been 'accepted'. For example, X offers Y £10,000 if Y will walk from London to Newcastle. Does Y accept the offer when he expresses an intention to accept the offer, when he reaches York or only when he gets to Newcastle? The general rule which English law has adopted was described by Goff LJ in *Daulia Ltd v Four Millbank Nominees Ltd* [1978] Ch 231, in the following terms:

> Whilst I think the true view of a unilateral contract must in general be that the offeror is entitled to require full performance of the condition which he has imposed and short of that he is not bound, that must be subject to one important qualification, which stems from the fact that there must be an implied obligation on the part of the offeror not to prevent the condition becoming satisfied, which obligation it seems to me must arise as soon as the offeree starts to perform.

The willingness of the courts to imply an obligation not to 'prevent the condition becoming satisfied' can be seen by contrasting the following two cases. The first is *Errington v Errington* [1952] 1 KB 290. A father bought a house for £750 and took out a mortgage for £500. His son and daughter-in-law moved into the house, and the father stated that if they paid off the mortgage the house was theirs. The couple moved into the house and began to pay off the mortgage, without promising to continue with the payments. The father died, and the father's personal representatives sought to revoke the arrangement. The Court of Appeal held that they could not do so because the 'father's promise was a unilateral contract', which could not be revoked once the couple had embarked upon performance provided that they did not leave performance 'incomplete and unperformed' (see also *Soulsbury v Soulsbury* [2008] EWCA Civ 969; [2008] Fam 1, [49]–[50]).

On the other hand, a different result was reached in the case of *Luxor (Eastbourne) Ltd v Cooper* [1941] AC 108. The claimant agreed with the defendants that if he introduced a purchaser who would buy the defendants' two cinemas for at least £185,000 each, he would be paid a commission. The claimant succeeded in introducing to the defendants a purchaser who was ready and willing to complete the purchase, but the defendants refused to proceed with the sale. It was held that the claimant was not entitled to the commission because it was only payable on completion of the sale. The House of Lords refused to imply a term that the defendants would do nothing to prevent the claimant from earning his commission, because it was contrary to the common understanding of the parties which was that the claimant took 'the risk in the hope of a substantial remuneration for a comparatively small exertion'.

3.14 Termination of the offer

There are five principal methods by which an offer may be terminated. The first is that the offer may be withdrawn. An offer can be withdrawn by the offeror at any time before it has been accepted. However, to withdraw an offer the notice of withdrawal must actually be brought to the attention of the offeree. There is no requirement that the offeror himself must be the one to bring the withdrawal to the attention of the offeree. Thus, in *Dickinson v Dodds* (1876) 2 Ch D 463, the defendant offered to sell a house to the claimant for £800, the offer to be left open until Friday. On Thursday the defendant sold the house to a third party, and the claimant was informed of this by another third party. Nevertheless, the claimant sent the defendant his letter of acceptance on the Friday. It was held that no contract had been concluded between the parties because the offer had been withdrawn before it was accepted (for critical evaluation of the case see Gilmore, 1974).

The rule that the withdrawal must be brought to the attention of the offeree has odd effects in relation to offers sent through the post. This can be seen in the case of *Byrne v Van Tienhoven* (1880) 5 CPD 344. The defendants sent the claimants an offer on 1 October 1879. This offer was received by the claimants on 11 October, and they sent off an immediate acceptance. However, in the meantime, the defendants had sent, on 8 October, a letter revoking their offer, which reached the claimants on 20 October. It was held that a contract was concluded between the parties on 11 October. To be effective the withdrawal must be drawn to the attention of the other party and, for this purpose, the postal rule does not apply, so that the revocation only takes effect when it actually reaches the other party. So the purported withdrawal could not take effect until 20 October but, by that time, a contract had already been concluded, and the withdrawal was therefore too late. This case is a good example of the objective approach which the courts adopt to the issue of agreement, because at no time were the parties actually subjectively agreed; by the time the claimants accepted the offer on 11 October, the defendants had already dispatched their 'withdrawal' of the offer.

Although it is clear that the revocation must be brought to the attention of the offeree, it is not entirely clear when the revocation is treated as being brought to his attention. It could be when the letter reaches his business, or it could be when he actually reads it. There is no clear English authority on this point, although in *The Brimnes* [1975] QB 929, the Court of Appeal held that, in the case of a notice of withdrawal of a vessel sent by telex during ordinary business hours, the withdrawal was effective when it was received on the telex machine. There was no requirement that it actually be read by any particular person within the organisation.

Secondly, an offer can be terminated by a rejection by the offeree. We have already seen how a rejection or a counter-offer has the effect of 'killing off' the original offer (*Hyde v Wrench* (see Section 3.7)).

Thirdly, an offer may be terminated by lapse of time. An offer which is expressly stated to last only for a specific period of time cannot be accepted after that date. An offer which specifies no time limit is deemed to last for a reasonable period of time.

Fourthly, an offer which is stated to come to an end if a certain event occurs cannot be accepted after that event has actually taken place.

Finally, an offer may be terminated by the death of the offeror, although the law is not entirely clear on this point. On one view, it could be said that death always terminates an offer because the parties cannot enter into an agreement once one of the parties is dead. However, it seems to be the case that an offeree cannot accept an offer once he knows that the offeror has died but that his acceptance may be valid if it is made in ignorance of the fact that the offeror has died, provided that the contract is not one for the performance of personal services. There is no authority on the position where it is the offeree who dies. The generally accepted view is that on the offeree's death the offer comes to an end by operation of law.

3.15 The limits of offer and acceptance

We have noted at various points in this chapter how difficult it is to fit many everyday transactions within the offer and acceptance framework. Simple examples which give rise to difficulty are boarding a bus, buying goods in a supermarket and making a contract through the post. The battle of the forms poses difficulties for the businessman. These difficulties have led some commentators to doubt the utility of the offer and acceptance model. It is true that there are difficulties with the offer and acceptance model, but these problems are often experienced because of the tension between the court's wish to give effect to the intention of the parties, their desire to achieve a just result on the facts of the case and the need to establish a clear rule which can be applied to all such cases in the future.

Some commentators argue that there is too much uncertainty within the present law. Certainty is an extremely important commodity in the law of contract. A greater degree of certainty could be provided by adopting legislative formulae to prescribe solutions for difficult and uncertain areas, such as the battle of the forms. An example of this approach is Article 19 of the Vienna Convention on Contracts for the International Sale of Goods, which provides that:

1. A reply to an offer which purports to be an acceptance but contains additions, limitations or other modifications is a rejection of the offer and constitutes a counter-offer.
2. However, a reply to an offer which purports to be an acceptance but contains additional or different terms which do not materially alter the terms of the offer constitutes an acceptance, unless the offeror, without undue delay, objects orally to the discrepancy or dispatches a notice to that effect. If he does not so object, the terms of the contract are the terms of the offer with the modifications contained in the acceptance.
3. Additional or different terms relating, among other things, to the price, payment, quality and quantity of the goods, place and time of delivery, extent of one party's liability to the other or the settlement of disputes are considered to alter the terms of the offer materially.

This type of approach seeks to achieve a solution which is practical, without being excessively rigid, and which is easy to apply. Yet Article 19 in turn has been criticised for being uncertain (see Vergne, 1985). For example, is any alteration proposed by the offeree an 'addition, limitation or other modification' or does some form of *de minimis* rule apply? Secondly, although the definition of 'materially' in paragraph (3) is helpful, it is clearly not exhaustive, but it is unclear how much further it goes. It is important to note that none of the many legislative solutions proposed for battle of the forms cases has escaped criticism (see McKendrick, 1988). The variety of battle of the forms cases is such that no single formula can provide an acceptable solution to all possible cases (another attempt to resolve the problem is to be found in Articles 2:208 and 2:209 of the Principles of European Contract Law). Absolute certainty of this type is unattainable because the intentions of parties vary too widely. It is submitted that English law is unlikely to be improved by the adoption of such formulae, which will still give rise to some uncertainty but at a price of an unacceptable level of rigidity.

Other commentators argue that the present rules can give rise to injustice in certain cases. This could be ameliorated by the adoption of Lord Denning's general approach in *Butler v Ex-Cell-O Corp (England) Ltd* [1979] 1 WLR 401 but, as we have noted (see Section 2.4), the general approach has its own problems because it gives rise to so much uncertainty.

It is submitted that the present law strikes a reasonable balance between the need for certainty and the desire to achieve a just result which is consistent with the intention of the parties. The offer and acceptance model has a core of well-established rules which are understood by lawyers and which are capable of being understood by the business community. At the same time, the model is applied with some degree of flexibility by the courts so that a conclusion can be reached which is consistent with the intention of the parties. The present state of the law cannot be said to be entirely satisfactory, but it is better than a system which imposes an unacceptable level of rigidity or a system which creates an unacceptable level of uncertainty.

Hot topic 3...

How is a contract concluded when parties enter into a transaction by email? The courts will look for an offer matched by a corresponding acceptance. So the first question to ask is whether the initial email was an offer or an invitation to treat. The answer to that question will depend upon the terms of the email, in particular whether it is drafted in sufficiently definite terms to amount to an offer. Assuming that it is held to be an offer, the next question is whether or not that offer has been accepted. To constitute an acceptance, it must mirror the terms of the offer and be communicated to the offeror. Whether or not the response mirrors the terms of the offer will depend upon a careful evaluation of the two emails. More difficult is the time at which the acceptance is communicated to the offeror. Is it when the email is sent or when it is received? The general rule requires communication of the acceptance which suggests that the appropriate time is the time of receipt, not the time of sending. On the other hand, an application of the postal rule would lead to the conclusion that the critical time is the time at which it was sent. However, it is unlikely that the English courts would apply the postal rule in this context, preferring the view that an exchange by email is to be equated with instantaneous communication so that acceptance takes place on receipt, not on sending (*Thomas v BPE Solicitors (a firm)* [2010] EWHC 306 (Ch)).

However, to state that the acceptance takes place on 'receipt' of the email does not answer all of the problems. Rather, it gives rise to a different problem, namely identifying the point in time at which the email is to be regarded as having been 'received'. In *Greenclose Ltd v National Westminster Bank plc* [2014] EWHC 1156 (Ch); [2014] 2 Lloyd's Rep 169, [132], Andrews J stated that

> 'The time at which an email is received is difficult to ascertain and is a recipe for argument – does one count receipt on the server, or receipt in the inbox? What if the recipient has a desktop computer and a handheld device such as a mobile phone to which emails are routed? Is the email received when it is loaded onto the first device or the second? What happens if the message is filtered out and never arrives but does not "bounce back"?'

She continued (at [137])

> 'If the parties are in an ongoing trading relationship where notices are routinely served by a particular method, such as a telex or fax, it makes sense to conclude that such a notice will be served when it is available to be read or seen during normal office hours. There may be many contexts in which a court would have no hesitation in deciding that an email was "received" when it was received on the other party's computer within ordinary business hours, or "delivered" when it is transmitted and no "message undeliverable" bounce-back arrives in the sender's inbox.'

Summary

▶ An offer is a statement by one party of a willingness to enter into a contract on stated terms, provided that these terms are, in turn, accepted by the party to whom the offer is addressed.

▶ An offer must be distinguished from an invitation to treat. A display of goods in a shop and advertisements are, subject to cases such as *Carlill v Carbolic Smoke Ball Co* [1893] 1 QB 256, regarded as invitations to treat. An auctioneer, by inviting bids to be made, makes an invitation to treat (except where the auction is to take place without a reserve price), and an invitation to parties to submit a tender is generally an invitation to treat.

▶ An acceptance is an unqualified expression of assent to the terms proposed by the offeror. An acceptance must generally be communicated to the offeror.

▶ A purported acceptance which does not mirror the terms of the offer is not an acceptance but a counter-offer which kills off the original offer.

▶ An offer cannot be accepted by someone who is ignorant of the existence of the offer or by someone who does not have the offer in his mind when he does the act which he alleges constitutes the acceptance.

▶ Where the offeror prescribes a specific method of acceptance, the general rule is that the offeror is not bound unless the terms of his offer are complied with.

▶ The general rule is that acceptance of an offer will not be implied from mere silence on the part of the offeree.

▶ A letter of acceptance takes effect whenever it is posted, provided that it was reasonable for the offeree to have used the post. This rule applies even where the letter gets lost in the post and never reaches the offeror. It is unclear what is the legal position where the offeree posts his acceptance and then sends a rejection by a quicker method so that the rejection reaches the offeror before the acceptance.

▶ In the case of a unilateral contract the offeror is only bound by full performance of the requested act but, in certain cases, the court will imply an obligation on the part of the offeror not to prevent completion of performance, which obligation arises as soon as the offeree starts to perform.

▶ An offer may be terminated by revocation, rejection by the offeree, lapse of time, the occurrence of a stipulated event and, possibly, the death of one or other of the parties. In the case of revocation the general rule is that the revocation must actually be brought to the attention of the offeree.

Exercises

3.1 Distinguish between an 'offer' and an 'invitation to treat'. Give examples to illustrate the distinction.

3.2 Do you think that *Lefkowitz v Great Minneapolis Surplus Stores* 86 NW 2d 689 (1957) would be followed in England? Give reasons for your answer.

3.3 In offer and acceptance cases do the courts 'reason forwards' or 'reason backwards'?

3.4 What is the 'postal rule'? Do you think it is a good rule?

3.5 Do you think Article 19 of the Vienna Convention is an improvement upon the principles established in *Butler v Ex-Cell-O Corp* [1979] 1 WLR 401? How would Article 19 apply to the facts of *Butler?*

3.6 Billy wishes to know whether or not he can refuse to carry out the following arrangements without finding himself in breach of contract. Advise him.

(a) Billy offered to sell his car to Jimmy for £5,000 and stated that he would assume that Jimmy had accepted his offer unless he informed Billy to the contrary. Jimmy has not been in contact with Billy but he has contacted his bank manager and agreed a loan to purchase the car.

(b) Billy offered to sell a consignment of bricks to Jimmy subject to his terms and conditions which stated that Jimmy would be responsible for collecting the bricks. Jimmy accepted the offer, subject to his terms and conditions which stated that Billy would be responsible for delivery of the bricks. Billy still possesses the bricks.

(c) Billy offered to sell his golf clubs to Jimmy. Jimmy immediately replied by letter accepting Billy's offer but, due to his carelessness in wrongly addressing the letter, the acceptance never reached Billy.

Certainty and agreement mistakes

In Chapter 2 we noted that the test for the existence of an agreement is objective rather than subjective. In this chapter we shall consider the application of the objective test in two areas, namely certainty and mistake.

4.1 Certainty

In order to create a binding contract, the parties must express their agreement in a form which is sufficiently certain for the courts to enforce. The traditional reason for this is that it is for the parties, and not the courts, to make the contract. The function of the court is limited to the interpretation of the contract which the parties have made, and it does not extend to making contracts on their behalf (Fridman, 1962). This sentiment was classically expressed by Viscount Maugham in *Scammell and Nephew Ltd v Ouston* [1941] AC 251 when he said that:

> in order to constitute a valid contract the parties must so express themselves that their meaning can be determined with a reasonable degree of certainty. It is plain that unless this can be done ... consensus ad idem would be a matter of mere conjecture.

The traditional stance has to be tempered, however, in its application to commercial contracts where business people wish to avoid rigid agreements which give them no room to manoeuvre in a fluctuating economy. For example, it is not uncommon for building and civil engineering contracts to contain terms which permit the contractor to vary the work which he is required to do, or which make provision for a variation of the time for performance or for the price to be recalculated in the light of events occurring during the agreement. A good example of such flexibility is provided by clause 51 of the Infrastructure Conditions of Contract, which states:

> 1. The Engineer:
>   (a) shall order any variation to any part of the Works that is in his opinion necessary for the completion of the Works and
>   (b) may order any variation that for any other reason shall in his opinion be desirable for the completion and/or improved functioning of the Works.
>
> Such variations may include additions omissions substitutions alterations changes in quality form character kind position dimension level or line and changes in any specified sequence method or timing of construction required by the Contract and may be ordered during the Defects Correction Period.

Such a clause is an important ingredient of any long-term construction contract because it obliges the contractor to carry out such additional work and it also entitles the contractor to be paid for that work under the terms of the contract. The desire to provide the parties with a degree of flexibility is not the only factor which impels the courts towards the conclusion that agreements are enforceable. The courts are also generally reluctant to find that no contract has been concluded where the parties have acted on the assumption that a contract has been entered into (*Percy Trentham Ltd v Archital Luxfer Ltd* [1993] 1 Lloyd's Rep 25, 27), although that reluctance has its limits (*Mathieson Gee (Ayrshire) Ltd v Quigley* 1952 SC (HL) 38, see Section 2.2). The courts are less likely to find the existence of a contract where the parties are in active disagreement over one or more essential term (*British Steel Corp v Cleveland Bridge and Engineering Co Ltd* [1984] 1 All ER 504, see Section 4.5) or the agreement is so incomplete as to amount to no more than an agreement to agree (*Barbudev v Eurocom Cable Management Bulgaria EOOD* [2012] EWCA Civ 548; [2012] 2 All ER (Comm) 963). But in the case where work has been done and the parties have reached agreement on essential terms, a court is more likely than not to find that the parties have entered into a contract (*RTS Flexible Systems Ltd v Molkerei Alois Müller GmbH & Co (UK Production)* [2010] UKSC 14; [2010] 1 WLR 753, [47]–[54], *Reveille Independent LLC v Anotech International (UK) Ltd* [2016] EWCA Civ 443; 116 Con LR 79). The word 'essential' is of vital significance in this context because it is in the case in which the parties have failed to reach agreement on what the court deems to be an essential term of the contract that the court is most likely to conclude that the parties have not in fact entered into a legally binding contract (for an example, see *Teekay Tankers Ltd v STX Offshore & Shipbuilding Co Ltd* [2017] EWHC 253 (Comm); [2017] 1 Lloyd's Rep 387 and *Morris v Swanton Care & Community Ltd* [2018] EWCA Civ 2763).

4.1.1   The competing policy considerations

This area of law is characterised by a tension between the traditional refusal of the courts to make a contract for the parties and the desire of the courts to put into effect what they believe to be the intention of the parties. The dominant judicial philosophy may be said to be one which leans in favour of upholding an agreement and treating it as a valid contract. Thus in *Hillas v Arcos* (1932) 147 LT 503, Lord Wright said:

> Businessmen often record the most important agreements in crude and summary fashion … It is … the duty of the court to construe such documents fairly and broadly, without being too astute or subtle in finding defects.

More recently in *Astor Management AG v Atalaya Mining plc* [2017] EWHC 425 (Comm); [2018] 1 All ER (Comm) 547, [64] Leggatt J stated that the role of the court in commercial disputes 'is to give legal effect to what the parties have agreed, not to throw its hands in the air and refuse to do so because the parties have not made its task easy.'

However, there are limits to the benevolence of the courts. Thus Lord Wright in *Hillas v Arcos* recognised that it is not the task of the court 'to make a contract for the parties'. In comparing these two statements of Lord Wright in *Hillas* we can see that he is making a contrast between 'construing' (or interpreting) a contract and 'making' a contract; the former being legitimate, the latter being illegitimate. Some academic commentators have accepted the existence of such a distinction (Fridman, 1962) but others have subjected it to heavy criticism (Samek, 1970; Ellinghaus, 1971). In application the distinction is by no means obvious. This is so for two reasons. The first is that the test for the existence of an agreement is objective and, as we have seen in cases such as *Gibson v Manchester City Council* [1979] 1 WLR 294 (see Section 3.1), the courts can and do differ in the application of this test to the facts of the case before the court. Secondly, as is clear from the judgment of Viscount Maugham in *Scammell v Ouston* (quoted above), the courts do not insist upon absolute certainty: 'a reasonable degree of certainty' will suffice. There is no hard and fast line between what is certain and what is uncertain. What is sufficiently certain to one judge may be uncertain to another. Thus, the distinction between 'construing' a contract and 'making' a contract is one of degree and not one of kind.

One consequence of this is that the approach which the courts have adopted has not been wholly consistent, with some judges being more willing than others to find the existence of a contract. This inconsistency was present in the cases at the time of the formulation of the rules in *Hillas v Arcos* (above) and it has continued to the present day. This can be demonstrated by reference to the following two pairs of contrasting decisions.

4.1.2   Illustrations of the competing policy considerations

The first pair consists of *May and Butcher v R* [1934] 2 KB 17 and *Hillas v Arcos*. In *May and Butcher* the parties entered into a written agreement under which the British government was to sell tentage to the claimant, and the agreement provided that the price and date of payment 'shall be agreed upon from time to time'. It was held that, the parties not having reached agreement on these matters, no contract had been concluded because, according to Lord Buckmaster: 'an agreement between two parties to enter into an agreement in which some critical part of the contract matter is left undetermined is no contract at all'. On the other hand, a different approach was adopted in the case of *Hillas v Arcos*. In 1930 the parties entered into a contract under which the claimants bought from the defendants 22,000 standards of 'softwood goods of fair specification'. The 1930 contract also contained a provision which stated that the claimants had an option 'of entering into a contract with sellers for the purchase of 100,000 standards for delivery in 1931'. When the claimants sought to exercise this option the defendants argued that the clause was too uncertain to be enforced. This argument was rejected by the House of Lords, who held that the words could be given a reasonable meaning and that therefore the option was binding. Lord Tomlin said that, before the conclusion that no contract has been completed is reached, 'it is necessary to exclude as impossible all reasonable meanings which would give certainty to the words'. But it should be noted that in *Hillas v Arcos* there was a prior contract between the parties which assisted the court in giving a meaning to the option clause.

The second pair of decisions demonstrates that the inconsistency is still present in the cases today. The two cases are *Queensland Electricity Generating Board v New Hope Collieries Pty Ltd* [1989] 1 Lloyd's Rep 205 and *Walford v Miles* [1992] 2 AC 128. In the former case the parties entered into a contract in 1978 under which New Hope Collieries agreed to supply the Board with coal for a period of 15 years. It is very difficult to draft a supply contract which is to last for such a long period of time. Some idea of the difficulties involved can be obtained by imagining a contract draftsman in 2018 seeking to assess the impact of possible events up to the year 2033 on the obligations contained in the contract. How can a contract draftsman possibly see into the future with any degree of accuracy? These difficulties are particularly acute when it comes to finding an acceptable formula for the price of the product over the lifetime of the contract. The contract in *Queensland Electricity* made provision, for the first five-year period of the contract, for a scale of base prices and the contract also contained elaborate 'escalation' or 'price variation' clauses for adjusting the base prices to reflect changes in New Hope's costs. Although provision was made for the general terms of the contract to continue beyond the initial five-year period, clause 2.5 of the agreement stated that '[t]he base price and provisions for variations in prices for changes in costs for purchases after 31 December 1982 shall be agreed by the parties thereto in accordance with clause 8' (which set out the broad criteria to be applied in setting the new pricing structure). The agreement also contained a comprehensive arbitration clause. One of the issues which arose before the Privy Council was whether or not the contract was enforceable after the first five years. It was argued that the contract was too uncertain because no price had been agreed for the supply of coal. The Privy Council rejected this argument in robust terms. Sir Robin Cooke stated:

> in cases where the parties have agreed on an arbitration or valuation clause in wide enough terms, the Courts accord full weight to their manifest intention to create continuing legal relations. Arguments invoking alleged uncertainty, or alleged inadequacy in the machinery available to the Courts for making contractual rights effective, exert minimal attraction … their Lordships have no doubt that here, by the agreement, the parties undertook implied primary obligations to make reasonable endeavours to agree on the terms of supply beyond the initial five-year period and, failing agreement and upon proper notice, to do everything reasonably necessary to procure the appointment of an arbitrator. Further, it is implicit in a commercial agreement of this kind that the terms of the new price structure are to be fair and reasonable as between the parties …

This liberal approach should, however, be contrasted with the more restrictive approach adopted by the House of Lords in *Walford v Miles* (above). The defendants were the owners of a company, and they entered into negotiations with the claimants for the sale of the company to the claimants. On 17 March 1987 the parties entered into an agreement under which the claimants promised to provide a comfort letter from their bank which confirmed that they had the financial resources to pay the price which was being asked for the company. In return the defendants agreed to deal exclusively with the claimants and to terminate any negotiations then current between the defendants and any other prospective purchasers of the company. The claimants complied with their side of the agreement, but the defendants subsequently decided not to deal with the claimants, and they agreed to sell the company to a third party on 30 March 1987. The claimants sought to recover damages in respect of the breach of the agreement of 17 March, while the defendants argued that the agreement was unenforceable on the ground that it was too uncertain.

The agreement of 17 March was both a 'lock-out' agreement (in that it sought to prevent the defendants from continuing negotiations with third parties) and a 'lock-in' agreement (in that it purported to oblige the defendants to negotiate exclusively with the claimants). Both aspects were held by the House of Lords to be unenforceable. The lock-out agreement could not be enforced, because it was not limited to a specified period of time, and the argument that a term should be implied that it was to last a reasonable period of time was decisively rejected. That argument had found favour with Bingham LJ in the Court of Appeal who stated that a reasonable time 'would end once the parties acting in good faith had found themselves unable to come to mutually acceptable terms'. But the House of Lords dismissed the argument on the ground that it 'would indirectly impose upon [the defendants] a duty to bargain in good faith'. The lock-in aspect of the agreement was also held to be unenforceable on the ground that an agreement to negotiate is not an enforceable contract, because it is too uncertain to have any binding force (in this respect following the decision of the Court of Appeal in *Courtney and Fairbairn Ltd v Tolaini Brothers (Hotels) Ltd* [1975] 1 WLR 297). The claimants sought to meet this argument by asserting that, in order to give 'business efficacy' to the agreement of 17 March, it was necessary to imply a term that the defendants were obliged to continue the negotiations in good faith, with the result that they were only entitled to terminate the negotiations if they had a 'proper reason', subjectively assessed, for doing so. Lord Ackner rejected this argument. He doubted whether a court could properly be expected to decide whether a contracting party subjectively had a good reason for terminating negotiations. He further stated that a 'concept of a duty to carry on negotiations in good faith is inherently repugnant to the adversarial position of the parties involved in negotiations' and that 'each party is entitled to pursue his (or her) own interest, so long as he avoids making misrepresentations'. Thus, he held, either party was entitled to withdraw from the negotiations at any time and for any reason, and the claimants' claim was therefore held to be without foundation.

It is suggested that the decision in *Walford v Miles* is a regrettable one because it makes it difficult to draft an enforceable 'lock-out' or 'lock-in' agreement, despite the commercial purposes which are served by such agreements in enabling contracting parties to buy time to put together a bid with no competition from a third party or to purchase a period of time in which to negotiate exclusively with a party in an effort to persuade him to conclude a contract. It is possible to draft an enforceable lock-out agreement provided that the duration of the agreement is confined to a limited period of time, such as 14 days (see *Pitt v PHH Asset Management Ltd* [1994] 1 WLR 327). But it may not be possible to draft an enforceable lock-in agreement because of the refusal of the House of Lords in *Walford v Miles* to recognise an obligation to negotiate in good faith for the period in which the parties are prohibited from conducting negotiations with third parties.

4.1.3 Assessment

So it can be seen from these cases that the approach adopted by the courts does seem to differ. The court in *Hillas v Arcos* and *Queensland Electricity* was more willing than the court in *May and Butcher* and *Walford v Miles* to uphold the agreement entered into by the parties. It is the more liberal approach in *Hillas v Arcos* and *Queensland* which has been followed with the greatest regularity in the cases (see, for example, *Foley v Classique Coaches* [1934] 2 KB 1). Judges generally do not want to 'incur the reproach of being the destroyer of bargains' (*Hillas v Arcos*, per Lord Tomlin) and therefore they tend to gravitate towards upholding and enforcing agreements. As Leggatt J recently observed in *Novus Aviation Ltd v Alubaf Arab International Bank BSC(c)* [2016] EWHC 1575 (Comm), [60] the conclusion that the contract is too uncertain to be enforceable should be one of 'last resort', at least when a document is intended by the parties to be legally binding, given that English law aims to uphold and give effect to the intentions of the parties, not to defeat them. Cases such as *May and Butcher* and *Walford v Miles* tend to be the exception. Indeed, courts in other jurisdictions have been reluctant to, or have refused to, follow these decisions (an example is the decision of the New Zealand Court of Appeal where the court declined to follow *May and Butcher*: see *Fletcher Challenge Energy Ltd v Electricity Corp of NZ Ltd* [2002] 2 NZLR 433, 446–47). Nevertheless, the distinction between 'construing' a contract and 'making' a contract is one of degree, and judges will continue to draw the line between the two categories in different places, with some judges being more cautious than others.

4.2　Vagueness

The uncertainty may arise from one of a number of different sources. In the first place, the terms of the agreement may be too vague for the courts to enforce. Such was the case in *Scammell and Nephew Ltd v Ouston* [1941] AC 251, where the parties entered into an agreement to buy goods on 'hire-purchase'. It was held that this agreement was too vague to be enforced because there were many different types of hire-purchase agreements in use, these agreements varied widely in their content and it was not clear what type of hire-purchase agreement was envisaged. *Scammell v Ouston* is, however, a 'rare case': in most cases the courts will 'strain to be the preserver and not the destroyer of bargains, especially where … the parties have acted upon their apparent agreement' (*Scammell v Dicker* [2005] EWCA Civ 405; [2005] 3 All ER 838, [31] and [41]).

However, as we have noted, the courts are reluctant to find that an agreement is so vague that it cannot be enforced. There are a number of devices available to a court which does not wish to find that an agreement is too vague to be enforced. The court may be able to ascertain the meaning of the phrase by reference to the custom of the trade in which the parties are contracting (*Shamrock SS Co v Storey and Co* (1899) 81 LT 413), or it may be able to enforce the agreement by severing a clause which is meaningless (*Nicolene Ltd v Simmonds* [1953] 1 QB 543) or, finally, the court may be able to interpret the vague phrase in the light of what is reasonable (*Hillas v Arcos* (1932) 147 LT 503).

4.3　Incompleteness

Alternatively, the agreement may be incomplete because the parties have failed to reach agreement upon a particular issue. It is at this point that cases such as *May and Butcher v R* [1934] 2 KB 17 and *Hillas v Arcos* (1932) 147 LT 503 become relevant. Once again, however, a number of devices are available to a court which wishes to avoid the conclusion that the agreement is incomplete and therefore cannot be enforced. The first is to invoke section 8(2) of the Sale of Goods Act 1979 which provides that where the price of goods in a contract of sale is not 'determined' by the contract (on which see s 8(1) of the Act) 'the buyer must pay a reasonable price' (see also Supply of Goods and Services Act 1982, s 15(1)). This section only comes into play where the contract is silent as to the price; where, as in *May and Butcher*, provision is made for calculating the price, but the provision is not implemented, then the section is inapplicable.

Secondly, where, as in *Hillas v Arcos*, the parties have agreed criteria by which an incomplete matter can be resolved, it is much easier for the court to uphold the agreement.

Thirdly, the contract itself may provide for machinery to resolve the dispute between the parties. It is possible for that machinery to be provided by one of the contracting parties. Thus, in *May and Butcher* Viscount Dunedin stated that 'with regard to price it is a perfectly good contract to say that the price is to be settled by the buyer'. Where the contract appears to confer a very broad discretion upon one of the contracting parties, the courts may cut down the scope of that discretion by implying into the contract a term to the effect that the discretionary power must not be exercised dishonestly, for an improper purpose, capriciously, arbitrarily or in a way in which no reasonable party would do (*Paragon Finance plc v Nash* [2001] EWCA Civ 1466; [2002] 1 WLR 685). Difficulties do, however, emerge where the machinery has, for some reason, failed to come into effect. It was once thought that such a failure was fatal to the existence of an enforceable contract because the court would not substitute its own, different machinery for that agreed by the parties. This view was, however, rejected by the House of Lords in *Sudbrook Estates Ltd v Eggleton* [1983] 1 AC 444. A lease gave to tenants (the lessees) an option to purchase the premises at a price to be agreed upon by two valuers, one to be nominated by the lessors and the other by the lessees and, in default of agreement, by an umpire to be appointed by the valuers. When the lessees sought to exercise the option, the lessors refused to appoint a valuer and claimed that the option clause was void for uncertainty. It was held by the House of Lords that the crucial question in each case was whether the machinery agreed upon by the parties was an essential factor in determining the price to be paid or whether it was simply a means of ensuring that a fair price was paid. It was only where the machinery was essential and had not been implemented that the agreement would be held to be incomplete and not binding. An example of machinery which may be held to be essential is the appointment of a particular valuer because of his special skill or his special knowledge (for another example see *Gillatt v Sky Television Ltd* [2000] 1 All ER (Comm) 461). On the facts of *Sudbrook* it was held, Lord Russell dissenting, that the reference to the valuers was an indication that the price was to be a reasonable and fair one and that the machinery for appointing the valuers was subsidiary to the main purpose of ascertaining a fair and reasonable price. Therefore, given that the machinery was not essential, the House of Lords was able to substitute its own machinery for ascertaining the price to be paid, and an inquiry was ordered into what was the fair value of the premises.

4.4   A general rule?

The general impression which is left by a study of the English case law on uncertainty is that the courts have adopted a rather piecemeal approach, which has resulted in a degree of inconsistency in the case law. The courts have not laid down a general rule which could provide a unifying basis for the law in this area. Such a general rule has been adopted in America in section 2-204 of the Uniform Commercial Code which states that:

> even though one or more terms are left open a contract for sale does not fail for indefiniteness if the parties have intended to make a contract and there is a reasonably certain basis for giving an appropriate remedy.

This rule could provide a basis for a coherent development of the law, but it would also bring its own problems of interpretation. For example, how would the courts decide whether the parties had an intention to contract, and what meaning would be given to the phrase a 'reasonably certain basis for giving an appropriate remedy'? It is a matter for consideration whether or not English law should adopt such a general rule.

4.5 A restitutionary approach?

It should not be assumed that the law of contract, and the law of contract alone, can resolve all the problems raised by agreements which appear to lack certainty. A role may be found for the law of restitution (or, to use the label which is probably now more commonly accepted, the law of unjust enrichment), as can be seen from the case of *British Steel Corp v Cleveland Bridge and Engineering Co Ltd* [1984] 1 All ER 504. The parties entered into negotiations for the manufacture by the claimants of steel nodes for the defendants. The defendants sent the claimants a letter of intent which stated their intention to place an order for the steel nodes and proposed that the contract be on the defendants' standard terms. The claimants refused to contract on these terms. Detailed negotiations then took place over the specifications of the steel nodes, but no agreement was reached on matters such as progress payments and liability for loss arising from late delivery, and no formal contract was ever concluded. After the final node had been delivered the defendants refused to pay for them. The claimants brought an action against the defendants, who counterclaimed for damages for late delivery or delivery of the nodes out of sequence. Robert Goff J discussed three possible analyses of the claimants' claim.

The first was to hold that an executory contract had come into existence after the letter of intent had been sent. But he rejected this solution on the ground that, since the parties were still negotiating and had not reached agreement, it was impossible to say what were the material terms of the contract. The second solution was to hold that there was a unilateral contract or a standing offer made by the defendants which, if acted upon before it was lawfully withdrawn, would result in a contract. But, because of the disagreement between the parties, Robert Goff J held that it could not be assumed from the fact that the claimants had commenced the work that a contract had thereby been created on the terms of the defendants' standing offer. The third solution, and the one which Robert Goff J adopted, was to allow the claimants to recover in a restitutionary action for the reasonable value of the work which they had done. He held that, because the defendants had requested the claimants to deliver the nodes, they had received a benefit at the expense of the claimants and that it was unjust that they retain that benefit without recompensing the claimants for the reasonable value of the nodes. The conclusion which was reached in the case was not altogether satisfactory because, no contract having been concluded, the defendants' counterclaim for damages for breach of contract fell away (although on the facts no injustice was caused, because the counterclaim was held to be without foundation in any event). On a different set of facts, if the defendants had argued that the claimants' *restitutionary* claim should have been reduced on the ground that the defects in the final product had reduced the value of the benefit which they had received as a result of the work done by the claimants, their argument might have been successful (see *Crown House Engineering Ltd v Amec Projects Ltd* (1990) 47 Build

LR 32 and, more generally McKendrick, 1988). So, instead of liberalising the rules relating to certainty (or possibly in addition to such liberalisation), an alternative approach would be to hold that no contract was concluded and look to the law of restitution for a solution (see, for example, *Whittle Movers Ltd v Hollywood Express Ltd* [2009] EWCA Civ 1189; [2009] 2 CLC 771). However, it should not be thought that a restitutionary claim will lie in all cases where work is done in anticipation of a contract materialising. In many cases the work will be done at the risk of the party who is doing the preparatory work, especially where the parties have conducted their negotiations on an express 'subject to contract' basis (see *Regalian Properties plc v London Dockland Development Corp* [1995] 1 WLR 212).

4.6   Mistake negativing consent

This is an extremely difficult area of law. It is important to distinguish at the outset between two different types of mistake. The first is called 'common' mistake and arises where both parties enter into the contract sharing the same mistake which nullifies their contract (see Sections 14.2–14.7). In this type of case the parties do initially reach agreement, but that agreement may subsequently be set aside on the ground of the parties' shared mistake. The second type of mistake, and the type with which we shall be concerned here, may be called an 'offer and acceptance' mistake because it negatives consent and prevents a contract coming into existence on the ground that one party is labouring under a mistake or the parties are at cross-purposes. Professor Goodhart has written (1941) that 'there is no branch of the law of contract which is more uncertain and difficult than that which is concerned with the effect of mistake on the formation of a contract'.

Despite this uncertainty, it is at least clear that the mere fact that one party to the contract is mistaken in his 'innermost mind' is not sufficient, of itself, automatically to render a contract void. This is because, as we have seen, the courts have adopted an objective rather than a subjective test of agreement (see Section 2.1). The objective test of agreement considerably reduces the scope of the doctrine of mistake, and this restriction is traditionally justified on the ground that it promotes certainty in commercial transactions. Despite these restrictions, mistakes can operate to negative consent in the following cases.

4.6.1   Latent ambiguity

The first case arises where the terms of the offer and acceptance suffer from such latent ambiguity that it is impossible reasonably to impute any agreement between the parties. The classic, if confusing, case in this category is *Raffles v Wichelhaus* (1864) 2 H & C 906. The defendants agreed to buy from the claimants a cargo of cotton to arrive 'ex Peerless from Bombay'. There were, unknown to the parties, two ships called 'Peerless' and both sailed from Bombay. The defendants meant the Peerless which sailed in October, whereas the claimants meant the Peerless which sailed in December. When the cotton eventually arrived, the defendants refused to accept delivery because they argued that the claimants were obliged to deliver the cotton on the Peerless which sailed in October, not the Peerless which sailed in December. The claimants therefore sued for the price of the cotton. The issue before

as to their intention. Not everyone accepts this distinction between written contracts and oral contracts. In *Shogun Finance Ltd v Hudson* the dissentients, Lord Nicholls and Lord Millett, rejected the distinction on the basis that the mistake in the two contexts is the same, namely that one party enters into the contract in the belief that his contracting party is X when in fact it is Y. In their view (at [33] in *Shogun Finance Ltd v Hudson*), the response of the law should not depend 'on the precise mode of communication of offer and acceptance' (that is, whether it is oral or written). While it is true that there are substantial similarities between the nature of the mistake made in the two cases, the law has chosen for the reasons given above to draw a distinction between contracts made in writing and contracts concluded orally in a face-to-face transaction. We must therefore consider the two situations separately.

4.6.5 Contracts entered into in writing

The leading case dealing with written contracts is the decision of the House of Lords in *Cundy v Lindsay* (1878) 3 App Cas 459 (a case which was affirmed by the majority in *Shogun Finance Ltd v Hudson*). A dishonest person called Blenkarn, who gave his address as 37 Wood Street, Cheapside, ordered handkerchiefs from the claimants. Blenkarn signed his name to make it look like Blenkiron & Co, a respectable firm who carried on business at 123 Wood Street and who were known by reputation to the claimants. The claimants duly sent the handkerchiefs to 'Blenkiron & Co, 37 Wood St' where Blenkarn received them. He did not pay for the goods but rather sold them to the defendants. When they discovered their mistake, the claimants sought to recover the goods from the defendants. The House of Lords found for the claimants and held that the contract between the claimants and Blenkarn was void for mistake because the claimants did not intend to deal with Blenkarn but with Blenkiron and Co, a firm which they knew. In deciding that the contract was void, the House of Lords had regard to the fact that the order form sent to the claimants was apparently signed 'Blenkiron and Co' and the fact that the claimants knew of a firm of that name and intended to deal with that firm.

However, it is not the case that a mistake will render a contract void in every case where the contract is reduced to writing. In *King's Norton Metal Co v Edridge Merrett & Co Ltd* (1897) 14 TLR 98 the claimants sent goods on credit to Hallam and Co, which purported to be a large firm in Sheffield but was in fact an impecunious rogue called Wallis. Wallis failed to pay for the goods and sold them to the defendants. The claimants, when they discovered their mistake, sought to recover the goods from the defendants. Their claim failed. It was held that they intended to contract with the writer of the letters, and they had simply made a mistake as to one of his attributes, namely his creditworthiness. The distinction between the two cases is that the mistake in *Cundy* was a mistake as to identity because the claimants intended to deal with an identifiable third party (Blenkiron & Co, a company which they knew), whereas in *King's Norton* the claimants had not heard of Hallam and Co and simply intended to contract with the writer of the letters. As Lord Phillips of Worth Matravers observed in *Shogun Finance Ltd v Hudson* (at [135]), the claimants in *King's Norton* 'intended to deal with whoever was using the name "Hallam & Co"'. It was necessary to resort to extrinsic evidence for the purpose of identifying the existence of 'Hallam & Co' but, 'once Wallis was identified as the user of that name, the party with whom the [claimants] had contracted was established' and they could not 'demonstrate that their acceptance of the offer was intended for anyone other than Wallis'. It is therefore permissible to have regard to extrinsic evidence for the purpose of ascertaining the identity of the person named in the contract, but not for the purpose of demonstrating that the party to the contract was not the party named in the contract but some third party. In the latter case, the function of the extrinsic evidence is to contradict the written terms of the contract (which the courts will not permit), whereas in the former case, resort is had to extrinsic evidence for the purpose of identifying, and giving effect to, the intention of the parties (which is permissible).

4.6.6 Contracts concluded in face-to-face dealings

Matters are rather more complex when we turn to contracts concluded between parties dealing face-to-face. A principal cause of the difficulty is that the cases are not at all easy to reconcile. In two of the leading cases the contract was held to be voidable (namely *Phillips v Brooks* [1919] 2 KB 243 and *Lewis v Averay* [1972] 1 QB 198), whereas in another case (*Ingram v Little* [1961] 1 QB 31) it was held to be void (support for the latter proposition may also be gleaned from the decision of the House of Lords in *Lake v Simmonds* [1927] AC 487, in particular in the speech of Lord Haldane). Here it will suffice to contrast *Ingram v Little* and *Lewis v Averay*.

The claimants in *Ingram v Little* were two sisters who were visited by a rogue who called himself Hutchinson and who wished to buy their car. He produced a cheque to pay for it, but one of the claimants said that they would not accept a cheque. The rogue then said that he was a certain P.G.M. Hutchinson of Stanstead House, Caterham. Neither of the claimants had heard of this person, but one of them went to the Post Office, checked in the telephone directory and confirmed that there was such a person. Believing the rogue to be P.G.M. Hutchinson, they allowed him to take the car on handing over the cheque, which later proved to be worthless. The rogue then sold the car to the defendants. When the claimants discovered their mistake they sought recovery of the car from the defendants. The Court of Appeal held that the contract between the claimants and the rogue was void because of a mistake as to identity. They held that, while there was a *prima facie* presumption that a party contracts with the person in front of him, the presumption was displaced on the facts of the case. The decisive factor appears to be that the claimants refused to accept the rogue's offer to enter into a contract on terms that he paid by cheque until they had checked his identity in the telephone directory, which showed that his identity was crucial to the creation of a contract and not simply to the method of payment under a contract which had already been concluded.

A different result was reached by the Court of Appeal in *Lewis v Averay*. A rogue, calling himself the actor Richard Greene, offered to buy the claimant's car. He signed a cheque, but the claimant did not want him to take the car away until the cheque had been cleared. In order to persuade the claimant to allow him to take the car away immediately, the rogue produced an admission pass to Pinewood Studios, bearing the name Richard A. Green, his address, his photograph and an official stamp. The claimant then let the rogue take the car in return for a cheque, which proved to be worthless. The rogue then sold the car to the defendant, from whom the claimant sought recovery when he discovered his mistake. In giving judgment for the defendant the Court of Appeal held that there was nothing to displace the *prima facie* presumption that the claimant intended to deal with the party in front of him, and they confined *Ingram v Little* to its 'special facts'.

How can *Ingram v Little* and *Lewis v Averay* be reconciled? One answer to this question is that there is no need to reconcile them because each case depends on its own facts. This was the position which was adopted by Waller J in *Citibank NA v Brown Shipley & Co Ltd* [1991] 2 All ER 690, 700 when he said that each case 'rests on its own facts'. While it is true that careful attention must be paid to the facts and circumstances of the individual case, the proposition that each case depends entirely on its own facts is not an attractive one. The law ought to be able to lay down some guidelines or principles which can be applied to the facts of any individual case. The guideline or principle which can be discerned from the case law takes the form of the presumption that a contracting party intends to deal with the party who is present in front of him. It is clear from *Shogun Finance Ltd v Hudson* that the presumption is a strong one. In particular, it will not suffice to rebut the presumption for a party to prove that he believed that the person in front of him was, in fact, somebody else. The strength of the presumption can also be inferred from the analysis of *Ingram v Little* which was adopted by their Lordships in *Shogun Finance Ltd v Hudson*. Thus, both Lord Millett (at [87]) and Lord Walker (at [185]) were of the view that *Ingram v Little* had been wrongly decided, while Lord Nicholls (at [20]–[22]) and Lord Phillips of Worth Matravers (at [142]–[147]) discussed the case in critical terms but, while they clearly preferred the reasoning of Devlin LJ, the dissenting judge in *Ingram v Little*, they did not state in express terms that *Ingram v Little* had been decided incorrectly. It is clear from *Shogun Finance Ltd v Hudson* that *Ingram v Little* is now under a cloud and that a court will be slow to infer that the presumption has been rebutted. What type of case will lead to the inference that the presumption has been rebutted? Some idea of the answer to this question can be gleaned from the speech of Lord Walker in *Shogun Finance Ltd v Hudson* when he referred (at [187]) to the case in which a rogue impersonates an individual with whom the claimant is acquainted (as in the biblical example where Jacob deceived his father Isaac by impersonating his brother Esau: see Genesis 27). In such a case the presumption may be rebutted, but such cases are likely to be few and far between.

The evident reluctance of the courts to conclude that the presumption has been rebutted in face-to-face transactions has the consequence that the divide between written contracts and oral contracts is of considerable potential significance. A court is more likely to conclude that the contract is void for mistake where the contract is reduced to writing than it is in the case where the contract is concluded face-to-face. One difficulty which is generated by this difference in treatment is that it may not always be a straightforward matter to determine whether the contract has been made face-to-face or in writing. This is particularly so where the contract is made through the medium of a third party (and it may also prove to be problematic given the growing incidence of contracts concluded through electronic means). The difficulty is in fact highlighted by the facts of *Shogun Finance Ltd v Hudson* itself. The claimant finance house entered into an agreement with a man who purported to be Mr Durlabh Patel. Under the agreement, the claimants agreed to supply Mr Patel with a car on hire-purchase terms. The rogue and the claimant finance house did not deal face-to-face. Instead, the rogue dealt with a car dealer who forwarded to the claimants the information (which included Mr Patel's driving licence which the rogue had obtained improperly) that the claimants needed in order to decide whether or not to enter into the contract with the rogue. The claimants ran a check on the credit status of Mr Patel and, it being clear, decided to provide finance in order to enable the rogue to acquire the car. The rogue defaulted on the hire-purchase transaction and sold the car to the defendant, who bought it in all good faith. The claimants brought an action in conversion against the defendant, and the claim succeeded. The defendant submitted that the rogue and the finance company had dealt face-to-face with the result that the presumption that a party intends to contract with the person in front of him was applicable. The basis for this submission was that the car dealer had acted as the claimants' agent when communicating information to the claimants. The submission was rejected by the majority in *Shogun Finance Ltd v Hudson*. The rogue had never had any face-to-face dealings with the claimants. He dealt with them in writing by submitting to them a written document for their acceptance or rejection. Nor could it be said that the car dealer had acted as an agent of the claimants in entering into the transaction. The car dealer was not an agent of the claimants for the purpose of entering into any contract on behalf of the claimants; rather, he was 'a mere facilitator serving primarily his own interests'. On this basis, the contract concluded between the rogue and the claimants was a written contract. One of the terms of that contract described Mr Patel as the customer, and it was not open to the defendant to lead evidence to contradict that written term and establish that the party to the contract was not in fact Mr Patel but the rogue. This being the case, the hirer under the contract was Mr Patel and, as he had not in any way authorised the conclusion of the contract, it was void. The defendant could not therefore make out any exception to the *nemo dat* rule, with the consequence that the claimants succeeded in their action against the defendant and were held to be entitled to recover from the defendant the value of the car which was in his possession.

Hot topic 4...

A recent example of the difficulties which the courts experience in deciding whether the parties have reached agreement on all essential matters is the decision of the Supreme Court in *Wells v Devani* [2019] UKSC 4; [2020] AC 129. The defendant undertook a development of a number of flats but had difficulty in selling them. He contacted the claimant estate agent and in a phone call agreed a commission rate of 2 per cent plus VAT. The flats were subsequently sold to a housing association introduced by the claimant. When the claimant sought to recover his commission, the defendant declined to pay and took the point that no contract had been concluded between the parties. The judge at first instance held that a contract had been concluded, but the Court of Appeal allowed the defendant's appeal and held that the parties had failed to reach agreement on an essential matter, namely the point in time at which the commission was payable. The Supreme Court allowed the claimant's appeal. Reflecting a reluctance to find that an agreement is too uncertain to be enforced where it is found that the parties had the intention of being contractually bound and have acted on their agreement, it was held that, while the parties had not discussed the point in time at which commission would be payable, there was no doubt that it would naturally be understood that payment would become due on completion and made from the proceeds of sale. This was held to be the only sensible interpretation of what the parties said to each other during their telephone conversation. Thus it was held that, having regard to the words used by the parties, their conduct and the context in which they dealt with one another, they intended commission to be payable on completion of the sale to a party who had been introduced by the claimant and for the fee to be paid from the proceeds of the sale. Had it been necessary for them to do so, the Supreme Court would also have been willing to imply a term into the contract that commission was to be paid on completion of the sale in order to make the contract work and to give it practical and commercial coherence. To leave the defendant without any obligation to make payment would be 'completely inconsistent with the nature of their relationship.' Had the parties failed to reach agreement on the rate at which commission was payable, the decision of the Court of Appeal would have been understandable. The rate at which commission is payable is likely to be an essential term. But it is far less likely that the date on which it is payable will be an essential term, particularly where the defendant is only obliged to make payment when it has received the performance which it requested. This being the case, the decision of the Supreme Court is much to be preferred to the conclusion which had been reached by the Court of Appeal.

Summary

- An agreement must be expressed with sufficient certainty before it will be enforced by the courts.

- The principal causes of uncertainty are vagueness and incompleteness.

- There are, however, a number of devices available to a court which wishes to avoid the conclusion that an agreement is too uncertain to be enforced.

- It should not be forgotten that a remedy may be found in the law of restitution where it is held that the agreement is too uncertain to constitute a contract. A mistake may negative consent and prevent a contract coming into existence where one party is labouring under a mistake or the parties are at cross-purposes.

- Mistake does, however, operate within very narrow confines. Mistake has been held to negative consent where the terms of the offer and acceptance suffer from such latent ambiguity that it is impossible reasonably to impute any agreement between the parties, where one party was under a mistake as to the terms of the contract and that mistake was known to the other party and where there was a mistake as to the identity of the other contracting party.

- When deciding whether or not a mistake as to identity renders a contract void, it is important to distinguish between contracts entered into in writing and contracts concluded orally. Where the parties deal with each other in a face-to-face transaction, the law presumes that each party to the transaction intends to deal with the party in front of him. The presumption is a strong one, and it will only be rebutted in exceptional cases. Where the contract has been reduced to writing, the courts will not generally allow extrinsic evidence to be led where that evidence seeks to contradict the written terms of the contract. Thus, where the contract describes one of the parties to the contract as X, it will not generally be open to the parties to lead evidence for the purpose of demonstrating that the party to the contract was not X but was in fact Y.

Exercises

4.1 Compare and contrast the decisions of the House of Lords in *May and Butcher v R* [1934] 2 KB 17 and *Hillas v Arcos* (1932) 147 LT 503.

4.2 List the devices which are available to a court which wishes to avoid the conclusion that an agreement is too uncertain to be enforced.

4.3 Would any advantage be obtained by introducing into English law a provision equivalent to section 2-204 of the American Uniform Commercial Code?

4.4 Distinguish between 'common mistake' and 'unilateral mistake'. Give some examples of the distinction.

4.5 What is the difference between a contract which has been held to be void and one which has been held to be voidable?

4.6 Compare and contrast the decisions of the Court of Appeal in *Ingram v Little* [1961] 1 QB 31 and *Lewis v Averay* [1972] 1 QB 198.

Chapter 5

Consideration and form

It is clear that no legal system treats all agreements as enforceable contracts. In every legal system there exist rules which identify the types of agreement that are to be treated as enforceable contracts. The function of these rules is to give what we shall call the 'badge of enforceability' to certain agreements. In English law that function is performed principally by the doctrine of consideration and, to a lesser extent, by a doctrine of formalities. Of course, it could be argued that the rules relating to duress, misrepresentation and illegality play a role in identifying those agreements which are to be treated as enforceable contracts (see Atiyah, 1986c) and, to some extent, this is true. But English law has, historically, viewed the requirements of consideration and form as being separate and distinct from doctrines such as duress, and this is the approach which we shall adopt in this chapter.

5.1 Requirements of form

A legal system may grant the 'badge of enforceability' only to those agreements which are entered into in a certain form. Historically, English law has placed considerable reliance upon requirements of form. The Statute of Frauds 1677 required that certain classes of contracts be evidenced in writing, but most of its provisions were repealed in 1954. Requirements of form are therefore no longer a significant feature of English contract law, except in a residual category of contracts. For example, a lease for more than three years must be by deed (Law of Property Act 1925, ss 52, 54(2)) and a unilateral gratuitous promise is only enforceable if it is made by deed. Compliance with this requirement is relatively straightforward: (i) there must be a document bearing the word 'deed', or having some other indication clearly on its face that it is intended to take effect as a deed (although an instrument shall not be taken to make it clear on its face that it is intended to be a deed merely because it is executed under seal); (ii) it must be signed by the individual maker of the deed; (iii) that signature must be attested by one witness if the deed is signed by the maker (there must be two witnesses if the deed is signed at his direction); and (iv) it must be delivered, that is to say, there must be some conduct on the part of the person executing the deed to show that he intends to be bound by it (Law of Property (Miscellaneous Provisions) Act 1989, ss 1(2), (3)). The requirement that the deed be under seal was abolished by section 1 of the Law of Property (Miscellaneous Provisions) Act 1989.

Bills of exchange (Bills of Exchange Act 1882, s 3(1)) and bills of sale (Bills of Sale Act 1878 (Amendment) Act 1882) must be in writing, while contracts for the sale or other disposition of an interest in land (Law of Property (Miscellaneous Provisions) Act 1989, s 2(1)) can only be made in writing. Contracts of guarantee (Statute of Frauds Act 1677, s 4) must be *evidenced* in writing. However, it is vital to note that, apart from the case of gratuitous promises made by deed, such formal requirements do not replace consideration; they are an additional requirement.

5.1.1   The advantages and disadvantages of formal requirements

Professor Atiyah has argued that 'insistence on form is widely thought by lawyers to be characteristic of primitive and less well-developed legal systems' (2006, 94). Yet many major legal systems in the world continue to place heavy reliance upon formal requirements. Many provinces in Canada and states in Australia are still governed by the Statute of Frauds, either in its original or a modified form. Scotland, which does not have a doctrine of consideration, places considerable emphasis upon formal requirements. Until relatively recently the law was archaic and out of step with the needs of modern commerce. For example, a contract of loan of a sum of money in excess of £8.33 could be created informally but had to be proved by the writ or oath of the party alleged to be bound. These old rules were swept away by the Requirements of Writing (Scotland) Act 1995, which attempts to provide a coherent framework for the modern law. The old rules relating to proof by writ or oath have been abolished (s 11(1)). As far as the constitution of contracts is concerned, the general rule is that writing is not required for the constitution of a contract or unilateral obligation (s 1(1)). There are exceptions, but they are few. Thus a written document (defined in s 2) is required for the constitution of a contract or unilateral obligation for the creation, transfer, variation or extinction of an interest in land (s 1(2)(a)(i)) and for the constitution of a gratuitous unilateral obligation except an obligation undertaken in the course of a business (s 1(2)(a)(ii)).

What are the functions of such formal requirements? Professor Fuller (1941) has identified three functions. The first is the evidentiary function; in cases of dispute a formal requirement, such as writing, provides evidence of the existence and content of the contract. For this reason, business people frequently reduce their contracts to writing, even though it is not mandatory to do so. Second, formalities have a cautionary function, 'by acting as a check against inconsiderate action'. A requirement that a contract be made by deed impresses upon the parties the importance of the transaction into which they are about to enter. This cautionary function has been recognised by Parliament in sections 60 and 61 of the Consumer Credit Act 1974 and in regulations made thereunder, which provide that a regulated consumer credit agreement is not 'properly executed' unless it complies with certain formal requirements which are designed to ensure, as far as possible, that the consumer is fully informed of the nature and consequences of the agreement before entering into it. Such formal, statutory, paternalistic requirements may become an increasingly common feature of English contract law, at least in the context of contracts concluded between a business and a consumer. The third function of formalities is the channelling function, that is to say, formalities provide a simple and external test of enforceability.

On the other hand, requirements of form are attended by considerable disadvantages. In the first place, formalities tend to be cumbersome and time-consuming. It would be ridiculous and impractical to insist that every contract be reduced to writing, so that every time I bought my morning newspaper I had to sign a written contract. This leads to a second difficulty which is that, given that it is impractical to apply formal requirements to all contracts, which contracts should be governed by requirements of form? For example, section 4 of the Statute of Frauds provides that contracts of guarantee must be evidenced in writing, but no such requirement applies to contracts of indemnity. Yet the two contracts are very similar and the cases have 'raised many hairsplitting distinctions of exactly that kind which bring the law into hatred, ridicule and contempt by the public' (*Yeoman Credit Ltd v Latter* [1961] 1 WLR 828, 835).

5.1.2 An illustration of the difficulties that can arise

A modern example of the significance of the distinction between a contract of guarantee and a contract of indemnity is provided by the case of *Actionstrength Ltd v International Glass Engineering In.Gl.EN.SpA* [2003] UKHL 17; [2003] 2 AC 541. Subcontractors, who were having great difficulty in obtaining payment from the main contractors, held a meeting with the employers (with whom the main contractors were in a contractual relationship) at which the subcontractors stated that they would withdraw from the project unless they were paid for their work. The subcontractors alleged that an oral agreement was reached at the meeting in terms that the subcontractors would not withdraw their labour, and the employers in turn agreed to ensure that the subcontractors would receive any amount due to them by the main contractors under the subcontract, if necessary by redirecting to subcontractors payments due by the employers to the main contractors. The content of this agreement was, however, disputed by the employers. They alleged that they had simply offered to help in the attempt to resolve the dispute between the subcontractors and the main contractors and they denied that they had assumed an express obligation to make payment direct to the subcontractors. Whatever the precise nature of the oral agreement, it was sufficient to persuade the subcontractors to continue with the project. Unfortunately, the practice of the main contractors did not change and their indebtedness to the subcontractors increased to £1.3 million, at which point the main contractors became insolvent. The subcontractors then looked to the employers to honour their oral agreement. The employers refused to do so. They claimed that it was, at best, an oral guarantee which was unenforceable because it was not evidenced in writing. The subcontractors submitted that the oral agreement was an indemnity which was not subject to requirements of form. A guarantee is a secondary liability which is dependent upon proof that another party, here the main contractors, had defaulted in their obligations, whereas an indemnity is a primary undertaking to make payment. The subcontractors claimed that the alleged undertaking to redirect payments to them had the consequence that the payment undertaking was primary in form. The judge at first instance thought it was arguable that this was so, but the Court of Appeal ([2002] BLR 44) held that the substance of the matter was that the undertaking given by the employers was a guarantee which was unenforceable because it was not evidenced in writing (before the House of Lords it was accepted that the undertaking was in the nature of a guarantee). The liability assumed by the employers was held to be a secondary liability because it was a liability that was contingent upon default by the main contractors of their obligations under the subcontract. The oral agreement was therefore held to be unenforceable because it had not been evidenced in writing. So the subcontractors were left with a worthless claim for £1.3 million against the main contractors who were insolvent.

The price of failure to comply with the formal requirements was a high one. Yet one cannot help but feel some sympathy for the subcontractors. On the facts it was not entirely clear at the outset whether the liability assumed by the employers was primary or secondary in nature, but the categorisation of the nature of the liability proved to be critical to the enforcement of the employers' alleged obligation. With the benefit of hindsight, we can see that the subcontractors should have ensured that the promise given by the employers was evidenced in writing. Given that the distinction between a guarantee and an indemnity is known to be a difficult one to draw, caution dictates that, in cases of doubt, the parties should ensure that the formal requirements for guarantees are satisfied. As the present case demonstrates, the price of a failure to comply with them can be a very high one (for another example of a case in which a high price was paid because the document in question was held to be a guarantee rather than an indemnity, see *Associated British Ports v Ferryways NV* [2009] EWCA Civ 189; [2009] 1 Lloyd's Rep 595).

5.1.3 Section 2(1) of the Law of Property (Miscellaneous Provisions) Act 1989

Section 2(1) of the Law of Property (Miscellaneous Provisions) Act 1989 (which provides that 'a contract for the sale or other disposition of an interest in land can only be made in writing and only by incorporating all the terms which the parties have expressly agreed in one document or, where contracts are exchanged, in each') has been almost equally productive in litigation terms as the courts have experienced some difficulty in deciding which terms have to be 'made in writing'. It is extremely difficult, if not impossible, to identify any rational theory which explains why certain contracts are subject to requirements of form while others are not. It is equally difficult to explain why some contracts must actually be made in writing, while others need only be evidenced in writing. Other difficult questions arise. What type of writing is required? Must the contract be signed? What constitutes a signature? Must all of the terms be contained in one document? These issues have all been the subject of extensive litigation under the Statute of Frauds 1677 (see Treitel, 2020, paras 5-020–5-026 and *Golden Ocean Group Ltd v Salgaocar Mining Industries PVT Ltd* [2012] EWCA Civ 265; [2012] 1 WLR 3674) and are an inevitable concomitant of a system based upon requirements of form. One issue which assumes considerable importance in the modern world is whether or not the need for 'writing' is satisfied by a communication in electronic form. Article 9(1) of the EC Directive on Electronic Commerce (2000/31 OJ L178/1) states that Member States 'shall ensure that their legal system allows contracts to be concluded by electronic means'. Section 8 of the Electronic Communications Act 2000 gives to Ministers the authority to review statutes and related legislation that require documents to be in writing and to amend them by way of secondary legislation 'in such manner as [the Minister] may think fit for the purpose of authorising or facilitating the use of electronic communications'. However it may be that judges can reach the conclusion that 'writing' includes electronic communications without the need for such amending legislation. This was the case in *J Pereira Fernandes SA v Mehta* [2006] EWHC 813 (Ch); [2006] 1 WLR 1543 where Judge Pelling QC held that an offer sent by email satisfied the requirement of 'writing' in the Statute of Frauds and that, when deciding whether or not an email has been 'signed', the same approach should be taken as would be adopted when deciding whether a hard copy of the same document had been signed (on the facts of the case, it was held that the email had not been signed by the offeror when his name did not appear in the body of the email but his email address had been automatically inserted by the internet service provider after the document had been transmitted by the offeror).

A final difficulty created by requirements of form arises where an 'innocent' party has acted to his detriment upon a 'contract' which did not comply with the relevant formalities (for a statutory attempt to strike a balance between the competing interests see ss 1(2)–(4) of the Requirements of Writing (Scotland) Act 1995). English law has not adopted a uniform approach to this problem. Prior to the enactment of section 2 of the Law of Property (Miscellaneous Provisions) Act 1989, the courts 'viewed with some disfavour those who made oral contracts but did not abide by them' and thus 'were prepared to interpret the statutory requirements generously to enable contracts to be enforced' (*Firstpost Homes Ltd v Johnson* [1995] 1 WLR 1567, 1575, per Peter Gibson LJ). But the courts have generally adopted a much stricter approach when seeking to interpret section 2 of the 1989 Act. A good illustration of the more generous approach which prevailed prior to the enactment of the 1989 Act is provided by cases concerning the (now repealed) section 40(1) of the Law of Property Act 1925. For example, in *Wakeham v Mackenzie* [1968] 1 WLR 1175 the deceased orally promised the claimant that he would leave his house to her if she moved into his house and looked after him until his death. She complied with his request but he failed to leave the house to her on his death. Could the claimant enforce the oral contract despite the fact that it did not comply with the formal requirements of section 40(1) of the Law of Property Act 1925 (which, it must be remembered, re-enacted part of s 4 of the Statute of Frauds 1677)? At common law the answer was 'no' because the defect in form rendered the contract unenforceable (but not void). But it was held that the contract was enforceable in equity under the doctrine of part performance. The doctrine of part performance was developed by equity in response to the hardships created by a strict application of the Statute of Frauds. The doctrine came into play where the acts of the claimant were referable to the alleged contract, it was a fraud for the defendant to rely on the Statute, the contract was specifically enforceable and there was proper evidence of the agreement. All these requirements were satisfied on the facts of *Wakeham*. It was not easy to reconcile the existence of the doctrine of part performance with the Statute of Frauds; in truth, it was incompatible with the Statute but it mitigated the hardships which would otherwise have been caused by its rigorous application.

Although section 40(1) of the 1925 Act has now been repealed by section 2(8) of the Law of Property (Miscellaneous Provisions) Act 1989, similar problems have arisen under the 1989 Act. But the courts have not generally taken such a benevolent approach under the new Act. As we have noted, section 2(1) requires that a contract for the sale or other disposition of an interest in land be 'made in writing'. An agreement which does not comply with the requirements of section 2(1) is therefore a nullity and part performance cannot breathe life into an agreement which is otherwise a nullity (*Keay v Morris Homes (West Midlands) Ltd* [2012] EWCA Civ 900; [2012] 1 WLR 2855, [47]). It follows from this that, where there is no writing, there is no contract and so nothing for part performance to bite on to. In *Firstpost Homes Ltd v Johnson* [1995] 1 WLR 1567, 1576 Peter Gibson LJ observed that the 1989 Act has a:

> new and different philosophy from that which the Statute of Frauds 1677 and Section 40 of the Act of 1925 had. Oral contracts are no longer permitted. To my mind it is clear that Parliament intended that questions as to whether there was a contract and what were the terms of the contract, should be readily ascertained by looking at the single document said to constitute the contract.

Further, in *McCausland v Duncan Lawrie Ltd* [1997] 1 WLR 38, 44 Neill LJ stated that Parliament 'intended to introduce new and strict requirements as to the formalities to be observed for the creation of a valid disposition of an interest in land'. This approach has been criticised for its 'propensity ... to allow people to escape from concluded agreements' (Thompson, 1995) but that is the price of taking formalities seriously and refusing to admit extrinsic evidence. The party who relies to his detriment on there being an enforceable contract for the sale of land when there is, in fact, no contract because it was not 'made in writing' is now in a rather precarious position. But he is not without any hope of salvation.

There are two principal options open to such a party. The first arises where the issue before the court is one that relates to the interpretation of section 2. In such a case the court may be willing to adopt a construction of the section which would 'prevent or mitigate the injustice of enabling genuine contracting parties to escape from their obligations' (*North Eastern Properties v Coleman* [2010] EWCA Civ 277; [2010] 1 WLR 2715, [45] and see also *Rabiu v Marlbray Ltd* [2016] EWCA Civ 476; [2016] 1 WLR 5147). On the facts of *North Eastern Properties v Coleman* the defendant purchasers resisted enforcement of a contract for the sale of 11 properties on the ground that not all the terms of the contract had been reduced to writing. As we have noted, section 2(1) requires the incorporation of 'all the terms which the parties have expressly agreed in one document or, where contracts are exchanged, in each'. Thus the defendants argued that the failure to include the term in question in the document had the consequence that 'all' the terms had not been incorporated so that the requirements of section 2(1) had not been satisfied. The Court of Appeal rejected this submission. The term in question was not a term in a contract for the sale of an interest in land but was part of a larger, composite transaction. Its omission did not therefore result in a failure to comply with the requirements of section 2. Briggs J stated (at [54]) that

> nothing in s 2 of the 1989 Act is designed to prevent parties to a composite transaction which includes a land contract from structuring their bargain so that the land contract is genuinely separated from the rest of the transaction in the sense that its performance is not made conditional upon the performance of some other expressly agreed part of the bargain.

It is important to note the robust language used by the court when dismissing the defendants' submission. Thus Briggs J stated (at [42]) that it was 'no part of Parliament's intention by enacting section 2 of the 1989 Act to make it easier for people who have genuinely contracted to escape their contractual obligations' (to similar effect see the judgment of Longmore LJ at [81]). This reluctance to permit section 2 to be used by a party as an escape route from its contractual obligations will not, however, provide any comfort for the party who fails to comply with the requirements of section 2. But, as the present case demonstrates, it may be used to support the finding that there has been no failure to comply with the requirements of section 2 in the first place.

Second, section 2(5) of the 1989 Act expressly states that 'nothing in this section affects the creation or operation of resulting, implied or constructive trusts'. While this subsection expressly preserves a role for the constructive trust (see *Matchmove Ltd v Dowding and Church* [2016] EWCA Civ 1233; [2017] 1 WLR 749), there is greater doubt whether proprietary estoppel has any role to play in this context. The principal source of doubt is the observation of Lord Scott in *Cobbe v Yeoman's Row Management Ltd* [2008] UKHL 55; [2008] 1 WLR 1752, [29] that proprietary estoppel cannot be invoked in order to render enforceable an agreement that section 2 has declared to be void. However, his observation was *obiter* and Lord Walker, who gave the other leading speech, reserved his view on the issue (at [93]). In *Thorner v Major* [2009] UKHL 18; [2009] 1 WLR 776, [99] Lord Neuberger stated that section 2 did not have any impact on 'a straightforward estoppel claim without any contractual connection'. It would therefore appear that proprietary estoppel has a very restricted role to play in the context of section 2, if it has any role at all. In particular, it is unlikely to be invoked by the courts where (i) the parties have not implemented their intention to make a formal document setting out the terms on which one party is to acquire an interest in property, (ii) the parties have failed to reach agreement with sufficient clarity on the property to be acquired or (iii) they did not expect their agreement to be immediately binding (*Herbert v Doyle* [2010] EWCA Civ 1095; [2011] 1 EGLR 119, [57]).

5.1.4   Is there a case for reform?

Judicial disquiet about the consequences that can flow from a failure to comply with formal requirements was expressed by Lord Bingham in *Actionstrength Ltd v International Glass Engineering In.Gl.EN.SpA* (above) where, as we have noted, the oral undertaking given by the employers to the subcontractors was held to be unenforceable because it was a guarantee which was not evidenced in writing. After noting that the reasons for requiring that guarantees be evidenced in writing related principally to the fact that guarantees are typically one-sided and the need to protect 'inexperienced people being led into undertaking obligations' which they do not 'fully understand', Lord Bingham continued:

> Whatever the strength of the reasons given … for retaining the old rule in relation to conventional consumer guarantees, it will be apparent that those reasons have little bearing on cases where the facts are such as those to be assumed here. It was not a bargain struck between inexperienced people, liable to misunderstand what they were doing. [The employers], as surety, had a very clear incentive to keep the [subcontractors'] workforce on site and, on the assumed facts, had an opportunity to think again. There is assumed to be no issue about the terms of the guarantee. English contract law does not ordinarily require writing as a condition of enforceability. It is not obvious why judges are more fallible when ruling on guarantees than other forms of oral contract. These were not small men in need of paternalist protection. While the familiar form of bank guarantee is well understood, it must be at least doubtful whether those who made the assumed agreement in this case appreciated that it was in law a guarantee. The judge at first instance was doubtful whether it was or not. The Court of Appeal reached the view that it was, but regarded the point as

interesting and not entirely easy ... Two members of the court discussed the question at a little length, with detailed reference to authority.

It may be questionable whether in relation to contracts of guarantee, the mischief at which section 4 was originally aimed, is not now outweighed, at least in some classes of case, by the mischief to which it can give rise in a case such as the present, however unusual such cases may be. But that is not a question for the House in its judicial capacity. Sitting judicially, the House must of course give effect to the law of the land of which (in England and Wales) section 4 is part.

Reform of the law is therefore a matter for Parliament and not for the judges, although it is probably unlikely that Parliament will find time to reconsider this issue.

There is no doubt that there are genuine difficulties experienced by legal systems which place heavy reliance upon requirements of form. But, as we have seen, formalities do perform useful evidentiary and cautionary functions. Although it is highly unlikely that Parliament will ever re-enact the Statute of Frauds, Parliament can usefully continue its practice of imposing requirements of form where it is satisfied that such requirements will 'provide a check against inconsiderate action' (as in the case of ss 60 and 61 of the Consumer Credit Act 1974 (above)). When it does so it can also devise a solution which will protect those who are in need of protection.

5.2 Consideration defined

Having largely rejected formal requirements, English law has developed a doctrine of consideration to play the principal role in selecting those agreements to be given the 'badge of enforceability'. However, the basis of the doctrine of consideration has been a battleground for leading contract scholars in recent years. The orthodox interpretation of consideration is that it is based upon the idea of 'reciprocity'; that a promisee should not be able to enforce a promise unless he has given or promised to give something in exchange for the promise or unless the promisor has obtained (or been promised) something in return. The classic definition was expressed in *Currie v Misa* (1875) LR 10 Ex 153 in the following terms:

> a valuable consideration, in the sense of the law, may consist either in some right, interest, profit or benefit accruing to the one party, or some forbearance, detriment, loss or responsibility given, suffered or undertaken by the other.

However, this orthodox interpretation has been subjected to a powerful challenge by Professor Atiyah (1986c). Atiyah argues that there is no coherent doctrine of consideration based upon reciprocity. He states that:

> the truth is that the courts have never set out to create a doctrine of consideration. They have been concerned with the much more practical problem of deciding in the course of litigation whether a particular promise in a particular case should be enforced ... When the courts found a sufficient reason for enforcing a promise they enforced it; and when they found that for one reason or another it was undesirable to enforce a promise, they did not enforce it.
>
> It seems highly probable that when the courts first used the word 'consideration' they meant no more than there was a 'reason' for the enforcement of a promise. If the consideration was 'good', this meant that the court found sufficient reason for enforcing the promise.

Professor Treitel has, in turn, launched a vigorous counter-attack on Atiyah's thesis. Treitel argues (2020, para 3-001) that English law does, in fact, recognise the existence of a 'complex and multifarious body of rules known as "the doc-trine of consideration"'. He rejects the argument that consideration means a rea-son for the enforcement of a promise and maintains (1976) that such a proposition is a 'negation of the existence of any applicable rules of law' because it does not tell us the circumstances in which the courts will find the existence of such a 'good reason'.

Yet even Treitel has to admit (1976) that in some cases the courts have 'invented' consideration, that is to say the courts 'have treated some act or forbearance as con-sideration quite irrespective of the question whether *the parties* have so regarded it'. This concession is necessary if the cases are to be reconciled with the traditional theory. Atiyah argues (1986c) that 'Professor Treitel has himself invented the con-cept of an invented consideration because he finds it the only way in which he is able to reconcile many decisions with what he takes to be the "true" or "real" doc-trine'. Although Atiyah challenges the orthodox interpretation of consideration, he does recognise that the presence of 'benefit or detriment is normally a good reason for enforcing a promise'. But, he argues '[it] does not in the least follow that the pres-ence of benefit or detriment is always a sufficient reason for enforcing a promise; nor does it follow that there may not be other very good reasons for enforcing a promise'.

The difference between the two schools of thought is that Treitel adheres to the benefit/detriment analysis (suitably expanded to encompass cases of 'invented con-sideration') while Atiyah maintains that there are other 'good reasons' for the enforcement of a promise. In the remaining sections of this chapter we shall con-sider whether the cases can be accommodated within a 'benefit/detriment' analysis or whether there are, as Atiyah argues, other reasons which support the enforce-ment of promises.

5.3 The many functions of consideration

As the law of contract has developed, so it would appear that the functions of the doctrine of consideration have gradually changed. Professor Simpson has argued (1975) that at an early stage in its development consideration played a multi-functional role within the law of contract. He states that:

> the old action for breach of promise catered for what we would call bilateral contracts – that is transactions involving both sides doing things – in terms of the doctrine of consid-eration and the concept of a condition.

He then recounts how, during the nineteenth century, the doctrines of offer and acceptance and intention to create legal relations were 'superimposed upon the six-teenth century requirement of consideration and made to perform some of the same functions' and concludes (at 263) that 'all this seems to me to have produced rather too many doctrines chasing a limited number of problems. To put my point differ-ently there is something to be said for throwing out old doctrine when importing new.' The refusal of English law to 'throw out' the doctrine of consideration gave rise to considerable problems in the twentieth century as the courts sought, largely without success, to ascertain the relationship between consideration and other emerging doctrines of the law of contract. This has proved to be a particularly pressing problem in relation to the rise of the doctrine of duress, particularly economic duress, and the willingness of the courts and some academics to re-analyse some of the old consideration cases in terms of duress rather than consideration (see Sections 5.13 and 17.2). This has led some of the judiciary to advocate a more 'flexible' approach to the doctrine of consideration. A good example of this process can be found in the judgment of Russell LJ in *Williams v Roffey Bros & Nicholls (Contractors) Ltd* [1991] 1 QB 1, 18 when he stated that:

> in the late twentieth century I do not believe that the rigid approach to the concept of consideration to be found in [the early nineteenth-century case of] *Stilk v. Myrick* is either necessary or desirable. Consideration there must still be but, in my judgment, the courts nowadays should be more ready to find its existence so as to reflect the intention of the parties to the contract where the bargaining powers are not unequal and where the finding of consideration reflects the true intention of the parties.

This 'watering-down' of consideration makes it very difficult to ascertain the purpose behind the modern doctrine of consideration, or to locate its function within the law of contract. The approach of Russell LJ appears to be that its function should be to 'reflect the intention of the parties to the contract', which suggests that it should, perhaps, become an aspect of the doctrine of intention to create legal relations. This is a controversial suggestion and not one which reflects the traditional understanding of the relationship between consideration and intention to create legal relations (see Section 5.29) but it does reflect the uncertainty which currently surrounds the role and functions of consideration within modern contract law.

5.4   Consideration and motive

Before we enter into a discussion of the substance of the doctrine of consideration, one further preliminary point must be made. That point relates to the distinction between consideration and motive. In *Thomas v Thomas* (1842) 2 QB 851 a testator, shortly before he died, expressed the desire that his widow should have the house for the rest of her life. After his death, his executors promised to carry out the testator's desire provided that the widow paid £1 per annum towards the ground rent and kept the house in repair. Now, although the testator's desire was the motive for the transaction, that desire was not the consideration; rather, the consideration was the widow's promise to pay £1 and to keep the house in good repair. It was only the latter which was of value in the eyes of the law.

5.5   The scope of the doctrine

The rules which make up the doctrine of consideration may be divided into three categories. The first is that consideration must be sufficient but it need not be adequate (Sections 5.6–5.17), the second is that past consideration is not good consideration (Section 5.18) and the third is that consideration must move from the promisee (Section 5.19). Once we have ascertained the scope of the doctrine of consideration, we shall consider the extent to which the law of contract protects those who rely to their detriment upon promises which are not supported by consideration (Sections 5.20–5.29).

5.6   Consideration must be sufficient but it need not be adequate

The first rule of the doctrine of consideration is that consideration must be sufficient but it need not be adequate. That is to say, the courts will not enforce a promise unless something of value is given in return for the promise. This is what is meant by saying that consideration must be 'sufficient'. On the other hand, the courts do not, in general, ask whether adequate value has been given in return for the promise or whether the agreement is harsh or one-sided (although here a significant role is played by the doctrines of duress and undue influence, on which see generally Chapter 17). This is what is meant by saying that consideration need not be 'adequate'. So if a house worth £250,000 is sold for £1, that is sufficient consideration, even though it is manifestly inadequate. In the following sections (5.7–5.17) we shall discuss in greater detail the scope of the rule that consideration must be sufficient but that it need not be adequate.

5.7   Trivial acts

The maxim that consideration must be sufficient but need not be adequate has resulted in very trivial acts being held to constitute consideration. The classic illustration is *Chappell & Co v Nestlé* [1960] AC 87. Nestlé offered for sale gramophone records in return for 1s 6d and three wrappers from their chocolate bars. The House of Lords held that the wrappers themselves, although of very trivial economic value, were nevertheless part of the consideration. This was so even though Nestlé threw away the wrappers. As Lord Somervell said: 'a contracting party can stipulate for what consideration he chooses. A peppercorn does not cease to be good consideration if it is established that the promisee does not like pepper and will throw away the corn.'

Atiyah has argued (1986c) that this case does not fit within the 'benefit/detriment' analysis because it would be 'ridiculous to assert that the sending or the receipt of the wrappers necessarily involved an actual detriment to the sender or a benefit to the defendants'. He argues that the receipt of the wrappers was not a benefit but was the motive which inspired the promise and that therefore this was a case in which a court would have enforced a promise despite the lack of benefit to the promisee. Treitel has replied (1976) by asserting that Atiyah has failed to take account of the principle that the courts will not investigate the adequacy of the consideration and that, once it is realised that consideration need only be of *some* value, 'there is no doctrinal difficulty in holding that a piece of paper or some act or forbearance of very small value can constitute consideration'.

The crucial question which must now be asked is: what does the law of contract recognise as 'value'? Treitel states (2020, para 3-027) that consideration must have 'some economic value', even though that value cannot be 'precisely quantified'. But, as we shall see, the courts have not adopted a consistent approach to the identification of 'value' or 'benefit'. In some cases (such as *Foakes v Beer* (1884) 9 App Cas 605, Section 5.15), they have ignored a factual benefit obtained by the promisor and held that no consideration was provided because, as a matter of *law*, the promisor was not benefited. In other cases (such as *Cook v Wright* (1861) 1 B & S 559, Section 5.9), the courts have found the existence of consideration despite the apparent lack of either benefit to the promisor or detriment to the promisee. Some cases have adopted an extremely subjective interpretation of benefit (see, for example, *Bainbridge v Firmstone* (1838) 8 A & E 743), but in other cases the courts have adopted an objective interpretation (see, for example, *White v Bluett* (1853) 23 LJ Ex 36, discussed in Section 5.8). The emphasis in the important decisions of the Court of Appeal in *Williams v Roffey Bros & Nicholls (Contractors) Ltd* [1991] 1 QB 1 (see Sections 5.11– 5.14) and *MWB Business Exchange Centres Ltd v Rock Advertising Ltd* [2016] EWCA Civ 553; [2017] QB 604 (see Section 5.15) was on the need to identify a 'practical benefit' to the promisor rather than 'a benefit in the eyes of the law' but this approach has not been carried through into all aspects of the doctrine of consideration (see *Re Selectmove Ltd* [1995] 1 WLR 474, also discussed in Section 5.15). One of the most difficult tasks in analysing the doctrine of consideration is to stabilise the concept of value or benefit (see Section 5.17).

5.8 Intangible returns

It is clear that 'natural affection of itself is not a sufficient consideration' (*Bret v JS* (1600) Cro Eliz 756). In *White v Bluett* (1853) 23 LJ Ex 36, a son's promise not to bore his father with complaints about the father's distribution of his property among his children was held not to be good consideration for the father's promise not to sue the son on a debt owed by the son to the father. Pollock CB said that the son had not provided any consideration as he had 'no right to complain' to his father (because it was for the father to decide how he wanted to distribute his property) and so, in giving up his habit of complaining, he had not provided any consideration. But the decision is open to attack on two possible grounds.

The first is that it ignored the 'practical benefit' which the father obtained in being freed from the complaints of his son. The emphasis on practical benefit in recent cases such as *Williams v Roffey Bros & Nicholls (Contractors) Ltd* [1991] 1 QB 1 (below) suggests that this aspect of *White* may be open to criticism. That this is so can be demonstrated by reference to the case of *Pitt v PHH Asset Management Ltd* [1994] 1 WLR 327. The defendants, acting as undisclosed agents of mortgagees, put a cottage on the market for £205,000. Both the claimant and a Miss Buckle were interested in purchasing the property and made competing bids. The claimant made a bid of £200,000 which the defendants accepted 'subject to contract'. The next day Miss Buckle increased her offer to £210,000 and the acceptance of the claimant's offer was withdrawn. Discussions then took place between the claimant and the defendants' agent. The claimant threatened to seek an injunction to halt the sale to Miss Buckle and also said that he would inform her of his loss of interest in the property so that she would be free to lower her offer in the absence of a rival bidder. The outcome of these negotiations was that it was agreed that the property should be sold to the claimant for £200,000 and that the vendors would not consider any further offers for the property provided that the claimant agreed to exchange contracts within two weeks of receipt of the contract. But in breach of the agreement the cottage was sold to Miss Buckle for £210,000. The claimant sued the defendants for damages for breach of contract. One of the defences which was invoked by the defendants was that the claimant did not provide any consideration for the promise not to consider other offers because he had only promised to be ready, willing and able to proceed to exchange of contracts, which he was already obliged to do. But the Court of Appeal held that the claimant had supplied consideration for the promise. In the first place, the claimant agreed not to apply for an injunction to restrain the sale to Miss Buckle. Peter Gibson LJ said that he could not see how the claimant could have succeeded with this claim but he held that the defendants were nevertheless freed from the 'nuisance value' of having to defend such a claim. Secondly, consideration was provided by the claimant agreeing not to carry out his threat to make trouble with Miss Buckle; once again, the removal of that 'nuisance' provided 'some consideration'. Finally, the promise of the claimant to proceed to exchange within two weeks was also held to amount to consideration. The court therefore held that 'these three items constituted valuable consideration sufficient to support the … agreement' and upheld the claimant's claim. The difficulty with the case is not so much in the result (as the third item seems clearly to constitute consideration) but the emphasis which the court placed upon the benefit which the defendants obtained by being free of 'nuisance claims'. This does not sit very easily with the refusal of the court to find consideration on the facts of *White* (although it must be said that, where the 'nuisance' consists of a threat of litigation (as in the case of the injunction), the courts have been particularly willing to find the existence of consideration, see Section 5.9).

The second ground on which *White* is open to attack is that the son did act to his detriment in refraining from making complaints. He was doing nothing wrong in complaining to his father, so in that sense he did have a 'right' to complain, and in giving up that right he provided consideration. This aspect of *White* should be contrasted with the American case of *Hamer v Sidway* (1891) 27 NE 256. An uncle promised to pay his nephew $5,000 if the nephew refrained from 'drinking liquor, using tobacco, swearing and playing cards or billiards for money' until he (the nephew) was 21. This promise was held to be enforceable because the nephew had a legal right to engage in such activities, and in giving up his rights he had provided consideration for the promise. Professor Atiyah has argued (1986c) that *Hamer* is a case which does not fit within the 'benefit/detriment' analysis because there was no benefit to the uncle (apart from the fact that he wanted his nephew to abstain from such practices, but that is a matter of motive, not benefit), nor was there a detriment to the nephew (on the ground that giving up smoking is a benefit rather than a detriment). Rather, Atiyah argues, this is a case in which the nephew was induced to act on the promise and the court thought it just to enforce the promise. But the court did not perceive matters in this way. It was of the opinion that the nephew had incurred a detriment because he had 'restricted his lawful freedom of action within certain prescribed limits upon the faith of the uncle's agreement' (see also Treitel, 1976).

Hamer is not at all easy to reconcile with *White*. It might be said that it is not necessary to reconcile them because *Hamer* is an American case and so not binding on an English court. While this is true, it is often assumed that *Hamer* does represent English law (see, for example, Beale, Bishop and Furmston, 2008, 102). It may be that the cases can be reconciled on the ground that the promise of the son in *White* was too uncertain to constitute consideration for the father's promise, or on the ground that there was no intention to create legal relations (Anson, 2020, 105). Alternatively, it could be said that the activities of the son in *White* were thought to be less socially valuable (bordering on duress?) and therefore less deserving of protection than the conduct of the nephew in *Hamer*. Even if *Hamer* does represent English law, it must be noted that there is a limit to the principle which it establishes, namely that, if the nephew had never intended to drink, smoke, swear or gamble because, for example, he had a religious objection to engaging in such practices, then he could not have enforced his uncle's promise. This is because 'it is not consideration to refrain from a course of conduct which it was never intended to pursue' (*Arrale v Costain Civil Engineering Ltd* [1976] 1 Lloyd's Rep 98, 106).

5.9   Compromise and forbearance to sue

A promise not to enforce a valid claim is good consideration for a promise given in return, as is a promise not to enforce a claim which is doubtful in law. On the other hand, it is clear that a promise not to enforce a claim which is known to be invalid is not good consideration for a promise given in return (*Wade v Simeon* (1846) 2 CB 548). The difficulty lies in the case where the claim is clearly bad in law but is believed to be good. In *Cook v Wright* (1861) 1 B & S 559, the claimants honestly believed that the defendant was under a statutory obligation to reimburse them in respect of certain expenditure which they had incurred in work on a street adjoining the house in which the defendant was residing. The defendant denied that he was under such an obligation, but he eventually promised to pay a reduced sum after he was threatened with litigation if he did not pay. When the defendant discovered that he was not in fact under a statutory obligation to pay, he refused to honour his promise. He maintained that his promise was not supported by consideration because the claimants had given nothing in return for it. But the court held that the promise was supported by consideration and that he was liable to pay the sum promised. Nevertheless, it is difficult to find the consideration supplied by the claimants. They had given up an invalid claim and in so doing they had suffered no detriment and the defendant was not benefited in any way by their promise to accept the reduced sum in full satisfaction of their invalid claim. It could be argued that the claimants' honest belief in the validity of their claim provided the consideration. But consideration must actually be of value in the eyes of the law and not merely something believed to be of value by the parties. Alternatively, it could be argued that the defendant benefited because he escaped the vexation which is inherent in litigation. Such a rationale proves too much because it would apply equally where the claim was known to be bad, and yet we know from *Wade v Simeon* that a promise not to enforce a claim which is known to be bad is not good consideration for a promise given in return (unless it is possible to confine *Wade v Simeon* on public policy grounds, namely that proceedings should not be instituted where the claim is known to be a bad one). *Cook v Wright* is therefore a case which is very difficult to accommodate within the 'benefit/detriment' analysis (although it should be noted that Treitel, 1976 includes the case within his category of 'invented' consideration).

5.10   Performance of a duty imposed by law

The question whether performance of a duty (or a promise to perform a duty) which one is already under an obligation to perform can constitute consideration for a promise given in return is currently a very controversial one in English contract law.

The orthodox position is clear: performance of an existing duty imposed by law and performance of a contractual duty owed to the promisor do not constitute consideration, while performance of a duty imposed by a contract with a third party does constitute consideration. But today the position is not so clear. The principal source of the problem is the decision of the Court of Appeal in *Williams v Roffey Bros & Nicholls (Contractors) Ltd* [1991] 1 QB 1, in which it was held that performance of an existing contractual duty owed to the promisor could constitute good consideration. Having reached this conclusion, the question which now arises is whether this approach can also be applied to performance of a duty imposed by law.

Prior to *Williams v Roffey Bros*, the law was relatively clear: performance of (or a promise to perform) a duty imposed by law was not good consideration for a promise given in return (*Collins v Godefroy* (1831) 1 B & Ad 950). The rule was generally supported on the ground that it prevented public officials extorting money in return for the performance of their existing legal duties or, to put the point more neutrally, on the basis that public officials, such as the police, owe a duty to the public to provide them with protection or other services without the need for payment (see *Michael v Chief Constable of South Wales Police* [2015] UKSC 2; [2015] AC 1732, [30]). But in other cases the rule could give rise to hardship because it ignored real benefits obtained by the promisor or real detriments incurred by the promisee. So it is no surprise to learn that the rule has come under some scrutiny.

The leading case is *Ward v Byham* [1956] 1 WLR 496. The father of an illegitimate child promised to pay the mother of the child £1 per week provided that the child was well looked after and happy. The mother was under a legal duty to look after the child. The mother sued the father when he stopped making the payments. The father argued that the mother had not provided any consideration for his promise because, by looking after the child, she was simply carrying out her existing legal duty. Denning LJ rejected this argument and launched a direct assault on the general rule. He held that the mother provided consideration by performing her legal duty to support the child. He stated that the father was benefited by the mother's promise to look after the child, just as he would have been benefited if a neighbour had promised to look after the child for reward. Lord Denning returned to this theme in *Williams v Williams* [1957] 1 WLR 148 when he said 'a promise to perform an existing duty is, I think, sufficient consideration to support a promise, so long as there is nothing in the transaction which is contrary to the public interest'.

Although this statement of principle has much to commend it, the other judges in the Court of Appeal in *Ward* did not expressly approve it. They were content simply to find that there was 'ample' consideration on the facts of the case. They attached significance to the letter written by the father in which he promised to pay the mother the weekly allowance 'provided you can prove that [the child] will be well looked after and happy and also that she is allowed to decide for herself whether or not she wishes to come and live with you'. It is not entirely easy to locate the consideration here. The letter could be interpreted as a waiver of the strict legal position between the parties (see Section 5.24), but a finding that there has been a waiver is not the same as a conclusion that consideration has been supplied. Alternatively, it could be said that the consideration is to be found in the fact that the mother promised to do more than her legal duty by promising to keep the child 'happy' and by promising to allow the child to decide for herself where she should live. The latter may be capable of constituting consideration but there is more doubt about the former. While a promise to do more than one is legally obliged to do is good consideration (*Glasbrook Ltd v Glamorgan CC* [1925] AC 270), there is some doubt about the application of this rule to the mother's promise to keep the child 'happy' because, as we have already noted, natural affection of itself is not a sufficient consideration (*Bret v JS* (1600) Cro Eliz 756, discussed in Section 5.8). Whatever doubts we may harbour about the validity of this approach, it should be noted that its focus is upon detriment to the mother in that it is argued that she did *more* than she was legally obliged to do. An alternative analysis of the case is to look at it in terms of benefit to the father. Thus in *Williams v Roffey Bros*, Glidewell LJ (at 13) interpreted *Ward* as a case in which the father obtained a *'practical benefit'* as a result of the mother's promise that the child would be well looked after and happy (although contrast the view of Purchas LJ at 20). Whatever might be said about this emphasis on practical benefit as a matter of principle (see Section 5.12) it is clear that it is not the approach which the court actually adopted on the facts of *Ward*. So, as a matter of authority, the rule that performance of a duty imposed by law does not constitute consideration remains intact, at least for now. But it may not be able to withstand the onslaught on the existing duty rule commenced by the Court of Appeal in *Williams v Roffey Bros* (see Section 5.11).

5.11　Performance of a contractual duty owed to the promisor

Until recently the rule which English law adopted was that performance of an existing contractual duty owed to a promisor was no consideration for a fresh promise given by that promisor. The rule was not a popular one: indeed, it was once stated that it has done the 'most to give consideration a bad name' (Patterson, 1958).

5.11.1　*Stilk v Myrick*

The origin of the rule can be traced back to the old case of *Stilk v Myrick* (1809) 2 Camp 317 and 6 Esp 129. Stilk was a seaman who agreed with the defendants to sail to the Baltic and back at a rate of pay of £5 per month. Originally, there were 11 men in the crew but two men deserted during the voyage. The master was unable to find replacements for the deserters and so he agreed with the remainder of the crew that he would share the wages of the two deserters between them if they would work the ship back to London. The crew members agreed. When they returned to London, Stilk demanded his share of the money but the master refused to pay. Stilk sued for the money. He was unsuccessful in his claim. The case was reported twice and, unfortunately, the two reports differ as to the reason for the failure of Stilk's claim (on which see generally Luther, 1999).

In the Espinasse report Stilk was unsuccessful on grounds of policy; the policy being that a successful claim would open up the prospect of sailors on the high seas making unreasonable and extortionate demands upon their masters as the price for performing their contractual duty to bring the ship back to the home port. In Campbell's report Stilk's claim failed, not on grounds of policy, but because he had provided no consideration for the master's promise as he had only done what he was already contractually obliged to do.

The difference between these two reports is crucial. If the former report is correct, it is possible to confine the rule to cases where there is a possibility of duress being exercised. Where such fear is absent, there is no objection to the enforcement of the promise. However, Espinasse is not highly regarded as a law reporter (although it might be pointed out that Campbell was not without his faults either: for a discussion of the problems of law reporting at this time see Luther, 1999, 528–37), and it was the second, wider rule derived from Campbell's report which was later accepted into English law (see *North Ocean Shipping Co v Hyundai Construction Co Ltd* [1979] QB 705).

But the existing duty rule laid down in Campbell's report of *Stilk v Myrick* has always been controversial. Thus Professor Atiyah has argued that cases such as *Stilk v Myrick* and *Ward v Byham* [1956] 1 WLR 496 (Section 5.10) cannot be accommodated within the 'benefit/detriment' analysis because, as a matter of fact, there was a benefit to the promisor and a detriment to the promisee but nevertheless there was held to be no consideration. In *Stilk v Myrick* there is little doubt that, as a matter of fact, the master of the ship was benefited by Stilk's promise to work the ship back home, yet the court concluded that no consideration had been provided. The defenders of the orthodox interpretation of consideration attempt to meet this argument by asserting that it is *legal* benefit or *legal* detriment which is important and not factual benefit or factual detriment. But, as Corbin has pointed out (1963), this does not explain *why* the courts have resorted to the concepts of legal benefit and detriment.

Given these criticisms of *Stilk v Myrick* it is perhaps surprising that it stood unchallenged for as long as it did. There are two possible reasons for this. The first is that the one case which appeared to be flatly inconsistent with *Stilk v Myrick* remained buried in the Law Reports, rarely being cited in the books or in the courts. That case is *Raggow v Scougall & Co* (1915) 31 TLR 564. The claimant was employed by the defendants for a period of two years at a certain salary. During the period of the contract, war broke out and the defendants' business was detrimentally affected. Rather than close the business the parties entered into a new agreement under which the claimant agreed to accept a lower salary until the end of the war, when the original agreement would be revived. The claimant accepted the reduced salary for a period of time but then brought an action claiming his salary at the old rate, arguing that the defendants had provided no consideration for his promise to accept a lower salary. Darling J held that the agreement was supported by consideration and that the action therefore failed. He held that the parties had in fact torn up the old agreement and made a new one by mutual consent, and stated that he was glad to be able to arrive at this conclusion because the claimant was seeking to do a 'very dishonest thing'. The case has been rarely cited since and it has never been used as the basis for an attack on the decision in *Stilk v Myrick* itself.

The second factor which contributed to the fact that *Stilk v Myrick* survived serious judicial assault consists of the two exceptions which exist to the original rule. The first arises where the promisee has done, or has promised to do, more than he was obliged to do under his contract. In *Hanson v Royden* (1867) LR 3 CP 47, the claimant was promoted from able seaman to second mate and it was held that, in carrying out the job of second mate, he had done more than he was obliged to do under his contract and so had provided consideration for the promise of extra pay. The second situation arises where, before the new promise was made, circumstances had arisen which entitled the promisee to refuse to carry out his obligations under his contract. In *Hartley v Ponsonby* (1857) 7 E & B 872, 17 of a crew of 36 deserted and only four or five of the remaining crew were able seamen. The desertion of such a large proportion of the crew rendered it unsafe to continue the voyage and would have entitled the remaining seamen to abandon the voyage. The seamen agreed to continue the voyage on being promised extra pay on its completion. The master refused to fulfil his promise on their return to the home port but it was held that the seamen were entitled to enforce the master's promise because, in agreeing to continue with the voyage when they were not obliged by the terms of their contract to do so, they had provided consideration.

5.11.2   *Williams v Roffey Bros & Nicholls (Contractors) Ltd*

However, a more wide-ranging attack on *Stilk v Myrick* was launched by the Court of Appeal in what is now the seminal case of *Williams v Roffey Bros & Nicholls (Contractors) Ltd* [1991] 1 QB1. The defendant contractors entered into a contract to refurbish a block of flats. They subcontracted the carpentry work to the claimant for a price of £20,000. The claimant ran into financial difficulties after having completed part of the work. The cause of his difficulties was partly attributable to the fact that he had underpriced the job and partly because of his own inability to supervise his workforce. It was in the interest of the defendants to ensure that the claimant completed the work on time because if, as a result of delay or non-performance by the claimant, the defendants were late in completing the work they would incur liability to their employers under the terms of a 'penalty' clause contained in the main contract. So the defendants called a meeting with the claimant in order to discuss the situation. At that meeting it was agreed that the defendants would pay to the claimant an extra £10,300 at the rate of £575 per flat on completion to ensure that the work was completed on time. The claimant subsequently finished eight more flats but the defendants paid him only a further £1,500. The claimant then ceased work on the flats and brought a claim against the defendants for the additional money. One of the grounds on which the defendants denied the existence of a liability to pay was that the claimant had provided no consideration for the promise of extra payment: he had simply promised to perform his existing contractual duties and that, according to *Stilk v Myrick*, did not constitute good consideration. The Court of Appeal rejected the defendants' argument and held that the claimant had provided consideration and that he was entitled to bring an action for damages (although it should be noted that the claimant was not awarded full expectation damages but only damages of £3,500, see Chen-Wishart, 1995).

The Court of Appeal adopted a very pragmatic approach to the issue. They held that the defendants had obtained a *practical benefit* as a result of the claimant's promise to complete the work on time and that practical benefit was, for this purpose at least, sufficient to constitute consideration. The proposition for which *Williams* stands as authority was summed up by Glidewell LJ in the following words:

> (i) if A has entered into a contract with B to do work for, or to supply goods or services to, B in return for payment by B and (ii) at some stage before A has completely performed his obligations under the contract B has reason to doubt whether A will, or will be able to, complete his side of the bargain and (iii) B thereupon promises A an additional payment in

return for A's promise to perform his contractual obligations on time and (iv) as a result of giving his promise B obtains in practice a benefit, or obviates a disbenefit, and (v) B's promise is not given as a result of economic duress or fraud on the part of A, then (vi) the benefit to B is capable of being consideration for B's promise, so that the promise will be legally binding.

The emphasis on 'practical benefit' is important. The case does not formally challenge the rule that a promise to perform an existing duty owed to the promisor does not constitute consideration, and cases can still be found in which the rule continues to be affirmed (see, for example, *WRN Ltd v Ayris* [2008] EWHC 1080 (QB); [2008] IRLR 889, [46]). But the reality is that the change in emphasis has substantially undermined the traditional rule and the courts today do not require much persuasion in order to find the existence of consideration. The latter proposition can be illustrated by reference to the decision of the Court of Appeal in *Attrill v Dresdner Kleinwort Ltd* [2011] EWCA Civ 229; [2011] IRLR 613 where it was held that an employee who continued to work after his employer had promised to establish a guaranteed minimum bonus pool had arguably provided consideration for the promise to set up the fund. But it might not have been the promise to perform his existing contractual duties that arguably provided the consideration; it could be said that the consideration was provided by the employee remaining in the employment of his employer and not exercising his right to terminate his contract of employment in order to find employment elsewhere at a time when the employer had particular need of his services (as indicated by Elias LJ at a subsequent stage of the litigation in *Attrill v Dresdner Kleinwort Ltd* [2013] EWCA Civ 394; [2013] 3 All ER 607, [95]). While it is too early to conclude that English law has abandoned the rule that a promise to perform an existing contractual duty does not amount to consideration, the width of the exception recognised in *Williams* suggests that little is left of the rule. Two immediate problems arise. The first is: what exactly was the practical benefit which the defendants obtained? The second is: how can this conclusion be reconciled with *Stilk v Myrick?* These issues must be examined with some care.

5.12 Practical benefit

There was no one practical benefit which the defendants in *Williams v Roffey Bros* were held to have obtained as a result of the claimant's promise. The court relied upon a number of factors in identifying the practical benefit obtained. The first was that the claimant continued with the work and did not breach his subcontract. The second was that the defendants were spared the 'trouble and expense of engaging other people to complete the carpentry work'. The third was that they avoided incurring a penalty under the main contract for delay in completion of the work. The fourth was that a 'rather haphazard method of payment' was replaced by a 'more formalised scheme involving the payment of a specified sum on the completion of each flat'. Finally, by directing the claimant to complete one flat at a time, the defendants 'were able to direct their other trades to do work in the completed flats which otherwise would have been held up until the claimant had completed his work'.

The first three factors are controversial. The first adopts a Holmesian conception of contract law so that 'the duty to keep a contract at common law means a prediction that you must pay damages if you do not keep it – and nothing else'. Thus Purchas LJ stated (at 23) that, although in 'normal circumstances the suggestion that a contracting party can rely on his own breach to establish consideration is distinctly unattractive', on the facts of the case, the claimant had given up his right to 'cut his losses' by deliberately breaching the contract with the defendants. To adopt such an approach is to refuse to recognise that the defendants under the original contract had bought not simply the right to damages in the event of non-performance, but the right to performance itself. The same approach can be adopted in relation to the second factor. The benefit of not having to look for alternative carpenters was a benefit which the defendants paid for under the original contract and were entitled to receive. The third factor is scarcely more convincing. If the defendants had been compelled to pay out under the 'penalty' clause because of the claimant's failure to complete on time they would have been entitled to recover that sum from the claimant by way of damages (although there was, admittedly, a risk that the claimant would not have been in a financial position to pay damages). The fourth and fifth factors do appear to be capable of constituting consideration (even on orthodox grounds) if the claimant did actually accept a new obligation to complete the flats one by one. Unfortunately, it is not clear from the judgments whether any new obligation was assumed because elsewhere in the judgments it is stated that the claimant simply performed his existing contractual duties. So the fourth and fifth factors are at best equivocal and it is not at all easy to pinpoint exactly what the practical benefit was on the facts. Are the factors cumulative or not? Does a promise to complete the work in itself confer a practical benefit, or must one show 'something more', such as the avoidance of a potential liability under a 'penalty' clause?

Williams v Roffey Bros has been applauded as a pragmatic decision, giving effect to the 'realities' of the situation. Modifications of contracts, it is argued, are in the public interest; both parties should be encouraged to bargain their way out of an unanticipated difficulty, and this can best be done by giving effect to the variations which the parties have agreed. But this is to tell only half of the story. Modifications are not necessarily in the public interest. There is a competing interest in holding parties to their original bargain. When I employ a subcontractor to do work for me for £20,000, I do not mean £20,000 plus whatever else he can extract from me by conduct short of duress. The deal is £20,000; not a penny more, not a penny less. In jumping on the practical benefit bandwagon, the judgments of the Court of Appeal are open to criticism not only on the ground that they failed to identify practical benefit with sufficient precision, but also on the basis that they failed to place sufficient weight on the need to hold contracting parties to the terms of their original bargain.

5.13   Consideration and duress

Even if the practical benefit hurdle can be overcome, we are left with our second problem. How can *Williams v Roffey Bros* be reconciled with *Stilk v Myrick*? The Court of Appeal in *Williams v Roffey Bros* was adamant that *Stilk v Myrick* had not been overruled: rather, it had been 'refined' and 'limited'. Yet the two cases are very similar. If the defendants in *Williams v Roffey Bros* received a practical benefit, can the same not be said of the master of the ship in *Stilk v Myrick*? He was practically benefited by the promise of Stilk to work the ship back home, yet that benefit was held not to constitute consideration. The Court of Appeal attempted to resolve this problem by explaining *Stilk v Myrick* as a duress case. This could have been done relatively easily. After all, Espinasse's report was explicitly based upon considerations of public policy and there were other cases in which the courts had relied upon public policy to hold that the sailors were not entitled to additional payment (see, for example, *Harris v Watson* (1791) Peake 102; contrast Luther (1999), who points out that Espinasse's report was not solely about duress and that account must be taken of the range of distinctive policy concerns which led the courts and Parliament to develop special rules both to protect and to regulate the conduct of merchant seamen). But this relatively straightforward approach was not for the Court of Appeal. The court chose to cite Campbell's report but in substance they followed Espinasse. Thus Purchas LJ stated (at 21) that *Stilk v Myrick* was a case arising out of:

> the extraordinary conditions existing at the turn of the 18th century under which seamen had to serve their contracts of employment on the high seas. There were strong public policy grounds at that time to protect the master and owners of a ship from being held to ransom by disaffected crews.

But where is the evidence for this on the facts of *Stilk v Myrick*? As Gilmore (1974) has pointed out, the contract in *Stilk v Myrick* was concluded on shore, not the high seas. We have no evidence that Stilk applied any pressure upon the master. The only real evidence of duress can be found in the Espinasse report but the Court of Appeal chose not to rely upon that evidence.

But even if *Stilk v Myrick* is now a duress case, what does this tell us about the case? Here we encounter the problem which we noted above (Section 5.3) of working out the relationship between consideration and duress. In *The Alev* [1989] 1 Lloyd's Rep 138, 147, Hobhouse J said that:

> now that there is a properly developed doctrine of the avoidance of contracts on the grounds of economic duress, there is no warrant for the Court to fail to recognise the existence of some consideration even though it may be insignificant and even though there may have been no mutual bargain in any realistic use of that phrase.

This approach advocates a more liberal approach to consideration, maintaining that the courts should be readier to find consideration now that they know that they can always set aside the contract on the ground of duress. On this analysis, there was consideration on the facts of *Stilk v Myrick* (because the master was practically benefited by Stilk's promise to work the ship back home). So a contract was initially concluded but that contract was then set aside on the ground of duress exerted by Stilk which prevented him from enforcing the contract.

Some commentators have gone even further than advocating a more liberal approach to the identification of consideration and argued that there are:

> good reasons why the doctrine of economic duress ought to *displace*, and not be in addition to, the doctrine of consideration in 'extortion situations', provided, of course, that it can be rationalised. (Phang, 1990)

Judicial support can also be found for this view. In *Adam Opel GmbH v Mitras Automotive UK Ltd* [2007] EWHC 3252 (QB); [2007] All ER (D) 272 (Dec), [42]

David Donaldson QC, sitting as a Deputy Judge of the High Court, stated that the:

> law of consideration is no longer to be used to protect a participant in such a variation. That role has passed to the law of economic duress, which provides a more refined control mechanism, and renders the contract voidable rather than void.

However, this view is not easy to understand. Duress cannot 'displace' consideration, because the two doctrines perform different functions. Consideration is relevant to the question whether or not a contract has been concluded. But duress is a vitiating factor; that is to say, it is a ground upon which an otherwise valid and subsisting contract can be set aside. The two issues cannot be collapsed into one.

So it is suggested that, after *Williams v Roffey Bros*, *Stilk v Myrick* should be interpreted as a case in which there was consideration but that the contract was set aside on the ground of duress. This view does not yet command universal support. For example, in *Anangel Atlas Compania Naviera SA v Ishikawajima-Harima Heavy Industries Co Ltd (No 2)* [1990] 2 Lloyd's Rep 526, 544–45 Hirst J, after expressing his approval of the emphasis upon practical benefit on the facts of *Williams v Roffey Bros*, stated that *Stilk v Myrick* still applied where there is 'a wholly gratuitous promise'. This is difficult to follow. Why was Stilk's promise wholly gratuitous, when the promise of the claimant in *Williams v Roffey Bros* was not? As has already been stated, there is very little to distinguish between the two cases. This failure to provide a coherent, fresh analysis of *Stilk v Myrick* in the light of *Williams v Roffey Bros* further underlines the confusion which currently exists in this area of the law.

5.14 Alternative analyses

We have now discussed the principal difficulties with, and analyses of, *Williams v Roffey Bros* and *Stilk v Myrick*. There are, however, three other theories which are worthy of brief mention.

5.14.1 A 'two contract' analysis?

The first was adopted by the Supreme Court of New Hampshire in *Watkin & Son Inc v Carrig* (1941) 21 A 2d 591. The parties entered into a written contract under which the claimant agreed to excavate a cellar for the defendant for a fixed price. Shortly after commencing the work the claimant discovered the presence of solid rock in the area which he had agreed to excavate. Discussions took place between the parties and the defendant agreed to pay a price which was approximately nine times the amount of the original contract price. The claimant did the work and then sued to recover the promised sum. The defendant argued that there was no consideration to support the promise to pay the additional sum. The argument was rejected. The trial judge found that the written contract between the parties had been superseded by a new agreement which was enforceable. In giving up their rights to sue each other under the original written contract, the parties provided consideration for their agreement to abandon that contract. The second contract was then supported by consideration. Applying this type of reasoning to *Stilk v Myrick* we can say that, if Stilk had been able to show that the original contract had been abandoned by the mutual agreement of the parties, then that abandonment would have been supported by consideration, and the agreement to pay the higher rate would then have been enforceable as a separate contract. But this is a very difficult test to apply in practice because how do the courts decide whether there is a variation of one contract or a replacement of one contract by another? The answer to the question is that it depends upon the intention of the parties. Where their intention is to rescind the first contract and replace it with a second contract, the rule in *Stilk v Myrick* has no application. On the other hand, the rule does apply where the intention of the parties is that the original contract should not be rescinded but rather should be varied. Admittedly, the distinction between the two cases can be difficult to draw, especially given the fact that there need be no interval in time between the rescission of the first contract and its replacement by a second contract. An instantaneous rescission of one contract followed by its immediate replacement can look very much like a variation of the original contract, but the courts have held that the former is nevertheless distinguishable from the latter (see *Compagnie Noga D'Importation et D'Exportation SA v Abacha (No 2)* [2003] EWCA Civ 1100; [2003] 2 All ER (Comm) 915, [57] and [60]). In cases of difficulty the court must try as best it can to elicit the intention of the parties. But a party who wishes to avoid the application of the rule in *Stilk v Myrick* would be well advised to make clear to his contracting party that what is taking place is not a variation of the original contract but a rescission of that contract followed immediately by the creation of a new contract in similar but not identical terms. In this way the new agreement should, absent duress, be enforceable.

5.14.2   A collateral unilateral contract?

The second analysis is that the original bilateral contract between the claimant and the defendants was supplemented by a 'collateral unilateral contract to pay more (or accept less) *if* actual performance is rendered' (Chen-Wishart, 2010a). According to this analysis,

> there is a unilateral offer by the promisor to pay more or to accept less, which is only binding when the other party accepts by actually performing the stipulated obligation. This unilateral contract would be collateral to the continuing original, main, bilateral contract. If the unilateral offer is not made binding by the acceptance of completed performance, then the original contract has full force. But, if the stipulated performance is completed, then the unilateral collateral contract can prevail over or qualify the original contract. (Chen-Wishart, 2010b)

Judicial support for this analysis can be found in the judgment of Arden LJ in *MWB Business Exchange Centres Ltd v Rock Advertising Ltd* [2016] EWCA Civ 553; [2017] QB 604, [90] (although Kitchin and McCombe LJJ chose not to base their judgments on this ground: see [49] and [67] respectively). On this view the consideration is provided not by the promise to perform an existing duty, but by the actual performance of that duty. It hinges on there being a difference between the *receipt* of performance and the right to contractual performance, with the former being more beneficial than the latter. This theory may also explain why the claimant in *Williams v Roffey Bros* was only paid for the work done and not for the work which had been promised but which remained undone. The explanation is neat and the results which it reaches are not unattractive in that the trigger for the obligation to make payment is the performance of the promised work and not the re-promise to perform an existing contractual obligation. But it suffers from three difficulties, although none of them is insurmountable. First, it is unlikely to be consistent with the intention of the parties. However, it may be that we should not be unduly concerned on this score. Given that the end result is probably consistent with the intention of the parties, does it really matter that the vehicle chosen by the law to give effect to that intention is one of which the parties were blissfully unaware? Second, it is a rather complex solution. On the facts of *Williams v Roffey Bros* it assumes that the defendants made '18 separate unilateral offers' to the claimant. Finally, it runs into difficulty in terms of identifying the point in time at which the offer of a unilateral contract can be revoked (see Section 3.13). In some cases the right to revoke will be lost once performance has begun but, as we have noted (Section 3.13), that is not an inevitable conclusion and much will depend upon the facts of the individual case.

5.14.3 Consideration should apply only to the formation of a contract, not its variation

The final analysis which can be offered of *Williams v Roffey Bros* is that it is moving English law in the direction of the conclusion that consideration should only be a requirement for the formation of a contract and that it should not be required for the modification of a contract. This point is not a new one. Sir Frederick Pollock stated (1950) that 'the doctrine of consideration has been extended, with not very happy results, beyond its proper scope, which is to govern the formation of contracts, and has been made to regulate the discharge of contracts'. The distinction between formation and modification has been recognised in America where section 2-209(1) of the Uniform Commercial Code dispenses with the requirement of consideration in the case of agreements to modify an existing contract. To some extent this view is based on the idea that variations of contracts are in the public interest (see Halson, 1990, 1991) and therefore it is open to the criticism that it does not place sufficient weight on the need to hold parties to the terms of their original bargain. If that bargain is subsequently altered by a fresh bargain, then there is obviously no objection to the enforcement of the fresh bargain. But if the original bargain is purportedly changed by what is no more than a gift, then there is a lot to be said for the argument that such a gift should be treated like any other gift and only enforced if it is in the form of a deed. For these and other reasons the Singapore Court of Appeal in *Ma Hongjin v SCP Holdings Pte* [2020] SGCA 106 rejected the proposition that the need for consideration should be dispensed with in the case of contractual variations. It is, however, possible to overstate the significance of this issue. The New Zealand Court of Appeal in *Antons Trawling Co Ltd v Smith* [2003] 2 NZLR 23 found it unnecessary to decide whether to adopt the more liberal approach to consideration which was articulated in *Williams v Roffey Bros* or to conclude that the doctrine of consideration was inapplicable to the variation of a contract. On either basis the court concluded that the agreement, as varied, was enforceable. But there is an obvious difference between the two views in legal theory, and that difference may have practical consequences in an exceptional case. This being the case, it would be helpful if the issue could be resolved conclusively. As it is, the position in England is that the doctrine of consideration continues to apply to the variation of a contract but the drift of modern authority, both judicial and academic, may support a further development in the law to the effect that consideration should cease to be necessary for the variation of a contract (see Coote, 2004).

5.15   Part payment of a debt

A close relation of the old rule that performance of an existing contractual duty owed to the promisor does not constitute consideration is the rule that a promise to accept part payment of a debt in discharge of the entire debt is not supported by consideration. The debtor is already contractually obliged to repay the entire debt and so provides no consideration for the creditor's promise to accept part payment (unless, for example, the debtor agrees to repay the debt at an earlier date, in which case he does provide consideration). This rule can be traced back to *Pinnel's Case* (1602) 5 Co Rep 117a and was upheld by the House of Lords in *Foakes v Beer* (1884) 9 App Cas 605 (although it should be noted that the rule is the subject of numerous common law limitations, see Treitel, 2020, paras 3-104–3-112, and has been substantially eroded by the intervention of equity, in particular the decision of the Court of Appeal in *Collier v P & M J Wright (Holdings) Ltd* [2007] EWCA Civ 1329; [2008] 1 WLR 643, on which see Section 5.25).

5.15.1   *Foakes v Beer*

In *Foakes v Beer* a creditor promised to abandon her claim to interest on the debt but it was held that her promise to forbear was unsupported by consideration. Although such an agreement is not supported by consideration, in many cases a creditor will, as a matter of fact, be benefited by receipt of part payment because, in the words of Corbin (1963) 'a bird in the hand is worth much more than a bird in the bush'. So how can this refusal to recognise the efficacy of a practical benefit in *Foakes v Beer* be reconciled with *Williams v Roffey Bros*? Curiously, *Foakes v Beer* was not cited to the court in *Williams v Roffey Bros* and, given that *Foakes v Beer* is a decision of the House of Lords, to the extent that the two cases cannot be reconciled it is *Williams v Roffey Bros* which should give way (see O'Sullivan, 1996). It is interesting to note that in *Foakes v Beer* Lord Blackburn registered his disagreement with the rule in *Pinnel's Case* on the basis of his:

> conviction that all men of business, whether merchants or tradesmen, do every day recognise and act on the ground that prompt payment of part of their demand may be more beneficial to them than it would be to insist on their rights and enforce payment of the whole. Even where the debtor is perfectly solvent, and sure to pay at last, this is often so. Where the credit of the debtor is doubtful it must be more so.

This is the same emphasis on practical benefit which was adopted by the Court of Appeal in *Williams v Roffey Bros*, yet it did not win the day in the House of Lords in *Foakes v Beer*. The majority of their Lordships decided that such a practical benefit did not constitute good consideration in law (for a defence of *Foakes v Beer* on its facts, see Treitel, 2002).

5.15.2 Distinguishing *Foakes*

While the House of Lords in *Foakes* rejected the proposition that a practical benefit in the form of a promise to pay, or payment of, part of a debt was sufficient to constitute consideration for the discharge of the entire debt, other forms of practical benefit received by the creditor would appear to be capable of amounting to the provision of consideration. Authority for the latter proposition can be derived from the decision of the Court of Appeal in *MWB Business Exchange Centres Ltd v Rock Advertising Ltd* [2016] EWCA Civ 553; [2017] QB 604 where a licensee of premises, who had fallen into arrears in the payment of the licence fees, entered into an agreement with the licensor under which it was agreed to re-schedule the licence fee payments on the basis that the licensee would pay less than the full licence fee in the early months of the revised agreement but would later repay the outstanding balance as its business developed. The licensor denied that the agreement was legally effective on the basis that no consideration had been supplied for its agreement to accept payment of a smaller sum by way of a licence fee. The Court of Appeal distinguished *Foakes v Beer* and held that the landlord had obtained a practical benefit which 'went beyond the advantage of receiving prompt payment of part of the arrears and a promise that it would be paid the balance of the arrears and any deferred licence fees over the course of the forthcoming months.' The principal practical benefit which it obtained from the revised agreement was the continued occupation of the premises by the licensee so that the licensor was not left with an immediate loss of income and the problem of finding another licensee to occupy the premises. The Court of Appeal therefore held that the trial judge had been entitled to conclude that the revised agreement was supported by consideration and that it would remain binding so long as the licensee continued to make payments in accordance with the revised payment schedule. On this basis *Foakes v Beer* stands for the proposition that the practical benefit obtained as a result of the promise to pay part of the debt does not suffice to constitute consideration. But the practical benefit obtained as a result of the preservation of the underlying relationship out of which the obligation to pay the debt has arisen would appear, on the basis of the *MWB* case, to be capable of constituting sufficient consideration. It is not immediately obvious why in principle the former practical benefit should be discounted as the provision of consideration, while the latter apparently suffices.

An alternative ground on which it might be possible to distinguish between *Foakes v Beer* and *Williams v Roffey Bros* is that a promise to release part of a debt is different from a promise to pay more for the performance of an existing contractual obligation. But it is hard to see the difference: in both cases less than full performance is accepted as full performance (see *Musumeci v Winadell Pty Ltd* (1994) 34 NSWLR 723). The fact that in one it is by receiving less and in the other it is by paying more should not be allowed to detract from that essential point.

5.15.3 The relationship between *Foakes v Beer* and *Williams v Roffey Bros*

The relationship between *Foakes v Beer* and *Williams v Roffey Bros* was also considered by the Court of Appeal in *Re Selectmove Ltd* [1995] 1 WLR 474. Peter Gibson LJ refused to extend *Williams v Roffey Bros* to the *Foakes v Beer* situation on the ground that:

> it would in effect leave the principle in *Foakes v. Beer* without any application. When a creditor and a debtor who are at arm's length reach agreement on the payment of the debt by instalments to accommodate the debtor, the creditor will no doubt always see a practical benefit to himself in so doing.

He continued:

> *Foakes* v. *Beer* was not even referred to in *Williams v. Roffey Bros*, and it is in my judgment impossible, consistently with the doctrine of precedent, for this court to extend the principle of the *Williams* case to any circumstances governed by the principle of *Foakes v. Beer*. If that extension is to be made, it must be by the House of Lords or, perhaps even more appropriately, by Parliament after consideration by the Law Commission.

This approach does not deny that there is an inconsistency between the two rules: it simply leaves it to the Supreme Court or to Parliament to sort out the mess (see to similar effect the judgment of the Court of Appeal in *Collier v Wright*). The Supreme Court was given the opportunity to resolve the issue in *Rock Advertising Ltd v MWB Business Exchange Centres Ltd* [2018] UKSC 24; [2019] AC 119 but it declined to do so (see [18]). This was so for a number of reasons. First, the issue was a 'difficult' one which required careful evaluation of cases such as *Williams v Roffey Bros, Selectmove* and *Foakes v Beer*. Second, while *Foakes* was stated to be 'probably ripe for re-examination' this should be done 'before an enlarged panel of the court'. In other words, for the Supreme Court to depart from *Foakes*, which has stood as authority for over 135 years, it is probably necessary to have a panel of more than five judges (and the appeal in *Rock* was heard by a panel of five judges). Third, and possibly most importantly, any reconsideration of *Foakes* by the Supreme Court in *MWB* would have been obiter, given that the appeal itself was decided on another ground. It was not desirable for a review of such a long-established authority to be conducted entirely by way of obiter dicta. While the refusal of the Supreme Court to grasp the nettle was understandable on the facts of the case, it is regrettable given that there is no immediate prospect of the Supreme Court having another opportunity to review the case law. The inconsistency therefore remains. A choice should be made between the different approaches: we ought not to have an emphasis on practical benefit in some cases (*Williams v Roffey Bros* and *MWB Business Exchange Centres Ltd v Rock Advertising Ltd*) but an emphasis on legal benefit in other cases (*Foakes v Beer*) with no rational explanation for the continued existence of such inconsistent rules. The English courts have not as yet made that choice with the result that both *Williams v Roffey Bros* and *Foakes v Beer* remain good law within their respective spheres of operation (*Forde v Birmingham City Council* [2009] EWHC 12 (QB); [2009] 1 WLR 2732, [85]–[89]).

5.16   Performance of a duty imposed by contract with a third party

Despite the difficulty which English law has experienced in recognising that performance of an existing contractual duty owed to a promisor is good consideration, performance of a contractual duty owed to a third party has been clearly recognised as good consideration for a long period of time. In *Shadwell v Shadwell* (1860) 9 CB

(NS) 159, the claimant, who was engaged to Ellen Nicholl, received a letter from his uncle, in which the uncle promised to pay the claimant £150 per year after he was married. The claimant sued to enforce the promise and it was held that he could do so because he had provided consideration for his uncle's promise by marrying Ellen (the nephew was at the time contractually bound to marry her). The proposition that performance of a contractual duty owed to a third party can constitute consideration has more recently been affirmed by the Privy Council in *The Eurymedon* [1975] AC 154 (see Section 7.2 for a full discussion of this case).

In *Jones v Waite* (1839) 5 Bing NC 341 it was held that a promise to perform (as opposed to actual performance of) a contractual duty owed to a third party did not constitute consideration. But in *Scotson v Pegg* (1861) 6 H & N 295 and *Pao On v Lau Yiu Long* [1980] AC 614 it was held that such a promise could constitute consideration, and the latter view is the one which is accepted by most scholars. It has always been difficult to explain why performance of an existing contractual duty owed to a third party can constitute consideration when the law has had such difficulty in recognising that performance of an existing contractual duty owed to a promisor does constitute consideration (although it should be noted that both *Shadwell v Shadwell* and *Scotson v Pegg* are treated by Treitel (1976) as examples of 'invented' consideration). It is here that the duress analysis may provide us with the key (and note, in this context, that the Court of Appeal in *Williams v Roffey Bros* derived some assistance from one of the three-party cases, namely *Pao On*). In the three-party cases such as *Shadwell v Shadwell*, there is not even a hint of duress. Indeed, it is difficult to see how the nephew in *Shadwell v Shadwell* could ever use the situation to apply pressure on the uncle. The fear of duress being absent, the courts saw no objection to the enforcement of a promise to pay in return for the performance of a duty imposed by contract with a third party (although it must be conceded that it is not easy to explain *Shadwell v Shadwell* even on the practical benefit test: in what sense did the uncle receive a practical benefit as a result of the marriage of his nephew to Ellen Nicholl?).

5.17 Conceptions of value

It can readily be seen from the cases which we have discussed that the courts adopt an inconsistent approach to the identification of a benefit or detriment. In *Foakes v Beer* (1884) 9 App Cas 605 the court ignored an obvious factual benefit to the creditor. Yet in *Cook v Wright* (1861) 1 B & S 559, *Shadwell v Shadwell* (1860) 9 CB (NS) 159 and *Scotson v Pegg* (1861) 6 H & N 295 the court found the existence of consideration upon the flimsiest of evidence. It will not do to say, as does Professor Treitel, that in some cases the courts have 'invented' consideration because that does not tell us why they have invented consideration, nor does it tell us when they are likely to invent it in the future. Nevertheless, it must be conceded that the courts do tend to employ the language of 'benefit' and 'detriment'. But their use of 'benefit' and 'detriment' is inconsistent, which suggests that, on occasions, the courts do, as Professor Atiyah argues, enforce a promise because there was a 'good reason' so to do. The most recent emphasis in *Williams v Roffey Bros* and *MWB Business Exchange Centres Ltd v Rock Advertising Ltd* (above) is upon 'practical benefit' but this has not been at the expense of *Foakes v Beer* where the focus of attention was on legal benefit and detriment. The inconsistency therefore remains unresolved and the conclusion which must be reached is that the English courts have built a theory of consideration upon the foundations of benefit and detriment without subjecting to stringent analysis the coherence of their conceptions of benefit and detriment (see further Atiyah, 1986c).

5.18 Past consideration

If I promise to reward you for acts which you have already performed prior to my promise, the general rule is that you cannot enforce my promise because the consideration which you have provided is past. By 'past consideration' lawyers mean that your consideration was already completed before I made my promise, so that you have not given anything new in return for my promise. The rule that past consideration is not good consideration is closely linked to the bargain theory of consideration. The fatal objection is that there is no reciprocity; the promisee does not give anything in return for the promise of the promisor. Thus it would appear that the past consideration rule is unaffected by the recent upheavals caused by *Williams v Roffey Bros* (above) because the point in the past consideration cases hinges, not on the distinction between legal benefit and practical benefit, but on the need to show that the promise was made as part of the bargain. The focus is upon the identification of a bargain, not upon the type of benefit received.

It follows from this that, as a general rule, if two parties have already made a binding contract and one of them subsequently promises to confer an additional benefit on the other party to the contract, that promise is not binding because the promisee's consideration, which is his entry into the original contract, is past. In *Roscorla v Thomas* (1842) 3 QB 234, the defendant agreed to sell a horse to the claimant. Shortly afterwards the defendant added a promise that he would give a warranty as to the soundness of the horse. It was held that the defendant's promise was unenforceable because the only consideration which the claimant had provided was his entry into the original contract of sale and that consideration was past. The courts do, however, have some degree of latitude in applying this rule and do not always take a strictly chronological view of the sequence of events. If the court is satisfied that the new promise and the act of the promisee which is alleged to be the past consideration are, in fact, part of the same overall transaction, the exact order in which the events occurred will not be decisive (*Classic Maritime Inc v Lion Diversified Holdings Berhad* [2009] EWHC 1142 (Comm); [2010] 1 Lloyd's Rep 59, [43]–[46]). In identifying whether consideration is actually past or not, the courts look, not to the wording of the contract, but to the actual sequence of events. Thus, in *Re McArdle* [1951] Ch 669, a promise made 'in consideration of your carrying out' certain work was held to be unenforceable as the consideration for it was past. Although the wording of the contract suggested that the work was to be done at some future time it had, as a matter of fact, been done prior to the making of the contract and was therefore past.

The rule as to past consideration is a harsh one. In *Eastwood v Kenyon* (1840) 11 A & E 438, the guardian of a young girl raised a loan to educate the girl and to improve her marriage prospects. After her marriage, her husband promised to pay off the loan. It was held that the guardian was unable to enforce this promise because the consideration which he had provided, which was bringing up and financing the girl, was past. The court conceded that the husband might have been under a moral obligation to pay, but that moral obligation could not be converted into a legal obligation because of the absence of consideration.

The harshness of the past consideration rule has been mitigated to some extent by the doctrine of implied assumpsit. Where the act of the promisee was performed at the request of the promisor and, subsequent to the performance of the act by the promisee, the promisor promises to pay for it, then such a promise may be enforceable. An early example is *Lampleigh v Brathwait* (1615) Hob 105. The defendant, who was under sentence of death, requested the claimant to ride to Newark to obtain a pardon from King James I. The claimant did so. The defendant then promised to pay the claimant £1,000. It was held that the claimant could enforce the contract. But the doctrine of implied assumpsit operates within narrow confines. The Privy Council in *Pao On v Lau Yiu Long* [1980] AC 614 held that three conditions must be satisfied by a promisee who wishes to invoke the doctrine. The first is that he must have performed the original act at the *request* of the promisor. The second is that it must have been clearly understood or implied between the parties when the act was originally requested that the promisee would be rewarded for doing the act. The third is that the eventual promise of payment after the act was completed must be one which, had it been made prior to or at the time of the act, would have been enforceable.

Parliament has also intervened to mitigate the hardships caused by the past consideration rule by providing that an antecedent debt or liability is good consideration for a bill of exchange (Bills of Exchange Act 1882, s 27(1)(b)) and by providing that a written acknowledgement of a debt by a debtor shall be deemed to have accrued on and not before the date of acknowledgement (Limitation Act 1980, s 27(5)).

5.19   Consideration must move from the promisee

At first sight the maxim that 'consideration must move from the promisee' can appear ambiguous. It could mean simply that a promise can only be enforced by a promisee if there is consideration for the promise (so that, on this view, the consideration need not be provided by the promisee himself). The objection to this view is that it is only another way of restating the basic requirement that a promise must be supported by consideration; it does not justify a separate maxim. The alternative understanding of the maxim, and the one which is generally shared, is that it means that a person to whom a promise is made can only enforce the promise if he himself provides consideration for that promise.

It should be noted that, while consideration must move from the promisee, there is no requirement that it must move to the promisor; thus the promisee can provide consideration by conferring a benefit on a third party at the request of the promisor (*Bolton v Madden* (1873) LR 9 QB 55). But the promisee himself must provide the consideration either by incurring some detriment or by conferring a practical benefit on the promisor (or a third party at the promisor's request). In *South Caribbean Trading Ltd v Trafigura Beheer BV* [2004] EWHC 2676 (Comm); [2005] 1 Lloyd's Rep 128 Colman J criticised the decision of the Court of Appeal in *Williams v Roffey*

Bros on the ground that it was, in his view, inconsistent with the 'long-standing rule' that consideration must move from the promisee. The answer to his criticism is that, in the view of the Court of Appeal in *Williams v Roffey Bros*, the promisee (the sub-contractor) did provide consideration for the promise of additional payment in that he continued with performance of the subcontract and did not breach it. While the consideration did not take the form of the assumption of an additional legal liability (the type of consideration for which Colman J was searching), the central point of *Williams v Roffey Bros* was, as we have noted, to mark a shift in emphasis from the existence or otherwise of a legal benefit or detriment towards an approach which focuses attention on the existence or otherwise of a *practical* benefit or detriment. Viewed through the lens of practical benefit and detriment, consideration did move from the promisee in *Williams v Roffey Bros*.

The requirement that the promisee must himself provide consideration can give rise to problems where A makes a promise to B which is for the benefit of C. Can C sue A if A fails to confer the promised benefit on C? The traditional answer which English law gave was that C could not sue because he was not a party to the contract between A and B. However, as a result of the enactment of the Contracts (Rights of Third Parties) Act 1999 (see Sections 7.5–7.13), English law now confers on third parties a much wider right to sue to enforce a term of a contract which has been concluded between two other parties. Assume that C comes within the scope of the new third-party right of action. Must C also comply with the rule that consideration must move from the promisee? The issue is a real one because on our facts C does not appear to have given anything in return for the promise made by A. The Act itself makes no formal change to the requirement that consideration must move from the promisee, but the fact that section 1 of the Act states in express terms that the third party, here C, 'may in his own right enforce a term of the contract' means that C can sue to enforce the term of the contract even where he has not provided any consideration. To the extent that C, as a gratuitous beneficiary, can sue to enforce a term of the contract, the rule that consideration must move from the promisee appears to have been reformed. But, technically, it can be argued that the rule has not been altered. C is not, in the language of the Act, made a party to the contract; he is simply given a right to sue to enforce a term of the contract. The promisee remains B and he must provide consideration for A's promise before C can acquire a right to enforce a term of the contract against A. In this sense, the rule that consideration must move from the promisee has not been reformed; but the substance of the matter is that the rule has been revised in that a third party who exercises his right to sue under the 1999 Act is not required to show that he has provided any consideration before he can enforce the third-party right which he has acquired.

5.20 Reliance upon non-bargain promises

A claimant who is able to establish the existence of consideration can, absent any other vitiating factor, bring an action on the contract to enforce the defendant's promise. But what of the claimant who relies to his detriment upon a promise of the defendant which is not supported by consideration? Can he enforce that promise or recover compensation for the extent to which he has detrimentally relied upon it? Once again, the debate between Treitel and Atiyah assumes enormous significance.

If Treitel is correct, and consideration is built upon reciprocity, then such a promise cannot be enforced because of the lack of consideration (although more limited effect may be given to the promise via the operation of estoppel). But, if Atiyah is correct and consideration means a reason for the enforcement of a promise, then such a promise may be enforceable where the court can find a 'good reason' for its enforcement.

A factual situation which will provide a useful backdrop to our discussion of these issues is provided by the American case of *Ricketts v Scothorn* 57 Neb 51 (1898). Scothorn was at work when her grandfather gave her a promissory note under which he promised to pay her $2,000 at 6 per cent per annum. On giving her the promissory note he told her that none of his other grandchildren worked and now 'you don't have to'. Scothorn gave up work in reliance upon his promise but, when her grandfather died, his executors refused to honour his promise. Could she enforce the promise? Her claim does appear to be a just one because she acted to her detriment in reliance upon the promise. But how do we reconcile such a claim with the doctrine of consideration which, as we have seen, requires that something of value be given in return for the promise? Two possible arguments suggest themselves. The first is that Scothorn did, in fact, provide consideration by giving up her work. The second is to challenge the rule that a promise is unenforceable if it is unsupported by consideration.

It may seem rather odd to canvass the first argument when purporting to discuss reliance upon promises which are unsupported by consideration. But claimants do, as a matter of practice, attempt to bring themselves within the fold of the doctrine of consideration before embarking upon the more hazardous task of seeking to persuade a court to enforce a promise which is unsupported by consideration. The issues are also related because, the wider the scope of the doctrine of consideration, the less need there is to find a substitute for consideration. So it is here that the liberal approach to consideration in *Williams v Roffey Bros* (Section 5.11) becomes important because it minimises the need for claimants to have resort to estoppel and hence diminishes the practical significance of the limitations from which estoppel presently suffers (such as the fact that it cannot be used to create a cause of action, see Section 5.22). In *Williams v Roffey Bros* itself, Russell LJ stated (at 17) that he:

> would have welcomed the development of argument … on the basis that there was … an estoppel and that the defendants, in the circumstances prevailing, were precluded from raising the defence that their undertaking to pay the extra £10,300 was not binding.

But it is not at all clear that the estoppel argument would have succeeded on the facts of *Williams v Roffey Bros* (see Section 5.22) and, for present purposes, that point is irrelevant. The point which is being made here is that there was no need for the claimant to resort to estoppel because he won on the consideration point. Why should a claimant make life difficult for himself by pleading estoppel (and possibly recovering less by way of compensation, see Section 5.28) when he can take the easy route and invoke the doctrine of consideration? It is sometimes argued that estoppel should be developed to play a much wider role, similar to that played by estoppel in America in section 90 of the Restatement (Second) of Contracts. But it is important to note that in America consideration operates within narrower confines and so the need for a more developed doctrine of estoppel is apparent. *Williams v Roffey*

Bros has chosen to develop English law in a different direction by expanding the doctrine of consideration and hence diminishing the practical need for a more elaborate doctrine of estoppel. On the other hand, should the more restrictive approach to consideration adopted in *Foakes v Beer* (1884) 9 App Cas 605 (Section 5.15) prevail, then the need for a broader doctrine of estoppel will become apparent (and note in this context the extent to which estoppel has already operated to limit the scope of the rule in *Foakes v Beer*, see Section 5.25). The relationship between the scope of consideration and the role of estoppel is therefore a close one.

5.21 The role of consideration

We have already seen that consideration is a rather elastic doctrine and that the courts have scope to 'invent' consideration. Could a court not find or invent consideration in a case such as *Ricketts v Scothorn* 57 Neb 51 (1898)? The difficulty is that the grandfather did not request Scothorn to give up her work and so there does not appear to be any bargain under which she promised to give up work in return for the promised sum of money. But could we not imply such a bargain? After all, the grandfather must have known that Scothorn would be likely to give up work as a result of his promise. Should a court not imply that, where it is foreseeable to a promisor that a promisee will act to her detriment in reliance upon his promise, the reliance of the promisee is at the request of the promisor and so constitutes consideration?

Such an approach was, however, rejected by the English Court of Appeal in *Combe v Combe* [1951] 2 KB 215. A husband promised to pay his wife £100 per annum on their separation. The husband did not make any of the payments and six years later the wife brought an action to recover the arrears. She argued that she had supplied consideration for her husband's promise because she had refrained from applying to court for a permanent maintenance order. But the Court of Appeal held that there was no request, express or implied, by the husband that the wife should refrain from applying to the court for maintenance. Therefore, no consideration was provided for the husband's promise and it was unenforceable.

But there were facts in *Combe v Combe* upon which the court could have implied a request by the husband that the wife forbear from applying for maintenance (see Goodhart, 1951, 1953, but contrast the alternative explanation of the case put forward by Denning, 1952, 2). Indeed, cases can be found in which a court has been prepared to make such an implication. For example, in *Alliance Bank v Broom* (1864) 2 Dr & Sm 289, the defendant owed £22,000 to the claimant bank. The bank demanded some security for the loan and this was promised by the defendant. The defendant failed to honour his promise and, when the bank sought to enforce it, he argued that his promise was not supported by consideration and was therefore unenforceable. The court held that the promise was enforceable because, as a result of the defendant's promise, the claimants had refrained from suing him to recover the debt and the defendant had therefore received 'the benefit of some degree of forbearance' (contrast *Miles v NZ Alford Estate Co* (1886) 32 Ch D 267). Although the defendant had not expressly requested the claimants to forbear, the court felt able to imply such a request. But why did the court imply a request on the facts of *Alliance Bank* but not in *Combe v Combe*? The answer to that question is unclear. It could be argued that the bank in *Alliance Bank* was much more likely to institute proceedings than was the wife in *Combe v Combe* and therefore it was easier for the court to imply such a request. Alternatively, it could be argued that the reason for the court's refusal to imply a request on the facts of *Combe v Combe* was that the 'justice of the case [did] not require that it should be' implied because the wife had an income in excess of that of her husband and she had delayed for six years in bringing her action (see Atiyah, 1986c). Whatever the precise ground of distinction between the two cases, it is clear that the courts do have considerable discretion in implying such a request. The readier they are to find a request, the wider will be the scope of the doctrine of consideration and hence the need to find a substitute for consideration will be radically diminished.

5.22　Estoppel

Where, as in *Ricketts v Scothorn* and *Combe v Combe*, the court is unable to find the existence of consideration, can the promise be enforced despite the absence of consideration? The orthodox answer is that such a promise will not be enforced. But limited effects may be given to the promise under the doctrine of estoppel. The essential ingredients of estoppel were defined by Lord Birkenhead in *Maclaine v Gatty* [1921] 1 AC 376, 386, in the following terms:

> where A has by his words or conduct justified B in believing that a certain state of facts exists, and B has acted upon such belief to his prejudice, A is not permitted to affirm against B that a different state of facts existed at the same time.

But the picture is in fact more complicated than this quotation from the judgment of Lord Birkenhead would suggest. In the first place, Lord Birkenhead was referring to estoppel by representation but, under the umbrella of 'estoppel', there are, in fact, many distinct doctrines: estoppel by representation, promissory estoppel, proprietary estoppel, estoppel by convention, contractual estoppel and related doctrines such as waiver and variation. It is not easy to identify the relationship between these different types of estoppel. The second difficulty lies in ascertaining whether there is a single unifying principle which unites these different estoppels (see Jackson, 1982; Lunney, 1992). The final difficulty lies in discerning the relationship between estoppel and the doctrine of consideration.

The latter point needs some amplification before we embark upon an analysis of the leading cases. If the courts were to hold that a promise was enforceable simply because a promisee had acted upon it to his detriment, then a great hole would arguably be blown in the doctrine of consideration (see Section 5.28). But, as Denning LJ stated in *Combe v Combe*, 'the doctrine of consideration is too firmly fixed to be overthrown by a sidewind' (see to similar effect the judgment of Lord Toulson in *Prime Sight Ltd v Lavarello* [2013] UKPC 22; [2014] AC 436, [30] when he stated 'consideration remains a fundamental principle of the law of contract and is not to be reduced out of existence by the law of estoppel'). So estoppel must be reconciled with consideration. The reconciliation achieved by the courts is a rather uneasy one and is summed up in the well-worn maxim that estoppel can be used as a 'shield but not as a sword'. The use of this metaphor has been criticised (Halson, 1999) on the ground that it 'can be confusing' and 'it conceals subtle shades of meaning'.

The sword/shield dichotomy suggests that a distinction need only be drawn between two cases when in fact the reality is that 'the use that can be made of an estoppel can be represented by a spectrum ranging from a defence to the creation of a new cause of action'.

At each end of this spectrum the position is clear. Estoppel can be used as a shield to defend a claim (see, for example, *Avon CC v Howlett* [1983] 1 WLR 603, discussed in Section 5.23) but it cannot be used to create a cause of action where none existed apart from the estoppel (as was the case in *Combe v Combe* where the wife had no basis for asserting a right against her husband other than the fact that she alleged that she had acted to her detriment in reliance upon his promise which was unsupported by consideration). Thus it is commonly stated that the estoppel must relate to the existing legal rights of the promisor; in other words, there must be a pre-existing legal relationship between the parties under which the promisor promises to give up some of his rights under that relationship. The effect of the estoppel is then to prevent the promisor from going back on his promise where the promisee has acted upon it to his detriment. But where there is no pre-existing legal relationship between the parties, as in *Combe v Combe*, then the promisee cannot invoke estoppel, because such an estoppel would create a completely new cause of action. To permit an estoppel to create a new cause of action would, on traditional analysis, undermine the doctrine of consideration.

In between these two extremes the position is less than clear-cut (see further Barnes, 2011). It is relatively clear that estoppel can be used by a claimant who can establish a recognised cause of action against the defendant in order to defeat a defence or a counterclaim which has been raised by the defendant. For example, a claimant brings a claim for breach of contract against the defendant. The claimant can establish the contract and the breach but the claim is time-barred. However, the defendant had previously represented to the claimant, within the limitation period, that he would not rely on any limitation defence. The claimant can rely on estoppel for the purpose of defeating the limitation defence (see *The Ion* [1980] 2 Lloyd's Rep 245). In this type of case the estoppel is being used actively by a claimant but the vital point to note is that it is not being used to establish a cause of action (the breach of contract has already been established) but to defeat a defence which would otherwise have succeeded. It is where the claimant relies on the estoppel for the purpose of establishing some or all of the elements of a recognised cause of action that we really encounter significant difficulties. Cases can be found in which estoppel appears to have been used in this way (see *The Henrik Sif* [1982] 1 Lloyd's Rep 456, 466–68) but other cases evince a more restrictive approach (see *Newport City Council v Charles* [2008] EWCA Civ 1541; [2009] 1 WLR 1884).

The extent to which estoppel can be used to establish elements of a cause of action has not been finally resolved in English law. A good example of the problem is provided by the fact situation in *Stilk v Myrick* (Section 5.11). How would estoppel apply on such facts? The answer is not entirely clear. There was a pre-existing contractual relationship between the parties. So, if estoppel had been invoked, would it have been used to create the cause of action or not? It is suggested that it would and so an argument based upon estoppel would have been rejected on the facts of the case. The original contract did not give Stilk the right to the promised extra pay. He could only establish the right to that money by relying upon the separate promise of the master to share the wages. The promise of the master to accept a more onerous obligation was not supported by consideration and so could not be enforced simply by proof that Stilk had relied upon it to his detriment (see also *Williams v Roffey Bros & Nicholls (Contractors) Ltd* [1991] 1 QB 1, 13, cf. 17–18). On the other hand, it could be argued that there was a contractual relationship between the parties so that it was not necessary to rely on the estoppel to create the cause of action; it was established by the contract. The resolution of this issue hinges ultimately on the answer to the question whether the modification of contracts should be treated differently from the formation of contracts. If it is right that they should be treated differently (see Halson, 1999) then estoppel should be allowed to operate on the facts of a case such as *Stilk v Myrick* because we are not creating a legal relationship where none existed before; we are simply recognising that that relationship has been modified. On the other hand, if it is the case that modification and formation should be treated in the same way (see Section 5.12) then the claimants in *Stilk v Myrick* should no more be entitled to rely on estoppel than the claimant in *Combe v Combe*. Note, however, that the essence of the latter argument is that both claimants must be treated in the same way; either both claims should succeed (if English law were to change course and decide that estoppel can, after all, create a cause of action) or they should both fail (as is suggested would happen in an English court applying the current law).

In the remaining sections of this chapter we shall consider the orthodox cases in which estoppel has been used other than in an attempt to create a new cause of action. We shall then discuss some cases in which it has been sought to use estoppel in order to create a new cause of action before we conclude by analysing the relationship between these cases and the doctrine of consideration.

5.23　Estoppel by representation

Estoppel clearly acts as a shield in the case of estoppel by representation. The basic principle is that a person who makes a representation of existing fact which induces the other party to act to his detriment in reliance on the representation will not be permitted subsequently to act inconsistently with that representation. It is a rule of evidence which *permanently* prevents a representor from averring or proving facts which are contrary to his own representation (see *Avon CC v Howlett* [1983] 1 WLR 603, 622, per Slade LJ). There are two particular features of this estoppel. First, the representation must be one of fact. This limitation was initially established at common law, but was extended to its equitable counterpart in the controversial decision of the House of Lords in *Jorden v Money* (1854) 5 HL Cas 185. Therefore, the doctrine does not apply to representations of intention. Although the courts have shown some inclination to construe a representation of fact from what appears to be a statement of intention (see Thompson, 1983), a promise is clearly beyond the scope of the doctrine. The second feature of this type of estoppel is that it operates as a defence; it does not create a cause of action. In *Avon CC v Howlett* the defendant was overpaid by his employers, the claimants. They sought to recover the money as paid under a mistake of fact. The defendant argued that the claimants were estopped from pursuing their claim because they had made a representation of fact to him that he was entitled to the money and he had spent some of the money in reliance upon their representation. The Court of Appeal upheld the defendant's argument. The effect of the estoppel was to act as a 'shield' and to defeat a claim which would otherwise have succeeded (on the facts of *Avon CC v Howlett* it was held that the effect of the estoppel was to give the defendant a complete defence to the claim brought by the claimant, but it would now appear that estoppel can operate as a partial defence where it would be clearly inequitable or unconscionable for the defendant to retain a balance in his hands, in which case the defendant will have a defence only to the extent that he has acted to his detriment in reliance on the representation made by the claimant: see *National Westminster Bank plc v Somer International (UK) Ltd* [2001] EWCA Civ 970; [2002] 1 All ER 198, and *Scottish Equitable plc v Derby* [2001] EWCA Civ 369; [2001] 3 All ER 818).

5.24 Waiver and variation

The role of estoppel as a shield can also be seen in cases where contracting parties agree to modify or abandon an existing contract. A preliminary point must be made here, which is that consideration applies to the discharge or variation of a contract as well as to its formation (although, as we have noted in Section 5.14, the extension of consideration to the discharge or variation of a contract is a controversial one and, after the decision of the Court of Appeal in *Williams v Roffey Bros* (above), it is arguable that consideration should no longer be applied to the modification of a contract). Where the discharge or variation is capable of benefiting either contracting party then the variation or discharge is supported by consideration and is enforceable (*WJ Alan & Co Ltd v El Nasr Export and Import Co* [1972] 2 QB 189). But where the variation or discharge can confer a benefit upon only one contracting party then the agreement is not supported by consideration. The classic example is the creditor who agrees to accept part payment of a debt in discharge of the entire debt (Section 5.15). In such a case, the variation can only operate to the benefit of the debtor and so is unsupported by consideration.

A variation which is unsupported by consideration has no contractual effect. But effect may be given to a promise to forgo rights under the doctrine of waiver. A variety of meanings has been attributed to the word 'waiver' (see *The Kanchenjunga* [1990] 1 Lloyd's Rep 391, 397–99 and Dugdale and Yates, 1976) and the present scope of the doctrine is a matter of some uncertainty. It is important to note the distinction between 'waiver by election' and 'waiver by estoppel' (see Section 20.8). Waiver by election arises where a contracting party has to choose between the exercise of two inconsistent rights (such as the right to affirm the contract or the right to terminate performance for breach, see Section 20.8) and has nothing to do with our present inquiry. Waiver by estoppel, on the other hand, is relevant in this context but it seems to be virtually indistinguishable from equitable estoppel and appears to have been subsumed within the larger doctrine of equitable or promissory estoppel (see, for example, *Prosper Homes v Hambro's Bank Executor & Trustee Co* (1979) 39 P & CR 395, 401). So we shall consider the elements of waiver within our discussion of promissory estoppel. Here it is sufficient to give one example of the operation of the doctrine of waiver.

In *Hickman v Haynes* (1875) LR 10 CP 598, the parties entered into a contract for the sale of goods. The buyer subsequently requested the seller to delay the delivery of the goods. The seller agreed and tendered delivery on the later date, but the buyer refused to accept delivery. The seller brought an action for damages against the buyer, who argued that the seller could not succeed, because he was in breach of contract in failing to deliver on time. The court held that the buyer had waived his right to demand delivery on time and that he could not subsequently reassert it without the giving of reasonable notice (see, on the giving of reasonable notice, *Charles Rickard Ltd v Oppenheim* [1950] 1 KB 616). It should be noted that, in contrast to *Avon CC v Howlett* (above), the estoppel in *Hickman* was invoked by the claimant and the effect of the waiver was to enable a claim to succeed which otherwise would have failed.

5.25   Promissory estoppel

As we have already noted, there is a very close relationship between the doctrines of waiver and promissory (or equitable) estoppel. The leading case on promissory estoppel is *Hughes v Metropolitan Railway Co* (1877) 2 App Cas 439. A landlord gave six months' notice to a tenant, requiring him to carry out certain repairs. The tenant responded by inquiring whether the landlord wished to purchase his interest in the premises for £3,000. The landlord entered into negotiations for the purchase of the lease but, when these negotiations broke down, he sought to forfeit the lease because the tenant had not carried out the repairs within six months of his original notice. The House of Lords held that the tenant was entitled to equitable relief against forfeiture of the lease on the ground that the running of the six-month period was suspended during the negotiations to purchase the lease and did not recommence until the negotiations broke down.

5.25.1   *High Trees*

Hughes v Metropolitan Railway Co lay in obscurity for many years until it was resurrected by Denning J in the famous case of *Central London Property Trust Ltd v High Trees House Ltd* [1947] KB 130. In 1937 the claimants let a block of flats in London to the defendants on a 99-year lease at an annual rent of £2,500. In 1940 the defendants discovered that, as a result of the outbreak of war and the evacuation of people from London, they were unable to let many of the flats. So the claimants agreed to reduce the rent to £1,250. This promise to accept a reduced rent was unsupported by consideration. At the end of the war in 1945 the property market had returned to normal and the flats were fully let. The claimants demanded that the defendants resume payment of the entire rent from 1945, but the defendants refused to pay. Denning J held that the claimants were entitled to demand the entire rent from the date when the flats became fully let early in 1945. The interest of this case lies in the new life which it breathed into promissory estoppel which, for present purposes, may be defined as follows:

> where, by words or conduct, a person makes an unambiguous representation as to his future conduct, intending the representation to be relied on and to affect the legal relations between the parties, and the representee alters his position in reliance on it, the representor will be unable to act inconsistently with the representation if by so doing the representee would be prejudiced.

This definition of promissory estoppel can be divided into five elements.

5.25.2 The elements of promissory estoppel

The first is that there must be a promise or a representation as to future conduct which is intended to affect the legal relations between the parties and which indicates that the promisor will not insist on his strict legal rights against the promisee. The promise or representation must be clear and unequivocal so that the promisor does not lose his rights simply because he has failed throughout to insist upon strict performance of the contract by the promisee. Although this requirement originated in estoppel by representation, it has since been extended to cases of promissory estoppel and waiver.

The second element is that the promise or representation must have been relied upon by the promisee. There are *dicta* which suggest that the promisee must have acted to his 'detriment' in reliance upon the promise but the better view is that it is sufficient to show that the promisee committed himself to a course of action which he would not otherwise have adopted. To the extent that it is necessary to demonstrate that a detriment has been suffered, the detriment often arises, not when the promise is made and relied upon, but when the promisor seeks to go back on its promise without giving reasonable prior notice of its intention to do so (*PM Project Services Ltd v Dairy Crest Ltd* [2016] EWHC 1235 (TCC), [40]).

The third requirement is that it must be 'inequitable' for the promisor to go back upon his promise. This will usually be satisfied by demonstrating that the promisee has acted in reliance upon the promise (although see *The Post Chaser* [1981] 2 Lloyd's Rep 693, where the promisee acted in reliance upon the promise but could not show that it was 'inequitable' for the promisor to go back upon his promise).

The fourth element is that the effect of promissory estoppel is generally suspensory; it does not extinguish the promisor's rights. In *Hughes v Metropolitan Railway Co* (above) the landlord's right to enforce the repairing covenant was not extinguished. It was suspended and could be resurrected by his giving reasonable notice. But in *High Trees* the estoppel had the potential to have permanent effects because Denning J was of the view that the lessors would not have been entitled to demand the rent waived between 1940 and 1945. Such a proposition is difficult to reconcile with *Foakes v Beer* (see Section 5.15) and has been criticised (see Treitel, 2020, para 3-115). But the better view is that, in cases of post-breach representations or where it is not possible or practicable to return the parties to their original position, then promissory estoppel may have permanent effects (*Collier v P & M J Wright (Holdings) Ltd* [2007] EWCA Civ 1329; [2008] 1 WLR 643, [37] and see Dugdale and Yates, 1976; Thompson, 1983). However, the precise effect of the estoppel will depend very much upon the facts of the individual case and upon the exercise by the trial judge of his or her discretion. The judge may conclude that it would be inequitable to permit the promisor to go back on its promise at all or the judge may conclude that it would be inequitable to permit the promisor to go back on its promise without giving reasonable notice (*MWB Business Exchange Centres Ltd v Rock Advertising Ltd* [2016] EWCA Civ 553; [2017] QB 604, [61]).

The final point is that promissory estoppel cannot act as a cause of action; in the words of the old metaphor, it acts as a shield but not as a sword (see *Combe v Combe* (above)).

5.25.3　The impact of promissory estoppel upon the doctrine of consideration

Promissory estoppel has the potential to make a significant impact upon the doctrine of consideration, as can be seen from a case such as *Collier v P & M J Wright (Holdings) Ltd* [2007] EWCA Civ 1329; [2008] 1 WLR 643. The applicant was one of three partners who owed £46,000 to the defendant. The liability of the partners was joint (that is to say, there was one liability for £46,000 so that one partner could be called upon to pay the entire debt and he would then have a claim for a contribution from his fellow partners). The applicant alleged that he made an oral agreement at the end of 2000 with the defendant under which it was agreed that his liability should be limited to one-third of the judgment debt and that the defendant would look to the other two partners and not to the applicant to recover their share of the debt. The applicant, over a period of five years commencing in 1999, paid £15,600 to the defendant. The defendant then claimed that he was entitled to recover the balance of the judgment debt from the applicant, who relied on the oral agreement he had reached with the defendant. The difficulty which the applicant faced was that, as a result of the rule in *Foakes v Beer*, the oral agreement was unsupported by consideration. However, the Court of Appeal held that the applicant had established an arguable case that promissory estoppel might afford him a defence to the claim of the defendant. It is important to note that the Court of Appeal was not asked to decide whether the applicant had a defence based on promissory estoppel or not: that was a matter for any trial of the action. All that the Court of Appeal had to decide, and did decide, was that promissory estoppel arguably afforded him a defence.

Two reasoned judgments were given. The first, given by Arden LJ, demonstrates the potential promissory estoppel has to undermine the rule in *Foakes v Beer*. Drawing upon the judgment of Lord Denning in *D & C Builders v Rees* [1966] 2 QB 617, 624–625 and upon an observation of Jessel MR in *Couldery v Bartrum* (1881) 19 Ch D 394, 399 she derived the following series of propositions:

> if (1) a debtor offers to pay part only of the amount he owes; (2) the creditor voluntarily accepts that offer, and (3) in reliance on the creditor's acceptance the debtor pays that part of the amount he owes in full, the creditor will, by virtue of the doctrine of promissory estoppel, be bound to accept that sum in full and final satisfaction of the whole debt. For him to resile will of itself be inequitable. In addition, in these circumstances, the promissory estoppel has the effect of extinguishing the creditor's right to the balance of the debt.

On this basis a debtor who pays (as distinct from one who merely promises to pay) the promised part of the debt will now be able to rely upon promissory estoppel in order to defeat a claim brought by the creditor to recover the balance of the debt. The significance of this conclusion should be noted. In *Foakes v Beer* itself the debtor had paid the promised part of the debt and so, on the reasoning of Arden LJ, ought to have been able to rely on promissory estoppel as a defence to the creditor's claim. If this approach is to be followed in subsequent cases, care will have to be taken to ensure that creditors do not inadvertently lose their rights to recover the full value of debts owed to them. In this respect, it is important to note the emphasis placed by Arden LJ on the need for a 'true accord' and for a 'voluntary' acceptance by the creditor.

These concerns surface much more clearly in the second reasoned judgment, given by Longmore LJ. He was much more hesitant in his approach and he doubted whether there was a 'true accord' on the facts of the case. In his view, the creditor may simply have intended to suspend his right to recover the entire sum from the debtor for a period of time and not to forgo it permanently. Thus he concluded that, if the approach advocated by Arden LJ is to be adopted, 'it is perhaps all the more important that agreements which are said to forgo a creditor's rights on a permanent basis should not be too benevolently construed'.

It is perhaps important not to read too much into the decision in *Collier*. As has been noted, the court was simply asked to decide whether or not the applicant had an arguable defence to the claim to recover the balance of the debt, and the robust analysis of Arden LJ was not entirely shared by Longmore LJ. To this extent, the authority of the case may be questioned. Further, in *MWB Business Exchange Centres Ltd v Rock Advertising Ltd* [2016] EWCA Civ 553; [2017] QB 604, [61] Kitchin LJ stated that, in his judgment, it was not the case that 'in every case where a creditor agrees to accept payment of a debt by instalments, and the debtor acts upon that agreement by paying one of the instalments, and the creditor accepts that instalment, then it will necessarily be inequitable for the creditor later to go back upon the agreement and insist on payment of the balance.' The effect of the estoppel will very much depend upon the facts of the case and so it cannot be said that extinction of the right is the inevitable consequence of the successful invocation of estoppel. Nevertheless, the fact that estoppel can have this extinctive effect adds further weight to the view of those who believe that, were *Foakes v Beer* to be reconsidered by the Supreme Court today, the case would be decided differently and the creditor would be prevented from recovering the balance of the debt (either on the ground that the agreement to pay part of the debt was supported by consideration or on the ground that the creditor was estopped from going back on her promise to accept part of the debt in discharge of the entire debt).

5.26   Estoppel by convention

So far we have been dealing with cases in which estoppel acted as a shield and did not create a new cause of action. But the effect of estoppel by convention may be to create a cause of action. The leading authority is *Amalgamated Investment and Property Co Ltd v Texas Commerce International Bank Ltd* [1982] QB 84, where estoppel by convention was defined in the following terms:

> when the parties have acted in their transaction upon the agreed assumption that a given state of facts is to be accepted between them as true, then as regards that transaction each will be estopped against the other from questioning the truth of the statement of facts so assumed.

In the *Texas Bank* case, the common assumption of the parties was that they had entered into a contract of guarantee under which the claimants had promised to guarantee loans made by a subsidiary of the defendants to a subsidiary of the claimants. In fact, the wording of the guarantee covered loans made by the defendants, but not loans made by the defendants' subsidiary. When the claimants went into liquidation the defendants applied money which they owed to the claimants in discharge of the claimants' alleged liability under the guarantee. The claimants sought a declaration that the defendants were not entitled to apply the money in such a way because the guarantee was not effective to cover the loans made by the subsidiary. But the court held that the parties had entered into the guarantee under the shared assumption that the guarantee did cover such loans, and the effect of the estoppel was to prevent the claimants from denying the efficacy of the guarantee. So the defendants used the estoppel as a shield to the claimants' claim for a declaration. But could they have sued on the guarantee to recover the sums which they alleged were due? The majority (Brandon LJ and Lord Denning) held that they could have done so, but Brandon LJ held that, in such a case, it would be the contract and not the estoppel which created the cause of action. This point is difficult to understand. The contract of guarantee was not enforceable. Only the estoppel could validate the contract and thereby render the guarantee enforceable. Thus stated, is it not the estoppel which creates the cause of action? That said, the generally accepted view seems to be that estoppel by convention cannot create a cause of action, a point affirmed by the Court of Appeal in *Smithkline Beecham plc v Apotex Europe Ltd* [2006] EWCA Civ 658; [2007] Ch 71, [107] and [110].

5.27 Proprietary estoppel

Whatever doubts we may harbour about the ability of estoppel by convention to create a cause of action, there can be no doubt that proprietary estoppel can be used to found a cause of action. Cases of proprietary estoppel have traditionally been divided into two broad categories. The first group of cases relate to the situation in which a landowner 'stands by' while another person improves his land in the mistaken belief that he is the owner of the land. In the second group of cases the promisee relies to his detriment upon the landowner's promise that he has or will be given an interest in the land.

5.27.1 Illustrative cases

The operation of proprietary estoppel can be illustrated by reference to the case of *Pascoe v Turner* [1979] 1 WLR 431. The claimant and the defendant lived together for a number of years. The claimant left the defendant and went to live with another woman, but he told the defendant that the house and everything in it were hers. In reliance upon this assurance, the defendant spent some £230 in repairs upon the house. The claimant subsequently decided that he wanted the house and he sued for possession. The defendant counterclaimed for a declaration that the house and everything in it were hers, and her counterclaim succeeded in the Court of Appeal. Although she had not provided any consideration for the claimant's promise, the defendant had acted to her detriment in reliance upon his promise. This created an equity in her favour and that equity could only be satisfied by an order that the claimant convey to her the fee simple in the house. The effect of the estoppel in *Pascoe v Turner* was clearly to create a new cause of action. There was no pre-existing legal relationship between the parties and yet the promise of the claimant was enforced, despite the absence of consideration.

In *Thorner v Major* [2009] UKHL 18; [2009] 1 WLR 776 Lord Walker identified the three principal ingredients of proprietary estoppel in the following terms: (i) a representation or assurance made to the claimant relating to the acquisition of an interest in property, typically an interest in land; (ii) reliance on that representation or assurance by the claimant and (iii) detriment to the claimant in consequence of his (reasonable) reliance on that representation or assurance. Two points should be noted about this definition. The first is that the representation or assurance must relate to the 'acquisition of an interest in property, typically an interest in land'. While authority supports the extension of the doctrine beyond land to other forms of property (*Western Fish Products Ltd v Penwith DC* [1981] 2 All ER 204, 218), it has never been extended beyond promises that concern the creation of an interest in property. This limitation is difficult to understand. Why is it that detrimental reliance upon a promise to create an interest in property can create a cause of action, but that detrimental reliance upon any other promise cannot do so? No convincing answer has ever been provided to this question. The second point relates to the role of 'reliance' and 'detriment'. In *Henry v Henry* [2010] UKPC 3; [2010] 1 All ER 988, [55] the Privy Council noted that the two requirements are often 'intertwined'. Any 'reliance' by the claimant must be assessed 'in the context of the nature and quality of the particular assurances which are said to form the basis of the estoppel' and the 'detriment' must be assessed 'in the context of the nature and quality of the particular conduct or course of conduct adopted by the claimant in reliance on those assurances'. On the facts of *Henry* a landowner promised the claimant that, if he cared for her until her death and cultivated the plot of land, she would leave her share of the plot to him on her death. The claimant performed the requested services but no share of the land was left to him. It was held that he had acted to his detriment in reliance upon the promise which had been made to him, notwithstanding the fact that he had lived effectively rent free on the plot of land for a significant period of time. He had given up the opportunity of a better life elsewhere and had 'opted for a hard life, in which he had to struggle to make ends meet and to provide for his family, in circumstances where more attractive prospects beckoned elsewhere'. An equity was held to have arisen in his favour under the doctrine of proprietary estoppel in respect of the half share of the plot.

5.27.2   A wider role for proprietary estoppel?

There was, however, a line of authority which seemed to envisage a much wider role for proprietary estoppel (albeit still in the context of promises relating to the acquisition of property). The classic expression of this view was to be found in the judgment of Oliver J in *Taylor Fashions Ltd v Liverpool Victoria Trustees Co Ltd* [1982] QB 133 when he stated that the inquiry in cases of proprietary estoppel is directed towards ascertaining:

> whether, in particular individual circumstances, it would be unconscionable for a party to be permitted to deny that which, knowingly or unknowingly, he has allowed or encouraged another to assume to his detriment rather than to inquiring whether the circumstances can be fitted within the confines of some preconceived formula serving as a universal yardstick for every form of unconscionable behaviour.

However, in *Cobbe v Yeoman's Row Management Ltd* [2008] UKHL 55; [2008] 1 WLR 1752 the House of Lords clearly established that 'unconscionable conduct' is not sufficient in itself to make good a proprietary estoppel claim. As Lord Scott observed:

> to treat a 'proprietary estoppel equity' as requiring neither a proprietary claim by the claimant nor an estoppel against the defendant but simply unconscionable behaviour is ... a recipe for confusion.

Rejection of the proposition that unconscionable conduct can suffice to establish a proprietary estoppel was accompanied by a strong message about the need to keep estoppel within proper bounds and that it should not be permitted to cause undue uncertainty in commercial transactions. Thus, Lord Walker affirmed the 'general principle that the court should be very slow to introduce uncertainty into commercial transactions by over-ready use of equitable concepts such as fiduciary obligations and equitable estoppel'.

5.27.3 The scope of proprietary estoppel

This leaves us with the difficulty of ascertaining the precise scope of the doctrine of proprietary estoppel. *Cobbe* at least makes it clear that the doctrine is narrower than many commentators previously believed it to be. This is so in at least three respects. First, as has been noted, unconscionability will no longer suffice of itself to trigger the operation of the doctrine. Second, the promisee must have an expectation of a 'certain interest in land'. If the expectation of the promisee is dependent upon the outcome of negotiations between the promisor and the promisee over the terms on which the promisee will acquire an interest in the land, it is unlikely that the expectation will be sufficiently 'certain' to establish an estoppel. Third, it is highly unlikely that a promisee will be able to invoke proprietary estoppel in the case where he knows that the promise on which he is basing his estoppel is not legally binding. This was the case in *Cobbe* itself where a property developer sought to claim an interest in land on the basis of proprietary estoppel. His claim was dismissed on the ground that he knew that the informal agreement which he had reached with the owner of the land was not legally binding because it failed to comply with the requirements of section 2 of the Law of Property (Miscellaneous Provisions) Act 1989. As Lord Walker observed, the claim of the property developer:

> seems to me to fail on the simple but fundamental point that, as persons experienced in the property world, both parties knew that there was no legally binding contract, and that either was therefore free to discontinue the negotiations without legal liability.

This amounts to a significant limitation upon the scope of the doctrine and will require the courts in future to focus careful attention on the beliefs of the claimant. A claimant who merely 'hopes' to acquire the property will not be able to establish an estoppel.

In order to do so, it will be necessary to go further and prove that he 'believed that the assurance on which he … relied was binding and irrevocable'. It may be possible for claimants to do this in 'domestic' cases such as *Pascoe v Turner* where the parties may well have limited appreciation of their legal rights and believe that a promise is 'binding and irrevocable' when in law it is not (a point subsequently confirmed by the House of Lords in *Thorner v Major*, above). But, in a commercial context, where parties can be expected to know when an agreement is binding and when it is not, this limitation will significantly curtail the operation of proprietary estoppel, as *Cobbe* itself demonstrates.

5.28 The relationship between estoppel and consideration

Finally, we turn to consider the relationship between estoppel and consideration. That relationship has been exhaustively analysed by the High Court of Australia in *Waltons Stores (Interstate) Ltd v Maher* (1988) 164 CLR 387. The parties were involved in the negotiation of a major leasing and construction project. The claimant was the owner of land which he hoped to lease to the defendants. It was also intended that the claimant would demolish the existing building on the site and erect a new building to the defendants' specifications. The negotiations reached an advanced stage and solicitors were instructed to prepare the formal documents. The claimant signed the requisite documents and they were forwarded to the defendants' solicitors for execution and exchange. He was informed by his solicitors that the contracts had been sent to the defendants and he believed that they would shortly exchange and complete. Because of this belief and because the project was one of extreme urgency, the claimant began to demolish the building on his land. Meanwhile, the defendants were beginning to have second thoughts about the deal and they instructed their solicitors to 'go slow', even though they knew that the claimant had commenced work on the site. After the claimant had completed a substantial amount of the work, the defendants informed him that they had decided to withdraw from the project. The claimant sought a declaration that a binding agreement existed between the parties and consequential relief. His difficulty was that no exchange had ever taken place. However, he argued that the defendants were estopped from withdrawing from their implied promise to complete the contract.

The defendants argued that the claimant could not use estoppel to create a cause of action. There was no pre-existing legal relationship between the parties and therefore nothing to which an estoppel could apply. The defendants' argument was rejected by the High Court who, by a majority, held that promissory estoppel could, in an appropriate case, create a cause of action; it could act as a sword as well as a shield. They held that such a proposition was not irreconcilable with the doctrine of consideration because the function of the estoppel was not 'to make a promise binding' or to make good the expectations engendered by a promise, but to 'avoid the detriment' which the promisee would suffer as a result of the unconscionable conduct of the promisor in departing from the terms of his promise (the differences between a contract and an equity created by an estoppel are fully set out in the judgment of Brennan J). A simple example will illustrate the distinction. Let us suppose that someone promises to pay me £500 and I act on that promise to my detriment by spending £300 which I would not otherwise have spent. Enforcement of the promise would give me £500 (and hence protect my expectation interest), whereas 'avoiding a detriment' would give me only £300 (thus protecting my reliance interest). The former is the province of the law of contract and hence demands consideration, the latter is the province of estoppel and so does not require consideration. To protect my reliance interest in this way does not necessarily undermine the doctrine of consideration. The High Court also rejected the argument that it was necessary to establish a pre-existing legal relationship between the parties before estoppel could be invoked. As *Waltons Stores v Maher* amply demonstrates, the action of the promisor in going back upon his promise can be as unconscionable where there is no pre-existing legal relationship between the parties as when there is such a relationship.

5.28.1 When is it unconscionable to go back upon a promise?

Three principal difficulties will lie ahead if the English courts choose to follow the lead taken in *Waltons Stores v Maher*. The first lies in ascertaining when it is unconscionable for a promisor to go back upon his promise where there is no pre-existing legal relationship between the parties. As was pointed out by Mason CJ and Wilson J in *Waltons Stores v Maher*, a failure to fulfil a promise does not of itself amount to unconscionable conduct. It therefore follows that mere reliance upon a promise will not suffice to bring promissory estoppel into play; something more must be established. That 'something more' they held could be:

> found, if at all, in the creation or encouragement by the party estopped in the other party of an assumption that a contract will come into existence or a promise will be performed and that the other party relied on that assumption to his detriment to the knowledge of the first party.

These factors were all present on the facts of *Waltons Stores v Maher*. It may be that there are other factors which will be found to be relevant but these will have to be worked out over time.

5.28.2 The available remedies

The second difficulty is much more fundamental and it relates to the remedies available to the court in estoppel cases. This debate takes us to the very heart of what estoppel is all about. The account of *Waltons Stores v Maher* makes clear that the aim of the remedy, according to Brennan J, was to protect the reliance interest of the claimant and not the expectation interest (see to similar effect *Commonwealth of Australia v Verwayen* (1990) 170 CLR 394, 413, 430, 454, 475 and 501). But this rationalisation of the remedy runs into difficulties when one looks to the remedy actually awarded in *Waltons Stores v Maher*, where damages were awarded on the basis that the defendants were estopped from going back on their promise that completion would take place, thus essentially protecting the claimant's expectation interest. Cases post-*Waltons Stores v Maher* have tended to protect the expectation interest rather than the reliance interest. Indeed, in *Giumelli v Giumelli* (1999) 196 CLR 101 the High Court of Australia expressly rejected an argument that the court could not grant relief which went beyond the reversal of any detriment suffered. This remedial confusion is also reflected in the academic literature where some commentators take the view that protection of the expectation interest should be the normal remedy in estoppel cases (see, for example, Cooke, 1997), while others maintain that it should be the protection of the reliance interest (see, for example, Robertson, 1998). Those who seek to defend the reliance model have to overcome the obvious difficulty that in many of the cases the remedy awarded has actually protected the claimant's expectation interest; they do so (see Robertson, 1998) on the ground that fulfilment of the claimant's expectation interest is often the only way of ensuring that the reliance interest is fully protected (usually because it is difficult for the claimant to calculate or to prove the extent of the reliance). But, where the reliance is disproportionate to the claimant's expectations (in the sense that the reliance is much less) then they claim that the court should only protect the reliance interest (a claim which draws some support from *Giumelli*).

This remedial debate raises two issues of importance. The first relates to the relationship between estoppel and consideration. If the remedy in estoppel cases does seek to protect the claimant's expectation interest then there is an obvious conflict with the doctrine of consideration which has to be sorted out. This leads on to the second, related point which concerns the function of estoppel and its location within the law of obligations. The reliance-based approach tends to locate estoppel essentially within the law of civil wrongs. The defendant has committed a wrong in acting unconscionably in (at the very least) making a promise which the claimant has, to his knowledge, relied upon (to his detriment). The location of estoppel within the law of wrongs explains why the remedy should be one which seeks to protect the claimant's reliance interest, consistently with most remedies in the law of wrongs (torts). Alternatively, it could be argued that estoppel should be located within the law of contract so that a contract would consist of a promise made by deed, promises supported by consideration and a promise which has been relied on in such a way that the claimant cannot go back on it and must honour it. If seen in this way, estoppel will act as an alternative to consideration. It is this role which *Combe v Combe* [1951] 2 KB 215 currently denies to estoppel. This issue is a very important one on which the English courts must make a choice. Estoppel presently seems more at home within the law of (equitable) wrongs and, if that is the case, it does not undermine the doctrine of consideration and the remedy should ordinarily seek to protect the claimant's reliance interest. On the other hand, if estoppel is to go further and become truly a part of the law of contract then it ought to be a genuine alternative to consideration, and the remedy should ordinarily aim to protect the claimant's expectation interest.

5.28.3 Is there a unified doctrine of estoppel?

The third point of difficulty is whether or not there is, or should be, a unified doctrine of estoppel. In England, it is clear that there is as yet no unified doctrine of estoppel nor any overarching principle (see, for example, *Republic of India v India Steamship Co Ltd (No 2)* [1998] AC 878, 914 per Lord Steyn), although the position is not so clear in Australia (the initial enthusiasm for the creation of a unified doctrine to be found in the judgment of Mason CJ in *Verwayen* (at 412) has since given way to a more cautious approach (see, for example, *Giumelli*)). If the estoppels are indeed separate then the need to explain the current differences between the estoppels might not be so pressing so that it becomes possible, for example, to accept that proprietary estoppel can create a cause of action while promissory estoppel cannot. The most obvious difference which justifies a difference in treatment is between estoppel by representation and promissory estoppel. Representations (or statements of fact) and promises are different (see Section 13.1) and should be treated differently. A representation invites reliance while a promisor goes further and undertakes an obligation to do or to refrain from doing a particular thing. This suggests that the remedy in estoppel by representation cases should be no more than the protection of the reliance interest, but it opens up the possibility that the remedy in cases of promissory estoppel should extend to the protection of the expectation interest. It has also been argued (Halson, 1999) that the different estoppels can be distinguished on the ground that estoppel by convention is a 'powerful tool to protect the reasonable expectations of negotiating parties' while promissory estoppel is concerned with the modification of contracts. The difficulty with this view is that there is no obvious distinctive policy basis for proprietary estoppel, and the claim that promissory estoppel is exclusively about contract modification is doubtful. Although most promissory estoppel cases are modification cases, this cannot be said of all of them (*Waltons Stores v Maher* being an obvious example). There is an obvious common theme running through the estoppel cases, and that relates to the rights of those who rely (to their detriment) on promises which are not otherwise enforceable. These rights should be analysed irrespective of whether the promise relates to the formation of a contract, the modification of a contract or the creation of an interest in land or other property. The basic choice which has to be made by the law is whether such protection as the law affords should be conferred within the law of wrongs (with the focus on any unconscionable conduct of the defendant and the remedy aiming to protect the claimant's reliance interest) or whether protection should be conferred within the law of contract (with the emphasis being placed on the promise and the (detrimental) reliance upon it by the claimant and the remedy aiming to protect the claimant's expectation interest).

5.29 Conclusion: the future of consideration

After the decision of the Court of Appeal in *Williams v Roffey Bros & Nicholls (Contractors) Ltd* [1991] 1 QB 1 (Section 5.11), the future of consideration in English contract law is somewhat uncertain. The Court of Appeal did not attempt expressly to throw out the doctrine; its stated aim was to 'limit' and 'refine' the rule in *Stilk v Myrick* by placing emphasis upon the need to identify practical benefit rather than legal benefit. But the inference which one draws from the tenor of the judgments is that the court, particularly Russell LJ, saw the doctrine as a technicality which, on occasions, could operate to prevent the court from giving effect to the intention of the parties. Far from being an essential ingredient of a contract, the courts appeared to regard consideration as a vitiating factor; that is to say, they perceived it as a doctrine which operated to set aside what was an otherwise valid and subsisting contract. More than that, they regarded it as a 'technical vitiating factor'; in other words, it was a vitiating factor which could not distinguish between modifications which were in the public interest and those which were not. That task, they thought, could be better achieved through the invocation of the doctrine of duress. The centrality of consideration to the creation of a contract was therefore thrown into doubt by the court. These doubts were raised once again by Lord Goff in his speech in *White v Jones* [1995] 2 AC 207, 262–63 when he said that 'our law of contract is widely seen as deficient in the sense that it is perceived to be hampered by the presence of an unnecessary doctrine of consideration'. These criticisms must be seen in their proper perspective. The argument is not that bargain promises should not be enforced, but that consideration draws the net of enforceability too tightly. As Professor Dawson has pointed out (1980):

> even the most embittered critics of bargain consideration do not really object to the enforcement of bargains. The objection has been to its transformation into a formula of denial, a formula that would deny legal effect to most promises for which there is nothing given or received in exchange.

The most significant recent judicial contribution to the debate about the future of consideration is to be found in the judgment of Andrew Boon Leong Phang JA in the Court of Appeal of Singapore in *Gay Choon Ing v Loh Sze Ti Terence Peter* [2009] SGCA 3; [2009] 2 SLR 332. The form of the contribution is unusual as it consisted of a 'coda' to the judgment of the court. In the coda he noted the 'basic weaknesses' of the doctrine of consideration and also drew attention to the rise of various possible 'alternative doctrines', such as promissory estoppel and economic duress. However, he also noted that these 'alternatives' are themselves in the course of development and have their own difficulties. This being the case, he stopped short of advocating the abolition of the doctrine of consideration and suggested that the 'most practical solution' might be to retain the doctrine of consideration in its current diluted form alongside the 'alternatives' such as promissory estoppel and duress. In his judgment, this combined approach would 'afford the courts a range of legal options to achieve a just and fair result in the case concerned'.

A more radical option would be to abolish the doctrine of consideration. Support for a step of this nature might be found by looking outside of English law. For example, there is no room for the doctrine of consideration in the Principles of European Contract Law. Article 2.101 states:

1) A contract is concluded if:
   (a) the parties intend to be legally bound; and
   (b) they reach a sufficient agreement without any further requirement.
2) A contract need not be concluded or evidenced in writing nor is it subject to any other requirement as to form. The contract may be proved by any means, including witnesses.

A similar approach has been taken in Article 3.1.2 of the UNIDROIT Principles of International Commercial Contracts, which states that 'a contract is concluded, modified or terminated by the mere agreement of the parties, without any further requirement'. The note to the Article states that consideration is of 'minimal practical importance' and that its elimination 'can only bring about greater certainty and reduce litigation'. While this may be true in the context of international commercial contracts, the task of limiting the scope of the law of contract must be entrusted to some set of rules. That task has traditionally been performed in English law by the doctrine of consideration which has required that there be a bargain between the parties; that is to say, both parties must contribute something to the transaction. In other words, there must be reciprocity. This insistence upon the centrality of reciprocity has recently been defended (Chen-Wishart, 2010c) on the ground that reciprocity 'enhances cooperation and division of labour, while preserving social equilibrium'. It 'represents the terms of engagement between equals who are deserving of respect' and 'keeps the state away from the private domain where external coercion would distort the practice of gift-giving and so destroy much which is valuable about it'. Admittedly, the task of identifying the existence of a bargain has not always been easy, but is English law really ready to abandon the requirement of a bargain in favour of the more nebulous requirement of 'mere agreement'?

A more limited argument is that the vital question in future cases should be: did the parties have an 'intention to contract'? The role of consideration would then be confined to answering this particular question. If the parties had an intention to contract, there would be consideration; if not, there would be none. This appears to be the approach of Russell LJ in *Williams v Roffey Bros* when he said that 'the courts nowadays should be more ready to find [the existence of consideration] so as to reflect the intention of the parties'. It also derives support from the judgment of Baragwanath J in *Antons Trawling Co Ltd v Smith* [2003] 2 NZLR 23 when he stated (at [93]) that:

> the importance of consideration is as a valuable signal that the parties intend to be bound by their agreement, rather than an end in itself. Where the parties who have already made such intention clear by entering legal relations have acted upon an agreement to a variation, in the absence of policy reasons to the contrary, they should be bound by their agreement.

The perception that consideration is not an 'end in itself' but rather performs an evidential function in terms of proving the parties' intention to create legal relations will take the doctrine of consideration into close proximity with the doctrine of intention to create legal relations (see Chapter 6) and may eventually lead to the latter subsuming the former. While this test may be relatively easy to operate in the commercial context, it is not at all obvious that the question whether the parties had an intention to contract will be any easier to answer than the question whether or not there was consideration (in the bargain sense) to support the agreement. It is the responsibility of those who advocate the abolition of the doctrine of consideration to formulate a precise set of alternative rules to mark out the limits of the law of contract.

Hot topic 5...

A particular source of difficulty in the modern law is the relationship between the decision of the House of Lords in *Foakes v Beer* and of the Court of Appeal in *Williams v Roffey Bros & Nicholls (Contractors) Ltd*. An indication of the difficulties created by the relationship between these two cases can be gleaned from the decision of the Court of Appeal in *MWB Business Exchange Centres Ltd v Rock Advertising Ltd*. The parties were alleged to have agreed to re-schedule the payment obligations of the defendant, under which the defendant would pay less to the claimant in the early months of the revised agreement. The claimant submitted that the defendant had provided no consideration for the revised agreement and relied on *Foakes v Beer* in making this submission. The defendant relied on *Williams v Roffey Bros* in support of its submission that the agreement was supported by consideration. The Court of Appeal held that the agreement was supported by consideration. It did not seek to challenge the decision in *Foakes* (and it could not do so given that the latter is a decision of the House of Lords). Kitchin and McCombe LJJ held that the consideration supplied was not the promise to pay part of the debt, or even payment of part of that debt, but in the continued occupation by the defendant of the premises, thus relieving the claimant of the need to find an alternative tenant. These practical benefits were sufficient to render the variation binding so long as the defendant continued to make payments in accordance with the revised payment schedule. Arden LJ adopted a rather different approach. She accepted what she termed the 'collateral unilateral contract' analysis of the case (an analysis originally developed by Professor Mindy Chen-Wishart), according to which the original bilateral contract between the parties was supplemented by a collateral unilateral contract according to which the claimant agreed to accept less by way of payment provided that the defendant complied with the revised payment schedule. On this basis the consideration was not the promise to pay in accordance with the revised schedule but actual payment in accordance with that schedule. In this way the Court of Appeal continued to respect *Foakes* but, at the same time, found the existence of consideration in the form of the practical benefits derived from the continuation of the underlying contractual relationship. In many ways the case demonstrates the willingness of modern courts to find the existence of consideration in order to give effect to agreements believed by the court to have been intended to be legally binding. While formally an essential part of contract law, the doctrine of consideration, when invoked before the courts, can be regarded by the judges as the invocation of a technical doctrine which attracts little judicial sympathy and the inclination of the judiciary would appear to be to find in such cases that the requirements of the doctrine have been satisfied. The Supreme Court did not deal with this issue when it heard an appeal from the decision of the Court of Appeal. The case was decided on another ground which relieved the Supreme Court of the need to reach a conclusion on the question whether consideration had been supplied on the facts of the case.

Summary

- English contract law does not generally insist upon requirements of form.

- The classical definition of consideration is that a promisee should not be able to enforce a promise unless he has given or promised to give something in exchange for the promise or unless the promisor has obtained (or been promised) something in return.

- Consideration must be sufficient but it need not be adequate, and it must be something which the law regards as being of value. Natural love and affection do not constitute value for this purpose.

- It is not clear when performance of an existing duty can constitute consideration. The orthodox view is that performance of a contractual duty owed to a third party does constitute consideration but that performance of an existing legal duty and performance of an existing contractual duty owed to the promisor do not constitute good consideration. The reason for the doubt relates to the scope of the decision of the Court of Appeal in *Williams v Roffey Bros & Nicholls* (Contractors) Ltd [1991] 1 QB 1 which suggests that performance of an existing (contractual) duty owed to the promisor can constitute consideration where it results in a 'practical benefit' to the promisor.

- Part payment of a debt does not constitute good consideration for the discharge of the entire debt. However, a court may find the existence of consideration where the creditor receives a practical benefit which goes beyond the advantage of receiving prompt payment of part of the arrears and a promise that it would be paid the balance of the arrears. The relationship between *Foakes v Beer* (1884) 9 App Cas 605 and *Williams v Roffey Bros* remains to be resolved.

- Past consideration is not good consideration. The harshness of this rule is mitigated by the doctrine of implied assumpsit.

- Consideration must move from the promisee.

- Where the act of the promisee can be shown to be at the request, express or implied, of the promisor, then the act of the promisee will constitute good consideration.

- A party may be estopped from going back on a promise or representation which he has made where (i) a clear and unequivocal promise or representation was made which was intended to affect the legal relations between the parties, (ii) the promise or representation has been relied upon by the promisee or representee (possibly to his detriment) and (iii) it would be inequitable to allow the promisor or representor to go back on his promise or representation. The effect of an estoppel is generally to suspend the rights of the promisor or representor.

Summary cont'd

▶ Estoppel can act as a shield but not as a sword. There must be a pre-existing legal relationship between the parties under which the promisor promises to give up some of his rights under that relationship. The effect of the estoppel is to prevent the promisor going back on his promise where the promisee has acted in reliance upon it.

▶ The maxim that estoppel acts as a shield but not as a sword operates in the case of estoppel by representation, waiver, promissory estoppel and estoppel by convention, but not in the case of proprietary estoppel.

▶ It is a matter for debate whether the English courts should follow the High Court of Australia and conclude that, in an appropriate case, promissory estoppel can create a cause of action.

Exercises

5.1 What is meant by the maxim 'consideration must be sufficient but it need not be adequate'? Give examples to illustrate your answer.

5.2 Can performance of an existing duty ever constitute consideration? Should it ever constitute consideration?

5.3 What is a 'practical benefit'?

5.4 Can *Williams v Roffey Bros & Nicholls (Contractors) Ltd* [1991] 1 QB 1 be reconciled with *Foakes v Beer* (1884) 9 App Cas 605?

5.5 If the Supreme Court in *Rock Advertising Ltd v MWB Business Exchange Centres Ltd* had considered the question of whether there was consideration to support the promise of the licensee to pay rent in accordance with the new schedule, how should they have decided the issue?

5.6 What is 'past consideration'? Do you think that the decision of the court in *Eastwood v Kenyon* (1840) 11 A & E 438 is (i) correct as a matter of principle and (ii) fair?

5.7 What is 'implied assumpsit'?

5.8 What is 'estoppel'? How many different types of estoppel are there and what is the relationship between them?

5.9 Describe the fact situation in the following two cases and explain their legal significance:

    (a) *Combe v Combe* [1951] 2 KB 215;

    (b) *Central London Property Trust Ltd v High Trees House Ltd* [1947] KB 130.

5.10 What is meant by the phrase 'estoppel can act as a shield but not as a sword'? Can estoppel ever act as a sword?

Chapter 6

Intention to create legal relations

6.1 Introduction

The fact that the parties have reached agreement does not necessarily mean that they have concluded a legally enforceable contract, even where the agreement is supported by consideration. The following fact situation will demonstrate the point. I promise to pay my wife £250 if she will type the manuscript of this chapter of the book. My wife agrees. Does this agreement create a legally enforceable contract? On the face of it there appears to be no reason why it should not. We have reached agreement and the agreement is supported by consideration. But it is likely that an English court would conclude that we had not entered into a legally binding contract because we lacked an 'intention to create legal relations', which has been held to be an essential element in any contract. Before examining the relevant case law, we must stop and contemplate the juristic basis of this doctrine of intention to create legal relations.

It could be said that the doctrine is based on the intention of the parties, objectively interpreted; that is to say, my wife and I did not intend that our agreement would have legal consequences. But my wife certainly expected to receive the £250 if she typed the manuscript, although it is unlikely that either of us intended that she would have to go to court in order to get her money. However, to say that we did not intend that she would have to go to court to get her money is not the same thing as saying that, if the case did go to court, we thought her action would fail.

Alternatively, it could be said that the doctrine is based upon public policy; that is to say that, as a matter of policy, the law of contract ought not to intervene in domestic situations because the courts would then be swamped by trifling domestic disputes. Thus, the Scottish Law Commission has stated (1977) that:

> it is, in general, right that courts should not enforce entirely social engagements, such as arrangements to play squash or to come to dinner, even though the parties themselves may intend to be legally bound thereby.

In such a case, it is for the court to decide, as a matter of policy, whether the agreement is 'entirely social' and hence not legally enforceable.

6.2 Balfour v Balfour

The approach which has been adopted in the English courts is best illustrated by reference to the case of *Balfour v Balfour* [1919] 2 KB 571. A wife sought to enforce a promise by her husband to pay her £30 per month while he worked abroad. The action failed because the wife had not provided any consideration for the promise of her husband and because it was held that the parties did not intend their agreement to 'be attended by legal consequences'. Atkin LJ said that:

> agreements such as these are outside the realm of contracts altogether. The common law does not regulate the form of agreements between spouses … The consideration that really obtains for them is that natural love and affection which counts for so little in these cold Courts.

But how did Atkin LJ know that the parties did not intend to create legal relations? Did he inquire into the intention of the parties or did he lay down this rule as a matter of policy? It appears from his judgment that he was more concerned with policy than with ascertaining the intention of the parties because he said that:

> it would be of the worst possible example to hold that agreements such as this resulted in legal obligations which could be enforced in the Courts … the small Courts of this country would have to be multiplied one hundredfold if these arrangements were held to result in legal obligations.

It was the need to prevent what was, in the opinion of the court, unnecessary litigation and the desire of the court to keep the law out of the marriage relationship ('each house is a domain into which the King's writ does not seek to run') which were the predominant factors behind the finding that there was no intention to create legal relations.

However, it does not necessarily follow from the fact that the judgment of Atkin LJ is based primarily upon considerations of policy that the intention of the parties is thereby completely irrelevant. The rule laid down in *Balfour* has been interpreted subsequently as a *presumption* that parties to a domestic agreement do not intend to create legal relations. Cases concerning intention to create legal relations are thus commonly divided into two categories; the first, concerning domestic and social agreements, where the presumption is that the parties did not intend to create legal relations, and the second, concerning commercial agreements, where the presumption is that the parties did intend to create legal relations. Both presumptions may be rebutted by evidence of contrary intention. But the fact that the initial presumption may be rebutted by evidence of contrary intention does not mean that the presumption itself is based upon the intention of the parties. Rather, as the judgment of Atkin LJ in *Balfour* makes clear, the initial presumption is a matter of policy. The policy which underpins these presumptions is one of 'keeping contract in its place; to keep it in the commercial sphere and out of domestic cases, except where the judges think it has a useful role to play' (Hedley, 1985). While this policy may have been appropriate for 'Victorian marriages' such as that of the Balfours, it is not entirely clear that it is appropriate for modern society in which family law 'has steadily embraced contract as its governing principle' and 'increasingly … extends to those in family relationships the power to regulate their own lives' (Freeman, 1996).

6.3 Rebutting the presumption

Although we have noted that evidence of intention is relevant to the rebuttal of the presumption, even here the role of intention is, at best, marginal. This is so for two reasons. The first is that in the case of many domestic and social agreements the parties have no discernible intention one way or the other. The second reason is that it is a very difficult task to rebut a presumption because of the strength of the initial presumption. In domestic agreements 'clear' evidence is required of an intention to create legal relations, whereas in commercial cases the presumption of legal relations is a 'heavy one' which is not discharged easily (*Edwards v Skyways* [1964] 1 WLR 349; *Attrill v Dresdner Kleinwort Ltd* [2013] EWCA Civ 394; [2013] 3 All ER 607, [80]). The marginal role of intention will be demonstrated by examining the scope of the two presumptions and then the factors which have been held to be relevant to the rebuttal of these presumptions.

6.4   Domestic and social agreements

As we have seen, an agreement between a husband and a wife is presumed not to be legally enforceable (*Balfour v Balfour*, Section 6.2). Similarly, agreements between parents and children are presumed not to be legally binding. In *Jones v Padavatton* [1969] 1 WLR 328, a mother persuaded her daughter, who was a secretary in Washington, DC, to give up her work and read for the English Bar by promising to pay her $200 maintenance per month. After the daughter had begun to read for the Bar, the agreement was varied. The mother bought a house in London so that the daughter could live there rent free, and the rent from letting out the other rooms to tenants would provide the daughter with her maintenance. Eventually, after the daughter had had more than one unsuccessful attempt at passing the Bar examinations, the mother and daughter fell out. The mother came to England and sought to gain possession of the house. The daughter relied upon their agreement as a defence to her mother's action. The Court of Appeal held that the agreement was not intended to be legally binding and that the mother was entitled to possession (see also *Hardwick v Johnson* [1978] 1 WLR 683).

Social arrangements are also presumed not to give rise to legal relations. In *Lens v Devonshire Social Club, The Times*, 4 December 1914, it was held that the winner of a competition held by a golf club could not sue for his prize because no one involved in the competition intended that legal consequences should flow from entry into the competition. Competitions can, however, give rise to legal relations between the organiser of the competition and the participants, an example being the competitions that are a regular feature of national newspapers (see, for example, *O'Brien v MGN Ltd* [2002] CLC 33).

The presumption may, of course, be rebutted by evidence of contrary intention, but a mere subjective intention to create legal relations will not suffice. There must be objective evidence of a contrary intent (although evidence of subjective intention is admissible in the case where one party actually knows that the other party has no intention to create legal relations given that 'a party who in fact knows that the other party does not intend to create legal relations cannot seek to contend otherwise by asserting that the evidence, objectively analysed, supports his case': *Attrill* v. *Dresdner Kleinwort Ltd* [2013] EWCA Civ 394; [2013] 3 All ER 607, [86]) . Although a complete list cannot be drawn up of the factors to which the court will have regard in considering whether or not the presumption has been rebutted, in practice the following three factors are among the most important.

The first is the context in which the agreement is made. If an agreement is entered into by family members in what the courts perceive to be a 'business context', the court will be readier to infer that the presumption has been rebutted. For example, the presumption may be rebutted where a husband and wife enter into an 'agreement to share the ownership or tenancy of the matrimonial home, bank accounts, savings or other assets' (*Granatino v Radmacher* [2010] UKSC 42; [2011] 1 AC 534, [142]). In *Snelling v John G Snelling Ltd* [1973] 1 QB 87, it was held that legal relations were created when three brothers, who were directors of a family company, entered into an agreement relating to the running of the company. Similarly, where a husband and a wife are about to separate or have separated, the presumption does not operate because in such a case the parties 'bargain keenly' and do not rely on 'honourable understandings' (*Merritt v Merritt* [1970] 1 WLR 1121, 1123 per Lord Denning and, more recently, *Soulsbury v Soulsbury* [2007] EWCA Civ 969; [2008] Fam 1, [35]).

Secondly, the court will have regard to any reliance which has been placed upon the agreement. Where one party has acted to his detriment on the faith of the agreement a court may be more willing to conclude that the agreement was intended to have legal consequences. Such was the case in *Parker v Clark* [1960] 1 WLR 286. The defendants, who were an elderly couple, suggested that the claimants, who were their friends, come to live with them. The claimants were agreeable to the proposal but pointed out that, if they were to live with the defendants, they would have to sell their own house. The defendants replied stating that the problem could be resolved by the defendants leaving to the claimants a share of their house in their will. The claimants accepted this offer, sold their house, lent the balance of the money to their daughter to enable her to purchase a flat and moved in with the defendants. However, the parties soon began to disagree over certain matters and the result was that the defendants asked the claimants to leave. The claimants left the house to avoid being evicted and brought an action against the defendants for breach of contract. The defendants argued that there was no contract between them because of a lack of intention to create legal relations. It was held that the parties had intended to create legal relations. Devlin J stated that:

> I cannot believe ... that the defendant really thought that the law would leave him at liberty, if he so chose, to tell the [claimants] when they arrived that he had changed his mind, that they could take their furniture away, and that he was indifferent whether they found anywhere else to live or not.

Similarly, there is some authority for the proposition that an agreement between workmates under which one is to provide the other with a lift to work in return for a contribution towards the petrol does not create legal relations with regard to journeys to be undertaken in the future (see *Coward v Motor Insurers' Bureau* [1963] 2 QB 259, 271, per Upjohn LJ) but that it does create legal relations with regard to journeys which have already been undertaken (see Lord Cross in *Albert v Motor Insurers' Bureau* [1972] AC 301, 340). In these cases the determining factor appears to be the fact that the parties have acted in reliance upon the agreement. The courts are reluctant to allow the parties to go back on their agreement once it has been acted upon.

Finally, the court will consider the certainty of the agreement which has been entered into by the parties. In *Vaughan v Vaughan* [1953] 1 QB 762, it was held that a promise by a husband to allow his deserted wife to stay in the matrimonial home did not have contractual force because its vagueness evidenced that it was neither intended to have, nor was understood as having, contractual force. The husband did not state how long she could live there, nor did he indicate the terms on which she could stay. Similarly, the uncertainty of the agreement in *Jones v Padavatton* (above) was a factor which persuaded the court to hold that there was no intention to create legal relations, despite the fact that the daughter had detrimentally relied upon the agreement. The daughter had been in London for six years and this was held to be long enough to complete her Bar exams. The mother's promise of support could not be treated as lasting indefinitely.

6.5 Commercial agreements

The presumption is that parties to commercial agreements do intend to create legal relations, and the presumption is a heavy one. The operation of the presumption can be seen in the case of *Esso Petroleum Ltd v Comrs of Customs and Excise* [1976] 1 WLR 1. Esso supplied garages with World Cup Coins in 1970, instructing the garages to give away one coin with every four gallons of petrol sold. It was sought to subject these coins to a purchase tax on the ground that they had been sold. On the facts, it was held that the coins were not supplied under a contract of sale. But the House of Lords divided on the issue of whether or not there was an intention to create legal relations. The majority, Lord Simon, Lord Wilberforce and Lord Fraser, held that there was an intention to create legal relations. They placed heavy reliance on the onus of proof in commercial transactions and on the fact that Esso envisaged a bargain of some description between the garage owner and the customer. But the minority, Lord Russell and Viscount Dilhorne, relying upon the language of the advertising posters which said that the coins were 'going free' and the minimal value of the coins, held that there was no intention to create legal relations (see also *J Evans & Son (Portsmouth) Ltd v Andrea Merzario Ltd* [1976] 1 WLR 1078).

The presumption may be rebutted by an express term of the contract which states that the parties do not intend to create legal relations. The parties must, however, make their intention clear. Thus, agreements for the sale of land are usually made 'subject to contract' and, on that ground, do not create legal relations. At common law a collective agreement entered into between trade unions and an employer was held not to give rise to legal relations (*Ford Motor Co Ltd v AEF* [1969] 1 WLR 339). This common law rule has been reinforced by a statutory presumption to the effect that a collective agreement is conclusively presumed not to have been intended by the parties to be a legally enforceable contract unless it is in writing and expressly provides to the contrary (see Trade Union and Labour Relations (Consolidation) Act 1992, s 179). The presumption may also be rebutted where an agreement is made between businessmen in a social context. In particular, the jocular context of a meeting and the vague terms of the alleged agreement may persuade a court that the parties did not intend to create legal relations. Thus in *Blue v Ashley* [2017] EWHC 1928 (Comm) a statement made by the defendant in a pub that he would pay the claimant £15 million if shares reached a specified price was held not to be a serious offer intended to create a legally binding agreement, given the jocular nature of the conversation in the pub that evening when those present regarded the statement as a joke, and not a binding contractual commitment. Similarly, in *MacInnes v Gross* [2017] EWHC 46 (QB) a highly informal dinner conversation in a restaurant followed by an email referring to 'headline terms' of agreement was held not to give rise to a legally binding commitment to pay to the claimant some 13 million euros for services which the claimant alleged that he had agreed to provide to the defendants.

The most interesting example in this category is, however, what is known as an honour clause. In *Rose and Frank Co v J R Crompton and Bros Ltd* [1925] AC 445, an agreement stated:

> this arrangement is not entered into as a formal or legal agreement, and shall not be subject to legal jurisdiction in the Law Courts but is only a definite expression and record of the purpose and intention of the parties concerned to which they each honourably pledge themselves.

The court held that this agreement was not a legally binding contract because it was not intended that it would have such an effect. The courts interpret such clauses restrictively and clear words must be used to create such an honour clause (see *Home Insurance Co v Administratia Asiguraliror* [1983] 2 Lloyd's Rep 674, 677).

Hot topic 6…

Blue v Ashley [2017] EWHC 1928 (Comm) arose out of a jocular conversation between three investment bankers in a pub on the evening of 24 January 2013 during the course of which the defendant, Mr Ashley, said that he would pay Mr Blue, the claimant, £15 million if Mr Blue could get the price of Sports Direct shares (then trading at around £4 per share) to £8. Mr Blue expressed his agreement to that proposal and everyone laughed. Thirteen months later the Sports Direct share price did reach £8. In these circumstances the claimant alleged that he was entitled to the promised £15 million. The defendant paid him £1 million but declined to make any further payment. The claimant brought an action to recover the balance of the promised payment. His claim failed. Leggatt ᴊ stated that the 'key issue' was whether, when the defendant said that he would pay the claimant £15 million if he could get the Sports Direct share price to £8 per share, this would reasonably have been understood as a serious offer capable of creating a legally binding contract. He decided that it was not an offer capable of creating a legally binding contract for the following reasons: (i) the setting for the meeting. Leggatt ᴊ stated that 'an evening of drinking in a pub with three investment bankers is an unlikely setting in which to negotiate a contractual bonus arrangement with a consultant'; (ii) the purpose of the meeting was not to discuss the position of the claimant but to meet with third parties; (iii) the jocular nature of the conversation at the pub; (iv) the defendant had no commercial reason to offer to pay the claimant £15 million as an incentive to do work aimed at increasing the Sports Direct share price; (v) the idea that the claimant could somehow, through his skills and contacts in corporate finance, get the share price to double its then level seemed plainly fanciful; (vi) the 'offer' was far too vague to have been seriously meant; (vii) none of the witnesses who took part in the conversation thought the defendant was being serious; and (viii) the claimant himself did not understand there to be such an intention at the time when the conversation in the pub took place or in the period immediately afterwards.

Summary

▶ An intention to create legal relations is an essential element in any contract.

▶ In cases of domestic and social agreements the presumption is that the parties did not intend to create legal relations. The presumption may be rebutted by 'clear' evidence to the contrary.

▶ Factors which may persuade a court to hold that the presumption has been rebutted include the context in which the agreement was made (that is, was it a business context?) and any reliance which has been placed upon the agreement.

▶ In cases involving commercial agreements the presumption is that the parties did intend to create legal relations. This presumption is also a 'heavy' one.

▶ Clear evidence is required to rebut the presumption. The presumption has been rebutted in cases of agreements to sell land 'subject to contract', collective agreements and 'honour clauses'.

Exercises

6.1. Is the doctrine of intention to create legal relations based on considerations of policy or does the court genuinely seek to discover the intention of the parties?

6.2. Reagan Ltd are considering inserting an 'honour clause' in their agreement with their major supplier, Jones Ltd. Advise them as to the advantages and disadvantages of such a course of action.

6.3. John offers £50 to anyone who will remove rubbish from his garden. The following people comply with the terms of his offer:

    (a)   his wife, Beatrice;

    (b)   his ex-wife, Brenda;

    (c)   his mistress, Belinda;

    (d)   his son, Billy;

    (e)   his nephew, Brian, whom he had never seen before;

    (f)   his god-child, Bernard; and

    (g)   his next-door neighbour, Benedict.

Advise John whether or not, in these circumstances, any legally enforceable contracts have been concluded.

Chapter 7
Third party rights

Introduction

The Contracts (Rights of Third Parties) Act 1999 has made a fundamental change to English contract law in that it enacts a substantial exception to the doctrine of privity of contract, which had long been a central, albeit controversial, part of English contract law. The doctrine of privity of contract consisted of two distinct general rules. The first rule has not been affected in any way by the 1999 Act. It is that a third party cannot be subjected to a burden by a contract to which he is not a party. This rule is not at all controversial. It would be wholly unreasonable for a legal system to enable two parties to subject a third party to a contractual obligation of which he was completely unaware. It is the second rule which was the controversial one and it is this aspect of the privity doctrine which has been reformed by the 1999 Act. The second rule was that a person who was not a party to a contract could not sue upon the contract in order to obtain the promised performance, even in the case where the contract was entered into with the very object of benefiting him.

The latter rule has had a somewhat chequered career. Prior to 1861, cases can be found in which third parties were held to be entitled to sue upon a contract entered into for their benefit (see, for example, *Dutton v Poole* (1677) 2 Lev 211 and, more generally, Flannigan, 1987). But that development was brought to a halt in 1861 in *Tweddle v Atkinson* (1861) 1 B & S 393 when it was held that the third party had no such right of action, and that decision was affirmed by the House of Lords more than 50 years later in *Dunlop Pneumatic Tyre Co Ltd v Selfridge* [1915] AC 847. In the twentieth century the rule in *Tweddle v Atkinson* and *Dunlop* survived a sustained attack by Lord Denning (launched in cases such as *Smith and Snipes Hall Farm Ltd v River Douglas Catchment Board* [1949] 2 KB 500 and *Beswick v Beswick* [1966] Ch 538). While the attack was ultimately rejected by the House of Lords (in cases such as *Scruttons Ltd v Midland Silicones Ltd* [1962] AC 446 and *Beswick v Beswick* [1968] AC 58), numerous expressions of disquiet about the state of the law continued to appear in the law reports (see, for example, *Scruttons Ltd v Midland Silicones* [1962] AC 446, 473, per Lord Reid; *Woodar Investment Development Ltd v Wimpey Construction UK Ltd* [1980] 1 WLR 277, 300, per Lord Scarman; *White v Jones* [1995] 2 AC 207, 262–63, per Lord Goff; *Darlington BC v Wiltshier Northern Ltd* [1995] 1 WLR 68, 77, per Steyn LJ; and *The Mahkutai* [1996] AC 650, 664–65, per Lord Goff). However, the difficulty was that the judiciary showed little inclination to act on their expressions of disquiet; in fact, Lord Denning apart, they tended to be remarkably orthodox in their interpretation and application of the doctrine of privity, even extending it in places (for example in *Scruttons Ltd v Midland Silicones*, discussed in more detail in Section 7.2) and at other times rejecting devices which would have enabled them to avoid some of the unfair consequences produced by its strict application (see, for example, *Woodar Investment Development Ltd v Wimpey Construction UK Ltd*, discussed in more detail in Section 7.14 below). So it was not until the 1999 Act was passed that significant reform of the rule was introduced.

It is this second aspect of the privity doctrine which forms the main subject-matter of this chapter (we shall return briefly to the first aspect of the doctrine in Section 7.23). We shall start by considering the way in which the doctrine operated prior to the 1999 Act (Section 7.2) and its relationship with the doctrine of consideration (Section 7.3) before turning to a more detailed analysis of the 1999 Act (Sections 7.5–7.13) and then a discussion of the various exceptions to the doctrine of privity which pre-date the 1999 Act (Sections 7.14–7.21).

7.2 Privity in operation

The rule that a person who was not a party to a contract could not sue upon the contract in order to obtain the promised performance, even in the case where the contract was entered into with the object of benefiting him, was capable of producing hardship. It applied both where the claimant was seeking to assert a positive right under the contract (for example, to be paid a sum of money) and where he was seeking to rely on a term in the contract as a defence to a claim brought by the claimant (for example, an exclusion clause contained in a contract between the claimant and a third party). Although many examples could be given in each category, it will suffice to provide one from the first category and two from the second category.

The case in the first category is *Beswick v Beswick* [1968] AC 58. Peter Beswick sold his coal round and the goodwill of his business to his nephew John Beswick in return for a promise to pay £6 10s a week to Peter Beswick for the rest of his life and thereafter £5 a week to Peter Beswick's widow for the rest of her life. The nephew ceased making payments to the widow shortly after Peter Beswick's death. The widow brought an action to compel the nephew to continue making the payments. She failed in the action in so far as it was brought in her own name because she was not privy to the contract between her husband and her nephew and so she was not entitled to sue on it. But she did succeed in another capacity in that she happened to be the administratrix of her husband's estate (when a person dies the administrator or administratrix of the estate, broadly speaking, acquires the rights of the deceased). So on the facts of the case no injustice was done and it was not necessary for the House of Lords to create an exception to the doctrine of privity in order to give the widow the remedy which it was thought she deserved. It was not necessary to create an exception to the doctrine of privity because in bringing a claim as the administratrix of her husband's estate it was as if Peter Beswick himself was suing and, of course, he was privy to the original agreement. But the fact that her third party claim was held to be without foundation demonstrated to many people that the privity doctrine was capable of giving rise to injustice.

Turning now to the second category of case, the doctrine of privity also made it very difficult for third parties to rely on an exclusion clause contained in a contract between two other parties. That this was so can be demonstrated by reference to the following two cases. The first case is *Scruttons Ltd v Midland Silicones Ltd* [1962] AC 446. The claimants, who were the owners of a drum of chemicals, entered into a contract with a firm of carriers for the transportation of the drum. Under the contract the carriers limited their liability to the claimants to $500. Stevedores, who were employed by the carriers to discharge the drum, negligently dropped it and the claimants brought an action in tort against them in respect of the resulting damage. The stevedores sought to rely on the limitation clause contained in the contract between the claimants and the carriers and in the contract between themselves and the carriers, but it was held that they could not do so because they were not privy to the same contract. The House of Lords held that English law knew of no doctrine of vicarious immunity (which would have enabled the stevedores, as agents, to claim the benefit of the immunity which had been negotiated by their principals) and that, in any case, the limitation clause only referred to the carriers and so was incapable of providing protection for the stevedores. This conclusion gave rise to considerable commercial inconvenience because it made it extremely difficult for an employer to give his employees and agents the benefit of an exclusion clause negotiated by the employer, even where the exclusion clause was a legitimate method of allocating the risks under the contract between the employer and the claimant.

Numerous attempts were made to get round this inconvenient ruling. Lord Reid provided the most hopeful route in *Scruttons Ltd v Midland Silicones* itself when he said that the stevedores might be able to claim the protection of an exclusion clause:

> if (first) the bill of lading makes it clear that the stevedore is intended to be protected by the provisions in it which limit liability, (secondly) the bill of lading makes it clear that the carrier, in addition to contracting for these provisions on his own behalf, is also contracting as agent for the stevedore that these provisions should apply to the stevedore, (thirdly) the carrier has authority from the stevedore to do that, or perhaps later ratification by the stevedore would suffice, and (fourthly) that any difficulties about consideration moving from the stevedore were overcome.

Lord Reid therefore envisaged that, at the moment the carrier signed the contract, two contracts would come into existence; the first between the owner and the carrier and the second between the owner and the stevedore. The difficulty with this analysis was that, at that moment in time, it was extremely difficult to find any consideration supplied by the stevedore; indeed, at the moment of signing the contract, it might not have been known which firm of stevedores was to unload the goods. Lord Reid's solution was therefore not entirely satisfactory.

The issue was reconsidered by the Privy Council in *NZ Shipping Co Ltd v AM Satterthwaite & Co Ltd (The Eurymedon)* [1975] AC 154, in which the stevedores were held to be entitled to take the benefit of the exclusion clause contained in the contract between the consignors and the carriers. The fact situation was similar to *Scruttons Ltd v Midland Silicones* except that the bill of lading was much more complex and clearly sought to give the stevedores the benefit of the exclusion clause. The first three of Lord Reid's four conditions were satisfied. The bill of lading expressly extended the benefit of the exclusion clause to any servants, agents and independent contractors employed by the carriers. The carriers had also contracted as the agents of the stevedores and they were authorised by the stevedores so to act. The principal problem lay in locating the consideration provided by the stevedores for the consignor's offer of immunity and in accommodating the solution within the offer and acceptance framework. The solution adopted by the Privy Council proceeded in the following stages. First, they held that when the consignors signed the bill of lading they made an offer to all the world that anyone who unloaded their goods at the port of discharge would be entitled to the benefit of the exclusion clause. Secondly, they held that this offer was accepted by the stevedores unloading the goods at the port of discharge and at that moment a binding contract came into existence. The consideration supplied by the stevedores was the performance of their contractual duty owed to the carriers and, as we noted in Section 5.16, performance of a contractual duty owed to a third party is good consideration for a promise given by the claimant.

The *Eurymedon* demonstrates that it was possible in some cases to get round the doctrine of privity of contract but only by considerable ingenuity and no doubt significant expense (in terms of employing lawyers to draft the clause and then to litigate the matter through the courts). And, while the clause worked on the facts of *The Eurymedon*, it did not appear to work in all cases. For example, it did not work where the stevedore damaged the goods before he started to unload them, because the acceptance of the owner's offer only took place when the stevedore began to unload the goods and by that time they had already been damaged (see *Raymond Burke Motors Ltd v Mersey Docks & Harbour Co* [1986] 1 Lloyd's Rep 155). In *The Mahkutai* [1996] AC 650 at 664–65 Lord Goff evaluated *The Eurymedon* critically and wondered whether its development was 'yet complete'. He noted that, while the solutions:

> are now perceived to be generally effective for their purpose, their technical nature is all too apparent; and the time may well come when, in an appropriate case, it will fall to be considered whether the courts should take what may legitimately be perceived to be the final, and perhaps inevitable, step in this development, and recognise in these cases a fully-fledged exception to the doctrine of privity of contract, thus escaping from all the technicalities with which courts are now faced in English law.

The law in this area had become too complex and too technical. The aim of the parties was simple, namely, to extend the benefit of an exclusion clause to a third party, but the law lacked the mechanism which enabled them to achieve that aim in a straightforward manner.

7.3   Privity and consideration

Before turning to consider the 1999 Act, it is necessary to discuss the relationship between the doctrine of privity and the doctrine of consideration because the historical development of privity is very closely linked with the doctrine of consideration. The link can be seen if we examine the two principal cases which established the doctrine of privity as we knew it prior to the enactment of the 1999 Act.

The first case is *Tweddle v Atkinson* (1861) 1 B & S 393. In this case John Tweddle and William Guy entered into an agreement under which each promised to pay a sum of money to William Tweddle on the occasion of William Tweddle's marriage to William Guy's daughter. The agreement between them further stated that 'it is hereby further agreed … that the said William Tweddle has full power to sue the said parties in any Court of law or equity for the aforesaid sums hereby promised and specified'. However, William Guy failed to pay the promised sum and, on his death, William Tweddle sued the executor of William Guy for the promised amount. It was held that he could not maintain such a cause of action. Now there was one obvious reason why he could not sue; he had provided no consideration for William Guy's promise. The consideration had been provided by John Tweddle. Indeed, Wightman, Crompton and Blackburn JJ all appeared to base their judgments on the rule that a stranger to the consideration cannot enforce the promise. There was therefore no need to explain the result in *Tweddle v Atkinson* on the basis of an independent doctrine of privity.

The second leading case is *Dunlop Pneumatic Tyre Co Ltd v Selfridge* [1915] AC 847. In this case the claimants attempted to operate a price-fixing ring. For this purpose they extracted a promise from dealers called Dew & Co that they in turn would obtain a written undertaking from any third party to whom they sold Dunlop products that the third party would not sell at a price below Dunlop's list price. The defendants, Selfridge, bought Dunlop products from Dew and gave the required undertaking to Dew but nevertheless sold Dunlop products at less than the list price. In these circumstances, Dunlop brought an action for an injunction and damages against Selfridge. The action failed. The majority held that the action failed because Dunlop had provided no consideration for the promise of Selfridge; the consideration had been provided by Dew. But Viscount Haldane, in a judgment which has since assumed considerable significance, held that, independently of the need for consideration, it was a fundamental principle of English law that 'only a person who is a party to a contract can sue on it' and that, because Dunlop were not a party to the contract between Dew and Selfridge, they could not sue on it.

Tweddle v Atkinson and *Dunlop* both demonstrate that there is a very close relationship between the doctrines of privity and consideration. Indeed, on one view, there is no difference between the doctrine of privity and the rule that consideration must move from the promisee (see Furmston, 1960). Privity then becomes swallowed up in the larger rule that consideration must move from the promisee. *Tweddle v Atkinson* and *Dunlop* are both consistent with this view because the majority view in each case was that the claimant could not sue because he had not provided consideration for the defendant's promise. Despite the strength of this argument, the more widely accepted view, and the one subsequently adopted by the House of Lords in the cases of *Scruttons Ltd v Midland Silicones Ltd* [1962] AC 446 and *Beswick v Beswick* [1968] AC 58, is that expressed by Viscount Haldane in *Dunlop*, namely, that the doctrine of privity is separate and distinct from the rule that consideration must move from the promisee. The following example is often used to illustrate the point. X makes a promise to Y and Z to pay £100 to Z in exchange for consideration provided by Y. In such a case Z is privy to the contract but cannot maintain an action against X unless he has provided consideration for X's promise. Privity and consideration constitute two hurdles for Z to surmount, not one (see *Kepong Prospecting Ltd v Schmidt* [1968] AC 810).

However, even those who maintain that privity and the rule that consideration must move from the promisee (on which see Section 5.19) are two separate rules, nevertheless concede that there is a very strong relationship between privity and consideration and that it is very difficult to reform the one without the other. For example, a rule which abolished the doctrine of privity but left intact the rule that consideration must move from the promisee would not avail the claimants in *Tweddle v Atkinson* and *Dunlop* because their claims would then be dismissed on the sole ground that they had not provided any consideration for the promise in respect of which they were bringing the claim. So when reforming privity it is necessary to take steps to ensure that the practical effects of the reform are not nullified by the doctrine of consideration (see Section 7.7).

The relationship between privity and consideration does, however, throw up a deeper issue and that relates to the justification for giving the *third party* a right of action in the first place (see Stevens, 2004). The difficulty is that the third party is, in most of the cases, a gratuitous beneficiary; he or she has given nothing in return for the promise. If the law does not generally allow a gratuitous beneficiary to bring a contractual claim (and the doctrine of consideration prevents him from doing so) why should we give a claim to a third party gratuitous beneficiary? The answer to that question is that in the third party case the consideration has been provided by the other contracting party and all that is happening is that the third party is, in effect, being allowed to take advantage of the consideration provided by that contracting party. So the case is distinguishable from a gratuitous promise where no one has provided consideration for the promise in respect of which the claim is being brought.

7.4 Criticisms of the doctrine of privity

By the end of the 1990s the doctrine of privity had few friends, at least that part of it which prevented third parties suing to obtain the benefit which the contracting parties had agreed to confer on them (privity is not, however, entirely devoid of friends: see Stevens, 2004, who mounts a robust defence of the pre-1999 law and maintains that the new Act may in fact create more problems than it solves). There were four principal criticisms levelled against the old law. The first was that it failed to give effect to the expressed intentions of the parties (see, for example, *Tweddle v Atkinson* (1861) 1 B & S 393, see Section 7.3). The second was that the law was unduly complex. A number of exceptions had grown up to the doctrine (some of which are set out below at Sections 7.14–7.21) and some of them were extremely artificial (as was the case with the trust of the promise device (see Section 7.17) and the use made of the collateral contract (see Section 7.15)). The contorted reasoning of the Privy Council in *The Eurymedon* (see Section 7.2) also demonstrated the unnecessary complexities which could arise in seeking to give effect to the intention of the contracting parties. The third deficiency was that the doctrine of privity was commercially inconvenient (see, for example, the difficulties which arose in *The Eurymedon* situation and, as we shall see (Section 7.21), commercial transactions such as insurance and carriage of goods by sea had to be put on a statutory footing in order to get round the privity problem). The final deficiency was that the application of the doctrine could sometimes lead to results which were regarded as fundamentally unjust (see *Tweddle v Atkinson* (Section 7.3)). It was therefore no real surprise when the Law Commission (1996) recommended substantial reform of this area of the law. These recommendations were finally implemented in the 1999 Act (on which see Burrows, 2000 and Beale, 2010).

7.5 The Contracts (Rights of Third Parties) Act 1999

It could be said that the Contracts (Rights of Third Parties) Act 1999 introduces into English law a limited third party right of action to enforce a term of a contract made between two other parties or, alternatively, that it carves out a further (substantial) exception to the doctrine of privity of contract. This may be no more than two ways of saying the same thing; on the other hand, the difference in emphasis may turn out to be important. The Act is based on a Law Commission Report (1996) and, in that Report, the Law Commission stated (at para 5.16) that, while their proposed reform:

> will give some third parties the right to enforce contracts, there will remain many contracts where a third party stands to benefit and yet will not have a right of enforceability. Our proposed statute carves out a general and wide-ranging exception to the third party rule but it leaves the rule intact for cases not covered by the statute.

Thus, the old rule of privity of contract and its exceptions remain intact (the exceptions are discussed in Sections 7.14–7.21) and, grafted on to the old law, is a new third party right of action which, in turn, has exceptions where the new third party right will not be available (see s 6 of the Act). While the Act has no doubt improved the law 'it has scarcely simplified' the law on this topic (Chitty, 2018, para 18-002).

The complexity arises in part from the fact that the new Act and the old law must coexist. Four distinct situations appear to be discernible. The first arises where the third party has a right of action under the Act but not at common law; in such a case the third party's right will be governed by the Act. The second situation is where the third party has no claim under the Act but does have a claim apart from the Act (that is to say at common law or by virtue of some other legislative provision). In such a case the third party's right will continue to be governed by that alternative provision. The third situation is where the third party has a right both under the Act and under the previous law. In such a case it would appear that the third party can choose which right to assert. The final case is where the third party has no rights under the Act or at common law. In such a case the third party will only be entitled to bring a claim if it can persuade a court that it ought to introduce a new exception to the doctrine of privity of contract (see Section 7.22). Here, it should be noted that the Law Commission explicitly state in their report (at para 5.10) that the courts should continue to be free to develop the common law where it is appropriate to do so. The Act should not have the effect of freezing the common law as at the date on which it came into force (11 May 2000).

7.6 The intention test

The scope of the third party right of action created by the Act is determined by the intention of the contracting parties themselves. The third party is given a right of action in two circumstances, the first being much more straightforward than the second.

7.6.1 The contract expressly confers the right to enforce a term

The first situation where the third party is given a right to enforce a term of the contract arises where 'the contract expressly provides that he may' (s 1(1)(a)). The right of action given to the third party may be a right to sue to enforce a positive claim, for example to payment, or it may be a right asserted by way of defence to rely on an exclusion or limitation clause contained in the contract between the two contracting parties (s 1(6)). Thus it applies both to the *Beswick v Beswick* type fact situation and to the fact situation in *The Eurymedon*. Gone are *The Eurymedon* days in which contracting parties had to express themselves in convoluted terms in order to confer the benefit of an exclusion or limitation clause on a third party. The need for complex drafting or judicial ingenuity in order to give effect to third party rights has been significantly reduced as a result of the enactment of the 1999 Act. It will suffice for the contracting parties to state that the third party shall have the right to enforce the contract (or a specified term of the contract) or that the third party shall be excluded from all liability towards the employer for damage caused in the performance of the contract.

It is, however, important to note that the intention test cuts both ways; that is to say, the contracting parties can make clear their intention *not* to confer a right of action on the third party or to subject the third party right of action to some sort of condition precedent. In other words, the third party cannot assert a right of action in the teeth of the terms of the contract. Furthermore, the contracting parties can exclude the third party right of action without having to worry about the potential impact of section 3 of the Unfair Contract Terms Act 1977 (UCTA, on which see Section 11.11). The Law Commission were of the view that to give a third party right of action was 'relatively uncontroversial' but that to prevent the contracting parties from contracting out of that third party right was to go too far. Where, however, the third party suffers loss or damage as a result of the negligence of one of the contracting parties, the proposition that UCTA does not apply to the exclusion of liability towards the third party requires some modification. If the claim is one in respect of death or personal injury caused by the negligence of one of the contracting parties, then section 2(1) of UCTA will operate to render the exclusion or limitation clause void (see Section 11.10). On the other hand, where the claim is one in respect of property damage or other loss caused by the negligence of one of the contracting parties, section 2(2) of UCTA will regulate the exclusion clause where the claim brought by the third party is one in the tort of negligence but not where the claim is that there has been a breach of a contractual duty of care owed to the third party (see s 7(2) of the 1999 Act: it should, however, be noted that UCTA can apply as between the two contracting parties so that, where the failure to confer a benefit on a third party also constitutes a breach of contract as between the contracting parties, UCTA applies in the usual way as between them).

7.6.2 The contract term purports to confer a benefit on the third party

Much more difficult is the case where the contracting parties do not make their intention express and the contract term 'purports to confer a benefit on' the third party (s 1(1)(b)). In such a case the third party may have a right to enforce the term. The words 'purports to confer a benefit' are important. A contract term does not 'purport to confer a benefit' on a third party simply because the position of the third party will be improved if the contract is performed. In order for a term to 'purport to confer a benefit' on the third party, one of the purposes of the parties' bargain (rather than one of its incidental benefits if performed) must have been to benefit the third party (*Dolphin Maritime & Aviation Services Ltd v Sveriges Angfartygs Assurans Forening* [2009] EWHC 716 (Comm); [2009] 2 Lloyd's Rep 123). However, the subsection does not require that the benefit to the third party 'shall be the predominant purpose or intent behind the term' (*Prudential Assurance Co Ltd v Ayres* [2007] EWHC

775 (Ch); [2007] 3 All ER 946). Equally, the fact that there is a 'benefit conferred on someone other than the third party' does not have the consequence that the requirements of the subsection cannot be met (*Cavanagh v Secretary of State for Work and Pensions* [2016] EWHC 1136 (QB); [2016] ICR 826). This approach suggests that it will not be a particularly difficult task to satisfy the requirements of section 1(1)(b) (as also evidenced by cases such as *Chudley v Clydesdale Bank plc (trading as Yorkshire Bank)* [2019] EWCA Civ 233; [2020] QB 284).

7.6.3 The parties did not intend the term to be enforceable by the third party

There is a further important limit on the right of the third party to enforce the term pursuant to section 1(1)(b), which is that the right of action is not triggered where 'on a proper construction of the contract it appears that the parties did not intend the term to be enforceable by the third party' (s1(2)). The difficulty here will of course lie in discerning the intention of the parties where they have not expressed it. The view of Professor Burrows (1996), the Law Commissioner primarily responsible for the preparation of the Report which led to the Act, is that the presumption of enforceability by the third party is 'a strong one'. He continues:

> I would anticipate that it would not normally be rebutted unless there is a term in the contract expressly negating the third party's legal rights, or an express term that is otherwise inconsistent with the third party having legal rights, or unless the parties have entered into a chain of contracts which gives the third party a contractual right against another party for breach of the promisor's obligations under the alleged 'third party' contract.

Thus the Law Commission were of the view that in *Beswick v Beswick* [1968] AC 58 (Section 7.2) Mrs Beswick would now have a claim in her own right under this second limb because the nephew would not be able to show that he and his uncle did not intend to give her the right to enforce the term (it is, of course, impossible to be sure on this point because we are applying a test which the courts at the time were never asked to apply; but the inference that this was the intention of the parties seems a reasonable one, although for a contrary view, see Treitel, 2002, 87).

Whatever doubts we may harbour about the application of the test to the facts of *Beswick*, the view of Professor Burrows has been borne out in the leading cases decided under the Act. In *Nisshin Shipping Co Ltd v Cleaves & Co Ltd* [2003] EWHC 2602 (Comm); [2004] 1 Lloyd's Rep 38, Colman J observed that the effect of section 1(2) was to put the onus on the party seeking to allege that section 1(1)(b) has been disapplied. Thus, if the contract is neutral, section 1(1)(b) is not disapplied and on the facts he held that section 1(1)(b) had not been disapplied with the consequence that the third party did have a right to enforce a term of the contract.

The conclusion in cases such as *Nisshin*, *Prudential* and *Cavanagh* underlines the importance of parties to the contract making clear their intention, particularly in the case where they do not wish the third party to have a right to enforce a term of the contract. In the case where the contract is silent, the party seeking to deny the existence of a third party right may be in some difficulty. Silence will often be neutral and so insufficient to displace the presumption that the third party has a right to enforce a term of the contract. The problem is compounded by a further aspect of the decision of Colman J in *Nisshin*. The defendants submitted that the claimant did not have a right to enforce the term of the contract under the Act because it had a right of action pursuant to one of the common law (or, more accurately, equitable) exceptions to the doctrine of privity, namely the device of a trust of the promise (on which see Section 7.17). Colman J rejected this submission and held that the 1999 Act provided a much simpler method by which the claimant could enforce its rights and, this being the case, it could not be inferred from the existence of an alternative cause of action that the parties had intended to take away the right which the claimant was held to have under the 1999 Act to enforce a term of the contract. If neither silence nor the existence of an alternative cause of action suffices to exclude the existence of a third party right to enforce a term of the contract, parties who wish to exclude the third party right would be well advised to say so expressly and clearly in their contract.

However, it would be going too far to say that the third party right can only be excluded by an express term of the contract. A court may be prepared to infer that the third party right of action has been excluded where the structure of the contracts set up by the parties demonstrates that the third party cannot, consistently with that structure, have a direct right to enforce a term of the contract concluded between two other parties. The reference by Professor Burrows (above) to 'a chain of contracts' suggests that the Law Commission did not intend that one party should be allowed to jump up a chain of related contracts in order to obtain an advantage which he could not obtain by suing his immediate contracting party. Take the typical example of a contract entered into between an employer and a main contractor, with the main contractor then subcontracting some of the work to a subcontractor. Can the subcontractor enforce against the employer a term in the contract between the main contractor and the employer or can the employer enforce against the subcontractor a term of the contract between the main contractor and the subcontractor? The answer in both cases would appear to be 'no'. In the latter case, the inference which is likely to be drawn by a court is that, on a true construction of the subcontract, interpreted in the light of the head-contract and the understanding and practice of the construction industry, the employer should not have a contractual right of action against the subcontractor but should rather be confined to its contractual right of action against the main contractor who should then pursue its claim on the contract against the subcontractor (thus, in a case such as *Junior Books v Veitchi & Co Ltd* [1983] 1 AC 520, discussed in Section 7.18, it is unlikely that the employer would be able to invoke the 1999 Act in order to entitle it to enforce a term of the contract against the subcontractor). The key to these examples is probably the understanding and the practice of the construction industry. Where contracts are linked sequentially but there is no proven understanding that the sequence of contracts prevents recourse to a third party right of action, the linked nature of the contracts will not of itself preclude the existence of a third party right of action under the 1999 Act (*Laemthong International Lines Co Ltd v Artis (The Laemthong Glory) (No. 2)* [2005] EWCA Civ 519; [2005] 1 Lloyd's Rep 688, at [52]–[54], *Great Eastern Shipping Co Ltd v Far East Chartering Ltd (The Jag Ravi)* [2012] EWCA Civ 180; [2012] 1 Lloyd's Rep 637).

Difficulties may also arise where the main contract contains a clause under which one of the parties assigns its rights under that contract to a third party. For example, in *Darlington BC v Wiltshier Northern Ltd* [1995] 1 WLR 68, Morgan Grenfell entered into a contract with the defendant construction company under which the defendants agreed to build a recreational centre for Darlington Borough Council. It was alleged that the construction work had been done defectively and the cost of repairs was estimated at £2 million. Could Darlington now bring a claim against the defendants under the 1999 Act? There is a case for saying that it should be able to do so. The only interest which Morgan Grenfell had in the performance of the contract was a financial one; they were not interested in performance of the work to a proper standard provided that they got their money back. The work was done to benefit Darlington and so the case seems to fall squarely within section 1(1)(b) of the Act. But, on closer analysis it is not at all obvious that Darlington would have had such a claim. There are two factors which make it difficult to assert with any confidence that Darlington would now have a right under the Act to enforce a term of the contract against the defendants. Firstly, Darlington did have a direct right of action against the defendants for liquidated damages for delay in the performance of the contract. Secondly, Morgan Grenfell assigned their interest under the contract with the defendants to Darlington and it was in its capacity as assignee that Darlington brought its claim for damages. Does it not therefore follow that the parties' intention was to give Darlington a direct right of action only for liquidated damages but that otherwise its rights were only those which it acquired by virtue of the assignment? Of course, it can be argued that, now that a direct right of action has been created under the 1999 Act, there is no longer any need for the inclusion of such a comprehensive assignment clause in a contract. But the parties may well prefer the certainty of a comprehensive assignment clause to the uncertainty of a direct right of action of doubtful scope. And, if they do include such an assignment clause in their contract, does this operate to exclude the third party right of action under the Act? The answer, ultimately, turns on the intention of the parties objectively ascertained. But there is a strong case for saying that the effect of the assignment may be to negative the intention to create a direct right of action in the third party, thereby confining the third party to its rights as an assignee of one of the contracting parties. This inference is not, however, an inevitable one. In *Nisshin Shipping Co Ltd v Cleaves & Co Ltd* (above), Colman J declined to infer from the existence of an alternative cause of action that the parties had thereby intended to exclude the application of the 1999 Act. So it cannot be said that the fact that the third party acquires rights as an assignee will inevitably lead to the inference that it was intended that he should not acquire any rights under the 1999 Act. The fact that no clear answer can be given to this question underlines the need for the parties to make their intention explicit on the face of the contract. If they fail to do so, their intention in relation to the third party may well be a matter of conjecture.

7.6.4 The third party must be expressly identified

One further limitation on the right of the third party to sue is that the third party 'must be expressly identified in the contract by name, as a member of a class or as answering a particular description but need not be in existence when the contract is entered into' (s 1(3)). This requirement applies to both limbs of the test for the existence of a third party right of action, and both where the third party wishes to enforce a positive right and where it seeks to rely on an exclusion or limitation clause in the original contract. The question whether there is 'express' identification of the third party as a member of a class or as answering a particular description is a process of construction of the contract as a whole. Although the requirement that the third party be expressly identified is a separate requirement from that to be found in s1(1)(b), the same term of the contract can be relied upon for the purpose of satisfying the requirements of both provisions (*Chudley v Clydesdale Bank plc (trading as Yorkshire Bank)* [2019] EWCA Civ 233; [2020] QB 284, [79]).

As far as positive rights are concerned, take the case where contracting party A enters into a construction contract with B under which B agrees to construct a building for A. At some later point in time A sells the building to C. It is subsequently discovered that the building requires extensive repair work caused by the failure of B to exercise reasonable care when constructing the building. Can C sue B? The answer, as far as the Act is concerned, is that it cannot do so because C was not 'expressly identified' in the contract (thus the Act would not give the third party a right of action on the facts of a case such as *Linden Gardens Trust Ltd v Lenesta Sludge Disposals Ltd* [1994] 1 AC 85 (see Section 7.14) because the third party was not identified in the contract). But suppose that the contract between A and B had stated that the warranty of quality given by B to A also extended to subsequent owners and/or tenants of the building. In such a case C, as a subsequent owner, has been described as a member of a class which has been identified in the contract, and so can bring a claim against B under the terms of the Act. The same point applies in the context of reliance by a third party on an exclusion clause in the main contract (as in *The Eurymedon* type case). If the contract between A and B contains a limitation clause but does not purport to extend the benefit of that clause to C (whether individually or as a member of a class) then C cannot rely on the limitation clause. It is therefore of fundamental importance to ensure that reference is made to the third party in the contract, either individually or as a member of a class. A failure to do so will mean that the third party will be unable to rely on the rights contained in the Act (see, for example, *Avraamides v Colwill* [2006] EWCA Civ 1533; [2007] BLR 76). Although the third party must be expressly identified in accordance with s 1(3), there is no requirement that the third party be aware of its right at the time that the contract was entered into. The right of the third party is not a reliance-based claim and so the question for the court is whether the third party has the right which it asserts, not whether it had knowledge of the right at the time of entry into the contract or at any particular time thereafter (*Chudley v Clydesdale Bank plc (trading as Yorkshire Bank)* [2019] EWCA Civ 233; [2020] QB 284, [80]).

7.7 No consideration required

The third party will be able to enforce the term of the contract notwithstanding the fact that he himself has not provided any consideration for his right to sue to enforce the term of the contract. The fact that the contract is supported by the consideration supplied by the original contracting parties is sufficient to give him a right of action. While it is true that the Act itself does not expressly deal with the doctrine of consideration, the fact that section 1 states that the third party may 'in his own right enforce a term of the contract' was thought to be sufficiently explicit to confer a right of action on the third party whether he had provided consideration or not. The fact that Parliament has expressly stated that the third party may in his own right enforce a term of the contract will make it practically impossible for the courts to qualify that right of action by adding in the requirement that the third party must himself have provided consideration. The wording of the Act should be sufficient to prevent it being outflanked by an argument based on lack of consideration. Indeed, it is the very fact that the third party can sue even where he has provided no consideration for his right of action that has been seized upon by those who are critical of the Act and its aims (see, for example, Kincaid, 2000; Stevens, 2004).

7.8 The remedies available to the third party

Where the third party does acquire a right to enforce a term of the contract under the Act, there 'shall be available to the third party any remedy that would have been available to him in an action for breach of contract if he had been a party to the contract (and the rules relating to damages, injunctions, specific performance and other relief shall apply accordingly)' (s 1(5)). The normal rules of contract law will therefore presumably apply to the third party's right of action (for example, the rules on remoteness of damage, mitigation etc. will be applicable to any action brought by the third party). The Law Commission intended to exclude termination of the contract from the scope of this provision on the ground that termination is not a judicial remedy. The Law Commission also believed that 'the third party should not be entitled to terminate the contract for breach as this may be contrary to the promisee's wishes or interests' (see para 3.33 of the report). It is therefore for the parties to the original contract to decide whether or not to terminate the contract in the event of a repudiatory breach by one party to the contract.

7.9 Variation and cancellation

Can the contracting parties between themselves divest the third party of his right of action on the contract? The general answer is that substantial limitations have been placed on the ability of the contracting parties to do so. This issue is addressed in section 2(1) of the Act which states:

> Subject to the provisions of this section, where a third party has a right under section 1 to enforce a term of the contract, the parties to the contract may not, by agreement, rescind the contract, or vary it in such a way as to extinguish or alter his entitlement under that right, without his consent, if –
>
> (a) the third party has communicated his assent to the term to the promisor,
> (b) the promisor is aware that the third party has relied on the term, or
> (c) the promisor can reasonably be expected to have foreseen that the third party would rely on the term and the third party has in fact relied upon it.

The easiest example is perhaps the case where the third party has communicated his assent to the promisor. Assent may be by words or conduct and, if sent to the promisor by post or other means, shall not be regarded as communicated to the promisor until received by him (s 2(2)). A third party who wishes to be secure in his third party right should assent expressly to the existence of the third party right of action and ensure that the assent is communicated to the promisor.

More controversial is the case where the third party has not communicated his assent to the promisor but has relied on the term. There is no requirement that the third party act to its detriment; reliance is enough in and of itself provided that the promisor is aware of it or could reasonably be expected to have foreseen that reliance would be placed on the term. The burden of proof will be on the third party to prove that he has relied on the term. The reliance must have been that of the third party; the reliance of another party, even if closely related to the third party, will not suffice. Rather curiously perhaps, the third party who has relied on the contract is not confined to the recovery of damages to protect his reliance outlay. The third party is entitled to recover its expectation damages in the ordinary way and so can recover its loss of net profit (provided it is not too remote) as well as its detrimental reliance. The 'reliance' provisions may well give rise to some difficulty in practice; for example, it may be no easy task for the third party to prove that the promisor was 'aware' of its reliance or that the promisor could reasonably be expected to have foreseen that the third party would so rely. It is in order to avoid these evidential difficulties that a third party should communicate his assent expressly to the promisor.

However, it is open to the contracting parties to agree to rescind or vary the contract without the consent of the third party by reserving to themselves in their contract the right to do so (s 2(3)(a)). Take a case in which a construction contract between an employer and a main contractor makes provision for variations of the works in certain circumstances. There is an obvious advantage in ensuring that any third party who acquires rights under the contract is bound by any such variation. The Act makes it possible for the contracting parties to ensure that such a party is bound by making appropriate provision in the contract itself. The inclusion of such a reservation will make the right of the third party rather vulnerable but, given that it is open to the contracting parties to exclude or limit the right of the third party, it was thought that it must follow that they ought to be able to withdraw or vary the right of the third party provided that the power to withdraw or to vary is set out in the contract itself. It is also open to the contracting parties to agree that the third party's right to enforce the term shall crystallise on the occurrence of an event other than those stated in section 2(1) of the Act (see s 2(3)(b)). For example, it is open to the contracting parties to provide in their contract that they can vary or cancel the contract until such time as the third party notifies them of his assent in writing.

The court (or, as the case may be, arbitral tribunal) is given a power to dispense with the third party's consent where that consent cannot be obtained because the whereabouts of the third party cannot reasonably be ascertained or he is mentally incapable of giving his consent (s 2(4)) or where it cannot be ascertained whether the third party has in fact relied on the contract (s 2(5)). The court or arbitral tribunal may impose conditions on any such dispensation including 'a condition requiring the payment of compensation to the third party' (s 2(6)).

7.10 The defences available to the promisor

The right which the third party acquires is essentially the right to enforce the term of the contract subject to the defences which would have been available to the promisor had he been sued on the contract by the promisee. The third party stands in no better situation than the promisee. Thus section 3(2) of the Act states that:

> the promisor shall have available to him by way of defence or set-off any matter that –
>
> (a) arises from or in connection with the contract and is relevant to the term, and
> (b) would have been available to him by way of defence or set-off if the proceedings had been brought by the promisee.

The Law Commission rejected the argument that section 3(2) should also apply to counterclaims on the ground that it would have been 'misleading and unnecessarily complex' to include counterclaims within the subsection. The reason for this is that a counterclaim may possibly exceed the value of the third party claim, in which case the effect of the counterclaim would be to impose a burden on the third party (in that its claim against the promisor would be subject to a counterclaim against the promisee which exceeded the value of the claim brought by the third party against the promisor). An example may illustrate the point. Suppose that A and B agree to confer a right of action on C. B fails to perform in accordance with the contract so that C now has a claim against B for £5,000 in consequence. Assume further that B has a counterclaim against A for £10,000. B cannot rely on that counterclaim in C's action to recover £5,000. The reason for this is that C would be worse off if B could do so (in that C would then be subject to a liability to pay £5,000 to B). The aim of the Act is to give the third party a right of action in certain circumstances; it is not to alter the rule that a burden cannot be imposed on a third party without the latter's consent. The counterclaim problem could have been dealt with by providing that B could rely on the counterclaim provided that it did not exceed the value of C's claim, but it was thought by the Law Commission to be too complex to insert such a provision into the Act. This exclusion of counterclaims from section 3(2) may make it important to distinguish between a set-off and a counterclaim.

Once again the contracting parties can contract out of this provision and they can do so in either direction. They can include within the contract an express provision to the effect that the promisor may not raise any defence or set-off that would have been available against the promisee (s 3(5)). Such a clause will have the effect of reducing the uncertainty for the third party, particularly in the context of a construction contract where there is a grant to subsequent owners of the building of contractual rights to have defects in the building repaired where the defect is attributable to the default of the contractor. The value of the right to the subsequent owner could be devalued significantly if the contractor was able to set-off against the third party claim any defences that the original contractor had against the employer. Thus, it may be possible for the employer, where it has the bargaining power to do so, to require the contractor to give to the third party a right of action which is not subject to any set-off or defences which the contractor has against the employer.

Conversely, it is open to the contracting parties to include in their contract an express term which makes the third party's claim subject to all defences and set-offs that the promisor would have had against the promisee (that is to say, whether or not they arise from or in connection with the contract and are relevant to the term) (s 3(3)). In this instance the third party's right is obviously much more vulnerable.

In addition to the third party's claim being subject to defences and set-offs which would have been available to the promisor in an action brought by the promisee, the third party's claim is also subject to the defences, counterclaims (not arising from the contract) and set-offs that would have been available to the promisor had the third party been a party to the contract (although it is also possible for the parties to agree on an express term that the promisor may not raise these matters against the third party) (s 3(4)). The promisor is entitled to bring counterclaims into account when the counterclaim is against the third party himself on the ground that there is no question here of making the third party worse off as a result of the counterclaim (in that, if the counterclaim succeeds, the third party owes the sum claimed to the promisor in any event).

Where the third party seeks to avail himself of an exclusion or limitation clause (or conceivably some analogous clause) in relation to proceedings brought against him, he may do so only to the extent that he could have done so had he been a party to the contract (s 3(6)). In other words, where the exclusion clause is invalid as between the two contracting parties, it will also be invalid when relied upon by the third party.

7.11 Avoiding double liability

As we shall see (Section 7.14), the Act does not impinge upon the promisee's rights under the contract. So both the promisee and the third party may now have an action against the promisor. Steps have therefore been taken to reduce, if not eliminate, the possibility of double liability on the part of the promisor. Where the third party has recovered damages from the promisor, the promisee's claim for damages is likely to fail on the ground that the promisee has suffered no loss. More difficult is the case where the promisee has sued and recovered damages from the promisor and the third party then brings an action against the promisor. The Act seeks to deal with this issue in section 5 which provides that where a term of the contract is enforceable by a third party in accordance with section 1 of the Act, and:

the promisee has recovered from the promisor a sum in respect of –

(a) the third party's loss in respect of the term, or
(b) the expense to the promisee of making good to the third party the default of the promisor,

then, in any proceedings brought in reliance on that section by the third party, the court or arbitral tribunal shall reduce any award to the third party to such extent as it thinks appropriate to take account of the sum recovered by the promisee.

The aim of this provision is clearly to protect the promisor against double liability. It does not deal with the question whether or not the promisee can be compelled to account to the third party for the sum which it has recovered from the promisor. That question will have to be answered by the courts applying common law (or equitable) principles.

7.12 Exceptions to the new third party right of action

In the absence of a saving provision, the 1999 Act had the potential to cause difficulty by cutting across some existing legislative schemes and so resulting in a distribution of rights and liabilities other than that intended by those who devised the original statutory scheme. In order to avoid this happening, a provision has been inserted into the Act which states that the third party right conferred by section 1 does not apply in certain situations (see s 6). For example, section 1 confers no rights on a third party in the case of a contract on a bill of exchange, promissory note or other negotiable instrument (s 6(1)). Nor does the section 1 right apply to contracts for the carriage of goods by sea except that a third party may in reliance on section 1 avail itself of an exclusion or limitation of liability in such a contract (ss 6(5), (6) and (7)). Equally, the Act does not apply to various contracts which are governed by certain international transport conventions (s6(8)).

7.13   Preserving existing exceptions

One further effect of the Act will be to reduce the practical significance of many of the pre-1999 exceptions to the doctrine of privity. But it is very important to note that the Act does not repeal or abolish these exceptions. On the contrary, section 7(1) of the Act states that section 1 'does not affect any right or remedy of a third party that exists or is available apart from this Act'. Equally, section 4 of the Act provides that the creation of the new third party right of action shall not 'affect any right of the promisee to enforce any term of the contract'. So the old exceptions together with the right of the promisee to bring a claim have been preserved, albeit that one might expect their practical significance to diminish somewhat. That said, there may still be cases in which it is necessary to consider the relative merits and demerits of the different ways of conferring enforceable rights on a third party. In the following sections (7.14–7.21), consideration will be given to the rights of the promisee and the existing exceptions to the doctrine of privity, and an attempt will be made, where appropriate, to assess their likely significance after the Act.

7.14   Rights of the promisee

As has been noted, section 4 of the 1999 Act expressly preserves the right of the promisee to enforce any term of the contract. Suppose that A and B enter into a contract under which, in return for some act to be performed by B, A agrees to pay £50 to C. A failure by A to pay the £50 to C will constitute a breach of contract between A and B. What remedies, if any, does B have against A in such a case? There are at least four possible actions which B could bring against A.

7.14.1   The contracting party sues to recover for its own loss

The first possibility is to bring an action for damages for breach of contract. The difficulty here is that B does not appear to have suffered any loss as a result of A's breach and so his damages are likely to be nominal (although if the £50 were to be paid to discharge a debt owed by B to C, then B might be entitled to more than nominal damages; see Windeyer J in *Coulls v Bagot's Executor* (1967) 119 CLR 460, 501–02 and see also the discussion of *Linden Gardens Trust Ltd v Lenesta Sludge Disposals Ltd* [1994] 1 AC 85 and *Darlington BC v Wiltshier Northern Ltd* [1995] 1 WLR 68, below). But even if B could recover substantial damages, this would be of no avail to C because the damages recovered by B would be held on his own behalf and not on

action against the defendant in relation to losses suffered by the third party? According to *Panatown*, it would seem that this is so. On the other hand, in *Darlington* the third party had a right to sue the defendant for liquidated damages for late completion of the works but the existence of that right was held not to deny to the claimant the right to sue and recover damages in respect of the loss suffered by the third party. In many ways *Darlington* is the critical case. It is under something of a cloud post-*Panatown*. The rule which emerges from *Panatown* is that the conferment of a contractual right of action upon the third party will generally operate to take away any right on the part of the claimant to recover damages in respect of the loss suffered by the third party. To the extent that *Darlington* is inconsistent with that rule, it must be regarded with suspicion.

7.14.5 Why can a claimant not generally sue in respect of a loss suffered by a third party?

One final issue relates to the juridical basis of the rule that a contracting party cannot sue and recover damages in respect of the loss suffered by a third party. In *Panatown* Lord Millett was of the view that the rule flowed directly from the proposition that compensation is 'compensation for loss'. Thus, he stated that it is:

> inherent in the concept of compensation that only the person who has suffered the loss is entitled to have it made good by compensation. Compensation for a third party's loss is a contradiction in terms. It is impossible on any logical basis to justify the recovery of compensatory damages by a person who has not suffered the loss in respect of which they are awarded unless he is accountable for them to the person who has.

Given the existence of the general rule that a contracting party cannot sue and recover damages in respect of a loss suffered by a third party, can the parties contract out of the rule? If A and B enter into a contract and they agree that any breach by A will have a detrimental effect on C, and that B should be entitled to sue and recover damages on behalf of C, why should the law refuse to give effect to that agreement? When privity was operated strictly by the courts, they may well have been reluctant to accede to an argument which effectively outflanked privity, and the House of Lords in *Woodar* appeared to be of the view that the rule could not be contracted out of in this way. But now that privity is seen by many to be a doctrine which is both commercially inconvenient and unjust, there seems little reason not to give effect to the agreement which A and B have voluntarily concluded. If A has agreed to pay damages to B on behalf of C, then it is suggested that effect should be given to the agreement. If it is the case that the parties can contract out of the general rule that a contracting party cannot sue and recover damages on behalf of a third party, how likely is it that the contracting parties will have such an intention and, further, be able to persuade a court that such was their intention? Where the parties are commercial parties who have been legally advised, such an intention may be discernible. But even in commercial contracts the creation of a direct contractual relationship between the third party and one of the contracting parties (as in *Panatown*) or a clause assigning to the third party the rights of one of the contracting parties (as in *Darlington*) will make it extremely difficult to persuade a court that the intention of the parties was that one contracting party should be entitled to sue and recover damages on behalf of the third party. In such a case it can be argued that the right of the third party is its right as assignee or its direct right of action; it is not a right to have a contracting party sue and recover damages on its behalf (although in *Darlington* the promisee was effectively allowed to recover in respect of the third party's loss, notwithstanding the assignment clause).

7.14.6 Specific performance

Thirdly, B could seek an order of specific performance against A (that is, an order of the court that the promisor carry out his promise). This was of course what happened in *Beswick v Beswick* [1968] AC 58 (Section 7.2). But, now that in a case such as *Beswick v Beswick* C is likely to bring an action for damages under the 1999 Act, it may be harder for the promisee to demonstrate that damages would not be an adequate remedy and, if damages are not inadequate, then specific performance may not be ordered (see Section 22.9). This being the case, one effect of the 1999 Act may be to diminish the likelihood of a promisee obtaining a specific performance order (although it could be argued that such a conclusion is, in fact, contrary to the clear words of s 4). But, even if B is entitled to specific performance, it should be noted that there does not appear to be any procedure by which C can compel B to sue A, so that B could refuse to sue A and thereby leave C without a remedy. If the promise which B seeks to enforce is a negative one then B can, in an appropriate case, claim an injunction to restrain the threatened breach of contract by A (see Section 22.10).

7.14.7 A stay of proceedings

Finally, if the promise made by A to B is a promise not to sue C, and A, in breach of contract with B, commences an action against C, B can ask the court, in its discretion, to stay the proceedings against C (*Snelling v John G Snelling* [1973] 1 QB 87, but contrast *Gore v Van Der Lann* [1967] 2 QB 31).

7.15 Collateral contracts

Turning now to the pre-1999 exceptions to the doctrine of privity, one exception which was employed on a number of occasions by the courts was the device of finding a collateral contract between the promisor and the third party. The mechanism now appears rather artificial and its practical significance is likely to reduce considerably in the light of the enactment of the 1999 Act. An example of the device in practice is provided by the case of *Shanklin Pier Ltd v Detel Products Ltd* [1951] 2 KB 854. Contractors employed by the claimants to paint the claimants' pier were instructed by the claimants to use paint manufactured by the defendants. The contract to purchase the paint was actually made between the contractors and the defendants but a representation was made by the defendants to the claimants that the paint would last for seven years. The paint only lasted three months. It was held that the claimants were entitled to bring an action for breach of contract against the defendants on the ground that there was a collateral contract between them to the effect that the paint would last for seven years, the consideration for which was the instruction given by the claimants to their contractors to order the paint from the defendants. A court will, however, be slow to find the existence of a collateral contract where the parties to the alleged collateral contract are experienced commercial parties who could easily have created a direct contractual relationship between themselves had they wished to do so. In such a case, a court is unlikely to be willing to 'supplement' the parties' contractual arrangements by creating a collateral contract (*Fuji Seal Europe Ltd v Catalytic Combustion Corp* [2005] EWHC 1659 (TCC); 102 Con LR 47).

The collateral contract device has also been usefully employed in cases of hire-purchase. In many cases consumers are unaware of the exact legal technicalities of a hire-purchase agreement. These technicalities are that the dealer will generally sell the goods to the finance house, who in turn will hire the goods to the consumer on hire-purchase terms. Thus the contracts are between the dealer and the finance house and between the finance house and the consumer; there is no contract between the dealer and the consumer (and indeed this is likely to remain the position under the 1999 Act so that the consumer will not generally have a right of action against the dealer under the 1999 Act). But in *Andrews v Hopkinson* [1957] 1 QB 229, it was held that the dealer's false warranty as to the roadworthiness of a car gave rise to a collateral contract between the dealer and the consumer, thereby enabling the consumer to bring an action against the dealer for breach of contract.

The limitation of the collateral contract device, however, is that the court must be able to find evidence upon which to imply such a contract and that consideration must be found to support the collateral contract. The latter requirement can give rise to some difficulty, as is illustrated by the case of *Charnock v Liverpool Corp* [1968] 1 WLR 1498. The claimant's car was damaged in an accident and he left the car to be repaired by the defendants' garage, the defendants having promised to do the repairs reasonably quickly. The car was repaired under a contract between the claimant's insurance company and the defendants. But it was held that the claimant could nevertheless bring an action in respect of the defendants' failure to carry out the repair reasonably quickly. It was held that there was consideration to support the collateral contract because, although there was no detriment to the claimant, the defendants were benefited by virtue of the opportunity given to them to enter into a contract with the insurance company for the repair of the car (note that Treitel, 1976, treats this as a case of 'invented' consideration and Atiyah, 1986c, 223 argues that this is a case of 'fictitious consideration' because the 'real' consideration was supplied by the insurers and not by the claimant).

7.16 Agency

It would cause great commercial hardship if a business that appointed an agent to enter into a contract on its behalf was prevented by the doctrine of privity from suing upon that contract itself. So the doctrine of agency exists to give the business such a right of action. An agency relationship arises where one party, the agent, is authorised by another, the principal, to negotiate and to enter into contracts on behalf of the principal. Once an agency relationship is created, the agent is thereby authorised to commit the principal to contractual relationships with third parties. Agency is now a specialised area of law and we will not deal with it in this book, except to give a very brief account of the relationship between agency and privity (for fuller consideration of the doctrine of agency see Treitel, 2020, ch 16).

When the agent discloses to the third party that he is acting as an agent of a principal and he concludes the contract within the scope of his authority, the general rule is that the contract is made between the principal and the third party, and the agent cannot sue or be sued on the contract. Such a transaction is not generally regarded as an exception to the doctrine of privity because the function of the agent is to negotiate the contract on behalf of his principal and once he has done that he 'drops out of the picture', leaving his principal as the true party to the contract.

However, there are certain aspects of the law of agency which appear to flout the traditional doctrine of privity. One such aspect is the rule that a principal may, in certain limited circumstances, sue upon the contract even though the agent has not disclosed to the third party that he is acting as an agent for the principal (see Treitel, 2020, paras 16-065–16-071). In these situations the third party can find himself in a contractual relationship with a person of whose existence he was blissfully unaware at the time that he entered into the contract. The ability of a principal to ratify the unauthorised act of his agent is also said to be an exception to the doctrine of privity (see Treitel, 2020, paras 16-049–16-061). It should be noted that the 1999 Act will not confer rights on the principal in either of these two cases because he has not been 'expressly identified' in the contract itself, so that both cases will continue to be governed by the common law rules.

Another case which does not come within the 1999 Act and which is extremely difficult to reconcile with the traditional doctrine of privity is the controversial case of *Watteau v Fenwick* [1893] 1 QB 346. In this case the agent, who was the manager of a public house, was prohibited by his principal (the owner of the public house) from purchasing cigars on credit for the purpose of the business. Despite this prohibition, the agent purchased cigars in his own name on credit from the claimants, who were unaware of the existence of the principal and therefore unaware of the prohibition placed upon the agent. It was held that the principal was nevertheless bound by the contract and was liable to the claimants. The rationale of the case appears to be that the principal, by employing the agent as his manager, was regarded as having given the agent the authority which was usually given to managers of a public house, which included the authority to purchase cigars. Further, the agreement between the principal and the agent, under which the agent's authority was restricted, was not binding on a third party who was unaware of that restriction. So the principal was bound. But *Watteau* demonstrates that agency and privity were always rather strange bedfellows. It was highly anomalous that the existence of an agency relationship could enable a claimant to sue a defendant who expressly disavowed any intention to benefit the claimant third party, whereas privity, in cases such as *Tweddle v Atkinson* (see Section 7.3), prevented a claimant third party from suing a defendant who had expressly declared an intention to benefit the claimant. The 1999 Act has largely removed this anomaly but it has not removed the need to rely on the rules of agency law because the latter rules confer rights of action on third parties (whether the third party be the principal or the person with whom the agent has dealt) in a wider range of circumstances than does the Act.

The importance of these statutory exceptions should not be underestimated. One commentator (Flannigan, 1987) has remarked that:

> but for the statutory exceptions, the doctrine of privity would undoubtedly have been abolished long ago upon it having become widely appreciated that, for example, third parties had no right to the proceeds of life insurance policies taken out for their benefit.

Thus section 11 of the Married Women's Property Act 1882 states that where a man has insured his life for the benefit of his wife and children, the policy shall create a trust in favour of the objects therein named. Third parties have been allowed, in certain circumstances, to sue on fire or marine insurance policies (Marine Insurance Act 1906, s 14(2)) and an injured third party may recover compensation from the insured's insurance company once he has obtained judgment against the insured (Road Traffic Act 1972, s 148(4)). Section 56 of the Law of Property Act 1925 provides that:

> a person may take an immediate or other interest in land or other property, or the benefit of any condition, right of entry, covenant or agreement over or respecting land or other property, although he may not be named as a party to the conveyance or other instrument.

Finally, under section 2 of the Carriage of Goods by Sea Act 1992, a person who becomes the lawful holder of a bill of lading shall, by virtue of becoming the holder of the bill, have transferred to and vested in him all rights of suit under the contract of carriage as if he had been a party to that contract from the outset (similar principles apply to sea waybills and to ships' delivery orders) (see also ss 6(5)–(7) of the 1999 Act).

7.22 A further common law exception?

Finally, is it still possible for the judiciary to create a further common law exception to the doctrine of privity? Given the enactment of the 1999 Act, the practical need for the creation of a further exception has diminished substantially but the Law Commission were careful to state in their report that the Act is not designed to freeze the common law in its pre-Act position. One area in which such judicial development may yet take place is in the *Eurymedon* type case (see Section 7.2). As we have noted, Lord Goff in *The Mahkutai* [1996] AC 650, 665 recognised that the development of the law may not yet be complete and that the courts may develop a 'fully - fledged exception to the doctrine of privity of contract' in these cases. This step was in fact taken by the Supreme Court of Canada in the seminal case of *London Drugs Ltd v Kuehne & Nagel International Ltd* (1992) 97 DLR (4th) 261, where the majority of the court chose not to adopt a *Eurymedon* type analysis but instead held that employees were entitled to take the benefit of a contractual limitation clause contained in a contract between their employer and the claimants if (i) the limitation of liability clause either expressly or impliedly extended its benefit to the employees seeking to rely on it and, (ii) the employees were acting in the course of their employment and had been performing the very services provided for in the contract at the time at which the loss was suffered (see further *Fraser River Pile & Dredge Ltd v Can-Dive Services Ltd* [2000] 1 Lloyd's Rep 199). There is much to be said for this approach, and the Supreme Court is not precluded from adopting it by virtue of the enactment of the 1999 Act.

7.23 Interference with contractual rights

Finally, it is necessary to return to a point made at the beginning of this chapter in relation to the general rule that a third party cannot be subjected to a burden by a contract to which he is not a party (a matter not regulated by the 1999 Act). Notwithstanding this rule, a contract between two parties may in fact impose certain obligations upon a third party. The first such obligation is that a third party must not seek to persuade one contracting party to break his contract with the other. Thus, it is a tort for a third party, without lawful justification, to interfere intentionally or recklessly with a contract between A and B, either by persuading A to break his contract with B or by preventing A from performing his contract with B by the use of some direct or indirect unlawful means. The case of *Lumley v Gye* (1853) 2 El & Bl 216 provides a useful illustration of the operation of this tort. The claimant was a theatre owner who entered into a contract with a famous opera singer, Ms Wagner, under which she was to sing only at his theatre for a period of time. The defendant, who was the owner of a rival theatre, procured Ms Wagner to break her contract with the claimant by promising to pay her more than she was receiving from the claimant. When Ms Wagner, in breach of contract, refused to continue to perform at the claimant's theatre, the claimant brought an action against the defendant alleging that the defendant had induced Ms Wagner to break her contract with him and that this had caused him loss. It was held that the defendant had indeed committed a tort and the claimant was therefore entitled to claim damages from the defendant to compensate him for his loss. The tort is one based on intention and is an example of accessory or secondary liability (*OBG Ltd v Allan* [2007] UKHL 21; [2008] 1 AC 1, [39]–[44]). In order to be liable the defendant must know that it is inducing a breach of contract. It does not suffice that the defendant knew that it was procuring an act which, as a matter of law or construction of the contract, was a breach: the defendant must actually realise that it will have this effect. Intention extends to recklessness but not to negligence (even gross negligence). But if the breach of contract is neither an end in itself nor a means to an end, but merely a foreseeable consequence, then it cannot be said to have been intended.

It has also been argued that a third party who acquires property in the knowledge that that property is affected by a contract between two other parties is bound by the terms of that contract and may be restrained from acting inconsistently with the terms of the contract. This indeed occurred in the case of *Tulk v Moxhay* (1848) 2 Ph 774. The claimant sold land subject to a restrictive covenant that the land must not be built upon but must be preserved in its existing condition. After a number of conveyances the land was eventually conveyed to the defendant, who had notice of the covenant but nevertheless sought to build on the land. It was held that the claimant was entitled to an injunction to restrain the proposed building. The defendant was therefore bound by an agreement to which he was not a party simply because he had notice of the covenant. The question which arises is whether this principle applies only within the rather rarefied atmosphere of land law and restrictive covenants or whether it is of general application. The answer is that it is a matter of land law and, even within the confines of land law, the scope of the principle has been narrowed; for example, the claimant must now show that he has retained ownership of other land in the immediate vicinity which is capable of being benefited by the covenant.

However, the prospect of extending the scope of *Tulk v Moxhay* beyond the province of restrictive covenants was held out by the Privy Council in *Lord Strathcona Steamship Co v Dominion Coal Co Ltd* [1926] AC 108. The owner of a ship chartered her to the claimants for a number of summer seasons. The owner sold the ship during the winter season. After a series of sales the ship was bought by the defendants who, although aware of the charterparty at the date of purchase, nevertheless refused to deliver the ship to the claimants for the summer season. The Privy Council held that the defendants were bound by the terms of the charterparty and granted the claimants an injunction to restrain the defendants from using the ship in any way inconsistent with the terms of the charterparty.

The result of the case does not seem to be entirely unfair. A person who buys property subject to the rights of third parties will generally pay a lower price for the property and, if he could then take advantage of the rules of privity to disregard those rights, he would thereby free the property and be able to sell it at a considerable profit. Nevertheless, it is difficult to reconcile *Strathcona* with the rule that a contract of hire only creates personal and not proprietary rights and that therefore the purchaser should be free to ignore the contract of hire. *Strathcona* is for this reason an extremely controversial case (see Gardner, 1982; Tettenborn, 1982) and, indeed, in the case of *Port Line Ltd v Ben Line Steamers Ltd* [1958] 2 QB 146, Diplock J said that he thought the case was wrongly decided and refused to follow it (contrast *Swiss Bank Corp v Lloyd's Bank Ltd* [1979] Ch 548 where Browne-Wilkinson J followed *Strathcona* on the ground that it was the equitable counterpart of the tort of knowing interference with contractual rights). The present standing of *Strathcona* is therefore unclear. In *Law Debenture Trust Corp v Ural Caspian Oil Corp Ltd* [1993] 1 WLR 138, 144, Hoffmann J accepted that *Strathcona* was still good law but stated that the real difficulty was that 'neither the *Strathcona* case nor the *Swiss Bank* case make it entirely clear when the principle applies and when it does not'. Only two things are clear. The first is that *Strathcona* 'does not provide a panacea for outflanking the doctrine of privity of contract' (*Law Debenture Trust Corp v Ural Caspian Oil Corp Ltd*). The second is that it can only apply where the purchaser has actual knowledge of the contract at the time of the purchase and the only remedy available is an injunction restraining the purchaser from acting inconsistently with the contract. The claimant cannot obtain a specific performance order requiring the purchaser to carry out the terms of the contract (*Port Line Ltd v Ben Line Steamers Ltd* (above); *Law Debenture Trust Corp v Ural Caspian Oil Corp Ltd* (above)).

7.24 Conclusion

A review of the 1999 Act concluded that is 'useful but still underused' (Beale, 2010). The reference to the relative lack of use of the Act reflects the fact that many commercial lawyers were initially hostile to the Act and systematically excluded its operation. Today a more reflective attitude is apparent and lawyers appear to be more willing to make use of the Act where it is, in their judgment, appropriate to do so. The 1999 Act has proved to be a useful tool where two contracting parties wish to confer an enforceable right of action upon a third party. It is now considerably easier to do so because a simple clause can be inserted into the contract giving the third party such a right of action. Where the contracting parties make their intention clear in relation to both the *existence* and the *scope* of the third party right, substantial difficulties should be few (for a more pessimistic view and a number of examples of situations which could prove to be difficult to resolve under the Act, see Stevens, 2004). On the other hand, where the parties fail to make their intention clear, difficulties will inevitably arise in deciding whether or not the parties had an intention to confer on the third party a right of action. In many respects, freedom of contract is one of the driving forces underneath the Act because of the degree of choice which is given to the contracting parties. Thus, parties who make their intention clear have little to fear from the Act. The Act does make an improvement to the law in that it reforms a doctrine which many parties regarded as unjust and commercially inconvenient, and the initial uncertainty has been outweighed by the benefits which the Act has brought for commercial parties.

Hot topic 7...

The practice of commercial parties has generally been to insert into their standard contract terms a term which excludes the operation of the Contracts (Rights of Third Parties) Act 1999 by providing that no third party shall have a right to enforce any term or terms of the contract. The advantage of doing this is that it makes the intention of the parties clear and the law will respect that choice by holding that the third party does not have a right to enforce a term of the contract. On the other hand, the failure to insert such a clause into the contract may result in a third party acquiring a right to enforce a term of the contract. Such was the case in *Chudley v Clydesdale Bank plc (trading as Yorkshire Bank)* [2019] EWCA Civ 233, [2020] QB 284. The claimants invested £990,000 in a scheme which turned out to have been a fraud. The claimants brought their claim not against the fraudsters but against the defendant bank. The claim was based on a letter of instruction ('LOI') signed by the defendant bank and sent to the company in which the claimants had invested their money and in which the defendant undertook to set up a segregated client account for the money invested in the scheme and not to pay it out except in very limited circumstances. The bank failed to comply with the terms of the LOI and paid the money out to the company so that it was no longer available to the claimants. In bringing their claim, the claimants relied upon the 1999 Act. The defendant denied that the Act was applicable but the Court of Appeal held that the claimants were entitled to rely on it. The LOI purported to confer a benefit on the claimants (in so far as it sought to protect their investments) and the reference to a 'Segregated Client Account' in the LOI was held to be sufficient to satisfy the requirements of s1(3) of the Act. The defendant bank was accordingly held liable to the claimants for the losses which they had suffered. The Supreme Court refused leave to appeal from the decision of the Court of Appeal. It is probably unlikely that the defendant bank intended to confer a right of action on the claimants when it signed the LOI. Its intention was no doubt to assume responsibility to the company to whom the letter was addressed. But the failure of the defendant expressly to exclude the possibility of a third party right of action left it exposed to a claim by the claimants who were held to be entitled to take the benefit of the LOI (and this was so even though they were unaware of its existence at the time at which they made their investments).

Summary

▶ The doctrine of privity consists of two distinct rules.

▶ The first is that a third party cannot be subjected to a burden by a contract to which he is not a party.

▶ The second was that a person who was not a party to a contract could not claim the benefit of it, even though the contract was entered into with the object of benefiting that third party. The latter rule has been substantially modified by the Contracts (Rights of Third Parties) Act 1999.

▶ The 1999 Act gives a third party a right to enforce a term of the contract where the contract expressly provides that he may or where the contract purports to confer a benefit on the third party. In the latter case the third party right is not triggered where, on a proper construction of the contract, it appears that the contracting parties did not intend the term to be enforceable by the third party. In both cases the third party must be expressly identified in the contract by name, as a member of a class or as answering a particular description but need not be in existence when the contract was entered into. The third party need not have provided consideration for his right of action.

▶ The contracting parties can rescind or vary the third party right unless the third party has communicated his assent to the term to the promisor or the promisor is aware that the third party has relied on the term or the promisor could reasonably be expected to have foreseen that the third party would rely and he has so relied.

▶ Unless otherwise agreed, the right which the third party acquires is essentially the right to enforce the term subject to the defences which would have been available to the contracting party had he been sued on the contract by the original contracting party.

▶ Where the promisee has already recovered damages in respect of the third party's loss, the third party's claim may be reduced to take account of the sum which has been recovered by the promisee. Where, in breach of contract with a promisee, a promisor has failed to confer a benefit on a third party, the promisee may bring an action for breach of contract against the promisor.

▶ The promisee may be able to obtain damages, specific performance or a stay of proceedings but the general rule is that a promisee cannot recover damages on behalf of a third party.

▶ There are a number of other situations in which English law does recognise the existence of enforceable third party rights and these have been preserved by the 1999 Act.

▶ In limited circumstances a court may be prepared to find the existence of a contract between the promisor and the third party which is collateral to the contract between the promisor and the promisee.

▶ An agent may bring into existence a contract between his principal and a third party. An agency relationship arises where one party, the agent, is authorised by another, the principal, to negotiate and to enter into contracts on behalf of the principal.

▶ Where an intention to create a trust can be shown to exist, a promisee may hold his right to sue the promisor on trust for the third party beneficiary, who can therefore sue to enforce the promise.

▶ In limited circumstances a third party may be able to bring an action in the tort of negligence against a negligent promisor.

▶ There are a significant number of statutory exceptions to the doctrine of privity.

▶ Provided that the relevant formalities are complied with, a promisee may assign his right to sue the promisor to a third party.

▶ A third party who intentionally seeks to procure a contracting party to break his contract with the claimant may be liable in tort to the claimant.

Exercises

7.1 Explain the relationship between the doctrine of privity and the rule that consideration must move from the promisee.

7.2 Rachel and Katie go out for a meal at Sam's restaurant. Katie pays for the meal. Rachel's meal is inedible. What remedies are available to Katie? If Katie refuses to sue, could Rachel sue? (See *Lockett v AM Charles Ltd* [1938] 4 All ER 170.)

7.3 Critically evaluate the Contracts (Rights of Third Parties) Act 1999. How would the following cases be decided under the Act:

(a) *Beswick v Beswick* [1968] AC 58;

(b) *Jackson v Horizon Holidays* [1975] 1 WLR 1468;

(c) *The Eurymedon* [1975] AC 154; and

(d) *White v Jones* [1995] 2 AC 207?

7.4 hat justification is there for giving a third party a right to sue to enforce a term of the contract when he has provided no consideration for that right?

7.5 When can the contracting parties deprive the third party of his right to enforce the term of the contract?

Part II

The content of a contract

Chapter 8

What is a term?

Having considered what the law recognises as a valid, enforceable contract and who is bound by that contract, we shall now consider the contents of a contract. This part is divided into four chapters. In this chapter we shall consider what constitutes a term of the contract; in Chapter 9 we shall discuss the sources of contractual terms; in Chapter 10 we shall consider the classification of contractual terms; and in Chapter 11 we shall analyse a particular type of contractual term, the exclusion or limitation clause.

8.1 What is a term?

A contract consists of a number of terms. However, not everything that is said or written during the course of negotiations constitutes a term of the contract. An example will illustrate the point. Suppose that I agree to sell my bicycle to my neighbour. During the course of negotiations he may ask me many things about it; its age, its size, how often it has been serviced, whether it has gears and, if so, how many, and so on. But the conclusion of the contract may consist simply of my statement 'I will sell you the bicycle for £200' and his statement 'I accept'. It is, however, highly unlikely that these two statements would be held to constitute the entirety of the contract. It is equally unlikely that all my answers to my neighbour's questions would be regarded as terms of the contract. My answers could, in fact, be classified in one of three ways.

The first is that some answers could be treated as mere statements of opinion or 'mere puffs' and will have no legal effect (for example, a statement that 'you will never regret buying a bicycle from me'; see Section 13.3). The principal distinction, however, is between the second and the third categories; that is, between a term and a mere representation (note that in some cases the distinction is drawn between 'warranties' and 'mere representations', but this terminology will not be used here, because it leads to confusion when, in Chapter 10, we seek to distinguish between a condition and a warranty (both of which are terms of a contract)). The distinction between a term and a mere representation is important because, if a statement is held to be a term of the contract, a failure to comply with it will be a breach of contract, entitling the innocent party to a remedy for breach of contract. On the other hand, if the statement is held to be a mere representation, the innocent party cannot claim that there has been a breach of contract, because the statement was not a term of the contract. His remedy, if any, is to seek to have the contract set aside or claim damages for misrepresentation (see Chapter 13).

Whether a statement is a contractual term or a mere representation depends, ultimately, on the intention with which the statement was made. In considering the intention with which a particular statement was made, the courts have, once again, adopted an objective approach to intention. The cases have established some principles (see Sections 8.2–8.4) to guide the court in deciding whether a statement is a term or a mere representation. No one principle is decisive; in every case the court must assess the relative importance of each principle (see *Heilbut, Symons & Co v Buckleton* [1913] AC 30, 50–51, per Lord Moulton).

8.2 Verification

A statement is unlikely to be a term of the contract if the maker of the statement asks the other party to verify its truth. In *Ecay v Godfrey* (1947) 80 Ll LR 286, a seller of a boat stated that the boat was sound but advised the buyer to have it surveyed. His statement was held to be a mere representation. On the other hand, in *Schawel v Reade* [1913] 2 IR 64, the claimant, while examining a horse with a view to buying it for stud purposes, was told by the defendant: 'You need not look for anything; the horse is perfectly sound. If there was anything the matter with this horse I should tell you.' In reliance upon this statement the claimant bought the horse without examining it. It was subsequently discovered that the horse was totally unfit for stud purposes and it was held that the defendant's statement was a term of the contract (contrast *Hopkins v Tanqueray* (1854) 15 CB 130).

8.3 Importance

A statement is likely to be a term of the contract where it is of such importance to the person to whom it is made that, had it not been made, he would not have entered into the contract. In *Couchman v Hill* [1947] KB 554, a heifer was put up for sale at an auction but no warranty was given as to its condition. The claimant asked the defendant whether the heifer was in calf and stated that he was not interested in purchasing it if it was. He was told that it was not in calf. Approximately seven weeks after the purchase the heifer suffered a miscarriage and died. The claimant brought an action for breach of contract. The statement that the heifer was not in calf was held to be a term of the contract because of the importance attached to it by the claimant (contrast *Oscar Chess Ltd v Williams* [1957] 1 WLR 370, discussed in Section 8.4).

8.4 Special knowledge

If the maker of a statement has some special knowledge or skill compared to the other party, the statement may be held to be a contractual term. On the other hand, if the parties' degrees of knowledge are equal or if the person to whom the statement is made has the greater knowledge, the statement may be held to be a mere representation. These propositions can be illustrated by reference to the following two cases.

The first is *Oscar Chess Ltd v Williams* [1957] 1 WLR 370 (Section 8.3), in which the defendant sold a car to the claimants for £290. The car was described as a 1948 Morris 10; in fact it was a 1939 model (which was worth only £175). The defendant had obtained the information that the car was a 1948 model in good faith from the car log book, but the log book was subsequently discovered to be a forgery. It was held that the defendant's statement as to the age of the car was not a term of the contract but a mere representation. The claimants, who were car dealers, were in at least as good a position as the defendant to know the true age of the car. On the other hand, in *Dick Bentley Productions Ltd v Harold Smith (Motors) Ltd* [1965] 1 WLR 623, the claimant asked the defendants, who were car dealers, to find him a 'well vetted' Bentley car. The defendants found a car which they sold to the claimant and which they stated had done only 20,000 miles since a replacement engine had been fitted. It had in fact done 100,000 miles. It was held that the defendants' statement as to the car mileage was a term of the contract; the defendants, being car dealers, were in a better position than the claimant to know whether their statement was true.

8.5 The consequences of the distinction between a term and a mere representation

Although the distinction between a term and a mere representation is important, it is not quite as fundamental as it used to be. At the beginning of the twentieth century, it was important because damages were only available for misrepresentation in a very narrow range of circumstances. But now, both at common law and under the Misrepresentation Act 1967, damages are available for misrepresentation in a much wider range of circumstances (see Section 13.9). The distinction is now primarily relevant to the *amount* of damages recoverable rather than to whether damages are recoverable at all (although there do remain cases in which damages are not recoverable for misrepresentation, see Section 13.9). If the statement is held to be a term, breach will generally entitle the innocent party to recover damages which will have the effect of putting him in the position which he would have been in had the contract been performed (called his 'expectation interest'), whereas if it is a representation, damages will generally be assessed on the basis of the extent to which the representee has incurred loss through reliance on the misrepresentation (the 'reliance interest') (see Chapter 21).

The distinction between a term and a representation is also relevant to the ability to set aside the contract. In the case of misrepresentation, the representee is always, in principle, entitled to set aside the contract (see Section 13.8), while in the case of a term the innocent party can only set aside the contract where the term which has been broken is a condition (see Section 10.3) or is an 'innominate term' and the consequences of the breach have been sufficiently serious (see Section 10.5). The meaning of 'set aside' also differs between the two contexts (see Section 13.8). In the case where the contract is set aside on the ground of misrepresentation, the contract is set aside both retrospectively and prospectively so that the aim of setting the contract aside is to restore both parties to their pre-contractual position. But in the case where a contract is set aside for breach, it is set aside prospectively only and the setting aside does not have retrospective consequences (see Section 20.7).

8.6 Can a representation be incorporated into a contract as a term?

This may seem a strange question to ask given that we have spent a chapter arguing that the two are separate and distinct. The issue can be illustrated by reference to the case of *Pennsylvania Shipping Co v Compagnie Nationale de Navigation* [1936] 2 All ER 1167. A tanker was chartered from the defendants by the claimants. Prior to the conclusion of the contract, the defendants provided the claimants with incorrect information about the heating of the ship. This information was subsequently incorporated into the contract. When the claimants discovered the true position, they sought, *inter alia*, to have the contract set aside on the ground of misrepresentation. Branson J held that the representation became 'merged in the higher contractual right' and that there was therefore no need to set aside the contract on the ground of misrepresentation; the claimants' claim was for breach of contract (contrast *Compagnie Française des Chemin de Fer Paris-Orleans v Leeston Shipping Co* (1919) 1 Ll LR 235). However, section 1(a) of the Misrepresentation Act 1967 now provides that a representee who has entered into a contract after a misrepresentation has been made to him may rescind the contract for misrepresentation, even though the misrepresentation is subsequently incorporated into the contract, provided that he would otherwise be entitled to rescind the contract. This may be of very great significance where the representee is unable to rescind the contract for breach because, for example, the term which has been broken is a warranty (see Section 10.3). In such a case, provided the relevant conditions for rescission for misrepresentation are satisfied (on which see Section 13.8), he may nevertheless be entitled to rescind for misrepresentation (see *Club Travel 2000 Holdings Ltd v Murfin* [2008] EWHC 2729 (Ch); [2008] All ER (D) 56 (Nov), [48]).

Summary

▶ A contract consists of a number of terms.

▶ A term must be distinguished from a statement of opinion or 'mere puff' (which has no legal effect) and a mere representation (which generates a claim for misrepresentation).

▶ The question whether a statement is a term or a mere representation depends upon the intention with which the statement was made. Factors to which the court will have regard in deciding this issue include whether the maker of the statement advised the other party to verify the truth of his statement, the importance of the statement and the respective states of knowledge of the parties.

▶ In certain circumstances the term/representation dichotomy may be crucial to the recoverability of damages, but it is more likely that it will be relevant to the amount of damages recoverable. Where a term of the contract has been broken, damages will generally protect the promisee's expectation interest but, in the case of a misrepresentation, damages will only protect the misrepresentee's reliance interest.

▶ A representee who has entered into a contract after a misrepresentation has been made to him may rescind the contract for misrepresentation, even though the misrepresentation is subsequently incorporated into the contract, provided that he would otherwise be entitled to rescind for misrepresentation.

Exercises

8.1 Why do lawyers distinguish between a 'term' and a 'mere representation'?

8.2 Distinguish between a 'term' and a 'mere representation'. What are the consequences of this distinction?

8.3 John, a specialist race-horse trainer, wished to buy a horse from Fred, who was a farmer who had little knowledge of horses. John believed that the horse was a potential champion and, during the course of negotiations, he asked Fred if he could inspect the horse. Fred said there was really no need as his stable-boy had assured him that the horse would make a 'brilliant race-horse'. In reliance on Fred's statement, John bought the horse. When the horse was delivered to John, he found it had a serious leg injury which made it useless as a race-horse. John wishes to know whether his remedy lies for breach of contract or for misrepresentation. Advise him.

8.4 What is the effect of section 1 (a) of the Misrepresentation Act 1967?

Chapter 9

The sources of contractual terms

9.1 Introduction

There are two principal sources of contractual terms: express terms and implied terms. Express terms are the terms which are agreed specifically by the contracting parties, and implied terms are those terms which are not specifically agreed by the contracting parties but which are implied into the contract by the courts or by Parliament. We shall deal with implied terms in Section 9.8. Here we shall focus our attention on express terms.

Express terms may be agreed orally or in writing. Where the contract is made orally the ascertainment of the contractual terms may involve difficult questions of fact, but the task of a judge is simply to decide exactly what was said by each of the parties. More difficulties arise in the case of written contracts. Three such difficulties will be dealt with here. The first and fundamental issue is whether the court can go beyond the written agreement in an attempt to discover the existence of additional terms to the contract (Section 9.2). The second is whether a person is necessarily bound by the terms of a contract which he has signed (Section 9.3). The third and final issue is whether written terms can be incorporated into a contract, either by notice (Section 9.4) or by a course of dealing (Section 9.5). Once we have discussed these issues we shall consider the approach which the courts adopt towards the interpretation of contracts (Section 9.6) and the circumstances in which rectification is available to correct a mistake which the parties have made in the recording of their agreement (Section 9.7).

9.2 The parol evidence rule

Once the contracting parties have elected to enshrine their contract in a written document, the courts have held that, as a general rule, the parties cannot adduce extrinsic evidence to add to, vary or contradict the written document; the document is the sole repository of the terms of the contract (*Jacobs v Batavia & General Plantations Trust Ltd* [1924] 1 Ch 287). This rule has been called the 'parol evidence rule'. The purpose behind this rule is said to be the promotion of certainty; that is to say, once the parties have gone to the trouble of drawing up a written document, one party should not be able to allege with impunity that there were, in fact, other terms which were, for some reason, not incorporated into the final written document. Thus Lord Hobhouse in *Shogun Finance Ltd v Hudson* [2003] UKHL 62; [2004] 1 AC 919 (on which see further Section 4.6) observed (at [49]) that the parol evidence rule 'is fundamental to the mercantile law of this country' and that 'the certainty of the contract depends on it'. In what may be thought to be something of an overstatement he concluded by saying that 'the rule is one of the great strengths of English commercial law and is one of the main reasons for the international success of English law in preference to laxer systems which do not provide the same certainty'.

On the other hand, if this rule were to be applied rigidly to all cases there is no doubt that it would produce considerable injustice. For example, the written document may have been procured by fraud and so one party would wish to lead extrinsic evidence to prove that fraud. So it is no surprise to find that the parol evidence rule is not an absolute rule, but is the subject of numerous exceptions. We will now consider the scope of these exceptions and then consider their implications for the status of the rule.

The first exception is that the rule does not apply where the written document was not intended to contain the whole of the agreement (*Allen v Pink* (1838) 4 M & W 140). As Lord Wedderburn has remarked (1959), this exception reduces the rule to 'no more than a self-evident tautology ... when the writing is the whole contract, the parties are bound by it and parol evidence is excluded; when it is not, evidence of the other terms must be admitted'.

The Law Commission in their report (1986) agreed with this observation, adding that the parol evidence rule is 'no more than a circular statement'. On this view, the parol evidence rule does not give rise to injustice because it will never prevent a party from leading evidence of terms which were intended to be part of the contract. On the other hand it must be remembered that the courts will presume that a document which looks like the contract is the whole contract. However, this presumption is rebuttable, and the presumption operates with less strength today than in former times, and it is therefore highly unlikely that the parol evidence rule will preclude a party from leading evidence of terms which were intended to be part of the contract. Parol evidence is also admissible to prove terms which must be implied into the agreement (*Gillespie Bros & Co v Cheney, Eggar & Co* [1896] 2 QB 59); to prove a custom which must be implied into the contract (*Hutton v Warren* (1836) 1 M & W 466); to show that the contract is invalid on the ground of misrepresentation, mistake, fraud or *non est factum* (on which see Section 9.3 and *Campbell Discount Co v Gall* [1961] 1 QB 431); to show that the document should be rectified (on which see Section 9.7); to show that the contract has not yet come into operation or that it has ceased to operate (*Pym v Campbell* (1856) 6 E & B 370); and to prove the existence of a collateral agreement (*Mann v Nunn* (1874) 30 LT 526). The latter exception is of particular significance because in one case extrinsic evidence was actually used to *contradict* the terms of the written agreement. In *City and Westminster Properties (1934) Ltd v Mudd* [1959] Ch 129, a lease entered into by the parties contained a covenant which stated that the tenant could use the premises for business purposes only. The tenant had been induced to sign the lease by an oral assurance given by the lessors' agent that the lessors would not raise any objection to the tenant continuing his practice of residing in the premises. In an action by the lessors to forfeit the lease on the ground that the tenant was using the premises for residential purposes, it was held that evidence of the assurance given by the lessors' agent was admissible to prove the existence of a collateral agreement, despite the fact that it contradicted the express terms of the written lease. This case has been subjected to some criticism and it does appear to be inconsistent with earlier cases such as *Angell v Duke* (1875) 32 LT 320 and *Henderson v Arthur* [1907] 1 KB 10. However, if the collateral agreement is truly a separate agreement, then there is no reason why it should not be contrary to the terms of the written agreement. That said, it must be conceded that the effect of the decision is largely to undermine the parol evidence rule.

The parol evidence rule has been subjected to considerable criticism. The exceptions are so wide that they largely subvert the purpose of the rule in promoting certainty. Indeed, the width of the exceptions is such that it must now be doubted whether there is a 'rule' in English law that parol evidence is not admissible to add to, vary or contradict the written document. In the light of these criticisms, the Law Commission provisionally recommended in a Working Paper (1976) that the parol evidence rule be abolished but, subsequently, they concluded in their report (1986) that no legislative action need be taken for two reasons. The first was that the rule did not preclude the courts from having recourse to extrinsic evidence where such a course was consistent with the intention of the parties. The second reason was that any legislative change would be more likely to confuse than clarify the law. Therefore the 'rule' remains in existence but it must be remembered that it is a rule which, because of the width of the exceptions, is unlikely to have significant effects in practice.

9.3   Bound by your signature?

Despite the existence of numerous exceptions to the parol evidence rule, English law does attach importance to the sanctity of written documents and this can be seen in the general rule that a person is bound by a document which he signs, whether he reads it or not. This proposition can be derived from the case of *L'Estrange v F Graucob Ltd* [1934] 2 KB 394. The claimant bought an automatic slot machine from the defendants. She signed an order form which contained a clause which excluded liability for all express and implied warranties. When the claimant discovered that the machine did not work she brought an action against the defendants for breach of an implied warranty that the machine was fit for the purpose for which it was sold. Judgment was given for the defendants on the ground that they had excluded their liability by virtue of the exclusion clause which was incorporated into the contract by the claimant's signature, even though the exclusion clause was in 'regrettably small print' and had not been read by the claimant. She was bound by her signature to the terms set out in the contract. Given the widespread use of contracts which rely heavily upon the use of small print, such a rule appears singularly unfortunate, especially in its application to consumers. The rule is, however, the subject of a number of limits or exceptions which mitigate its impact.

9.3.1   The limits of the rule

The first limit is to be found in the decision of the Court of Appeal in *Grogan v Robin Meredith Plant Hire* [1996] CLC 1127. There the document signed by the defendants was a time sheet for the hire of machinery which stated, at the bottom of the page, that 'All hire undertaken under CPA conditions. Copies available on request.' It was held that the indemnity clause contained in the CPA conditions had not been incorporated into the contract as a result of the signature on the time sheet. Auld LJ stated that it was 'too mechanistic' a proposition to state that the mere signature on a document which contains or incorporates by reference contractual terms has the effect of incorporating these terms into the contract. The court must consider whether the document which has been signed could be regarded as a contractual document having contractual effect or whether it was simply an administrative document designed to enable the parties to give effect to their prior agreement. In deciding whether the document purports to have contractual effect the court must consider, not only the nature and purpose of the document, but also the circumstances surrounding its use by the parties and their understanding of its purpose at the time. On the facts of *Grogan*, the time sheet was held not to have contractual effect. The focus of the court was therefore on the nature of the document which had been signed. Where the document which has been signed is not one which would ordinarily have contractual effect, the signature of the party alleged to be bound is likely to add little. He is not entrapped by his signature.

The second is that, while affirming the general rule that a party is bound by his or her signature, the courts have been careful to recognise the possibility of an exception to the general rule, albeit the precise limits of any such exception remain to be established. So, for example, in *Cargill International Trading Pte Ltd v Uttam Galva Steels Ltd* [2019] EWHC 476 (Comm), [89] Bryan J stated that 'there are exceptional cases in which the signing party was under undue pressure or had no real opportunity to read and consider the contract before signing, such as an individual at an airport presented with a car rental agreement.' The case where 'undue pressure' is applied to the signatory is relatively straightforward in so far as the pressure applied amounts to duress (which is a recognised ground on which a contract can be set aside, see Section 17.2). More difficult is the proposition that a party can claim not to be bound by his signature because he had 'no real opportunity to read and consider the contract before signing.' As a general rule, a party should find the time to read the document before signing it (*Higgins & Co Lawyers Ltd v Evans* [2019] EWHC 2809 (QB); [2020] 1 WLR 141). The reference to an individual who is presented with a car rental agreement at an airport is probably to the decision of the Ontario Court of Appeal in *Tilden Rent-a-Car Co v Clendenning* (1978) 83 DLR (3d) 400 where it was held that the defendant was not bound by a term in a contract for the hire of a car at an airport which had the effect of imposing on him liability for damage done to the car. The court held that a signature could only be relied upon as evidence of genuine consent when it was reasonable for the party relying on the signed document to believe that the signer did assent to the onerous terms proposed and that this test had not been satisfied on the facts of the case. Would an English court follow *Clendenning*? The dicta of Bryan J in *Cargill International Trading Pte Ltd* might be taken to suggest that English law is moving in that direction. But there have been other signs of a resurgence in judicial support for the rule in *L'Estrange*. The lead has been taken in this respect by the High Court of Australia in *Toll (FGCT) Pty Ltd v Alphapharm Pty Ltd* (2004) 219 CLR 165 where a significant challenge to the rule was rejected in robust terms (albeit that the court was not required to address the specific issue which arose on the facts of *Clendenning*). Further, in *Peekay Intermark Ltd v Australia and NZ Banking Group Ltd* [2006] EWCA Civ 386; [2006] 2 Lloyd's Rep 511 Moore-Bick LJ stated (at [43]) that the rule in *L'Estrange* is 'an important principle of English law which underpins the whole of commercial life; any erosion of it would have serious repercussions'. Thus, it cannot be assumed that *Clendenning* would be followed in an English court, although it is not impossible that it might be.

In the absence of a clearly established common law principle which can attack clauses of the type used in *L'Estrange*, the focus of attention has largely shifted towards Parliament. The Unfair Contract Terms Act 1977 (see Sections 11.9–11.15) places significant controls upon exclusion clauses of the type found in *L'Estrange*. Part 2 of the Consumer Rights Act 2015 (on which see Chapter 18) will also have a role to play in the consumer context in regulating the use of unfair terms in the small print of contracts. Two of its provisions appear to be of relevance in this context. The first is paragraph 10 of Schedule 2 to the Consumer Rights Act which states that a term which has the object or effect of 'irrevocably binding the consumer to terms with which the consumer has had no real opportunity of becoming acquainted before the conclusion of the contract' is indicatively unfair. This provision attacks the *L'Estrange* rule in the consumer context, not by challenging the effect of signature, but by regulating the term which seeks to incorporate the onerous terms into the contract. Its focus is upon the 'incorporation term' rather than the terms which it is sought to incorporate into the contract. The second provision is paragraph 2 of Schedule 2 which applies to terms which have the object or effect of:

> inappropriately excluding or limiting the legal rights of the consumer in relation to the trader or another party in the event of total or partial non-performance or inadequate performance by the trader of any of the contractual obligations.

This time the focus is upon the term which it is sought to incorporate and, had *L'Estrange* been a consumer contract, then it seems clear that the exclusion clause would have fallen within the scope of paragraph 2 and so would have been indicatively unfair.

Aside from the possible impact of the Unfair Contract Terms Act 1977 and the Consumer Rights Act 2015, the rule in *L'Estrange* does not apply where the signature has been procured by fraud or misrepresentation or where the defence of *non est factum* is made out. Fraud and misrepresentation will be dealt with in Chapter 13. Here we shall discuss the defence of *non est factum*.

9.3.2   *Non est factum*

The defence of *non est factum* is a defence of respectable antiquity in English law. It was originally applied to the case where an illiterate person signed a deed which had been read to him incorrectly by another person. In such a case, the illiterate person was not bound by the deed; to put it in technical terms, he could plead *non est factum*, which means 'this is not my deed'. The effect of *non est factum* is to render the deed void so that a third party cannot obtain good title under it (see further on the issue of third party rights the discussion at Section 4.6). As the doctrine has developed, it has had to grapple with the problem that it is seeking to reconcile two competing policies. These policies are, firstly, the injustice of holding a person to a bargain to which he has not brought a consenting mind and, secondly, the necessity of holding a person to a document which he has signed, especially where innocent third parties rely to their detriment upon the validity of the signature.

These two competing policies can be seen at work in the important decision of the House of Lords in *Saunders v Anglia Building Society* (also referred to as *Gallie v Lee*) [1971] AC 1004. A widow of 78 made a will in which she left her house to her nephew. However, the nephew wished to raise money immediately on the security of the home. The widow was prepared to help her nephew to raise the money provided that she was permitted to live in her home for the rest of her life rent free. The difficulty for the nephew was that he did not want to raise the loan in his own name because he was afraid that his wife would get her hands on the money. So he arranged that a friend of his should raise the money on the security of the house. The nephew arranged for the preparation of a document assigning the house to the friend for £3,000. The widow did not read the document because her glasses were broken, but she signed it after the friend told her that it was a deed of gift to the nephew. The friend raised money on a mortgage with the respondent building society but he made no payment to the building society, the nephew or the widow. The building society sought to recover possession of the property from the widow, who invoked the defence of *non est factum*. Here we have the clash of the competing policies which we noted above. On the one hand, there is the injustice of holding the widow to an agreement to which she had not brought a consenting mind; but on the other hand, there is the need to protect the building society which had innocently relied to its detriment upon the widow's signature. The House of Lords gave greater weight to the latter policy and held that the defence of *non est factum* was not made out on the facts of the case. As Scott LJ stated in *Norwich and Peterborough Building Society v Steed (No 2)* [1993] QB 116, 125, the law almost invariably protects the innocent third party because 'the signer of the document has, by signing, enabled the fraud to be carried out, enabled the false documents to go into circulation'. It is the signer of the document who must therefore bear the consequences and, to further that goal, *non est factum* is kept within very narrow confines (*CF Asset Finance Ltd v Okonji* [2014] EWCA Civ 870, [27]). Its scope can best be considered by asking ourselves three questions.

The first question is: to whom is the plea available? As originally conceived, the doctrine only applied to those who were unable to read. However in *Saunders* it was held that the doctrine was not confined to those who are blind or illiterate. It extends to those 'who are permanently or temporarily unable through no fault of their own to have without explanation any real understanding or purport of a particular document, whether that be from defective education, illness or innate incapacity'. Their Lordships did not say that the defence could never be available to a person of full capacity, but it would only be available to him in the most exceptional of cases and would not be available simply because he was too busy or too lazy to read the document.

The second question is: for what type of mistake is the defence available? Initially it was held that the defence was available if the mistake went to the heart of the transaction (*Foster v MacKinnon* (1869) LR 4 CP 704). But in *Howatson v Webb* [1907] 1 Ch 537, Warrington J drew a distinction between a mistake as to the 'character' of the document and a mistake as to its 'content', only the former being sufficient to support a plea of *non est factum*. However, this distinction was rejected by the House of Lords in *Saunders* on the ground that it was 'arbitrary'. Instead, it was held that the difference between the document as it was and as it was believed to be must be radical or substantial or fundamental. This test was not satisfied on the facts of *Saunders* because the widow wished to benefit her nephew by enabling him to raise money on the security of the house and the document which she signed was in fact intended to do this, although it was designed to do it by a different route, namely by assignment to the friend instead of by gift to the nephew.

The third and final question is: in what circumstances is a person precluded from relying on the defence? The principal circumstance in which the defence is not available arises where there is carelessness on the part of the person who signs the document. In *United Dominions Trust Ltd v Western* [1976] QB 513, the defendant signed a loan agreement with the claimant company in connection with the purchase of a car and he left it to the garage owner to fill in the details, including the price. The garage owner increased the price of the car and the claimant company paid over the money to the garage owner in good faith. The court held that the onus was on the defendant to show that, in allowing the form to be filled in by the garage owner, he had acted carefully. It was held that he had wholly failed to discharge that onus and therefore could not invoke the defence of *non est factum* (see also *Norwich and Peterborough Building Society v Steed* (No 2) at 128).

It is clear that English law has given considerable weight to the idea that a person should be able to rely on the signature of a contracting party. Such protection would be undermined by a wide defence of *non est factum* because it would render agreements void and thus detrimentally affect third party rights. However, it should not be assumed that, where the defence of *non est factum* fails, the person who signs the document will therefore be left without a remedy. He may have a remedy in misrepresentation, fraud or undue influence (see, for example, *Avon Finance Co v Bridger* [1985] 2 All ER 281). But the important point to note is that misrepresentation, fraud and undue influence only render the contract voidable and so greater protection is thereby afforded to third party rights (on which see Section 4.6).

9.4 Incorporation of written terms

Contracting parties may agree to incorporate a set of written terms into their contract. Three hurdles must be overcome before such terms can be incorporated. The first is that notice of the terms must be given at or before the time of concluding the contract. It is therefore crucial to determine the *precise* moment at which the contract was concluded. In *Olley v Marlborough Court Ltd* [1949] 1 KB 532, a notice in the bedroom of a hotel, which purported to exempt the hotel proprietors from any liability for articles lost or stolen from the hotel, was held not to be incorporated into a contract with a guest, whose furs were stolen from her bedroom, because the notice was not seen by the guest until after the contract had been concluded at the hotel reception desk.

Secondly, the terms must be contained or referred to in a document which was intended to have contractual effect. It is a question of fact whether or not a document was intended to have contractual effect and the issue must be decided by reference to current commercial or consumer practices. In *Chapleton v Barry UDC* [1940] 1 KB 532, the claimant hired a deck chair from the defendants. On paying his money he was given a ticket which, unknown to him, contained a number of conditions, including an exclusion clause. The claimant was injured when he sat in the deck chair and it gave way beneath him. He sued the defendants, who relied by way of defence on the exclusion clause contained in the ticket. It was held that they could not rely on the exclusion clause because it was contained in a mere receipt which was not intended to have contractual effect.

Thirdly, and finally, reasonable steps must be taken to bring the terms to the attention of the other party. In *Parker v South Eastern Railway* (1877) 2 CPD 416, it was established that the test is whether the defendant took reasonable steps to bring the notice to the attention of the claimant, not whether the claimant actually read the notice. Thus, in *Thompson v London, Midland and Scottish Railway Co Ltd* [1930] 1 KB 41, an exclusion clause contained in a railway time-table was held to be validly incorporated despite the fact that the claimant was illiterate and therefore unable to read the clause. The result may be different, however, where the party seeking to rely on the exclusion clause knows of the disability of the other party (*Richardson, Spence and Co Ltd v Rowntree* [1894] AC 217).

What amounts to reasonable notice is a question which depends upon the facts and circumstances of the individual case. In *Thompson*, the defendants were held to have taken reasonable steps to bring the exclusion clause to the attention of the claimant, even though it was contained on page 552 of the time-table and the time-table cost one-fifth of the price of the railway ticket. It is doubtful whether such a liberal view would be taken today (see, for example, *The Mikhail Lermontov* [1990] 1 Lloyd's Rep 579, 594). If the clause is not referred to on the front of the ticket (*Henderson v Stevenson* (1875) LR 2 Sc & Div 470) or if the reference to the clause is obliterated (*Sugar v London, Midland and Scottish Railway Co* [1941] 1 All ER 172) the clause is less likely to be incorporated into the contract. Reference to terms on a website may amount to the giving of reasonable notice, at least in the case where it is a straightforward matter to find the document in question (*Impala Warehousing and Logistics (Shanghai) Co Ltd v Wanxiang Resources (Singapore) Pte Ltd* [2015] EWHC 25 (Comm), [16]). On the other hand, the more unusual or unreasonable the clause, the greater the degree of notice required by the courts. In *J Spurling Ltd v Bradshaw* [1956] 1 WLR 461, Denning LJ famously said that some clauses would need to be printed in red ink on the face of the document with a red hand pointing to it before the notice could be held to be sufficient.

All of the 'incorporation' cases which we have considered so far are concerned with attempts to incorporate exclusion clauses into a contract. They generally evince a restrictive approach to incorporation, particularly in cases such as *Spurling v Bradshaw* (above) where Lord Denning enunciated his 'red hand rule'. It could be argued that such a restrictive approach is confined to exclusion clauses and, indeed, that, since the enactment of the Unfair Contract Terms Act 1977, which gives the courts considerable power to control exclusion clauses (see Sections 11.9–11.14), there is little need for such a restrictive approach, even in the case of exclusion clauses. But the restrictive approach is very much alive and, further, it is not confined to exclusion clauses.

In *Interfoto Picture Library Ltd v Stiletto Visual Programmes Ltd* [1989] QB 433 (see further Macdonald, 1988a) the defendants ordered photographic transparencies from the claimants, not having dealt with them before. The claimants duly sent them 47 transparencies, together with a delivery note which contained a number of conditions. Condition 2 stated that a holding fee of £5 per day was payable for every day the transparencies were kept in excess of 14 days. The defendants put the transparencies to one side and forgot about them. They eventually returned them after approximately one month. The claimants then sent the defendants an invoice for £3,783.50, which the defendants refused to pay. In an action by the claimants to recover the

£3,783.50, the Court of Appeal held that condition 2 was not incorporated into the contract because insufficient notice had been given to the defendants of its terms and that, in the absence of express provision in the contract, the claimants were only entitled to an award of £3.50 per transparency per week on a *quantum meruit* basis. It was held that a party who seeks to incorporate into a contract a term which is particularly onerous *or* unusual must prove that the term has been fairly and reasonably drawn to the attention of the other party. Bingham ʟᴊ stated that cases on sufficiency of notice are concerned with the question 'whether it would in all the circumstances be fair (or reasonable) to hold a party bound by any conditions … of an unusual and stringent nature'. The utility of this general principle must surely be debatable and its application to the present facts even more so. The defendants were business people and were surely capable of reading the conditions on the delivery note. If they did not do so, they must be deemed to have accepted the risk that the terms might prove to be unacceptable to them. The objection that the terms were particularly onerous could possibly have been dealt with by arguing that condition 2 was a penalty clause, a point suggested by Bingham ʟᴊ. The difficulty with this argument is that the penalty clause rule applies to sums payable on a breach of contract (see Section 22.6) and the defendants might not have been in breach of contract in retaining the transparencies beyond 14 days (for example, the claimants could have operated a two-tier price structure, with one fee being payable for the first 14 days and a different fee thereafter). But even if the penalty clause rule was inapplicable, any unfairness in the terms sought to be incorporated into a contract should be dealt with directly, through a general doctrine of unfairness or unconscionability or, in the consumer context, by the Consumer Rights Act 2015 (see Chapter 18) and not by distorting the rules relating to the incorporation of terms into a contract. Nevertheless, English law continues to demand that greater notice be given of a term which is either onerous or unusual in order for that term to be incorporated into the contract.

The continued use of a special test for the incorporation of onerous or unusual terms has given rise to some practical difficulties in determining which clauses are caught by this rule. The words 'onerous or unusual' are not 'terms of art' (*O'Brien v MGN Ltd* [2002] CLC 33, [23], per Hale ʟᴊ) and, as a consequence, the courts have not always been able to agree whether a particular term is or is not 'onerous or unusual'. This point divided the Court of Appeal in *AEG (UK) Ltd v Logic Resource Ltd* [1996] CLC 265, where the majority held that a clause requiring the purchaser to return defective goods at his own expense had not fairly and reasonably been drawn to the attention of the purchaser. Hobhouse ʟᴊ dissented and warned that:

> if it is to be the policy of English law that in every case those clauses are to be gone through with, in effect, a toothcomb to see whether they were entirely usual and entirely desirable in the particular contract, then one is completely distorting the contractual relationship between the parties and the ordinary mechanisms of making contracts. It will introduce uncertainty into the law of contract.

The point was well-made because the clause at issue was already subject to attack under the Unfair Contract Terms Act 1977 and, in the view of Hobhouse ʟᴊ, it was 'under the provisions of that Act that problems of unreasonable clauses should be addressed and the solution found'. All that the majority succeeded in doing was adding yet another layer of uncertainty. There is no need to apply different standards on the issue of incorporation according to the severity of the term sought to be incorporated; the same test should be applied to all terms, regardless of their severity. However, notwithstanding the difficulties which they have experienced in deciding which terms fall within the scope of the rule, the courts continue to apply a special rule to the incorporation of 'onerous or unusual' terms in both consumer and commercial transactions (*Kaye v Nu Skin UK Ltd* [2009] EWHC 3509 (Ch); [2011] 1 Lloyd's Rep 40) and the common law rules have not been altered by the enactment of the Unfair Contract Terms Act 1977 (*Goodlife Foods Ltd v Hall Fire Protection Ltd* [2018] EWCA Civ 1371; [2018] BLR 491, [35] and [106]).

9.5 Incorporation by a course of dealing

Terms may also be incorporated into a contract by a course of dealing. The courts have never defined course of dealing with any degree of precision, but some useful guidance was given by the House of Lords in *McCutcheon v David MacBrayne Ltd* [1964] 1 WLR 125. There it was held that the course of dealing must be both regular and consistent. What constitutes a 'regular' course of dealing depends upon the facts of the particular case. Thus, in *Henry Kendall Ltd v William Lillico Ltd* [1969] 2 AC 31, the House of Lords held that 100 similar contracts over a period of three years constituted a course of dealing. But in *Hollier v Rambler Motors (AMC) Ltd* [1972] 2 QB 71, three or four contracts over a period of five years were held not to be a course of dealing between a consumer and a garage (see to similar effect *Transformers & Rectifiers Ltd v Needs Ltd* [2015] EWHC 269 (TCC); [2015] BLR 33). The position may, however, be different where the contracting parties are commercial parties of equal bargaining power. In *British Crane Hire Corp Ltd v Ipswich Plant Hire Ltd* [1975] QB 303, a clause was incorporated into the contract on the basis of two previous transactions and the custom of the trade. The court placed emphasis on the fact that the parties were of equal bargaining power, they were both in the trade and such conditions were habitually incorporated into these contracts.

The course of dealing must not only be regular; it must also be consistent. In *McCutcheon v David MacBrayne Ltd* (above) a ferry belonging to the defendants sank and the claimant's car was lost. In the resulting action by the claimant, the defendants sought to rely on an exclusion clause contained in a risk note which, contrary to their usual practice, they had not asked the claimant's brother-in-law (who made the arrangement for the shipping of the claimant's car) to sign. The defendants' argument failed in the House of Lords because it was held that there was no consistent course of dealing on the basis of which the exclusion clause could be incorporated into the contract. Lord Pearce said that there was no consistent course of dealing because the previous transactions had always been in writing (that is, by the signing of the risk note) and in the present case the transaction was entirely oral. But this is surely to take the requirement of consistency too far because the only reason for the defendants' reliance upon the course of dealing argument was that they had forgotten to ensure that the risk note was signed. If that forgetfulness, of itself, also had the effect of precluding them from relying upon the course of dealing argument, cases of incorporation by a course of dealing will be very rare (see further Macdonald, 1988b). It is suggested that the better view of the case is that the evidence failed to establish a consistent course of dealing because, although on some occasions the brother-in-law had been asked to sign the risk note, there were other occasions when he had not been asked to sign. On this basis there was clearly no consistent course of dealing.

Knowledge of the conditions will be inferred from the regularity and consistency of the course of dealing. In *McCutcheon* Lord Devlin said that previous dealings were only relevant if they proved actual knowledge of the terms and assent to them, but this view was not shared by other judges in the case and appears to have been rejected by the House of Lords in *Henry Kendall Ltd v William Lillico Ltd* (above).

9.6 Interpretation

Once the terms of the contract have been ascertained, they must be interpreted to establish their 'true' meaning. Many contractual disputes arise out of disagreements over the proper interpretation of a particular phrase in a contract and most of them hinge upon the precise wording and context of the contract. When it comes to the interpretation of contracts, precedents are of relatively limited value: 'a decision on a different clause in a different context is seldom of much help on a question of construction' (*Surrey Heath BC v Lovell Construction Ltd* (1990) 48 Build LR 113, 118). The limited precedent value of cases concerned with the interpretation of contracts has not, however, had the effect of reducing the volume of case law on the subject. In recent years the House of Lords and the Supreme Court have had a steady stream of cases raising questions of interpretation in which they have sought to state (or restate) the principles which should guide the courts when seeking to interpret contracts (leading cases include *Investors Compensation Scheme Ltd v West Bromwich Building Society* [1998] 1 WLR 896, *Chartbrook Ltd v Persimmon Homes Ltd* [2009] UKHL 38; [2009] 1 AC 1101, *Rainy Sky SA v Kookmin Bank* [2011] UKSC 50; [2011] 1 WLR 2900, *Arnold v Britton* [2015] UKSC 36; [2015] AC 1619 and *Wood v Capita Insurance Services Ltd* [2017] UKSC 24; [2017] AC 1173). Although differences of emphasis can be detected between these various restatements, a number of propositions can be derived from them with a substantial degree of certainty.

9.6.1 The objective nature of the test

The first is that the task of the court is to ascertain the objective meaning of the language which the parties have chosen in which to express their agreement. The courts are not concerned with the subjective understanding of the parties to the contract (*Scottish Power UK Plc v BP Exploration Operating Co Ltd* [2015] EWHC 2658 (Comm), [21]). The general rule is that the intention of the parties is to be ascertained from an *objective* assessment of the wording of the contract and of the surrounding circumstances. The 'methodology' of the common law is 'not to probe the real intentions of the parties … Intention is determined by reference to expressed rather than actual intention' (*Deutsche Genossenschaftsbank v Burnhope* [1995] 1 WLR 1580, 1587, per Lord Steyn).

9.6.2 The factual matrix

The second is that the courts have expanded the range of materials on which they can draw when seeking to interpret a contract. This is the so-called 'factual matrix' which has been defined as 'all the background knowledge which would reasonably have been available to the parties in the situation in which they were at the time of the contract' and which includes 'absolutely anything which would have affected the way in which the language of the document would have been understood by a reasonable man' (*Investors Compensation Scheme Ltd v West Bromwich Building Society* [1998] 1 WLR 896, 912-913 per Lord Hoffmann). This emphasis on the 'factual matrix' can be traced back to the speech of Lord Wilberforce in *Prenn v Simmonds* [1971] 1 WLR 1381 but it has been criticised (see Staughton, 1999) on the ground that 'counsel have wildly different ideas as to what a matrix is and what it includes' and that it has had the effect of increasing unnecessarily the cost of commercial litigation by requiring the court to have regard to evidence of very little value. Lord Hoffmann responded to these criticisms in *Bank of Credit and Commerce International SA v Ali* [2001] UKHL 8; [2002] 1 AC 251 when he stated (at [39]) that:

> I did not think it necessary to emphasise that I meant anything which a reasonable man would have regarded as *relevant*. I was merely saying that there is no conceptual limit to what can be regarded as background. It is not, for example, confined to the factual background but can include the state of the law (as in cases in which one takes into account that the parties are unlikely to have intended to agree to something unlawful or legally ineffective) or proved common assumptions which were in fact quite mistaken … I was certainly not encouraging a trawl through 'background' which could not have made a reasonable person think that the parties must have departed from conventional usage.

This 'qualification' is rather limited in its scope but it does at least send out a signal to judges that the factual matrix does have its limits, difficult though it may be to find them, and that these limits should be used to curb the excesses of overenthusiastic counsel who seek to use the factual matrix in an attempt to adduce evidence of dubious relevance to the issue that the court must resolve. Although there are few formal limits on the scope of the factual matrix, the weight attributed to evidence derived from the background to the contract is likely to be less where the issue before the court is one that relates to a standard form contract which is in use throughout a particular industry (*Re Sigma Finance Corp (in administrative receivership)* [2009] UKSC 2; [2010] 1 All ER 671) or to a public document which is available for inspection (*Cherry Tree Investments Ltd v Landmain Ltd* [2012] EWCA Civ 736; [2013] Ch 305). In the latter case the focus of the court is not so much on the particular contractual relationship between the parties but on the understanding of the market or the general user of the contract form in question.

9.6.3   Pre-contractual negotiations and conduct subsequent to the making of the contract

Third, notwithstanding the breadth of the factual matrix, there are limits to the materials which the courts can take into account when seeking to interpret the contract. Two such limitation are worthy of note: the first is pre-contractual negotiations and the second is the conduct of the parties subsequent to the making of the contract. In relation to pre-contractual negotiations, the House of Lords in *Chartbrook Ltd v Persimmon Homes Ltd* [2009] UKHL 38; [2009] 1 AC 1101 affirmed the general rule that evidence of pre-contractual negotiations is inadmissible when seeking to interpret a contract. In so deciding, their Lordships attached importance to the promotion of certainty and the need to avoid an unacceptable addition to the cost of litigation by increasing still further the volume of material that is admissible in evidence. Thus Lord Hoffmann stated that the law of contract is 'designed to enforce promises with a high degree of predictability' and 'the more one allows conventional meanings or syntax to be displaced by inferences drawn from background, the less predictable the outcome is likely to be'. Further, Lord Rodger stated that, if there is to be a change to the general rule, it should be 'on the basis of a fully informed debate in a forum where the competing policies can be properly investigated and evaluated'. Although it would be open to the Law Commission to provide such a forum, in the absence of such an intervention, the general rule which excludes evidence of pre-contractual negotiations is now firmly entrenched in English contract law.

It is, however, important to note the scope of the exclusionary rule. Lord Hoffmann addressed the scope of the rule in the following passage from his speech in *Chartbrook Ltd v Persimmon Homes Ltd* [2009] UKHL 38; [2009] 1 AC 1101. He observed that:

> [t]he rule excludes evidence of what was said or done during the course of negotiating the agreement for the purpose of drawing inferences about what the contract meant. It does not exclude the use of such evidence for other purposes: for example, to establish that a fact which may be relevant as background was known to the parties, or to support a claim for rectification or estoppel. These are not exceptions to the rule. They operate outside it.

In this passage, Lord Hoffmann identifies three situations which are outside the scope of the exclusionary rule. The first is that it is possible to have regard to pre-contractual negotiations for the purpose of establishing that 'a fact which may be relevant as background was known to the parties'. It would thus appear to be possible to refer to pre-contractual negotiations in so far as they are part of the factual matrix. As Lord Clarke observed in *Oceanbulk Shipping and Trading SA v TMT Asia Ltd* [2010] UKSC 44; [2011] 1 AC 662, [40] the factual matrix 'may well include objective facts communicated by one party to the other in the course of the negotiations'. However, the admissibility of evidence does not extend to the negotiating position of the parties (*Northrop Grumman Missions Systems Europe Ltd v BAE Systems (Al Diriyah C41) Ltd* [2015] EWCA Civ 844; [2015] BLR 657, [31]). The distinction between 'objective facts' (which are admissible) and statements in the course of pre-contractual negotiations which are, in the words of Lord Hoffmann in *Chartbrook*, 'drenched in subjectivity' ([38]) (and therefore inadmissible) will not always be easy to draw (*Merthyr (South Wales) Ltd v Merthyr Tydfil County Borough Council* [2019] EWCA Civ 526, [55] where it was acknowledged that there 'may be borderline cases' where the line 'may be hard to draw'). An example of a case in which the court inclined against admissibility is provided by *Scottish Widows Fund and Life Assurance Society v BGC International* [2012] EWCA Civ 607; (2012) 142 Con LR 27 where the Court of Appeal declined to rely upon pre-contractual negotiations for the purpose of establishing the 'general object of the transaction' or as evidence of the 'genesis and objective of the transaction'. Arden LJ stated that 'judges should exercise considerable caution before treating as admissible communications in the course of pre-contractual negotiations relied on as evidencing the parties' objective aim in completing the transaction', while Davis LJ stated that counsel for the respondents had 'impermissibly' delved into the pre-contractual negotiations 'with a view to

meaning of what the parties said in the document with what they meant to say but did not say'. In short, it brings into the interpretative process issues which may be said properly to relate to the remedy of rectification. There is little doubt that there is now a 'close relationship' between interpretation and rectification (see *Oceanbulk Shipping and Trading SA v TMT Asia Ltd* [2010] UKSC 44; [2011] 1 AC 662, [45]) in that the courts today can achieve results as a matter of interpretation which in previous generations would have been reached (if at all) via rectification (see Section 9.7). The modern courts appear to be willing to engage in a measure of 'rewriting' the contract under the guise of interpretation, referred to by Arden LJ as 'corrective interpretation' (*Cherry Tree Investments Ltd v Landmain Ltd* [2012] EWCA Civ 736; [2013] Ch 305, [62]). However, this exercise takes place within relatively narrow confines and it is more likely to be undertaken where the punctuation has 'gone awry' than in the case where one party has submitted that the court should insert into the contracts words that are not there (*Vitol E&P Ltd v New Age (African Global Energy) Ltd* [2018] EWHC 1580 (Comm), [28]). As Lord Hoffmann observed in *Chartbrook Ltd v Persimmon Homes Ltd* [2009] UKHL 38; [2009] 1 AC 1101, it 'requires a strong case to persuade the court that something must have gone wrong with the language'. It is highly unlikely that a party will be able to make such a 'strong case' by demonstrating that the contract is unduly favourable to one party. The fact that the contract is particularly favourable to one party does not show that something must have gone wrong with the language; on the contrary, it shows that one party has made a good deal. Similarly, the fact that the person responsible for drafting the clause has not thought through its consequences does not suffice to demonstrate that 'something has gone wrong with the language' (*Prophet plc v Huggett* [2014] EWCA Civ 1013; [2014] IRLR 797). It is not the function of the court to rewrite the contract in order to save a party from the improvident bargain into which it has entered. But, in the case where the results are startling and at times haphazardly favour one party and at other times the other, the court may, as in *Chartbrook*, conclude that the contract document does not mean what it literally says, and it will then adopt a construction which gives effect to what the court perceives to be the objective intention of the parties. In such a case, the court can go to considerable lengths in order to give effect to the intention of the parties. In *Chartbrook*, Lord Hoffmann stated that there is no 'limit to the amount of red ink or verbal rearrangement or correction which the court is allowed'. However, before the court can embark on this exercise it must be 'clear that something has gone wrong with the language' and, crucially, it must be 'clear what a reasonable person would have understood the parties to have meant'. In other words, both the problem ('something has gone wrong with the language') and the solution (it must be 'clear what a reasonable person would have understood the parties to have meant') must be clear. This dual requirement should limit the uncertainty which might otherwise be generated (see *Scottish Widows Fund and Life Assurance Society v BGC International* [2012] EWCA Civ 607; (2012) 142 Con LR 27). As Rix LJ observed in *ING Bank NV v Ros Roca SA* [2011] EWCA Civ 353; [2012] 1 WLR 472, [110] 'judges should not see in *Chartbrook* an open sesame for reconstructing the parties' contract, but an opportunity to remedy by construction a clear error of language which could not have been intended'. Provided that this point is understood, construction will not be 'pushed beyond its proper limits in pursuit of remedying what is perceived to be a flaw in the working of a contract'.

9.7 Rectification

Once the contract has been interpreted, one of the parties may argue that the written agreement, as interpreted, fails to reflect the agreement which the parties actually reached. In such a case, the court may be asked to rectify the document so that it accurately reflects the agreement which the parties did reach. Such was the case in *Lovell & Christmas Ltd v Wall* (1911) 104 LT 85 where the claimant asked the court to adopt a particular interpretation of the contract and, when that argument failed, sought to have the contract document rectified.

The precise nature of the relationship between interpretation and rectification has, however, proved to be a somewhat vexed issue (see Davies, 2016). On one view there is a clear distinction to be drawn between the two. Interpretation is the process of ascribing a meaning to a term of the contract which the parties have agreed. Rectification, on the other hand, is a process whereby a document, the meaning of which has already been ascertained, is rectified so that it gives effect to the intention of the parties. In *Tartsinis v Navona Management Co* [2015] EWHC 57 (Comm), [13] Leggatt J described interpretation and rectification as two 'very different exercises'. He drew attention to two principal differences. The first is that the law adopts an objective approach when seeking to identify the intention of the parties as part of the process of interpreting a contract (see Section 9.6). In the case of rectification, by contrast, there are situations in which the courts will have regard to the subjective intentions of the parties, although this point has been one of some controversy which has not been finally resolved (on which see below). The second difference is that, while pre-contractual negotiations are generally inadmissible when seeking to interpret a contract (see Section 9.6 above), they are admissible where the claim is one to rectify the contract. This difference can have an important practical consequence. A party seeking to demonstrate that something has gone wrong with the language of the contract may find that the best evidence is to be found in the pre-contractual negotiations which may enable a court to identify with some precision the point in time at which the error crept into the documents. A court which is only concerned with the proper interpretation of the contract cannot, as the law presently stands, admit such evidence for the purpose of deciding whether something has gone wrong with the contract and so may not be able to see that something has indeed gone wrong. But, if a claim is made to rectify the contract, the admissibility of such evidence may persuade a court to conclude that something has in fact gone wrong with the language of the contract and grant rectification accordingly (for an example see *LSREF III Wight Ltd v Millvalley Ltd* [2016] EWHC 466 (Comm); 165 Con LR 58).

An alternative view of the relationship between interpretation and rectification is that it is much closer than the above would suggest and that there is a substantial degree of overlap between the two doctrines. Thus cases can be found in which the courts have corrected minor errors in the expression of a document by a process of construction rather than by rectification. For example, in *Nittan (UK) Ltd v Solent Steel Fabrication Ltd* [1981] 1 Lloyd's Rep 633, the Court of Appeal read 'Sargrove Electronic Controls Ltd' as if it read 'Sargrove Automation' and thereby avoided the need to rectify the document. One effect of the modern principles by which contracts are interpreted has been to increase the number of cases in which mistakes in the language of the contract are corrected as part of the interpretation of the contract (a process described by Arden LJ in *Cherry Tree Investments Ltd v Landmain Ltd* [2012] EWCA Civ 736; [2013] Ch 305, [62] as 'corrective interpretation'). As we have noted, the modern approach to the interpretation of contracts has given the courts greater freedom to conclude that the parties have used the wrong words to give effect to their intention and then to adopt an interpretation of these words which gives effect to that intention without the need formally to resort to the remedy of rectification. A court may resort to 'corrective interpretation' in the case where the parties have made a mistake of language or syntax but it is less likely to be appropriate in the case where the parties have failed to provide for a particular circumstance or have mistakenly omitted a particular clause (*Cherry Tree Investments Ltd v Landmain Ltd*). In the latter case, rectification is more likely to be the more appropriate remedy.

Rectification is therefore a remedy which is concerned with defects not in the making, but in the recording, of a contract. This distinction can be illustrated by reference to the case of *Frederick E Rose (London) Ltd v William H Pim Jnr & Co Ltd* [1953] 2 QB 450. The claimants were asked to supply certain buyers of theirs with a quantity of 'Moroccan horsebeans known here as feveroles'. The claimants did not know what feveroles were and so they asked the defendants, who replied that they were simply horsebeans. So the parties entered into a contract for the supply by the defendants to the claimants of 'horsebeans'. At the time of making the contract both parties believed that 'horsebeans' were 'feveroles'. It later transpired that 'feveroles' were a more expensive variety of horsebean than the type which had been supplied to the claimants under the contract. When the claimants' buyers claimed damages from the claimants on the ground that the horsebeans which had been supplied to them were not 'feveroles', the claimants sought to have the contract with the defendants rectified by the insertion of the word 'feveroles'. The Court of Appeal refused to rectify the contract. This was not a case in which the document failed to record the intention of the parties. The document did reflect their prior agreement; it was simply the case that the parties were under a shared misapprehension that 'horsebeans' were 'feveroles'.

Rectification is an equitable discretionary remedy (its equitable nature is a further ground on which interpretation and rectification can be distinguished: *Daventry District Council v Daventry & District Housing Ltd* [2011] EWCA 1153; [2012] 1 WLR 1333, [198]). As such, it is only available in the discretion of the court. Originally the courts were reluctant to exercise this discretion but gradually they have become more willing to do so. In deciding whether to rectify a document a court will have regard to the following considerations.

The first is that a court will only rectify a document where 'convincing proof' is provided that the document fails to record the intention of the parties (*Joscelyne v Nissen* [1970] 2 QB 86; *George Wimpey UK Ltd v VI Components Ltd* [2005] EWCA Civ 77; [2005] BLR 135). A high degree of proof is needed so that certainty is not undermined (*The Olympic Pride* [1980] 2 Lloyd's Rep 67, 73). The test to be applied when seeking to identify the common intention of the parties has been a subject of considerable controversy. In *Chartbrook Ltd v Persimmon Homes Ltd* [2009] UKHL 38; [2009] 1 AC 1101, Lord Hoffmann concluded that, where the document of which rectification is sought is a written contract, the intention of the parties is to be assessed objectively and not subjectively so that the court is concerned with what the reasonable observer with knowledge of the background facts and prior communications between the parties would have thought their common intention at the time of entry into the contract to have been. This conclusion had both its supporters and its detractors, and there were early signs of judicial disquiet about the focus on the objective rather than the subjective intention of the parties (see, for example, *Tartsinis v Navona Management Co* [2015] EWHC 57 (Comm), [87]–[99]). The controversy came to a head in *FSHC Group Holdings Ltd v GLAS Trust Corporation Ltd* [2019] EWCA Civ 1361; [2020] Ch 365 where the Court of Appeal sought to divide the cases into two groups. The first group consists of cases where the parties have made a binding agreement to execute a document containing particular terms but instead execute a document containing different terms. In this instance the terms of the initial agreement must be objectively determined and this proposition is one that is generally accepted. More difficult is the second group of cases which consists of those in which there is no prior binding agreement between the parties but simply a continuing common intention. Here the Court of Appeal held, contrary to the view of Lord Hoffmann in *Chartbrook*, that the intention of the parties in relation to that continuing common intention is to be ascertained subjectively. The reason for this is said to be that it is only in the case where the contract document fails to give effect to what both parties in fact intended and mutually understood each other to intend that there exists a sufficient justification for departing from the objective meaning of the document which they have concluded. In other words, it is only when the document fails to give effect to their common subjective intention that it is unconscionable for both parties to be bound by the terms of the document which they have concluded. In this second group of cases, in order to obtain rectification, it is necessary to show not only that each party to the contract had the same actual intention with regard to the relevant matter, but also that there was an 'outward expression of accord'; that is to say that, as a result of the communication between the parties, they understood each other to share that common intention. While the judgment of the Court of Appeal in *FSHC* contains a long and careful analysis of the authorities, it rests for its validity on the proposition that Lord Hoffmann's conclusion in *Chartbrook* in relation to the objective nature of the test to be applied was not part of the *ratio* of the case (see [133]) because the point was 'academic' given that the case had been decided on other grounds. However, as the Court of Appeal also acknowledged, the judgment of Lord Hoffmann did command the unanimous agreement of the House of Lords and so it cannot be lightly cast aside. It is unlikely that the decision of the Court of Appeal will be the last word on this contested issue.

The second is that the document must fail to record the intention of *both* parties. Unilateral mistake is insufficient of itself to base a claim to rectification (*Riverlate Properties v Paul* [1975] Ch 133). But where one party mistakenly believes that the document correctly expresses the parties' common intention, and the other party is aware of that mistake, rectification may be available (*A Roberts and Co Ltd v Leicestershire CC* [1961] Ch 555). Where the defendant has been guilty of unconscionable conduct then the claimant may be entitled to rectification. An example of such unconscionable conduct was provided by Stuart-Smith LJ in *Commission for the New Towns v Cooper (Great Britain) Ltd* [1995] Ch 259, 280 in the following terms:

> where A intends B to be mistaken as to the construction of the agreement, so conducts himself that he diverts B's attention from discovering the mistake by making false and misleading statements, and B in fact makes the very mistake that A intends, then notwithstanding that A does not actually know, but merely suspects, that B is mistaken, and it cannot be shown that the mistake was induced by any misrepresentation, rectification may be granted.

Thus the mere fact that a party has made a mistake, even a serious mistake, will not entitle that party to seek rectification of the contract. It is necessary to go further and prove that the other party to the contract knew of the mistake so that it can be said to have behaved dishonestly or unconscionably (*George Wimpey UK Ltd v VI Components Ltd* [2005] EWCA Civ 77; [2005] BLR 135).

Thirdly, as we have noted, the document must have been preceded either by a concluded contract or by a 'continuing common intention'. The case where there is a prior enforceable contract between the parties is generally straightforward; more difficult is the case where there has been simply a 'common continuing intention in regard to a particular provision or aspect of the agreement' (*Crane v Hegeman-Harris* [1970] 2 QB 86). The particular difficulty has been whether the 'continuing common intention' must be accompanied by evidence of 'an outward expression of accord'. In *FSHC Group Holdings Ltd v GLAS Trust Corporation Ltd* (above), the Court of Appeal affirmed (at [73]) that an outward expression of accord is a necessary ingredient of a rectification claim in a 'continuing common intention' case and that it does not suffice to demonstrate that the relevant intentions of the parties were 'locked separately in the breast of each other' without being communicated by each party to the other. An example of rectification being granted in a case of a continuing common intention is provided by the case of *Joscelyne v Nissen*. A father and daughter agreed that the daughter would purchase the father's business and would, in return, pay all the expenses of the father's home, including the gas, electricity and coal bills. The formal contract signed by the parties made no mention of the fact that the daughter had agreed to pay these bills. There was no prior contract to which the court could have regard but it was held that there was sufficient evidence of a continuing common intention that the daughter pay the gas, electricity and coal bills to enable the court to rectify the agreement to give effect to their common intention.

Finally, rectification will not be granted in favour of a claimant who has been guilty of excessive delay in seeking rectification, nor will it be granted against a *bona fide* purchaser for value without notice.

9.8 Implied terms

In addition to the terms which the parties have expressly agreed, a court may be prepared to hold that other terms must be implied into the contract. Such terms may be implied from one of three sources.

9.8.1 Terms implied by statute

The first is statute. Parliament has, in numerous instances, seen fit to imply terms into contracts. It is clear that these statutorily implied terms are not based upon the intention of the parties but on rules of law or public policy. As an illustration of statutorily implied terms we shall give very brief consideration to sections 12 to 15 of the Sale of Goods Act 1979 (and see also the equivalent terms which are implied into a contract under which a trader supplies goods to a consumer in sections 9–18 of the Consumer Rights Act 2015). It is an implied condition of a contract for the sale of goods that the seller has the right to sell the goods (s 12(1)) and there is an implied warranty that the goods are free from charges or incumbrances in favour of third parties (s 12(2)). There is also an implied condition that goods sold by description shall correspond with the description (s 13(1)) and that goods sold by sample shall correspond with the sample (s 15). In the case of a seller who sells goods in the course of a business, there is an implied condition that the goods supplied under the contract are of satisfactory quality (s 14(2)), except in relation to defects drawn to the buyer's attention before the contract was concluded or, in the case where the buyer examines the goods, as regards defects which that examination ought to reveal (s 14(2C)). Finally, where the seller sells goods in the course of a business and the buyer makes known to the seller any particular purpose for which the goods are being bought, there is an implied condition that the goods supplied under the contract are reasonably fit for that purpose (s 14(3)). The function of these implied terms is not to give effect to the intention of the parties but to provide some protection for the expectations of purchasers, particularly, in the case of the Consumer Rights Act 2015, consumer buyers. This element of 'consumer protection' is further evidenced by the fact that both the Unfair Contract Terms Act 1977 and the Consumer Rights Act place severe restrictions upon the ability of sellers to exclude the operation of these implied terms and, indeed, as against a consumer, many of them cannot be excluded (see Section 11.11; section 31 of the Consumer Rights Act 2015).

9.8.2 Terms implied by custom

The second source of implied terms is terms implied by custom. A contract may be deemed to incorporate any relevant custom of the market, trade or locality in which the contract is made (*Hutton v Warren* (1836) 1 M & W 466), unless the custom is inconsistent with the express terms of the contract or its nature (*Palgrave, Brown & Son Ltd v SS Turid (Owners)* [1922] 1 AC 397). A custom will generally be implied into a contract where it can be shown that the custom was generally accepted by those doing business in the particular trade in the particular place and was such that an outsider making inquiries could not fail to discover it (*Kum v Wah Tat Bank Ltd* [1971] 1 Lloyd's Rep 439). A custom which satisfies these requirements binds both parties, whether they actually knew of it or not.

9.8.3 Terms implied at common law

The third source of implied terms is terms implied at common law. There are, broadly speaking, two types of terms which are implied at common law (the distinction was recognised by Lord Bridge in *Scally v Southern Health and Social Services Board* [1992] 1 AC 294, 306–07). The first type are sometimes called terms 'implied in fact'. This nomenclature seeks to convey the idea that the term is being implied as a matter of fact to give effect to what the court perceives to be the unexpressed intention of the parties to the particular contract. The second type are known as terms 'implied in law' and are implied into all contracts of a particular type. Given the more general nature of the implication, terms implied in law are less directly linked to the unexpressed intention of the parties to the particular contract. Thus terms are frequently implied into contracts of employment and into contracts between landlords and tenants, not on the basis of the relationship between the particular parties, but as a general incidence of the relationship of employer and employee or landlord and tenant. To take the employment relationship as an example, a term is generally implied that an employee will serve his employer faithfully and that he will indemnify his employer for liabilities incurred as a result of his wrongful acts in the course of his employment (*Lister v Romford Ice & Cold Storage Co Ltd* [1957] AC 555). Equally, it has been held that there is an implied term to the effect that the employer must not 'without reasonable and proper cause conduct [himself] in a manner calculated or likely to destroy or seriously damage the relationship of confidence and trust between the parties' (*Mahmud v Bank of Credit and Commerce International SA* [1998] AC 20, 44–45, per Lord Steyn).

9.8.4　Terms implied in fact: controversy in the development of the law

The test which must be satisfied before a term will be implied into a contract has been the subject of considerable controversy in recent years. Traditionally, the courts relied upon a range of tests which all expressed, albeit in slightly different terms, the idea that a term will only be implied into a contract where it is necessary to make the implication. One such test is known as the 'officious bystander' test, the origin of which lies in the following statement:

> *Prima facie* that which in any contract is left to be implied and need not be expressed is something so obvious that it goes without saying; so that, if, while the parties were making their bargain an officious bystander were to suggest some express provision for it in the agreement, they would testily suppress him with a common 'Oh, of course' (MacKinnon LJ in *Shirlaw v Southern Foundries Ltd* [1939] 2 KB 206, 207).

Another way of expressing the same, or very similar idea is to say that the implication must be 'necessary to give the transaction such business efficacy as the parties must have intended' (*The Moorcock* (1889) 14 PD 64). These tests were drawn together and summarised by Lord Simon in *BP Refinery (Westernport) Pty Ltd v Shire of Hastings* (1978) ALJR 20, 26 in the following terms:

> for a term to be implied, the following conditions (which may overlap) must be satisfied:(1) it must be reasonable and equitable; (2) it must be necessary to give business efficacy to the contract, so that no term will be implied if the contract is effective without it; (3) it must be so obvious that 'it goes without saying'; (4) it must be capable of close expression; (5) it must not contradict any express term of the contract.

This established line of case-law was thrown into some disarray by the judgment of Lord Hoffmann in *A-G of Belize v Belize Telecom Ltd* [2009] UKPC 10; [2009] 2 All ER 1127 where he sought to bring the law relating to the implication of terms into line with the principles applied when seeking to interpret a contract. Thus he stated that the implication of a term into a contract is an exercise in the construction of the contract as a whole where the court is concerned only to discover what the instrument means. He continued:

> it follows that in every case in which it is said that some provision ought to be implied in an instrument, the question for the court is whether such a provision would spell out in express words what the instrument, read against the relevant background, would reasonably be understood to mean. … There is only one question: is that what the instrument, read as a whole against the relevant background, would reasonably be understood to mean?

In Lord Hoffmann's judgment the tests traditionally applied by the courts were best regarded

> not as a series of independent tests which must each be surmounted, but rather as a collection of different ways in which judges have tried to express the central idea that the proposed implied term must spell out what the contract actually means, or in which they have explained why they did not think that it did so.

Lord Hoffmann's rationalisation of the case-law gave rise to two principal difficulties. The first was whether his intention was to liberalise the rules relating to the implication of terms into a contract, in effect lowering the threshold which has to be overcome in order to imply a term into a contract. The second concerned his suggestion that the implication of a term into a contract is part of an exercise in the construction of the contract, a proposition at variance with the traditional understanding of the relationship between the interpretation of an express term of the contract and the implication of a term into that contract. These two issues will be considered in turn.

9.8.5   Orthodoxy restored

In relation to the first issue it is unlikely that Lord Hoffmann intended to liberalise the rules relating to the implication of terms into a contract. This was also the view of Lord Clarke in *Mediterranean Salvage & Towage Ltd v Seamar Trading & Commerce Inc (The Reborn)* [2009] EWCA Civ 531; [2009] 2 Lloyd's Rep 639, [15] when he stated that Lord Hoffmann was 'not in any way resiling from the often stated proposition that it must be necessary to imply the proposed term. It is never sufficient that it should be reasonable.' Whatever Lord Hoffmann's actual intention, the Supreme Court has since affirmed in *Marks and Spencer plc v BNP Paribas Securities Services Trust Co (Jersey) Ltd* [2015] UKSC 72; [2016] AC 742, [17] that 'a term will only be implied if it satisfies the test of business necessity.' In so concluding the Supreme Court expressly affirmed the continued validity of the traditional tests, such as the 'officious bystander' test, albeit Lord Neuberger noted that the test is not one of 'absolute necessity' but of 'business necessity'. Thus, the question to be asked is whether, without the term, 'the contract would lack commercial or practical coherence' or whether the implication is necessary 'to make the contract work'. It is important to note that it is not sufficient that the term is a reasonable one for the court to be able to imply it into the contract, nor is it sufficient that the term proposed is 'fair'. The fairness or reasonableness of the term may be a necessary requirement, but it is not sufficient. Thus it is not appropriate for a court to apply hindsight and to seek to imply a term in a commercial contract merely because it appears to be fair or because one considers that the parties would have agreed to it if it had been suggested to them (*Bou-Simon v BGC Brokers LP* [2018] EWCA Civ 1525; [2019] 1 All ER (Comm) 955, [12]) The reason for this more restrictive approach is that it is not the task of the court to make the contract for the parties. Rather, the task of the court is to give effect to the agreement into which the parties have entered and this requires that the term be 'necessary' in order to make the contract work or to give effect to the parties' intention.

The essence of the modern approach to the implication of terms as a matter of fact was summed up by Lord Hughes in *Ali v Petroleum Company of Trinidad and Tobago* [2017] UKPC 2; [2017] ICR 531 in the following terms (at [5]):

> It is enough to reiterate that the process of implying a term into the contract must not become the re-writing of the contract in a way which the court believes to be reasonable, or which the court prefers to the agreement which the parties have negotiated. A term is to be implied only if it is necessary to make the contract work, and this it may be if (i) it is so obvious that it goes without saying (and the parties, although they did not, ex hypothesi, apply their minds to the point, would have rounded on the notional officious bystander to say, and with one voice, 'Oh, of course') and/or (ii) it is necessary to give the contract business efficacy. Usually the outcome of either approach will be the same. The concept of necessity must not be watered down. Necessity is not established by showing that the contract would be improved by the addition. The fairness or equity of a suggested implied term is an essential but not a sufficient pre-condition for inclusion. And if there is an express term in the contract which is inconsistent with the proposed implied term, the latter cannot, by definition, meet these tests, since the parties have demonstrated that it is not their agreement.

Therefore a high standard must be satisfied before a term will be implied into a contract. Attempts to imply a term have therefore failed where one of the parties did not know of the term which it was alleged must be implied (*Spring v NASDS* [1956] 1 WLR 585) and where it was not clear that both parties would in fact have agreed to the term (*Luxor (Eastbourne) Ltd v Cooper* [1941] AC 108). The courts are also reluctant to imply a term where the parties have entered into a carefully drafted written contract containing detailed terms agreed between them: in such a case a court is likely to presume that the written contract constitutes a complete code and so refuse to imply any term into it (*Marks and Spencer plc v BNP Paribas Securities Services Trust Co (Jersey) Ltd* [2015] UKSC 72; [2016] AC 742, [21]). Further, as Lord Simon stated in *BP Refinery (Westernport) Pty Ltd v Shire of Hastings* (above), a term will not be implied into a contract if it would be inconsistent with the express wording of the contract (see also *Duke of Westminster v Guild* [1985] QB 688). Inconsistency can take one of two forms (*Irish Bank Resolution Corporation Ltd v Camden Markets Holding Corp* [2017] EWCA Civ 7; [2017] 2 All ER (Comm) 781, [35]). The first, and most obvious, is direct linguistic inconsistency where the term sought to be implied cannot be reconciled with or contradicts one of the express terms of the contract. The second, less obvious form of inconsistency is substantive inconsistency which does not involve any linguistic inconsistency but arises where the term sought to be implied does not fit with the substance or the essence of the express terms of the contract or the parties' allocation of risk under the contract.

9.8.6 Terms implied in law

The 'business necessity' test is directed to the implication of terms as a matter of fact (*Marks and Spencer plc v BNP Paribas Securities Services Trust Co (Jersey) Ltd*

[2015] UKSC 72; [2016] AC 742, [15]). It does not directly address terms implied as a matter of law. So, what test do the courts apply when deciding whether to imply a term into a contract as a matter of law? It would appear that the implication is not based on the 'officious bystander' test but on some less stringent test which reflects the court's perception of the nature of the relationship between the parties and whether such an implied term is suitable or 'reasonable' for incorporation in all contracts of the particular type in question (for example, in the context of a landlord and tenant relationship see *Liverpool CC v Irwin* [1977] AC 239). As Lord Bridge put it in *Scally v Southern Health and Social Services Board* at 306, there is:

> a clear distinction between the search for an implied term necessary to give business efficacy to a particular contract and the search, *based on wider considerations*, for a term which the law will imply as a necessary incident of a definable category of contractual relationship.

These 'wider considerations' have proved to be difficult to identify with any precision but, as Dyson LJ observed in *Crossley v Faithful & Gould Holdings Ltd* [2004] EWCA Civ 293; [2004] IRLR 377, the better view is that the courts in cases involving terms implied in law ought not to 'focus on the elusive concept of necessity' which is 'somewhat protean' but rather should 'recognise that, to some extent at least, the existence and scope of standardised implied terms raise questions of reasonableness, fairness and the balancing of competing policy considerations' (see further Peden, 2001). *Crossley* itself provides evidence of the difficulties involved in taking these 'wider considerations' into account. The principal issue at stake in the case was whether or not there was an 'implied term of any contract of employment that the employer will take reasonable care for the economic well-being of his employee'. The Court of Appeal refused to make the implication because it held that it was not appropriate for it to imply such a broad term into contracts of employment when the House of Lords in cases such as *Scally* had chosen not to formulate an implied term in broad terms but rather had chosen to formulate a narrowly drawn implied term which was devised with the facts of the particular case very much in mind. More importantly, the Court of Appeal held that 'such an implied term would impose an unfair and unreasonable burden on employers'. The interests of employers and employees can and do conflict and, in such cases, it was held that it would be 'unreasonable' to require the employer 'to have regard to the employee's financial circumstances when he takes lawful business decisions which may affect the employee's economic welfare'. Further, it was held not to be the function of an employer to 'act as his employee's financial adviser'. This being the case, it was held that there were 'no obvious policy reasons to impose on an employer the general duty to protect his employee's economic wellbeing'.

9.8.7   Interpretation and implication

The second difficulty created by Lord Hoffmann's judgment in *Belize* arose from the suggestion that the process of implying a term into a contract is part of the exercise of interpreting a contract. The Supreme Court in *Marks and Spencer plc v*

Chapter 10

The classification of contractual terms

10.1 The classification of terms

Not all contract terms are of equal significance; some are more important than others. For example, if a company were to enter into a contract to buy a new car, the make of the car, its roadworthiness and the price would probably be much more important to it than its colour. This fact has long been reflected in contract law in the distinction which has traditionally been drawn between a condition and a warranty.

A condition is an essential term of the contract which goes to the root or the heart of the contract. Thus, in the example of the purchase of a new car, the terms as to the make of the car, its roadworthiness and the obligation to pay the price would likely be conditions. A warranty, on the other hand, is a lesser, subsidiary term of the contract, such as the term relating to the colour of the car (unless it was part of the description of the car, in which case it could be treated as a condition under the Sale of Goods Act 1979, s 13(1); see Section 9.8). The distinction between a condition and a warranty is vital in the event of a breach of contract. A breach of a condition enables the party who is not in breach of contract ('the innocent party') *either* to terminate performance of the contract and obtain damages for any loss suffered as a result of the breach *or* to affirm the contract and recover damages for the breach. A breach of a warranty only enables the innocent party to claim damages; that is to say he cannot terminate performance of the contract and must therefore continue to perform his obligations under the contract. So if, in our example, the company wished to terminate the contract to purchase the car and to return the car to the sellers, it would be essential for it to show that the sellers had broken a condition of the contract because, if the sellers had only broken a warranty, it would be confined to a remedy in damages.

It may seem odd to discuss the classification of contractual terms at this stage in the book if the primary significance of the classification relates to breach of contract. However, the justification for doing so lies in the fact that the distinction is an important one in contract law and we shall encounter it on a number of occasions before we reach the chapter on breach of contract (Chapter 20).

10.2 What is a 'condition'?

Before embarking upon a more detailed discussion of the distinction between a condition and a warranty, it is necessary to deal with a preliminary point relating to the meaning of the word 'condition'. The word 'condition' can be used in a number of different senses and it is important to have a clear grasp of the meanings which contract lawyers ascribe to this word. In the first place it could mean some event upon which the existence of the contract hinges. Such conditions are commonly called contingent conditions. A contingent condition may be either a condition precedent or a condition subsequent. A condition precedent provides that the contract shall not become binding until the occurrence of a specified event (*Pym v Campbell* (1856) 6 E & B 370). For example, I enter into an agreement to buy a car but the agreement provides that it shall not become binding until the car passes a road test; if the car fails the road test no contract comes into existence. A condition subsequent provides that a previously binding contract shall come to an end on the occurrence of a stipulated event. So if I enter into a binding contract, supported by consideration, under which I promise to pay £100 a month to my granddaughter Emma until she gets married, the occurrence of her marriage will determine the contract between us. In both cases the effect of the occurrence of the condition is to terminate the agreement without either party being in breach of contract because, in the case of the condition precedent, neither party promised that the condition would be fulfilled and, in the case of the condition subsequent, neither party promised that the condition would not occur.

However, we are not concerned here with such contingent conditions; we are concerned with promissory conditions. A promissory condition is a term of a contract under which one party promises to do a particular thing, and a failure on his part to perform the promised act constitutes a breach of contract.

10.3 Distinguishing between a condition and a warranty

Having established that we are discussing promissory conditions, it is now necessary to explain how it is decided whether a term is a condition or a warranty. We shall approach this issue by examining the situations in which a term has been held to be a condition. A term may be held to be a condition in one of three ways: by statutory classification, by judicial classification or by the classification of the parties.

10.3.1 Classification by statute

Firstly, a term may be classified as a condition by statute. We have already noted (see Section 9.8) that sections 12 to 15 of the Sale of Goods Act 1979 imply certain terms into contracts for the sale of goods (other than a contract of sale between a trader and a consumer which falls within the scope of the Consumer Rights Act 2015). These sections also classify these implied terms; thus the implied terms as to satisfactory quality, fitness for purpose and compliance with description and sample are declared to be conditions, whereas the implied term that the goods are free from charges and incumbrances in favour of third parties is stated to be a warranty.

10.3.2 Classification by the courts

Secondly, a term may be classified as a condition by the courts. There are two grounds, apart from the stipulation of the parties, on which courts may decide that a term is a condition. The first is where performance of the term goes to the root of the contract so that, by necessary implication, the parties must have intended that the term should be treated as a condition, breach of which would entitle the other party to treat himself as discharged (see *Couchman v Hill* [1947] KB 544, discussed in Section 8.3). Although the term must go to the root of the contract, it need not be the case that every breach of the term should deprive the innocent party of substantially the whole benefit which it was intended that he would obtain from the contract (*Bunge Corp v Tradax Export SA* [1981] 1 WLR 711). When seeking to ascertain the significance of the term which has been broken, the courts will have regard to the views and practices of the commercial community. As Kerr LJ has stated, the court is, in the absence of any other 'more specific guide', making 'what is in effect a value judgment about the commercial significance of the term in question' (*State Trading Corp of India Ltd v M Golodetz Ltd* [1989] 2 Lloyd's Rep 277, 283). In particular, where a decision has been made by an experienced trade arbitrator or tribunal as to the status of a particular term and that decision is based upon the commercial significance of the term, the courts will be extremely reluctant to interfere with the finding of that arbitrator or tribunal (*State Trading Corp of India Ltd v M Golodetz Ltd* [1989] 2 Lloyd's Rep 277, 284 and *The Naxos* [1990] 1 WLR 1337, 1348).

The second ground on which a court may decide that a term is a condition is that binding authority requires the court to hold that the term is a condition. In some industries, parties trade on standard terms, and a decision that a particular standard term is a condition will affect not only that contract, but also all subsequent contracts of that type. Thus, a stipulation in a voyage charterparty relating to the time at which the vessel is expected ready to load is generally treated as a condition (*The Mihalis Angelos* [1971] 1 QB 164). The governing factor here is the need for certainty. But certainty carries with it a price. That price is that, in some cases, a party has been held to be entitled to terminate for breach of a condition, even though the breach has caused him little or no hardship. The most infamous example is, perhaps, *Arcos Ltd v E A Ronaasen & Son* [1933] AC 470. Timber, described in the contract as half an inch thick, was bought to be used in making cement barrels. The timber, as delivered, was 9/16 inch thick but this did not impair its utility for making cement barrels. Nevertheless, the buyers were held to be entitled to reject the timber, even though their motive in doing so was clearly that the market price for timber had fallen. As Professor Brownsword has stated (1992):

> the objection to the decision in *Arcos* is not so much that the buyers were allowed to act unreasonably or inefficiently by rejecting goods which they could use, but that they were allowed to reject such goods in order to take advantage of a falling market. In short, the objection is that the buyers acted in bad faith.

The buyers can be said to have acted in bad faith because the reason which they gave for exercising the right to terminate (the thickness of the timber) was not the 'real reason' and further that the 'real reason' was not attributable to the consequences of the breach but to the fact that they had entered into what had turned out to be a bad bargain. The courts are not presently concerned to ascertain the 'real reason' for the decision to terminate: as long as the party asserting the right to terminate does actually possess it, the courts will not inquire into the motives behind its assertion. Arguably, the courts are right to adopt this approach because of the cost and uncertainty which would be created by inquiries into the actual motives of the party seeking to exercise the right to terminate.

10.3.3 Classification by the parties

The third method of classification is the parties' own classification of the contractual term. Thus, if a contract states that a particular term is a condition, the term will generally be regarded as a condition. This ability to classify a term as a condition gives an extremely powerful weapon to contracting parties, as can be seen from the case of *Lombard North Central plc v Butterworth* [1987] QB 527. A contract for the hire of computers stated in clause 2 of the agreement that it was of the essence of the contract that the hirer should pay each instalment promptly. The hirer failed to pay certain instalments promptly, whereupon the owners retook possession of the computers and sued the hirer for damages. The Court of Appeal held that making punctual payment of the essence of the contract was sufficient to turn the failure to pay a single instalment into a repudiation of the contract, thus entitling the claimant owners to terminate the contract and recover, not only in respect of arrears as at the date of termination, but also the loss of future instalments (subject to a discount for accelerated receipt of the future rentals). The court held that there was no restriction upon the right of the parties to classify the relative importance of the terms of their contract. It has been objected that such a principle 'does not always lead to a desirable result' (Bojczuk, 1987) but Mustill LJ refused to subject such terms to the control of the penalty clause jurisdiction (see Section 22.5) on the ground that to do so would be 'to reverse the current of more than 100 years' doctrine, which permits the parties to treat as a condition something which would not otherwise be so'.

However, the court must be satisfied that the parties intended to use the word 'condition' in its technical sense. In *Schuler AG v Wickman Machine Tool Sales Ltd* [1974] AC 235, clause 7(b) of a four-year distributorship agreement stated that 'it shall be [a] condition of this agreement that [Wickman] shall send its representatives to visit [six named United Kingdom manufacturers] at least once in every week for the purpose of soliciting orders'. Wickman failed to make some visits to the named manufacturers. Schuler claimed that they were therefore entitled to terminate the agreement because Wickman had broken a 'condition' of the agreement. This argument was rejected by the House of Lords. Lord Reid held that the use of the word 'condition' was an 'indication', perhaps even a 'strong indication', that the parties intended the term to be a condition in the technical sense, but it was by no means 'conclusive' evidence. He held that the more unreasonable the consequences of treating a term as a condition in its technical sense, the less likely it was that the parties intended to use the word 'condition' in such a way. On the facts, the consequence that a 'failure to make even one visit' would entitle Schuler to terminate the contract 'however blameless Wickman might be' was so unreasonable that it compelled Lord Reid to interpret 'condition' in clause 7(b) in its non-technical sense. Lord Wilberforce dissented. He attacked the majority approach on the ground that it assumed, 'contrary to the evidence, that both parties … adopted a standard of easy-going tolerance rather than one of aggressive, insistent punctuality and efficiency'. There is much force in this criticism and *Schuler* has subsequently been referred to as the 'high-water mark' of the courts' reluctance to classify a term as a condition (*Heritage Oil and Gas Ltd v Tullow Uganda Ltd* [2014] EWCA Civ 1048; [2014] 2 CLC 61, [33]). Perhaps, at the end of the day, the vital factor in the case was that the contract was 'poorly drafted' so that the majority were able to employ this lack of clarity to justify their decision to refuse to adopt a construction which produced what was, in their view, an 'unreasonable' or 'absurd' result. Had the parties used the term 'condition' once and provided that 'it is a condition of this agreement that…' it is likely that the court would have concluded that the parties had used the word 'condition' in its technical sense (*Personal Touch Financial Services Ltd v Simplysure Ltd* [2016] EWCA Civ 461; [2016] Bus LR 1049, [28]).

Although contracting parties are free to create conditions by stipulating that performance of a particular obligation shall be of the essence of the contract, it is vital to note that *both parties* must agree to this classification before the term will enjoy the status of a condition. The position is entirely different where *one party* serves a notice on the other party purporting to make performance of a particular obligation 'of the essence of the contract'. Let us suppose that one party fails to comply with the terms of a warranty, thus giving rise only to a claim for damages. Can the innocent party give the party in breach notice requiring him to perform the obligation within a certain period of time, stating that a failure to do so will be regarded as a repudiatory breach giving rise to a right to terminate (thus making performance 'of the essence of the contract')? Two issues must be distinguished here. The first relates to the entitlement of the innocent party to serve such a notice; the second concerns the effect of the notice. In relation to the first issue, the innocent party is entitled to serve such a notice because the right to give notice is not confined to essential terms of the contract but can be exercised in relation to any term of the contract (*Behzadi v Shaftesbury Hotels Ltd* [1992] Ch 1). Notice can be served at the moment of breach: it is not necessary to wait for a reasonable time to elapse before serving it (see *Behzadi* (above)). The period of notice given must, however, be reasonable; an issue which depends upon all the facts and circumstances of the case. The vital issue is therefore the second one, namely the effect of such a notice. In *Re Olympia & York Canary Wharf Ltd (No 2)* [1993] BCC 159, Morritt J rejected the argument that a failure to comply with a 'time of the essence' notice was of itself sufficient to constitute a repudiation of the contract. It is suggested that this is correct because, if failure to comply did of itself amount to a repudiation it would, in effect, give to one party the power unilaterally to turn a non-essential term into an essential term. As Sir Terence Etherton C observed in *Urban 1 (Blonk Street) Ltd v Ayres* [2013] EWCA Civ 816; [2014] 1 WLR 756, [44] 'it is contrary to all principle for one party to be able unilaterally to transform one type of contractual provision (namely, an innominate term or a warranty in the strict sense) into something different (namely, a condition in the strict sense)'. There is therefore all the difference in the world between a term which both parties agree to classify as a condition and a term which both parties agree to classify as a warranty but one party purports unilaterally to elevate to the status of a condition. A breach of the former will give to the innocent party a right to terminate the contract, whereas a breach of the latter will not (*Samarenko v Dawn Hill House Ltd* [2011] EWCA Civ 1445; [2013] Ch 36, [65]). The function of a 'time of the essence' notice is therefore limited: a failure to comply in respect of a non-essential term will not constitute a repudiation of the contract but at most will provide evidence from which a court may be prepared to infer that a repudiatory breach has occurred.

10.4 The need for change?

It can be seen that the primary emphasis in these cases has been upon the importance of the *term* which has been broken rather than upon the importance of the *consequences of the breach* of that term. The result has been that, in cases such as *Arcos Ltd v E A Ronaasen & Son* (above), a term has been classified as a condition even though the consequences of breach were insignificant. The justification for this approach is, firstly, that the parties must be free to classify the relative importance of their own contractual terms (see *Lombard North Central v Butterworth* (above)) and, secondly, the need for certainty in commercial transactions. Certainty can be achieved most effectively by deciding whether or not a term is a condition according to the nature of the term broken, not by requiring the parties to wait and examine the consequences of the breach before deciding whether or not they are sufficiently serious to justify the classification of the term as a condition. The cause of certainty is further advanced by the fact that, once a term is classified as a condition, the innocent party is, unless barred by estoppel, by his election to affirm the contract (on which see Section 20.8), or by statute (see section 15A of the Sale of Goods Act 1979, below), automatically entitled to terminate performance of the contract. But it is important not to overstate the certainty which is achieved by classifying a term as a condition. It is true that, once a term has been classified as a condition a significant measure of certainty is thereby achieved, but uncertainty can still arise in relation to the prior question of whether the term which has been broken is actually a condition. For example, in *The Naxos* [1990] 1 WLR 1337 a majority of the House of Lords held that the obligation of the seller to have the cargo ready for delivery at any time within the contract period was a condition, whereas a majority of the Court of Appeal and the first instance judge were of the opinion that it was not. This uncertainty is, however, largely confined to previously unclassified terms and, while it should not be ignored, it should not detract from the principal point which is that the classification of a term as a condition does give rise to a greater degree of certainty in commercial transactions.

But the cost of this emphasis on the need to promote certainty is an element of injustice, in cases such as *Arcos v Ronaasen* (above), where the motive for terminating the contract was that the contract had turned out to be a bad bargain for the innocent party. Such injustice could be largely avoided if the critical factor in deciding whether a term was a condition (and hence whether the innocent party was entitled to terminate performance of the contract) was to become the consequences of the breach (a point acknowledged by Beatson LJ in *Heritage Oil and Gas Ltd v Tullow Uganda Ltd* [2014] EWCA Civ 1048; [2014] 2 CLC 61, [33]). Then the innocent party would only be entitled to terminate performance of the contract where the consequences to him of the breach were sufficiently serious (indeed there was authority for such a proposition in the early case of *Boone v Eyre* (1777) 1 H Bl 273, before the emphasis switched to the importance of the term which had been broken in cases such as *Behn v Burness* (1863) 3 B & S 751 and *Bettini v Gye* (1876) 1 QBD 183). Yet the cost of such a shift in emphasis would be the sacrifice of a degree of certainty.

A further criticism which has been levelled against too great a willingness to classify a term as a condition is that it encourages termination of contracts rather than their performance. As Roskill LJ stated in *The Hansa Nord* [1976] QB 44:

> in principle, contracts are made to be performed and not to be avoided according to the whims of market fluctuation and where there is a free choice between two possible constructions I think the court should tend to prefer that construction which will ensure performance, and not encourage avoidance of contractual obligations.

The Hansa Nord was a case, like *Arcos v Ronaasen*, where the buyer was searching for a way out of a bad bargain and it is true that, in this context, a refusal to classify a term as a condition is more likely to lead to contractual performance. But in other contexts this is not so. The classification of a term as a condition can give an incentive to a would-be contract-breaker to perform his obligations under the contract because breach will expose him to a claim for loss of bargain damages. The hirer in *Lombard North Central plc v Butterworth* (above) will, presumably, take greater steps to perform his obligations under any future contract of hire he may conclude, knowing the draconian consequences which can follow from breach of a condition. In this sense, classification of a term as a condition could be said to act as an incentive to performance rather than termination. So this argument, ultimately, is not convincing and it is the apparent injustice of cases such as *Arcos v Ronaasen* which is the real basis for arguments for reform.

So, in this context, what we have is, essentially, a conflict between the interests of 'certainty' and the interests of 'justice' or 'fairness'. 'Certainty' requires the focus to be upon the nature of the term broken and demands a high degree of remedial rigidity. 'Justice', on the other hand, requires the focus to be on the consequences of the breach and demands a high degree of remedial flexibility. The generally accepted view was that, in cases such as *Arcos v Ronaasen*, the pendulum had swung too far in favour of the promotion of certainty and that it was time to redress the balance.

10.4.1 Limiting the number of terms that may be classified as conditions

In seeking to redress the balance, three approaches have been adopted. The first is to seek to limit the number of terms which are classified as conditions. Thus, in *Reardon Smith Line Ltd v Hansen Tangen* [1976] 1 WLR 989, Lord Wilberforce stated that some of the authorities which we have discussed were 'excessively technical and due for fresh examination' by the House of Lords. But these cases still await 'fresh examination' and it is unlikely that this line of approach will be further developed.

10.4.2 Section 15A of the Sale of Goods Act 1979

The second approach has been to address the fact situation in *Arcos v Ronaasen* directly and place a statutory restriction upon the right of a buyer to reject goods. This has been done by section 15A of the Sale of Goods Act 1979 which states in subsection (1) that where the buyer would, apart from this subsection, have the right to reject goods by reason of a breach on the part of the seller of a term implied by sections 13 to 15 of the Sale of Goods Act 1979, but the breach is so slight that it would be unreasonable for him to reject them, the breach is not to be treated as a breach of a condition but may be treated as a breach of warranty. Thus the buyer in such a case would be confined to a claim in damages. It is for the seller to show that the breach is slight so as to preclude the buyer from rejecting the goods (s 15A(3)). At first sight this provision seems apt to encompass the fact situation in *Arcos v Ronaasen*, but in fact it all depends upon the meaning to be given to the word 'slight'. As Treitel points out (2020, para 18-060) 'the difference between half an inch and 9/16 of an inch is by no means obviously "slight" (at least as a proportion)' and if it is not slight the buyer is not deprived of his right to reject no matter how unreasonable his decision to reject. This new provision is also limited in that it only applies to a breach by the seller of one of the terms implied by sections 13 to 15 of the 1979 Act: it has no application to a breach by the seller of section 12 of the Act, to the breach of an express term of the contract and it has no application whatsoever to the seller's right to terminate following a breach by the buyer. Some attempt has been made to preserve certainty by enacting that the new restriction shall apply 'unless a contrary intention appears in, or is to be implied from the contract' (s 15A(2)). The meaning to be given to section 15A(2) is not initially obvious, but it is intended to exclude from the reform clauses such as time clauses where it is generally accepted that a breach should give rise to a right to terminate (see Section 10.5). Notwithstanding the inclusion of section 15A(2), the effect of this reform is to take away a degree of certainty in commercial transactions but the limits to which it is subject (particularly the exclusion of seller termination following buyer breach) make it hard to resist the conclusion of Treitel (2020, para 18-061) that the section is 'an unfortunate provision which manages to fall between two stools' in that it 'undermines' certainty but 'scarcely goes far enough to promote justice'.

10.4.3 Focus attention on the consequences of the breach

The third approach is one of more general application and it has been to focus more attention on the consequences of the breach and thereby to give the courts greater remedial flexibility. This has been achieved through the recognition of the fact that the distinction between a condition and a warranty is not an exhaustive one.

10.5 Innominate terms

A third classification has now been recognised in English law: the intermediate or the innominate term. The origin of this development can be found in the judgment of Diplock LJ in *Hong Kong Fir Shipping Co Ltd v Kawasaki Kisen Kaisha Ltd* [1962] 2 QB 26, 70 when he said:

> There are many ... contractual undertakings ... which cannot be categorised as being 'conditions' or 'warranties'. ... Of such undertakings all that can be predicated is that some breaches will and others will not give rise to an event which will deprive the party not in default of substantially the whole benefit which it was intended that he should obtain.

An innominate term can be distinguished from a condition on the ground that breach of an innominate term does not automatically give rise to a right to terminate performance of the contract and it can be distinguished from a warranty on the ground that the innocent party is not confined to a remedy in damages. Thus the court is given a greater degree of remedial flexibility and it can focus attention on the consequences of the breach by allowing a party to terminate performance of the contract only where the breach of the innominate term has had serious consequences for him. Yet it is this remedial flexibility which is, itself, problematic because one can never be entirely sure whether one has the right to terminate when faced with a breach by the other party. In deciding whether or not the breach was of a sufficiently serious character the courts will have regard to all the relevant circumstances of the case. Carter (2012) has helpfully identified the following factors which are relied upon by the courts: (i) any detriment caused, or likely to be caused, by the breach; (ii) any delay caused, or likely to be caused, by the breach; (iii) the value of any performance received by or tendered to the party not in breach; (iv) the cost of making any performance given or tendered by the party in breach conform with the requirements of the contract; (v) any opportunity 'enjoyed' by the party in breach to remedy the discrepancies in its performance; (vi) the consequences of any prior breach of the contract by the party in breach and whether further breaches were a likely consequence of the breach at issue; and (vii) whether the party not in breach will be adequately compensated by an award of damages in respect of the breach. Not only is this list of factors extremely broad, but the weight which is accorded to each one must depend, to a large extent, on the facts of the case. The uncertainty thereby caused is important because, if a contracting party gets it wrong and purports to terminate when he was not in fact entitled to do so (because the breach was not repudiatory), he will be held to have repudiated his obligations under the contract and may be liable to pay substantial damages in consequence. Uncertainty can carry with it a real price.

10.5.1 Making the wrong call

A case in which that price was paid is *Ampurius Nu Homes Holdings Ltd v Telford Homes (Creekside) Ltd* [2013] EWCA Civ 577; [2013] 4 All ER 377. The parties entered into a development contract in 2008 under which the defendant undertook to procure that the works were carried out with due diligence. As a result of the financial downturn in 2009, the defendant was unable to obtain the finance required to develop two of the four blocks. It therefore stopped work on these blocks in June 2009 and was not able to resume the works until 4 October 2010 when it obtained the necessary funding. The claimant purported to terminate the contract on 22 October 2010 but it was held that it was not entitled to do so.

Although the defendant had breached its duty to procure that the works were carried out with due diligence, the consequences of the breach were held not to be sufficiently serious to entitle the claimant to terminate the contract. The Court of Appeal acknowledged that the bar is 'set high' when deciding whether the consequences of the breach are sufficiently serious to entitle the innocent party to terminate the contract and that the claimant had failed to clear the bar on the facts of the case. When deciding whether the claimant had been deprived of substantially the whole benefit of the contract, consideration was to be given to the circumstances as at the date on which the claimant purported to terminate the contract (that is, 22 October 2010). The court considered the benefits it was intended that the claimant would obtain from performance of the contract and the effect of the defendant's breach on the claimant. As at 22 October 2010 the defendant had resumed work on the project so that the effect of the breach was not to postpone the contract indefinitely but to delay the project by a number of months, the consequences of which could be made good by an award of damages. The benefit which it was intended that the claimant would obtain from performance of the contract was the grant of a 999-year lease. Viewed from the perspective of that long-term benefit, the delay which had occurred was not particularly significant and it certainly did not deprive the claimant of substantially the whole benefit of the contract. This being the case, the claimant had itself repudiated the contract in purporting to terminate the contract when it was not entitled to do so and it was liable in damages accordingly. In a case such as *Ampurius* it is important to distinguish between two different types of loss that are said to flow from the breach. The first is the loss suffered at the time of the purported termination. This is capable of proof as a matter of fact. The second is loss subsequent to the date of the purported termination, for example the loss of profit that the innocent party claims it would have made on the contract had it run for its full term. Given that the existence or otherwise of loss of the latter type depends upon future events, it cannot be proved as a matter of historical fact but will depend upon the evidence as to the likely future course of events. In the case where the loss at the date of the purported termination is not sufficiently serious of itself to entitle the innocent party to terminate the contract, its entitlement to terminate will depend upon proof of the likely future course of events and their impact on the innocent party. In such a case, it is no easy task for such a party to prove its entitlement to terminate the contract (particularly in the case where the other party leads evidence to the effect that it would have performed its future obligations in accordance the terms of the contract had it not been terminated), although it is not impossible (*Phones 4U Ltd (in administration) v EE Ltd* [2018] EWHC 49 (Comm); [2018] 1 Lloyd's Rep 204).

10.5.2 Distinguishing between an innominate term, a condition and a warranty

The creation of this new category of innominate terms leaves us with the further difficulty of distinguishing between an innominate term, a condition and a warranty. In practice, classification of a term as a warranty is rare but such a classification is not entirely without significance. A party who is in breach of contract may wish to argue that the term which has been broken is a warranty rather than an innominate term so as to restrict the innocent party to a remedy in damages and to deprive him of the ability to terminate. Contracting parties are free to classify terms as warranties, just as they are free to classify terms as conditions, but if they wish to confine a term to the status of a warranty, they should 'make it plain from the contract as a whole' that that is their intention (*Re Olympia & York Canary Wharf Ltd (No 2)* [1993] BCC 159, 166). If the contract states that the term is a condition then, subject to *Schuler AG v Wickman Machine Tool Sales Ltd* [1974] AC 235, it will be treated as a condition. A term will also be regarded as a condition where it is classified as such by statute. Where the term has been previously classified by the judiciary as a condition, then it is likely that the term will generally continue to be regarded as a condition. The principal difficulty is likely to arise in connection with previously unclassified terms.

At this point we return to the conflict which we have noted between the interests of 'certainty' and 'justice'. If primary attention is given to considerations of fairness, this will favour classification of terms as innominate terms because the remedy can be tailored to the facts of the case. On the other hand, an approach which gives primary attention to considerations of certainty will favour classification as a condition because the remedial consequences will then be clear. It cannot be said that the courts have resolved this conflict in clear terms and, indeed, it may not be appropriate for them to do so. Rather, what is called for is a balancing exercise which requires the court to evaluate the competing policy considerations and to assess their weight on the facts and circumstances of the individual case (see, for example, *Grand China Logistics Holding (Group) Co Ltd v Spar Shipping AS* [2016] EWCA Civ 982; [2016] 2 Lloyd's Rep 447). There are signs that the courts do engage in such a balancing exercise and further that they do sometimes disagree when doing so (a good example is provided by *Ark Shipping Company LLC v Silverburn Shipping (IoM) Ltd* [2019] EWCA Civ 1161; [2019] 2 Lloyd's Rep 603 where Carr J, at first instance, concluded that the term in issue between the parties was a condition term but the Court of Appeal held that it was an innominate term).

10.5.3 A term is innominate unless the contrary is made clear

In so far as it is possible to detect a general pattern in the cases it can be said that the courts have been rather reluctant to find that a term is a condition unless there is clear evidence to justify such a conclusion. Support for this proposition can be gleaned from the leading case of *Bunge Corp v Tradax Export SA* [1981] 1 WLR 711 (above), albeit that, on the facts of the case, the House of Lords concluded that the term was a condition on the basis that the courts have generally taken a strict approach to time stipulations in commercial contracts and held them to be of the essence of the contract. Notwithstanding this conclusion on the facts of the case, Lord Wilberforce said that 'the courts should not be too ready to interpret contractual clauses as conditions'. As Hamblen LJ observed in *Grand China Logistics Holding (Group) Co Ltd v Spar Shipping AS* [2016] EWCA Civ 982; [2016] 2 Lloyd's Rep 447, [93] 'the modern approach is that a term is innominate unless a contrary intention is made clear.' This suggests that, apart from terms which are commercially vital where the need for certainty is greatest, greater consideration will be given to the interests of 'justice' by classifying contract terms as innominate terms in order to give the courts flexibility in granting the appropriate relief (*Heritage Oil and Gas Ltd v Tullow Uganda Ltd* [2014] EWCA Civ 1048; [2014] 2 CLC 61, [33]).

A good example is provided by *The Hansa Nord* [1976] QB 44, a case which bears some resemblance to *Arcos Ltd v E A Ronaasen & Son* [1933] AC 470 (and which would now fall within the Sale of Goods Act 1979, s 15A if the consequences of the breach were 'slight': see Section 10.4). Buyers of citrus pulp purported to reject the cargo on the ground that shipment was not made in 'good condition'. The price of the cargo was £100,000. The sellers were compelled to sell the cargo, and the buyers, acting through an agent, managed to repurchase it for £30,000 and they were able to use the citrus pulp for its original intended purpose. The Court of Appeal held that the term which had been broken was not a condition and, applying *Hong Kong Fir*, they concluded that the term was an innominate one and that the consequences of the breach were not sufficiently serious to give rise to a right to reject the goods. The buyers were therefore confined to a claim in damages to reflect the loss in value of the cargo caused by its defective state. On this approach, the injustice of cases such as *Arcos v Ronaasen* need no longer occur.

Hot topic 9...

Why might it be important for a party to draft a term of a contract as a condition? There are two principal reasons. First, any breach of a condition gives to the innocent party a right to terminate further performance of the contract. Second, a breach of a condition is a repudiatory breach which will entitle the innocent party to recover damages on a loss of bargain basis. The importance of these points can be seen from the recent decision of the Court of Appeal in *Grand China Logistics Holding (Group) Co Ltd v Spar Shipping AS* [2016] EWCA Civ 982; [2016] 2 Lloyd's Rep 447. The defendant failed to pay hire as it fell due under a time charterparty. One of the issues before the court was whether the failure to pay hire punctually was a breach of a condition. The Court of Appeal, having regard to a range of factors, concluded that it was not. The parties had not expressly described it as a condition and the modern approach is to treat a term as innominate unless a contrary intention has been made clear. A further factor is that time of payment is not generally a condition of the contract and it is for this reason that commercial parties frequently insert into their contract a term making time of payment of the essence of the contract (although this was not done on the present facts). Thus a failure to pay a single instalment of hire did not amount to a repudiatory breach. However, the claimant was able to establish that the defendant had renounced the contract as a result of its repeated inability to pay hire on time in the past and its prospective inability to pay on time in the future. Of course, the task of proving a renunciation was much more onerous than proving a failure to pay a single instalment of hire. Had the claimant taken the time to ensure that the time of payment of hire was a condition of the contract its route to establishing a repudiatory breach would have been much easier than in fact proved to be the case.

Summary

- ▶ Contract terms can be classified either as conditions, warranties or innominate terms.

- ▶ A condition is an essential term of the contract which goes to the root or the heart of the contract. This is a promissory condition which must be distinguished from a contingent condition, which is some event upon which the existence of the contract hinges. A contingent condition may be either a condition precedent or a condition subsequent.

- ▶ A term may be classified as a promissory condition by statute, by judicial classification or by the classification of the parties. In the latter category the court must be satisfied that the parties intended to use the word 'condition' in its technical sense.

- ▶ Breach of a promissory condition entitles the innocent party either to terminate performance of the contract and claim damages or to affirm the contract and claim damages.

- ▶ A warranty is a lesser, subsidiary term of the contract. Breach of a warranty only gives a remedy in damages.

- ▶ The category of innominate terms was recognised by the Court of Appeal in *Hong Kong Fir Shipping Co Ltd v Kawasaki Kisen Kaisha Ltd* [1962] 2 QB 26.

- ▶ An innominate term can be distinguished from a condition on the ground that breach of an innominate term does not automatically give rise to a right to terminate performance of the contract, and it can be distinguished from a warranty on the ground that the innocent party's remedy is not confined to damages. Classification as an innominate term therefore gives the court an important degree of remedial flexibility.

Exercises

10.1 Distinguish between a 'promissory condition' and a 'contingent condition'.

10.2 When will a term be classified as a promissory condition?

10.3 What are the remedial consequences of classifying a term as

(a)   condition;

(b)   a warranty; and

(c)   an innominate term?

Chapter 11

Exclusion clauses

An exclusion clause may be defined as a 'clause in a contract or a term in a notice which appears to exclude or restrict a liability or a legal duty which would otherwise arise' (Yates, 1982, 1). Exclusion clauses are a common feature of contracts today and may take a number of different forms. The most frequently encountered types of exclusion clauses are those which seek to exclude liability for breach of contract or for negligence or which seek to limit liability to a specified sum. Another type of clause commonly encountered is an indemnity clause, under which one contracting party promises to indemnify or reimburse the other for any liability incurred by him in the performance of the contract (for a description of other types of exclusion clauses see Yates, 1982, 33–41).

11.1 Exclusion clauses: defence or definition?

Despite the common occurrence of exclusion clauses in contracts, differing views remain as to their essential nature. Let us take an example to illustrate the point. John, who presently lives in Colchester, wishes to have his furniture transported to his new house in Preston and for this purpose he contracts with Peter. Peter, who is self-employed, offers a price which is substantially lower than any other removal firm because he offers no insurance cover for the goods while they are in transit; instead he relies on the owner of the goods either to use his existing insurance policy (if it is applicable) or to take out his own special insurance policy. In order to give effect to his pricing policy Peter inserts a clause into his contracts to the following effect: 'no liability is accepted for any damage, howsoever caused, to any goods during the course of transit'. Two views may be adopted as to the function of such a clause.

One view holds that this clause simply defines the obligations which the contracting parties have chosen to accept. Peter has only accepted a limited obligation to transmit the goods and has never accepted any liability for damage to the goods during the course of transit. On this view, the function of the exclusion clause is to assist in *defining* the obligations of the parties. This view is not, however, the one which the courts have traditionally adopted. Courts have traditionally seen exclusion clauses as performing a defensive function. On this view a failure by Peter to deliver the goods safely to Preston constitutes a breach of contract and the role of the exclusion clause is to provide Peter with a *defence* to John's action for breach of contract.

Yet a closer examination of this traditional view reveals a serious difficulty. The difficulty is that Peter has not accepted an absolute obligation to deliver John's goods; such a conclusion could only be reached by ignoring the exclusion clause when defining Peter's obligations. But why should the exclusion clause be ignored in defining Peter's obligations, when it is via the exclusion clause that Peter has sought to define the extent of his obligations and it is only by this means that he can offer a service at a price lower than that of his competitors? There can surely be no justification for ignoring the exclusion clause in this manner. The clause is simply one means, albeit an important one, by which Peter has attempted to *define* his obligations. If this view of exclusion clauses is accepted, the justification for subjecting exclusion clauses to distinct regulation largely disappears because such clauses then become functionally indistinguishable from every other term of the contract which assists in defining the obligations which the parties have accepted towards each other (this theory was initially developed by Coote, 1964, and is also supported by Yates, 1982).

The argument that exclusion clauses define the obligations of the parties has been attacked by Adams and Brownsword (1988a) on the ground that it is 'elegantly formalistic' and that it ignores 'both the historical development of the problem, and the realities of the situation'. The 'historical development' is that the growth in the use of standard form contracts has been accompanied by a growth in the use of exclusion clauses and the 'realities' of the situation are that such terms are offered on a 'take it or leave it basis'. In short, these standard form contracts, which so often include sweeping exclusion clauses, are imposed on the weaker party to the transaction. They take away the rights of the weaker party and nullify his expectations rather than define the obligations of the parties. But it is only by looking outside the contract for the initial existence of these 'rights' or 'expectations' that exclusion clauses can be said to 'take away' the 'rights' of the weaker party or nullify his 'expectations'. These 'rights' and 'expectations' must exist outside the contract because the contract as a whole certainly did not confer them upon the weaker party. How then are we to ascertain the scope of these 'rights' or 'expectations'? Are they to be found in some conception of 'public policy'? Proponents of the 'defensive' view of exclusion clauses do not tell us. Surely the evil which we are seeking to eradicate is not the existence of exclusion clauses or even simply the existence of 'unreasonable exclusion clauses', but the existence of 'unfair' terms in a contract. If this is so, then the correct approach must be to deal with exclusion clauses as part of a general doctrine of inequality of bargaining power or 'unconscionability' (see further Chapter 17) and not by the artificial and misleading process of subjecting exclusion clauses to distinct regulation on the basis that they are a defence to a breach of an obligation. Notwithstanding the force of this criticism, the courts and Parliament have generally treated exclusion clauses as a defence to a breach of an obligation.

11.2 The functions of exclusion clauses

Before embarking upon an analysis of the detailed rules of law, we must identify the different functions of exclusion clauses. Exclusion clauses perform a number of useful functions. First, they help in the allocation of risks under the contract. In our example involving Peter and John the risk of damage to the goods is clearly allocated to John and there is no need for Peter to take out insurance cover; double insurance is thereby avoided. Secondly, exclusion clauses can help reduce litigation costs by making clear the division of responsibility between the parties. Thirdly, exclusion clauses are often used in standard form contracts which, by enabling people, such as Peter, to mass-produce their contracts, helps reduce the cost of negotiations and of making contracts.

On the other hand, exclusion clauses can perform a function which is socially harmful in that, as we have already seen, they can be used by the powerful in society to exclude liability towards the weaker party, thereby leaving the weak without a remedy. It is this socially undesirable function of exclusion clauses which has provided significant impetus for reform of this area of law and which explains the restrictive approach which the courts have adopted in their treatment of exclusion clauses.

11.3　An outline of the law

A contracting party who wishes to include an exclusion clause in a contract must overcome three hurdles before he can do so. First, it must be shown that the exclusion clause is properly incorporated into the contract (Section 11.4). Secondly, it must be shown that, properly interpreted, the exclusion clause covers the loss which has arisen (Sections 11.5–11.7). Thirdly, there must be no other rule of law which would invalidate the exclusion clause (Sections 11.8–11.14).

Historically, it was the first two of these three stages which were important. The principal explanation for this is that, although at common law the court has power to strike down contract terms which are 'contrary to public policy' (see Sections 15.6–15.16), it did not have the power to hold exclusion clauses invalid because they were unreasonable (despite arguments to the contrary by Lord Denning in cases such as *Levison v Patent Steam Carpet Cleaning Co Ltd* [1978] QB 68). Deprived of the ability to strike down unreasonable exclusion clauses by such direct means, the courts sought to achieve such a goal by the indirect means of adopting a restrictive approach towards the incorporation (Sections 9.4 and 11.4) and the interpretation (Sections 11.5–11.7) of exclusion clauses. Lord Denning recognised this in *Gillespie Bros v Roy Bowles Ltd* [1973] 1 QB 400, 415 when he said that

> judges have ... time after time, sanctioned a departure from the ordinary meaning. They have done it under the guise of 'construing' the clause. They assume that the party cannot have intended anything so unreasonable. So they construe the clause 'strictly'. They cut down the ordinary meaning of the words and reduce them to reasonable proportions. They use all their skill and art to that end.

But now that the courts have been given power under the Unfair Contract Terms Act 1977 (UCTA) and the Consumer Rights Act 2015 to regulate exclusion clauses, there is less need for them to use the first two stages to control unreasonable exclusion clauses. However, as we shall see, the first two stages still have the potential to create difficulty for a party seeking to rely upon an exclusion or a limitation clause.

11.4　Incorporation

At the first stage it must be shown that the exclusion or limitation clause was validly incorporated into the contract. Here the reader should refer to the discussion of incorporation in Section 9.4. Of particular note in this context is the principle set out in *Interfoto Picture Library Ltd v Stiletto Visual Programmes Ltd* [1989] QB 433 relating to the incorporation of onerous or unusual terms. While not every exclusion or limitation clause is an onerous or an unusual term (see *Shepherd Homes Ltd v Encia Remediation*

Ltd [2007] EWHC 70 (TCC); [2007] BLR 135), the principle does have the potential to apply to widely drafted exclusion or limitation clauses. Has this principle survived the enactment of the Unfair Contract Terms Act 1977? The Court of Appeal answered this question in the affirmative in *Goodlife Foods Ltd v Hall Fire Protection Ltd* [2018] EWCA Civ 1371; [2018] BLR 491, [35] where Coulson LJ observed that the incorporation of a term at common law and the reasonableness of a term under the 1977 Act are 'separate' and 'distinct' issues, albeit there 'may be some overlap in the matters that fall to be considered under each principle'. For this reason, a contracting party who wishes to incorporate an exclusion or limitation clause into a contract would be well advised to take care to ensure that the term is properly incorporated, given that a failure to incorporate the term will have the consequence that there is no limit on the liability of that party in the event of it being in breach of contract.

11.5 Construction of exclusion clauses

At the second stage it must be shown that the exclusion or limitation clause, properly interpreted or properly construed, covers the damage which was caused. Had the courts adopted a definitional approach to exclusion clauses then such clauses would have been subject to the same rules of interpretation as any other term of the contract. But one consequence of the courts' adoption of the defensive approach to exclusion clauses has been that exclusion clauses have not been interpreted in the same way as other terms of the contract; they have been interpreted more rigorously or restrictively.

The traditional approach which the courts adopted to the interpretation of exclusion clauses was a restrictive one, under which the exclusion clause was interpreted strictly against the party seeking to rely on it. This rule is called the *contra proferentem* rule. The effect of the rule is that any ambiguity in the exclusion clause is resolved against the party seeking to rely on it. Although the *contra proferentem* rule is applicable to any ambiguous term in a contract, it was in the past applied particularly stringently to exclusion clauses. However, the future of the *contra proferentem* rule may be in some doubt. In *The Federal Republic of Nigeria v JP Morgan Chase Bank NA* [2019] EWHC 347 (Comm); [2019] 1 CLC 207, [34] three reasons were given for the limited role now played by the rule in English law. The first is that there is some doubt about who, for this purpose, is the *proferens*? Is it the party who drafted the clause or simply the party who is relying on the clause? The answer would appear to be the latter (see *Scottish Special Housing Association v Wimpey Construction UK Ltd* 1986 SLT 173) but the point is not entirely free from doubt. The second is that 'the modern objective and contextual approach to the meaning of words, with business common sense and purpose also being relevant in some cases, renders it unnecessary to regard there as being a separate *contra proferentem* rule.' The third is that 'the force of what was the *contra proferentem* rule is embraced by recognising that a party is unlikely to have agreed to give up a valuable right that it would otherwise have had without clear words.' Thus the modern emphasis may be on the need to use clear words if liability is effectively to be excluded rather than insistence upon the continued existence of the *contra proferentem* rule. .

One consequence of the application of the traditional, restrictive approach to the interpretation of exclusion and limitation clauses has been a game of 'cat and mouse' between contract draftsmen and the courts, as draftsmen have sought to evade the restrictive interpretations adopted by the courts. This can be illustrated by reference to the following two cases. In *Wallis, Son and Wells v Pratt and Haynes* [1911] AC 394, a contract for the sale of seeds contained a clause which stated that the sellers gave 'no warranty express or implied' as to the description of the seeds. The seeds did not correspond with the description so the buyers brought an action for damages against the sellers, who sought to rely on the exclusion clause. It was held that they could not do so because it only covered breach of a 'warranty' and, in failing to provide seeds which corresponded with the description, the sellers had broken a condition (the distinction between a condition and a warranty is discussed in Section 10.1). The impact of this ruling can be seen in *Andrews Bros (Bournemouth) Ltd v Singer and Co Ltd* [1934] 1 KB 17. This time the exclusion clause stated that 'all conditions, warranties and liabilities *implied* by statute, common law or otherwise are excluded'. The claimants contracted with the defendants to buy some 'new Singer cars'. One of the cars delivered by the defendants was a used car. The claimants sued for damages and the defendants sought, unsuccessfully, to rely on the exclusion clause. Greer LJ said that the defendants were probably trying to escape the effect of *Wallis* but the only problem was that, although they had included the word 'condition', they had omitted the word 'express' and this was fatal because the court held that the defendants had broken an express term of the contract.

It continues to be a dangerous practice to rely upon a clause which states that 'the seller gives no warranty express or implied …' or that 'the goods are not warranted free from defect …' because such a term may be held not to encompass a breach of a condition. An illustration of these dangers is provided by the decision of the Court of Appeal in *KG Bominflot Bunkergesellschaft Für Mineralöle mnH & Co v Petroplus Marketing AG (The 'Mercini Lady')* [2010] EWCA Civ 1145; [2011] 1 Lloyd's Rep 442 where the words 'no guarantees, warranties or representations, express or implied, [of] merchantability, fitness or suitability of the oil' were held not to be effective to exclude liability for breach of the implied condition that goods be of satisfactory quality. But there is no rule of law which requires the use of the word 'condition' in order to exclude liability for breach of a condition. In each case it is a question of construction of the particular clause and, where the words are broad enough to encompass a breach of a condition (for example, 'all other … obligations … or liabilities express or implied arising by law'), a court may conclude that the term is effective to exclude liability for breach of a condition notwithstanding the failure to make express reference to the word 'condition' (see *Air Transworld Ltd v Bombardier Inc* [2012] EWHC 243 (Comm); [2012] 1 Lloyd's Rep 349). Nevertheless, the safest course remains to make express reference to the exclusion of liability for breach of a condition if the intention is to exclude liability for such a breach.

While it remains the case that it is necessary to draft clearly when drafting an exclusion or limitation clause, there are signs that the strict approach of former years has been largely abandoned, at least in cases where the parties to the contract are experienced commercial organisations who have access to skilled legal advice (see *Transocean Drilling UK Ltd v Providence Resources plc* [2016] EWCA Civ 372; [2016] 2 Lloyd's Rep 51; *Persimmon Homes Ltd v Ove Arup & Partners Ltd* [2017] EWCA Civ 373; [2017] BLR 417, [52]). In *Ailsa Craig Fishing Co Ltd v Malvern Fishing Co Ltd* [1983]

1 WLR 964, the House of Lords held that, in the case of limitation clauses, the *contra proferentem* rule did not apply with the same rigour as in the case of exclusion clauses. Lord Fraser and Lord Wilberforce said that limitation clauses were not viewed with the same hostility as exclusion clauses because of their role in risk allocation and because it was more likely that the other party would agree to a limitation clause than an exclusion clause. This approach is open to the objection that it ignores the risk allocation function of exclusion clauses and it is by no means certain that the other party would be more willing to agree to a limitation clause, especially where the limit is derisory (see Palmer, 1982). As Evans LJ observed in *BHP Petroleum Ltd v British Steel plc* [2000] 2 Lloyd's Rep 277, 285:

> I think it is unfortunate if the present authorities cannot be reconciled on the basis that no categorization is necessary and of a general rule that the more extreme the consequences are, in terms of excluding or modifying the liability which would otherwise arise, then the more stringent the Court's approach should be in requiring that the exclusion or limit should be clearly and unambiguously expressed. Indeed, if the requirement is of a clear and unambiguous provision, then it is not easy to see why degrees of clarity and lack of unambiguity should be recognised.

This approach seems preferable in that it avoids rigid categorisation and instead adopts a sliding-scale. However, it would appear that the distinction between a limitation clause and an exclusion clause remains part of English law because the decision in *Ailsa Craig* was followed by the House of Lords in *George Mitchell (Chesterhall) Ltd v Finney Lock Seeds Ltd* [1983] 2 AC 803. On the other hand, the High Court of Australia in *Darlington Futures Ltd v Delco Australia Pty Ltd* (1987) 61 ALJR 76, has refused to differentiate between exclusion clauses and limitation clauses in this manner. Instead the court held that:

> the interpretation of an exclusion clause is to be determined by construing the clause according to its natural and ordinary meaning, read in the light of the contract as a whole, thereby giving due weight to the context in which the clause appears including the nature and the object of the contract and, where appropriate, construing the clause *contra proferentem* in case of ambiguity.

This approach is to be welcomed in so far as it adopts a more natural interpretation of exclusion clauses.

Some support for a more clement approach can also be found in some English cases. As we have already noted (Section 9.6), in *Photo Production Ltd v Securicor Transport Ltd* [1980] AC 827, Lord Diplock said that 'the reports are full of cases in which what would appear to be very strained constructions have been placed upon exclusion clauses'. He noted that many of these cases involved consumer contracts and continued, 'any need for this kind of judicial distortion of the English language has been banished by Parliament's having made these kinds of contract subject to the Unfair Contract Terms Act 1977'. Lord Hoffmann adopted a similar approach in *Bank of Credit and Commerce International SA v Ali* [2001] UKHL 8; [2002] 1 AC 251 (Section 9.6) when he stated (at [60]) that

> the lesson which I would draw from the development of the rules for construing exemption clauses is that the judicial creativity, bordering on judicial legislation, which the application of that doctrine involved is a desperate remedy, to be invoked only if it is necessary to remedy a widespread injustice. Otherwise there is much to be said for giving effect to what on ordinary principles of construction the parties agreed.

Further in *McGee Group Ltd v Galliford Try Building Ltd* [2017] EWHC 87 (TCC), [25] Coulson J stated:

> In summary, a clause which seeks to limit the liability of one party to a commercial contract, for some or all of the claims which may be made by the other party, should generally be treated as an element of the parties' wider allocation of benefit, risk and responsibility. No special rules apply to the construction or interpretation of such a clause although, in order to have the effect contended for by the party relying upon it, a clause limiting liability must be clear and unambiguous.

While *Photo Production, Darlington Futures, BCCI v Ali* and *McGee* all support the adoption of a more natural approach to the interpretation of exclusion and limitation clauses, they all affirm the need to use clear and unambiguous language if liability is effectively to be excluded (see also *Transocean Drilling UK Ltd v Providence Resources plc* [2016] EWCA Civ 372; [2016] 2 Lloyd's Rep 51, [20]).

However, there remain at least two situations in which particular rules of construction are employed by the courts. These rules apply where one party seeks to exclude liability for his own negligence (Section 11.6) or where he seeks to exclude liability for a 'fundamental breach' (Section 11.7). We shall now discuss these two special rules of construction.

11.6 Negligence liability

The first relates to the situation where a contracting party seeks to exclude liability for his own negligence (note that UCTA contains severe restrictions on the ability of a contracting party to exclude liability for his own negligence even where it is clear that the clause, on its proper construction, covers negligently inflicted damage; see Section 11.10). The courts regard it as inherently unlikely that one party will agree to allow the other contracting party to exclude liability for his own negligence. To give effect to this, the courts evolved specific rules or guides of construction which find their origin in the speech of Lord Morton of Henryton in *Canada Steamship Lines Ltd v The King* [1952] AC 192.

11.6.1 The three limbs of the rule

The first rule or guide is that if a clause contains language which expressly exempts the party relying on the exclusion clause from the consequences of his own negligence then (subject to UCTA) effect must be given to the clause. This test may be fulfilled by using a word which is a synonym for negligence (*Smith v UBM Chrysler (Scotland) Ltd* 1978 SC (HL) 1) such as 'any act, omission, neglect or default' (*Monarch Airlines Ltd v London Luton Airport Ltd* [1998] 1 Lloyd's Rep 403, 409). The safest course, however, is to use the word 'negligence' expressly. The words 'loss whatsoever or howsoever occasioned' do not count as an express reference to negligence (*Shell Chemicals UK Ltd v P&O Roadtanks Ltd* [1995] 1 Lloyd's Rep 297, 301). If the first rule or guide is not satisfied the court will then proceed to apply the remaining limbs of Lord Morton's test (although, as we shall see, there is some doubt about the continuing validity of the third limb of the test). It is important to understand that, while the first limb stands alone, the second and the third limbs have traditionally operated in combination so that both elements must be satisfied if a party is effectively to exclude liability in respect of its own negligence. The second limb is that the court must consider whether the words are wide enough, in their ordinary meaning, to cover negligence on the part of the party relying on the exclusion clause. If a doubt arises as to whether the words are wide enough, the doubt must be resolved against the party relying on the clause. Exclusion clauses which have been held wide enough to satisfy this test include clauses which exclude liability for 'any act or omission' or 'any damage whatsoever'.

Once the second limb has been satisfied, the third limb of Lord Morton's test requires the court to consider whether the exclusion clause may cover some kind of liability other than negligence. If there is such a liability, the clause will generally be confined in its application to that alternative source of liability and will be held not to extend to negligently inflicted loss. It was once thought that the mere existence of a possible alternative source of liability meant that the clause could not cover negligence, but the point has since been reconsidered by the Court of Appeal in *The Raphael* [1982] 2 Lloyd's Rep 42 (see Palmer, 1983). In that case it was held that the rules laid down in *Canada Steamship* were merely aids to be used by the courts in identifying the intention of the parties and it was emphasised that where the alternative source of liability was 'fanciful or remote' it would not prevent the exclusion clause covering liability in negligence. But what if the alternative source of liability was sufficiently realistic for the parties to intend the clause to apply to that other source of liability? Does such an alternative source of liability mean that the clause cannot apply to negligence? Stephenson LJ thought so. On the other hand, Lord Donaldson and May LJ held that the point was ultimately one of construction, but even they said that in such a case the clause would generally be interpreted as not excluding liability for negligence.

11.6.2 Criticisms of the rule

The combination of the second and the third limbs can produce results which are unsatisfactory and contrary to the probable intention of the parties. Two particular problems can be identified. The first is that the two limbs make contradictory demands of the draftsman. The second limb demands that the clause be drafted as widely as possible so that it will be held to encompass negligently inflicted damage. But the third limb demands that the clause be narrow in scope because the wider it is, the more likely it is that it will encompass some source of liability other than negligence and so be confined in its scope to that alternative source of liability. A number of clauses have been caught by this dilemma: they surmount the second limb, only to fall at the third because the clause is held to be confined to the alternative, non-negligent source of liability (see, for example, *Dorset CC v Southern Felt Roofing Co Ltd* (1989) 48 Build LR 96).

The second problem is that the parties may intend the same clause to apply both to negligently inflicted damage and to non-negligently inflicted damage. In our example involving Peter and John (see Section 11.1), Peter may wish the exclusion clause to cover not only negligence on his part, but also any liability which he may incur for late delivery of the furniture through no fault of his own (for example, his van may break down and John may incur expenses living in a hotel in Preston while waiting for the furniture to arrive). In such a case, the application of the *Canada*

Steamship test would be more likely to frustrate that intention than give effect to it, and rules which so frustrate the intention of the parties should be abandoned at the first opportunity. It is therefore suggested that the courts should no longer apply the *Canada Steamship* rules but should leave the issue as one of construction, with the courts simply having to decide, as a matter of construction, whether or not the exclusion clause covered negligently caused damage. Such a step was taken by the Supreme Court of Victoria in *Schenker & Co (Aust) Pty Ltd v Malpas Equipment and Services Pty Ltd* [1990] VR 834, 846, where McGarvie J stated that the strained approach to construction adopted in *Canada Steamship* was inconsistent with the more natural and ordinary rules of construction adopted by the High Court of Australia in *Darlington Futures Ltd v Delco Australia Pty Ltd* (1987) 61 ALJR 76 (above). He justified this departure from strained rules of construction on the following ground:

> To construe commercial contracts as they would be understood by business people serves primary aims of both the law and commerce. The law serves the community best if citizens understand it and are able to resolve their dispute themselves by reference to it, without resorting to lawyers or courts.

English law has not, as yet, taken this stance. Indeed, cases can be found in which the courts have chosen to affirm the *Canada Steamship* rules in robust terms. The best example is provided by the judgment of Hobhouse J in *EE Caledonia Ltd v Orbit Valve Co Europe* [1993] 4 All ER 165, 173 where he stated that:

> it has to be borne in mind that commercial contracts are drafted by parties with access to legal advice and in the context of established legal principles as reflected in the decisions of the courts. Principles of certainty, and indeed justice, require that contracts be construed in accordance with the established principles. The parties are always able by the choice of appropriate language to draft their contract so as to produce a different legal effect. The choice is theirs.

While certainty is indeed an important commodity in the law of contract, the approach of Hobhouse J is open to criticism on a number of grounds. The first is that parties do not always have access to legal advice. Secondly, the fact that parties can contract out of the rule does not justify the rule itself. Finally, the continued existence of an unsatisfactory rule imposes costs on commerce because the parties must bear the cost of negotiating their way out of an inconvenient rule. Notwithstanding these points, the Court of Appeal has endorsed the *Canada Steamship* rules in clear terms on a number of occasions (see, for example, *EE Caledonia Ltd v Orbit Valve Co Europe* [1994] 1 WLR 1515 and *The Fiona* [1994] 2 Lloyd's Rep 506).

The House of Lords, however, adopted a more clement approach in *HIH Casualty and General Insurance Ltd v Chase Manhattan Bank* [2003] UKHL 6; [2003] 2 Lloyd's Rep 61. Their Lordships emphasised that the paramount task of the court is to give effect to the intention of the parties (see Lord Bingham at [11], Lord Hoffmann at [61]–[63], Lord Hobhouse at [95] and Lord Scott at [116]). Further, in *Persimmon Homes Ltd v Ove Arup & Partners Ltd* [2017] EWCA Civ 373; [2017] BLR 417, [55] Jackson LJ observed that 'over the last 66 years there has been a long running debate about the effect of [the three guidelines] and the extent to which it is still good law'. Further, he noted that, with the benefit of hindsight, it can be seen that 'it is not satisfactory to deal with exemption clauses and indemnity clauses in one single compendious passage'. He continued by stating that 'it is one thing to agree that A is not liable to B for the consequences of A's negligence. It is quite another thing to agree that B must compensate A for the consequences of A's own negligence.'

11.6.3 Guidelines and giving effect to the intention of the parties

Given these criticisms, the weight to be attached to Lord Morton's guidelines seems to have diminished substantially. They should therefore be seen as tools to be used by the courts and not as their masters (*Lictor Anstalt v Mir Steel UK Ltd* [2012] EWCA Civ 1397; [2013] 2 All ER (Comm) 54 and *Greenwich Millennium Village Ltd v Essex Services Group plc* [2014] EWCA Civ 960; [2014] 1 WLR 3517). To the extent that the guidelines do not give effect to the intention of the parties they should not, presumably, be applied. Secondly, their Lordships appeared to recognise that there are some contexts, such as the fact situation in *HIH Casualty and General Insurance* itself, where the courts will more readily infer that the intention of the parties, or the purpose behind their contractual structure, was to entitle one party to exclude or limit liability for his own negligence or the negligence of those who act on his behalf.

An example in the latter category, albeit it involved an indemnity clause rather than an exclusion clause, is provided by the decision of the Court of Appeal in *Greenwich Millennium Village Ltd v Essex Services Group plc* [2014] EWCA Civ 960; [2014] 1 WLR 3517. A party who had been guilty of 'passive negligence' (that is to say, it had failed to detect a defect in work done by its contracting party) was held to be entitled to claim an indemnity from that party (who was the party 'actively' responsible for the defect) notwithstanding the fact that the indemnity clause did not contain an express reference to negligence. The effect of holding that the claimant was entitled to be indemnified was that liability was then able to flow down the chain of contracts until it rested with the party who was actually responsible for the loss and this was held to be consistent with the intention of the parties.

But this is not to say that the guidelines set out by Lord Morton are to be entirely discarded. On the contrary, they have been retained and they will continue to be applied by the courts when they appear to give effect to the intention of the parties. That this is so can be seen from the speech of Lord Bingham in *HIH Casualty and General Insurance* when he stated (at [11]) that:

> There can be no doubting the general authority of [Lord Morton's principles], which have been applied in many cases, and the approach indicated is sound. The courts should not ordinarily infer that a contracting party has given up rights which the law confers upon him to an extent greater than the contract terms indicate he has chosen to do; and if the contract terms can take legal and practical effect without denying him the rights he would ordinarily enjoy if the other party is negligent, they will be read as not denying him those rights unless they are so expressed as to make clear that they do.

On this basis, the rules may express no more than a judicial reluctance to conclude that one party has willingly agreed to exclude the other party from the consequences of his negligence. This reluctance is not unreasonable but it does not justify Lord Morton's guidelines, in particular the operation of the second and the third limbs. These rules or guides, particularly the third limb, should be dispensed with and be replaced by the ordinary rules applicable to the interpretation of contracts (on which see Section 9.6). As it is, the courts in more recent years seem to pay lip-service to the

Canada Steamship guidance but the substance of their decisions suggests that the rules have little or no positive or helpful contribution to make to the resolution of the case (see *National Westminster Bank v Utrecht-America Finance Co* [2001] EWCA Civ 733; [2001] 3 All ER 733). In these circumstances it would be better if the *Canada Steamship* rules or guidelines were quietly laid to rest.

11.7 Fundamental breach

The second situation in which the courts have evolved specific rules of interpretation is where the breach of contract by the party relying on the exclusion clause is of a fundamental nature. Two distinct approaches have been adopted here and it is vital to understand the difference between the two. The first approach may be called the rule of law approach, under which it was not possible by a clause (however widely drafted) to exclude liability for certain breaches of contract which were deemed to be fundamental. This approach grew under the guiding hand of Lord Denning as a means of control over exclusion clauses which were thought to be unreasonable. The second approach may be called the rule of construction approach. According to this approach, the question whether an exclusion clause covered a fundamental breach was a question of construction, under which the clause was interpreted against the party seeking to rely on it.

In *Suisse Atlantique Société d'Armament Maritime SA v NV Rotterdamsche Kolen Centrale* [1967] 1 AC 361, the House of Lords held that the latter approach was the correct one but, unfortunately, their Lordships' judgments were not a model of clarity and their ambiguities were seized upon in cases such as *Harbutt's Plasticine Ltd v Wayne Tank Pump Co Ltd* [1970] 1 QB 477, to resurrect the rule of law approach. However, the rule of law approach was finally laid to rest by the House of Lords in *Photo Production Ltd v Securicor Transport Ltd* [1980] AC 827. The claimants, who were factory owners, entered into a contract with the defendants under which the defendants contracted to provide periodic visits to the claimants' factory during the night for the purpose of checking that the factory was secure. During one of these visits an employee of the defendants started a fire, apparently to keep himself warm, but which got out of control and burnt down the factory.

The claimants sought to recover damages of £648,000 from the defendants, but the defendants relied on an exclusion clause which stated that 'under no circumstances' were they 'to be responsible for any injurious act or default by any employee ... unless such act or default could have been foreseen and avoided by the exercise of due diligence on the part of [the defendants]'. The House of Lords held that it was a question of construction whether or not the exclusion clause covered a fundamental breach and that, on the facts, the defendants were not liable because the exclusion clause did, in fact, cover the damage which had arisen.

It is undoubtedly the case that much mystique surrounds the doctrine of fundamental breach. This is largely due to the difficulties and confusion created by the rule of law approach. Now that the rule of law approach has been laid to rest, the 'doctrine' simply exists as a rule of construction, according to which the more serious the breach, or the consequences of the breach, the less likely it is that the court will interpret the exclusion clause as applying to the breach. As

Neill LJ stated in *Edmund Murray Ltd v BSP International Foundations Ltd* (1993) 33 Con LR 1, 16,

> it is always necessary when considering an exemption clause to decide whether as a matter of construction it extends to exclude or restrict the liability in question, but, if it does, it is no longer permissible at common law to reject or circumvent the clause by treating it as inapplicable to 'a fundamental breach'.

Although the rule of law approach has gone, great care must still be taken when drafting a clause which seeks to exempt one party from the consequences of a particularly serious breach. Therefore if a contracting party wishes to exclude liability for (i) breach of a fundamental term of the contract (that is a term which goes to the root of the contract or forms the essential character of the contract, see *Karsales (Harrow) Ltd v Wallis* [1956] 1 WLR 936), (ii) a deliberate refusal to perform his obligations under the contract (*Sze Hai Tong Bank Ltd v Rambler Cycle Co Ltd* [1959] AC 576) or (iii) a breach which will have particularly serious consequences for the other party, then he must use clear words to such an effect if he is to achieve his purpose. Yet even here, as we have already noted, the House of Lords in *Photo Production* stated that a strained construction should not be put upon words in an exclusion clause which are clearly and fairly susceptible of only one meaning and there is no presumption against a clause being construed so as to cover a deliberate, repudiatory breach (*Astrazeneca UK Ltd v Albemarle International Corp* [2011] EWHC 1574 (Comm); [2011] 2 CLC 252).

11.8　Other common law controls upon exclusion clauses

There are certain additional controls over exclusion clauses which exist at common law. The common law limitations are of much less significance since the intervention of Parliament (see Section 11.9). A party cannot rely on an exclusion clause, the effect of which he has misrepresented to the other party (*Curtis v Chemical Cleaning and Dyeing Co Ltd* [1951] 1 KB 805). Similarly, an exclusion clause which is contained in a written document can be overridden by an express inconsistent undertaking given at or before the time of contracting (*Couchman v Hill* [1947] KB 554). Finally, it must be remembered that the courts have no power at common law to strike down an exclusion clause simply because it is unreasonable (see Section 11.3).

11.9　The Unfair Contract Terms Act 1977

Parliament has now assumed the major role in regulating the use of exclusion clauses in contracts. The principal legislation which it has enacted in pursuance of this role is the Unfair Contract Terms Act 1977 (UCTA). The Act is a complex and technical piece of legislation. It is important to bear in mind that here we are dealing with an Act of Parliament and the *exact* words used by the Act must be studied and applied. Until the enactment of the Consumer Rights Act 2015 (on which see Chapter 18), UCTA applied to certain contracts entered into by consumers. Contracts concluded between a trader and a consumer have now been removed from the scope of UCTA so that UTCA now only applies to contracts concluded between parties acting in the course of a business.

While UCTA gives the courts considerable power to regulate exclusion clauses, it is vital to note that English law still does not recognise the existence of a general doctrine of unfairness or unconscionability (see Section 17.4). It is only particular types of clause, such as exclusion or limitation clauses, which are picked out for regulation by UCTA. One consequence of this approach is that Parliament must define what constitutes an exclusion or a limitation clause and the courts must in turn interpret that definition. The focus is therefore upon the *form* of *the clause* which is the subject of the control rather than upon the *substance* of *the contract* taken as a whole. The result is that difficult threshold questions can arise in deciding whether or not the clause in the contract falls within the scope of UCTA. If it does, it will be subjected to the reasonableness test (unless it is declared by the Act to be void), but if it falls outside the scope of the Act then there is no general doctrine of unfairness or unreasonableness to which the party seeking to set aside the term can appeal (unless, in the case of a contract to which a consumer is a party, it falls within the scope of Part 2 of the Consumer Rights Act 2015). This has given rise to various jurisdictional difficulties as contracting parties have sought to evade the clutches of the Act by arguing that the clause at issue does not fall within the scope of the Act. In the following sections of this chapter we shall look at the various clauses which fall within the scope of the Act and explore one or two of the 'jurisdictional' issues which have arisen.

11.10 Negligence liability

The first issue which the Act deals with are attempts to exclude or restrict liability for negligently inflicted loss. Section 2 provides that:

(a) A person cannot by reference to any contract term or to a notice given to persons generally or to particular persons exclude or restrict his liability for death or personal injury resulting from negligence.
(b) In the case of other loss or damage, a person cannot so exclude or restrict his liability for negligence except in so far as the term or notice satisfies the requirement of reasonableness.
(c) Where a contract term or notice purports to exclude or restrict liability for negligence a person's agreement to or awareness of it is not of itself to be taken as indicating his voluntary acceptance of any risk.

A number of points should be noted about this section. The first is that it only applies to 'negligence', so that it does not apply to attempts to exclude or restrict liability which is strict (that is to say, liability which arises irrespective of fault). 'Negligence' is defined in section 1(1) as:

the breach –

(a) of any obligation, arising from the express or implied terms of a contract, to take reasonable care or exercise reasonable skill in the performance of the contract;
(b) of any common law duty to take reasonable care or exercise reasonable skill (but not any stricter duty);
(c) of the common duty of care imposed by the Occupiers' Liability Act 1957 or the Occupiers' Liability Act (Northern Ireland) 1957.

An act is not prevented from being an act of negligence on the ground that the breach of duty was intentional rather than inadvertent, or because liability for it arose vicariously rather than directly (s 1(4)).

The second point to note about section 2 is that it applies only to attempts to exclude or restrict 'liability' and that liability for this purpose is confined to 'business liability'. Business liability is defined in section 1(3) as:

liability for breach of obligations or duties arising

(a) from things done or to be done by a person in the course of a business (whether his own business or another's) or
(b) from the occupation of premises used for business purposes of the occupier.

'Business' is defined in section 14 as including a profession and the activities of any government department or local or public authority.

The third point to note is that the section is not confined in its application to contracts: it also extends to non-contractual notices which purport to exclude or restrict liability for negligence.

Fourthly, it should be noted that section 2 adopts two methods of control. The first, contained in section 2(1), is that any contract term or notice which attempts to exclude or restrict liability for negligence causing death or personal injury is *void*. Personal injury is defined in section 14 as including 'any disease and any impairment of physical or mental condition'. The second method of control, contained in section 2(2), is that attempts to exclude or restrict liability for negligence causing loss or damage other than death or personal injury are valid only if they satisfy the requirement of *reasonableness* (the reasonableness test is discussed in Section 11.13).

Finally, we must turn to the 'jurisdictional' issues which have arisen, or may arise, under section 2. As has been noted, the section refers to a party attempting to 'exclude or restrict his liability' for negligence, and negligence itself is defined in section 1 as the 'breach' of an obligation or a duty. Section 2 is therefore drafted in defensive terms; that is to say, it assumes that there has been a *breach* of duty and so does not appear to extend to clauses which define the obligations of the parties. So how would a court respond to the argument that the clause which is the subject matter of the litigation simply defined the obligations of the parties and therefore fell outside the scope of section 2?

11.10.1 *Phillips Products Ltd v Hyland and Hamstead Plant Hire Co Ltd*

Such an argument was put to the Court of Appeal in *Phillips Products Ltd v Hyland and Hamstead Plant Hire Co Ltd* [1987] 2 All ER 620. The defendants 'hired' a JCB excavator and driver to the claimants. Condition 8 of the contract stated that the driver was to be regarded as the employee of the claimants and that the claimants alone should be responsible for all claims arising in connection with the driver's operation of the excavator. Owing to the negligence of the driver, the JCB excavator crashed into the claimants' factory wall. The claimants sued for damages and the defendants sought to rely upon condition 8. The claimants argued that condition 8 was caught by section 2(2) of UCTA and that it failed to satisfy the requirement of reasonableness. The defendants argued that condition 8 was not caught by section 2(2) on the ground that there was no negligence within the meaning of section 1(1)(b) because there had been no breach of their obligations as they had never accepted any liability for the acts of the driver. This argument was rejected by the Court of Appeal. Slade LJ asserted that, in considering whether there has been a breach of duty under section 1(1), the court must leave out of account the clause which is relied on by the defendants to defeat the claimants' claim. But why should condition 8 be left out of account when it was via that clause that the defendants had sought to define their obligations? Slade LJ claimed to find further support for his analysis in section 13(1) of the Act which extends the scope of section 2 to encompass 'terms and notices which exclude or restrict the relevant obligation or duty'. It is clear that the function of this provision is to extend the scope of section 2 to certain duty-defining clauses. The aim of the provision is probably to prevent evasion of the Act by clever draftsmen employed by the more powerful party to the contract. But the difficulty which it causes lies in ascertaining the *extent* to which it applies to duty-defining clauses. Section 13(1) does not give any criteria by reference to which we can decide which duty-defining clauses are caught by the Act and which are not.

The scope of section 13 was discussed by the House of Lords in *Smith v Eric S Bush* [1990] 1 AC 831. Lord Templeman stated that the Act subjected to regulation 'all exclusion notices which would in common law provide a defence to an action for negligence'. Lord Griffiths interpreted section 13 as 'introducing a "but for" test in relation to the notice excluding liability'; that is to say, a court must decide whether a duty of care would exist 'but for' the exclusion clause. Lord Jauncey stated that the wording of section 13 was 'entirely appropriate to cover a disclaimer which prevents a duty coming into existence'. But surely the Act does not catch all duty-defining clauses? Ridiculous conclusions would be reached if it did (for some examples, see Palmer and Yates, 1981; Palmer, 1986). One example will suffice to illustrate the point: 'an overworked accountant says to a potential investor "this is all I can remember about Company X but I may be wrong so don't rely on me"' (Palmer, 1986). Is such a statement caught by the Act? The answer is not clear. But if it is, how can a person qualify his obligations without being caught by the Act? This lack of clarity is almost certain to result in confusion in the courts, although there are signs that the courts may be willing to depart from the 'but for' test and so permit a party to qualify its obligations without attracting the application of the Act (see, for example, *Titan Steel Wheels Ltd v Royal Bank of Scotland plc* [2010] EWHC 211 (Comm); [2010] 2 Lloyd's Rep 92, [104]), at least where there is no attempt retrospectively to alter the character of what has gone before or to rewrite the history of the transaction (*Avrora Fine Arts Investment Ltd v Christie, Manson & Woods* [2012] EWHC 2198 (Ch); [2012] PNLR 35). Although the courts must share some responsibility for the creation of this confusion, the confusion lies, ultimately, at the heart of UCTA in its misconception of the function of exclusion clauses (see Sections 11.1 and 11.15), and until that issue is resolved the courts will continue to experience considerable difficulty in identifying the clauses which fall within the scope of the Act.

11.10.2 *Thompson v T Lohan (Plant Hire) Ltd*

A further example of these difficulties is provided by *Thompson v T Lohan (Plant Hire) Ltd* [1987] 2 All ER 631, a case which can be usefully contrasted with *Phillips v Hyland*. Once again the case concerned the hiring of an employee and a JCB excavator and a claim arising out of the negligence of the driver. The contract term which was the subject of the dispute was a new version of condition 8 (the variation is of no significance for present purposes). But this time it was held that condition 8 was not caught by section 2 of UCTA. In *Thompson* the driver's negligence led to the death of Mr Thompson. Mr Thompson's widow recovered damages from the general employers who then sought to recover an indemnity from the hiring employers under condition 8. The hiring employers argued that condition 8 was caught by section 2(1) of the Act and was therefore ineffective. However, it was held that condition 8 was not caught by section 2(1) and so was effective to transfer liability to the hiring employer. The vital issue which divides these two cases is whether or not it is sought to *exclude* liability towards the *victim* of the negligent act. In *Thompson* condition 8 did not attempt to exclude liability towards the victim of the driver's negligence (Mr Thompson), because his widow had recovered from the general employers and the issue was whether that liability could be *transferred* from the general employers to the hiring employers. On the other hand, condition 8 in *Phillips v Hyland* was relied upon in an effort to *exclude* liability towards the *victim* of the driver's negligence (the claimants) and therefore was caught by section 2(2) (see further Adams and Brownsword, 1988b). This distinction between an *exclusion* and a *transfer* of liability can lead to haphazard results in practice. Suppose that the driver in *Phillips v Hyland*, instead of damaging a wall belonging to the claimants, had damaged a wall belonging to a third party, who sought and recovered damages from the general employer. In any action brought by the general employer against the hirers to recover the sum paid to the third party, section 2 would be irrelevant because there would then be no attempt to exclude a liability towards the victim of the negligence (the third party). Such a conclusion makes it impossible for a lawyer to state in advance whether the clause will be caught by section 2 because it all depends upon whose wall is damaged and whether the person who is seeking to recover damages is the victim of the negligence. But should it not be the case that, whether the property which is damaged belongs to the claimants or not, the result in each case should be the same? Either the risk has been fairly allocated or it has not. Distinctions of the type drawn in *Phillips v Hyland* and *Thompson v Lohan (Plant Hire)* are incoherent in policy terms and reflect the apparent focus of the Act upon considerations of form rather than substance.

This 'form or substance' debate is of great significance for the future of the Act. Notwithstanding the decisions in *Phillips v Hyland* and *Thompson v Lohan (Plant Hire)*, the courts have not always made it clear which approach they will follow. In *Johnstone v Bloomsbury HA* [1992] QB 333, 346, Stuart-Smith LJ, relying in part upon the judgment of Slade LJ in *Phillips v Hyland*, stated that 'when considering the operation of section 2 of the Act the court is concerned with the substance and not the form of the contractual provision'. On the other hand, it must be said that *Phillips v Hyland* itself would appear to have fallen foul to reasoning of form rather than substance, as can be seen when *Phillips v Hyland* is compared with *Thompson v Lohan (Plant Hire)*. The issue therefore remains to be resolved by the courts, notwithstanding its importance for the future of the Act (see Section 11.15).

11.11 Liability for breach of contract

The Act also regulates clauses which seek to exclude or restrict liability for breach of contract. The principal section which performs this role is section 3. The section applies where one party 'deals … on the other's written standard terms of business'.

No definition is provided of this phrase. A number of questions arise here. Does the requirement that the terms be 'written' exclude a contract which is partly written and partly oral? How much of a variation is needed before the terms cease to be 'standard'? What is meant by the word 'deals'? And, finally, what does the word 'other's' mean? The courts have recently begun to provide answers to these questions. The first question awaits judicial resolution but the other three questions have been considered by the courts and we shall discuss them in turn.

11.11.1 'deals…on the other's written standard terms of business'

The first relates to the meaning of the word 'standard'. This was considered by Judge Stannard in *Chester Grosvenor Hotel Co Ltd v Alfred McAlpine Management Ltd* (1991) 56 Build LR 115, 131. He stated that the question was 'one of fact and degree' and continued:

> what is required for terms to be standard is that they should be so regarded by the party which advances them as its standard terms and that it should habitually contract in those terms. If it contracts also in other terms, it must be determined in any given case, and as a matter of fact, whether this has occurred so frequently that the terms in question cannot be regarded as standard, and if on any occasion a party has substantially modified its prepared terms, it is a question of fact whether those terms have been so altered that they must be regarded as not having been employed on that occasion.

This pragmatic approach has much to commend it and it will reduce the ability of parties effectively to contract out of section 3 by regularly changing their standard terms in minor respects. It is not the case that all contract terms have to be fixed in advance before the contract can be considered 'standard' but the greater the negotiation of important terms of the contract, the more likely it is that the contract will fall outside the scope of section 3 (*The Flamar Pride* [1990] 1 Lloyd's Rep 434; *The Salvage Association v CAP Financial Services Ltd* [1995] FSR 655).

The second issue relates to the meaning of the word 'deals'. It has been held that it means '"makes a deal", irrespective of any negotiations that may have preceded it'. Thus, negotiations over standard terms of business do not of themselves take the case outside the scope of section 3 provided that the contract is in fact entered into on those standard terms (*St Albans City and District Council v International Computers Ltd* [1996] 4 All ER 481, 491). But matters are otherwise if the negotiations do result in alterations to the proffered 'standard terms'. As Edwards-Stuart J observed, 'if there is any significant difference between the terms proffered and the terms of the contract actually made, then the contract will not have been made on one party's written standard terms of business' (*Yuanda (UK) Co Ltd v WW Gear Construction Ltd* [2010] EWHC 720 (TCC); [2010] BLR 435, [26]). The word 'significant' may be important here. Some differences may be so insignificant as to make it possible to conclude that the contract has been made on the other party's standard terms, notwithstanding the alterations that have been made (*University of Wales v London College of Business Ltd* [2015] EWHC 1280 (QB), [93]). But if the negotiations have resulted in substantial variations, it has been held that it is 'unlikely to be the case' that the party relying on the Act will have discharged the burden on him to show that the contract has been made on the other's written standard terms of business (*African Export-Import Bank v Shebah Exploration & Production Co Ltd* [2017] EWCA

Civ 845; [2017] BLR 469, [25]). The fact that the party relying upon the exclusion clause is willing to negotiate about other terms of the contract does not prevent the exclusion clause from amounting to a standard term on which the parties have dealt in the case where the exclusion clause itself is not negotiable (*Commercial Management (Investments) Ltd v Mitchell Design and Construct Ltd* [2016] EWHC 76 (TCC); 164 Con LR 139).

The third issue relates to the meaning of the word 'other's'. In *British Fermentation Products Ltd v Compair Reavell Ltd* [1999] BLR 352 the contract between the parties was concluded on the Institution of Mechanical Engineers Model Form of General Conditions of Contract. The defendants successfully argued that section 3 of the Act did not apply to the exclusion clause contained in the contract on the ground that the claimants had failed to prove that these terms were *the defendants'* written standard terms of business. This conclusion is obviously one of great significance for Model Forms of contract which are prevalent in industries such as the construction industry. It may be the case that these Forms now fall completely outside the scope of section 3. Judge Bowsher did suggest that it might be possible to prove that a defendant has by practice or by express statement adopted a Model Form as his standard terms of business (a suggestion supported by Phillips J in *African Export-Import Bank v Shebah Exploration & Production Co Ltd* [2016] EWHC 311 (Comm); [2016] 2 All ER (Comm) 307, [24]) but he expressly left open the question whether such proof, either alone or with other features, would make section 3 applicable in such a case. In many ways this conclusion is a surprising one because it takes so many contracts outside the scope of section 3, and the only beneficiary of this restrictive approach to the interpretation of the section is an exclusion or limitation clause which would not pass the reasonableness test. Had Judge Bowsher adopted a more liberal approach to the interpretation of 'other's' so that it encompassed Model Form contracts, it would not have resulted in the automatic invalidation of exclusion clauses contained in such Forms. All that would have happened is that they would have been subjected to the reasonableness test in the usual way. As it is, it would appear to be the case that those responsible for the drafting of Model Forms contracts no longer have to worry about the reasonableness of an exclusion or limitation clause, at least as far as section 3 of the Act is concerned.

11.11.2 Section 3(2)

Once over the section 3(1) hurdle we come to the substance of the section. Section 3(2)(a) is relatively straightforward, but section 3(2)(b) is more problematic. As against the party who deals on the other's written standard terms of business, the other party cannot by reference to any contract term 'when himself in breach of contract, exclude or restrict any liability of his in respect of the breach except in so far as the contract term satisfies the requirement of reasonableness' (s 3(2)(a)). Note that liability once again means business liability and that the subsection is cast in defensive terms, that is to say it assumes the existence of a breach of contract. This time, however, section 13(1) is not available to apply to duty-defining clauses because it states that it only extends the scope of sections 2, 6 and 7 of the Act.

Duty-defining terms may, however, be caught by section 3(2)(b) which states that the other party cannot by reference to any contract term claim to be entitled –

(a) to render a contractual performance substantially different from that which was reasonably expected of him, or
(b) in respect of the whole or any part of his contractual obligation, to render no performance at all,

except in so far as ... the contract term satisfies the requirement of reasonableness.

This subsection must apply to situations other than a breach of contract because, if there was a breach of contract, it would be caught by section 3(2)(a). The type of situation the draftsman would appear to have in mind arises where a holiday company reserves the right to change the destination of the holiday or the hotel booked (without breaking the contract) and the alternative which it provides is less than the other contracting party reasonably expected (*AXA Sun Life Services plc v Campbell Martin Ltd* [2011] EWCA Civ 133; [2011] 2 Lloyd's Rep 1, [50]). But how can a court identify the other party's 'reasonable expectations'? Presumably the exclusion clause will be ignored in identifying his reasonable expectations, but how many other terms will be disregarded in identifying his reasonable expectations? Some indication of the potential scope of the subsection was provided by the Court of Appeal in the case of *Timeload Ltd v British Telecommunications plc* [1995] EMLR 459. Clause 18 of the contract gave to BT the right 'at any time' to terminate the contract with the claimants on giving one month's notice. The claimants argued that the clause fell within the scope of section 3(2)(b). BT argued that the claimants could not reasonably expect that which the contract did not purport to offer, that is to say, the enjoyment of the service for an indefinite period. But Sir Thomas Bingham MR stated that:

if a customer reasonably expects a service to continue until BT has substantial reason to terminate it, it seems to me at least arguable that a clause purporting to authorise BT to terminate it without reason purports to permit partial or different performance from that which the customer expected.

Perhaps as important, he stated that, even if the case did not fall within the precise terms of section 3(2)(b), the subsection could nevertheless be used as a 'platform for invalidating or restricting the operation of an oppressive clause in a situation of the present, very special, kind' (contrast the approach of the House of Lords in *National Westminster Bank plc v Morgan* [1985] AC 686, where Lord Scarman, far from perceiving the Act as a kind of springboard, was of the opinion that the courts should draw back now that Parliament has intervened, see Section 17.5). This expansive interpretation of section 3(2)(b) is questionable. There was nothing particularly onerous about the clause in issue in *Timeload*: it gave to both parties the right to terminate the contract on the giving of a period of notice. If the courts are to place so little emphasis upon the terms of the contract in identifying the expectations of the parties, then it is difficult, if not impossible, to identify the limits of the subsection.

A more cautious approach to the interpretation of section 3(2)(b) was, however, adopted by the Employment Appeal Tribunal in *Peninsula Business Services Ltd v Sweeney* [2004] IRLR 49. A term in a contract of employment stated that 'an employee has no claim whatsoever to any commission payments that would otherwise have been generated and paid if he is not in employment on the date when they would normally have been paid'. The claimant resigned his post with the defendants and, as a consequence, he had to forgo substantial commission payments to which he would have been entitled had he remained in employment. He sought to challenge the entitlement of the defendants to withhold the commission on the ground that the clause purported to entitle the defendants to render a contractual performance substantially different from that which was reasonably expected of them. The EAT rejected the submission on the basis that the defendants were simply operating the contract in accordance with its terms. Rimer J stated that the clause 'simply defined the limits' of the claimant's rights and did not purport to 'cut down or restrict his rights in any way'. This contrast is open to the criticism that it appears to ignore the point that the aim of section 3(2)(b) is to extend the scope of the Act to certain contract terms which define the rights of the parties, so the fact that the term assisted in the definition of the claimant's rights should not, of itself, have taken the term outside the scope of the subsection. A stronger ground for rejecting the claimant's reliance on section 3(2)(b) was that it was held that there was 'no basis on which [the claimant] could ever have reasonably expected any rights greater than' those that the contract conferred on him. On this basis it would appear that the distinction between this case and *Timeload* lies principally in the weight given by the court to the terms of the contract when seeking to ascertain the reasonable expectations of the parties. It is suggested that the approach of the EAT in *Peninsula* is the preferable approach and that a court ought to attach considerable weight to the terms of the contract when identifying the reasonable expectations of the parties unless it can be demonstrated that the party relying on the term of the contract either knew, or ought to have known, that the other party to the contract was unaware of the term of the contract and could not reasonably be expected to have been familiar with it.

11.11.3 Sections 6 and 7

The Act also regulates other terms which seek to exclude or restrict liability for breach of contract. In contracts for the sale or hire-purchase of goods, the implied terms as to title cannot be excluded or restricted by reference to any contract term (s 6(1)); and the sellers' implied undertakings as to the conformity of goods with the description or sample, or as to their quality or fitness for a particular purpose, cannot be excluded or restricted by reference to a contract term except in so far as the term satisfies the requirement of reasonableness (s 6 (1A)). Two additional points should be noted here. The first is that all attempts to exclude or restrict these implied terms are caught by UCTA, not simply those which seek to exclude or restrict a business liability under section 1(3) (s 6(4)). It should, however, be remembered that the implied terms relating to quality and fitness for purpose apply only where the seller sells the goods in the course of a business (see Section 9.8). The second is that the Act directs the courts to have regard to specific matters in considering whether such a term is reasonable (s 11(3) and Schedule 2).

In the case of a contract of hire or a contract of exchange, any term of the contract which purports to exclude or restrict liability for breach of an obligation arising by implication from the nature of the contract in respect of the goods' correspondence with their description or sample or their quality and fitness for any particular purpose must satisfy the reasonableness test (s 7(1A)). Liability for breach of the obligations contained in section 2 of the Supply of Goods and Services Act 1982 cannot be excluded or restricted by reference to any contract term (s 7(3A)), and liability in respect of the right to transfer ownership of the goods or give possession or the assurance of quiet possession to a person taking goods in pursuance of the contract cannot be excluded or restricted by reference to any such term except in so far as the term satisfies the requirement of reasonableness (s 7(4)).

11.12 Attempts at evasion

The Act contains a number of controls upon attempts to evade the application of the Act. Two are worthy of note here. The first is section 13(1), the existence of which we have already had cause to note (see Section 11.10). The subsection states:

> To the extent that this Part of this Act prevents the exclusion or restriction of any liability it also prevents –
>
> (a) making the liability or its enforcement subject to restrictive or onerous conditions;
> (b) excluding or restricting any right or remedy in respect of the liability, or subjecting a person to any prejudice in consequence of his pursuing any such right or remedy;
> (c) excluding or restricting rules of evidence or procedure;
>
> and (to that extent) sections 2, 6 and 7 also prevent excluding or restricting liability by reference to terms and notices which exclude or restrict the relevant obligation or duty.

The principal point which should be noted is that this subsection does not have independent effect: its function is to extend the scope of sections 2, 6 and 7. It does not, of itself, render any contract term void, nor does it subject any contract term to the reasonableness test. That task is performed by sections 2, 6 and 7 and a court ought always to refer back to whichever of these sections is applicable when applying the reasonableness test or declaring that the term is void. We have already noted that section 13(1) is open to criticism in that it fails to provide guidance as to the extent to which it applies to duty-defining clauses (see Section 11.10). But, in other respects, the extensions which it makes are useful ones. For example, purporting to exclude a right of set-off falls within its scope (*Stewart Gill Ltd v Horatio Myer & Co Ltd* [1992] QB 600) as would setting a short time-limit within which a claim must be made or excluding a particular remedy (such as termination) while leaving other remedies (such as damages) intact.

The second section which is worthy of note in this connection is section 10, which states that a term excluding or restricting liability, which is contained in a separate contract rather than in the contract giving rise to the liability, is ineffective in so far as it attempts to take away a right to enforce a liability which under the Act cannot be excluded or restricted. The mischief at which the section is aimed is the practice of seeking to evade the Act by the use of another contract, for example where a term in a contract between a manufacturer of a product and a purchaser purports to affect the rights of the purchaser against the vendor under the Sale of Goods Act 1979. The section therefore applies to attempts to evade the provisions of the Act by the introduction of an exclusion clause in a contract with a third party, but it does not apply to genuine compromises of existing claims (*Tudor Grange Holdings Ltd v Citibank NA* [1992] Ch 53).

11.13   The reasonableness test

The reasonableness test is central to the operation of the Act and therefore requires separate discussion. Section 11(1) provides that:

> in relation to a contract term, the requirement of reasonableness … is that the term shall have been a fair and reasonable one to be included having regard to the circumstances which were, or ought reasonably to have been, known to or in the contemplation of the parties when the contract was made.

It is important to note that reasonableness is to be assessed at the date of making the contract, not the date of breach. The onus lies on the party relying on the exclusion clause to show that it is reasonable (s 11(5)). The courts have taken into account a number of factors in deciding whether an exclusion clause is reasonable: the respective bargaining power of the parties, whether the exclusion clause was freely negotiated, the extent to which the parties were legally advised, the availability of insurance, the availability of an alternative source of supply to the innocent party and the extent to which the party seeking to rely on the exclusion clause sought to explain its effect to the other party (see also the factors listed in Schedule 2 to the Act which the court is specifically directed to take into account in the case of a contract which falls within the scope of section 6 or 7 of the Act).

11.13.1   An illustration

An example of the operation of the reasonableness test can be provided by reference to the case of *Phillips v Hyland* (discussed in Section 11.10). There it was held that condition 8 of the contract failed the reasonableness test because the claimants did not generally hire JCB excavators and their drivers, the hire was for a very short period of time, there was little opportunity for the claimants to arrange any insurance cover and the claimants had no control over the choice of driver. The defendants were in the best position to take out insurance and to bear the loss. All these factors combined to suggest that condition 8 was not reasonable. But the question of the reasonableness of a particular clause depends on a careful evaluation of a range of factors and so much depends on the facts of the individual case. The courts have not been wholly consistent in their evaluation of the relevant factors and the weight to be attached to them. Some judges have been more interventionist than others (see Adams and Brownsword, 1988a). The consequence of this is an element of unpredictability and inconsistency in the case law. Appellate courts have largely abdicated their role as the guardians of predictability and consistency by holding that an appellate court must treat the trial judge's finding on the issue of reasonableness with the utmost respect and refrain from interference unless satisfied that the lower court proceeded on some 'erroneous principle or was plainly and obviously wrong' (*George Mitchell (Chesterhall) Ltd v Finney Lock Seeds Ltd* [1983] 2 AC 803; *Cleaver v Schyde Investments Ltd* [2011] EWCA Civ 929; [2011] 2 P & CR 21). Given this approach, it is likely that inconsistency will continue to be a feature of cases decided under the reasonableness test of UCTA and, to that extent, the interest in preserving commercial certainty has been sacrificed.

11.13.2 The meaning of the clause

Although much depends upon the facts of the individual case, there are a number of propositions which can be advanced with a degree of certainty. The first is that the court must ascertain the meaning of a clause before deciding whether or not it passes the reasonableness test (*Watford Electronics Ltd v Sanderson CFL Ltd* [2001] 1 All ER (Comm) 696). A wide interpretation of the clause may incline a court towards the conclusion that the clause is unreasonable, whereas a narrower interpretation may lead it to conclude that the clause is reasonable (see, for example, *Regus (UK) Ltd v Epcot Solutions Ltd* [2008] EWCA Civ 361; [2009] 1 All ER (Comm) 586 and *University of Wales v London College of Business Ltd* [2015] EWHC 1280 (QB)).

11.13.3 Look at the clause as a whole

The second proposition is that the court will have regard to the clause as a whole in deciding whether or not it is reasonable: the court does not have regard only to that part of the clause which is being relied upon by the party seeking to exclude or restrict liability (see *Stewart Gill Ltd v Horatio Myer & Co Ltd* [1992] QB 600). This proposition flows from the fact that section 11(1) states that the time for assessing the reasonableness of the clause is the time at which the contract was made (at which point it will not be known which part of it will be relied upon by the defendant) and not the time of the breach. However, when considering the possible scope of a clause, the court 'should not be too ready to focus on remote possibilities or to accept arguments that a clause fails the test by reference to relatively uncommon or unlikely situations' (*FG Wilson (Engineering) Ltd v John Holt & Co (Engineering) Ltd* [2012] EWHC 2477 (Comm); [2012] BLR 468, [96]). The court should focus attention on events that would have been contemplated by the parties at the time of contracting as 'realistic and not unlikely'.

11.13.4 No power of severance

The third point is that the court does not have the power to sever the unreasonable parts of an exclusion clause from the reasonable parts, leaving the latter in force (*Stewart Gill Ltd v Horatio Myer & Co Ltd*). This conclusion has important drafting consequences. It is now extremely unwise to rely upon a single all-embracing exclusion clause because, should it go too far at one particular point, it may fail in its entirety. That said, there are signs that the courts may be willing to make use of severance where a lengthy contractual term is capable of being broken down and considered in its constituent elements, at least in the case where the different parts of the clause are held to be 'independent' of one another (see, for example, *Regus (UK) Ltd v Epcot Solutions Ltd*) or where 'the different parts are performing different functions' (*Murphy & Sons Ltd v Johnston Precast Ltd* [2008] EWHC 3024 (TCC); [2008] All ER (D) 114 (Dec)).

11.13.5 Equality of bargaining power

The fourth point relates to the importance of equality of bargaining power: the greater the equality of the bargaining power of the parties, the more likely it is that the clause will pass the reasonableness test. The importance of the bargaining power of the parties was set out in forthright terms by Chadwick LJ in *Watford Electronics Ltd v Sanderson CFL Ltd* when he stated (at [55]):

> Where experienced businessmen representing substantial companies of equal bargaining power negotiate an agreement, they may be taken to have had regard to the matters known to them. They should, in my view be taken to be the best judge of the commercial fairness of the agreement which they have made; including the fairness of each of the terms in that agreement. They should be taken to be the best judge on the question whether the terms of the agreement are reasonable. The court should not assume that either is likely to commit his company to an agreement which he thinks is unfair, or which he thinks includes unreasonable terms. Unless satisfied that one party has, in effect, taken unfair advantage of the other – or that a term is so unreasonable that it cannot properly have been understood or considered – the court should not interfere.

Other judges have been more restrained (see, for example, *Britvic Soft Drinks Ltd v Messer UK Ltd* [2002] 1 Lloyd's Rep 20, 57–58). However, the balance of judicial opinion attaches considerable weight to this factor, and a number of judges have expressed a reluctance to strike down a term which has been freely agreed between large commercial parties who are regarded as the best judges of their own interests (see, for example, *Granville Oil & Chemicals v Davis Turner* [2003] EWCA Civ 570; [2003] 2 Lloyd's Rep 356, [31]; *Raiffeisen Zentralbank Osterreich AG v Royal Bank of Scotland plc* [2010] EWHC 1392 (Comm); [2011] 1 Lloyd's Rep 123, [321]; and *Air Transworld Ltd v Bombardier Inc* [2012] EWHC 243 (Comm); [2012] 1 Lloyd's Rep 349, [133]). As Gross LJ observed in *Goodlife Foods Ltd v Hall Fire Protection Ltd* [2018] EWCA Civ 1371; [2018] BLR 491, [103] 'at least in the case of commercial contracts between parties of broadly equal bargaining power, considerations of party autonomy and freedom of contract remain potent'.

11.13.6 The importance of insurance and abandon widely drafted exclusion clauses

Fifthly, it is clear that the insurance consequences of the clause should always be brought before the court. It is the availability of insurance at the time at which the contract was concluded which is important, not the actual insurance position of the parties (see *The Flamar Pride* [1990] 1 Lloyd's Rep 434). Thus, the fact that the defendant has chosen to insure itself for a sum substantially in excess of the limitation clause in the contract does not of itself establish that the limitation clause is unreasonable (*Moores v Yakeley Associates Ltd* (1999) 62 Con LR 76). Sixthly, contracting parties should abandon widely drafted exclusion clauses. In particular, the courts are unlikely to look favourably upon exclusion clauses which undermine the express promises which have been made under the contract (see *Lease Management Services Ltd v Purnell Secretarial Services Ltd* [1994] Tr LR 337).

11.13.7 Enforcement in practice

The seventh point relates to the way in which the clause is enforced in practice. The fact that the defendant has not always enforced the clause in practice does not mean that the clause is inevitably unreasonable. In *Schenkers Ltd v Overland Shoes Ltd* [1998] 1 Lloyd's Rep 498, the Court of Appeal, in finding a clause to be reasonable, had regard to the fact

that the clause was in common use and was well known and that there was no significant inequality of bargaining power between the parties, and concluded that in that
context the give-and-take practised by the parties, where the clause was not always
rigorously enforced, did not prevent the defendant from relying on the clause. The position is otherwise where there is a recognition in the industry that reliance on the clause
is unreasonable. In such a case, a court is likely to infer from the fact that the clause was
not enforced in practice that this was because the clause was unreasonable (see *George
Mitchell (Chesterhall) Ltd v Finney Lock Seeds Ltd* [1983] 2 AC 803).

11.13.8 Two different forms of loss

The eighth point is that it is not advisable to include two very different types of loss
within the same limitation clause. In *Overseas Medical Supplies Ltd v Orient Transport
Services Ltd* [1999] 2 Lloyd's Rep 273 the defendant freight forwarders failed to insure
the claimants' goods as they were required to do under the terms of the contract. The
defendants' liability was limited to £600. It was held that, while a limitation of £600
would have been reasonable for a claim for direct loss suffered by the claimants (for
example, caused by the default of the defendants when transporting the goods), it was
not reasonable for a failure to insure. The reason for this conclusion is to be found in the
different consequences which flow from the two breaches. A failure to insure the goods
meant that the claimants could only recover £600 from the defendants, whereas, had the
goods been insured but damaged as a result of the default of the defendants, the claimants could have recovered the first £600 of their loss from the defendants and the balance from their insurance policy. In seeking to include two very different losses within
the same limitation clause, the defendants made it very difficult for themselves to show
that the limitation clause was reasonable and, indeed, on the facts they failed to do so
and they were liable to the claimants in the sum of £8,500.

11.13.9 Limitation clauses

The final point relates to the advantages which can be obtained by the use of limitation clauses rather than exclusion clauses. In many cases a sensibly drawn limitation
clause is more likely to pass the reasonableness test than a total exclusion of liability.
But there is no guarantee that it will pass. In *St Albans City and District Council v
International Computers Ltd* [1996] 4 All ER 481, a clause in a computer contract which
limited liability to £100,000 was held to be unreasonable. In that case, the trial judge
([1995] FSR 686), whose judgment was upheld by the Court of Appeal, attached
importance to the fact that the parties were of unequal bargaining power, the
defendants had not justified the figure which they had inserted into the contract, the
defendants were insured and he thought that the party who stood to make the profit
(the defendants) should also take the risk of loss. It would seem that, where a limitation clause is inserted into the contract, an attempt should be made to provide some
objective justification for the selection of that figure (in terms of the turnover of the
party relying on the clause, the insurance cover available, the value of the contract
or the financial risk to which the claimants are exposed). A failure to adduce such
evidence might incline a court towards the conclusion that the clause is unreasonable (see *The Salvage Association v CAP Financial Services Ltd* [1995] FSR 655).

11.14 Excepted contracts

Finally, it should be noted that the Act does not apply to certain contracts, such as contracts of insurance and contracts which concern the transfer of an interest in land (see generally Sch 1).

Section 26 of the Act provides that the limits imposed by the Act on the extent to which a person may exclude or restrict liability by reference to a contract term do not apply to liability arising under an international supply contract, nor are the terms of such a contract subject to the reasonableness requirement under section 3. An international supply contract is defined in sections 26(3) and (4). It is defined as a contract for the sale of goods or one under or in pursuance of which the possession or ownership of goods passes and which is made by parties whose places of business (or, if they have none, habitual residences) are in the territories of different States (s 26(3)). In addition, at least one of the following further conditions must be satisfied: either (a) the goods in question are, at the time of the conclusion of the contract, in the course of carriage, or will be carried from the territory of one State to the territory of another, or (b) the acts constituting the offer and acceptance have been done in the territories of different States, or (c) the contract provides for the goods to be delivered to the territory of a State other than the State within whose territory the acts constituting the offer and acceptance were done. Section 26(4)(a) does not require a seller or hirer to have undertaken an obligation to deliver the contractual goods to another state; it suffices that, at the time of the conclusion of the contract, the goods in question will be carried from the territory of one state to the territory of another (*Trident Turboprop (Dublin) Ltd v First Flight Couriers Ltd* [2009] EWCA Civ 290; [2010] QB 86, [28]). The reference to 'the acts constituting the offer and acceptance' in section 26(4)(b) is a reference to the 'totality of the acts which constitute the offer and acceptance, including the making and receiving of each' (*Air Transworld Ltd v Bombardier Inc* [2012] EWHC 243 (Comm); [2012] 1 Lloyd's Rep 349, [82]). However, in the case of section 26(4)(c), it is not sufficient to prove that the goods have been delivered 'in' the territory of a State other than the State within whose territory the acts constituting the offer and acceptance were done. The goods must be delivered 'to' that country; in other words, the goods must have been delivered from a country which was outside that territory (*Amiri Flight Authority v BAE Systems plc* [2003] EWCA Civ 1447; [2004] 1 All ER (Comm) 385). The phrase 'made by parties' in section 26(3) is a reference to the principals to the contract in question and not to the agents (*Ocean Chemical Transport Inc v Exnor Craggs Ltd* [2000] 1 Lloyd's Rep 446, 453).

Nor does the Act purport to regulate any contractual provision which is authorised or required by the express terms or by necessary implication of an enactment, or any contractual provision which is necessary in order to secure compliance with an international agreement to which the United Kingdom is a party (s 29(1)). Relevant statutes and international conventions include those relating to carriage of goods by sea and carriage of passengers, goods and luggage by air and by land. Furthermore, a contract term will be assumed to have satisfied the requirement of reasonableness if it is incorporated or approved by, or incorporated pursuant to a decision or ruling of, a competent authority (that is, any court, arbitrator or arbiter, government department or public authority) acting in the exercise of any statutory jurisdiction or function and is not a term in a contract to which the competent authority is itself a party.

Finally in this context section 27(1) states that, where the law applicable to a contract is the law of any part of the United Kingdom only by choice of the parties, sections 2 to 7 of the Act do not operate as part of the law applicable to the contract. Thus, foreign parties who choose English law as the law applicable to their contract do not thereby subject themselves to sections 2 to 7 of UCTA (but the rules which regulate attempts to exclude liability for misrepresentation are applicable to such contracts). However, there are limits on the extent to which it is possible to evade the clutches of the Act by resort to a choice of law clause and these limits are to be found in section 27(2). The subsection provides that the controls contained in the Act cannot be evaded by the choice of a law outside the UK as the governing law if it appears that the choice of law was imposed wholly or mainly to enable the party imposing it to evade the operation of the Act.

11.15 Conclusion

The Unfair Contract Terms Act 1977 is a major attempt to regulate the use of exclusion clauses in Britain. It cannot claim to be a wholly satisfactory piece of legislation. The main difficulty lies in identifying the essential nature of an exclusion clause: does it define the nature and extent of the contractual obligation or is it a defence to a breach of an obligation? As we have noted, the courts have traditionally seen exclusion clauses in defensive terms and, although UCTA is cast primarily in defensive terms, section 13(1) and section 3(2)(b) do extend the Act to certain duty-defining clauses. But, once it is conceded that the Act does apply to duty-defining clauses, on what basis can it be decided which duty-defining terms are caught by the Act and which are not? This has become a question of some importance as contract draftsmen have sought to evade the clutches of the Act. Yet, it is a question to which those who support the defensive view of exclusion clauses have provided no answer.

It is suggested that the only solution, however unpalatable it may be, lies in a reconsideration of the whole basis of the Act, in recognising that exclusion clauses perform duty-defining functions and treating them like any other term of the contract and only intervening to control them where they are shown to be 'unfair' or 'unconscionable'. However, with the enactment of the Consumer Rights Act 2015, it is unlikely that there will be significant further interest in the reform of UCTA. The creation of a separate body of legislation for consumer contracts (which adopts a more expansive definition of the type of contract term that falls within its scope, see Chapter 18) has largely satisfied the lobby for further reform. The confinement of UCTA principally to business-to-business contracts will have the effect of increasing the significance of the definitional debates about what does and does not constitute an exclusion or limitation clause for the purposes of the Act. If the term is held to fall within the scope of the Act, it will be subject to review. If it does not, the Act will not apply and freedom of contract will apply unless the party seeking to challenge the validity of the contract term can claim the protection of some other common law doctrine (such as misrepresentation, mistake or duress).

Hot topic 10...

One

How should the courts go about the interpretation of an exclusion clause? In the past the courts approached exclusion clauses with a degree of suspicion and adopted restrictive rules (such as the *contra proferentem* rule) which they then applied to the interpretation of such clauses. The modern approach is less hostile to exclusion clauses (or at least certain forms of them). A recent illustration is *Transocean Drilling UK Ltd v Providence Resources plc* [2016] EWCA Civ 372; [2016] 2 Lloyd's Rep 51 where the contract between the parties contained a detailed and sophisticated scheme for apportioning responsibility for loss and damage of all kinds, backed by insurance, the effect of which was to exclude liability for 'consequential loss', including the loss suffered by the defendant. In holding that the clauses were effective, as a matter of interpretation, to exclude liability in respect of these consequential losses, the Court of Appeal held that it was no part of their function to adjust the contract in order to render it fairer in their eyes. The task of the court is to give effect to the intention of the parties and that will generally be done by giving to the words they have used their natural and ordinary meaning. Thus the court could see no reason in principle why commercial parties should not be free to embark on a venture of this kind on the basis of an agreement that losses arising in the course of the work will be borne in a certain way and that neither should be liable to the other for consequential losses, however they chose to define them. Further, the Court of Appeal declined to apply the *contra proferentem* rule on the ground that the meaning of the disputed clause was clear and the term was not 'one-sided' but applied to both parties equally and they were both of 'equal bargaining power'. The case strongly suggests that modern courts will give the words in an exclusion clause their natural and ordinary meaning, at least in the case where the parties are of equal bargaining power and have 'entered into mutual

undertakings to accept the risk of consequential loss flowing from each other's breaches of contract'.

Two

How do the courts go about deciding whether or not an exclusion or limitation clause is reasonable? Much depends upon the facts of the particular case. A recent illustration is *Goodlife Foods Ltd v Hall Fire Protection Ltd* [2018] EWCA Civ 1371; [2018] BLR 491. Losses in excess of £6 million were caused by a fire at the claimant's factory. The claimant brought an action against the defendant in which it was alleged that the fire suppression system supplied and installed some ten years previously by the defendant had failed. The defendant relied on an exclusion clause by way of defence. In reaching the conclusion that the exclusion clause was reasonable the Court of Appeal, following in this respect the decision of the first instance judge, attached particular weight to (i) the fact that the exclusion clause had been freely agreed by parties of broadly equal size and status, (ii) the ease with which the parties could obtain insurance in respect of the losses which had been caused, (iii) the fact that the claimant was in the best position to take out insurance against the losses in question and had in fact taken out such insurance, (iv) the fact that the defendant had offered the claimant the option of additional insurance cover in return for the offer of increased liability, which offer had not been taken up by the claimant and (v) the fact that this was a 'relatively low value contract' (the contract price was £7,490) but the potential liability of the defendant was very high (some £6 million) and liability could arise sometime after performance of the contract (on the facts, ten years later). The Court of Appeal also emphasised the narrow limits within which appellate courts will review the conclusion of a first instance judge on the reasonableness or unreasonableness of an exclusion or limitation clause.

Summary

▶ Exclusion clauses may be seen either as defining the obligations of the parties or as a defence to a breach of an obligation. The latter is the view which the courts have primarily adopted.

▶ Exclusion clauses must be validly incorporated into the contract. Incorporation may take place either by the party who is not relying on the exclusion clause signing the contract containing the exclusion clause, by giving reasonable notice of the exclusion clause to that party or by a course of dealing.

▶ The exclusion clause, properly interpreted, must cover the damage which has arisen.

▶ In recent years the courts have been more willing to apply to exclusion and limitation clauses the same principles as they would apply to the interpretation of any other contract term, although they will generally insist that the term be clearly worded if it is to be effective to exclude or restrict liability.

▶ In relation to an attempt by a contracting party to exclude liability for his own negligence, three specific rules have been devised by Lord Morton in *Canada Steamship Lines Ltd v The King* [1952] AC 192. However, these rules are only aids to be used by the court in identifying the intention of the parties.

▶ The doctrine of 'fundamental breach' is a rule of construction, according to which the more serious the breach, or the consequences of the breach, the less likely it is that the court will interpret the exclusion clause as covering the breach.

▶ The Unfair Contract Terms Act 1977 is now one of the major sources of control of exclusion and limitation clauses.

▶ Attempts by reference to a contract term or notice to exclude or restrict liability for negligence causing death or personal injury are void. In relation to other loss or damage caused by negligence, such attempts are only valid if they are held to be reasonable.

▶ Where one party deals on the other's written standard terms of business, the other party cannot exclude or restrict business liability for his own breach of contract or claim to be entitled to render a contractual performance substantially different from that which was reasonably expected of him or render no performance at all, except in so far as the contract term satisfies the requirement of reasonableness.

▶ Reasonableness is to be assessed as at the date of making the contract and the onus is upon the party relying on the exclusion clause to show that it is reasonable.

▶ The court has a wide discretion in deciding whether or not an exclusion clause is reasonable and will consider a number of different factors in reaching its conclusion.

Exercises

Consider the example involving Peter and John set out in Section 11.1 on the assumption that it includes the following exclusion clause: 'no liability is accepted for any damage, howsoever caused, to goods during the course of transit'.

What is the function of such a clause?

11.1 Peter wishes to know how he can incorporate such a clause into his contracts. How would you advise him?

11.2 Does the exclusion clause cover the damage done in the following cases?

    (a)   Some of John's furniture is damaged as it is loaded into Peter's van;

    (b)   John's furniture is damaged when Peter's van crashes because of Peter's negligent driving;

    (c)   John's furniture is totally destroyed when Peter's van is destroyed by fire;

    (d)   Peter sells John's furniture before he gets to Preston.

11.3 How does the Unfair Contract Terms Act 1977 affect the exclusion clause in the situations described in Exercise 11.2(a)–(d) (on the assumption that neither party is entering into the contract as a consumer)?

Part III

Policing the contract

Chapter 12
A duty to disclose material facts?

In this part of the book we shall consider various ways in which the law of contract regulates the agreement concluded by the parties and allocates the risk of unforeseen events between the parties. In Chapters 12 and 13 we shall discuss the obligations which are imposed upon contracting parties during the process of contractual negotiation. In Chapter 14 we shall analyse the methods by which the courts allocate the risk between contracting parties when they enter into a contract under a common fundamental mistake or an unforeseen event occurs after they have entered into the contract which destroys the basis on which they entered into the contract. In Chapters 15 and 16 we shall consider the limitations which are placed upon the enforceability of contracts by the doctrine of illegality and by the rules relating to capacity to enter into contracts. In Chapter 17 we shall discuss the doctrines of duress, undue influence and inequality of bargaining power and consider the extent to which the law of contract is concerned with the fairness of the bargain concluded by the parties. Finally, in Chapter 18 we shall discuss the regulation of unfair terms in consumer contracts in Part 2 of the Consumer Rights Act 2015 (previously found in the Unfair Terms in Consumer Contracts Regulations 1999 (SI 1999/2083)).

12.1 Introduction

In terms of disclosing information during the process of contractual negotiation, there are essentially two types of obligation which could be imposed by the courts upon contracting parties. The first is a duty to disclose all known material facts to the other contracting party. The second is a duty to refrain from making active misrepresentations: that is to say, a contracting party is not compelled to disclose information, but once he does disclose, he must do so truthfully. English law has adopted the latter approach and does not recognise the existence of a general duty to disclose material facts known to one contracting party but not to the other (*Keates v Cadogan* (1851) 10 CB 591).

A number of reasons can be identified for this refusal to countenance the existence of a general duty of disclosure. An instructive example provided by Professor Fried (2015, 79) will help us to appreciate these reasons:

> An oil company has made extensive geological surveys seeking to identify possible oil and gas reserves. These surveys are extremely expensive. Having identified one promising site, the oil company (acting through a broker) buys a large tract of land from its prosperous farmer owner, revealing nothing about its survey, its purposes or even its identity. The price paid is the going price for farmland of that quality in that region.

An English court would uphold the validity of such a contract and would not require the buyer to disclose his information to the seller prior to the making of the contract. A number of justifications can be provided for such a rule. The first is the simple proposition that the information acquired by the buyer has a financial value and to expect him to disclose it to the seller without compensation is to deprive him unfairly of his valuable information, to provide a disincentive to the acquisition of such information and to unjustly enrich the seller. The second is that contractual obligations are generally voluntarily assumed by parties who deal 'at arm's length', seeking to make the best bargain they can. In such a context contracting parties are not expected to share information with each other. The third justification is that, if such a duty were to be recognised, then questions would have to be resolved as to when it would arise and what would be its content. This justification may be called the floodgates argument. These are compelling justifications for the refusal of the law to recognise the existence of a *general* duty of disclosure.

But strong arguments can be adduced to support the recognition of a duty of disclosure in certain *particular* cases. For example, few would support a rule which enabled a car dealer to sell a car which he knew to be dangerous without revealing that fact to the purchaser. Thus we find that, in certain exceptional cases, a particular duty of disclosure is held to exist. We shall now consider these exceptions and conclude by considering whether they have any coherent rationale.

12.2 Snatching at a bargain

The first example of a limited duty of disclosure arises from the rule, which we have already noted (see *Hartog v Colin and Shields* [1939] 3 All ER 566, discussed in Section 2.2), that a claimant will be prevented from snatching at a bargain which he knew was not intended by the defendant. Thus, in *Smith v Hughes* (1871) LR 6 QB 597, the principle was established that a seller who knows that the buyer has misunderstood the terms of his offer is under an obligation to inform the buyer of the true nature of his offer in the sense that the contract will be set aside on the ground of mistake if he does not disclose. In other words, he is under a duty to disclose the existence of the mistake. But, where the buyer makes a mistake and that mistake does not relate to the terms of the seller's offer, then the seller, even if he is aware of the buyer's mistake, is not under an obligation to disclose the mistake to the buyer (see, for example, *Statoil ASA v Louis Dreyfus Energy Services LP* [2008] EWHC 2257 (Comm); [2008] 2 Lloyd's Rep 685). It is the responsibility of the buyer to discover his mistake and he cannot escape from his bad bargain by arguing that it was the responsibility of the seller to inform him of his mistake (see further, Kronman, 1978a; Brownsword, 1987; Beale, 2012).

12.3 Representation by conduct

The second group of exceptions all concern liability for misrepresentation (Sections 12.3–12.5). A misrepresentation consists of a false statement of fact (see Section 13.2) but the courts have, in limited circumstances, been flexible in their identification of a 'statement' of fact so that, in effect, they have imposed a limited duty of disclosure by the back door. For example, a contracting party does not have to open his mouth to make a statement; he can make it by his conduct. In *Walters v Morgan* (1861) 3 D F & J 718, Campbell LC said that, while simple reticence does not amount to a legal fraud, 'a nod or a wink, or a shake of the head, or a smile from the purchaser intended to induce the vendor to believe the existence of a non-existing fact, which might influence the price of the subject to be sold' would be a sufficient ground for refusing to enforce a contract.

The refusal to draw a rigid distinction between statements and conduct seems eminently sensible in the examples given by Campbell LC in *Walters*. Conduct can be as misleading as words. An apparently straightforward example of the imposition of liability on the basis of the conduct of the defendant is provided by *Gordon v Selico* (1986) 11 HLR 219 (see Gleeson and McKendrick, 1987). An independent contractor, employed by the defendants, was asked to bring a flat, which was infected with dry rot, up to a very good standard for the purpose of selling it. The independent contractor simply covered up the dry rot and made no attempt to eradicate it. The claimants purchased the flat and later discovered the presence of the dry rot. It was held that, in concealing the dry rot, the independent contractor had knowingly made a false representation to the claimants that the flat did not suffer from dry rot and that he and the vendors were therefore liable to the claimants in damages.

But, once it is recognised that a representation may be made by conduct, difficulties arise in identifying the meaning to be ascribed to the conduct and in ascertaining the situations in which the defendant is under an obligation to correct the meaning conveyed by his conduct (see *Spice Girls Ltd v Aprilia World Service BV* [2002] EWCA Civ 15; [2002] EMLR 27). For example, in a case such as *Gordon v Selico*, what would have been the position if the independent contractor had papered the dining-room prior to selling the house, partly because it needed redecorating anyway and partly to hide the defective state of the plaster? What is the meaning to be attributed to such conduct and is such a vendor under a duty to disclose the reasons why he has papered the room? In the High Court in *Gordon v Selico* (1985) 275 EG 899, 903, Goulding J said that:

> the law must be careful not to run ahead of popular morality by stigmatising as fraudulent every trivial act designed to make buildings or goods more readily saleable even if a highly scrupulous person might consider it dishonest.

The vagueness of this principle highlights the fact that, in the absence of a general duty of disclosure, it is extremely difficult to mark out the limits of any particular duty of disclosure.

12.4 Representation falsified by later events

A person may also be guilty of misrepresentation where he fails to correct a representation which, when made was true, but which subsequently, to his knowledge, has become false or which, at the time of making it he believed to be true, but which he has subsequently discovered to be false. In *With v O'Flanagan* [1936] Ch 575, negotiations for the sale of a medical practice began at a time when the practice was valued at £2,000. But when the contract of sale was concluded, the practice had become worthless because of the ill-health of the vendor in the intervening period. It was held that the vendor was under an obligation to disclose the change of circumstances to the buyer. The justification for this rule appears to be that a representation, once made, is deemed to be a continuing representation so that, once it becomes false to the knowledge of the representor and he fails to correct it, it becomes a misrepresentation (*Shankland & Co v Robinson and Co* 1920 SC (HL) 103, per Lord Dunedin). However, where the representation relates to a statement of intention and the contracting party changes his intention before the conclusion of the contract, then there is no obligation to communicate that change of intention (*Wales v Wadham* [1977] 1 WLR 199).

12.5 Statement literally true but misleading

A further situation in which a court may conclude that a misrepresentation has been made is where the statement is literally true but is nevertheless misleading because the maker of the statement has failed to disclose all the relevant information. In *Notts Patent Brick and Tile Co v Butler* (1866) 16 QBD 778, a purchaser of land asked the vendor's solicitors whether the land was subject to restrictive covenants. The solicitor replied that he was not aware of any, but he did not say that the reason for his ignorance was that he had not bothered to check. It was held that, although the solicitor's statement was literally true, it nevertheless amounted to a misrepresentation.

12.6 Contracts uberrimae fidei

There are a group of contracts which are known as contracts *uberrimae fidei* or contracts of the utmost good faith. These are typically contracts in which only one party to the contract has knowledge of the material facts and the law imposes on that party a duty to disclose these facts to the other party. A failure to do so renders the contract voidable. The classic example of a contract in this category was contracts of insurance but legislation has recently intervened to modify the extent to which it can meaningfully be said that insurance contracts are based on the utmost good faith. Principal among these legislative interventions are the Consumer Insurance (Disclosure and Representations) Act 2012 and the Insurance Act 2015. The latter Act provides in s 14(1) that 'any rule of law permitting a party to a contract of insurance to avoid the contract on the ground that the utmost good faith has not been observed by the other party is abolished.' The duty of the insured under the 2015 Act is now described as a duty of 'fair presentation' which, in broad terms, imposes on the insured an obligation to disclose material circumstances known to the insured in a manner which would be reasonably clear and accessible to a prudent insurer in which every material representation as to a matter of fact is substantially correct and every material representation as to a matter of expectation is made in good faith (s 3).

12.7 Fiduciary relationships

There is also a limited class of fiduciary relationships in which the party in whom the trust is reposed is placed under an obligation to disclose information to the person who has placed his trust in him (a good example is provided by the cases in which the presumption of undue influence is held to arise, see Section 17.3). Where such a fiduciary relationship exists, the parties do not bargain 'at arm's length' and the objection to the imposition of a duty of disclosure largely disappears.

12.8 A duty of disclosure in tort?

Rather than seek a remedy in contract, a claimant may argue that the defendant committed the tort of negligence in failing to disclose the information to the claimant. But the law of tort does not impose a general duty of disclosure; indeed, Lord Keith has reaffirmed that a person who sees 'another about to walk over a cliff with his head in the air, and forbears to shout a warning' incurs no liability in the tort of negligence

(*Yuen Kun Yeu v A-G of Hong Kong* [1988] AC 175, 192). On the other hand, a failure to speak may give rise to liability in the tort of negligence where the defendant has voluntarily assumed a responsibility to disclose information to the claimant and the claimant has relied upon that assumption of responsibility (*Banque Keyser Ullmann SA v Skandia (UK) Insurance Co Ltd* [1990] 1 QB 665, 794). A duty of disclosure may also be imposed by the law of tort in certain other exceptional cases. But these remain exceptions to the general rule and the law of tort has not taken, and is unlikely to take, the step of imposing a duty on contracting parties to disclose information to each other.

12.9 The role of the Sale of Goods Act 1979 and the Consumer Rights Act 2015

We have already noted (see Section 9.8) that both the Sale of Goods Act 1979 and the Consumer Rights Act 2015 imply certain terms into contracts for the sale of goods. Two of these terms to be found in the Sale of Goods Act 1979 are of particular significance here (similar terms are to be found in sections 9 and 10 of the Consumer Rights Act 2015). Firstly, where a seller sells goods in the course of a business, there is an implied condition that the goods supplied under the contract are of satisfactory quality, except in relation to defects drawn to the buyer's attention before the contract was concluded or, in the case where the buyer examines the goods, as regards defects which that examination ought to reveal (ss 14(2) and (2C)). Secondly, where the seller sells goods in the course of a business and the buyer makes known to the seller any particular purpose for which the goods are being bought, there is an implied condition that the goods supplied under the contract are reasonably fit for that purpose (s 14(3)). In many ways the rights conferred by these provisions are greater than any protection afforded by the imposition of a duty of disclosure upon the seller. This is because it suffices for the buyer to prove that the goods were not of satisfactory quality or were not reasonably fit for their purpose: it is not necessary for the buyer to assume the additional burden of proving that the seller was aware of the defect and had failed to disclose it to the buyer. The Supply of Goods and Services Act 1982 and, to a lesser extent, Part I of the Consumer Protection Act 1987 (which imposes strict liability for defective products) further extend the scope of such regulatory legislation and lessen the need for the creation of a general duty of disclosure because they protect the 'consumer' irrespective of whether the supplier of the goods, the provider of the services or the manufacturer of the product, knew of the relevant defect.

12.10 Conclusion

In *Interfoto Picture Library Ltd v Stiletto Visual Programmes Ltd* [1989] QB 433, 439, Bingham LJ noted that in many legal systems in the world 'the law of obligations recognises and enforces an overriding principle that in making and carrying out contracts parties should act in good faith'. A duty of good faith is, of course, wider in scope than a duty of disclosure because it is not necessarily confined to pre-contractual behaviour but can extend to the way in which the parties behave during performance of the contract and even to its termination. A case which might have been caught by a duty of good faith is *Arcos Ltd v E A Ronaasen & Son* [1933] AC 470 (discussed in more detail in Section 10.3), where the buyers under a contract of sale rejected goods ostensibly on the ground that they did not conform with description but in reality because the market price for the goods had fallen. As Professor Brownsword has noted (1992), the real objection is that the buyers 'acted in bad faith'. But English law currently recognises no general principle that a party must exercise his contractual rights 'reasonably' or 'in good faith' and so there was no way in which an English court could at that time challenge the buyers' actions on this ground (they could now possibly be challenged under Sale of Goods Act 1979, s 15A on which see Section 10.4). The traditional hostility towards the recognition of a doctrine of good faith can be seen in the decision of the House of Lords in *Walford v Miles* [1992] 2 AC 128, 138 (discussed in more detail in Section 4.1), where Lord Ackner refused to imply a term that the parties would continue to negotiate in good faith on the ground that a 'concept of a duty to carry on negotiations in good faith is inherently repugnant to the adversarial position of the parties when involved in negotiations'. He maintained that each party 'is entitled to pursue his (or her) own interest, so long as he avoids making misrepresentations'.

12.10.1 The experience of other jurisdictions

At present, English law appears to stand out from the many other jurisdictions which recognise the existence of a doctrine of good faith. In America, the Uniform Commercial Code states in section 1–304 that 'every contract or duty within [the UCC] imposes an obligation of good faith in its performance and enforcement' and, for this purpose, section 1–201 defines good faith as 'honesty in fact and the observance of reasonable commercial standards of fair dealing'. Further, the recognition of a duty of good faith and fair dealing in the performance and enforcement of contracts in section 205 of the US Restatement (Second) of Contracts (note that it does not extend to the negotiation of contracts) has been hailed by Professor Summers (1982) as a reflection of 'one of the truly major advances in American contract law during the past fifty years'. Article 242 of the German BGB states that 'the debtor is bound to effect performance according to the requirements of good faith, giving consideration to common usage'. Article 1104 of the revised French Civil Code states that contracts must be negotiated, formed and performed in good faith. Article 7(1) of the Vienna Convention on Contracts for the International Sale of Goods states that in the interpretation of the Convention regard is to be had, *inter alia*, to the 'observance of good faith in international trade'. Article 1.7 of the UNIDROIT Principles of International Commercial Contracts (see Section 1.7) states that 'each party must act in accordance with good faith and fair dealing in international trade' and further that 'the parties may not exclude or limit this duty'. The comment to the article states that 'good faith and fair dealing may be considered to be one of the fundamental ideas underlying the Principles'. Article 1.106(1) of the Principles of European Contract Law states that 'These Principles should be interpreted and developed in accordance with their purposes. In particular, regard should be had to the need to promote good faith and fair dealing, certainty in contractual relationships and uniformity of application.' Further, Article 1.201 states that 'each party must act in accordance with good faith and fair dealing' and that the 'parties may not exclude or limit this duty'.

This contrast between English law and other jurisdictions can, however, be overstated. In the first place, while English law does not presently recognise a duty of good faith, it can be very firm (possibly even harsh) in its treatment of those who act in bad faith. Specific examples of bad faith, such as telling lies (see Chapter 13), using illegitimate pressure (see Section 17.2), exploiting the weakness of others and abusing positions of confidence (see Sections 17.3 and 17.4), all constitute grounds upon which a contract can be set aside. Those who make false statements, even innocently, will find little to cheer them in English law (see Section 13.8). However, it may be that it is when we turn from the negative (not telling lies) to the positive (requiring disclosure of the whole truth) that English law may be found wanting. Secondly, many if not most of the rules of English contract law do in fact conform with notions of good faith. The individual bricks which could be used to create a general principle of good faith and fair dealing can already be identified. The existence of contracts *uberrimae fidei* and the limited duty of disclosure which English law recognises (see Sections 12.2–12.6), the operation of the doctrines of promissory estoppel (Section 5.25) and estoppel by convention (Section 5.26), the law applicable to fiduciaries (Section 12.7), the rules which the courts apply when seeking to interpret contracts (see Section 9.6) and the willingness of the courts to imply terms into a contract in particular situations (Sections 9.8 and 12.9) could, with varying degrees of persuasiveness, be rationalised in terms of good faith. As Professor Clarke has acknowledged (1993), the 'foundations of a general rule of good faith can be discerned in the common law dust' but the courts have not been prepared to use these particular rules 'as the piles for the building of a principle of good faith'. Finally, civilian lawyers may well use the doctrine of good faith to reach results which English law would reach by a more narrowly defined doctrine. For example, English law has developed a distinct doctrine of frustration to deal with impossibility and impracticability in performance (see Sections 14.8–14.17) rather than rely on a doctrine of good faith to deal with these issues. The difference may be more one of technique than result.

12.10.2 The reluctance to recognise a doctrine of good faith

Why then has English law been reluctant to recognise a doctrine of good faith or a general duty of disclosure? A number of reasons can be identified. The first is that English law starts from a premise of rugged individualism, in which the parties are expected to look after their own interests and to bargain to obtain the best terms which they can for themselves. But, as we have noted, this is not the complete picture: the commitment to individualism is not an absolute one. The piecemeal exceptions which we have noted represent a limited attempt by the courts and Parliament to protect the expectations of contracting parties, and in particular consumers, and to impose a limited duty of co-operation in an effort to avoid the unfairness and the excesses which would arise from an absolute refusal to recognise the existence of any duty of disclosure or a duty to bargain in good faith (for an alternative explanation of these exceptions in terms of a liberal theory of contract, see Fried, 2015, 77–85). In this connection, it should also be noted that a commitment to good faith does not require the complete abandonment of individualism. A duty to act in good faith qualifies or limits the pursuit of self-interest but it does not outlaw it. So, while a good faith duty might require the parties to act in a way that will permit both of them to enjoy the anticipated benefits of their contract, it does not require either party to give up a freely negotiated financial advantage clearly embedded in the contract (*Gold Group Properties Ltd v BDW Trading Ltd* [2010] EWHC 1632 (TCC); [2010] All ER (D) 18 (Jul), [91]). Those who argue that the recognition of a duty of good faith will make arm's length commercial bargaining impossible overstate their case. The second reason for the failure to recognise a doctrine of good faith or a general duty of disclosure is that English law is reluctant to embrace broad general principles, such as a duty of good faith. It prefers to develop incrementally and by analogy to existing precedents rather than by reference to broad statements of general principle (see McKendrick, 1999b). As Bingham LJ noted in *Interfoto*, while English law recognises no 'overriding principle' that parties must act in good faith, it has 'developed piecemeal solutions in response to demonstrated problems of unfairness'. It could be said that English law prefers to mark out on an incremental basis what constitutes 'bad faith' but that it refuses to lay down a broad principle that parties must act in good faith.

The third reason, closely related to the second, is that a broad general principle would generate too much uncertainty. When would a duty of good faith arise and what would be its content? Is good faith a subjective standard or an objective one? Should it apply to all contracts, or only in a non-commercial context where the need for certainty is less pressing? These are difficult questions which the proponents of a doctrine of good faith must answer.

12.10.3 The case for change

But the arguments are not all one way. There are arguments which can be deployed to support the existence of a duty of good faith and fair dealing. The first is that, to the extent that contracting parties choose to use the language of good faith, both freedom of contract and sanctity of contract suggest that effect should be given to their agreement and that the courts should not lightly conclude that an obligation to act in good faith is unenforceable. The courts seem to have accepted the argument that effect should be given to expressly assumed obligations to act in good faith, at least in relation to an obligation to act in good faith in the performance of a contract (*Compass Group UK and Ireland Ltd v Mid Essex Hospital Services NHS Trust* [2013] EWCA Civ 200; [2013] BLR 265) and in relation to a dispute resolution clause in an existing and enforceable contract which required the parties to seek to resolve a dispute by friendly discussions in good faith and within a limited period of time (*Emirates Trading Agency LLC v Prime Mineral Exports Private Ltd* [2014] EWHC 2104 (Comm); [2014] 2 Lloyd's Rep 457). More difficult is the case where the parties accept an express obligation to negotiate a contract in good faith. However, the difficulty experienced by English law in this context would appear to relate more to the validity of an obligation to negotiate than to the validity of an obligation to act in good faith. Thus a bare agreement to negotiate is not enforceable as a matter of English law and this would appear to be so whether the duty to negotiate is unqualified or is qualified by words such as 'good faith' or 'reasonable endeavours' (see *Shaker v Vistajet Group Holding SA* [2012] EWHC 1329 (Comm); [2012] 2 Lloyd's Rep 93 and *Jet2.com Ltd v Blackpool Airport Ltd* [2012] EWCA Civ

417; [2012] 2 All ER (Comm) 1053). However, even here there are some signs of judicial willingness to give effect to an expressly assumed obligation to negotiate in good faith. So, for example, in *Petromec v Petroleo Brasileiro SA Petrobas* [2005] EWCA Civ 891; [2006] 1 Lloyd's Rep 121 Longmore LJ (at [115]–[121]) adopted a narrow interpretation of *Walford v Miles* and stated that an express obligation to negotiate in good faith may be enforceable on the ground that it would be 'a strong thing to declare unenforceable a clause into which the parties have deliberately and expressly entered' (to similar effect see *Knatchbull-Hugessen v SISU Capital Ltd* [2014] EWHC 1194 (QB), [23]). It cannot be said that English law presently recognises the validity of an express obligation to negotiate in good faith but it may develop in that direction if greater weight is given to freedom of contract and sanctity of contract over arguments that such an obligation is too uncertain to be enforceable.

Second, the arguments deployed against the recognition of a duty of good faith may be overstated. Such was the conclusion of Leggatt J in *Yam Seng Pte Ltd v International Trade Corporation Ltd* [2013] EWHC 111 (QB); [2013] 1 All ER (Comm) 1321. He rejected the proposition that recognition of such a duty was inconsistent with the incremental nature of common law development, noting (at [147]) that there was 'no need for common lawyers to abandon their characteristic methods' given that the content of the duty is heavily dependent on context and the proper interpretation of the contract. In relation to the claim that English contract law is said to embody 'an ethos of individualism' he concluded (at [148]) that the aim of a good faith duty was to give effect to the presumed intention of the parties and it therefore did not amount to 'an illegitimate restriction on the freedom of the parties to pursue their own interests'. Finally, in relation to the claim that a duty of good faith will generate excessive uncertainty, Leggatt J (at [152]) dismissed this objection on the ground that it was 'unjustified' and that there was 'nothing unduly vague or unworkable about the concept' and that its application would involve 'no more uncertainty than is inherent in the process of contractual interpretation'.

Third, as we have seen, there are a number of rules of English law which conform with notions of good faith. Examples given by Leggatt J in *Yam Seng* include the implied term that a discretionary power must be exercised honestly and in good faith and not arbitrarily, capriciously or irrationally, and the implied term which requires contracting parties to co-operate with each other in the performance of the contract. Given that a number of rules of English contract law can be explained consistently with a duty of good faith, should English law not take the step of making explicit that which is currently implicit?

Fourth, English law is very much in the minority to the extent that it declines to recognise the existence of a general duty of good faith. This is not to say that English law should slavishly follow the views of the majority, but the fact that the majority take such a different view of the matter does at least suggest that English law might wish to review its current stance.

The final argument in favour of the recognition of a doctrine of good faith is that the present rules can create hardship in individual cases. While English law is currently *influenced* or *shaped* by notions of good faith it does not recognise the existence of a *doctrine* of good faith. The point was well-made by Steyn LJ in *First Energy*

(UK) Ltd v Hungarian International Bank Ltd [1993] 2 Lloyd's Rep 194, 196, when he said:

> a theme that runs through our law of contract is that the reasonable expectations of honest men must be protected. It is not a rule or a principle of law. It is the objective which has been and still is the principal moulding force of our law of contract. It affords no licence to a Judge to depart from binding precedent. On the other hand, if the *prima facie* solution to a problem runs counter to the reasonable expectations of honest men, this criterion sometimes requires a rigorous re-examination of the problem to ascertain whether the law does indeed compel demonstrable unfairness.

In this way, notions of good faith may be said to inform our law of contract. One of the aims of the law of contract is to produce fair and workable rules which conform to the standards of fair and reasonable people (see Steyn, 1997). To the extent that a rule appears to encourage bad faith, it will be the subject of 'rigorous re-examination' by the courts. But those who advocate the introduction of a doctrine of good faith argue that this is not sufficient because, as Steyn LJ acknowledges, it does not enable judges to depart from 'binding precedent'. Thus good faith could not be used to overrule a case such as *Arcos v Ronaasen*, nor to give effect to the agreement of the parties in *Walford v Miles*. It can therefore be argued that the influence of good faith is at times rather muted and that judges require stronger weapons to combat bad faith, which can only be done by elevating good faith to the status of a legal doctrine or a principle of law.

12.10.4 Where are we now?

Given these competing considerations, where does English law currently stand? This is not an easy question to answer. But the following propositions are suggested.

First, an express term in a contract which requires the parties to act in good faith in the performance of a contract will be upheld and enforced by the courts (and contracting parties who wish to be subject to a duty to act in good faith in the performance of the contract would be well advised to say so in express terms: *Chelsfield Advisers LLP v Qatari Diar Real Estate Investment Co* [2015] EWHC 1322 (Ch), [80]). Where the express term requires the parties to act in good faith in the negotiation of a contract, the enforceability of the term is more doubtful. The orthodox view is that it is not enforceable but that view, as we have seen, has come under some judicial challenge recently.

Second, the courts may imply a term into a contract that requires the parties to act in good faith in the performance of a contract. Courts are most likely to make this implication where the parties have entered into what has come to be referred to as a 'relational' contract (see *Al Nehayan v Kent* [2018] EWHC 333 (Comm); [2018] 1 CLC 216, [167]–[174]; *Bates v Post Office Ltd (No.3: Common Issues)* [2019] EWHC 606 (QB), [711] and [725]–[726]). In broad terms a 'relational' contract may be said to have two principal characteristics (for a more elaborate and non-exhaustive list of the characteristics of a 'relational' contract see *Bates v Post Office Ltd*, [725]). The first is the long-term nature of the agreement between the parties and the second is the high degree of trust and co-operation that is inherent in their relationship. It is the latter element that is most important. Long-term contracts can be entered into on an arm's length basis by contracting parties who are intent on looking after their own interests. Such contracts are not relational in nature and there is no need to imply a duty of good faith into them (see *UTB*

LLC v Sheffield United Ltd [2019] EWHC 2322 (Ch), [202]–[204]). The case for the implication of a good faith term is at its strongest where the relationship between the contracting parties is a collaborative one, in which the parties repose trust and confidence in one another. In such a case, where the emphasis of the parties is on loyalty, integrity, co-operation and the spirit of the deal rather than the letter of the contract, a duty of good faith may be more likely to give effect to the presumed intention of the parties. Although there is authority post *Bates* which supports the implication of a good faith term into 'relational' contracts (see, for example, *Essex County Council v UBB Waste (Essex) Ltd (No 2)* [2020] EWHC 1581 (TCC), [106]), there is also some hostility towards the proposition (*Russell v Cartwright* [2020] EWHC 41 (Ch), [87]). It is suggested that the better approach may be to dispense with the inquiry into whether the contract is properly to be classified as a 'relational' contract from which a duty of good faith is then derived. Instead, the courts should examine all the facts and circumstances of the case, including the alleged 'relational' nature of the contract, and then decide whether a reasonable reader of the contract would consider an obligation of good faith to be so obvious as to go without saying or whether such an obligation is necessary for the proper working of the contract between the parties (*Cathay Pacific Airways Ltd v Lufthansa Technik AG* [2020] EWHC 1789 (Ch), [185]–[218]).

Although it is possible to imply a duty of good faith into a contract, it is suggested that, except in the cases where the contract between the parties has the indicia attributed to a 'relational' contract as set out above, the courts will be slow to do so, particularly in detailed contracts where the parties could have, but did not, make use of the language of good faith (*Fujitsu Services Ltd v IBM United Kingdom Ltd* [2014] EWHC 752 (TCC)) or in the case where the arm's length nature of the relationship between the parties makes it inappropriate to imply a good faith duty (*Myers v Kestrel Acquisitions Ltd* [2015] EWHC 916; [2016] 1 BCLC 719 (Ch)). The courts will also decline to make the implication where its effect is to cut down the scope of an obligation which the parties have expressed in absolute terms (*Greenclose Ltd v National Westminster Bank plc* [2014] EWHC 1156 (Ch); [2014] 2 Lloyd's Rep 169), where the term is perceived to impose an unduly onerous obligation on the parties to the contract (*Hamsard 3147 Ltd v Boots UK Ltd* [2013] EWHC 3251 (Pat)) or where the implication of a general good faith duty would duplicate or render redundant other clauses of the contract (*Portsmouth City Council v Ensign Highways Ltd* [2015] EWHC 1969 (TCC); [2015] BLR 675). Appellate courts in particular have expressed hesitations about the development of a general good faith principle which may have far-reaching and unintended consequences (see, for example, *MSC Mediterranean Shipping Co SA v Cottonex Anstalt* [2016] EWCA Civ 789; [2016] 2 Lloyd's Rep 494, [45]).

Third, the meaning of good faith, and thus the extent of the obligation which its acceptance imposes on contracting parties, will depend upon its context. Good faith has been described as a 'modest' requirement (*Astor Management AG v Atalaya Mining plc* [2017] EWHC 425 (Comm); [2018] 1 All ER (Comm) 547, [98]). At its core it demands that the parties act honestly in their dealings with one another. But it is capable of demanding more of contracting parties. Thus it may require parties to adhere to the spirit of the contract, to observe reasonable commercial standards of fair dealing, to be faithful to the agreed common purpose and to act consistently with the justified expectations of the parties (*Health & Case Management Ltd v The Physiotherapy Network Ltd* [2018] EWHC 869 (QB), [128]). The latter duties are more likely to be found in long-term, relational contracts where the parties' relationship is a deep one and where such a duty is more likely to be reflective of their intention (*Al Nehayan v Kent* [2018] EWHC 333 (Comm); [2018] 1 CLC[167]–[174]; *Bates v Post Office Ltd*, [710]). In other contracts, good faith may require no more than honesty. But even here there is room for disagreement as to what honesty requires of the parties. At a minimum it demands that the parties refrain from telling lies. The more difficult question is the extent to which it will require parties to disclose the truth. Traditionally, as we have seen, English law has refrained from imposing such a duty on parties to a contract or parties negotiating a contract. One consequence of the possible recognition of a duty of good faith may be to increase the pressure for the recognition of a duty of disclosure, at least between contracting parties and possibly between negotiating parties.

Hot topic 11...

The question whether English law does or should recognise that contracting parties are subject to a duty of good faith is currently a very controversial one. The immediate cause of the controversy was the judgment of Leggatt J in *Yam Seng Pte Ltd v International Trade Corporation Ltd* which can justly claim to be the most controversial first instance decision on English contract law for many years. A recent example of its application is to be found in the judgment of Fraser J in *Bates v Post Office Ltd*, a judgment at first instance which has also given rise to a considerable amount of debate.

Bates was a case in which the contracts between the Post Office and its sub-postmasters were held to be 'relational' contracts which imposed an implied duty of good faith on both parties. In deciding that the contracts were relational, Fraser J identified a number of characteristics of a relational contract, namely (i) there must be no specific express terms in the contract that prevents a duty of good faith being implied into the contract, (ii) the contract will be a long-term one, with the mutual intention of the parties being that there will be a long-term relationship, (iii) the parties must intend that their respective roles be performed with integrity and with fidelity to their bargain, (iv) the parties will be committed to collaborating with one another in the performance of the contract, (v) the spirits and objectives of their venture may not be capable of being expressed exhaustively in a written contract, (vi) they will each repose trust and confidence in one another, but of a different kind to that involved in fiduciary relationships, (vii)

the contract in question will involve a high degree of communication, co-operation and predictable performance based on mutual trust and confidence, and expectations of loyalty, (viii) there may be a significant investment by one party (or both) in the venture, and this significant investment may be, in some cases, more accurately described as substantial financial commitment and (ix) exclusivity of the relationship may also be present.

But not everyone is convinced of the validity of this approach. The judgment of Fancourt J in *UTB LLC v Sheffield United Ltd* contains a clear warning in relation to the use of the term 'relational' contract, and in particular, he highlights the fact that not every long-term contract is to be regarded as a relational contract. Thus he stated that 'it is self-evidently not all long-term contracts that involve an enduring but undefined, cooperative relationship between the parties that will, as a matter of law, involve an obligation of good faith.' In each case it is necessary to consider whether an obligation of good faith is necessary to the proper working of the contract. Further, it is necessary to pay careful attention to the express terms of the contract when considering whether or not it is necessary to imply a good faith duty because such a duty may not sit comfortably with the express terms of the contract and, in such a case, the implication of a good faith duty will not be made.

The debate about relational contracts and good faith remains to be resolved, and we await an authoritative decision of an appellate court on the issue.

Summary

▶ English law does not recognise the existence of a general duty to disclose material facts known to one contracting party but not to the other.

▶ A defendant who knows that the claimant has misunderstood the terms of his offer is under an obligation to inform the claimant of the true nature of his offer.

▶ A representation may be made by conduct.

▶ A person is under a duty to disclose material facts which come to his notice before the conclusion of a contract if they falsify a representation previously made by him.

▶ A person may be guilty of misrepresentation if his statement is literally true but is in fact misleading.

▶ A duty to disclose material facts is imposed in the case of contracts *uberrimae fidei* (of the utmost good faith) and in the case of certain fiduciary relations.

▶ Exceptionally a duty of disclosure may be imposed by the law of tort.

▶ The existence of the 'satisfactory quality' and 'fitness for purpose' provisions in the Sale of Goods Act 1979 mitigates the hardships which would otherwise be caused by the refusal of English contract law to recognise the existence of a general duty of disclosure. Similar obligations are now contained in the Supply of Goods and Services Act 1982.

Exercises

12.1 Why does English law not recognise the existence of a general duty of disclosure? Do you think it should recognise the existence of such a duty?

12.2 List the exceptional situations in which English law does recognise the existence of a particular duty of disclosure. Do these exceptions have any coherent rationale?

12.3 In Professor Fried's illustration concerning the oil company and the farmer (see Section 12.1), should the oil company be required to disclose its information to the farmer? Give reasons for your answer. Can you distinguish this illustration from the case of *Gordon v Selico* (1986) 11 HLR 219?

12.4 Joe papered his dining-room prior to selling the house, partly because it needed redecorating anyway and partly to hide the defective state of the plaster. Emma bought the house and later discovered that the defective state of the plaster was in fact caused by a serious structural fault in the dining-room wall. Has she a cause of action against Joe?

12.5 It is a noticeable feature of the duty of disclosure cases which have arisen in the twentieth century that they concern contracts which fall outside the scope of regulatory legislation, such as the Sale of Goods Act 1979. Can we learn any lessons from this fact?

Chapter 13

Misrepresentation

13.1 Introduction

Although English law does not recognise the existence of a general duty to disclose information during the process of contractual negotiation, the process of contractual negotiation is not left unregulated. Rather, a duty is imposed not to make any false statements of fact or law to the other contracting party and thereby to induce him to enter into the contract. As we shall see, the law relating to misrepresentation does have a crucial role to play in the policing of contractual negotiations (see Section 13.3).

At the outset a fundamental distinction must be drawn between a promise and a representation. A promise may be defined as a statement by which the maker of the statement accepts or appears to accept an obligation to do or not to do something. A representation, on the other hand, is a statement which simply asserts the truth of a given state of facts. The distinction can be illustrated by reference to the case of *Kleinwort Benson Ltd v Malaysia Mining Corp Berhad* [1989] 1 WLR 379. The claimants agreed to make available to a subsidiary company of the defendants a £10 million credit facility. The defendants refused to act as guarantors but they gave to the claimants a letter of comfort which stated that 'it is our policy to ensure that the business of [the subsidiary company] is at all times in a position to meet its liabilities to you under the above arrangements'. The subsidiary company ceased to trade after the collapse of the tin market at a time when its indebtedness to the claimants was £10 million. The defendants refused to honour their undertaking in the letter of comfort and so the claimants took proceedings against them, arguing that the defendants were in breach of contract in failing to pay. But the Court of Appeal held that the letter of comfort did not amount to a contractual promise by the defendants. Therefore, they were not liable to the claimants. It was held that the letter of comfort was simply a representation of fact as to the defendants' policy at the time when the statement was made. The defendants did not promise that they would not change their policy for the future; they did not state that 'it is *and will at all times continue to be* our policy to ensure that the subsidiary will at all times be in a position to meet its liabilities to you'.

Thus promises and representations are functionally different and have different legal consequences. A representation is a statement of fact which induces the other party to enter into a contract or otherwise act to his detriment. The representor does not promise anything; he simply asserts the truth of his statement and invites reliance upon that statement. If his statement of fact is false then it is a misrepresentation and the most appropriate remedy is to put the other party in the position which he would have been in had he not acted upon the misrepresentation to his detriment. Thus, on the facts of *Kleinwort Benson*, had the defendants' policy, at the time at which they made the statement, not been to ensure that the subsidiary would at all times be in a position to meet its liabilities, then their statement would have amounted to an actionable misrepresentation (see Section 13.3). A promise, on the other hand, creates an expectation that the promise will be fulfilled and the promisor accepts (or is deemed to accept) an obligation to carry out his promise. Having accepted such an obligation, the law will call upon the promisor to fulfil that obligation and will seek, by the remedy granted, to protect the expectation so created (see Section 21.3). Although promises and representations are functionally different, it can be very difficult to tell whether a particular statement is a promise or a representation. For example, in *Kleinwort Benson* the trial judge, Hirst J, held that the letter of comfort was a contractual promise, whereas the Court of Appeal held that it was a representation of fact. But any difficulty experienced in drawing the line should not blind us to the fact that representations and promises are fundamentally different types of statement.

One final point must be made before we consider the substance of the law relating to misrepresentation. That point is that misrepresentation lies on the boundary of contract, tort and restitution (or unjust enrichment). A party who has been induced to enter a contract by a misrepresentation may seek a remedy in contract, tort or restitution. Therefore, at various points in the chapter, we shall have to consider liability in all three branches of the law. Additionally, consumers have been given rights of redress against traders in respect of various unfair commercial practices (which include misleading actions taking the form of the giving of false information) under Part 4A of the Consumer Protection from Unfair Trading Regulations 2008 (SI 2008/1277). These rights include the right to unwind the contract in certain circumstances, the right to a discount and the right to damages. These rights are additional to the rights available to a consumer at common law or in equity but cannot be exercised in combination with these rights.

Our analysis will proceed in four stages. At the first stage we will define a misrepresentation; at the second stage we shall discuss the different types of misrepresentation; at the third stage we shall consider the remedies for misrepresentation; and at the final stage we shall discuss the exclusion of liability for misrepresentation.

13.2 What is a misrepresentation?

A misrepresentation may be defined as an unambiguous, false statement of fact or law which is addressed to the party misled, which is material (although this requirement is now debatable) and which induces the contract. This definition may be broken down into three distinct elements. The first is that the representation must be an unambiguous false statement of fact or law (Section 13.3), the second is that it must be addressed to the party misled (Section 13.4) and the third is that it must be an inducement to entry into the contract and possibly it must also be material (Section 13.5).

13.3 A statement of existing fact or law

The rule was traditionally stated in the form that a representation must be an unambiguous false statement of existing fact. However, it is now clear that a misrepresentation of law can constitute an actionable misrepresentation. This was not always so. For many years a misrepresentation of law did not suffice to create a cause of action. The mistake of law bar was first broken by the House of Lords in *Kleinwort Benson Ltd v Lincoln City Council* [1999] 2 AC 349 where it was held that money paid under a mistake of law could be recovered on essentially the same basis as money paid under a mistake of fact. Building on the foundation laid in *Kleinwort Benson* the courts have subsequently held that a mistake of law can, in an appropriate case, entitle the mistaken party to set aside a contract entered into as a result of the mistake (*Brennan v Bolt Burden (a firm)* [2004] EWCA Civ 1017; [2005] QB 303) and that a misrepresentation of law can found a cause of action (*Pankhania v London Borough of Hackney* [2002] EWHC 2441 (Ch)). Thus, a misrepresentation of law should now give a representee a cause of action on the same basis as if the misrepresentation had been of an existing fact.

Misrepresentations of law apart, the representation must be an unambiguous false statement of existing fact. The need for a statement underlines the point that a failure to disclose information will not generally constitute a representation, although, as we have noted, the courts have been flexible in their identification of a 'statement' so that, for example, a statement can be made by conduct as well as by words (see Sections 12.3–12.5). The statement must also be one of *existing fact*. The following three categories of statement have been held *not* to constitute statements of existing fact and therefore cannot amount to actionable misrepresentations.

The first is a 'mere puff'. We have already noted (see Section 8.1) that a commendatory statement may be so vague as to be neither a promise which is incorporated into the contract as a term, nor a statement of fact. In *Dimmock v Hallett* (1866) LR 2 Ch App 21, Turner LJ said that a representation that land was 'fertile and improveable' would not, except in an extreme case, be considered such a misrepresentation as to entitle the innocent party to rescind the contract. But there are limits to this principle. The more specific the statement, the less likely it is to be treated as a mere puff (*Carlill v Carbolic Smoke Ball Co* [1893] 1 QB 256, discussed in more detail in Section 3.3).

Secondly, a statement of opinion or belief which proves to be unfounded is not a false statement of fact. In *Bisset v Wilkinson* [1927] AC 177, a vendor of a farm in New Zealand, which had not been used for sheep farming before, represented to a prospective purchaser that, in his judgment, the land could carry 2,000 sheep. In fact it could not carry 2,000 sheep and the purchaser, when he discovered this, sought to set aside the contract on the ground of the vendor's misrepresentation. He was unable to do so because the vendor's statement was not a false statement of fact but a statement of opinion which he honestly held.

Bisset was distinguished, however, in the important case of *Esso Petroleum Ltd v Mardon* [1976] QB 801. Esso represented to the defendant, a prospective tenant of a petrol filling station which was in the process of construction, that the throughput of petrol at the station was likely to reach 200,000 gallons per year. However, the local authority refused planning permission for the petrol pumps to front on to the main street. Instead, the station had to be built back to front with the forecourt at the back of the station and the only access to the petrol pumps being from a side street. Esso, through their experienced officials, assured the defendant that this change would not affect the projected throughput of petrol. In fact, as a result of the change, the throughput only reached 78,000 gallons per year. The defendant incurred considerable losses in operating the station and he eventually reached the position where he could no longer pay Esso for his petrol. Esso consequently sought to repossess the station and to recover the money owed to them by the defendant. The defendant counterclaimed for damages for breach of contract and for negligent misrepresentation. Esso argued that their statement as to the throughput of petrol was a statement of opinion and hence was not actionable. But the Court of Appeal held that the statement was actionable. Lord Denning distinguished *Bisset* on the ground that there 'the land had never been used as a sheep farm and both parties were equally able to form an opinion as to its carrying capacity'. Esso, on the other hand, had special knowledge and skill in the forecasting of the throughput of petrol and they were held to represent that they had made the forecast with 'reasonable care and skill'. On the facts it was held that they had not exercised reasonable care and skill and they were therefore liable to the defendant in damages. A similar approach to that adopted in *Esso* was espoused by Bowen LJ in *Smith v Land and House Property Corp* (1884) 28 Ch D 7, when he said that where:

> the facts are equally known to both parties, what one says to the other is frequently nothing but an expression of opinion … But if the facts are not equally well known to both sides, then a statement of opinion by one who knows the facts best involves very often a statement of material fact, for he impliedly states that he knows facts which justify his opinion.

Combining the principles established in *Esso* and *Smith* we can deduce the following proposition: where the representor has greater knowledge than the representee, the courts will imply that the representation must be made with reasonable care and skill (*Esso*) and that the representor knows facts which justify his opinion (*Smith*). In effect, these cases impose upon negotiating parties who have special skill a duty to take reasonable care in the preparation of forecasts and opinions.

Finally, a statement of intention is not a statement of fact. Nor is a promise a statement of fact. A person who fails to carry out his stated intention does not thereby make a misrepresentation (*Wales v Wadham* [1977] 1 WLR 199). But a person who misrepresents his present intention does make a false statement of fact because the state of his intention is a matter of fact. In *Edgington v Fitzmaurice* (1885) 29 Ch D 459, directors of a company invited the public to subscribe for debentures on the basis that the money so raised would be used to expand the business. In fact, the real purpose in raising the money was to pay off company debts. It was held that the directors were guilty of misrepresentation because they had misrepresented their actual intention.

13.4 Addressed to the party misled

Secondly, it must be shown that the representation was addressed to the party misled. There are two ways in which a representation may be addressed to the party misled. The first and most obvious method is by the direct communication of the misrepresentation to the claimant by the representor. Alternatively, the misrepresentation may be addressed by the representor to a third party with the intention that it be passed on to the claimant. In *Commercial Banking Co of Sydney v RH Brown and Co* [1972] 2 Lloyd's Rep 360, the defendant bank misrepresented to the claimants' bank the financial standing of one of the claimants' customers. The claimants' bank communicated the information to the claimants, who acted on it to their detriment.

It was held that the defendants were liable to the claimants because they knew that the claimants' bank did not want the information for their own purposes and that it was to be passed on to a customer who was proposing to deal with a client of the defendant bank.

13.5 Inducement

Finally, the representation must be an inducement to entry into the contract and possibly it must also be a material misrepresentation. The materiality requirement can be taken first because of the controversy which currently surrounds it. In the old cases, frequent references can be found to the requirement that the misrepresentation must be material (see, for example, *Mathias v Yetts* (1882) 46 LT 497, 502, per Jessel MR). The precise meaning of materiality was not always clear but it seems to have meant that the misrepresentation must have been such as would affect the judgment of a reasonable man in deciding whether or not to enter into the contract on these terms. Today the requirement that the misrepresentation be material is commonly doubted. The reality would appear to be that the modern courts tend not to distinguish carefully between materiality and inducement. Rather, an inference of inducement is often drawn from a finding of materiality, so that materiality ceases to be a distinct requirement and becomes a part of the inquiry into whether or not the misrepresentation induced entry into the contract. On this basis the law can be stated in the following propositions. If the misrepresentation would have induced a reasonable person to enter into the contract, then the court will presume that it did induce the representee to enter into the contract, and the onus of proof is then placed on the representor to show that the representee did not in fact rely on the representation (see *Museprime Properties Ltd v Adhill Properties Ltd* (1991) 61 P & C R 111, 124, per Scott J and *County NatWest v Barton* [2002] 4 All ER 494). On the other hand, where the misrepresentation would not have induced a reasonable person to enter into the contract, then the onus of proof is upon the representee to show that the misrepresentation did in fact induce him to enter into the contract (*Dadourian Group International Inc v Simms* [2009] EWCA Civ 169; [2009] 1 Lloyd's Rep 601, [99]–[101]). These propositions may well strike a reasonable balance between the interests of the parties. The difficult case is where an innocent and immaterial misrepresentation does actually induce a representee to enter into a contract. Should such a representee be entitled to set aside the contract? It is not at all obvious that he should. In practice it is, of course, extremely unlikely that a representee would be able to prove that he was induced to enter into a contract by an immaterial misrepresentation. But the possibility that a representee could do so might suggest that the courts ought to exercise caution before abandoning the materiality requirement (fraud, of course, constitutes an exception here because a person who has been fraudulent cannot be heard to argue that the representation was immaterial: *Ross River Ltd v Cambridge City Football Club Ltd* [2007] EWHC 2115 (Ch); [2008] 1 All ER 1004).

Whatever doubts we may harbour about the materiality requirement, there is no doubt that the representation must induce the contract, that is to say, it must induce or cause the claimant to enter into the contract. The onus of proof is upon the representee to prove that it was induced to enter into the contract by the misrepresentation, at least in cases where the misrepresentation was made innocently or negligently (*BV Nederlandse Industrie van Eiprodukten v Rembrandt Enterprises Inc* [2019] EWCA Civ 596; [2020] QB 551, [15]). Matters are more difficult where the misrepresentation was made fraudulently. In such a case it would appear that there is an evidential presumption of fact (not law), which is very difficult to rebut, that a representee was induced by a fraudulent misrepresentation that was intended to cause him to enter the contract (*BV Nederlandse Industrie van Eiprodukten v Rembrandt Enterprises Inc*, [43]). But, even in the case of a fraudulent misrepresentation, it remains the case that the representee must have acted on the misrepresentation. If the representee would have acted in exactly the same way in the absence of the misrepresentation, an attempt to bring a claim on the basis of misrepresentation will fail (*Versloot Dredging BV v HDI Gerling Industrie Versicherung AG* [2016] UKSC 45; [2017] AC 1, [29]).

Whether a particular representation induced a party to enter into a contract is a question of fact (*Zurich Insurance Co plc v Hayward* [2016] UKSC 48; [2017] AC 142, [25] and [63]). In *Edgington v Fitzmaurice* (1885) 29 Ch D 459 (above) it was held that the misrepresentation need not be the sole inducement, nor must it have been 'decisive'. On the other hand, it is not sufficient for the claimant to demonstrate that 'he was supported or encouraged in reaching his decision by the representation in question' (*Raiffeisen Zentralbank Osterreich AG v Royal Bank of Scotland plc* [2010] EWHC 1392 (Comm); [2011] 1 Lloyd's Rep 123, [153]). The claimant must go further and establish that the representation played a 'real and substantial' part in inducing him to enter into the contract. In order to prove that a representation played a 'real and substantial' part, the claimant must prove that 'but for such representation' he 'would not have entered into the contract on the terms on which he did, even though there were other matters but for which he would not have done so either' (*Raiffeisen Zentralbank Osterreich AG v Royal Bank of Scotland plc* at [170]). When deciding whether a claimant was induced by the representation to enter into the contract, a court will generally ask what the claimant would have done if no representation had been made to him; it is not generally necessary for the claimant to establish that he would have acted differently if he had known the truth (*Raiffeisen Zentralbank Osterreich AG v Royal Bank of Scotland plc* at [179]–[187]) nor is it necessary to prove that the representee believed that the representation was true (*Zurich Insurance Co plc v Hayward* [2016] UKSC 48; [2017] AC 142). Instead the vital question to be answered is whether the representation induced the representee to enter into the contract.

There are at least three situations in which a claimant will be unable to show that the representation induced the contract. The first is where the claimant was unaware of the existence of the representation (*Horsfall v Thomas* (1862) 1 H & C 90), the second is where the claimant knew (and not simply suspected) that the representation was untrue and the third is where the claimant did not allow the representation to affect his judgment. A claimant does not allow a representation to affect his judgment where he regards the representation as being unimportant (*Smith v Chadwick* (1884) 9 App Cas 187) or where he relies upon his own judgment. In *Atwood v Small* (1838) 6 Cl & F 232, Atwood contracted to sell his mine to Small, but exaggerated its earning capacity. Small appointed agents to verify Atwood's representations and they reported that his statements were true. After the contract was concluded, Small discovered the exaggerations and sought to rescind the contract. He was unable to do so because he had relied upon his agents' report rather than upon Atwood's representation. It should be noted that this rule does not apply to the claimant who has the opportunity to discover the truth himself but does not take it. In such a case, the claimant remains entitled to relief against the misrepresentor (*Redgrave v Hurd* (1881) 20 Ch D 1; although, in the light of the decision of the House of Lords in *Smith v Eric S Bush* [1990] 1 AC 831, *Redgrave* may no longer apply where it was reasonable to expect the representee to make use of the opportunity and he fails to do so: Treitel, 2020, para 9-033). Thus, it will not suffice for the representor to show that the person to whom the misrepresentation was made could have discovered the true situation; he must go further and prove that he did discover it in order to show that the misrepresentation did not induce entry into the contract. A similar rule applies in the case where the representor 'corrects' his misrepresentation prior to reliance upon it by the representee; in such a case the representor, in order to negate the inducement, must generally show that the correction was actually brought to the attention of the representee prior to reliance upon it (*Peekay Intermark Ltd v Australia and NZ Banking Group Ltd* [2006] EWCA Civ 386; [2006] 2 Lloyd's Rep 511, where the 'correction' was to be found in the detailed contents of the contract which were sent to the claimant: in this case the initial representations had been cast in rather vague terms and the claimant could reasonably be expected to examine the terms of the contract which had been sent to him prior to signing its terms).

13.6 The types of misrepresentation

There are four different types of misrepresentation. It is important to distinguish between the different types of misrepresentation because they may give rise to different remedial consequences. We shall see that all types of misrepresentation entitle the representee to rescind the contract but not all types of misrepresentation give rise to an action for damages.

13.6.1 Fraud

The first type of misrepresentation is fraudulent misrepresentation. Fraudulent misrepresentation, in addition to being a ground on which a contract may be set aside, constitutes the tort of deceit. Although the word 'fraud' bears a wide meaning in common parlance, its meaning in law is much narrower as a result of the decision of the House of Lords in *Derry v Peek* (1889) 14 App Cas 337. In *Derry v Peek*, Lord Herschell established the following three propositions. The first is that there must be proof of fraud and nothing short of that is sufficient. The second is that fraud is proved when it is shown that a false representation has been made (i) knowingly or (ii) without belief in its truth or (iii) recklessly, careless whether it be true or false. Unreasonableness of belief does not of itself constitute fraud; it simply provides evidence of dishonesty on the part of the maker of the statement (*Angus v Clifford* [1891] 2 Ch 449). Thirdly, if fraud is proved the motive of the person guilty of it is immaterial. In *Polhill v Walter* (1832) 3 B & Ad 114, the representor knew that his statement was false but his motive in making the statement was to benefit his principal and not to benefit himself, nor to injure anyone else. Notwithstanding his good motives, he was held liable in the tort of deceit. Deceit is a difficult matter to prove and it should not be alleged unless there are good grounds to believe that fraud has indeed been practised. Thus fraud is not lightly invoked in the courts.

13.6.2   Negligence

The second type of misrepresentation is negligent misrepresentation at common law. In the period immediately after *Derry v Peek*, it was thought that negligent misrepresentation was not actionable in tort because liability in tort arose only in cases of fraudulent misrepresentation (*Le Lievre v Gould* [1893] 1 QB 491). However, this view was rejected by the House of Lords in *Nocton v Lord Ashburton* [1914] AC 932. Although the House recognised that negligent misrepresentation could be actionable, they held that it was actionable only where there was a preexisting contractual relationship between the parties or where the parties were in a 'fiduciary relationship'. This restrictive approach prevailed in England as late as 1951 (see *Candler v Crane, Christmas and Co* [1951] 2 KB 164, but contrast the powerful dissenting judgment of Denning LJ).

However, in 1964 in *Hedley Byrne v Heller* [1964] AC 465, the House of Lords finally expanded the ambit of liability for negligent misrepresentation. The claimants were advertising agents who booked substantial advertising space on behalf of their clients, Easipower Ltd, on terms that they were personally liable if Easipower defaulted. The claimants became concerned about the financial standing of Easipower and, through their bank, sought from the defendants, who were Easipower's bankers, a reference on the financial soundness of Easipower. The defendants replied that Easipower were 'considered good for its ordinary business transactions'. In reliance upon the reference, the claimants placed orders which, because of the subsequent default of Easipower, resulted in a loss to them of £17,000. The claimants alleged that the defendants were negligent in the preparation of the reference and were therefore liable to them in damages. Their claim failed because the defendants had provided the reference 'without responsibility'. However the importance of *Hedley Byrne* lies, not in the fact that the claim failed because of the disclaimer, but in the fact that the House of Lords would have allowed the claim to succeed had it not been for the disclaimer. In so concluding, their Lordships significantly widened the scope of liability in tort for negligent misrepresentation. The important task which now remains for us is to ascertain the limits of *Hedley Byrne*.

This is not an entirely straightforward task. As Lord Sumption observed in *Playboy Club London Ltd v Banca Nazionale del Lavoro SpA* [2018] UKSC 43; [2018] 1 WLR 4041, [7], the principle established in *Hedley Byrne* has 'undergone considerable development since 1964'. Key elements in establishing what has come to be known as *Hedley Byrne* liability are reasonable reliance by the representee on a statement made by the representor and for that reliance to have been reasonably foreseen by the representor who is thereby deemed to have assumed responsibility for the statement (*NRAM Ltd v Steel* [2018] UKSC 13; [2018] 1 WLR 1190, [19]). Thus the two critical ingredients of *Hedley Byrne* liability are an assumption of responsibility by the representor (and typically that assumption of responsibility is a voluntary one) and reasonable reliance thereon by the representee (*Spring v Guardian Assurance plc* [1995] 2 AC 296 and *Henderson v Merrett Syndicates Ltd* [1995] 2 AC 145). It is the assumption of responsibility by the representor which has been held to be the 'foundation' of this form of liability and it typically serves to limit liability to 'an identifiable (although not necessarily identified) person or group of persons' so that it does not extend to 'the world at large or to a wholly indeterminate group' (*Playboy Club London Ltd v Banca Nazionale del Lavoro SpA* [2018] UKSC 43; [2018] 1 WLR 4041, [7] and *Caparo Industries plc v Dickman* [1990] 2 AC 605).

A key element of *Hedley Byrne* liability is therefore the knowledge of the representor at the time at which the statement was made. The greater the knowledge which the representor has of the representee and of the purposes for which the representee is likely to rely upon his statement, the more likely it is that the representor will be held to owe a duty of care to the representee. It is important to note that the knowledge of the representor must relate both to the identity of the representee (whether as a specific, identified person or as a member of a limited group) and to the purpose for which the information will be used (typically to enter into a transaction). So, for example, on the facts of *Hedley Byrne* the representor understood that the credit reference would be relied upon by an unidentified, but readily identifiable, client on whose behalf the bank had made the inquiry. The representor also knew that the proposed transaction was an advertising contract for some £9,000, although it would probably have sufficed for it to know (which it did) that someone was proposing to enter into a business transaction with Easipower Ltd.

13.6.3 Section 2(1) of the Misrepresentation Act 1967

Negligent misrepresentation at common law must be distinguished from the liability which may arise under section 2(1) of the Misrepresentation Act 1967. This is the third type of misrepresentation. Section 2(1) provides that:

> Where a person has entered into a contract after a misrepresentation has been made to him by another party thereto and as a result thereof he has suffered loss then, if the person making the misrepresentation would be liable to damages in respect thereof had the misrepresentation been made fraudulently, that person shall be so liable notwithstanding that the misrepresentation was not made fraudulently, unless he proves that he had reasonable grounds to believe and did believe up to the time that the contract was made that the facts represented were true.

Section 2(1) operates independently of the *Hedley Byrne* line of authority and has been described as 'a statutory tort' (*First Tower Trustees Ltd v CDS (Superstores International) Ltd* [2018] EWCA Civ 1396; [2019] 1 WLR 637, [98]). The section is drafted in rather clumsy and unusual terms because it imposes liability by reference to liability for fraudulent misrepresentation, even though the misrepresentor has not been fraudulent (for a discussion of the possible consequences of the 'fiction of fraud' see Atiyah and Treitel, 1967, 372–75). But, stripped of its convoluted drafting, the general effect of the section is clear; where a misrepresentation has been made by one contracting party to another, the party making the misrepresentation is liable to the other in damages unless he can prove that he had reasonable grounds to believe and did believe up to the time that the contract was made that his statement was true. The section is concerned with the liability of the 'other party' to the contract and not with the liability of an agent of that party (*Resolute Maritime Inc v Nippon Kaiji Kyokai, The Skopas* [1983] 1 WLR 857).

This statutory right has three advantages over a common law negligence claim. The first is that the Act does not require that there be a *Hedley Byrne* relationship between the parties, thus avoiding the difficulties inherent in establishing the existence of such a relationship. This was of crucial significance in *Gosling v Anderson* [1972] EGD 709. The defendant, who was selling her flat, represented to the claimant, through her estate agents, that planning permission had been obtained for building a garage when, in fact, it had not been obtained. In the Court of Appeal Roskill LJ stated that, had the action been heard before 1967, the claimant's action would have failed unless she had been able to prove fraud, but that she was now able to rely on section 2(1) of the 1967 Act and was entitled to damages for the misrepresentation.

The second advantage of a claim under section 2(1) is that the representor is liable unless he proves that he had reasonable grounds to believe and did believe up to the time that the contract was made that the facts represented were true, whereas at common law it is for the representee to prove that the representor was negligent. It is the belief of the representor that is relevant for this purpose, not the belief of an agent of the representor. Thus it will not suffice for a representor to show that an agent had reasonable grounds to believe and did believe that the representation was true. The subsection is concerned with the liability of the 'other party' to the contract and so it is only the belief of a party who can be identified with the company itself that is relevant (*MCI WorldCom International Inc v Primus Telecommunications Inc* [2003] EWHC 2182 (Comm); [2004] 1 All ER (Comm) 138). It is no easy task for a representor to discharge the onus of proof under section 2(1), as can be seen from the case of *Howard Marine v Ogden* (above). The defendants wished to hire barges from the claimants and, during the course of the negotiations, the claimants' manager represented that the deadweight capacity of each barge was 1,600 tonnes when, in fact, it was only 1,055 tonnes. The defendants used the barges for six troublesome months but, when they discovered the true deadweight capacity of the barges, they refused to continue to pay the hire. The claimants sued for the hire charges and the defendants counterclaimed, *inter alia*, for damages under section 2(1) of the 1967 Act. The representation of the claimants' manager as to the deadweight capacity of the barges was based upon his recollection of the figures in Lloyd's Register (Lord Denning stated that Lloyd's Register 'was regarded in shipping circles as the bible'). The manager's recollection was correct but, unusually, Lloyd's was wrong. The Court of Appeal held, Lord Denning dissenting, that the claimants had not discharged the burden of proof upon them of showing that they had reasonable grounds to believe that the statement was true. This was because the accurate figures were contained in the ships' documents and the claimants had failed to show any 'objectively reasonable ground' for disregarding the figure in these documents and preferring the figure in Lloyd's Register. The burden upon the representor is therefore a heavy one and it is likely to enable a representee to recover where at common law he would have failed (for example, in *Howard Marine v Ogden* itself, only Shaw LJ was of the opinion that a common law claim would have succeeded).

The third advantage is that the measure of damages recoverable under section 2(1) is the measure of damages for the tort of deceit. Authority for this proposition is derived from the controversial case of *Royscot Trust Ltd v Rogerson* [1991] 2 QB 297. The claimant finance company was induced to enter into a hire-purchase transaction with Mr Rogerson as a result of a misrepresentation by the defendant car dealers. As the defendants knew, it was the claimants' policy not to enter into a hire-purchase transaction unless 20 per cent of the purchase price of a car was paid to the dealer by the customer. Mr Rogerson agreed with the defendants to put down a deposit of £1,200 on a car, the price of which was £7,600. But that produced a deposit of only some 16 per cent of the purchase price. So the defendants falsely stated that the price of the car was £8,000 and that Mr Rogerson had paid a deposit of £1,600; thus producing the required 20 per cent deposit (it is vital to note here that there was no allegation that the defendants were guilty of fraud in making these changes: the case proceeded upon the assumption that the defendants had not been fraudulent). On this basis, the claimants agreed to enter into the transaction but Mr Rogerson subsequently, in breach of contract, sold the car and ceased to pay the hire-purchase instalments. The Court of Appeal held that damages under section 2(1) were to be assessed as if the defendants had been fraudulent, so that the claimants were entitled to recover their actual loss directly flowing from the misrepresentation, whether or not that loss was reasonably foreseeable. The remoteness rule applicable was that derived from the tort of deceit, not the tort of negligence (see Section 13.9). The court held that the action of Mr Rogerson in dishonestly selling the car was a direct result of the defendants' misrepresentation, in the sense that there was no break in the chain of causation between the misrepresentation and the loss. The claimants were therefore entitled to recover damages of £3,625, namely the difference between the £6,400 they advanced to Mr Rogerson and the instalments of £2,775 they received from him before his default. While there may remain some circumstances in which a representee will gain an advantage by bringing a claim in the tort of deceit rather than under section 2(1) (on which see Hooley, 1992), the effect of *Royscot* must surely be to reduce the practical significance of the tort of deceit. After all, why go to the trouble of proving that the representor was fraudulent when you can recover the same measure of damages under section 2(1) without even having to prove that the representor was negligent?

Yet, there is something distinctly odd about the result in *Royscot*. The defendants were not fraudulent, but they were treated as if they had been. The point becomes even more apparent when applied to the facts of *Howard Marine v Ogden* (above). What justification can there possibly be for treating the claimants in *Howard Marine* as if they had been fraudulent, when it was not even proved that they had been guilty of negligence?

These anomalies could have been avoided if the court in *Royscot* had accepted that the reference to fraud in section 2(1) was simply a 'fiction'. But Balcombe LJ rejected this argument on the ground that it was inconsistent with the authorities and contrary to the 'plain words of the subsection'. While the intention of Parliament in enacting section 2(1) may well have been to incorporate, by analogy, the rules for the tort of deceit (see Cartwright, 1987a, 429–33), it is almost certain that Parliament could not have foreseen the anomalies which would arise as a result of the analogy drawn. But *Royscot* makes the anomaly plain for all to see. There is no justification for treating an innocent party as if he had been fraudulent. In *Smith New Court Securities Ltd v Scrimgeour Vickers (Asset Management) Ltd* [1997] AC 254, 283 Lord Steyn noted that *Royscot* had been the subject of 'trenchant academic criticism' (by Hooley, 1991) and expressed 'no concluded view' on the correctness of the decision

(Lord Browne-Wilkinson also 'expressed no view' (267) on the correctness of *Royscot*). So the point remains an open one, at least at the level of the Supreme Court. Below that level it is binding, notwithstanding the substantial judicial criticism of the decision in *Royscot* (see, for example, *Cheltenham BC v Laird* [2009] EWHC 1253 (QB); [2009] IRLR 621, [524] and Leggatt J in *Yam Seng Pte Ltd v International Trade Corporation Ltd* [2013] EWHC 111 (QB); [2013] 1 All ER (Comm) 1321, [206]). If the Supreme Court does not overrule *Royscot*, or is not given the opportunity to do so, then it is suggested that legislation is required to remove this anomaly. The rules applicable to the assessment of damages should be derived from the tort of negligence, not deceit (and cases can be found in which the analogy drawn by the court has been with the tort of negligence: see, for example, *Gran Gelato Ltd v Richcliff (Group) Ltd* [1992] Ch 560, discussed further in Section 13.9 and *Taberna Europe CDO II plc v Selskabet AF1 (formerly Roskilde Bank A/S)* [2016] EWCA Civ 1262; [2017] QB 633, [52]).

Notwithstanding the advantages which the statutory cause of action affords, there remain certain situations in which a claimant must have recourse to a common law claim. The first situation arises where, as in *Hedley Byrne*, the representation is made by a third party who is not party to the contract. Section 2(1) only applies where the representation has been made by the other party to the contract and it only entitles the representee to recover such damages as flow from the representee having entered into a contract with the representor. It does not extend to losses suffered as a result of entry into a contract with a third party (*Taberna Europe CDO II plc v Selskabet AF 1.September 2008* [2016] EWCA Civ 1262; [2017] QB 633). The second situation in which it may be necessary to have recourse to the common law arises where the contract between the parties is void *ab initio* (for example, on the ground of *non est factum*). In such a case, there is no contract to which section 2(1) can apply. Thirdly, a court may hesitate to find the existence of a misrepresentation in a case brought under section 2(1) given the draconian consequences that flow from a finding of liability under the subsection (*Avon Insurance plc v Swire Fraser Ltd* [2000] 1 All ER (Comm) 573, 633 and *Raiffeisen Zentralbank Osterreich AG v Royal Bank of Scotland plc* [2010] EWHC 1392 (Comm); [2011] 1 Lloyd's Rep 123, [85]). Fourthly, it may be the case that section 2(1) cannot be applied to a case in which the misrepresentation is to be found in the contract itself but was not made before the contract was entered into (*Leofelis SA v Lonsdale Sports Ltd* [2008] EWCA Civ 640; [2008] All ER (D) 87 (Jul), [141]). In such a case the claimant cannot state that it has entered into a contract 'after' a misrepresentation has made been made to it. Finally, a claimant who has a right to redress under Part 4A of the Consumer Protection from Unfair Trading Regulations 2008 (SI 2008/1277) is not entitled to be paid damages under section 2(1) in respect of conduct constituting the misrepresentation (section 2(4) of the Misrepresentation Act 1967).

13.6.4   Innocent misrepresentation

The final type of misrepresentation is innocent misrepresentation. An innocent misrepresentation is a misrepresentation which is neither fraudulent, nor negligent.

13.7 Remedies

Once the existence of a misrepresentation has been established, consideration must be given to the remedies available for misrepresentation. There are two principal remedies. The first is the setting aside of the contract induced by the misrepresentation (this is called 'rescission' by lawyers). There is a debate, which it is not necessary for us to resolve, as to whether rescission is a contractual remedy or a restitutionary remedy. It is contractual in the sense that it enables the representee to escape from the contract and to set it aside for all purposes. But it can also be characterised as a restitutionary remedy in that, upon its exercise, the claimant is entitled to recover the value of the enrichment which the defendant has received under the contract prior to it being set aside, and the claimant must in turn make restitution to the defendant for any benefit which the claimant has obtained at the expense of the defendant. However, a claimant may not be satisfied with rescission and may also want compensation for the financial loss which he has suffered. A claim for damages does not lie in contract when the contract has been rescinded but a claim for damages may lie in tort or under statute and so we must consider the relationship between these claims.

In addition consumers have been given certain rights of redress against traders where they are the victims of misleading actions and these rights include the right to unwind the contract, the right to a discount and the right to damages (see Part 4A of the Consumer Protection from Unfair Trading Regulations 2008 (SI 2008/1277)). These statutory rights will not be discussed further in this chapter and the discussion of the remedial consequences of a misrepresentation is therefore confined to rights which arise at common law or in equity.

13.8 Rescission

Rescission is, in principle, available for all types of misrepresentation (subject to the discretion of the court to award damages in lieu of rescission under the Misrepresentation Act 1967, s 2(2); see Section 13.9). It is, however, very important to be clear about the precise meaning of the word 'rescission'. Atiyah and Treitel (1967) helpfully distinguish two types of rescission. The first type, entitled 'rescission for misrepresentation', arises where the contract is set aside for all purposes, that is to say, the contract is set aside both retrospectively and prospectively. Here the aim is to restore, as far as possible, the parties to the position which they were in before they entered into the contract and in particular to ensure that the claimant is not unjustly enriched at the defendant's expense. The second type of rescission, called 'rescission for breach', arises where one contracting party terminates performance of the contract because of the breach by the other party. In the latter case, the effect of rescission is to release the parties from their obligations to perform in the future but the contract is not treated as if it had never existed. Therefore, rescission for breach does *not* operate retrospectively (see Section 20.6). In this chapter we shall discuss only rescission for misrepresentation. Rescission does not occur automatically when a misrepresentation is made. Misrepresentation renders a contract voidable. Therefore, the representee can elect either to rescind or to affirm the contract. If he decides to rescind, the general rule is that he must bring his decision to rescind to the notice of the representor. This can be done in a number of ways: for example, by seeking a declaration that the contract is invalid, by restoring what he has obtained under the contract or by relying upon the misrepresentation as a defence to an action on the contract (*Redgrave v Hurd* (1881) 20 Ch D 1 (above)). In *Islington LBC v UCKAC* [2006] EWCA Civ 340, Dyson LJ stated that a voidable contract continues to exist 'until and unless it is set aside by an order of rescission made by the court at the instance of a party seeking to terminate it or bring it to an end'. The requirement of a court order seems unwarranted. The decision whether or not to rescind the contract is one that resides initially with the contracting parties, not the court. The court can validly decide whether or not a party was entitled to rescind a contract and, in this sense, can review the decision which has been made. But the court itself does not actually rescind the contract by virtue of the order which it makes. In the case where the representor deliberately absconds and so makes it impossible for the representee to give him notice of his decision to rescind, then it is sufficient that the representee evidences his intention to rescind by some overt means, falling short of communication, which is reasonable in the circumstances. So, where a thief persuades an owner to part with his car by a fraudulent misrepresentation and the thief cannot subsequently be traced, the owner can validly rescind by notifying the police or the Automobile Association (*Car and Universal Finance Co v Caldwell* [1965] 1 QB 525, but contrast the Scottish case of *MacLeod v Kerr* 1965 SC 253).

There are, however, certain limits to the right to rescind. The right to rescind may be lost by affirmation of the contract by the claimant after he discovered the truth, by the intervention of innocent third party rights where the third party acted in good faith and gave consideration, or by lapse of time of such a length that it would be inequitable in all the circumstances to grant rescission (*Leaf v International Galleries* [1950] 2 KB 86, as explained in *Salt v Stratstone Specialist Ltd* [2015] EWCA Civ 745; [2015] 2 CLC 269, although lapse of time does not, of itself, bar rescission in cases of fraudulent misrepresentation). The principal ground on which the right to rescind may be lost arises where it is impossible to restore the parties to their pre-contractual position. A claimant who wishes to recover the value of a benefit which he has conferred upon the defendant must be prepared to make restitution to the defendant for any benefit which he has received at the expense of the defendant. In other words, a claimant cannot both get back what he has parted with and keep what he has received in return. The aim of this rule is to ensure that the claimant is not unjustly enriched as a result of rescission: it does not have as its aim the avoidance of loss on the part of the defendant (*McKenzie v Royal Bank of Canada* [1934] AC 468; *Halpern v Halpern (No. 2)* [2007] EWCA Civ 291; [2008] QB 195). At common law the courts insisted upon precise restitution, but the harshness of this rule is mitigated by the intervention of equity. In equity a party who can make substantial, but not precise, restitution can rescind the contract if he returns the subject-matter of the contract in its altered form and gives an account of any profits made through his use of the product together with an allowance for any deterioration in the product (*Erlanger v New Sombrero Phosphate Co* (1878) 3 App Cas 1218). The emphasis of the court is on the need to achieve a 'practically just' outcome so that, where it is impossible physically to restore the parties (or the subject matter of their contract) to the pre-contract position, the court should consider whether a monetary award can restore the parties in substance to that position (*Salt v Stratstone Specialist Ltd* [2015] EWCA Civ 745; [2015] 2 CLC 269). So, for example, where the claimant has made use of the asset which he obtained from the defendant under the contract, the claimant obviously cannot return the use which he has made of the chattel but he can make a money payment to the defendant which represents the use which he has made of the chattel. Given that almost any use or alteration to a product can be valued in money terms, it may be that the law should recognise that, provided the claimant is prepared to restore to the defendant the benefit which he has obtained at the defendant's expense, the transaction should be set aside (provided that no other bar to rescission is applicable on the facts).

We have already noted that the effect of rescission is to set aside the contract for all purposes. A consequence of this is that *contractual* damages cannot be claimed because the contract has been set aside for all purposes and so there is no basis for any claim on the contract. But rescission may give rise to a personal restitutionary claim. In *Whittington v Seale-Hayne* (1900) 82 LT 49, the claimants took a lease of premises for the purpose of breeding prize poultry. They were induced to do so by representations of the defendant's agent that the premises were in good sanitary condition. Under the lease, the claimants covenanted to execute all such works as might be required by the local authority. The premises were not, however, in a sanitary condition and were in a state of disrepair. The water supply was poisoned and, as a result, the poultry died or became valueless and the manager of the farm became ill. The local authority declared the premises unfit for habitation and required the claimants to renew the drains. It was held that the claimants were entitled to an indemnity in respect of the rates which they had paid and the cost of carrying out the repairs ordered by the local authority because these were obligations which were actually created by the lease. It was expenditure on their part which resulted in a benefit to the defendant and he would have been unjustly enriched had he not been required to pay for these benefits when the premises were returned to him. On the other hand, the claimants were not entitled to recover in respect of the value of the lost stock or their loss of profit because these were not losses on their part which resulted in a benefit to the defendant. Such losses can, in principle, be recovered in a damages action in tort but, on the facts, a claim in damages was not available.

13.9 Damages

A contractual claim for damages does not lie for misrepresentation, unless the misrepresentation has been subsequently incorporated into the contract as a term, in which case damages can be claimed for breach of contract (see Sections 8.1 and 8.6). But damages may be recoverable in *tort* where the misrepresentation was made fraudulently or negligently. Sections 2(1) and 2(2) of the Misrepresentation Act 1967 also make provision for the recovery of damages for misrepresentation. Provided there is no element of double recovery, a claimant may rescind and claim damages (except under the Misrepresentation Act 1967, s 2(2); see below). When considering the entitlement of a claimant to damages for misrepresentation, it is vital to give separate treatment to each type of misrepresentation.

13.9.1 Fraud

Where the misrepresentation is fraudulent then damages may be recovered in the tort of deceit. The aim of an award of damages in deceit is to put the claimant in the position which he would have been in had the tort not been committed; that is to say, it aims to protect his reliance interest. The defendant is also liable for all the damage directly flowing from the fraudulent inducement which was not rendered too remote by the claimant's own conduct, whether or not the defendant could have foreseen such consequential loss (*Doyle v Olby* [1969] 2 QB 158, as approved by the House of Lords in *Smith New Court Securities Ltd v Scrimgeour Vickers (Asset Management) Ltd* [1997] AC 254). Exemplary (or punitive) damages can potentially be recovered for fraudulent misrepresentation (*Kuddus v Chief Constable of Leicestershire Constabulary* [2001] UKHL 29; [2002] 2 AC 122). Aggravated damages may be awarded to compensate the claimant for the injury to his feelings (*Archer v Brown* [1985] QB 401).

13.9.2   Negligence

In the case of negligent misrepresentation at common law, the misrepresentor has committed a tort and damages can therefore be claimed. Once again the award of damages seeks to put the claimant in the position which he would have been in had the tort not been committed. The representor will be liable for all losses which are a reasonably foreseeable consequence of the misrepresentation (*The Wagon Mound (No. 1)* [1961] AC 388). Where the representee has also been at fault, the damages payable may be reduced on the ground of contributory negligence (Law Reform (Contributory Negligence) Act 1945, s 1; *Gran Gelato Ltd v Richcliff (Group) Ltd* [1992] Ch 560). In an exceptional case, a court may be prepared to award exemplary damages in a negligence action, although the likelihood of a court doing so is extremely small (*A v Bottrill* [2002] UKPC 44; [2003] 1 AC 449).

13.9.3   Section 2(1) of the Misrepresentation Act 1967

In the case of a claim under section 2(1) of the Misrepresentation Act 1967, there was initially some controversy relating to the measure of damages recoverable. Some argued that damages should seek to put the claimant in the position he would have been in had the representation not been made (thus protecting the reliance interest), while others argued that damages should put the claimant in the position he would have been in had the representation been true (thus protecting the expectation interest). In *Gosling v Anderson* [1972] EGD 709 and *Jarvis v Swan's Tours* [1973] QB 233, Lord Denning appeared to suggest that the measure of recovery was the expectation measure and this view was followed by Graham J in *Watts v Spence* [1976] Ch 165. But this view has since been rejected and it is now clear that the measure of recovery is the reliance measure (*Royscot Trust Ltd v Rogerson* [1991] 2 QB 297 and *Sharneyford Supplies Ltd v Barrington Black and Co* [1987] Ch 305, 323). It is suggested that this is the correct approach because, as we have already noted (Section 13.1), promises and representations are functionally different. A representor does not promise anything; he simply asserts the truth of his statement and invites *reliance* upon that statement. It is therefore appropriate that the measure of damages should be the reliance measure (see Taylor, 1982). The reliance measure can encompass the loss of profit which the claimant would have obtained from entering into some other transaction if the misrepresentation had not been made (*Yam Seng Pte Ltd v International Trade*

Corporation Ltd [2013] EWHC 111 (QB); [2013] 1 All ER (Comm) 1321, [217]). Although damages are confined to the reliance measure, it must be remembered that damages are assessed as if the representor had been fraudulent (*Royscot Trust Ltd v Rogerson*), so that the remoteness rules applicable are those pertaining to the tort of deceit, not the tort of negligence. It has also been held that damages payable under section 2(1) may be reduced on the ground of the representee's contributory negligence (*Gran Gelato Ltd v Richcliff (Group) Ltd*), although it should be noted that Sir Donald Nicholls vc reached his conclusion by drawing an analogy with the tort of negligence. This reasoning does not appear to be consistent with the approach of the Court of Appeal in *Royscot*, where it was held that the appropriate analogy was with the tort of deceit. The point is an important one because contributory negligence is not available as a defence to an action in deceit (see *Standard Chartered Bank v Pakistan National Shipping Corp (No. 2)* [2002] UKHL 43; [2003] 1 AC 959), and so, on the reasoning in *Royscot*, it should not have been in issue in *Gran Gelato* as a possible defence to the section 2(1) claim.

In cases of innocent misrepresentation, the traditional common law rule was that damages were not available. Innocent misrepresentation is not a tort and therefore the only remedy was rescission and an indemnity. In practice the courts tended to mitigate the rigours of this rule, either by finding that the representation was in fact not a representation at all but a contractual term (see Sections 8.1–8.4), or by finding that the representation was enforceable as a 'collateral contract'. The latter technique can be illustrated by reference to the case of *De Lassalle v Guildford* [1901] 2 KB 215. The claimant was induced to enter into a lease by an oral statement made by the defendant that the drains were in good order. The drains were not in good order but the lease contained no reference to the drains. It was held that the defendant's representation was enforceable as a warranty which was collateral to the lease. Thus, there were two contracts between the parties. The first one was the written lease and the second consisted of the oral statement that the drains were in good order, the consideration for which was the entry by the claimant into the lease. However, the courts were not able to find the existence of such a collateral contract in every case (see *Heilbut Symons & Co v Buckleton* [1913] AC 30).

13.9.4 Section 2(2) of the Misrepresentation Act 1967

The need to seek out the existence of a collateral contract has been reduced by section 2(2) of the Misrepresentation Act 1967 which provides that:

> where a person has entered into a contract after a misrepresentation has been made to him otherwise than fraudulently, and he would be entitled, by reason of the misrepresentation, to rescind the contract, then, if it is claimed in any proceedings arising out of the contract, that the contract ought to be or has been rescinded, the court or arbitrator may declare the contract subsisting and award damages in lieu of rescission, if of opinion that it would be equitable to do so, having regard to the nature of the misrepresentation and the loss that would be caused by it if the contract were upheld, as well as to the loss that rescission would cause to the other party.

Thus, the courts now have a discretion to award damages in lieu of rescission in the case of innocent misrepresentation. The following points should be noted about section 2(2).

The first is that the power to award damages is discretionary. The representee has no right to damages, in contrast to section 2(1) where damages are available as of right. The second point is that damages are in lieu of rescission, so that if the claimant wishes to rescind he cannot recover damages as well (although he may be able to recover the value of any benefits which he has conferred upon the defendant, see Section 13.8).

Thirdly, the discretion which has been conferred upon the court is a 'broad one, to do what it is equitable' (*William Sindall plc v Cambridgeshire CC* [1994] 1 WLR 1016, 1036, per Hoffmann LJ). The courts are directed by the wording of section 2(2) to consider the nature of the misrepresentation, the loss that would be caused by the misrepresentation if the contract were upheld and the loss which would be caused to the misrepresentor by rescission, but the weight to be attached to these factors very much depends upon the facts of the case. The courts are most likely to invoke section 2(2) in a case where a representee has been induced by a misrepresentation to enter into what has turned out to be a bad bargain for him. Such was the case in *William Sindall* itself where the value of the land which the claimants had purchased had dropped dramatically in value and they alleged that they were entitled to withdraw from the contract because the defendant had innocently failed to disclose the existence of a private foul sewer running across the land. On the facts of the case, the Court of Appeal found that there had been no misrepresentation by the defendant, but, had there been, they would have exercised their discretion to grant the claimants damages in lieu of rescission because the loss caused to the claimants by the (relatively insignificant) innocent misrepresentation was trifling in comparison to the loss which the defendant would have experienced had the contract been rescinded (see also *UCB Corporate Services Ltd v Thomason* [2005] EWCA Civ 225; [2005] 1 All ER (Comm) 601, especially at [36]).

This leads us on to the fourth problem, which is the measure of damages to be awarded in lieu of rescission under section 2(2). This is a difficult issue. The measure should be less than the measure available under section 2(1) because the representor is less culpable. The temptation is simply to award the representee some protection for his reliance interest, but the court must proceed carefully here because the award of full reliance damages might have the effect of protecting the representee from his bad bargain, which the court has just refused to sanction by its decision not to grant rescission. In the event, the Court of Appeal in *William Sindall* failed to provide clear guidance on this point. Hoffmann LJ thought that damages under section 2(2) should never exceed a sum which would have been awarded if the representation had been a warranty, while Evans LJ was of the view that the correct measure was the contract measure, that is to say, the difference between the actual value received and the value which the property would have had if the representation had been true. The position may be that damages are limited to the loss in value of what is bought under the contract and that damages for consequential loss are not recoverable (*Thomas Witter Ltd v TBP Industries Ltd* [1996] 2 All ER 573, 591). Finally, a claimant who has a right to redress under Part 4A of the Consumer Protection from Unfair Trading Regulations 2008 (SI 2008/1277) is not entitled to be paid damages under section 2(2) in respect of conduct constituting the misrepresentation (section 2(4) of the Misrepresentation Act 1967).

The final point relates to the situation where the claimant had the right to rescind but has lost it. Does such a claimant also lose the right to claim damages under section 2(2)? The point was the subject of a conflict of authority for a period of time but the conflict was recently resolved by the Court of Appeal in *Salt v Stratstone Specialist Ltd* [2015] EWCA Civ 745; [2015] 2 CLC 269 where it was confirmed that the jurisdiction of the court to award damages in lieu of rescission under s 2(2) is confined to the case where rescission is available or was available at the time the contract was rescinded. This conclusion was held to follow from the words 'if it is claimed … that the contract ought to be or has been rescinded the court … may declare the contract subsisting and award damages in lieu of rescission'. The words 'in lieu of rescission' were held to carry with them the implication that rescission is available (or was available at the time the contract was rescinded) in order for the jurisdiction of the court to be triggered. On this basis, if rescission is not available because of affirmation, the intervention of third party rights or some other reason, damages cannot be awarded under s2(2). The unavailability of rescission thus deprives the court of the jurisdiction to award damages under s2(2).

13.10 Excluding liability for misrepresentation

At common law a person could not exclude liability for his own fraudulent misrepresentation (*S Pearson & Son Ltd v Dublin Corp* [1907] AC 351 and *HIH Casualty and General Insurance Ltd v Chase Manhattan Bank* [2003] UKHL 6; [2003] 2 Lloyd's Rep 61), but he could exclude liability for negligent or innocent misrepresentation, although such exclusion clauses were subject to strict rules relating to incorporation and construction (see Sections 9.4 and 11.4–11.7). However, section 3(1) of the Misrepresentation Act 1967 (as amended by the Unfair Contract Terms Act 1977, s 8) limits the freedom of the parties to exclude liability for the consequences of a misrepresentation. It provides that:

> If a contract contains a term which would exclude or restrict –
>
> (a) any liability to which a party to a contract may be subject by reason of any misrepresentation made by him before the contract was made; or
> (b) any remedy available to another party to the contract by reason of such a misrepresentation,
>
> that term shall be of no effect except in so far as it satisfies the requirement of reasonableness as stated in section 11(1) of the Unfair Contract Terms Act 1977; and it is for those claiming that the term satisfies that requirement to show that it does.

This section does not apply to a term in a consumer contract within the meaning of Part 2 of the Consumer Rights Act 2015. It should be noted that, once again, the Act is drafted in defensive terms (see Section 11.1) so that it attacks attempts to 'exclude or restrict' a 'liability' or a 'remedy'. As Moore-Bick LJ observed in *Taberna Europe CDO II plc v Selskabet AF 1.September 2008* [2016] EWCA Civ 1262; [2017] QB 633, [20] section 3 is 'concerned with attempts to exclude liability for misrepresentation after the event' and 'is not concerned with the question whether there has actually been a misrepresentation'. This might be taken to suggest that it is not a difficult task to avoid the clutches of section 3 by drafting a clause in such a way as to deny the existence of a misrepresentation. A frequently encountered clause which seeks to do this is a so-called 'no reliance clause' whereby one party acknowledges that he has not relied on any statement made to it by the other party. However, the aim of avoiding section 3 via a clause such as a no-reliance clause was dealt a severe below by the decision of the Court of Appeal in *First Tower Trustees Ltd v CDS (Superstores International) Ltd* [2018] EWCA Civ 1396; [2019] 1 WLR 637. Lewison LJ there stated (at [51]) that section 3 'must be interpreted so as to give effect to its evident policy' which was 'to prevent contracting parties from escaping from liability for misrepresentation unless it is reasonable for them to do so' and further that 'how they seek to avoid that liability is subsidiary' (see *Cremdean Properties v Nash* [1977] 2 EGLR 80 and *Raiffeisen Zentralbank Osterreich AG v The Royal Bank of Scotland plc* [2010] EWHC 1392 (Comm); [2011] 1 Lloyd's Rep 123). Any other conclusion would enable section 3 to be by-passed with relative ease and, as Leggatt LJ observed (at [99]), 'no rational legislator could have intended that the need for a contract term to satisfy a test of reasonableness could be avoided simply by felicity in drafting the contract term'. This broad, purposive approach is likely to make it very difficult for contracting parties to evade the operation of section 3 and the justification given by the Court of Appeal for the adoption of this expansive approach to the interpretation of section 3 is that 'the freedom of parties to contract on whatever terms they choose depends crucially on the assumption that their consent to the terms of the contract has been obtained fairly'. This is obviously not the case where consent has been induced by a misrepresentation and so, to the extent that a contract term purports to remove the right of a party to complain that its consent to the terms of the contract was obtained by misrepresentation, it will be caught by section 3. Given the severe difficulties involved in any attempt to avoid the application of section 3 after the decision of the Court of Appeal in *First Tower Trustees*, contracting parties would be well advised to focus their efforts on ensuring that any clause which seeks to exclude liability for what would otherwise be a misrepresentation is reasonable (for the factors which the courts take into account when assessing the reasonableness of a clause, see Section 11.13).

Hot topic 12...

In *Monde Petroleum SA v Westernzagros Ltd* [2016] EWHC 1472 (Comm); [2016] 2 Lloyd's Rep 229, [214] Mr Richard Salter QC, sitting as a Deputy Judge of the High Court, noted the academic criticisms which have been levelled against the decision of the Court of Appeal in *Royscot Trust Ltd v Rogerson* [1991] 2 QB 297 but concluded that, unless and until it was over-ruled, he was bound by the decision. While *Royscot* has been the subject of considerable criticism, it can only be over-ruled by the Supreme Court and the likelihood that a suitable case can be found to test the point in the Supreme Court is probably low (at least in the near future). It is also unlikely that Parliament will find the time to amend section 2(1) of the Misrepresentation Act 1967 in order to remove the fiction of fraud (and it is the reference to fraud which is at the root of some of the difficulties). This being the case, we appear to be stuck with the ruling in *Royscot* and to the proposition that in the circumstances of s 2(1) English law treats a party who fails to show he had reasonable grounds to believe the truth of his statement as if he had been fraudulent, a proposition which is extremely unattractive.

Summary

▶ A misrepresentation may be defined as an unambiguous false statement of fact or law which is addressed to the party misled, which is material (although this requirement is now debatable) and which induces the contract.

▶ Mere puffs, statements of opinion and statements of intention are not statements of fact.

▶ A representation does not induce the contract if the representation was unimportant, the representee was unaware of its existence or he did not allow it to affect his judgment.

▶ A fraudulent misrepresentation is made when it is proved that a false representation has been made (i) knowingly or (ii) without belief in its truth or (iii) recklessly, careless whether it be true or false.

▶ Negligent misrepresentation is actionable at common law where there is a *Hedley Byrne v Heller* [1964] AC 465 relationship between the claimant and the defendant. The existence of such a relationship depends upon a number of factors, including the knowledge of the representor, the purpose for which the statement was made and the reasonableness of the reliance by the representee.

▶ Section 2(1) of the Misrepresentation Act 1967 states that where a misrepresentation has been made by one contracting party to another, the party making the misrepresentation is liable to the other in damages unless he can prove that he had reasonable grounds to believe and did believe up to the time that the contract was made that his statement was true.

▶ The principal remedies for misrepresentation are rescission and damages. Rescission is in principle available for all types of misrepresentation. The effect of rescission is generally to put the parties as far as possible into the position which they would have been in had the contract not been concluded and in particular to ensure that the claimant is not unjustly enriched at the defendant's expense.

▶ Damages can be claimed for fraudulent and negligent misrepresentation and under section 2(1) of the 1967 Act. In all cases the measure of damages is the reliance measure. In the case of innocent misrepresentation the court has a discretion to award damages in lieu of rescission under section 2(2) of the 1967 Act.

▶ The ability of a contracting party to exclude liability for misrepresentation is controlled by section 3 of the Misrepresentation Act 1967 which subjects any term which purports to exclude or restrict liability or a remedy for misrepresentation to the reasonableness test.

Exercises

13.1 What is a 'misrepresentation'?

13.2 What is a 'statement of existing fact'? Give examples to illustrate your answer.

13.3 Distinguish between 'fraudulent', 'negligent' and 'innocent' misrepresentation.

13.4 What are the advantages to a claimant in invoking section 2(1) of the Misrepresentation Act 1967 rather than the common law of negligent misrepresentation? Are there any disadvantages?

13.5 What are the principal remedies for misrepresentation? What is the difference between damages and an indemnity?

13.6 Can a defendant exclude liability for misrepresentation?

Chapter 14
Common mistake and frustration

Introduction

Parties occasionally enter into a contract on the basis of a common assumption which they later discover was false. Alternatively, events occur after the formation of the contract which were not within the contemplation of the parties when they entered into the contract. In these circumstances, are the parties bound to carry out their contract according to its terms, even though the events which have occurred were not within their contemplation when they entered into the contract? The answer to this question is that the courts may, in certain circumstances, release the parties from their obligations to perform. But it is very important to understand the basis of the intervention of the courts in these cases. The basis is not that the parties failed to reach agreement. These cases are not like the mistake cases which we discussed in Section 4.6, where one party is claiming relief on the basis that he was mistaken and that mistake negatived his consent and so prevented a contract coming into existence.

Here the parties do actually reach agreement. But an event occurs which was unforeseen by the parties and which destroys the basis upon which they entered into the contract. In such a case the courts must decide who bears the risk of such an unforeseen event. Where the courts intervene to grant relief they do so on the ground that it is no longer fair or just to hold the parties to their agreement in such radically changed and unforeseen circumstances.

Where the common misapprehension is present *at the date of entry* into the contract, the contract may be set aside on the ground of common (or, as it is sometimes called, 'mutual') mistake. On the other hand, where events have occurred *after* the making of the contract which render performance of the contract impossible, illegal or something radically different from that which was in the contemplation of the parties at the time at which they entered into the contract, then the contract may be discharged on the ground of 'frustration' (on which see generally Treitel, 2013).

Common mistake is often treated separately from frustration on the ground that the latter is concerned with the discharge of a contract, whereas mistake relates to the formation of a contract. It is true that mistake relates to events which exist or occur prior to the making of the contract, and frustration applies to events which occur after the making of the contract. But there is, in fact, a strong link between these two doctrines, as can be seen from a brief analysis of the following case.

In *Amalgamated Investment and Property Co Ltd v John Walker & Sons Ltd* [1977] 1 WLR 164, the defendants sold property to the claimants for £1,710,000. The property was advertised as being suitable for occupation or redevelopment and the defendants knew that the claimants wished to redevelop the property. In their pre-contract enquiries the claimants asked the defendants whether the property was designated as a building of special historic or architectural interest. The defendants replied that it was not but, unknown to both parties, officials at the Department of the Environment had, on 22 August 1973, unconditionally included the property in a list of buildings to be designated as buildings of special architectural or historical interest. The parties signed the contract of sale on 25 September 1973. On the following day the Secretary of State wrote to the defendants informing them that the building had been listed and that the listing would take effect the next day when signed by the Secretary of State. The effect of the listing was to cause the value of the property to drop by £1,500,000 to approximately £200,000.

In these circumstances, the claimants sought to have the contract set aside. They argued that the contract should be set aside on the ground of mistake or, alternatively, that the contract was frustrated by the listing of the building. But into which category did the case fall? If the listing took effect before the contract was signed on 25 September 1973 the ground on which the claimants sought relief was common mistake, but, if the listing took effect after the contract had been signed on 25 September, the ground upon which relief was sought was frustration. The Court of Appeal held that the building did not become a listed building until it was signed by the Secretary of State on 27 September. The ground on which relief was sought was therefore frustration. But the court held that the contract was not frustrated because the claimants knew of the risk that the building could be listed, as was evidenced by their pre-contract enquiries and it was a risk which they had to bear. The listing of the building was not an unforeseen event which rendered the performance of the contract something radically different from that which had been contemplated by the parties (see Section 14.9).

This case demonstrates that there is a strong relationship between common mistake and frustration. The point at issue in the case was: who should bear the risk of the listing of the building? Whether the case is treated as one of common mistake or frustration, the issue is exactly the same. In the remaining sections of this chapter we shall give separate treatment to the doctrines of common mistake and frustration, and conclude by identifying the relationship between the two doctrines.

14.2 Common mistake

Where the mistake is common to both parties, the parties have reached agreement, but that agreement is based upon a fundamental mistaken assumption. In such a case the court may nullify the consent of the parties and set aside the contract which they concluded. The leading case on common mistake is *Bell v Lever Brothers Ltd* [1932] AC 161. The defendants, Bell and Snelling, entered into a contract with the claimants under which they agreed to serve for five years as chairman and vice-chairman, respectively, of a subsidiary company of the claimants. One of the terms of their service agreements was that they must not make any private profit for themselves, by doing business on their own account, while working for the subsidiary. But the defendants, unknown to the claimants, did engage in business on their own account and did not disclose their profits to the claimants. The claimants later decided that they wished to terminate the defendants' contracts because of a reorganisation of their business. So they entered into compensation agreements with the defendants under which they agreed to pay Bell £30,000 and Snelling £20,000 in exchange for their consent to the termination of their service agreements. After the money had been paid, the claimants discovered the breaches by the defendants of their service agreements. The significance of the breaches by the defendants was that they would have entitled the claimants to terminate the service agreements without the payment of any compensation. In these circumstances the claimants sought to recover the money which they had paid to the defendants. A crucial feature of the case was the finding of the jury that, when they entered into the compensation agreements, the defendants did not have their breaches of duty in mind. The parties therefore entered into the compensation agreements under a common mistake that the service agreements were valid when they were, in fact, liable to be set aside by the claimants without the payment of compensation.

The House of Lords held, by a majority of three to two, that the claimants could not recover the money. Lord Atkin and Lord Thankerton held that the mistake was not sufficiently fundamental to avoid the contract. Lord Blanesburgh held that the claimants could not recover because they had not pleaded common mistake, but he also expressed his 'entire accord' with the judgments of Lord Atkin and Lord Thankerton. The test established by the majority was well expressed by Lord Thankerton when he said that the common mistake must 'relate to something which both [parties] must necessarily have accepted in their minds as an essential element of the subject matter'. Yet, even applying this test, why was the claimants' mistake not fundamental? They had paid £50,000 to the defendants, which in 1929 must have been a colossal sum of money, when they could have dismissed them without paying any compensation. The answer to this question is not entirely clear.

A partial answer is that the House of Lords did not want to lay down a principle which would enable parties to escape from what was merely a bad bargain. They wanted to hold men to their bargains and to emphasise the exceptional nature of the jurisdiction of the court to set aside a contract on the ground of mistake. But why did they not recognise that this was, in fact, such an exceptional case? After all, the claimants had made a spectacular mistake. One view, adopted by Steyn J in *Associated Japanese Bank (International) Ltd v Crédit du Nord* [1989] 1 WLR 255, is that the mistake may not have been as significant as it appears at first sight because the claimants were very anxious to carry through the reorganisation and to secure the defendants' consent to the termination of their service agreements and so they *might* have entered into the same agreements, even if they had known of the defendants' breaches of duty.

A careful examination of the facts conducted more recently by MacMillan (2003) suggests that such a hypothesis is unlikely. She points out that the claim was brought by the claimants as a matter of principle and so it is extremely unlikely that they would have made the payments had they known the true state of affairs. Rather, she attributes the failure of the claim to a number of different factors. The first is that the principal claim brought by the claimants was one based on fraud and the mistake claim was added as something of an afterthought. This had the consequence that the consideration given to the mistake claim was not as complete as it might have been. Second, the claimants' fraud claim failed on the facts. Third, it was found that Bell and Snelling had in fact made significant contributions to the success of the company and that the profits which they had made from their wrongdoing were trifling in comparison with the benefits which the claimants had obtained from their services. These factors combined to suggest to the majority that the mistake was insufficiently fundamental to entitle the claimants to set aside the compensation agreements.

The proposition of law for which *Bell v Lever Brothers* stands as authority, namely that a mistake must be fundamental in order to entitle a party to set aside a contract, must therefore be seen against the background of the particular facts of the case. Nevertheless, it must be said that the test adopted by the majority is a relatively open-textured one and that it can admit of varying interpretations. This is demonstrated by the judgments in *Bell v Lever Brothers* itself because the minority, Lord Warrington and Lord Hailsham, held that the claimants' mistake *was* sufficiently fundamental to avoid the contract. In the following sections (Sections 14.3–14.6), we shall seek to ascertain the circumstances in which the courts have held a common mistake to be sufficiently fundamental to avoid a contract.

14.3 Mistake as to the existence of the subject-matter of the contract

A mistake may be sufficiently fundamental to avoid a contract where both parties are mistaken as to the existence of the subject-matter of the contract. For example, in *Galloway v Galloway* (1914) 30 TLR 531, the defendant, assuming his wife to be dead, married the claimant. The defendant and the claimant later separated and entered into a deed of separation under which the defendant promised to pay a weekly allowance to the claimant. The defendant subsequently discovered that his first wife was still alive and he fell into arrears. When the claimant sued to recover the arrears it was held that she could not do so because the separation agreement was void on the ground that it was entered into under the common mistake that the parties were, in fact, married.

Greater difficulties arise in the case of a contract for the sale of non-existent goods. Section 6 of the Sale of Goods Act 1979 provides that:

> where there is a contract for the sale of specific goods, and the goods without the knowledge of the seller have perished at the time when the contract is made, the contract is void.

This section was thought to give effect to the decision of the House of Lords in *Couturier v Hastie* (1856) 5 HLC 673. The parties entered into a contract for the sale of a cargo of corn, which was believed to be in transit from Salonica to the United Kingdom. But, before the contract was made and unknown to both parties, the corn had deteriorated to such an extent that the master of the ship sold it. The seller argued that the buyer remained liable for the price of the corn because he had bought an 'interest in the adventure' or such rights as the seller had under the shipping documents. The House of Lords rejected the seller's argument, holding that the subject-matter of the contract was not the rights of the seller under the shipping documents but the corn and that, since the corn did not exist, there was a total failure of consideration and the buyer was not liable to pay the price. But the precise legal basis of the decision of the House of Lords in *Couturier* has been the subject of some debate and controversy among lawyers. We shall now consider the principal interpretations which have been placed upon *Couturier*.

The first interpretation is that a mistake as to the existence of the subject-matter of a contract inevitably renders a contract void. This appears to be the interpretation placed upon *Couturier* by the draftsman of section 6 of the Sale of Goods Act 1979. However, the word 'mistake' was not used in any of the judgments in *Couturier*. The court was principally concerned with the construction of the contract and the question whether the consideration had totally failed. The court did not establish such an all-embracing proposition.

The second interpretation, adopted by Denning LJ in *Solle v Butcher* [1950] 1 KB 671, 691, is that the contract in *Couturier* was void because there was an implied condition precedent that the contract was capable of performance. In *Couturier*, the parties proceeded upon the assumption that the goods were capable of being sold when, in fact, they were not and the effect of the implied condition precedent was to render the contract void. The difficulty with this interpretation is that it does not tell us when, or on what basis, the courts will imply such a condition precedent.

The third interpretation is that the question whether or not a contract is void depends upon the construction of the contract. Such an interpretation was placed upon *Couturier* by the High Court of Australia in *McRae v Commonwealth Disposals Commission* (1951) 84 CLR 377. In this rather bizarre case the defendants purported to sell to the claimants the wreck of a tanker which was lying on the Jourmand Reef and was said to contain oil. The claimants embarked upon an expedition in an attempt to salvage the vessel but no tanker was found and, indeed, no such tanker had ever existed. The claimants succeeded in their action for damages for breach of contract. The defendants had argued that there could be no liability for breach of contract because the alleged contract was void owing to the non-existence of the subject-matter of the contract. This argument was rejected by the court on the ground that the defendants had promised that such a tanker was in existence and they were liable for breach of that promise. *Couturier* was distinguished on the ground that there the parties had entered into the contract under the shared assumption that the corn was still in existence and could be sold by the seller; that assumption proved to be unfounded and the contract was held to be void. But in *McRae*, the defendants had actually promised that the tanker was in existence. They had assumed the risk of the non-existence of the tanker and for the breach of their promise they were held liable in damages.

But would an English court follow *McRae*? It seems clear that it is factually distinguishable from *Couturier* for the reasons already given. The result in *McRae* seems perfectly just because the defendants assumed the risk of the non-existence of the tanker and the effect of the decision was to place that risk upon the defendants. In policy terms there is little doubt that *McRae* should be followed and the Court of Appeal so concluded in *Great Peace Shipping Ltd v Tsavliris Salvage (International) Ltd* [2002] EWCA Civ 1407; [2003] QB 679, [77]–[81]. The difficulty lies in reconciling *McRae* with the wording of section 6 of the Sale of Goods Act 1979 (above). Section 6 does not provide an insuperable obstacle, however, because it can be argued that a case such as *McRae* is not caught by the actual wording of section 6 since the tanker never existed and therefore it could not have 'perished'. On this interpretation, only contracts for the sale of goods which once existed but have since perished would be governed by section 6. Contracts for the sale of goods which never existed would not be caught by section 6 but would instead be governed by the more flexible approach adopted in *McRae*. But such a distinction has little to commend itself in policy terms.

Alternatively, it could be argued that section 6 is only a rule of construction which can, in a case such as *McRae*, be ousted by proof of contrary intention (see Atiyah, 1957). The difficulty with this argument is that many sections of the Sale of Goods Act 1979 explicitly state that they are subject to contrary agreement, but there is no such provision in section 6. Finally, it could be argued that, although the main contract in a case such as *McRae* is void, the defendants could be liable to the claimants under a collateral contract, the terms of which would be that the tanker was in existence. The consideration provided by the claimants would be the entry into the void contract. It is doubtful whether entry into a void contract can constitute consideration (but see *Strongman (1945) Ltd v Sincock* [1955] 2 QB 525 and see the more flexible approach to consideration adopted in *Williams v Roffey Bros & Nicholls (Contractors) Ltd* [1991] 1 QB 1, see Section 5.11). Even if the consideration hurdle could be overcome, such a solution would be inelegant and horribly artificial. The contortions which are required to evade section 6 and to achieve a satisfactory solution in a case such as *McRae* suggest that English contract law would be improved by the reform of section 6 of the Sale of Goods Act 1979.

14.4 Mistake as to identity of the subject-matter

A mistake as to the identity of the subject-matter of the contract may be sufficiently fundamental to avoid a contract if both parties thought that they were dealing with one thing when in fact they were dealing with another. There is no English case on this point (but see the discussion in the Canadian case of *Diamond v British Columbia Thoroughbred Breeders' Society* (1966) 52 DLR (2d) 146).

14.5 Mistake as to the possibility of performing the contract

A mistake may be sufficiently fundamental to avoid a contract where both parties believe that the contract is capable of being performed when, in fact, it is not. Treitel (2020) helpfully divides these cases into three categories.

The first category is physical impossibility. In *Sheikh Brothers Ltd v Ochsner* [1957] AC 136, the appellants granted to the respondents a licence to enter and cut sisal growing on their land and in return the respondents agreed to deliver to the appellants 50 tons of cut sisal per month. Unknown to both parties, the land was incapable of producing an average of 50 tons of sisal per month throughout the term of the licence. The Privy Council held that the contract was void because the mistake of the parties related to a matter which was essential to the agreement and neither party had assumed the risk of the land being incapable of producing such a yield.

The second type of impossibility is legal impossibility, that is to say, the contract provides for something to be done which cannot, as a matter of law, be done. In *Cooper v Phibbs* (1867) LR 2 HL 149, the appellant agreed to take a lease of a salmon fishery which both parties believed to be the property of the respondents. It was subsequently discovered that the appellant, as the tenant in tail, was the owner of the fishery. The contract was set aside, albeit, as the Court of Appeal pointed out in *Great Peace Shipping Ltd v Tsavliris Salvage (International) Ltd* [2002] EWCA Civ 1407; [2003] QB 679, [109], 'it is not easy to analyse the precise principles that led the House of Lords to set aside the agreement'. One explanation for the case is that the agreement was set aside on the ground that it was legally incapable of performance because the appellant was already the owner of the fishery (see *Great Peace* [110]: 'the type of mistake under consideration was one whereby a party agrees to purchase a title which he already owns').

The third type of impossibility is commercial impossibility. In *Griffith v Brymer* (1903) 19 TLR 434, the parties entered into a contract for the hire of a room for the purpose of viewing the coronation procession of Edward VII. The procession was cancelled because of the illness of Edward VII. The parties had concluded their contract at 11 am but, unknown to both parties, the decision to operate on Edward VII was taken at 10 am. It was held that the contract was void because the mistake of the parties went to the root or the heart of their agreement. Although the contract was still physically and legally capable of performance, the cancellation of the procession had undermined the commercial object of the contract.

14.6 Mistake as to quality

A mistake as to the quality of the subject-matter of the contract may be sufficiently fundamental to avoid a contract. But the courts are extremely reluctant to conclude that a mistake as to quality renders a contract void, as can be seen from *Bell v Lever Brothers Ltd* itself (see Section 14.2). A further difficulty is created by the fact that the cases are not easy to reconcile. A brief account will be given of some of the leading cases and then an attempt will be made at some reconciliation.

In *Leaf v International Galleries* [1950] 2 KB 86, the Court of Appeal stated that a contract for the sale of a picture would not be set aside on the ground of mistake if both parties entered into the contract erroneously believing the picture to be a Constable. In *Harrison and Jones v Burton and Lancaster* [1953] 1 QB 646, the parties entered into a contract for the sale of a particular brand of kapok which was believed to be pure kapok whereas, in fact, it also contained some brush cotton which made it a commercially inferior product. It was held that the mistake was not sufficiently fundamental to avoid the contract. In *Oscar Chess Ltd v Williams* [1957] 1 WLR 370 (see Section 8.4) both parties entered into a contract for the sale of a car under the belief that the car was a 1948 model when in fact it was a 1939 model. Once again the mistake was not sufficiently fundamental to avoid the contract.

In *Solle v Butcher* [1950] 1 KB 671, the defendant agreed to lease a flat to the claimant for seven years at an annual rental of £250. The parties entered into this agreement under the mistaken assumption that the flat was free from rent control. When the claimant discovered that the flat was subject to rent control and that the rent payable under the legislation was only £140, he sought to recover the rent which he had overpaid. The defendant counterclaimed for rescission of the lease on the ground of mistake. The Court of Appeal held that the landlord was entitled to set aside the lease 'on terms' (on which see Section 14.7) but the ratio of the case is not easy to discern because the judges all took different approaches. Jenkins LJ dissented on the ground that the mistake was one of law, not fact, and a mistake of law at that time did not entitle the landlord to set aside the lease (although today a mistake of law might entitle the landlord to seek relief: see *Brennan v Bolt Burden (a firm)* [2004] EWCA Civ 1017; [2005] QB 303). Denning LJ held that the contract was valid at law but voidable in equity. The judgment of Bucknill LJ is more difficult. He held that the landlord was entitled to set aside the lease on the ground that 'there was a mutual mistake of fact on a matter of fundamental importance, namely, as to the identity of the flat'. Some have concluded that Bucknill LJ was of the view that the contract was void at law, but that view cannot be reconciled with the fact that Bucknill LJ agreed with Denning LJ as to the terms on which the lease was to be set aside. Although the matter is not free from doubt, it is suggested that *Solle v Butcher* can best be understood as a case in which the lease was valid at law but voidable in equity (but see now Section 14.7). One particularly noteworthy feature of *Solle v Butcher* is that Lord Denning clearly wished to restrict the scope of the doctrine of common mistake at law because of the drastic effect which nullity has both for the parties themselves and for innocent third parties (see Section 4.6).

Finally, in *Great Peace Shipping Ltd v Tsavliris Salvage (International) Ltd* [2002] EWCA Civ 1407; [2003] QB 679 the defendant salvors agreed to provide salvage services for a vessel which was in serious difficulties in the South Indian Ocean. The defendants were informed that the Great Peace was close to the vessel which was in difficulty and so they contacted the claimants, the owners of the Great Peace, by telephone and agreed to hire it for a minimum of five days. It subsequently transpired that the Great Peace was not as close to the stricken vessel as the defendants had believed (it being 410 miles away rather than 35 miles). When they discovered the true situation the defendants sought to obtain the services of another vessel which was not as far away and, once they had done so, they purported to terminate the contract of hire with the claimants.

The claimants sued to recover the hire. The defendants resisted the claim on the ground that the contract to hire the Great Peace was vitiated by a common mistake as to the true location of the vessel. The Court of Appeal held that the mistake was not sufficiently fundamental to set aside the contract. While the vessels were 410 miles apart and it would have taken them some 22 hours to meet, this was not such a time delay as to render performance 'essentially different from those which the parties had envisaged when the contract was concluded'.

On the basis of these cases it would appear to be extremely difficult, if not impossible, to establish that a common mistake as to quality renders a contract void. But there are cases in which a mistake as to quality has been held to be sufficiently fundamental to avoid the contract. One such case is *Scott v Coulson* [1903] 2 Ch 249. A contract for the sale of a life assurance policy was held to be void when, unknown to both parties, the assured had died and the value of the policy had consequently increased from £460 to £777. But, as the Court of Appeal pointed out in *Great Peace* ([87]), the decision is 'by no means easy to reconcile' with *Bell v Lever Brothers*. Secondly, in *Nicholson and Venn v Smith-Marriott* (1947) 177 LT 189, the defendants put up for auction table napkins 'with crest of Charles I and authentic property of that monarch'. In reliance upon this description, the claimant bought the napkins for £787. It was later discovered that the napkins were Georgian and were worth only £105. Hallet J held that the claimant was entitled to damages for breach of contract but he also held that the claimant could have avoided the contract on the ground of mistake. The authority of this case has been weakened, however, by doubts cast upon its correctness by Denning LJ in *Solle v Butcher* (above).

How can these cases be reconciled? The general test can be identified reasonably easily. As Lord Thankerton stated in *Bell v Lever Brothers* (above), the mistake of the parties must relate to an 'essential and integral element of the subject matter of the contract'. The difficulty lies in applying that test to the facts of any given case. Treitel (2020, para 8-020) has put forward the following test: imagine that you can 'ask the parties, immediately after they made the contract, what its subject-matter was. If, in spite of the mistake, they would give the right answer the contract is valid at law.' Such a test works satisfactorily in most cases and helps explain the difference between cases such as *Oscar Chess* and *Nicholson and Venn*. But it does not appear to explain *Leaf*, where the parties would surely have said that they were purchasing a Constable and not simply a painting. Treitel (at para 8-021) concedes this point, but counters that the *dicta* in that case are not conclusive because the claimant 'did not claim that [the contract] was void for mistake'. It is also difficult to apply this test to *Scott* where it is arguable that the parties would have given the correct answer, namely an insurance policy. Although this test cannot reconcile all the cases, it does provide some useful guidance in considering whether a mistake as to quality relates to an 'essential and integral element of the subject matter of the contract'.

A different approach was adopted by the Court of Appeal in *Great Peace* where it was suggested (at [76]) that the following elements must be present before a common mistake can avoid a contract: '(i) there must be a common assumption as to the existence of a state of affairs, (ii) there must be no warranty by either party that that state of affairs exists, (iii) the non-existence of the state of affairs must not be attributable to the fault of either party, (iv) the non-existence of the state of affairs must render performance of the contract impossible, (v) the state of affairs may be the existence, or a vital attribute, of the consideration to be provided or circumstances which must subsist if performance of the contractual adventure is to be possible.' The relationship between these different factors is not made clear but the thrust of the analysis is clear: the doctrine of common mistake operates within very narrow limits.

Courts post-*Great Peace* have kept the doctrine of common mistake within these narrow limits, although the precise ambit of the doctrine remains to be finally established (*Lehman Bros International (Europe) (in administration) v Exotix Partners LLP* [2019] EWHC 2380 (Ch); [2020] 1 All ER (Comm) 635, [190]). The narrowest version of the doctrine is that the common mistake must be such as to render performance of the contract impossible (*Brennan v Bolt Burden (a firm)* [2004] EWCA Civ 1017; [2005] QB 303). But it is doubtful whether this insistence on impossibility is necessary. The analogy with frustration suggests that the doctrine should not be so confined and that it should extend to cases where performance in the circumstances would be something radically different from what the parties had in contemplation at the time of entry into the contract and there is now authority which supports this slightly broader conception of the doctrine of common mistake (*Triple Seven MSN 27521 Ltd v Azman Air Services Ltd* [2018] EWHC 1348 (Comm); [2018] 2 Lloyd's Rep 424, [76]; *Apvodedo NC v Collins* [2008] EWHC 775 (Ch); [2008] All ER (D) 246 (Apr), [43] and [46]). The acceptance of such an extension will not lead to a radical expansion of the doctrine of mistake and it has the great merit of bringing the doctrine of common mistake into closer alignment with the doctrine of frustration. A party will not, however, be entitled to invoke common mistake in the case where the contract has made provision in the event that the common assumption was mistaken (*Triple Seven MSN 27521 Ltd v Azman Air Services Ltd* [2018] EWHC 1348 (Comm); [2018] 2 Lloyd's Rep 424).

14.7   Mistake in equity

The decision of the House of Lords in *Bell v Lever Brothers Ltd* [1932] AC 161 gave birth to an extremely narrow doctrine of common mistake in English law. For many years the narrow approach adopted in *Bell v Lever Brothers* was 'supplemented by the more flexible doctrine of mistake in equity' (*Associated Japanese Bank (International)*

Ltd v Crédit du Nord [1989] 1 WLR 255, per Steyn J). The origin of the wider doctrine of mistake in equity was the decision of the Court of Appeal in *Solle v Butcher* [1950] 1 KB 671, where *Bell v Lever Brothers* was held to be an authority only on the scope of the doctrine of mistake at law. In so confining *Bell v Lever Brothers* the Court of Appeal was able to develop a wider doctrine of mistake in equity.

Mistake in equity differed in three major respects from mistake at law. First, the scope of the doctrine was wider (see Cartwright, 1987b). In *Solle v Butcher* (above) Denning LJ stated that in equity the mistake must be 'fundamental' and that the party seeking to set the contract aside must not himself be 'at fault'. But he also asserted that the court had power to set aside a contract which is valid at law 'whenever it is of the opinion that it is unconscientious for the other party to avail himself of the legal advantage which he has obtained'. While judges in subsequent cases did not always use the language of 'unconscientiousness' it was at least clear that the test applied in equity was less stringent than that applied at law (see, for example, *Grist v Bailey* [1967] Ch 532 and *Magee v Pennine Insurance Co* [1969] 2 QB 507). This wider test was always controversial because it had the effect of undermining the emphasis placed upon the promotion of certainty in *Bell v Lever Brothers*, and in some cases it appeared that the doctrine of mistake in equity was invoked successfully by a party who had entered into a bad bargain and was looking for a way out of the transaction (see, in particular, the decision of the Court of Appeal in *Grist v Bailey* (above)).

The second difference between mistake in equity and mistake at law was that mistake in equity rendered a contract voidable and not void, so that when a contract was set aside on the ground of mistake in equity, innocent third party rights could be protected. The third difference was that in equity the courts had greater remedial flexibility because they could set aside the contract 'on terms' (that is to say, they could attach conditions to the entitlement of one party to set aside the initial contract).

The existence of this wider, more flexible doctrine of mistake in equity was, however, brought to an end by the decision of the Court of Appeal in *Great Peace*. The refusal of the Court of Appeal in *Great Peace* to follow the decisions of the Court of Appeal in *Solle v Butcher*, *Grist v Bailey* and *Magee v Pennine Insurance* has given rise to some controversy. The Court of Appeal cannot generally refuse to follow its own decisions. But the Court of Appeal in *Great Peace* concluded that it was entitled to refuse to follow *Solle v Butcher* and the line of cases which it generated on the ground that it was 'impossible to reconcile *Solle v Butcher* with *Bell v Lever Brothers*' which is, of course, a decision of the House of Lords. They held that the effect of *Solle v Butcher* was not 'to supplement or mitigate the common law' but that it was 'to say that *Bell v Lever Brothers* was wrongly decided'. They stated that 'if coherence is to be restored to this area of our law, it can only be by declaring that there is no jurisdiction to grant rescission of a contract on the ground of common mistake where that contract is valid and enforceable on ordinary principles of contract law'.

It is suggested that the decision of the Court of Appeal in *Great Peace* is correct and that *Solle v Butcher* has been effectively overruled (a point acknowledged by Lord Walker in *Pitt v Holt* [2013] UKSC 26; [2013] 2 AC 108, [115]). *Solle* could not stand with *Bell v Lever Brothers* and, as the Court of Appeal pointed out in *Great Peace*, it is simply not 'conceivable that the House of Lords [in *Bell v Lever Brothers*] overlooked an equitable right in Lever Bros to rescind the agreement, notwithstanding that the agreement was not void for mistake at common law'. The House of Lords in *Bell v Lever Brothers* intended to conclude that the agreement was valid and binding and this was so whether the claim was brought at law or in equity.

The narrow doctrine of mistake at law has therefore triumphed over the more flexible doctrine that had been developed in equity post-*Solle v Butcher*. Some will mourn this loss of flexibility. As the Court of Appeal observed in *Great Peace* (at [161]):

> We can understand why the decision in *Bell v Lever Brothers Ltd* did not find favour with Lord Denning. An equitable jurisdiction to grant rescission on terms where a common fundamental mistake has induced a contract gives greater flexibility than a doctrine of common law which holds the contract void in such circumstances. Just as the Law Reform (Frustrated Contracts) Act 1943 was needed to temper the effect of the common law doctrine of frustration, so there is scope for legislation to give greater flexibility to our law of mistake than the common law allows.

The likelihood of legislation of this type being introduced in the near future appears to be remote. In any event, the analogy drawn with the Law Reform (Frustrated Contracts) Act 1943 seems misplaced given that the 1943 Act is concerned to regulate the remedial consequences of a contract that has already been set aside, whereas in the present case the issue is the prior one of whether or not the contract should be set aside at all. It is perhaps rather ironic that the Court of Appeal in *Great Peace* lamented the loss of flexibility given that they are the ones responsible for this loss of flexibility. But it may be an error to see *Great Peace* as a decision which favours certainty over flexibility. In many ways the aim of the Court of Appeal was to restore a degree of coherence to this area of law. They were not prepared to tolerate the continued existence of an equitable doctrine which, in effect, undermined the decision of the House of Lords in *Bell v Lever Brothers*. Their essential point is that there should only be one law of mistake and not two (for a similar approach see *Statoil ASA v Louis Dreyfus Energy Services LP* [2008] EWHC 2257 (Comm); [2008] 2 Lloyd's Rep 685, [97]–[105] where, in the context of a claim to set aside a contract on the ground of unilateral mistake, Aikens J rejected the submission that there was a wider equitable jurisdiction than that which existed at common law). The law must therefore choose between a narrow doctrine of mistake which favours certainty and a more liberal regime which favours flexibility. For better or for worse, English law made that choice in favour of certainty in *Bell v Lever Brothers*, and that decision can only be reversed by a subsequent decision of the Supreme Court or by legislation. It could not be made by the Court of Appeal in *Solle v Butcher*. In many ways the effect of *Great Peace* is simply to take the law back to the position that it was in post-*Bell v Lever Brothers* and prior to the decision of the Court of Appeal in *Solle v Butcher*.

14.8 Frustration

A contract can only be set aside on the ground of common mistake where the parties were labouring under the mistake at the time at which they entered into the contract. Unforeseen events which occur after the contract has been concluded cannot form the basis of a claim for relief on the ground of mistake, but, in such a situation, a court may hold that the contract has been discharged by operation of the doctrine of frustration. A contract is frustrated where, *after* the contract was concluded, events occur which make performance of the contract impossible, illegal or something radically different from that which was in the contemplation of the parties at the time they entered into the contract. A contract which is discharged on the ground of frustration is brought to an end automatically by the operation of a rule of law, irrespective of the wishes of the parties (*Hirji Mulji v Cheong Yue SS Co* [1926] AC 497).

It has been argued (Section 14.1) that the principal difference between common mistake and frustration relates to the *time* at which the misapprehension or unforeseen event occurs. Yet, it must be conceded that the time at which the misapprehension or unforeseen event occurs does have significant consequences; that is to say, it is easier to discover the true facts at the moment of entry into the contract than it is to foresee future events. Therefore, it is to be expected that a court will be readier to discharge a contract on the ground of frustration than it will be to avoid a contract on the ground of mistake. But when one looks at the cases, that expectation is not clearly fulfilled because the doctrine of frustration presently operates within very narrow confines. What is it that explains the reluctance of the courts to invoke the doctrine of frustration?

14.9   Frustration, force majeure and hardship

It is suggested that there are two principal reasons which help to explain the reluctance of the courts to invoke the doctrine of frustration. The first is that the courts do not want to allow parties to find an easy escape route from what has turned out to be an improvident contract. The second is that the parties can insert into their contract terms which make provision for the impact of catastrophic events beyond the control of the parties, and it can be said that they are better placed to allocate the risk of the occurrence of such events than is the general law of contract. We shall examine these reasons in turn.

14.9.1   No escape from a bad bargain

The courts do not wish the doctrine of frustration to act as an escape route for a party for whom the contract has simply become a bad bargain. The attitude of the modern courts was well summed up by Lord Roskill when he said that the doctrine of frustration was 'not lightly to be invoked to relieve contracting parties of the normal consequences of imprudent bargains' (*The Nema* [1982] AC 724, 752). An example of this approach at work is provided by the case of *Davis Contractors Ltd v Fareham UDC* [1956] AC 696. The claimant contractors agreed to build 78 houses for the defendants for £94,000. The work was scheduled to last for eight months but, owing to shortages of skilled labour, the work took an extra 14 months to complete and cost £115,000. The claimants, in an attempt to recover a sum of money in excess of the contract price, argued that the contract had been frustrated. Their argument was rejected by the House of Lords. Lord Radcliffe stated that it was not:

> hardship or inconvenience or material loss itself which calls the principle of frustration into play. There must be as well such a change in the significance of the obligation that the thing undertaken would, if performed, be a different thing from that contracted for.

Davis can be said to be the paradigm example of a bad bargain. The deal had undoubtedly turned out to be a poor one for the claimants but the courts refused to rescue them. The decision may seem harsh but, had it gone the other way, it would have created a new principle of uncertain ambit which would have denied to the defendants the fruits of the good deal which they had negotiated. The hardship which *Davis* possibly creates is more than offset by the clear rule which it establishes and the signal which it gives to contracting parties that the courts will not lend their assistance to a party who is looking for a way out of a bad bargain.

However, the combined impact of the economic downturn in 2008/2009, worries about the possible consequences of Brexit and the COVID-19 global pandemic have caused some to question the wisdom of having such a narrow doctrine of frustration. Although the economic downturn of over a decade ago caused some contracting parties to lose substantial sums of money, it did not result in judicial re-consideration of the scope of the doctrine of frustration. Nor has Brexit (at least thus far) led to any widening of the doctrine of frustration. On the contrary, the leading case to date concerned with the impact of Brexit affirmed the narrow scope of the doctrine of frustration in clear and unequivocal terms (*Canary Wharf (BP4) T1 Ltd v European Medicines Agency* [2019] EWHC 335 (Ch), [21]–[24]). Whether the COVID-19 pandemic will result in judicial re-consideration of the scope of frustration remains to be seen. It is likely that the impact of COVID-19 will lead to the frustration of a number of contracts, at least in the case of contracts entered into before there was any general awareness of the existence of the virus. Contracts likely to be frustrated include those where performance has become illegal or impossible as a result of lockdowns imposed by governments in response to the pandemic. But the fact that performance is delayed, supplies are more difficult to obtain, or performance has become considerably more expensive will not result in the frustration of the contract. This strict approach is likely to create significant difficulties for businesses who are currently experiencing serious cash flow problems as a result of the pandemic and who may not survive if left to shoulder the losses themselves. In this environment, it is not surprising to find that there have been calls for a more responsive, co-operative approach to the problems created by COVID-19 for contracting parties. These calls include guidance issued by the Cabinet Office (2020) in which it sought to encourage 'responsible and fair behaviour' in 'performing and enforcing contracts where there has been a material impact' from COVID-19. This responsible and fair behaviour was stated to include 'making, and responding to…frustration.' The guidance issued by the Cabinet Office is not legally binding and so will not result in any formal changes to the doctrine of frustration. But it may in time lead to judicial re-consideration of aspects of the scope of the current doctrine, in particular whether contracting parties should be required to co-operate with one another in order to address the problems (and, possibly, share the losses) created by a pandemic of the gravity of the current COVID-19 pandemic.

The present approach of the courts, when deciding in a particular case whether or not a contract has been frustrated, is to adopt what has been termed a 'multifactorial' approach (see *Edwinton Commercial Corp, Global Tradeways Limited v Tsavliris Russ (Worldwide Salvage & Towage) Ltd (The 'Sea Angel')* [2007] EWCA Civ

547; [2007] 2 Lloyd's Rep 517, [111]). Factors which the courts should take into account include:

> [i] the terms of the contract itself, [ii] its matrix or context, [iii] the parties' knowledge, expectations, assumptions and contemplations, in particular as to risk, as at the time of contract, at any rate so far as these can be ascribed mutually and objectively, and then [iv] the nature of the supervening event, and [v] the parties' reasonable and objectively ascertainable calculations as to the possibilities of future performance in the new circumstances.

These factors can be divided into two groups. Factors [i]–[iii] can be described as '*ex ante* factors', while factors [iv]–[v] are post-contractual (*Islamic Republic of Iran Shipping Lines v Steamship Mutual Underwriting Association (Bermuda) Ltd* [2010] EWHC 2661 (Comm); [2011] 1 Lloyd's Rep 195, [105]). While this multi-factorial approach has injected a degree of flexibility into the law in terms of the range of factors which a court can take into account when deciding whether or not a contract has been frustrated (*Bunge SA v Kyla Shipping Co Ltd* [2013] EWCA 734; [2013] 3 All ER 1006, [7]), the doctrine continues to operate within very narrow limits. The essence of the doctrine remains that there must be a break in identity between the contemplated and the new performance and the courts will not lightly conclude that there has been such a break (see also *CTI Group Inc v Transclear SA* [2008] EWCA Civ 856; [2008] 2 Lloyd's Rep 526).

14.9.2   The significance of force majeure and hardship clauses

The second reason for the narrowness of the doctrine of frustration is that we all know that the future is uncertain; prices may suddenly increase, inflation may rise, labour disputes break out. Contracting parties are expected to foresee many such possibilities when entering into a contract and guard against them in the contract. Contracts today often make provision for the impact of unexpected events upon contractual performance. A clause which is frequently employed for this purpose is known as a 'force majeure' clause. In *Channel Island Ferries Ltd v Sealink UK Ltd* [1988] 1 Lloyd's Rep 323, the contract between the parties contained the following force majeure clause:

> A party shall not be liable in the event of non-fulfilment of any obligation arising under this contract by reason of Act of God, disease, strikes, lock-outs, fire, and any accident or incident of any nature beyond the control of the relevant party.

Another clause which is found in commercial contracts is known as a 'hardship clause'. Such a clause will generally define what constitutes 'hardship' (usually of an economic variety) and will lay down a procedure to be adopted by the parties in the event of such hardship occurring. Generally, the clause will purport to impose an obligation on both parties to use best endeavours to renegotiate the contract in good faith in an attempt to alleviate the hardship which has arisen. A further type of clause which is found in commercial contracts is an 'intervener clause'. Such a clause is similar to a 'hardship clause' except that it gives to a third party such as an arbitrator (the 'intervener') the authority to resolve the dispute which has arisen between the parties and to adjust the terms of their contract in the light of the changed circumstances. Intervener clauses are employed as a sanction to be invoked in the event of the parties themselves failing to negotiate their way out of a hardship event.

What advantages can be obtained by the use of such clauses? It is suggested that there are a number of advantages (see McKendrick, 1995). The first is the provision of a degree of certainty. It is often difficult to know whether or not a contract has been frustrated. To an extent this uncertainty can be reduced by the parties agreeing a list of events which are to constitute force majeure or hardship events. The second is that frustration operates within very narrow limits (both in terms of the events which constitute frustrating events and the width of doctrines such as self-induced frustration which deny to a party the ability to claim that the contract was frustrated, see Section 14.16). On the other hand, force majeure and hardship clauses give to the parties the opportunity, should they want to avail themselves of it, to agree that a wider class of events shall constitute force majeure or hardship events. For example, an unexpected increase in prices does not constitute a frustrating event (see *Davis Contractors v Fareham UDC* (above)) but a commercial contract may state that an 'abnormal increase in prices and wages' shall constitute a force majeure event.

The third advantage is that the parties can make provision for the consequences of the occurrence of a force majeure or hardship event. Frustration operates too drastically because it terminates the contract, irrespective of the wishes of the parties (see Section 14.8). Very often the parties want to continue their relationship but to adapt the terms to meet the new situation. This cannot be done under the doctrine of frustration. But force majeure clauses often provide for a period of suspension of the contract (to allow more time for performance or to enable the parties to wait for the supervening event, such as bad weather or a strike, to subside) before resorting to the more drastic remedy of termination. Hardship and intervener clauses are particularly well suited to contracting parties who wish their relationship to continue through changing circumstances. The remedial rigidity of the doctrine of frustration contrasts unfavourably with the flexibility which can be obtained by drafting an appropriate force majeure or hardship clause.

It is suggested that the ability of contracting parties to make such provision in their contracts has had a significant impact upon the development of the doctrine of frustration. Indeed, at one point in its history, supervening or unforeseen events were not regarded as an excuse for non-performance because the parties could provide against such accidents in their contract. Once a party had assumed an obligation he was 'bound to make it good' (*Paradine v Jane* (1647) Aleyn 26, 27). This absolutist approach was gradually relaxed during the latter half of the nineteenth century and, commencing with *Taylor v Caldwell* (1863) 3 B & S 826 and culminating in cases such as *Jackson v Union Marine Insurance Co Ltd* (1874) LR 10 CP 125 and *Krell v Henry* [1903] 2 KB 740, the courts developed a wider role for the doctrine of frustration and it became significantly easier to invoke the doctrine. Today, the courts have reverted to a more restrictive approach and it is rare to find frustration being pleaded successfully. For this reason, contracting parties frequently include force majeure and hardship clauses in their contracts so that they can allocate the risk of the occurrence of such unforeseen events (see Section 14.16). It is often said that English law does not encourage the adjustment of bargains in the event of contractual performance becoming more onerous. This is not entirely accurate. The issue should not be seen as whether or not English law permits adjustment. The real issue is: who should do the adjusting? Is it the courts or is it the parties? The answer which English law gives is that it is for the parties to do the adjusting. While the courts will not adjust the bargain for the parties, they will be reluctant to place significant obstacles in the way of attempts by the parties to adjust their bargain to meet changing circumstances.

14.10 Frustration: a sterile doctrine?

Although frustration is a difficult defence to invoke, it should not be thought that it has become a sterile doctrine which is incapable of development. The scope of the doctrine was, in fact, expanded by the decision of the House of Lords in *National Carriers v Panalpina (Northern) Ltd* [1981] AC 675. For many years it was thought that the doctrine of frustration could not apply to a lease because a lease created an interest in land and that interest in land was unaffected by the alleged frustrating event. But in *Panalpina* it was held that, as a matter of principle, a lease could be frustrated, although, as a matter of practice, it would be rare for a court to conclude that a lease had been frustrated. Many leases run for a long period of time, such as 99 or even 999 years, and it is difficult to conceive of such a lease being frustrated because the parties must anticipate that major changes will occur during the period and so, to a large extent, they will have assumed the risk of supervening events. The type of lease which might be frustrated is a lease of a holiday flat or some other lease of short duration. Although the practical significance of *Panalpina* may be minimal, the decision does display a willingness, in an appropriate case, to expand the horizons of the doctrine of frustration.

14.11 Impossibility

A contract which, without the fault of either party to the contract, has become impossible of performance is frustrated. In *Taylor v Caldwell* (1863) 3 B & S 826, the defendants granted to the claimants a licence to use the 'Surrey Gardens and Music Hall' for a series of concerts at a fee of £100 per concert. After the contract had been concluded, but before the first concert was performed, the music hall was accidentally destroyed by fire so that it became impossible to stage the concerts. The claimants argued that the defendants were in breach of contract in failing to supply the hall and sought to recover their wasted advertising expenditure. But the court held that the contract was frustrated because the destruction of the music hall rendered performance of the contract impossible. The frustrating event released both parties from their obligations under the contract and so the defendants were no longer under an obligation to supply the hall and were not in breach of contract. Partial destruction of the subject-matter may also frustrate a contract where it renders performance of the contract impossible. For example, in *Taylor v Caldwell* the contract was for the hire of the music hall and the 'Surrey Gardens', but it was only the music hall which was destroyed. Nevertheless, because the destruction of the music hall rendered performance of the contract impossible the contract was frustrated.

Contracts for personal services, such as contracts of employment and contracts of apprenticeship, are frustrated by the death of either party to the contract. Similarly, a contract of employment may be frustrated if the ill-health of an employee renders him permanently unfit for work.

A contract may also be frustrated where the subject-matter of the contract is unavailable for the purpose of carrying out the contract. For example, a charterparty was held to be frustrated when the ship was requisitioned and so was unavailable to the charterer (*Bank Line Ltd v Arthur Capel & Co Ltd* [1919] AC 435). Temporary unavailability of the subject-matter may also frustrate a contract. In *Jackson v Union Marine Insurance Co Ltd* (1874) LR 10 CP 125, a ship was chartered in November 1871 and was required to proceed with all possible dispatch from Liverpool to Newport, and there load a cargo for carriage to San Francisco. On her way to Newport in early January 1872, the ship ran aground and was not fully repaired until the end of August 1872. It was held that the contract was frustrated because the ship was not available for the voyage for which she was chartered. A voyage to San Francisco in late August 1872 was performance radically different from that originally contemplated.

Where the contract is one of fixed duration and the unavailability of the subject-matter is only temporary, the court must, in deciding whether the contract has been frustrated, consider the ratio of the likely interruption in contractual performance to the duration of the contract. The higher the ratio, the more likely it is that the contract will be frustrated. In *The Nema* [1982] AC 724 (above) a charterparty was frustrated when a long strike closed the port at which the ship was due to load so that, of the six or seven voyages contracted to be made between April and December, no more than two could be completed (see also *Morgan v Manser* [1948] 1 KB 184).

14.12 Frustration of purpose

Where the common purpose for which the contract was entered into can no longer be carried out because of some supervening event the contract may be frustrated. Examples of frustration of purpose are, however, extremely rare. The reason for this is that the courts do not wish to provide an escape route for a party for whom the contract has simply become a bad bargain. A rare case in which a plea of frustration of purpose succeeded is *Krell v Henry* [1903] 2 KB 740. The defendant hired a flat in Pall Mall from the claimant for two days. The object in entering into the contract was to view the coronation procession of Edward VII, although this was not actually expressed in the contract. After the contract had been concluded, the coronation of Edward VII was postponed because of the illness of the King. The Court of Appeal held that the contract was frustrated. *Krell* must, however, be contrasted with *Herne Bay Steam Boat Co v Hutton* [1903] 2 KB 683, in which the defendant hired a ship from the claimant 'for the purpose of viewing the naval review and for a day's cruise around the fleet'. After the contract had been concluded, the naval review was cancelled because of the illness of Edward VII. Nevertheless, the court held that the contract was not frustrated. What is the difference between this case and *Krell*?

In answering this question, it is necessary to refer to an example considered by Vaughan Williams LJ in *Krell*. It was put to Vaughan Williams LJ that, if the contract was frustrated on the facts of *Krell*, then it:

> would follow that if a cabman was engaged to take someone to Epsom on Derby Day at a suitably enhanced price for such a journey ... both parties to the contract would be discharged in the contingency of the race at Epsom for some reason becoming impossible.

But Vaughan Williams LJ was of the opinion that such a contract would not be frustrated because he did not think that 'the happening of the race would be the foundation of the contract'. In *Krell*, on the other hand, the 'foundation of the contract' was the viewing of the coronation. However, the contract in *Krell* was an extremely unusual one. The rooms were hired out by the day, excluding the night. In the words of Marcus Smith J in *Canary Wharf (BP4) T1 Ltd v European Medicines Agency* [2019] EWHC 335 (Ch), [37] the common purpose of the parties was the buying and selling of 'a room with a view'. This being the case, the only purpose which *both* parties had in entering into such an unusual contract was to hire the rooms for the purpose of viewing the coronation. So interpreted, the contract was frustrated. On the other hand, in *Herne Bay Steam Boat Co v Hutton* the defendant could still see the fleet and, although the defendant's motive in entering into the contract might have been to see the naval review, it could not be said that that was the 'common foundation of the contract'. Similar reasoning explains the example of the cancellation of the Derby. Although the motive of the hirer might have been to see the Derby, that was not of itself sufficient to render the happening of the Derby the 'common foundation' of the contract. The taxi driver in such a case has been stated to be 'entirely indifferent as to the purpose of the journey and indeed its destination' (*Canary Wharf (BP4) T1 Ltd v European Medicines Agency* [2019] EWHC 335 (Ch), [37]). A potential difficulty with this analysis is the significance of the agreement to pay 'a suitably enhanced price' for the journey. The enhanced price could be said to be evidence of the fact that the taxi driver had accepted that the purpose of the journey was to secure transport to the Derby. An alternative analysis, and the one adopted by Marcus Smith J in *Canary Wharf (BP4) T1 Ltd v European Medicines Agency* [2019] EWHC 335 (Ch), [37] is that the enhanced price had 'nothing to do with a common purpose' but was 'simply a reflection of market forces' and of the 'opposing interests of cab driver and passenger'. Whatever the precise analysis of, and explanation for, the taxi driver case, it is clear that *Krell* is a very narrow decision whose scope will not be extended (*North Shore Ventures Ltd v Anstead Holdings Inc* [2010] EWHC 1485 (Ch), [310]) and so it is not surprising that it has been distinguished (rather than followed) in modern cases such as *Amalgamated Investment and Property Co Ltd v John Walker & Sons Ltd* [1977] 1 WLR 164 (Section 14.1).

14.13 Illegality

Supervening illegality can operate to frustrate a contract. In *Fibrosa Spolka Akcyjna v Fairbairn Lawson Combe Barbour Ltd* [1943] AC 32, the respondents agreed to manufacture machines for the appellants and to deliver them to Gdynia in Poland. However, before the respondents had completed the manufacture of the machines, Gdynia was occupied by the German army. It was held that the contract was frustrated because in time of war it is against the law to trade with the enemy. The public interest in ensuring that no assistance was given to the enemy in time of war outweighed the fact that it remained physically possible to manufacture and deliver the machines. In this context the concern of the court is not simply with the allocation or distribution of the loss caused by the supervening event, but with public policy considerations, particularly in ensuring that the law is observed (*Islamic Republic of Iran Shipping Lines v Steamship Mutual Underwriting Association (Bermuda)*

Ltd [2010] EWHC 2661 (Comm); [2011] 1 Lloyd's Rep 195, [100]). Where the illegality is only temporary or partial, the contract will be frustrated only if the illegality affects the performance of the contract in a substantial or fundamental way (contrast *Denny, Mott & Dickinson v James B Fraser & Co Ltd* [1944] AC 265 and *Cricklewood Property Investment Trust Ltd v Leighton's Investment Trust Ltd* [1945] AC 221).

14.14 Express provision

There are a number of limitations upon the scope of the doctrine of frustration. Three such limitations will be considered here (Sections 14.14–14.16). The first is that a contract is not frustrated where the parties have made express provision for the occurrence of the alleged frustrating event in their contract (*Joseph Constantine Steamship Line Ltd v Imperial Smelting Corp Ltd* [1942] AC 154, 163). A frustrating event is a supervening, unforeseen event; it is not an event which has been anticipated in the contract itself. But where the contract is frustrated on the ground that further performance of the contract is against the law, because it involves trading with the enemy in time of war, the operation of the doctrine of frustration cannot be excluded by express provision in the contract. Overriding considerations of public policy deny effect to such a clause (*Ertel Bieber and Co v Rio Tinto Co Ltd* [1918] AC 260).

The express provision rule has important consequences for force majeure clauses and hardship clauses. The effect of such clauses may be to exclude the operation of the doctrine of frustration because the contract, on its proper construction, will be held to have covered and made its own provision for the event which has occurred. But the courts have generally subjected to a narrow interpretation clauses which, it is alleged, make provision for what would otherwise be a frustrating event. In particular, the fact that the contract deals with events of the same general nature as the alleged frustrating event does not mean that the clause deals with every event in that class. A good example of this approach is provided by the decision of the House of Lords in *Metropolitan Water Board v Dick, Kerr and Co* [1918] AC 119. Here contractors agreed to construct a reservoir in six years. The contract provided that, in the event of delay 'whatsoever and howsoever occasioned', the contractors were to apply to the engineer for an extension of time. When the contractors were required by Government Order to stop the work and sell their plant, it was held that the contract was frustrated because the delay clause was not intended to apply to such a fundamental change of circumstances. It was held that the clause was intended to cover only temporary difficulties and did not cover fundamental changes in the nature of the contract (see too *Jackson v Union Marine Insurance Co Ltd* (above)).

So the courts insist that provision for the event be 'full and complete' before frustration is excluded, and the greater the magnitude of the event, the less likely it is that it will be held to fall within the scope of the contract. One consequence of this approach is that it is extremely difficult, if not impossible, to draft a force majeure clause which will exclude the operation of the doctrine of frustration completely. As the *Metropolitan Water Board* case demonstrates, even the widest of clauses may be held not to encompass a particularly catastrophic event. Similarly, the fact that a force majeure clause makes provision for a temporary suspension of the contract on the occurrence of a force majeure event is likely to be interpreted by the court as an indication that the scope of the clause is confined to temporary interruptions in performance and that it does not apply to an event which renders further performance of the contract 'unthinkable' (*The Playa Larga* [1983] 2 Lloyd's Rep 171, 189).

14.15 Foreseen and foreseeable events

Given that a frustrating event is a supervening, unforeseen event, the doctrine ought logically not to apply to an event which is within the contemplation of the parties at the time the contract is concluded. In *Walton Harvey Ltd v Walker and Homfrays Ltd* [1931] 1 Ch 274, the defendant granted to the claimant the right to display an advertising sign for seven years on the defendant's hotel. Before the seven years had elapsed, the local authority compulsorily purchased the hotel and demolished it. The court held that the contract between the parties was not frustrated by the compulsory purchase and demolition of the hotel because it was within the contemplation of the defendant, at the time that the contract was concluded, that the property might be the subject of a compulsory purchase order. The proposition that a foreseeable event cannot frustrate a contract has been challenged, however, by Lord Denning in *The Eugenia* [1964] 2 QB 226 (see too *WJ Tatem Ltd v Gamboa* [1939] 1 KB 132). The status of these *dicta* is uncertain. On the one hand, they suggest that the general rule requires reconsideration, but, on the other hand, they can be reconciled with the orthodox analysis on the ground that the events in these cases were not sufficiently foreseeable to satisfy the very high test of foreseeability which is applicable here. An event is foreseeable and will prevent frustration of the contract only where it is one which 'any person of ordinary intelligence would regard as likely to occur' (see Treitel, 2020, para 19-085, and contrast Hall, 1984). In other words, the question would appear to be one of fact and degree, and much will depend on the extent to which the event in question was foreseeable by the parties. As Rix LJ stated in *The Sea Angel* [2007] EWCA Civ 547; [2007] 2 Lloyd's Rep 517, [127], 'the less that an event, in its type and its impact, is foreseeable, the more likely it is to be a factor which, depending on other factors in the case, may lead on to frustration'. Rix LJ also warned against the 'over-refinement' of submissions on this issue, further reinforcing the view that much here depends upon the facts and circumstances of the individual case. Whatever doubts we may harbour about the precise role of foreseeability within the doctrine of frustration, it is at least clear that a contract can be frustrated by supervening illegality even in the case where the war which has brought about the frustrating event was foreseeable. In such cases, overriding considerations of public policy lead to the conclusion that the contract was frustrated.

14.16 Self-induced frustration

A party cannot invoke the doctrine of frustration where the alleged frustrating event is brought about through his own conduct or the conduct of those for whom he is responsible. This inability to invoke frustration is generally referred to as 'self-induced frustration'. It is, however, important to be clear about the consequences of concluding that the 'frustration' was 'self-induced'. Frustration is generally invoked by a defendant who has not performed his contractual obligations as a defence to an action for breach of contract. But where the 'frustration' is held to be 'self-induced', the consequence is that the defendant is unable to rely on frustration and so, in the absence of any other defence, will be found to be in breach of contract.

Although the concept of self-induced frustration is clearly established in the cases, the courts have never established its limits with any degree of clarity. In *J Lauritzen AS v Wijsmuller BV (The 'Super Servant Two')* [1989] 1 Lloyd's Rep 148, Hobhouse J defined self-induced frustration as a 'label' which has been used by the courts to describe 'those situations where one party has been held by the courts not to be entitled to treat himself as discharged from his contractual obligations'. On his analysis, frustration was self-induced where the alleged frustrating event was caused by a breach or an anticipatory breach of contract by the party claiming that the contract has been frustrated, where an act of the party claiming that the contract has been frustrated broke the chain of causation between the alleged frustrating event and the event which made performance of the contract impossible, and where the alleged frustrating event was not a supervening event, by which he meant 'something altogether outside the control of the parties'. Thus a negligent act by the defendant will generally amount to self-induced frustration because such an event is not 'altogether outside the control' of the defendant. On the contrary, it is within his control, notwithstanding the fact that his negligence is a result of his unreasonable failure to exercise that control (see *Joseph Constantine Steamship Line Ltd v Imperial Smelting Corp Ltd* [1942] AC 154).

Some insight into the scope of self-induced frustration can be gleaned from an analysis of the following two cases. The first case is *Maritime National Fish Ltd v Ocean Trawlers Ltd* [1935] AC 524. The defendants chartered a ship from the claimants but the vessel could only be used for its intended purpose if it was fitted with an otter trawl. An otter trawl could only be used under licence and, although the defendants applied for licences for the five vessels which they operated, they were allocated only three licences. They elected to apply the licences to the trawlers which they owned directly or indirectly rather than to the vessel chartered from the claimants. The claimants sued for the hire due under the terms of the contract but the defendants denied liability to pay on the ground that the contract had been frustrated by their failure to obtain a licence. The Privy Council held that the contract was not frustrated as a result of the defendants' failure to obtain a licence for the vessel; this was a case of self-induced frustration. But the ratio of the decision remained unclear. On the one hand, it could be argued that it was the fact that the defendants elected to allocate the licences to their own vessels which led the Privy Council to conclude that this was a case of self-induced frustration. On the other hand, it could be maintained that the mere fact that the defendants had a choice as to the distribution of the licences was sufficient to constitute self-induced frustration.

Our second case is *J Lauritzen AS v Wijsmuller BV (The 'Super Servant Two')* [1990] 1 Lloyd's Rep 1, where the Court of Appeal adopted the latter of our two possible interpretations of the *Maritime National Fish* case. The defendants agreed to transport the claimants' oil rig using, at their option, either Super Servant One or Super Servant Two (both of which were self-propelling barges especially designed for the transportation of rigs). Prior to the time for performance of the contract the defendants made a decision, which they admitted was not irrevocable, to allocate Super Servant Two to the performance of the contract with the claimants and to allocate Super Servant One to the performance of other concluded contracts. Unfortunately, after the contract had been concluded but before the time fixed for performance, Super Servant Two sank while transporting another rig. The contract could not be performed by Super Servant One because of its allocation to the performance of other concluded contracts, and so the contract was eventually performed by another, more expensive method of transportation. The claimants brought an action for damages against the defendants, alleging that they were in breach of contract in failing to transport the rig in the agreed manner. The defendants denied liability on two grounds. The first was that they argued that the contract had been frustrated as a result of the sinking of Super Servant Two. This argument was rejected. The Court of Appeal held that the cause of the non-performance of the contract was not the sinking of Super Servant Two but the choice of the defendants to allocate Super Servant One to the performance of other contracts. The existence of such a choice was held to be sufficient to turn the case into one of self-induced frustration. The difficulty with this analysis is that the defendants had no *real* choice as to the allocation of Super Servant One. It was impossible to allocate it to the performance of all concluded contracts and so the sinking of Super Servant Two *compelled* them to make such a decision. The conclusion of the Court of Appeal appears to leave a seller or supplier of goods in an impossible position where his source of supply partially fails due to an unforeseen event.

But at this point it is important to turn to the defendants' second defence, which was that they were entitled to terminate performance of the contract without incurring any liability under the terms of a force majeure clause contained in the contract. One of the force majeure events listed in the contract was 'perils or dangers and accidents of the sea' and the Court of Appeal held that this phrase was apt to encompass the sinking of Super Servant Two *provided that* its sinking was not attributable to negligence on the part of the defendants or their employees. So, provided there was no negligence on the part of the defendants, the force majeure clause gave to the defendants an effective defence to the claimants' claim for damages.

Super Servant Two is an interesting and important case because it provides us with an excellent example both of the narrow confines within which the doctrine of frustration currently operates and of the advantages which can be obtained by the incorporation of a suitably drafted force majeure clause in a contract. Indeed, the latter point was made abundantly clear by Hobhouse J at first instance when he said that if a promisor wished protection in the event of a partial failure of supplies 'he must bargain for the inclusion of a suitable force majeure clause in the contract'. The responsibility for adjusting and regulating the bargain is thus clearly allocated to the parties and not to the courts. Given the narrow confines within which frustration currently operates, *Super Servant Two* demonstrates that a contracting party who wishes to be released from his obligations to perform in a wider range of circumstances must bargain for the inclusion of a force majeure, hardship or intervener clause in the contract (see Section 14.9).

14.17 The effects of frustration

As we have already noted (Section 14.8), a contract which is discharged on the ground of frustration is brought to an end automatically at the time of the frustrating event. For the purposes of ease of exposition, we shall consider separately the effects of frustration upon a claim to recover money paid prior to the frustrating event and its effects upon a claim to recover the value of goods supplied or services provided prior to the frustrating event.

14.17.1 The common law rules

At common law it was held in *Fibrosa Spolka Akcyjna v Fairbairn Lawson Combe Barbour Ltd* [1943] AC 32 (overruling *Chandler v Webster* [1904] 1 KB 493 where it had been held, essentially, that the loss lay where it fell) that money paid prior to the frustration of the contract was recoverable upon a total failure of consideration. A total failure of consideration arises where the party seeking recovery has got no part of what he has bargained for. In *Fibrosa* (see Section 14.13), the appellants sought to recover the £1,000 they had paid to the respondents on the signing of the contract. The House of Lords held that the consideration for the payment had wholly failed because the machines had not been delivered to the appellants and that they were entitled to the recovery of their prepayment. While it is true to say that *Fibrosa* represented an improvement upon the old common law rule established in *Chandler v Webster*, it did not leave the law in an entirely satisfactory state. Two principal defects remained. The first was that the payer could only recover money paid upon a total failure of consideration; where the failure was only partial he could not recover (*Whincup v Hughes* (1871) LR 6 CP 78, see further Section 21.6). The second defect was that the payee could not set off against the money to be repaid any expenditure which he had incurred in the performance of the contract. For example, on the facts of *Fibrosa*, the respondents had incurred expenditure in making the machines (although it was, admittedly, unclear whether that expenditure had been wasted), yet they were unable to retain any portion of the £1,000 which represented their expenditure upon the machines.

14.17.2 Section 1(2) of the Law Reform (Frustrated Contracts) Act 1943

This position has been rectified by the enactment of section 1(2) of the Law Reform (Frustrated Contracts) Act 1943. The effect of this subsection is threefold. The first is that moneys paid prior to the frustrating event are recoverable. The second is that sums payable prior to the time of discharge cease to be payable. The third is that the payee may be entitled to set off against the sums so paid expenses which he has incurred before the time of discharge in, or for the purpose of, the performance of the contract. Section 1(2) meets the two deficiencies of the common law in that the right to recover money is not confined to a total failure of consideration and the payee can set off against the sums repayable any reliance expenditure which he had incurred in the performance of the contract. But certain deficiencies remain (for fuller consideration see McKendrick, 1995). The first is that the section does not make clear the basis upon which the court is to calculate the amount of expenditure which a payee is entitled to retain. Is it all of it, half of it, some other portion of it, or none of it? In *Gamerco SA v ICM/Fair Warning (Agency) Ltd* [1995] 1 WLR 1226, Garland J considered the various possibilities and concluded (at 1237) that he could see 'no indication in the Act, the authorities or the relevant literature that the court is obliged to incline towards either total retention or equal division'. Rather, he thought that his task was to do 'justice in a situation which the parties had neither contemplated nor provided for, and to mitigate the possible harshness of allowing all loss to lie where it has fallen'. The emphasis is thus placed on the 'broad nature' of the discretion which the court enjoys and the imperative to do justice on the facts of the case. While this apparent reluctance to structure the discretion of the courts is unfortunate, it is preferable to a rigid insistence upon equal division of the loss (as has been done by legislation in British Columbia: see Frustrated Contracts Act (British Columbia) 1974, s 5(3)). The only point which can be established with any degree of certainty in the present context is that the onus of proof is upon the payee to show that it is just in all the circumstances of the case for him to retain any part of the prepayment (see *Gamerco*, at 1235). The second difficulty created by section 1(2) is that the payee cannot recover or retain more than the value of the prepayment, so that any reliance expenditure incurred which is in excess of the prepayment cannot be recovered under section 1(2), although it may be recoverable under section 1(3) where the expenditure results in a valuable benefit being obtained by the other party (see below).

14.17.3 Section 1(3) of the Law Reform (Frustrated Contracts) Act 1943

We must now consider the effects of frustration upon a claim to recover the value of goods supplied or services provided prior to the frustrating event. At common law the leading case was *Appleby v Myers* (1867) LR 2 CP 651. The claimants contracted to make and erect machinery in the defendants' factory and to maintain the machinery for two years. Payment was to be upon completion of the work. After part of the machinery had been erected, an accidental fire destroyed the factory and machinery and frustrated the contract. It was held that the claimants could not recover in respect of their work because they were only entitled to payment when performance was completed (called the 'entire obligations' or 'entire contracts' rule, see Section 22.2) and, as the fire had prevented completion of the work, they were not entitled to payment. This rule caused obvious hardship to the provider of services under a frustrated contract and it has since been replaced by section 1(3) of the Law Reform (Frustrated Contracts) Act 1943. Section 1(3) states that:

> where any party to the contract has, by reason of anything done by any other party thereto in, or for the purpose of, the performance of the contract, obtained a valuable benefit (other than a payment of money to which the last foregoing subsection applies) before the time of discharge, there shall be recoverable from him by the said other party such sum (if any), not exceeding the value of the said benefit to the party obtaining it, as the court considers just, having regard to all the circumstances of the case and, in particular –
>
> (a) the amount of any expenses incurred before the time of discharge by the benefited party in, or for the purpose of, the performance of the contract, including any sums paid or payable by him to any other party in pursuance of the contract and retained or recoverable by that party under the last foregoing subsection, and
> (b) the effect, in relation to the said benefit, of the circumstances giving rise to the frustration of the contract.

This subsection is an unnecessarily complex provision (for details see McKendrick, 1995). Its basic effect is that, where one party to the contract has conferred upon the other party a 'valuable benefit' (other than a payment of money which is governed by s 1(2)) before the time of discharge, he shall be entitled to recover a 'just sum' which shall not exceed the value of the benefit which he has conferred upon the other party. In *BP v Hunt* [1979] 1 WLR 783, Robert Goff J concluded that there were two steps involved in a section 1(3) claim. The first was the identification and valuation of the benefit. The subsection does not define what is to count as a benefit: it could be either the value of the services performed or it could be the end product of the services. In *BP v Hunt* (above) Robert Goff J stated that in 'an appropriate case' it was the end product which was to be regarded as the benefit. He appeared to envisage two circumstances in which a court could have regard to the value of the services in identifying the benefit; the first arising where the service by its very nature does not result in an end product (for example, the transportation of goods) and the second where the service results in an end product which has no objective value (for example, a claimant who commences 'the redecoration, to the defendant's execrable taste, of rooms which are in good decorative order'). But he held that, where the end product is destroyed by the frustrating event, the provider of the services has no claim under section 1(3) because the value of the benefit (namely, the end product) has been reduced to zero by the frustrating event. This interpretation of 'benefit' has unfortunate consequences. It means that the result in *Appleby v Myers* would be unaffected by the Act because the claimants' work was destroyed by the fire and so did not result in any end product. Although this interpretation of 'benefit' has been heavily criticised (see Treitel, 2020, para 19-113 and Haycroft and Waksman, 1984), such an interpretation has also been adopted in the Commonwealth (*Parsons Bros Ltd v Shea* (1966) 53 DLR (2d) 86) and it appears to accord closely with the structure of section 1(3), which draws a distinction between the claimant's performance and the defendant's benefit, and so it cannot be said that the defendant's benefit is the value of the claimant's performance.

The second step in a section 1(3) claim is the assessment of a 'just sum'. Here it must be remembered that the value of the benefit obtained acts as a ceiling on the 'just sum'. Robert Goff J held that the contractual allocation of risk will always be a relevant factor in deciding what is a just sum. But it is very difficult to predict what a court will award as a just sum. Robert Goff J sought to provide a measure of certainty by stating that the aim of the court in assessing the just sum ought to be 'the prevention of the unjust enrichment of the defendant at the [claimant's] expense' and that the assessment should therefore be similar to that undertaken by a court in a *quantum meruit* claim. But this approach seems to have been rejected by the Court of Appeal when Lawton LJ stated that 'what is just is what the trial judge thinks is just' and that an appellate court is not entitled to interfere with the assessment of the just sum by the trial judge 'unless it is so plainly wrong that it cannot be just' (*BP v Hunt* [1982] 1 All ER 925, 980). This leaves the issue to the almost untrammelled discretion of the trial judge. It is regrettable that the Court of Appeal did not establish guidelines to assist trial judges in the exercise of their discretion to ensure a measure of consistency in decided cases and out-of-court settlements.

It must be concluded that section 1(3) is poorly drafted and that it produces results which are, in principle, undesirable. A benefit should be identified as the value of the services and not as the end product of the services. The focus of the Act is upon the prevention of unjust enrichment (*BP v Hunt* [1979] 1 WLR 783, 799, per Robert Goff J) and, consequently, it does not address itself to the recovery of reliance losses which do not result in a benefit to the other party, nor does it seek to apportion the losses between the parties. In failing to address itself to these issues, the 1943 Act is sadly deficient and it is no surprise to learn that its restricted approach has been rejected in the Commonwealth (see, generally, McKendrick, 1991).

14.18 Conclusion

In this chapter we have sought to argue that in cases of common mistake and frustration the courts are dealing with the same issue; namely the allocation of risk of an unforeseen event. In both groups of cases the courts are faced with an issue of construction: did the contract make provision for the events which have happened? If it has, then the contract governs the situation. But if it has not, then the court must consider whether it has jurisdiction to intervene and grant relief on the basis of mistake or frustration, depending on the point in time at which the event occurred. Both mistake (post-*Great Peace Shipping Ltd v Tsavliris Salvage (International) Ltd* [2002] EWCA Civ 1407; [2003] QB 679) and frustration operate within very narrow confines and emphasise the need to hold people to their bargains. Their concern is with the preservation of certainty and the desire to prevent the doctrine from being used as an escape route by those who are looking for a way out of a bad bargain (the point that both jurisdictions employ the 'same concept' has been made by Evans LJ in *William Sindall plc v Cambridgeshire CC* [1994] 1 WLR 1016, 1039).

The link between mistake and frustration is also apparent from the judgment of the Court of Appeal in *Great Peace*. The court stated that 'consideration of the development of the law of frustration assists with the analysis of the law of common mistake'. They deduced a number of lessons for the law relating to mistake from the law relating to frustration: the first is that the theory of an implied term is as unrealistic when considering common mistake as when considering frustration; the second is that, in considering whether performance of the contract is impossible, it is necessary to identify what it is that the parties agreed would be performed; the third is that, just as the doctrine of frustration only applies if the contract contains no provision that covers the situation, the same should be true of common mistake.

Although it has been argued in this chapter that there is a very close relationship between common mistake and frustration, it is important to acknowledge that this analogy is not accepted by everyone. Thus, Treitel (2020, para 19-132) has described the analogy between common mistake and frustration as an 'interesting and sometimes helpful' one but argues that it 'should not be pressed too far'. In particular, Treitel argues that mistake and frustration are '"different juristic concepts"; the one relating to the formation and the other to the discharge of contracts'. Although it is true that one relates to formation and the other to discharge, they both relate to the same issue, as can be seen from the *Amalgamated Investment* case (Section 14.1) and a comparison of *Griffith v Brymer* (1903) 19 TLR 434 (Section 14.5) and *Krell v Henry* [1903] 2 KB 740 (Section 14.12). Secondly, Treitel argues that events which frustrate a contract may not be sufficient to set aside a contract on the ground of mistake. This point I have already conceded, but the difference is a matter of degree, not kind. Finally, Treitel points out that the effects of frustration and mistake are different; frustration cases being subject to the Law Reform (Frustrated Contracts) Act 1943. This is true. But the 1943 Act was enacted as a response to the particular problems which had emerged in the law relating to the remedial consequences of frustration as a result of the decision of the Court of Appeal in *Chandler v Webster* [1904] 1 KB 493. The Act was not extended to mistake because it was based on a report prepared by the Law Revision Committee, whose terms of reference were confined to a reconsideration of *Chandler v Webster* (see McKendrick, 1991). The fact that Parliament did not or could not see fit to draw the analogy between common mistake and frustration in 1943 should not prevent us from drawing the analogy today. The same principles should be applicable to the remedial consequences of both common mistake and frustration. In both cases unjust enrichments should be reversed and, if this is thought to be insufficient to achieve a satisfactory result in all cases, consideration should be given to the principles upon which any loss caused by the mistake or the frustrating event should be apportioned between the parties. There is no need to provide a different remedial regime for the consequences of common mistake and frustration.

Hot topic 13...

The question of the impact of Brexit on a long-term contract was considered by Marcus Smith J in *Canary Wharf (BP4) T1 Ltd v European Medicines Agency* [2019] EWHC 335 (Ch). The claimant landlords entered into a 25 year underlease with the defendant in 2014. The defendant is an agency of the EU. The defendant's case was that the departure of the UK from the EU would operate to frustrate the agreement between the parties. Two particular grounds were relied upon by the defendant.

The first was that the continued occupation of the premises would be illegal because the defendant could no longer lawfully occupy premises in London, or pay rent in respect of these premises, after the UK's departure from the EU. Marcus Smith J held that there was no illegality involved in the defendant's continued occupation of the premises. While there were political reasons which led to the relocation of the EMA to Amsterdam, there was no rule of law which prevented it from occupying premises outside of the EU. In any event, any illegality was a matter of EU law, but the underlease was governed by English law and, as a matter of English law, there was no illegality

involved in the defendant remaining in occupation of the premises.

Second, it was argued that the purpose of the underlease had been frustrated. This submission was also rejected. The EMA had entered into a bad bargain in so far as it had entered into a long-term contract without a break clause, but that did not have the consequence that the contract was frustrated. Nor could it be said that the parties had entered into the underlease on the basis that the defendant would occupy the premises for the entire 25 years. The provisions in the agreement dealing with the assignment of the underlease and sub-letting demonstrated that the parties had anticipated the possibility that EMA might wish to vacate the premises. This being the case, the way out of the contract for the EMA was to rely on these provisions in the contract and not to attempt to invoke frustration.

The present case does not stand for the proposition that Brexit can never have the effect of frustrating a contract. But it does demonstrate that the fact that Brexit has caused the contract to become an improvident one for one of the parties does not give that party a passport to abandon the contract.

Summary

▶ Where both parties enter into a contract under a common fundamental mistake which relates to an essential element of the subject-matter of the contract, then the contract is void at law.

▶ A mistake may be sufficiently fundamental to avoid a contract where both parties are mistaken as to the existence (or possibly the identity) of the subject-matter of the contract. Despite the enactment of section 6 of the Sale of Goods Act 1979, a mistake as to the existence of the subject-matter may not inevitably render a contract void; it may depend upon the construction of the contract (see *McRae v Commonwealth Disposals Commission* (1951) 84 CLR 377).

▶ A mistake may be sufficiently fundamental to avoid a contract where both parties believe that the contract is capable of being performed when, in fact, it is not. The impossibility may be physical, legal or commercial.

▶ A mistake as to the quality of the subject-matter of the contract may be sufficiently fundamental to avoid a contract. But the courts are extremely reluctant to hold a contract void on such a ground. The mistake must relate to an 'essential and integral element of the subject matter' of the contract. There is no longer a wider doctrine of common mistake in equity.

▶ A contract is frustrated where, after the contract was concluded, events occur which make performance of the contract impossible, illegal or something radically different from that which was in the contemplation of the parties at the time they entered into the contract.

▶ A contract is not frustrated where the parties have made express provision for the consequences of the alleged frustrating event in their contract, where the alleged frustrating event was a foreseeable one or where the frustration was 'self-induced'. But express provision for, and foreseeability of, the frustrating event are irrelevant in cases of trading with the enemy.

▶ A contract which is discharged on the ground of frustration is brought to an end automatically by the operation of a rule of law, irrespective of the wishes of the parties.

▶ Sums paid prior to the frustrating event are recoverable, sums payable prior to the time of discharge cease to be payable and the payee may be entitled to set off against the sums so paid expenses which he has incurred before the time of discharge in, or for the purpose of, the performance of the contract (Law Reform (Frustrated Contracts) Act 1943, s 1(2)).

▶ Where one party to the contract has conferred upon the other party a 'valuable benefit' (other than a payment of money which is governed by s 1 (2)) before the time of discharge, he shall be entitled to recover from that other party a 'just sum' which shall not exceed the value of the benefit which he has conferred upon the other party (1943 Act, s 1(3)).

Exercises

14.1 What is the scope of the doctrine of common mistake at law?

14.2 What is the proper interpretation to be placed upon the decision of the House of Lords in *Couturier v Hastie* (1856) 5 HLC 673?

14.3 When will a mistake as to the quality of the subject-matter of the contract render a contract void?

14.4 Why did the Court of Appeal in *Great Peace Shipping Ltd v Tsavliris Salvage (International) Ltd* [2002] EWCA Civ 1407; [2003] QB 679 reject the proposition that mistake in equity is broader and more flexible than the doctrine of mistake at common law?

14.5 When will the courts hold that a contract has been frustrated? Illustrate your answer.

14.6 What is 'self-induced frustration'?

14.7 What are the effects of frustration upon a contract?

14.8 What is the relationship, if any, between common mistake and frustration?

Chapter 15

Illegality

15.1 Introduction

In this chapter we turn to consider substantive limitations upon the enforceability of contracts, in particular in relation to contracts that involve the performance of illegal acts or are contrary to public policy. This area of law has proved to be the subject of considerable controversy in recent years, particularly at the level of the Supreme Court. The most recent decision of the Supreme Court is its decision in *Patel v Mirza* [2016] UKSC 42; [2017] AC 467. It is a decision that is notable for the sharp divergence of view between the members of the court as to the way in which the law should be developed. The claimant paid to the defendant £620,000 in connection with an illegal agreement to trade in shares in Royal Bank of Scotland (known as insider dealing). The agreement was not implemented because the expected information did not materialise. The claimant sued to recover his payment. The Supreme Court held, unanimously, that he was entitled to its return (although the reasoning which led the Supreme Court Justices to that conclusion diverged sharply). It should be noted that the claimant did not attempt to recover the profit that he expected to make from the illegal transaction. His claim was confined to one to reverse the transaction by restoring the parties to the position they were in prior to entry into the illegal contract.

Let us assume, however, that the claimant in *Patel* had sought to enforce the illegal contract and to obtain the benefits which he expected to get from its performance. What objections might there be to the enforcement of such a contract? There are a number of possible objections. The first is that the court is concerned to preserve the integrity and consistency of the legal system by avoiding a conclusion that conduct which is illegal can at the same time give rise to a right to enforce the contract. It would be inconsistent for the law both to apply criminal sanctions to the claimant in *Patel* for entering into an unlawful arrangement and at the same time give him his expected profit under the transaction by way of a claim for damages. The second, which may be no more than another way of making substantially the same point, is that the court should not be called upon to aid a willing party to an illegal contract or to a contract which is contrary to public policy. The third is that justice would be tainted and the dignity of the court offended by enforcement of the contract. The fourth is that the law should not permit a person to profit from his or her wrongdoing. The fifth is that a refusal to grant relief will make entry into illegal contracts a hazardous enterprise and will thus deter people from entering into such contracts.

But these arguments are not always persuasive. Not all claimants are willing participants in an illegal contract. What is to be done in the case where the claimant was unaware at the time of entry into the contract of the fact that the contract was illegal or that it was to be performed in a way that is illegal? Nor is the dignity of the court always offended by intervention on behalf of a party to an illegal contract; there is a vast difference between a contract involving gross immorality or a contract to rob a bank and a contract which innocently infringes a piece of regulatory legislation. The deterrence argument rests upon the rather dubious assumption that everyone knows the law and will take heed of its deterrent effect. Deterrence is also properly the function of the criminal law, not the civil law.

There are other competing policies which must be considered. The first is the argument from freedom of contract; that the parties should be as free as possible to regulate their own affairs. This suggests that the law should be slow to characterise a contract as illegal or contrary to public policy but it does not address the question which has most troubled the courts, namely the remedial response which should be adopted when a contract has been classified as illegal or contrary to public policy. But it is important to note that the readier the courts are to conclude that a contract is illegal or contrary to public policy, the greater the problem in practical terms of dealing with the consequences of an illegal contract. A further matter to be taken into account is the need to prevent unjust enrichment. This concern was reflected in the decision of the Supreme Court in *Patel v Mirza* where it was held that the defendant was not entitled to retain the payment which he had received from the claimant. Thus the effect of *Patel* appears to be to widen the right to recover payments made or property transferred pursuant to an illegal contract (at least in the case where the contract has not been performed) and to turn the question of the enforcement of the contract into a discretionary exercise. On this basis there is a difference between the reversal of an illegal contract by returning the parties to the position which they were in prior to entry into the illegal contract and the enforcement of an illegal contract. Reversal of the contract does not encounter the same public policy objections as enforcement, given that the real concern of the law is not to give effect to, or enforce, contracts which the law has declared to be illegal, at least where to do so would be to permit a party to profit from its own wrongdoing and where it would commit the law to incoherence by 'giving with the left hand what it takes with the right hand'.

The principal issue which divided the majority and the minority in *Patel v Mirza* was whether the remedial consequences of entry into an illegal contract should be decided by the court in the exercise of a discretion or whether this is an area which should be characterised by rules of law. In *Les Laboratoires Servier v Apotex Inc* [2014] UKSC 55; [2015] AC 430, [23] Lord Sumption, giving the judgment of the majority of the Supreme Court, concluded that this was an area of law which should be governed by rules of law and that the general rule was one of 'judicial abstention' which 'precludes the judge from performing his ordinary adjudicative function in a case where that would lend the authority of the state to the enforcement of an illegal transaction or to the determination of the legal consequences of an illegal act'. But this approach was not to last for long. In *Patel v Mirza*, with Lord Sumption dissenting in vigorous terms, the Supreme Court adopted a more discretionary approach, at least in relation to the possible enforcement of an illegal contract, concluding that a court should have regard to the underlying purpose of the rule which has rendered the contract illegal and to the nature and circumstances of the illegality in determining whether the public interest in preserving the integrity of the justice system should result in the law denying redress or other form of relief to the claimant. The scope, and the merits, of this more discretionary approach will be considered at a later point in this chapter (see Sections 15.17 and 15.18). For now it suffices to note that the law relating to illegality has entered into a new chapter in its history and that the key feature of this new regime will be a greater emphasis on the exercise of discretion and on the development of a proportionate remedial response to the consequences of entry into an illegal contract.

15.2 Some difficulties of classification

Illegal contracts come in different shapes and sizes. Some involve gross immorality or a calculated attempt to break the law, while others involve innocent infringement of regulatory legislation. A contract to rob a bank has little in common with a contract which is performed by one of the parties in such a way that a statutory instrument is innocently infringed. Indeed, illegal contracts come in so many different shapes and sizes that it is difficult to find an appropriate classification for all the cases (see Furmston, 1965). Treitel (2020) distinguishes between contracts which involve the 'commission of a legal wrong' and 'contracts contrary to public policy'. Cheshire, Fifoot and Furmston (2017) distinguish between contracts which are 'rendered void by statute', contracts which are 'illegal by statute or at common law' and contracts which are 'void at common law on grounds of public policy'. No two commentators appear to adopt the same classification. But these different classifications do not reflect radical disagreement as to the content of the relevant rules of law. Rather, the categorisation is undertaken largely for the purpose of ease of exposition.

The approach which will be adopted in the present chapter is, first, to discuss illegality in the performance of a contract, and then to distinguish between statutory illegality and common law illegality. The latter division should not be taken to suggest that it is easier to establish the existence of statutory illegality than common law illegality. The function of this division is to emphasise that the techniques employed by the courts in each case are rather different. In the case of statutory illegality, the courts are seeking to discern the intention of Parliament and the effect of the breach of the statute upon the contract. But in the case of common law illegality, the courts have greater scope to identify their own conceptions of public policy. The limiting feature, however, is that the courts do not wish to be seen to be employing their own idiosyncratic conceptions of public policy and, at the same time, they are aware that Parliament now has the principal role to play in establishing the limits of public policy.

15.3 Illegality in performance

Illegality may affect a contract in two principal ways. In the first place, the illegality may relate to the formation of the contract, so that the contract is illegal at the moment at which it is formed. Such a contract is void *ab initio* because it is infected with the illegality from the very outset. Secondly, the illegality may arise in the performance of an otherwise valid and enforceable contract. Here the contract is valid at the moment of formation and it is only infected with the illegality when it occurs during the performance of the contract. An example will illustrate the point. Two parties enter into a contract for the transportation of goods. At the moment of formation the contract is good and enforceable. But let us suppose that, while transporting the goods, the carrier commits a criminal offence by speeding. Does such an illegal act, committed in the course of the performance of the contract, invalidate the contract? In *St John Shipping Corp v Joseph Rank Ltd* [1957] 1 QB 267, 281, Devlin J rejected the argument that violation of the speed limit in the course of performance of the contract would, of itself, render the contract unenforceable by the party guilty of the offence. This must be right. The criminal courts will pass judgment on the offence committed; the civil courts should enforce the contract. But what are the limits of this rule? When will an illegal act committed in the course of performance of the contract invalidate the contract? This is not an easy question to answer. Separate consideration must be given to the position of the party who committed the criminal offence and the position of the other, 'innocent' party.

In deciding whether the party who committed the criminal offence can enforce the contract it is necessary to examine the judgment of Devlin J in *St John Shipping Corp v Joseph Rank Ltd*. A shipowner committed a statutory offence when he over-loaded his ship in the performance of certain contracts for the carriage of goods. The shipowner was held to be entitled to sue to recover the freight, despite the illegality. Devlin J held that the purpose behind the statute was to penalise the conduct which led to the contravention of the statute and not to prohibit the contract itself. The contract therefore remained enforceable. Similarly, in *Shaw v Groom* [1970] 2 QB 504, a landlord committed an offence by failing to give his tenant a rent-book. It was held that the landlord was nevertheless entitled to sue for the rent because the purpose behind the legislation was to punish his failure to issue a rent-book but not to invali-date the tenancy agreement (contrast the more restrictive approach adopted in the earlier case of *Anderson v Daniel* [1924] 1 KB 138, where the 'guilty' party was held to be unable to enforce the contract). Although both of these cases concern statutory illegality, it is suggested that the question which should be asked in all cases is: was it the purpose of the statute (or the common law rule) that the illegal act committed in the course of the performance of a contract should invalidate the contract? This purposive approach may glean some support from the more discretionary approach to the consequences of illegality adopted by the Supreme Court in *Patel v Mirza* [2016] UKSC 42; [2017] AC 467 (see further Sections 15.18 and 15.19).

The claim by the innocent party to enforce the contract is a much stronger one, especially where he does not know of or consent to the illegality. This was recognised by the court in *Archbolds (Freightage) Ltd v S Spanglett Ltd* [1961] 2 QB 374. A contract was made for the carriage of a consignment of whisky and, in performing the con-tract, the carrier committed a criminal offence because the vehicle which he used to transport the whisky was not licensed to carry goods belonging to a third party. It was held that the claimant could nevertheless sue for breach of the contract of carriage because he was unaware of the illegality and so was not tainted by it (see too *Marles v Philip Trant & Sons Ltd* [1954] 1 QB 29). Devlin LJ stated that he thought that:

> the purpose of this statute is sufficiently served by the penalties prescribed for the offender; the avoidance of the contract would cause grave inconvenience and injury to members of the public without furthering the object of the statute.

But where the 'innocent' party has knowledge of the commission of the illegality, then it is more likely that he will be unable to enforce the contract. In *Ashmore, Benson, Pease & Co Ltd v AV Dawson Ltd* [1973] 1 WLR 828, the parties entered into a contract for the transportation of tube banks. The defendants sent articulated lorries which could not lawfully be used to carry the load. The load was damaged in transit. The claimant sued for damages. The action failed because there was evidence that the claimants' transport manager knew of the illegal performance and that, by sanctioning the illegal performance of the contract, he had 'participated' in the illegality. The crucial role played by the knowledge of the innocent party appears, at first sight, to be inconsistent with the maxim that ignorance of the law is no excuse (*Nash v Stevenson Transport Ltd* [1936] 2 KB 128). It is true that, where at the moment of formation, a contract is declared to be illegal, the knowledge of the parties is of more limited relevance. Where, on the other hand, the illegality occurs in the performance of a contract which is capable of lawful performance, the knowledge of the innocent party is a relevant consideration because his ignorance relates, not to the *law*, but to the *fact* that the other contracting party has performed the contract in an illegal manner. His knowledge of the illegality is therefore a relevant consideration.

15.4 Statutory illegality

A contract is illegal if its formation is expressly or impliedly prohibited by statute. Where the making of the contract is expressly prohibited, no difficulties arise; the contract is illegal. Greater difficulties arise where it is alleged that Parliament has impliedly prohibited the *making* of such a contract (see Buckley, 1975). The function of the court in such a case is to interpret the statute to discern whether, on its proper construction, the Act prohibits the making of such a contract. The difficulty is that Parliament has often not addressed itself to this issue. So the process of 'finding' the 'intention' of Parliament is frequently an extremely artificial one.

In *Re Mahmoud and Ispahani* [1921] 2 KB 716, the Seeds, Oils and Fats Order 1919 stated that 'a person shall not ... buy or sell or otherwise deal in' linseed oil without a licence. The defendant misrepresented to the claimant that he had a licence. The defendant later refused to accept delivery of the order. The claimant sued the defendant for damages. The defendant argued that the contract was illegal because he did not have a licence. The court held that the claimant could not maintain his action for damages because such an action would undermine the purpose behind the statute. Bankes LJ stated that the Order was 'a clear and unequivocal declaration by the Legislature in the public interest that this particular type of contract shall not be entered into'. Yet the consequences for the claimant were extremely harsh and it may be questioned whether the court correctly identified the intention of Parliament. In an effort to avoid the possibility of a court misinterpreting the intention of Parliament, Acts of Parliament now frequently specify the consequences for a contract which has been entered into in breach of the Act. However, the courts are generally reluctant to conclude that a statute impliedly prohibits the making of a contract (see *Archbolds (Freightage) Ltd v S Spanglett Ltd* (above) and *St John Shipping Corp v Joseph Rank Ltd* [1957] 1 QB 267, 289).

15.5 Gaming and wagering contracts

Parliament will occasionally declare a particular type of contract to be 'void'. The traditional example cited in this context was section 18 of the Gaming Act 1845 which stated that 'all contracts or agreements, whether by parole or in writing, by way of gaming or wagering shall be null and void'. The section further provided that no action could be maintained in any court for the recovery of 'any money or valuable thing alleged to be won upon any wager'. Finally, the section provided that no action could be brought to recover any money or valuable thing which had been deposited in the hands of any stakeholder, although the interpretation placed upon this part of the section was that a deposit could be recovered before it had been paid over to the winner (*Diggle v Higgs* (1877) 2 Ex D 442). However, section 18 was repealed on the coming into force of the Gambling Act 2005 on 1 September 2007 which transformed the regulation of gambling activities in the United Kingdom. Section 335(1) of the Act provides that the 'fact that a contract relates to gambling shall not prevent its enforcement'. This is, however, without prejudice 'to any rule of law preventing the enforcement of a contract on the grounds of unlawfulness (other than a rule relating specifically to gambling)' (s 335(2)). So, in the case where the outcome of the bet depends upon the commission of a criminal act, the contract will be avoided by section 335(2) and will not be enforced. Section 336 also confers a power upon the Gambling Commission to make an order the effect of which will be to render any contract or other arrangement in relation to the bet void and to order the repayment of money paid in relation to the bet. However, the Commission can only issue such an order where it is satisfied that the bet was 'substantially unfair' (as defined in s 336(4)).

15.6　Illegality at common law

A contract may be illegal at common law. The scope of the doctrine of illegality at common law is extremely wide and encompasses contracts which are 'contrary to public policy'. 'Illegality' at common law therefore goes beyond contracts to commit a crime and extends, for example, to contracts which are contrary to good morals and contracts which are prejudicial to the institution of marriage. Some commentators seek to divide the cases into two distinct compartments (see Cheshire, Fifoot and Furmston, 2017), namely, contracts which are 'illegal' at common law on grounds of public policy and contracts which are 'void' at common law on grounds of public policy. But this division is a troublesome one because of the difficulty in deciding which contracts are 'illegal' and which are simply 'void'. In this chapter we shall not attempt to divide the cases up in such a manner. Rather, we shall analyse the cases under the title of contracts which are 'illegal' at common law because they are 'contrary to public policy' (often referred to, for the sake of brevity, as 'illegal' contracts) and we shall seek to identify the scope of the doctrine of public policy at common law.

In deciding whether a particular contract is 'contrary to public policy', the courts cannot shelter behind the argument that they are simply giving effect to the intention of Parliament. They must evolve their own conceptions of public policy. Here the courts are open to the charge of usurping the function of Parliament and of giving effect to their own personal opinions on what is, and what is not, morally justifiable. Thus, we find that Burroughs J once described public policy as 'a very unruly horse, and when once you get astride it you never know where it will carry you' (*Richardson v Mellish* (1824) 2 Bing 229, 252). On the other hand, Lord Denning has argued that: 'with a good man in the saddle, the unruly horse can be kept in control.

It can jump over obstacles' (*Enderby Town Football Club Ltd v The Football Association Ltd* [1971] Ch 591, 606).

The courts have, in fact, been extremely cautious and conservative in their formulation of public policy. We shall now survey the different grounds upon which the courts have held a contract to be contrary to public policy and conclude with an examination of the scope of the doctrine of public policy at common law.

15.7 Contracts contrary to good morals

A contract to promote sexual immorality is illegal on the ground that it is contrary to public policy. In *Pearce v Brooks* (1866) LR 1 Ex 213 it was held that a contract to supply goods to a prostitute to be used by her in the furtherance of her profession was illegal. Similarly, a promise by a man to pay a woman if she will become his mistress is illegal (*Franco v Bolton* (1797) 3 Ves 368). At one point in time, contracts between cohabiting couples who were not married were contrary to public policy. But the attitude adopted by the courts towards extramarital relationships has gradually changed to reflect the growing incidence of such relationships in society. Where the parties are living together in a 'stable' extramarital relationship, it is no longer conceivable that a court today would conclude that an agreement entered into by them in relation to the purchase of property is contrary to public policy (so for example in *Tinsley v Milligan* [1994] 1 AC 340, it was not argued that the parties' agreement to purchase property was unenforceable on the ground that they were lovers, see Section 15.18).

15.8 Contracts prejudicial to family life

Contract law is also protective of family relationships. Contracts which are prejudicial to the institution of marriage are contrary to public policy; thus a contract which restrains a party from marrying (*Lowe v Peers* (1768) 2 Burr 2225) or a contract under which one person undertakes to procure the marriage of another in return for a fee is illegal (*Hermann v Charlesworth* [1905] 2 KB 123, although it is questionable whether this case would be followed today as society's attitude to introduction agencies has changed considerably). But a promise to pay a sum of money to a person for as long as they remain single is valid (*Gibson v Dickie* (1815) 3 M & S 463). In *Spiers v Hunt* [1908] 1 KB 720, a promise by a man to marry the claimant after the death of his wife was held to be contrary to public policy because it encouraged sexual immorality and was likely to encourage the break-up of his marriage (although it should be noted that the action for breach of promise to marry has been abolished by section 1 of the Law Reform (Miscellaneous Provisions) Act 1970). More difficult has been the question of the validity of pre-nuptial and post-nuptial agreements. The attitude of the courts to this issue has changed over time. At one time it was 'contrary to public policy for a married couple, or a couple about to get married, to make an arrangement that provided for the contingency that they might separate' (*Granatino v Radmacher* [2010] UKSC 42; [2011] 1 AC 534, [31]). Matters were otherwise where husband and wife had separated at the time of entry into the agreement. In such a case, there is no public policy objection to enforcement of the agreement. The concern of the law was with agreements made by parties who were still living together as husband and wife at the time of entry into the agreement or who were about to get married. But even here the attitude of the courts has gradually relaxed over time. A post-nuptial agreement making provision for future separation is now valid and enforceable in the same way as any other contract between spouses (*MacLeod v MacLeod* [2008] UKPC 64; [2010] 1 AC 298), although the agreement cannot oust the jurisdiction of the court to make financial orders should the parties separate or divorce. A similar position now obtains in relation to pre-nuptial agreements. While the majority of the Supreme Court in *Granatino v Radmacher* (above, but note the strongly worded dissenting judgment of Baroness Hale) stopped short of formally according a pre-nuptial agreement the status of a contract (see [62]), they concluded (at [75]) that the following proposition should in future be applied to both pre-and post-nuptial agreements:

> the court should give effect to a nuptial agreement that is freely entered into by each party with a full appreciation of its implications unless in the circumstances prevailing it would not be fair to hold the parties to their agreement.

The Law Commission (2014) has since recommended that 'qualifying nuptial agreements' should be enforceable between the parties subject to certain procedural safeguards and it remains to be seen whether this recommendation will be implemented by the government (attempts have been made to effect reform via a Bill started in the House of Lords but it has never made its way on to the statute book). A parent cannot by contract transfer to another adult his rights and duties in relation to a child (although, in an appropriate case, an adoption order can be made by a court).

15.9 Contracts to commit a crime

A contract to commit a crime is illegal on the ground that it is contrary to public policy. In *Bigos v Bousted* [1951] 1 All ER 92, the parties entered into a contract which was contrary to the exchange control regulations. The contract was held to be unenforceable. Similarly, contracts to defraud the revenue are contrary to public policy (*Miller v Karlinski* (1945) 62 TLR 85). In *Alexander v Rayson* [1936] 1 KB 169, the parties entered into a contract to defraud the rating authority by showing the value of the property at less than its actual value. The contract was held to be illegal and unenforceable. A contract is also illegal where it makes provision for the payment of money to a person as a result of his commission of an unlawful act. In *Beresford v Royal Exchange Assurance* [1938] AC 586, a person who had insured his life for £50,000 committed suicide. It was held that his estate was not entitled to enforce the policy even though it expressly covered death by suicide because, at that time, suicide was a criminal offence (the reasoning is now practically obsolete because suicide is no longer a crime). To permit a person, or his estate, to benefit from his own crime was held to be contrary to public policy.

A contract to indemnify a person against criminal liability is illegal where the criminal offence is committed with a guilty intent, but the position is unclear where the crime is committed with no guilty intent.

15.10 Contracts prejudicial to the administration of justice

Contracts which are prejudicial to the administration of justice are illegal. Thus a contract to stifle a prosecution may be illegal and a contract under which one party promises to give false evidence in criminal proceedings is illegal (*R v Andrews* [1973]

QB 422). Agreements to obstruct bankruptcy proceedings are illegal (*Elliott v Richardson* (1870) LR 5 CP 744). Agreements which tend to abuse the legal process by encouraging litigation which is not *bona fide* are contrary to public policy.

Also contrary to public policy are contracts which seek to oust the jurisdiction of the courts by stipulating that a contracting party is not entitled to access to the courts in the event of a dispute between the parties. But contracting parties may validly provide that a dispute must be referred to arbitration before it can be brought to court (*Scott v Avery* (1855) 5 HLC 811). The scope of judicial control over arbitration proceedings has now been radically reduced. While a party to an arbitration remains entitled to apply to the court to challenge an award in the arbitral proceedings 'on the ground of serious irregularity affecting the tribunal, the proceedings or the award' (Arbitration Act 1996, s 68(1)), the entitlement to appeal to a court on a point of law has been severely curtailed (see Arbitration Act 1996, s 69). The parties to the arbitration can even contract out of this limited right of appeal to the court, although in the case of a 'domestic arbitration agreement' such an agreement can only be made after the commencement of the arbitration (see s 87 of the Act).

15.11 Contracts prejudicial to public relations

Contracts which are prejudicial to foreign friendly countries are contrary to public policy and unenforceable. Thus, a contract to facilitate the forcible overthrow of the government of a friendly country is unenforceable (*De Wutz v Hendricks* (1824) 2 Bing 314). A similar rule applies to contracts which are prejudicial to the interests of the State; trading with the enemy is declared to be illegal under the Trading with the Enemy Act 1939. Contracts which seek to further or promote corruption in public life are illegal. Thus, a contract to sell a public office or a public honour is illegal. In *Parkinson v College of Ambulance Ltd* [1925] 2 KB 1, the parties entered into a contract under which one party promised to procure a knighthood for the other. The contract was held to be contrary to public policy.

15.12 Contracts in restraint of trade

A contract or a covenant in restraint of trade is an undertaking whereby one party agrees to restrict his freedom to trade or his freedom to conduct his profession or business in a particular locality for a specified period of time. A contract which is in restraint of trade is void and unenforceable unless it can be shown to be reasonable. The doctrine of restraint of trade is based upon considerations of public policy. But every contract contains an element of restraint of trade. Let us suppose that I enter into a contract to give a course of 50 lectures over a two-year period. The contract restricts my freedom to trade during the hours in which I have agreed to give the lectures. But such a contract is not caught by the restraint of trade doctrine.

What types of contract are caught by the doctrine? The question is an important one because, while the courts have no general power to review contract terms in the name of reasonableness, the restraint of trade doctrine gives them the power to strike down a clause unless the party relying upon it can show affirmatively that it is reasonable. The doctrine is a powerful one and the question of its scope is therefore one of fundamental importance (see Smith, 1995). Given that it is a doctrine that is based on public policy, its scope has been adjusted by the courts over time in response to social change (*Egon Zendher Ltd v Tillman* [2019] UKSC 32; [2020] AC 154, [26]).

However, it is generally accepted that there are two principal types of contract to which the doctrine applies. The first is a covenant by an employee not to compete with his employer either during or after his employment, and the second is a covenant by the seller of a business and its goodwill not to carry on a business which will compete with the business bought by the purchaser. The doctrine can also apply to other contracts but it is extremely difficult to define its limits. As Arden LJ remarked in *Proactive Sports Management Ltd v Rooney* [2011] EWCA Civ 1444; [2012] 2 All ER (Comm) 815, [55] the 'boundary between contracts that are contrary to public policy as being in restraint of trade and that will not be enforced, and contracts that contain acceptable restrictions is an uncertain and porous one'. In *Esso Petroleum Co Ltd v Harper's Garage (Stourport) Ltd* [1968] AC 269, the doctrine was applied to a contract under which a garage agreed to accept all of its petrol from one supplier for a considerable period of time. Lord Reid stated that he 'would not attempt to define the dividing line between contracts which are and contracts which are not in restraint of trade' and that the better approach was 'to ascertain what were the legitimate interests of the [suppliers] which they were entitled to protect and then to see whether these restraints were more than adequate for that purpose'. Further, in *Proactive Sports Management Ltd v Rooney* (above) the restraint of trade doctrine was held to be applicable to an Image Rights Representation Agreement to which the footballer Wayne Rooney was a party. The agreement regulated the use of Rooney's name in connection with sponsorship and other promotional activities. The agreement was entered into when Rooney was 17, was stated to last for eight years and provided that commission was payable to the defendant at a rate of 20 per cent. The Court of Appeal held that the trial judge had been entitled to conclude that the doctrine of restraint of trade had been engaged on the facts having regard to the inexperience and youth of Rooney, the lack of independent legal advice available to him, the duration of the agreement (measured against the likely length of his career as a footballer), the rate of commission payable to the defendant, the fact that the rate of commission did not taper at any point, the significant restrictions which the agreement placed upon Rooney's ability to exploit his talent, and the fact that the terms of the agreement were effectively dictated by the defendant and were 'not in any sense a standard form which had been tried and tested in this particular field of commerce'. On the contrary, the agreement was held to be 'unusual in many respects and unique in its duration'. The contract was thus sufficiently 'out of the norm' or 'oppressive' to fall within the scope of the restraint of trade doctrine.

Once it is decided that the contract is subject to the doctrine then it is for the party who is seeking to rely on the clause to show that it is reasonable in two respects. The first is that it must be reasonable as between the parties and the second is that it must be reasonable in the public interest (although the latter requirement has been criticised by Smith, 1995). In analysing the reasonableness requirements, we shall discuss separately covenants in contracts of employment, covenants in contracts for the sale of a business and, finally, other contracts to which the doctrine applies.

15.13 Contracts of employment

A contract of employment may contain a covenant which purports to restrict the freedom of the employee to work either during or after the termination of his employment. Such covenants are scrutinised with great care by the courts. In deciding whether the restraint clause is reasonable as between the parties, two factors are particularly relevant. The first is that the covenant must seek to protect some legitimate interest of the employer. Lord Parker stated in *Herbert Morris Ltd v Saxelby* [1916] 1 AC 688 that an employer must establish that he has 'some proprietary right, whether in the nature of a trade connection or in the nature of trade secrets, for the protection of which such a restraint is ... reasonably necessary'. Thus, an employer can legitimately restrain an employee who has come into contact with customers of the employer in such a way as to acquire influence over them (*Fitch v Dewes* [1921] 2 AC 158) or who has acquired trade secrets or confidential information belonging to the employer (*Forster and Sons v Suggett* (1918) 35 TLR 87). But an employer is not entitled to protect himself against the use of the 'personal skill and knowledge' acquired by the employee in the course of the employer's business. Such skills belong to the employee and he is free to exploit them in the marketplace.

The second factor is that the restraint must be reasonable in terms of subject-matter, locality and time. An employer is not generally entitled to restrain an employee from carrying on a business which is different from that in which he was employed. Similarly, the restraint must not be wider in area than is necessary to protect the employer's interest (see *Mason v Provident Clothing and Supply Co* [1913] AC 724, in which a clause restraining an employee from working in a similar business within 25 miles of London was held to be unreasonable). The restraint must also be reasonable in terms of time, although it is possible for the restraint clause to be unlimited in time and still be reasonable (*Fitch v Dewes* (above)).

Once it is demonstrated that the restraint is reasonable as between the parties, it must also be demonstrated that it is reasonable in the interests of the public. However, the courts are extremely reluctant to conclude that an agreement, which is reasonable as between the parties, is unenforceable because it is contrary to the interests of the public, especially in the case of a restraint clause in a contract of employment (but see *Wyatt v Kreglinger and Fernau* [1933] 1 KB 793).

15.14 Contracts for the sale of a business

A contract for the sale of a business frequently contains a clause under which the vendor of the business agrees not to set up a similar business in the immediate vicinity for a period of time. The purchaser has bought the goodwill in the business and he is entitled to protect his purchase by an appropriately drawn restraint clause. Such a clause is not viewed with the hostility of a restraint clause in a contract of employment.

The restraint clause must be reasonable as between the parties and two factors are of particular relevance here. The first is that the buyer must establish a proprietary interest which the clause is seeking to protect. That is to say, when a buyer purchases a business and pays for the goodwill of the business, he is entitled to take reasonable steps to protect that interest. The second factor is that the clause must be reasonable in the light of all the circumstances of the case. It will be unreasonable if it goes further than reasonably necessary for the protection of his interest in point of space, time or subject-matter. The reasonableness of a clause depends upon all the facts of each case (see *Nordenfelt v Maxim Nordenfelt* [1894] AC 535, in which a world-wide restraint was upheld because of the limited number of manufacturers in the particular industry). Once the clause is shown to be reasonable as between the parties, it must be shown to be reasonable in the public interest. The courts have, once again, been reluctant to conclude that an agreement which is reasonable as between the parties is unenforceable because it is contrary to the public interest.

15.15 Restrictive trading and analogous agreements

We have already noted that it is extremely difficult to define the limits of the doctrine of restraint of trade. For example, it was once thought that exclusive dealing agreements were not within the scope of the doctrine or, if they were, they were valid because they were not contrary to the public interest. But that view received a fatal blow as a result of the decision of the House of Lords in *Esso Petroleum Co Ltd v Harper's Garage (Stourport) Ltd* (above). A garage company, which owned two garages, entered into a solus agreement with Esso under which it agreed to buy all its petrol from Esso, to keep the garage open at all reasonable hours and not to sell the garage without ensuring that the purchaser entered into a similar agreement with Esso. One agreement was to last for five years and the other for 21 years. In effect, the garage owners were tied to Esso for 21 years. It was held that the agreements fell within the scope of the restraint of trade doctrine, that the five-year agreement with Esso was valid but that the 21-year agreement was invalid.

A further illustration of the uncertain scope of the restraint of trade doctrine is provided by the decision of the Supreme Court in *Peninsula Securities Ltd v Dunnes Stores (Bangor) Ltd* [2020] UKSC 36; [2020] 3 WLR 521. The issue before the court was whether the restraint of trade doctrine applied to a restrictive covenant entered into between a developer of a shopping centre and a well-known retail company, Dunnes Stores, according to which, in return for Dunnes Stores agreeing to take a long lease of premises at the centre, the developer agreed not to permit any shop of a significant size to be built which would compete with Dunnes Stores. After the passage of some 30 years the shopping centre had entered into a period of decline and the assignees of the developer wished to bring into the centre new shops and, in order to do so, it sought to challenge the validity of the restrictive covenant on the ground that it was an unreasonable restraint of trade. In *Esso Petroleum Co Ltd v Harper's Garage (Stourport) Ltd* the House of Lords had held that such a restrictive covenant was subject to the restraint of trade doctrine only if the land subject to the restrictive covenant was in the ownership of the person bound by it at the time of the imposition of the covenant. If, however, the land was acquired subject to the restrictive covenant, the doctrine had no application on the basis that, in such a case, the acquirer has simply obtained a limited interest and there has been no impairment of its existing freedom to trade. The Supreme Court in *Peninsula Securities* rejected this distinction and departed from this aspect of the decision in *Esso*. In doing so it concluded that the 'pre-existing freedom' test adopted in *Esso* lacked any basis in principle and so it replaced it by the so-called 'trading society' test according to which the terms of a contract which reflect 'the accepted and normal currency of commercial relations' are not subject to the restraint of trade doctrine because they have already satisfied the test of public policy contained within the restraint of trade doctrine. Applying this new test to the facts of the case, it was held that the restrictive covenant was not subject to the restraint of trade doctrine because it has 'long been accepted and normal' for the grant of a long lease in part of a shopping centre to include a restrictive covenant on the part of the lessor in relation to the use of other parts of the shopping centre. The Supreme Court further found that there was no basis for re-considering the acceptability of such covenants, and, this being the case, it was held that the restrictive covenant did not engage the restraint of trade doctrine.

Although the courts have been prepared to extend the scope of the doctrine of restraint of trade to certain exclusive dealing contracts, they have not subjected them to stringent scrutiny (but contrast the more interventionist approach adopted by the House of Lords in *Schroeder Music Publishing Co Ltd v Macaulay* [1974] 1 WLR 1308, where there was a considerable disparity in bargaining power between the parties). The courts are generally willing to find the existence of a legitimate interest which such exclusive dealing agreements seek to protect, such as maintaining retail outlets or protecting a competitive position in the marketplace, and they have adopted a *laissez-faire* approach to the reasonableness requirements (see *Alec Lobb (Garages) Ltd v Total Oil (GB) Ltd* [1985] 1 WLR 173). The consequence of this *laissez-faire* approach has been that the courts have played a secondary role in the regulation of anti-competitive practices and the primary role is now played by Parliament (see the Competition Act 1998) and, at least until 31 December 2020, by European Union law (see Articles 101 and 102 of the Treaty on the Functioning of the European Union). There is little doubt that Parliament is better equipped than the common law to engage in the regulation of such allegedly anti-competitive practices (see Trebilcock, 1976, where he subjects the decision of the House of Lords in *Schroeder v Macaulay* to substantial criticism).

15.16 The scope of public policy

The doctrine of public policy at common law is an extremely conservative one and operates within relatively rigid confines. Indeed, Lord Halsbury once stated that the courts cannot 'invent a new head of public policy' (*Janson v Driefontein Consolidated Mines Ltd* [1902] AC 484). Such a restrictive approach is no longer generally accepted. The courts are prepared gradually to adapt the existing categories to reflect changing social and moral values (see, for example, the discussion of contracts between cohabiting couples at Section 15.7), although they remain extremely reluctant to extend the doctrine to a contract of a type to which the doctrine has never been applied before. Such a rigidly controlled doctrine has the merit of limiting the ability of individual judges to develop their own idiosyncratic conceptions of public policy. The task of placing limits upon freedom of contract in the name of public policy is therefore left largely to Parliament. A judge in a modern case would not conclude that a contract which was supported by 'inadequate consideration' was void because it was 'contrary to public policy'. But he might be able to say that the contract was voidable because it had been procured by undue influence or by unconscionable conduct (see

Sections 17.3 and 17.4). Doctrines such as undue influence, the rules relating to contractual capacity (Chapter 16), the legal regulation of exclusion clauses (Chapter 11) and the penalty clause rule (Section 22.7) can all be regarded as 'disguised extensions or applications of the doctrine of public policy' (Treitel, 2020, para 11-036). While the courts remain reluctant to expand the doctrine of 'public policy' beyond the contracts to which it has traditionally been applied, the influence of 'public policy' in English law is more likely to be found in cases of alleged undue influence or unconscionability than in the cases which we have discussed in this chapter.

15.17 The effects of illegality

Prior to the decision of the Supreme Court in *Patel v Mirza* [2016] UKSC 42; [2017] AC 467, the general rule of English law was that an illegal contract would not be enforced by the courts. Although this was the general rule, circumstances could be found in which the courts were prepared to give to the 'innocent party' a remedy on some alternative basis. In *Strongman (1945) Ltd v Sincock* [1955] 2 QB 525, the defendant stated that he would obtain the necessary licences to enable the claimant builders lawfully to modernise his house. The defendant failed to obtain all the licences and he refused to pay for some of the work which the claimants had done, arguing that the contract was illegal. The claimants were unable to sue on the building contract because of the failure to obtain all the licences, but they were able to recover the value of the work which they had done on the ground that the defendant had breached a *collateral warranty* that he would obtain the necessary licences. In *Shelley v Paddock* [1980] QB 348, it was also recognised that an innocent party to an illegal contract could recover damages for fraudulent misrepresentation. By searching out the existence of remedies other than on the contract itself, the court was able to take steps to protect an innocent party who had relied to his detriment upon a contract which he subsequently discovered to be illegal.

In the light of the decision of the Supreme Court in *Patel v Mirza* it can no longer be said that there is a general rule to the effect that the courts will not enforce an illegal contract. Instead, much will depend upon the facts and circumstances of the individual case. The factors which in future will be taken into account by a court when deciding whether it would be contrary to public policy to allow a claim which is tainted in some way by illegality will include the underlying purpose of the prohibition which has been transgressed, any other relevant public policies which might be rendered ineffective by denial of the claim and the proportionality of any decision to grant or withhold a remedy. This new approach requires the courts to take account of multiple policy considerations and to apply a proportionate approach to the cases that come before them. The standard of review to be applied by an appellate court remains to be determined. In *Singularis Holdings Ltd v Daiwa Capital Markets Europe Ltd* [2018] EWCA Civ 84; [2018] 1 WLR 2777, [65] the Court of Appeal held that an appellate court should only interfere with the decision of a first instance judge if he or she has 'proceeded on an erroneous legal basis, taken into account matters that were legally irrelevant, or failed to take into account matters that were legally relevant.' However, when the case was appealed to the Supreme Court, Lady Hale, giving the judgment of the court, expressed her 'reservations about the view expressed by the Court of Appeal' (*Singularis Holdings Ltd v Daiwa*

Capital Markets Europe Ltd [2019] UKSC 50; [2019] 3 WLR 997, [21]) on the basis that 'an appellate court is as well placed to evaluate the arguments as is the trial judge'. The matter therefore remains to be resolved. However, it is likely that much will continue to depend on the evaluation conducted by the trial judge.

This injection of a substantial degree of discretion into this area of the law has not been without controversy. On the one hand, Professor Burrows (2017) has described the decision of the Supreme Court in *Patel* as a 'triumph' but, on the other hand, the Singapore Court of Appeal in *Ochroid Trading Ltd v Chua Siok Lui (trading as VIE Import & Export)* [2018] SGCA 5; [2018] 1 SLR 363, declined to follow it on the ground that it involved 'an unnecessarily broad balancing process' and was 'unnecessary to achieve remedial justice'.

Why did the Supreme Court adopt this discretionary approach? Three reasons can be suggested. First, the existing law was thought by many to be unsatisfactory and lacking in certainty. So this is not an example of the courts creating uncertainty where none existed before. Second, the range of factors to which a court can legitimately have regard when considering its response to the impact of illegality on the rights and obligations of the parties is so broad that they cannot meaningfully be subsumed within a single clearly defined legal rule. Third, the claim of the parties that they are entitled to the protection of a set of clearly defined legal rules is not strong given that, as Lord Kerr acknowledged in *Patel*, certainty or predictability of outcome 'is not a premium to which those engaged in disreputable conduct can claim automatic entitlement'.

Notwithstanding the adoption of this discretionary approach, it is suggested that, for the reasons given in Section 15.1 above, it is extremely unlikely, if not impossible, to conceive of a court giving an award of damages on the facts of *Patel* to compensate the claimant for the loss of his bargain. Any such award would be inconsistent with the policy which rendered the contract illegal. But in other cases, perhaps where the illegality is trivial and the claimant was unaware of the illegality, a court may be willing to allow a claimant to enforce its rights under the contract. However, this is likely to be an exceptional response and for the most part courts can be expected not to permit claimants to enforce their rights under illegal contracts because it would lead to inconsistency with the law that rendered the contract illegal.

15.18 The recovery of money or property

Matters may be otherwise in relation to the recovery of benefits which have been conferred upon the other party to an illegal contract, where there may now be a broader right of recovery. Prior to the decision of the Supreme Court in *Patel v Mirza*, the general rule was that the courts would not permit the recovery of benefits transferred under an illegal contract (*Holman v Johnson* (1775) 1 Cowp 341). However, the rule which prevented recovery was not absolute. It was the subject of a number of exceptions.

15.18.1 The law prior to *Patel v Mirza*

First, a claimant could recover the value of a benefit conferred where the parties were not *in pari delicto* (that is to say, they were not equally to blame or equally at fault). So, for example, a claimant could recover a benefit conferred under an illegal contract where he was operating under a mistake of fact which rendered him unaware of the illegal nature of the contract (*Oom v Bruce* (1810) 12 East 225). Similarly, a claimant could recover where he was induced to enter into the illegal transaction by the fraudulent representation of the defendant which had the effect of concealing the illegal nature of the transaction from him (*Hughes v Liverpool Victoria Legal Friendly Society* [1916] 2 KB 482) or the claimant was induced to enter into the contract under some form of compulsion amounting to oppression (*Smith v Cuff* (1817) 6 M & S 160). Another aspect of the *in pari delicto* rule was that recovery was permitted where a transaction was rendered illegal under a statute which was enacted in an effort to protect parties in the position of the claimant (*Kasumu v Baba-Egbe* [1956] AC 539 and *Kiriri Cotton v Dewani* [1960] AC 192).

Second, a claimant was entitled to recover a benefit conferred under an illegal contract if he repudiated the illegal purpose before performance under the contract had commenced (in the case of partial performance it was difficult to identify the precise point in time at which the right to withdraw was lost). The payer was said to have a *locus poenitentiae* (a space or time for repentance) and could withdraw from the illegal contract and recover his payment (see *Taylor v Bowers* (1876) 1 QBD 291 and *Kearley v Thomson* (1890) 24 QBD 742, usefully discussed by Beatson, 1975). It was this exception to the general rule of no-recovery which was in issue in the lower courts in *Patel v Mirza*.

Third, a claimant was able to recover money paid or property transferred under an illegal contract if he could establish his right to the money or the property without relying upon the illegal nature of the contract (*Bowmakers Ltd v Barnet Instruments Ltd* [1945] KB 65, *Belvoir Finance v Stapleton* [1971] 1 QB 210, *Tinsley v Milligan* [1994] 1 AC 340). So, for example, in *Bowmakers* the claimants bought machine tools in contravention of the Defence Regulations and they delivered the tools to the defendants under three illegal hire-purchase agreements. The defendants, in breach of the agreements, sold some of the tools and refused to return the remainder. The claimants sued successfully for damages in the tort of conversion. The defendants' right to possess the goods terminated on their breach of the hire-purchase agreements and so the claimants were able to establish their title to the machine tools without placing any reliance upon the illegal transactions. The difficulty with this exception was that it was rather arbitrary in its operation because the ability to recover depended entirely on the chance of whether the claimant could establish its right to the property without relying upon the illegality (see, for example, *Collier v Collier* [2002] EWCA Civ 1095; [2002] BPIR 1057). The other criticism levelled against *Bowmakers* was that, by awarding damages assessed by reference to the value of the machine tools, the result was *de facto* enforcement of the contract. On the other hand, to refuse a remedy would have been to confer a *de facto* gift upon the defendants. As Coote has pointed out (1972): 'the real difficulty lies in the arbitrary, all-or-nothing character of the common law governing illegal contracts.'

15.18.2 *Patel v Mirza*

The general rule of no-recovery and the exceptions to that rule were swept away by the majority of the Supreme Court in *Patel v Mirza* in favour of what appears to be a broader right of recovery. Lord Toulson sought to develop the law in a different direction by holding that a claimant who satisfies the ordinary requirements of a claim in unjust enrichment will not prima facie be debarred from recovering money paid or property transferred simply because the consideration which has failed was an unlawful consideration. In this way the majority sought to free the law from what it saw as the arbitrary consequences which flowed from the existing common law, in particular the rule that a claimant can recover money paid or property transferred under an illegal contract if he can establish his right to the money or the property transferred without relying upon the illegal nature of the contract. The recognition of a wider right to recover benefits conferred was held not to undermine the policy behind the rule which rendered the contract illegal because, in granting a right of recovery, the court was not seeking to enforce the contract, nor was the claimant seeking to profit from the illegality. On the contrary, the aim was to put the parties back into the position which they would have been in had no illegal transaction ever been entered into.

Although the right to recover benefits or property transferred under an illegal contract appears to have been widened, its precise scope remains to be worked out. Some uncertainties still exist. First, there may be circumstances where the nature of the illegality is such that the court will not permit the claimant to recover the value of any benefit or property transferred to the defendant. The example raised by the Supreme Court was a contract which involved drug trafficking where the seriousness of the illegality may deprive the claimant of the entitlement it would otherwise have to reverse an unjust enrichment. While it was not necessary for the Supreme Court to decide this point, the likelihood is that the courts will not permit recovery in exceptional cases of this type. Second, the meaning of the phrase 'a person who satisfies the ordinary requirements of a claim in unjust enrichment' requires further elucidation. Some cases are clear. For example, it will encompass a case where the claimant's mistake was such that it was unaware of the illegality or the case in which the claimant withdrew from the illegal transaction before any performance had taken place. However, there was a right of recovery in such circumstances prior to *Patel*. More difficult is the case where there has been substantial performance under the contract or performance is complete. So, for example, what would have been the case if the contract in *Patel* had been fully performed? It is unlikely that there would be a right of recovery in such a case because the consideration has not failed and so the claimant would not be able to satisfy the ordinary requirements of a claim in unjust enrichment. But what about the case where there has been partial performance? As we shall see (see Section 21.6) the law does not generally recognise a right to recover a benefit transferred upon a partial failure of consideration and so it could be said that the claimant in such a case has not satisfied the ordinary requirements of a claim in unjust enrichment. On the other hand, there are indications in the judgments in *Patel* that there might be a right of recovery in such circumstances. The issue therefore remains to be resolved.

It is clear that the Supreme Court in *Patel* has set the law on a new track but it is not entirely clear where it will lead. Two points would, however, appear to be clear. First, there has been a re-statement of, and a potential widening of, the right to recover benefits or property transferred under an illegal contract. Second, the courts now enjoy a considerable degree of discretion when deciding the remedial consequences of entry into an illegal contract and it largely remains to be seen how the courts will exercise that discretion. Enforcement of the contract by way of an award of damages which puts the claimant in the position it would have been in had the contract been performed according to its terms is likely to be exceptional because such an award risks inconsistency with the rule that renders the contract illegal and might enable a party to profit from its own wrongdoing. More likely is a greater readiness to unwind an illegal contract so as to restore the parties to the position they were in prior to entry into the illegal contract.

15.19 Severance

Finally, it may be possible to 'sever' the illegal part of the contract and enforce the remainder. If the illegal part of the contract can be separated from the rest of the contract, without rendering the remainder of the contract radically different from the contract which the parties originally concluded, then the court may be prepared to sever the illegal part, provided that severance is not contrary to the public policy which rendered the contract illegal (see further Treitel, 2020, paras 11-156–11-169). The application of the doctrine of severance to a covenant in restraint of trade was considered by the Supreme Court in *Egon Zendher Ltd v Tillman* [2019] UKSC 32; [2020] AC 154 where a three-stage approach was adopted. At the first stage, the unenforceable provision must be capable of being removed without the need to add to or modify the remaining wording of the clause. Severance is therefore confined to 'cutting things up and does not extend to adding things in'. This was held to be inherent in the word 'severance' so that the courts do not have jurisdiction to re-write a restraint so as to turn it into a reasonable restraint. Second, the remaining terms must continue to be supported by consideration. Third, and finally, the court must consider whether the removal of the offending provision would generate any major change in the overall effect of the restraints in the contract. If it would effect such a change, then severance will not be available.

Hot topic 14...

In his judgment in *Patel v Mirza* Lord Sumption, in the minority on this point, stated that the court 'would be doing no service to the coherent development of the law' if it 'simply substituted a new mess for the old one' and that the test proposed by the majority was 'far too vague and potentially far too wide to serve as the basis on which a person may be denied his legal rights'. The majority resisted this charge on the ground that the common law pre-*Patel v Mirza* was itself uncertain and unpredictable, uncertainty has not been a source of serious problems in those jurisdictions which have adopted a flexible approach of the type developed by the majority in *Patel* and, in any event, people who contemplate unlawful activity do not have a strong case for maintaining that they need to be sure of their legal ground. The essence of the reasoning of the majority is to be found in the following passage from the judgment of Lord Toulson in *Patel*:

the essential rationale of the illegality doctrine is that it would be contrary to the public interest to enforce a claim if to do so would be harmful to the integrity of the legal system (or, possibly, certain aspects of public morality, the boundaries of which have never been made entirely clear and which do not arise for consideration in this case). In assessing whether the public interest would be harmed in that way, it is necessary a) to consider the underlying purpose of the prohibition which has been transgressed and whether that purpose will be enhanced by denial of the claim, b) to consider any other relevant public policy on which the denial of the claim may have an impact and c) to consider whether denial of the claim would be a proportionate response to the illegality, bearing in mind that punishment is a matter for the criminal courts. Within that framework, various factors may be relevant, but it would be a mistake to suggest that the court is free to decide a case in an undisciplined way. The public interest is best served by a principled and transparent assessment of the considerations identified, rather by than the application of a formal approach capable of producing results which may appear arbitrary, unjust or disproportionate.

Summary

▶ As a general rule the courts have refused to enforce a contract which is illegal or which is otherwise contrary to public policy but now the courts enjoy a greater degree of remedial flexibility when considering the consequences of entry into an illegal contract.

▶ Where the illegality arises in the performance of a contract which was valid at the moment of formation, the contract can be enforced by the guilty party only when it was not the purpose of the statute broken or the common law rule violated that the contract should be invalidated. In the case of the innocent party, the contract can generally be enforced by him where he had no knowledge of the illegality.

▶ A contract is illegal if its formation is expressly or impliedly prohibited by statute. The function of the court is to interpret the statute to discern whether, on its proper construction, the Act prohibits the making of such a contract.

▶ A contract may be illegal at common law on the ground that it is contrary to public policy. Contracts which are contrary to public policy include contracts which are contrary to good morals, contracts which are prejudicial to family life, contracts to commit a crime or a civil wrong, contracts which are prejudicial to the administration of justice, contracts prejudicial to public relations and contracts in unreasonable restraint of trade.

▶ A contract which is in restraint of trade is void and unenforceable unless it can be shown to be reasonable. The doctrine applies principally to a covenant by an employee not to compete with his employer either during or after his employment and to a covenant by the seller of a business and its goodwill not to carry on a business which will compete with the business bought by the purchaser. A clause which is caught by the doctrine is void unless it is reasonable as between the parties and reasonable in the public interest.

▶ Although the courts are prepared gradually to adapt the doctrine of public policy to reflect changing social and moral values, they remain extremely reluctant to extend the doctrine to a contract of a type to which the doctrine has never been applied before.

▶ The courts will not enforce an illegal contract where the consequences of doing so would be to enable a party to profit from its own wrongdoing or the effect of doing so would be inconsistent with the policy which underpins the rule that rendered the contract illegal. Otherwise the remedy very much lies in the discretion of the court and the court in exercising that discretion will have regard to the underlying purpose of the prohibition which has been transgressed, any other relevant public policies which might be rendered ineffective by denial of the claim and the proportionality of any decision to grant or withhold a remedy.

▶ A claimant who satisfies the ordinary requirements of a claim in unjust enrichment will not prima facie be debarred from recovering money paid or property transferred simply because the consideration which has failed was an unlawful consideration.

Exercises

15.1 Will the courts ever enforce an illegal contract? Should the courts ever enforce an illegal contract?

15.2 Compare and contrast the decisions in *Re Mahmoud and Ispahani* [1921] 2 KB 716 and *Archbolds (Freightage) Ltd v S Spanglett Ltd* [1961] 2 QB 374.

15.3 What impact does illegality in performance have on the enforceability of a contract?

15.4 When will a contract be held to be contrary to public policy? Does the doctrine of public policy reflect any values other than the idiosyncratic values of the judiciary?

15.5 A 35-year-old employee agrees with his employer that he will not work for the rest of his life if the employer pays him a lump sum of £1 million. The employer pays the money but the employee has now decided that he wishes to return to work. Discuss. (See *Wyatt v Kreglinger and Fernau* [1933] 1 KB 793.)

15.6 Joe employs six travelling salesmen. They sell insurance policies. Joe wishes to insert a restraint of trade clause in their contracts of employment. Advise him and draft a clause which will be suitable to his needs.

15.7 Can the value of benefits conferred under an illegal contract be recovered? Why might the law be more willing to permit the recovery of benefits than to enforce the contract?

Chapter 16

Capacity

Introduction

Adults of sound mind have full contractual capacity. On the other hand, minors, the mentally incapacitated and companies have limited contractual capacity. In the case of minors and the mentally incapacitated, contract law seeks to protect such persons from the consequences of their own inexperience or inability. The limitations placed upon the contractual capacity of companies raise rather different issues, to which we shall return at Section 16.4.

Although contract law seeks to play a role in protecting minors and the mentally incapacitated, a competing policy is that the law does not wish to expose to hardship those who deal fairly and in all good faith with such persons. We shall see that the rules of law reflect an uneasy compromise between these competing policies. We shall begin our analysis by a consideration of the contractual capacity of minors (Section 16.2), then we shall discuss the contractual capacity of the mentally incapacitated (Section 16.3) and, finally, we shall analyse the contractual capacity of companies (Section 16.4).

16.2 Minors

A minor is a person under the age of 18. The law adopts a particularly protective attitude towards minors, often at the expense of those who deal with them in all good faith. The general rule is that a minor is not bound by a contract which he enters into during his minority. But this general rule is subject to three principal exceptions.

16.2.1 Contracts for 'necessaries'

The first is that a contract to supply a minor with 'necessaries' is binding upon the minor where the contract as a whole is for the benefit of the minor; where its terms are harsh or onerous it is not binding upon the minor. The definition of 'necessaries' is a wide one. In the case of a contract for the sale of goods, necessaries have been defined in section 3(3) of the Sale of Goods Act 1979 as 'goods suitable to the condition in life of the minor ... and to his actual requirements at the time of the sale and delivery'. At common law a wide definition of necessaries has also been adopted. Regard must be had to the station in life of the minor; the higher the status, the greater the range of necessaries. So in *Peters v Fleming* (1840) 6 M & W 42, rings, pins and a watch chain were held to be necessaries for an undergraduate who had a rich father. But there is a trap for the trader here because, in deciding whether a particular article is a necessary, a court will have regard to the status of the minor and his actual needs at the time of entry into the contract. Thus, in *Nash v Inman* [1908] 2 KB 1, a tailor sold 11 fancy waistcoats to a minor, who was a Cambridge undergraduate. The minor refused to pay for them. The tailor's action for payment failed because he could not establish that the defendant was not already amply supplied with clothing; the waistcoats were not therefore necessaries. Although a minor is bound by an executed contract for necessaries, it remains unclear whether a minor is bound by an executory contract for necessaries (contrast *Nash v Inman* and *Roberts v Gray* [1913] 1 KB 520).

16.2.2   Contracts for the benefit of minors

Secondly, a minor is bound by a contract of employment if that contract is generally for his benefit (*Fisher v Brooker* [2009] UKHL 41; [2009] 1 WLR 1764, [23] and contrast *Clements v L & NW Rly* [1894] 2 QB 482 and *De Francesco v Barnum* (1890) 45 Ch D 430). This principle, however, is confined to contracts of employment and analogous contracts (such as a contract to give publishers the exclusive rights to publish the minor's memoirs, see *Chaplin v Leslie Frewin (Publishers) Ltd* [1966] Ch 71). But there is no general principle of law that a contract with a minor is binding simply because it is for his benefit.

16.2.3   Voidable contracts

Thirdly, certain contracts with minors are not void but are only voidable; that is to say, the contract is valid and binding upon the minor unless he repudiates liability before majority or within a reasonable time thereafter. Only the minor can repudiate; the adult is bound by the contract. For example, a contract under which a minor acquires an interest in land or shares in a company is voidable, as is a partnership agreement to which a minor is a party. The effect of the repudiation is to release the minor from his obligations to perform in the future. But the minor can only recover money paid under such a contract where there has been a total failure of consideration (*Steinberg v Scala (Leeds) Ltd* [1923] 2 Ch 452). A total failure of consideration arises where the basis upon which the minor paid the money has wholly failed, that is to say, he has received no part of the performance for which he has bargained.

16.2.4   Cases in which a minor may incur liability

Outside these three categories, the general rule is that, as we have noted, minors are not bound by the contracts into which they enter. However, a minor may incur liability to an adult in a number of other ways. In the first place, the minor will be liable on the contract if he ratifies it after he has reached majority. Secondly, where a contract is unenforceable against the minor or he has repudiated it, the court may, 'if it is just and equitable to do so', require the minor to transfer to the other party any 'property acquired' by the minor under the contract, or any 'property representing it' (Minors' Contracts Act 1987, s 3(1). It should be noted in this context that the Act contains no definition of 'property'; in particular, it is unclear whether 'property' includes money. The aim of this section is to prevent the unjust enrichment of the minor in cases such as *Nash v Inman*, by enabling the court to order the minor to restore to the vendor the fancy waistcoats. But the court cannot order the minor to return the property where he has disposed of it and obtained nothing in return for it. This limitation has been criticised on the ground that it should be irrelevant that the benefits conferred are no longer identifiable in the minor's hands. Nevertheless, this provision is to be welcomed in so far as it reduces the possibility of the unjust enrichment of the minor. But it should be noted that the 1987 Act did not abolish the existing common law rules (see *Stocks v Wilson* [1913] 2 KB 235 and *Bristow v Eastman* (1794) 1 Esp 172), so that the adult may still have resort to these rules where, for some reason, a remedy is not available to him under the Act. However, it is unlikely that an adult will wish, in future, to have resort to the pre-1987 common law because section 3(1) of the Act generally improves the position of the adult *vis-à-vis* the minor.

Thirdly, a minor who has actually performed his side of the contract may be unable to recover the benefits which he has conferred upon the other party. At first sight this seems rather anomalous. The foolish minor enters into improvident bargains; the very foolish minor actually carries through his side of the bargain. The courts have, however, approached this issue from a different perspective. Their approach has been to allow minority to act as a *defence* to a claim brought against the minor by an adult (as in *Nash v Inman*), but they have refused to allow that same minority to be used as the foundation for an *active* claim by the minor: that is to say, they have refused to recognise that minority can act as a factor rendering the conferral of a benefit unjust so as to trigger an unjust enrichment claim. On the contrary, a minor who seeks to recover the value of a benefit which he has conferred upon an adult must satisfy the same requirements as an adult making a restitutionary claim (except that, where the claim is based on a total failure of consideration, the minor can make out a restitutionary claim even though the adult was ready and willing to perform his side of the bargain). It is for this reason that we find in the cases that minors have relied upon traditional grounds of restitution, such as total failure of consideration (see, for example, *Steinberg v Scala (Leeds) Ltd*). The failure to recognise minority as a ground of restitution presents an odd contrast with the case of mental incapacity (see Section 16.3), where it is clear that it is the incapacity (together with the knowledge of the other party) which constitutes the factor which renders the enrichment unjust. There is much to be said for the view that minority should also constitute a ground of restitution subject to the requirement that the minor make counter-restitution to the adult (that is to say, the minor must restore to the adult any benefit which he has obtained at the expense of the adult). Indeed, this may have been the view that English law originally adopted in *Valentini v Canali* (1889) 24 QBD 166, before the case was (wrongly) interpreted as an authority for the proposition that the minor must establish the existence of a total failure of consideration.

Fourthly, a contract with a minor is effective to pass property to the minor (Minors' Contracts Act 1987, s 3(1)); similarly it is effective to pass property from the minor to the adult. Finally, a minor may incur liability in tort or in restitution, but, where the effect of the tort action or the restitutionary action would be to undermine the protection afforded by the law of contract, then the tort or restitutionary action will also be barred. In *R Leslie Ltd v Sheill* [1914] 3 KB 607, a minor obtained a loan of £400 by fraudulently misrepresenting his age. It was held that the minor could not be sued in the tort of deceit because the effect of granting damages in the tort action would be indirectly to enforce the contract and thus undermine the protection afforded by the law of contract. But it must be doubted whether *Leslie* would be followed today. It has been sharply criticised (for example, by Burrows, 2010, 581–82) on the ground that a restitutionary action to recover the value of a benefit conferred is not the same thing as an action to enforce the contract of loan, a point recognised in another context by the House of Lords in *Westdeutsche Landesbank Girozentrale v Islington London BC* [1996] AC 669, 718. The measure of recovery in a restitutionary claim is the value of the benefit conferred (here the loan) subject to the defence of change of position, whereas in the contractual claim it is the principal sum together with the contractually agreed rate of interest.

Despite the enactment of the Minors' Contracts Act 1987, the law relating to the contractual capacity of minors remains in a confused state (the common law rules were described by Baroness Hale as 'complex and confusing' in *Fisher v Brooker* [2009] UKHL 41; [2009] 1 WLR 1764, [21]). The rules relating to necessaries can act as a trap for persons who deal in all good faith with minors. On the other hand, given that in the vast majority of cases a minor can avoid liability without the need to repudiate, it is difficult to understand why certain contracts are treated as voidable so that the minor can only avoid liability by a timely repudiation. The rules of law remain in need of further rationalisation in an effort to provide a better balance between, on the one hand, the protection of minors and, on the other hand, the interests of those who deal in all good faith with them.

16.3 Mental incapacity and drunkenness

The law relating to mental incapacity underwent significant change as a result of the coming into force of the Mental Capacity Act 2005. The law is here seeking to strike a delicate balance. On the one hand, we do not wish to deprive people of their contractual freedom unless it is strictly necessary to do so. On the other hand, we do not want to leave the weak and vulnerable to potential exploitation by those who would take advantage of them. A further consideration is the desire to provide a protective regime within which the assets of an incapable person can be properly administered. Section 1(2) of the Act places the initial emphasis on capacity rather than incapacity. It provides that a person must be assumed to have capacity unless it is established that he does not. Lack of capacity is the subject-matter of section 2 of the Act. A person is stated to lack capacity 'in relation to a matter if at the material time he is unable to make a decision for himself in relation to the matter because of an impairment of, or a disturbance in the functioning of, the mind or brain' (s 2(1), as further defined in s 3). The impairment or disturbance can be temporary or permanent (s 2(2)). A person is not to be treated as unable to make a decision unless all practicable steps to help him to do so have been taken without success (s 1(3)); nor is he to be treated as unable to make a decision merely because he makes an 'unwise decision' (s 1(4)). Further, a lack of capacity cannot be established merely by reference to a person's age or appearance or by a condition of his, or an aspect of his behaviour, which might lead others to make unjustified assumptions about his capacity (s 2(3)). If necessary goods or services are supplied to a person who lacks capacity to contract for the supply, he must pay a reasonable price for them (and necessaries, for this purpose, are defined to mean 'suitable to a person's condition in life and to his actual requirements at the time when the goods or services are supplied') (s 7). The Act also makes provision, in Part 2, for the Court of Protection which has wide powers to make decisions in relation to the conduct of life of a person who lacks capacity.

At common law mental incapacity is not a ground for the setting aside of a contract or for the return of benefits conferred under a contract, unless the incapacity is known to the other party to the contract (*Imperial Loan Co v Stone* [1892] 1 QB 599) or the other party ought to have known of it (*Dunhill v Burgin (Nos 1 and 2)* [2014] UKSC 18; [2014] 1 WLR 933, [25]). Where the incapacity is not known to the other party, the contract cannot be set aside, unless the contract is of such a nature as to attract the equitable jurisdiction to relieve against unconscionable bargains between two persons of sound mind (*Hart v O'Connor* [1985] AC 1000). This requirement that the other party be aware of the incapacity should be contrasted with the case of minors, where there is no requirement that the other party be aware of the minority and, indeed, the minor may be relieved even when he has misrepresented his age. In Scotland, the rule is that knowledge of the insanity is not a relevant consideration (*John Loudon & Co v Elder's CB* 1923 SLT 226). It is therefore no surprise to learn that the requirement that the other party be aware of the incapacity has been subjected to severe criticism (see Hudson, 1986), although its harshness may be mitigated in practice by the existence of the equitable jurisdiction to set aside an improvident bargain made with a poor and ignorant person (*Cresswell v Potter* [1978] 1 WLR 255, on which see Section 17.4).

Drunkenness is treated in the same way as mental incapacity, so that the contract may only be set aside by the drunken party where the drunkenness prevented him from understanding the transaction, and the other party to the contract knew of his incapacity (*Gore v Gibson* (1843) 13 M & W 623). Finally, it should be noted that in the case of a contract for the sale of goods, 'where necessaries are sold and delivered to a person who by reason of drunkenness is incompetent to contract, he must pay a reasonable price for them' (Sale of Goods Act 1979, s 3(2)).

16.4 Companies

A company is a legal person which is separate and distinct from its shareholders. But the capacity of the company is limited by the objects for which the company is set up and which are contained in the company's memorandum of association. If the company acts beyond its objects then it has acted *ultra vires*, that is to say, it has acted beyond its capacity. In *Ashbury Railway Carriage and Iron Co v Riche* (1875) LR 7 HL 653, it was held that a contract which was *ultra vires* the company was void. One of the principal justifications for the *ultra vires* rule is that it gives protection for shareholders who can learn from the objects clause 'the purposes to which their money can be applied' (*Cotman v Brougham* [1918] AC 514, 520, per Lord Parker of Waddington). In theory, it also provides protection for those who lend money to the company because they can infer from the objects clause the extent of the company's powers. But, in practice, a strict application of the rule caused hardship to innocent third parties who entered into a contract with a company, unaware of the *ultra vires* nature of the contract.

So it is not surprising to learn that the courts have created a number of exceptions to the rule in an effort to provide some protection for innocent third parties who deal in all good faith with the company. The most significant protection is provided by statute in section 39(1) of the Companies Act 2006 which states that:

> The validity of an act done by a company shall not be called into question on the ground of lack of capacity by reason of anything in the company's constitution.

The effect of the intervention of Parliament is to abolish the *ultra vires* rule as regards innocent third parties who deal in all good faith with the company (see further ss 40(1)–(3)), while retaining it for internal purposes concerning the relationship between the shareholders and the company (ss 40(4) and (5)). The effective abolition of the *ultra vires* rule in relation to third parties who deal in all good faith with the company has the consequence that the contract between the company and the third party remains valid and enforceable.

Summary

▶ The general rule is that a minor is not bound by a contract which he enters into during his minority.

▶ But a minor is bound by a contract to supply him with 'necessaries' where the contract as a whole is for the benefit of the minor, and he is also bound by a beneficial contract of employment. Certain contracts involving minors are voidable and the minor can escape liability only by a timely repudiation.

▶ However, a minor may incur liability in a number of other ways. He may incur liability on the contract if he ratifies it after attaining majority, he may incur liability in tort, he may be ordered to restore any property he has acquired under the contract or any property representing it (Minors' Contracts Act 1987, s 3(1)) and it is more difficult for a minor to obtain a remedy where the contract has been performed.

▶ At common law mental incapacity is not a ground for the setting aside of a contract, unless the incapacity is known to the other party to the contract. The Mental Capacity Act 2005 states that a person is assumed to have capacity unless it is established otherwise, but provides that a person lacks capacity in relation to a matter if at the material time he is unable to make a decision for himself in relation to the matter because of an impairment of, or a disturbance in the functioning of, the mind or brain.

▶ The rule established in *Ashbury Railway Carriage and Iron Co v Riche* (1875) LR 7 HL 653 was that a contract which is *ultra vires* a company is void. However, as a result of statutory intervention, the doctrine of *ultra vires* is effectively abolished in relation to third parties who deal in all good faith with the company.

Exercises

16.1 Alfie, who is aged 17, agrees to buy a motor bike from Trike Ltd for £2,500. He takes delivery of the bike but refuses to pay for it. Advise Trike Ltd.

16.2 In what circumstances may a minor incur liability to an adult as a result of entering into a contract?

16.3 John, who suffers from dementia, agrees to sell a portrait to Brian for £5,000. Brian does not know that John is suffering from dementia. It is later discovered that the portrait is, in fact, an original nineteenth-century painting, which is worth £125,000. Advise John whether he has any rights against Brian.

16.4 What does *ultra vires* mean? What effect does it have on a contract with a party who is unaware of the *ultra vires* nature of the transaction?

Chapter 17

Duress, undue influence and inequality of bargaining power

17.1 Introduction

The law of contract has always placed limits upon the exercise of economic power by contracting parties (see Reiter, 1981). This role has traditionally been played by the doctrines of duress and undue influence, although recent years have also witnessed a (largely abortive) attempt to introduce into the common law a doctrine of inequality of bargaining power. In this chapter we shall give separate consideration to each of these issues and conclude by discussing the extent to which the law of contract is concerned with the fairness of the bargain reached by the parties.

17.2 Common law duress

The doctrine of duress has been a relatively late developer in English contract law. Although the courts have had little difficulty in setting aside a contract on the ground of duress to the person, they have had more difficulty in recognising the existence of more subtle forms of duress, such as duress to goods and economic duress (see below). Historically, some of the work was done by the doctrine of consideration (see Sections 5.3, 5.6 and 5.11). For example, if X puts a gun to Y's head and extracts from Y a promise to pay him £10,000, then Y's promise is unenforceable because of the absence of any consideration provided by X. But the doctrine of consideration was never well equipped to deal with duress and this is largely because of the rule that consideration must be sufficient but need not be adequate (see Section 5.6). So if X agrees to give Y his pen worth £1 in return for the promise to pay £10,000, the consideration hurdle is overcome.

The role of consideration in regulating duress-type situations is likely to diminish still further as a result of the decision of the Court of Appeal in *Williams v Roffey Bros & Nicholls (Contractors) Ltd* [1991] 1 QB 1 (discussed in more detail in Sections 5.11–5.14). The approach of the Court of Appeal strongly suggests that the modern courts will be more willing to find the presence of consideration in the renegotiation of a contract and leave it to duress to regulate the fairness of the renegotiation. Indeed, one of the factors which was relied upon in adopting a more liberal approach to consideration was the fact that the court could always set aside the renegotiated contract on the ground of duress where the ingredients of duress were established. Thus, a case such as *Stilk v Myrick* (1809) 2 Camp 317 and 6 Esp 129 (see Sections 5.11 and 5.13) was reclassified as a duress case rather than a consideration case. So, post-*Williams v Roffey Bros*, it is clear that the doctrine of duress assumes greater significance. The difficulty is that duress has been bedevilled by conceptual confusion, with the result that it is not easy to identify its limits and it is not obvious that it is ready to play the role which has been allocated to it. Having set duress in its context, we must now turn to consider the scope of the doctrine of duress at common law.

17.2.1   Duress to the person

There are three types of duress at common law. The first, and least controversial, is duress to the person. This may consist of actual violence to the claimant or to members of his family or threats of such violence. To constitute duress to the person, the threat must be one that relates to physical wellbeing and not economic wellbeing. A threat to inflict financial ruin on a party will therefore be regarded as a potential case of economic duress (see below) and not as duress to the person (*Holyoake v Candy* [2017] EWHC 3397 (Ch), [233]). In *Barton v Armstrong* [1976] AC 104, the Privy Council held that the threats need not be the sole reason for entry into the contract; it was sufficient that the threats were a factor influencing the victim to enter into the contract.

17.2.2   Duress to goods

The second type of duress is duress to goods, that is, a threat of damage to the victim's goods rather than to his person. Here the development of the law was hindered by the old case of *Skeate v Beale* (1840) 11 Ad & E 983, in which it was held that the unlawful detention of another's goods does not constitute duress. On the other hand, there was authority for the proposition that money paid to release goods which had been unlawfully detained could be recovered back in an action for money had and received (*Astley v Reynolds* (1731) 2 Str 915). The decision in *Skeate v Beale* has come under heavy academic criticism (see Beatson, 1974) and in *The Siboen and The Sibotre* [1976] 1 Lloyd's Rep 293, Kerr J declined to follow it. Given the development of the doctrine of economic duress (see below), it can be predicted with some confidence that *Skeate v Beale* will not be followed today and in *The Evia Luck* [1992] 2 AC 152, Lord Goff stated that the limitation in *Skeate v Beale* that only duress to the person would entitle a party to avoid a contract had been 'discarded'. So it is now clear that duress to goods can, in an appropriate case, form the basis of a claim for relief.

17.2.3   Economic duress

The third type of duress, and the most difficult to stabilise, is economic duress. This type of duress arises where one party uses his superior economic power in an 'illegitimate' way so as to coerce the other contracting party to agree to a particular set of terms. The existence of this doctrine was first recognised in England by Kerr J in *The Siboen and The Sibotre* and its existence has been affirmed in a number of subsequent cases. In *R v A-G for England and Wales* [2003] UKPC 22 Lord Hoffmann stated that there were two elements to the 'wrong of duress'. The first was 'pressure amounting to compulsion of the will of the victim and the second was the illegitimacy of the pressure'. Each of these elements requires separate consideration.

17.2.4   Coercion of the will

The phrase which Lord Hoffmann uses to encapsulate the first element is 'compulsion of the will of the victim'. The more traditional formula is that there must have been a 'coercion of the will' of the victim which was such as to 'vitiate' his consent. The 'coercion of the will' theory was particularly apparent in the early economic duress cases such as *The Siboen and The Sibotre*. However, the difficulties inherent in the 'coercion of the will' theory were convincingly exposed by Professor Atiyah (1982). The principal difficulty is that duress does not deprive a person of all choice, but merely presents him with a choice between evils. For example, if a man forces me at gun point to enter into a contract, I do in fact consent to entering into the contract. Indeed, the more real the pressure, the more real is my willingness to enter into the contract, even if it is only to extricate myself from my predicament. What is wrong with the contract is not the absence of consent, but the wrongful nature of the threats which have been used to bring about the consent.

Given these criticisms of the 'coercion of the will' test it is not surprising to find that the courts have begun to distance themselves from it. In *The Evia Luck* (above) Lord Goff, giving the principal judgment of the House of Lords, noted (at 165) the criticisms which have been levelled against the theory and doubted whether 'it is helpful to speak of the [claimant's] will having been coerced'. However, as the judgment of Lord Hoffmann in *R v A-G for England and Wales* makes clear, the courts have not, as yet, abandoned the language of 'compulsion of the will' entirely. Hopefully, the courts will, ultimately, abandon the test completely and have regard to the consent of the claimant only for the purpose of ensuring that there is a sufficient causal link between the pressure applied by the defendant and the entry into the contract. That said, there is some uncertainty as to the test which is to be applied by the courts when seeking to determine whether or not there is a sufficient causal link between the two. In the context of duress to the person, the threat need only be a cause of the claimant acting as he did and there is even a suggestion in *Barton v Armstrong* that the onus of proof switches to the defendant to show that the illegitimate pressure would not have influenced the claimant in any event. On the other hand, it is clear that this generous approach to the claimant does not apply in cases of economic duress because it would lead to relief being given too readily (in particular, it could make it too easy for a claimant to set aside a renegotiation of a contract which he has since decided is definitely disadvantageous for him). As Leggatt LJ observed in *Al Nehayan v Kent* [2018] EWHC 333 (Comm), [190] 'the test of causation differs according to the nature of the duress'. So a claimant must overcome a more serious hurdle in the case of economic duress than in the case of duress to the person. While there is some authority for the proposition that, in cases of economic duress, the claimant must prove that the pressure applied was a 'significant cause' inducing him to enter into the contract (see *The Evia Luck* [1992] 2 AC 152, 165, per Lord Goff and *Huyton SA v Peter Cremer GmbH & Co Inc* (above) at 636–37, per Mance J), the weight of modern authority supports the application of the traditional 'but for' test (*Kolmar Group AG v Traxpo Enterprises Pty Ltd* [2010] EWHC 113 (Comm); [2010] 2 Lloyd's Rep 653, [92]; *Times Travel (UK) Ltd v Pakistan International Airlines Corporation* [2017] EWHC 1367 (Ch), [253]; *Al Nehayan v Kent* [2018] EWHC 333 (Comm), [190]). The courts are also likely to consider whether or not there was an alternative open to the claimant. In *Huyton SA v Peter Cremer GmbH & Co Inc*, Mance J stated (at 638) that, while it was 'not necessary to go so far as to say that it is an inflexible third essential ingredient of economic duress that there should be no or no practical alternative course open to the innocent party', it seemed to him

it mean 'pressure' or is it a more subtle, continuing form of domination? The courts have not provided clear answers to these questions. There are two principal views in play. The first is that the focus in undue influence cases is upon the position of the claimant and that the basis on which the court gives relief is the impairment of the claimant's decision-making process caused by his excessive reliance or dependence upon the defendant (see Birks and Chin Nyuk Yin, 1995). The second view looks rather to the position of the defendant and requires some 'wrongful' conduct on the part of the defendant. Thus the emphasis is placed on the need for an 'abuse' of a position of confidence, the 'exploitation' of the weaker party or some other form of 'advantage taking'. The courts have not, as yet, committed themselves to one view to the exclusion of the other. In some recent cases judges have placed emphasis on the need for some 'wrongful' conduct on the part of the defendants. Thus in *R v A-G for England and Wales* [2003] UKPC 22, [21] Lord Hoffmann stated:

> Like duress at common law, undue influence is based upon the principle that a transaction to which consent has been obtained by unacceptable means should not be allowed to stand. Undue influence has concentrated in particular upon the unfair exploitation by one party of a relationship which gives him ascendancy or influence over the other.

The combination of the analogy drawn with duress and the emphasis on the need for 'unacceptable means' and 'unfair exploitation' gives the analysis of undue influence a very strong defendant focus. A similar approach was taken by Lord Millett in *National Commercial Bank (Jamaica) Ltd v Hew* [2003] UKPC 51, [29]–[31] when he defined undue influence in the following terms:

> Undue influence is one of the grounds on which equity intervenes to give redress where there has been some unconscionable conduct on the part of the defendant ... the doctrine involves two elements. First, there must be a relationship capable of giving rise to the necessary influence. And secondly the influence generated by the relationship must have been abused.

To similar effect, in *Davies v AIB Group (UK) plc* [2012] EWHC 2178 (Ch); [2012] 2 P & CR 19 Norris J stated that undue influence 'does not protect against folly, but against victimisation' and that it has a 'connotation of impropriety'. However, the cases do not speak with one voice. In *Pesticcio v Huet* [2004] EWCA Civ 372; [2004] All ER (D) 36 (April), Mummery LJ mounted the following defence of a doctrine of undue influence which does not insist on wrongdoing on the part of the defendant as an essential ingredient of any claim (to similar effect see also *Hammond v Osborn* [2002] EWCA Civ 885 and *Macklin v Dowsett* [2004] EWCA Civ 904). Mummery LJ stated (at [20]):

> Although undue influence is sometimes described as an 'equitable wrong' or even as a species of equitable fraud, the basis of the court's intervention is not the commission of a dishonest or wrongful act by the defendant, but that, as a matter of public policy, the presumed influence arising from the relationship of trust and confidence should not operate to the disadvantage of the victim, if the transaction is not satisfactorily explained by ordinary motives: *Allcard v Skinner* (1887) 36 Ch D 145 at 171. The court scrutinises the circumstances in which the transaction, under which benefits were conferred on the recipient, took place and the nature of the continuing relationship between the parties, rather than any specific act or conduct on the part of the recipient. A transaction may be set aside by the court, even though the actions and conduct of the person who benefits from it could not be criticised as wrongful.

Still other cases can be found in which the courts appear to have looked at both the position of the claimant and the conduct of the defendant and not made an explicit choice between the two schools of thought (see, for example, *Randall v Randall* [2004] EWHC 2258 (Ch) and *Turkey v Ahwad* [2005] EWCA Civ 507). Most cases of undue influence do involve some conduct on the part of the defendant which can properly be described as wrongful, in the sense that the defendant has exploited or otherwise taken advantage of the vulnerability of the claimant. However, not every case can be so described. As Mummery LJ observes, there was no finding of any wrongdoing on the part of the Mother Superior in *Allcard v Skinner*. The only criticism which could be levelled against her conduct was that she had failed to ensure that the claimant, who was a novice in a religious order, had access to independent advice before deciding to give away all her property on entering the order. The ground of relief in *Allcard* would therefore appear to relate to the claimant's excessive dependence on the defendant and not to any suggestion of impropriety on the part of the defendant. This being the case, it would be unwise to shut the door on the possibility that undue influence can be established without showing any wrongful conduct on the part of the defendant (see Birks, 2004). It is unlikely that the House of Lords in *Royal Bank of Scotland v Etridge (No. 2)* [2001] UKHL 44; [2002] 2 AC 773 intended to shut the door completely on a claimant-sided version of undue influence. While the predominant emphasis in the speeches is upon the conduct of the defendant, their Lordships were careful to emphasise that it is always important to have regard to the facts and circumstances of the case and that undue influence can take many different forms (for example, coercion, domination, victimisation and other 'unacceptable forms of persuasion'). If it be the case that undue influence does assume different forms, we should not rule out the possibility that one of these forms is a claimant-sided version which does not require some form of wrongful conduct on the part of the defendant.

The traditional approach is to divide undue influence into two distinct categories, namely presumed and actual undue influence. The significance of the distinction between these two categories has been much reduced as a result of the decision of the House of Lords in *Etridge*. The distinction used to be one of considerable significance because a 'manifest disadvantage' requirement applied in the case of presumed undue influence (*National Westminster Bank plc v Morgan* [1985] AC 686) but not in the case of actual undue influence (*CIBC Mortgages plc v Pitt* [1994] 1 AC 200). A disadvantage was said to be 'manifest' if 'it would have been obvious as such to any independent and reasonable persons who considered the transaction at the time with knowledge of all the relevant facts' (*Bank of Credit and Commerce International SA v Aboody* [1990] 1 QB 923). However, the 'manifest disadvantage' requirement underwent judicial reconsideration in *Etridge* and it did not emerge unscathed. While their Lordships did not conclude that the reformulated manifest disadvantage requirement applies in cases of actual undue influence, Lord Nicholls pointed out that 'the exercise of undue influence is unlikely to occur, where the transaction is innocuous'.

17.3.1 Actual undue influence

Cases of actual undue influence appear to overlap with common law duress. As Lord Nicholls observed in *Etridge*, actual undue influence 'comprises overt acts of improper pressure or coercion such as unlawful threats' and thus there is today 'much overlap with the principle of duress as this principle has subsequently developed'. An example of this is the old case of *Williams v Bayley* (1866) LR 1 HL 200. A father sought to rescind a mortgage which he had executed in favour of a banker. He proved that he had executed the mortgage because he was frightened by the banker's warning or threat that he had it in his power to prosecute his son for forgery. It was held that he was entitled to rescind the mortgage on the ground of undue influence. Today *Williams v Bayley* could be analysed as a duress case. Where the actual undue influence takes the form of the application of illegitimate pressure then it is suggested that there ought to be no need for a claimant to prove that the transaction cannot reasonably be accounted for on ordinary motives of friendship or the like (on which requirement, see below). There is no such requirement in cases of common law duress and there does not appear to be any justification for imposing it on its equitable counterpart. In the case where there is a clear overlap between duress and actual undue influence, it may be that undue influence will be held not to add anything to the duress claim. As Nugee J observed in *Holyoake v Candy* [2017] EWHC 3397 (Ch), [408] if pressure is not illegitimate for the purposes of the law of duress, it is equally not undue influence for the purposes of the equitable doctrine of undue influence.

More difficult is the case where the actual undue influence takes a form other than the application of illegitimate pressure. It seems clear that cases of actual undue influence extend beyond 'pressure' cases. Thus Lord Hobhouse in *Etridge* defined actual undue influence as 'an equitable wrong committed by the dominant party against the other which makes it unconscionable for the dominant party to enforce his legal rights against the other'. This broader notion of actual undue influence would appear to encompass cases in which the claimant can prove that the defendant has in fact taken advantage of, or abused, a relationship of trust that existed between the parties. In this example it may be the case that the claimant must also prove that the transaction cannot be accounted for by ordinary motives because of the strong resemblance that exists between this case and a case of presumed undue influence.

17.3.2   Presumed undue influence

Cases of presumed undue influence are even more problematic. Until recently, the presumption was regularly invoked in litigation in the courts. But the House of Lords in *Etridge* has introduced a note of caution into this area of the law and has, in effect, discouraged too much reliance upon the presumption of undue influence. This scepticism in relation to the utility of the presumption was particularly apparent in the speech of Lord Clyde. He stated that 'there is … room for uncertainty whether the presumption is of the existence of an influence or of its quality as being undue', and he stated that 'at the end of the day, after trial, there will either be proof of undue influence or that proof will fail and it will be found that there was no undue influence'. In other words, lawyers must pay careful regard to the facts and circumstances of the case and to the proof of the matters alleged by the claimant and they ought not to hide these matters behind so-called 'presumptions'. But it does not follow from this that the 'presumption' of undue influence has been abandoned.

It has been retained but it is now clear that it takes the form of a shift in the evidential onus of proof (and that the presumption is generally one of influence and not abuse). Thus Lord Nicholls stated that 'proof that the complainant placed trust and confidence in the other party in relation to the management of the complainant's financial affairs, coupled with a transaction which calls for explanation, will normally be sufficient, failing satisfactory evidence to the contrary, to discharge the burden of proof'.

This being the case, there would appear to be three elements to a case of 'presumed undue influence' (in so far as this terminology can still safely be used). First, the claimant must prove that he placed trust and confidence in the defendant in relation to the management of his affairs or that he was in a position of vulnerability or dependence in relation to the defendant. In the case of some relationships the law presumes the existence of a relationship of trust and confidence. Thus in *Etridge* Lord Nicholls stated that there are certain relationships where 'the law presumes, irrebuttably, that one party had influence over the other' (and this 'irrebuttable presumption' must be distinguished from the evidential nature of the presumption of undue influence, see *Etridge* at [18]). Relationships within this class are 'parent and child, guardian and ward, trustee and beneficiary, solicitor and client, and medical adviser and patient'. The presumption may also arise between a spiritual adviser and disciple (*Curtis v Curtis* [2011] EWCA Civ 1602; [2012] All ER (D) 46 (Jan)). The relationship of husband and wife is not, however, within this category. In cases outside this category the claimant must prove that he actually reposed trust and confidence in the defendant.

Secondly, the claimant must prove that the transaction 'calls for explanation'. This is the reformulation of the 'manifest disadvantage' requirement which first made its appearance in the speech of Lord Scarman in *National Westminster Bank plc v Morgan* [1985] AC 686. Lord Nicholls in *Etridge* noted that 'experience has ... shown that this expression [i.e. manifest disadvantage] can give rise to misunderstanding' and has been 'causing difficulty'. He therefore returned to the test originally adopted by Lindley LJ in *Allcard v Skinner* (1887) 36 Ch D 145, 185, namely whether the gift is so large that it cannot be accounted for on the ground of friendship, relationship, charity or other ordinary motives on which ordinary men act. It may be that this departure from the language of 'manifest disadvantage' will have little effect in practice. It may be a change of label rather than substance. The courts are simply seeking a label that will serve to denote a transaction or a gift that calls for an explanation. As Lord Nicholls observed, it:

> would be absurd for the law to presume that every gift by a child to a parent, or every transaction between a client and his solicitor or between a patient and his doctor, was brought about by undue influence unless the contrary is affirmatively proved. Such a presumption would be too far-reaching. The law would be out of touch with everyday life if the presumption were to apply to every Christmas or birthday gift by a child to a parent, or to an agreement whereby a client or patient agrees to be responsible for the reasonable fees of his legal or medical adviser. The law would be rightly open to ridicule, for transactions such as these are unexceptionable. They do not suggest that something may be amiss. So something more is needed before the law reverses the burden of proof, something which calls for an explanation. When that something more is present, the greater the disadvantage to the vulnerable person, the more cogent must be the explanation before the presumption will be regarded as rebutted.

The third stage in a case of presumed undue influence will generally consist of the defendant's attempt to rebut the inference of undue influence that has arisen from proof by the claimant of the existence (actual or presumed) of a relationship of trust and confidence and a transaction which requires explanation. There is no finite list of the ways in which the presumption can be rebutted. For example, it may be rebutted by showing that the donor acted independently of any influence of the recipient and with full appreciation of what he was doing. The most usual, although not the only way of rebutting the presumption, is to show that the donor had competent and independent advice before acting. But the presumption may also be rebutted by showing that the act of the donor in making the gift had been a 'spontaneous and independent act' (*Re Brocklehurst* [1978] Ch 14). However, it will not suffice to rebut the presumption to show that there was a reasonable explanation for the transaction (*Smith v Cooper* [2010] EWCA Civ 722; [2010] 2 FLR 1521).

The general effect of *Etridge* may be to reduce the practical significance of the presumption of undue influence and to focus the attention of lawyers on the need for the claimant to prove his case (see *Annulment Funding Co Ltd v Cowey* [2010] EWCA Civ 711; [2010] All ER (D) 205 (Jun)). A claimant can prove a case of relational undue influence in one of two ways. Either he can prove that he reposed trust and confidence in the defendant and, where necessary, that the defendant abused or took advantage of that trust or he can prove the existence of a relationship of trust and confidence between himself and the defendant and a transaction that cannot be accounted for on ordinary motives, and the evidential burden will then shift to the defendant to rebut the inference of undue influence that has arisen. But in both cases the claimant must prove that undue influence has been exercised. The difference between the two cases is simply that, in the second case, 'the court has drawn appropriate inferences of fact upon a balanced consideration of the whole of the evidence at the end of a trial in which the burden of proof rested upon' the claimant.

17.3.3 The causal link

Finally, there must be a sufficient causal link between the undue influence and the decision to enter into the impugned transaction but the influence need not have been the 'principal reason' for entry into the transaction (*UCB Corporate Services Ltd v Williams* [2002] EWCA Civ 555; [2002] 3 FCR 448). The causal test would appear to be weakest where there has been some fraudulent act on the part of the stronger party and in general it would appear that it must be established that the undue influence was 'part of the process' by which consent was obtained (*The Libyan Investment Authority v Goldman Sachs International* [2016] EWHC 2530 (Ch), [157]–[158]).

17.4 Inequality of bargaining power

The issue whether a doctrine of inequality of bargaining power exists in English law has been one of some controversy. The primary source of this controversy lies in the seminal judgment of Lord Denning in *Lloyds Bank v Bundy* [1975] QB 326. The facts of the case were, in many ways, unremarkable. Mr Bundy, an elderly man not well versed in business affairs, gave his bank a guarantee regarding his son's business debts and mortgaged his house to the bank as security for the guarantee. In entering into this transaction Mr Bundy relied implicitly on his bank manager as his adviser, but the bank manager was also acting on behalf of the son, thereby creating a conflict of interest. When the bank sought to enforce the guarantee against old Mr Bundy and obtain possession of the house, Mr Bundy defended the action on the ground that the mortgage had been improperly obtained. The majority of the court decided the case on orthodox grounds, holding that the bank had failed to rebut the presumption of undue influence because they could not show that Mr Bundy had been independently advised. All this, however, was not for Lord Denning. He set out the following general principle:

> English law gives relief to one who without independent advice enters into a contract upon terms which are very unfair or transfers property for a consideration which is grossly inadequate, when his bargaining power is grievously impaired by reason of his own needs and desires, or by his own ignorance or infirmity, coupled with undue influence or pressures brought to bear on him by or for the benefit of the other.

Lord Denning envisaged that this new general principle would unify hitherto discrete areas of law and provide a basis for a solution to a wide range of problems. But it has since received a rather frosty reception in the appellate courts. In *Pao On v Lau Yiu Long* [1980] AC 614, Lord Scarman, giving the judgment of the Privy Council, said that agreements were not voidable simply because they had been 'procured by an unfair use of a dominant bargaining position'. A much more severe rebuff was handed out by Lord Scarman, giving the judgment of the House of Lords in *National Westminster Bank plc v Morgan* [1985] AC 686. He specifically disapproved of Lord Denning's principle of inequality of bargaining power and questioned whether there was any need for such a doctrine, given that Parliament, in statutes such as the Consumer Credit Act 1974, has undertaken the task of placing 'such restrictions upon freedom of contract as are necessary' to protect the most likely victims of inequality of bargaining power. As Rose J observed in *The Libyan Investment Authority v Goldman Sachs International* [2016] EWHC 2530 (Ch), [132] 'generally speaking the law will not intervene to save people from making improvident bargains'.

However, although Lord Denning's principle of inequality of bargaining power has been rejected, it should not be assumed that courts will stand by and allow the strong 'to push the weak to the wall' (*Alec Lobb (Garages) Ltd v Total Oil (GB) Ltd* [1985] 1 WLR 173, 183). Even in *National Westminster Bank v Morgan*, Lord Scarman recognised the existence of an equitable jurisdiction to grant relief against an unconscionable (or unfair) bargain. He refused to confine the jurisdiction of equity within rigid limits, saying that the 'court in the exercise of this equitable jurisdiction is a court of conscience'. Thus we find that equity intervenes to relieve against unconscionable bargains (*Earl of Chesterfield v Janssen* (1751) 2 Ves Sen 125), to set aside an agreement made with an expectant heir (*Earl of Aylesford v Morris* (1873) LR 8 Ch App 484), to set aside an improvident bargain made with a poor and ignorant person (*Cresswell v Potter* [1978] 1 WLR 255) and to grant relief where there has been an abuse of a relationship of confidence (*Demarara Bauxite Co Ltd v Hubbard* [1923] AC 673). The jurisdiction to set aside an improvident bargain made with a poor and ignorant person has been stated to be 'in good heart and capable of adaptation to different transactions entered into in changing circumstances' (*Credit Lyonnais Bank Nederland NV v Burch* [1997] 1 All ER 144, 151, per Nourse LJ) and examples can still be found of contracts set aside by the courts on the ground that they constitute unconscionable bargains (see, for example, *Boustany v Piggott* (1995) 69 P & CR 298). There are two principal objections to this development.

The first is that the failure of the courts to define the basis of their jurisdiction leads to uncertainty and inconsistency. Is the basis of these doctrines the inequality between the parties, the unfair nature of the terms, the knowing taking advantage of the weakness of another or some combination of these factors? It would appear that the answer is that the courts look for a combination of factors. The combination which was required by Blair J in *Strydom v Vendside Ltd* [2009] EWHC 2130 (QB); [2009] All ER (D) 135 (Aug), [36] was as follows: 'one party has to have been disadvantaged in some relevant way as regards the other party, that other party must have exploited that disadvantage in some morally culpable manner, and the resulting transaction must be overreaching and oppressive'. The advantage of this approach is its flexibility. The disadvantage is that it can generate uncertainty. An example of the uncertain state of the current law is provided by *Boustany v Piggott*, where the precise reason for the lease being set aside does not emerge from the advice of the Privy Council with any clarity. A further example is provided by the case of *Portman Building Society v Dusangh* [2000] 2 All ER (Comm) 221 where the Court of Appeal distinguished the decision in *Burch* and, in doing so, appeared to place greater emphasis on the need to show 'morally reprehensible' conduct on the part of a defendant before a claimant can set aside a transaction. This insistence on the need for some positive advantage-taking by the more powerful party has been the subject of some criticism on the ground that it fails to encompass the case in which the terms of the contract are substantively unfair and the claimant was, to the knowledge of the defendant, vulnerable but the defendant was a mere passive recipient of the benefit (see Capper, 2010). A restricted doctrine of unconscionability permits a defendant to benefit from the known vulnerability of the claimant provided that the defendant does not take active steps to procure the benefit in a manner which can be characterised as 'morally reprehensible'. On the other hand, to extend the scope of the doctrine to include the case of a 'passive recipient' may generate even more uncertainty.

The second objection is that, although there is no general principle of inequality of bargaining power, it remains to be seen how far these residual equitable doctrines will be resurrected to play the role which Lord Denning envisaged would be played by his doctrine of inequality of bargaining power. In this way the courts may achieve covertly what they refuse to do overtly and such subterfuge should not be encouraged in the law.

17.5 The role of Parliament

Parliament has also had a role to play in regulating contracts in an effort to protect the most likely victims of inequality of bargaining power. For the future, at least as far as consumers are concerned, that role will be played in large part by the Consumer Rights Act 2015 (on which see Chapter 18). Looking backwards, that role has been played by statutes such as the Consumer Credit Act 1974.

For example, section 140A of the latter Act gives to the court the power to make an order:

> if it determines that the relationship between the creditor and the debtor arising out of the agreement … is unfair to the debtor because of one or more of the following: (a) any of the terms of the agreement or of any related agreement; (b) the way in which the creditor has exercised or enforced any of his rights under the agreement or any related agreement; or (c) any other thing done (or not done) by, or on behalf of the creditor (either before or after the making of the agreement or any related agreement).

In *Plevin v Paragon Personal Finance Ltd* [2014] UKSC 61; [2014] 1 WLR 4222, [10] Lord Sumption noted that section 140A is 'deliberately framed in wide terms.' He identified the following 'general points' that are worthy of note. First, what must be unfair is the relationship between the debtor and the creditor. Second, that, although the court is concerned with hardship to the debtor, matters relating to the creditor or the debtor may be relevant to the court's inquiry. Third, the alleged unfairness must arise from one of the three categories of cause listed at sub-paragraphs (a) to (c). Finally, although the great majority of relationships between commercial lenders and private borrowers are probably characterised by large differences of financial knowledge and expertise and so are inherently unequal, it cannot have been Parliament's intention that the generality of such relationships should be liable to be reopened for that reason alone.

Section 140B confers broad powers on the courts in order to remedy the unfairness in the relationship between these parties. Thus they can, for example, order repayment of sums paid, reduce or discharge any sum payable by the debtor or alter the terms of the agreement.

Consumers have also been given rights of redress against traders in respect of certain forms of unfair commercial practices, including misleading and aggressive actions (which could encompass actions which amount to duress at law or undue influence in equity). The rights given to the consumer include the right to unwind the contract, the right to a discount and the right to damages (see Part 4A of the Consumer Protection from Unfair Trading Regulations 2008 (SI 2008/1277)). These rights are additional to the rights available to a consumer at common law or in equity but may not be exercised in combination with those rights.

Other examples of statutes enacted in an attempt to protect the most likely victims of inequality of bargaining power include the Unfair Contract Terms Act 1977 (on which see Chapter 11). Parliament has also intervened to regulate the employment relationship and the relationship between landlords and tenants in an effort to provide greater protection for employees and tenants (see Sections 1.2 and 1.3). But, as we have already noted, Lord Scarman in *National Westminster Bank plc v Morgan* [1985] AC 686 used the existence of such legislation as a justification for refusing to create a doctrine of inequality of bargaining power (contrast the approach of the Court of Appeal in *Timeload Ltd v British Telecommunications plc* [1995] EMLR 459, where section 3 of the Unfair Contract Terms Act was used as a 'platform' from which the court could reach out to regulate clauses which fell outside the ambit of the Act). But the better approach would surely have been to create such a doctrine and follow the policy being pursued by Parliament. Instead, the common law has been left pursuing an individualistic policy which is in opposition to the policies being pursued by Parliament in statutes such as the Consumer Credit Act 1974 and the Unfair Contract Terms Act 1977.

17.6 A general doctrine of unconscionability?

Despite the efforts of Parliament, any discussion of the desirability of a general doctrine of unconscionability may seem rather academic, given the rejection of Lord Denning's doctrine of inequality of bargaining power. At first sight, English contract law seems unconcerned with the fairness of the contract concluded by the parties. The courts have rejected a doctrine of inequality of bargaining power and, as we have already noted (Section 5.6), the general rule is that consideration must be sufficient but need not be adequate. Freedom of contract reigns and the adequacy of the consideration is irrelevant.

But, despite initial appearances to the contrary, the rules which make up English contract law are concerned with the fairness of the bargain reached by the parties. We have seen the hostility which the courts have displayed towards exclusion clauses, both in terms of the interpretative devices adopted (Section 11.5) and their reluctance to incorporate exclusion clauses and other onerous clauses into a contract (Section 9.4). Innominate terms (Section 10.5) were created to give the courts greater remedial flexibility, so that the injustice of cases such as *Arcos Ltd v E A Ronaasen & Son* [1933] AC 470 need no longer occur (see also Sale of Goods Act 1979, s 15A). We have also noted the protective attitude which the courts have adopted towards minors (see Section 16.2). Later in this book we shall see that the courts are reluctant to order specific performance of a contract which is unfair (Section 22.9), they have an equitable jurisdiction to grant relief against forfeiture (Section 22.7) and they have developed a penalty clause jurisdiction, under which a court will not enforce a term of a contract which requires a party who is in breach of contract to pay a sum of money which is extravagant or unconscionable in comparison with the legitimate interest of the innocent party (Section 22.6). Surely, conceptions of fairness must underpin, to a greater or lesser extent, these rules and doctrines (see Waddams, 1976). If these conceptions of fairness permeate the law of contract, would it not be better to acknowledge these considerations openly by the creation of a general doctrine of unconscionability?

Four principal objections can be raised against the creation of such a doctrine. The first is that the courts have difficulty in identifying contracts which are unfair because the adversarial nature of litigation does not make it easy for them to set the transaction which is before them in the context of the market in which the parties are operating. A fuller understanding of that market may suggest that the transaction is not, in fact, unfair (see Trebilcock, 1976). The second is that such a general doctrine would create an unacceptable degree of uncertainty. The third is that English law has a general aversion to the creation of broad, general principles; the courts in particular prefer to reason incrementally and by analogy to existing categories rather than by reference to a general, overarching principle. The fourth is that it is not the function of contract law to engage in the redistribution of wealth (Fried, 1981, contrast Kronman, 1980 who defends 'the view that the rules of contract law should be used to implement distributional goals whenever alternative ways of doing so are likely to be more costly or intrusive').

These are powerful objections to the creation of such a general doctrine. But they are not necessarily conclusive. We have already noted (Section 1.3) the conflicting ideologies which run through the law of contract and it is here that market-individualism and consumer-welfarism are in conflict (although contrast Tiplady, 1983). Given that these conceptions of fairness run throughout the law of contract, they cannot be dismissed as an insignificant aspect of contract law. Although Parliament must continue to play the principal role in regulating the economy and placing necessary restrictions upon freedom of contract, a residual role can nevertheless be played by the courts and that role can best be recognised by the creation of a general doctrine of unconscionability. Uncertainty can be reduced by the recognition of the fact that unfairness can take different forms. Broadly speaking, two types of unfairness can be recognised. The first may be called procedural unfairness and the second substantive unfairness (although it should be noted that the distinction between the two has been doubted by Atiyah (1986d), who maintains that the two 'feed upon each other'). The first is concerned with the process by which the contract is negotiated. The second is concerned with the fairness of the terms or the substance of the contract. It is easier to identify the procedural tactics which are unacceptable as part of the process of contractual negotiation than it is to define substantive unfairness (see Thal, 1988). It is also easier to provide a sound justification for the law's concern with the fairness by which the contract was concluded than it is to identify the principle which explains why the law is concerned with the fairness of the terms of the contract (but see Smith, 1996). Unacceptable tactics might include threats to commit a crime, a tort or a breach of contract and the courts might recognise that there are certain bargaining weaknesses, such as infirmity and necessity, which should not be exploited. More difficulty is experienced in defining substantive unfairness; all that can be said is that it should only be a ground of relief in the very rare case where the consideration is manifestly and totally inadequate and that the courts must be left to work out the principles on a case-by-case basis. Such a narrowly drawn doctrine of unconscionability would not create an unacceptable level of uncertainty, but it would prevent injustice arising in the few cases in which it was needed.

Hot topic 15...

Should lawful acts ever constitute illegitimate pressure for the purpose of the doctrine of economic duress? This issue was most recently considered by the Court of Appeal in *Times Travel (UK) ltd v Pakistan International Airlines Corporation* [2019] EWCA Civ 828; [2020] Ch 98. The claimant travel agents sought to set aside an agreement into which they had entered with the defendant airline. The claimants' business consisted almost entirely of the sale of tickets for flights to Pakistan, and the defendant was, at the time, the only carrier who flew direct between the UK and Pakistan. The claimants alleged that they had been pressurised by the defendant to enter into an agreement not to participate as claimants in proceedings brought against the defendant by other travel agents in the Association of Pakistani Travel Agents and instead to enter into a fresh agreement with the defendant. Under this new agreement the claimants agreed to give up all accrued claims for commission under the previous contractual arrangements between the parties.

The Court of Appeal held that the claimants were not entitled to set aside this agreement on the ground that they had entered into it as a result of the application of economic duress. The pressure applied by the defendant was held in all respects to be lawful. It was neither a breach of contract nor a tort or other actionable wrong or an offence for the defendant to reduce the claimants' ticket allocation, to give notice of termination of the existing contractual arrangements between the parties or to insist on the inclusion of the waiver of past claims in the new agreement.

It was therefore held that the claimants had not established a case of economic duress because the pressure applied by the defendant was lawful and the claimants had not demonstrated that the defendant did not have a genuine belief in its entitlement to take the steps which it had taken.

The Supreme Court has given the claimants leave to appeal and the appeal was heard in November 2020. The Supreme Court will therefore be given the opportunity to decide whether or not English law recognises a principle of lawful act duress and, if it does, the scope of any such principle. The Court of Appeal sought to strike a careful balance which recognised the principle but sought to confine it within narrow limits. The Supreme Court could affirm the decision of the Court of Appeal or it could depart from it. And it could depart from it in one of two principal ways: either by rejecting any role for lawful act duress or by giving it a more expansive role which encompasses a case in which the party applying the pressure has no reasonable grounds for holding the view that it was entitled to apply the pressure which it did. The outcome of the case is keenly awaited.

Summary

▶ A contract may be set aside on the ground of duress. The duress may be to the person, to his goods or economic duress.

▶ Duress can be shown to exist where the consent of the victim has been obtained by the application of illegitimate pressure.

▶ Undue influence is an equitable doctrine. Actual undue influence may consist of the application of illegitimate pressure but it also extends to other forms of wrongdoing.

▶ The essence of presumed undue influence is that one party has taken advantage of a relationship of trust and confidence to the substantial detriment of the party who has reposed trust and confidence in him. The presumption is no more than a shift in the evidential onus of proof and it arises where the claimant proves: (i) the existence of a relationship of trust and confidence and (ii) a transaction that is not explicable in terms of the ordinary motives on which ordinary people act. The presumption is a rebuttable one. It can be rebutted by showing that entry into the transaction was the result of the free exercise of an independent will by the party seeking to set aside the transaction.

▶ English law does not recognise the existence of a general doctrine of inequality of bargaining power. But equity may intervene to set aside unconscionable bargains, agreements made with expectant heirs, improvident bargains made with poor and ignorant persons and contracts procured by an abuse of a relationship of confidence.

▶ Parliament has also intervened, in statutes such as the Consumer Credit Act 1974 and the Unfair Contract Terms Act 1977, in an effort to protect the most likely victims of inequality of bargaining power.

Exercises

17.1 A threatens B that he (A) will shoot the next person he sees unless B pays him £10. B pays the £10. Can he recover it? Would your answer be the same if A had threatened to burn one of B's old family heirlooms unless he paid the £10?

17.2 What is the relationship between the doctrines of consideration and duress? (See *Stilk v Myrick* (1809) 2 Camp 317 and 6 Esp 129 (Section 5.11) and *D & C Builders v Rees* [1966] 2 QB 617.)

17.3 What is 'economic duress'? What are its limits?

17.4 What is 'undue influence'? How does it differ from duress?

17.5 Does English law recognise the existence of a doctrine of inequality of bargaining power? Should it?

17.6 Do you think that the courts are concerned with the fairness of the bargain reached by the parties?

17.7 An old lady is 'induced by her solicitor under strong pressure to sell him a large and inconvenient family home at full market value'. Can the transaction be set aside by the old lady? If so, on what grounds?

Chapter 18

Unfair terms in consumer contracts

Having examined the extent to which English contract law recognises a general doctrine of unconscionability (see Section 17.6) and noted some examples of legislative provisions which have a role to play in regulating contracts in an effort to protect the most likely victims of inequality of bargaining power (see Section 17.5), it is now time to examine Part 2 of the Consumer Rights Act 2015 which is entitled 'Unfair Terms' and, as its title suggests, it regulates unfair terms in consumer contracts concluded between a consumer and a trader. Thus section 62(1) of the Act provides that 'an unfair term of a consumer contract is not binding on the consumer'. This apparently straightforward statement contains within it a number of difficult issues. What, for this purpose, is a 'consumer contract'? When is a term in such a contract 'unfair'? What does it mean to say that a term is not 'binding' on the consumer? In seeking to answer these questions it is important to set Part 2 of the Act in its context and to examine its origins and its predecessors.

18.1 The background to the Act

The origins of Part 2 of the Consumer Rights Act 2015 are to be found in a European Directive on Unfair Terms in Consumer Contracts (93/13/EEC). The transposition of the Directive into domestic law has proved to be somewhat problematic. Part 2 of the Consumer Rights Act represents the third attempt by the UK to implement the Directive into domestic law. The first attempt is to be found in the Unfair Terms in Consumer Contracts Regulations 1994 (SI 1994/3159) which came into force on 1 July 1995 (although the Directive itself came into force on 1 January 1995). The 1994 Regulations were subsequently revoked by the Unfair Terms in Consumer Contracts Regulations 1999 (SI 1999/2083) which in turn came into force on 1 October 1999. The 1999 Regulations have now been revoked by Part 2 of the Consumer Rights Act.

18.1.1 The drafting of the Directive

The European origin of the legislation is important for a number of reasons. The first is that the drafting of the original Directive is not a model of clarity and has been the subject of a number of criticisms (see Hartley, 1996). Unfortunately, Parliament has not always been willing to grapple with these difficulties. Indeed, the 1999 Regulations adopted a technique known as the 'copy-out' technique so that the Regulations largely copied out the text of the Directive without attempting to remove the ambiguities or deal with difficulties of interpretation. This approach has advantages in so far as it minimises the potential liability of the State for failure to implement the Directive properly and, in not departing from the text of the Directive, it appears to promote the cause of uniformity in Europe. But this approach also had its disadvantages in so far as it has at times left the law in an unsatisfactory state and triggered litigation the outcome of which was difficult to predict.

18.1.2 The approach to interpretation

The second point of significance which flows from the fact that the legislation has been enacted in implementation of a European Directive relates to the approach which should be adopted when seeking to interpret the legislation. Domestic legislation has traditionally been interpreted literally, with close attention being paid to the precise words which Parliament has chosen to use, and rather less emphasis is placed on the purpose or spirit behind the legislation. In contrast, the Court of Justice of the European Union ('CJEU') adopts a much more purposive or teleological approach to interpretation which, at times, seems to do some violence to the words which have actually been used in the texts that are being interpreted. An English lawyer must therefore learn to approach the interpretation of the legislation with a less finely tuned linguistic fork and pay greater attention to the purposes which lie behind the Directive and to the other language versions of the Directive. An illustration of this point is provided by a question which arose initially under the 1994 Regulations, namely whether they applied to contracts for the sale of land. At first sight the answer seemed to be 'no' because the Regulations referred only to sellers and suppliers of 'goods' or 'services', and land, as far as English lawyers are generally concerned, is neither a good nor a service. The reference to 'goods' and 'services' was then deleted in the 1999 Regulations but their deletion did not have the necessary consequence that land thereafter fell within the scope of the Regulations. The Regulations were simply silent on the point. But the French text of the Directive uses the words 'vendeur de biens', words which can encompass a seller of both movable and immovable property. The French text therefore includes land and it would have undermined the goal of uniformity if the Directive were to apply to contracts for the sale of land in France but not to contracts for the sale of land in the United Kingdom. The Court of Appeal in *London Borough of Newham v Khatun* [2004] EWCA Civ 55; [2005] QB 37, after referring to the background to the Directive and to the use of the word 'biens' in the French text, concluded that the Directive and the Regulations do apply to contracts relating to land and the same conclusion now follows under Part 2 of the Consumer Rights Act. In other cases the UK courts have been criticised for their unwillingness to adopt a purposive approach and instead have placed greater emphasis on a careful construction of the wording of the text (see, in particular, the decision of the Supreme Court in *Office of Fair Trading v Abbey National plc* [2009] UKSC 6; [2010] 1 AC 696, discussed below, which has been criticised on the ground that it took a rather literal approach to the interpretation of the provision in dispute and gave insufficient attention to the purpose of the Directive).

18.1.3 The role of the CJEU

The third point relates to the role of the CJEU in the interpretation of the Directive. There are two issues here. The first relates to the obligation of national courts to make a reference to the CJEU under Article 267 of the Treaty on the Functioning of the European Union if a decision on the correct interpretation of the Directive is necessary to enable the court to give judgment and the matter is not *acte clair*. Both the House of Lords and the Supreme Court have declined to make a reference in cases concerned with the interpretation of the Regulations/Directive, and their failure to do so has been the subject of some criticism (see Dean, 2002). The second concerns the extent to which the CJEU will see fit to conclude that certain words or phrases in the Directive have an 'autonomous' or 'independent' meaning to be established by the Court. In *VB Pénzügyi Lizing Zrt v Ferenc Schneider* (Case C-137/08); [2011] 2 CMLR 1 the CJEU affirmed that its jurisdiction extended to the interpretation of 'unfair term' in Article 3(1) of the Directive and that it could also determine the criteria which a national court may or must apply when assessing the fairness of a contractual term. It is then for the national court to apply these criteria to the facts of the case and to decide whether a particular contract term is or is not 'unfair' (see also *Kásler v OTP Jelzálogbank Zrt* Case C-26/13; [2014] 2 All ER (Comm) 443). The interpretation of the Directive and the Regulations has therefore been a partnership between the CJEU and national courts.

The form of this partnership has, of course, changed now that the UK has left the EU. First, section 6(1)(b) of the European Union (Withdrawal) Act 2018 provides that a court or tribunal in the UK will not be able to refer any matter to the CJEU on or after 'exit day' (which has now been extended through to the end of the transition period on 31 December 2020). Second, the authority of the case law of the CJEU has been altered. Decisions of the CJEU made on or after the end of the transition period will not be binding on UK courts or tribunals, although UK courts or tribunals in their discretion may have regard to such decisions in so far as they are relevant to any matter before them (s 6(1)(a) and (2) of the European Union (Withdrawal) Act 2018). Judicial comity would seem to require that some weight be given to the decisions of the CJEU but, in the post-Brexit world, the courts may come under pressure to plough their own furrow and assert their independence from the CJEU. In relation to decisions of the CJEU which pre-date the end of the transition period, they will continue to carry authority as now with the exception of the Supreme Court who will no longer be bound by any retained EU case law and, when deciding whether to depart from any retained EU case law, it must apply the same test as it would apply when deciding whether or not to depart from its own case law (s 6(3) and (4)).

18.1.4 The means chosen to implement the Directive

A significant criticism of the means chosen to implement the Directive into English law was that no attempt was made initially to integrate either the 1994 or the 1999 Regulations with existing legislation (in particular, the Unfair Contract Terms Act 1977 (UCTA), on which see Sections 11.9–11.15). The decision not to attempt integration created some confusion because there were important differences between UCTA, on the one hand, and the 1994 and the 1999 Regulations on the other hand. The most important one for present purposes is that UCTA is confined in its application to particular types of clause (essentially exclusion and limitation clauses, see Section 11.15), while the Regulations were not confined to any particular type of term in a consumer contract. Thus, the jurisdictional problems which we noted under UCTA (see, for example, Section 11.10) did not arise under the Regulations. But the co-existence of UCTA and the Regulations did create some difficulties and apparent inconsistencies. For example, paragraph 1(a) of Schedule 2 to the 1999

Regulations gave as an example of a term which was indicatively unfair, a term which had the object or effect of 'excluding or limiting the legal liability of a seller or supplier in the event of the death of a consumer or personal injury to the latter resulting from an act or omission of that seller or supplier' notwithstanding the fact that section 2(1) of UCTA provides that any attempt to exclude or restrict business liability for death or personal injury caused by negligence is of no effect (see Section 11.10). Thus such a term was void by virtue of section 2(1) of UCTA but was only indicatively unfair as far as the Regulations (a subsequent statutory instrument) were concerned. While it was highly unlikely that a court would have taken the view that the Regulations had impliedly repealed section 2(1) of UCTA (see Reynolds, 1994), the procedure adopted by Parliament had little to commend it.

It was the desire to produce a more coherent set of rules that led the Law Commission and the Scottish Law Commission (2005) to recommend that the Regulations and UCTA be replaced by a single, unified regime. This recommendation has not been enacted in the form originally envisaged by the Law Commissions but there is little doubt that the work of the Law Commissions has been extremely influential in relation to the enactment of Part 2 of the Consumer Rights Act. Rather than produce a single, unified regime, the approach which has been adopted is to take consumer contracts out of UCTA, leaving the latter to deal principally with contracts concluded between parties both of whom are acting in the course of a business. The regulation of unfair terms in consumer contracts will henceforth be governed by Part 2 of the Consumer Rights Act and not by UCTA. Having set out the background to Part 2, we shall now turn to consider its principal provisions.

18.2 What is a consumer contract?

Part 2 of the Act applies to a contract between a 'trader' and a 'consumer' (s 61(1)). A trader is defined in section 2(1) of the Act as a 'person acting for purposes relating to that person's trade, business, craft or profession, whether acting personally or through another person acting in the trader's name or on the trader's behalf' (which definition is applicable to Part 2 of the Act by virtue of s 76(2)). A 'business' for this purpose includes the activities of any government department or local or public authority (s 2(7)). The definition of trader is therefore wide enough to encompass charities and other not-for-profit organisations where they are acting for the purpose of their business in, for example, selling goods to the general public.

A 'consumer' is defined in section 2(3) as 'an individual acting for purposes that are wholly or mainly outside the individual's trade, business, craft or profession' (which definition is applicable to Part 2 of the Act by virtue of s 76(2)). There are a number of points to note here. The first is that a consumer must be an 'individual'. A company cannot, for this purpose, claim to be a consumer (in this respect differing from the approach which had been taken in the now repealed section 12 of UCTA). Second, the definition of a consumer is broad. An individual will be a consumer provided that he or she was acting for purposes 'wholly or mainly' outside his or her trade, business, craft or profession. The words 'wholly or mainly' have been added into the Act and were not to be found in the previous Regulations, nor are they contained in the Directive itself. The principal effect of the extension will be, for example, to permit an individual who purchases a computer which is used occasionally for business purposes to claim the protection of Part 2 of the Act. Third, it is for a trader to prove that an individual was not acting for purposes wholly or mainly outside the individual's trade, business, craft or profession (s 2(4)). Fourth, the Act excludes certain contracts entered into by consumers from its scope. Thus section 61(2) provides that contracts of employment or apprenticeship do not fall within the scope of Part 2. However, the Act does include within its scope a 'consumer notice' which is defined as a notice which relates to rights or obligations as between a trader and a consumer or which purports to exclude or restrict a trader's liability to a consumer (s 61(4)).

Both the Regulations and the Directive contained a further requirement which had to be satisfied before a term could be challenged on the ground that it was unfair. That requirement was that the term in the contract must not have been 'individually negotiated'. A term was not individually negotiated where it had been drafted in advance and the consumer had therefore not been able to influence the substance of the term (see regulation 5(2) of the 1999 Regulations and Article 3(2) of the Directive). This requirement has now been removed so that the consumer is entitled to claim the protection of Part 2 even when the term has been individually negotiated with the trader. It is difficult to assess the significance of this extension. While consumers may well seek to negotiate the price that is payable, it is less likely that they will seek to negotiate the type of term likely to fall within the scope of Part 2. But, where they do, the term will still fall within the scope of Part 2 and the fact that the term has been negotiated will only be of relevance in so far as it is a factor which may be relied upon by the trader for the purpose of demonstrating that the term was fair.

18.3 When is a contract term unfair?

The core of the legislation is to be found in the definition of 'unfair term' which is contained in section 62(4) in the following terms:

> A term is unfair if, contrary to the requirement of good faith, it causes a significant imbalance in the parties' rights and obligations under the contract, to the detriment of the consumer.

A virtually identical test is applied to a consumer notice (see s 62(6)). It can be seen that there are two key components to the definition of an 'unfair term'. The first is that the term must cause a 'significant imbalance' in the rights and obligations of the parties to the detriment of the consumer and the second is that a term is unfair if it is 'contrary to the requirement of good faith'. What is the relationship between these two components? Earlier drafts of the Directive distinguished clearly between significant imbalance and incompatibility with the requirement of good faith: they were alternative rather than cumulative grounds of unfairness. Thus, a draft of the Directive stated that a contract term was unfair if:

> it causes to the detriment of the consumer a significant imbalance in the parties' rights and obligations arising under the contract, or

> it causes the performance of the contract to be unduly detrimental to the consumer, or

> it causes the performance of the contract to be significantly different from what the consumer could legitimately expect, or

> it is incompatible with the requirements of good faith.

But in the final version of the Directive and the Act, the test appears to be cumulative. In *Director General of Fair Trading v First National Bank plc* [2001] UKHL 52; [2002] 1 AC 481 the House of Lords emphasised both elements in the equation so that a consumer will have to show both an absence of good faith and significant imbalance before a court will conclude that a term is 'unfair', albeit that, as Lord Steyn observed, there is a 'large area of overlap between the concepts of good faith and significant imbalance' (see also *UK Housing Alliance (North West) Ltd v Francis* [2010] EWCA Civ 117; [2010] 3 All ER 519, [21]).

18.3.1 Good faith

The reference to 'the requirement of good faith' had the potential to be problematic for English lawyers because, as we have already noted (see Section 12.10), good faith is not a standard which is generally employed in English contract law, although it is more familiar to our civilian counterparts. Nevertheless, the House of Lords in *Director General of Fair Trading v First National Bank* (above) did not experience undue difficulty in giving a meaning to the words 'good faith' when called upon to interpret the 1994 Regulations. They emphasised its connection to fair and open dealing and it is likely that the courts will use the good faith standard in order to promote fair and open dealing, to create an expectation that the trader will draw the existence of the term and its principal effects to the consumer and to prevent unfair surprise (see *West v Ian Finlay & Associates (a firm)* [2014] EWCA Civ 316; [2014] BLR 324, [58]). To similar effect the CJEU in *Aziz v Caixa d'Estalvis de Catalunya, Tarragona i Manresa (Catalunyacaixa)* (C-415-11); [2013] 3 CMLR 5 stated that, when seeking to decide whether the imbalance has arisen contrary to the requirement of good faith, the court must consider whether the seller or supplier, dealing fairly and equitably with the consumer, could reasonably have assumed that the consumer would agree to the term had they been the subject of individual contract negotiations. The 1994 Regulations contained some further guidance as to the meaning of 'good faith'. Schedule 2 to these Regulations stated that in making an assessment of good faith particular regard should be had to the strength of the bargaining positions of the parties, whether the consumer had an inducement to agree to the term, whether the goods or services were sold or supplied to the special order of the consumer, and the extent to which the seller or supplier had dealt fairly and equitably with the consumer. These factors bore a strong resemblance to the factors taken into account by the courts when assessing the reasonableness of an exclusion clause under UCTA and so had a familiar resonance for English lawyers. However Schedule 2 to the 1994 Regulations was deleted from the 1999 Regulations and has not been re-enacted in the Consumer Rights Act. This does not mean that these factors are no longer relevant. They are all mentioned in the preamble to the Directive and so a court may still make reference to them notwithstanding the fact that they no longer appear on the face of the Act.

18.3.2 Significant imbalance

In relation to the meaning of 'significant imbalance', it should be noted that it is not sufficient to show that there is an imbalance. It is necessary to go further and show that the imbalance is 'significant' (*Office of Fair Trading v Ashbourne Management Services Ltd* [2011] EWHC 1237 (Ch); [2011] ECC 31, [174]). This reference to imbalance is clearly directed towards substantive unfairness (that is, unfairness in the terms or the substance of the contract) rather than procedural unfairness (that is, unfairness in the procedure by which the contract was concluded). As Lord Bingham observed in *Director General of Fair Trading v First National Bank,* [17] the requirement of significant imbalance 'is met if a term is so weighted in favour of the supplier as to tilt the parties' rights and obligations under the contract significantly in his favour'.

18.3.3 How do the courts decide whether a term is unfair?

However, the inquiry into the fairness of a term does not depend entirely on the meaning of the words 'significant imbalance' and 'contrary to the requirement of good faith'. Further guidance can be derived from section 62(5) which states that the fairness of a contract term shall be assessed 'taking into account the nature of the subject matter of the contract' and 'by reference to all the circumstances existing when the term was agreed and to all of the other terms of the contract or of any other contract on which it depends'. It should be noted that the time at which the assessment is to be conducted is the time at which the term was agreed, not the time at which it is challenged. But these tests are set at a high level of abstraction and will not easily yield predictable results when applied to the facts of individual cases. Rather more concrete guidance may be gleaned from the following two sources.

The first is to be found in Part 1 of Schedule 2 to the Act which provides 'an indicative and non-exhaustive list of terms of consumer contracts that may be regarded as unfair' for the purposes of Part 2 of the Act (s 63(1)). It should be noted that inclusion in the list does not mean that the term is unfair. It only means that it may be unfair: in this sense it is a grey list rather than a black list. The grey list goes beyond attempts to exclude or limit liability for negligence or breach of contract and encompasses, for example, terms which purport to make 'disproportionately high' sums payable by the consumer who fails to fulfil his obligations under the contract, terms which enable the trader to alter the terms of the contract unilaterally without a valid reason which is specified in the contract, and terms which have the effect of irrevocably binding the consumer to terms with which he had no real opportunity of becoming acquainted before the conclusion of the contract. The legislation therefore has a broad reach and its reach was broadened with the enactment of the Consumer Rights Act 2015, where the opportunity was taken to add three more contract terms to the grey list.

The second source is to be found in a number of decided cases in which the courts have considered what constitutes an unfair term. Although these cases were decided under the 1994 or the 1999 Regulations, the approach adopted in these cases would appear to be applicable under the 2015 Act given the similarity in language between the provisions. When deciding whether a term is or is not unfair, the identity of the party putting forward the term would appear to be of considerable significance. Where the term is put forward by the consumer, or by the consumer's professional advisers, the term is unlikely to be unfair (*Bryen & Langley Ltd v Boston* [2005] EWCA Civ 973; [2005] BLR 508), unless, perhaps, the adviser did not inform the consumer of the drawbacks of the clause. But where the term is put forward by the contractor, the term may be held to be unfair, although the inference is by no means inevitable. In such a case, a contractor must be prepared to assume the burden of proving the fairness of the term, and in particular that the term has been brought to the attention of the consumer and that the consumer has understood its implications. A court may be more willing to find that a term is not unfair where the consumer has substantial business experience and so should be expected to understand the significance of the term which he or she is seeking to challenge (*West v Ian Finlay & Associates (a firm)* [2014] EWCA Civ 316; [2014] BLR 324).

The leading case is the decision of the Supreme Court in *ParkingEye Ltd v Beavis* [2015] UKSC 67; [2016] AC 1172. The defendant parked his car in a car park operated by the claimant. There were signs at the car park which it was accepted were reasonably large, prominent and legible which provided that the maximum stay in the car park was 2 hours and that a failure to comply with the time limit would 'result in a Parking Charge of £85'. The defendant exceeded the time limit by 56 minutes but declined to pay the £85. When sued by the claimant he submitted that the term requiring him to pay this amount was an unfair term (within what was then the Unfair Terms in Consumer Contracts Regulations 1999). The Supreme Court held that the term was not unfair (and they also rejected the submission that it was a penalty clause, on which see Section 22.5). In so concluding, the majority of the Supreme Court held that the claimant had a legitimate interest in imposing a charge of this size in order to support its business model which enabled members of the public to park free of charge for up to two hours. Further, following *Aziz v Caixa d'Estalvis de Catalunya, Tarragona i Manresa (Catalunyacaixa)* (C-415-11); [2013] 3 CMLR 5, the majority held the claimant, dealing fairly and equitably with the consumer, could reasonably assume that the consumer would have agreed to the £85 charge. The majority conceded that there was an element of artificiality in relation to the proposition that there could be a negotiation with the consumer over access to the car park, but they nevertheless accepted that the reasonable motorist would have accepted an entitlement to two hours of free parking in return for a risk that he or she would be charged £85 if the two hour limit was exceeded. They also held that the notice displayed by the claimant was clear, the sum charged was not disproportionately high and it had not been imposed on the consumer contrary to the requirement of good faith. Lord Toulson dissented. He pointed out that £85 was by most people's standards 'a substantial sum of money' and he was not persuaded that the claimant had demonstrated that it had shown grounds for assuming that a party who was in a position to bargain individually, and who was advised by a competent lawyer, would have agreed to the £85 charge. But his was a minority view. The decision will come as a disappointment to many consumer groups who may see in the decision a reluctance on the part of the Supreme Court fully to protect the interests of consumers.

18.3.4 Sections 71 and 72

Section 71 of the Act provides that in relation to proceedings before a court which relate to a term of a consumer contract, the court must consider whether the term is fair even if none of the parties to the proceedings has raised the issue or indicated that it intends to do so provided that the court has before it sufficient legal and factual material to enable it to consider the fairness of the term. In this way a duty has been imposed upon the courts to consider the fairness of a term in a consumer contract. The intent here is to give effect to case law of the CJEU which has emphasised this proactive duty of the court so that the onus is not left entirely with the consumer, who may be unaware of his or her rights, to raise the point that the term which is in dispute between the parties may be unfair.

In order to reduce the possibility of evasion, section 72 of the Act provides for the application of Part 2 of the Act to 'secondary contracts' which comes into play where a term of a contract reduces the rights or remedies or increases the obligations of a person under another contract, which is defined as 'the main contract'. Take, for example, the case in which the manufacturer of a product includes a term in a direct contract with the consumer which purports to restrict the consumer's rights against the retailer who sells the goods to the consumer. In such a case the term of the secondary contract between the manufacturer and the consumer is subject to the controls to be found in Part 2 of the Act.

18.4　Exclusion from assessment of fairness

Not all terms in consumer contracts are subject to assessment for their fairness. Some terms are exempt from assessment. Thus Part 2 of the Consumer Rights Act is stated not to apply to a term of a contract, or to a notice, to the extent that it reflects mandatory statutory or regulatory provisions or the provisions or principles of an international convention to which the United Kingdom or the EU is a party (s 73). The reason for this exclusion is that, in such cases, the trader has no option but to include the term in its contract and it is therefore exempt from review.

18.4.1　The exclusion of core terms

The most difficult exemption in practice has proved to be the exemption that relates to what have been called the 'core terms' of the contract. These 'core terms' may be described broadly as terms which define the main subject-matter of the contract and which determine the price payable. While it may seem odd at first sight to exclude such 'core terms' from assessment in this way, it has been suggested that the object of the exemption is 'to exclude from assessment for fairness that part of the bargain that will be the focus of a customer's attention when entering into a contract' (*Office of Fair Trading v Abbey National plc* [2009]; [2009] UKSC 6; [2010] 1 AC 696, [79]). In other words, the aim behind the Directive is to prevent the 'unfair surprise' of the consumer. While consumers tend to be aware of the price of the goods or services and the definition of the main subject-matter of the contract provided that they are set out in clear terms, they tend to be unfamiliar with, and hence surprised by, the myriad of terms found in the small print of consumer contracts. It is the latter clauses, generally to be found in the small print of the contract, which are the subject of regulation. Although the general idea behind the exclusion can be readily understood, it has proved to be more difficult to translate it into a clear legal rule, as can be seen from the different ways in which the rule has been expressed and the litigation which the exemption has triggered in the courts. In seeking to explain the applicable rules we shall start with the Directive and then consider the evolution of its transposition into English law.

Article 4(2) of the Directive provides that:

> assessment of the unfair nature of the terms shall relate neither to the definition of the main subject matter of the contract nor to the adequacy of the price and remuneration, on the one hand, as against the services or goods supplied in exchange, on the other, in so far as these terms are in plain intelligible language.

Article 4(2) of the Directive was implemented into English law initially in Regulation 3(2) of the 1994 Regulations and then by Regulation 6(2) of the 1999 Regulations. The latter provided:

> In so far as it is in plain intelligible language, the assessment of fairness of a term shall not relate –
>
> (a) to the definition of the main subject matter of the contract, or
> (b) to the adequacy of the price or remuneration, as against the goods or services supplied in exchange.

The equivalent provision in the Consumer Rights Act is section 64(1) which provides that:

> A term of a consumer contract may not be assessed for fairness under section 62 to the extent that –
>
> (a) it specifies the main subject matter of the contract, or
> (b) the assessment is of the appropriateness of the price payable under the contract by comparison with the goods, digital content or services supplied under it.

Section 64(2) continues by providing that s 64(1) excludes a term from an assessment under section 62 only if it is 'transparent and prominent'. A term that is included in the grey list in Part 1 of Schedule 2 cannot fall within the scope of section 64.

Although expressed in slightly different language, the essence of these provisions is to exclude from review terms which define the main subject-matter of the contract or which determine the price as long as they are in plain intelligible language (or, to use the language of the Consumer Rights Act 2015, are transparent and prominent). Thus stated, there appear to be three issues to be resolved (although there is a degree of inter-relationship between them). The first relates to the identification of the term that is excluded from assessment (the term which defines the main subject-matter of the contract and the price term). The second relates to the nature of the exclusion from assessment: is it the case that the term is excluded from assessment entirely or is it only excluded from certain forms or types of assessment? The final issue relates to the requirement that the term be expressed in 'plain intelligible language' or that it be 'transparent and prominent'. We shall consider the first two issues in relation to the main subject matter of the contract and the price term before turning to the requirement that these terms be expressed in plain intelligible language or are transparent and prominent

18.4.2 The main subject matter of the contract

The first exclusion relates to terms which define or specify the 'main subject matter of the contract'. It can be seen that the language used in the Directive, the Regulations and the Consumer Rights Act in this context is virtually identical. In *Kásler v OTP*

Jelzálogbank Zrt (Case C-26/13); [2014] 2 All ER (Comm) 443 the CJEU held that this
exclusion encompassed those terms that 'lay down the essential obligations of the
contract and, as such characterise it' and not terms that are 'ancillary to those that
define the very essence of the contractual relationship'. The distinction between an
'essential' and an 'ancillary' term is a question of interpretation which requires the
court to examine the disputed term in its legal and factual context. But the fact that
we are here concerned with a 'derogation' from the general fairness test requires the
court to adopt a 'strict' construction of the exemption. A court can therefore be
expected to examine a contract term with some care in order to ascertain whether or
not it defines or specifies the main subject-matter of the contract. A term which is
held to fall within this category would appear to be an exempt term so that it cannot
be examined for unfairness at all (although contrast *Office of Fair Trading v Ashbourne
Management Services Ltd* [2011] EWHC 1237 (Ch); [2011] ECC 31, [153] where Kitchin
J held that the term was not exempt from any assessment of its fairness and that the
assessment which was precluded was one that related to 'the definition of the main
subject matter of the contract, that is to say its meaning, description and clarity').

18.4.3 The adequacy of the price

The second exclusion relates to the 'adequacy' or 'appropriateness' of the price or
remuneration 'as against' or 'by comparison with' the goods or services supplied in
exchange. The change from 'adequacy' to 'appropriateness' made in the Consumer
Rights Act is probably not a change of substance given that, as Lord Mance observed
in *Office of Fair Trading v Abbey National plc* [2009] UKSC 6; [2010] 1 AC 696, [94],
'adequacy' here means 'appropriateness or reasonableness (in amount)'. However,
the nature of this exemption and whether the term is excluded from assessment for
fairness in its entirety or is only excluded from certain forms of assessment has
proved to be an issue of some controversy. That controversy is best illustrated by
reference to the leading cases concerned with the interpretation of this particular
exemption.

The first such case is the decision of the House of Lords in *Director General of Fair
Trading v First National Bank plc* [2001] UKHL 52; [2002] 1 AC 481, [34] where Lord
Steyn stated that the definition of a 'core term' must be interpreted 'restrictively' so
that the main purpose of the scheme is not 'frustrated by endless formalistic arguments as to whether a provision is a definitional or an exclusionary provision'.
On the facts of *Director General of Fair Trading v First National Bank* the defendant
bank argued that a term in a loan agreement which provided that, should the customer default on repayments to the bank, the bank would be entitled to recover
from the customer the whole of the balance on the customer's loan account together
with outstanding interest and the costs of seeking judgment was part of the bank's
remuneration so that the court was not entitled to scrutinise the term in the name of
fairness. The House of Lords rejected this submission. Lord Bingham stated that the
term did not concern the adequacy of the interest earned by the bank as its remuneration but was designed to ensure that the bank's entitlement to interest did not
come to an end on the entry of judgment. It was not a term which expressed the
substance of the bargain between the parties. Rather it was a default provision
which was not directly related to the price charged for the loan or to its adequacy. It

was therefore no more than an incidental (possibly an important incidental) term of the agreement between the parties.

The second case is the decision of the Supreme Court in *Office of Fair Trading v Abbey National plc* [2009] UKSC 6; [2010] 1 AC 696, where the issue before the court concerned a number of terms in contracts between banks and their customers. In broad terms, the litigation raised the question whether the fairness of bank charges levied on personal current account holders in respect of what may be termed 'unauthorised overdrafts' could be challenged under the 1999 Regulations. To the surprise of many, the Supreme Court held that they could not be so challenged. It held that Regulation 6(2)(b) excluded from assessment not only 'essential' price or remuneration terms but that it extended to 'any monetary price or remuneration payable under the contract'. The width of this exclusion can be demonstrated by the outcome of the litigation itself. The Supreme Court held that the various bank charges constituted part of the price or remuneration for the banking services provided by the banks and, given that the terms were found to be in plain, intelligible language, any assessment of the fairness of those terms which related to their adequacy as against the services supplied was excluded by Regulation 6(2)(b). It was held that the words 'related to their adequacy as against the services supplied' are important because they emphasise the fact that it is not the term itself which is excluded from assessment. Instead, the term is excluded from certain forms of assessment (namely, on grounds of price/quality ratio) but can be subject to challenge on other grounds (for example, on the ground that it is unfair because of its other, discriminatory effects). The latter point is not unimportant given that it holds out the prospect that the terms could be open to challenge on grounds other than the price/quality ratio.

How can the decision in *Director General of Fair Trading v First National Bank* be reconciled with the decision of the Supreme Court in *Office of Fair Trading v Abbey National plc*? The answer given by the Supreme Court in *Office of Fair Trading v Abbey National plc* was that the term in question in *Director General of Fair Trading v First National Bank* was a 'default provision' ([43]) or concerned an 'ancillary payment' ([113]) which was not part of the price or remuneration for the goods or services to be supplied. However, notwithstanding these explanations, the line of distinction between the two cases is not at all clear. While in formal terms it may be possible to distinguish the two cases, it is more difficult to distinguish them in substantive terms. There was a fear that the spirit of *Director General of Fair Trading v First National Bank* had been undermined by the Supreme Court in *Office of Fair Trading v Abbey National plc* and that the decision in the latter case threatened to emasculate the legislation. The decision of the Supreme Court in *Abbey National* has been criticised on a number of grounds, principally: (i) it adopted a literal approach to the interpretation of the Regulations; (ii) it failed to pay sufficient attention to the purpose behind the Directive; (iii) it failed to protect consumers against unfair surprise; and (iv) the scope of the decision was not clear and it thus introduced considerable uncertainty into the law.

The third and final case is the decision of the CJEU in *Kásler v OTP Jelzálogbank Zrt* (Case C-26/13); [2014] 2 All ER (Comm) 443 where it was held that this exclusion was 'limited in scope' because it concerned 'only the adequacy of the price or remuneration as against the services or goods supplied in exchange' (see also *Matei v SC*

Volksbank România SA (Case C-143/13); [2015] 1 WLR 2385). Thus the exclusion is not of the term itself (as it is in the case of a term which defines the main subject-matter of the contract) but only an exclusion from certain forms of assessment, namely in relation to the 'adequacy of the price and the remuneration on the one hand as against the services or goods supplied on the other'. On this basis, a contract term, whether essential or ancillary, cannot be assessed for fairness by comparing the adequacy of the price against the services or goods supplied in exchange. If the term relates to aspects of the price other than the amount, such as the time at which payment is to be made, the term may be assessed for fairness provided that the amount of the price is not assessed as part of this process. The relationship between the decision of the Supreme Court in *Office of Fair Trading v Abbey National plc* and the jurisprudence of the CJEU is uneasy, with the CJEU seeming to take a more restrictive view of the exclusion than that taken by the Supreme Court. Given this apparent disparity, the submission was made in *Casehub Ltd v Wolf Cola Ltd* [2017] EWHC 1169 (Ch) that *Office of Fair Trading v Abbey National plc* had been wrongly decided and should not be followed. This submission was rejected because the court was bound by the decision of the Supreme Court (and doubt was also expressed as to whether the decisions of the CJEU had the effect for which the claimant contended). The decision of the Supreme Court in *Office of Fair Trading v Abbey National plc* therefore remains good law as a matter of English law.

18.4.4 Plain intelligible language

It is, however, important to remember that the term is only excluded from assessment if it is in 'plain intelligible language' (as required by the Directive) or is 'transparent and prominent' (as required by the Consumer Rights Act). The terminological change which was introduced in the Consumer Rights Act was heavily influenced by the work of the Law Commissions (2012 and 2013) who were asked to review the exclusion in Regulation 6(2) of the 1999 Regulations after the decision of the Supreme Court in *Office of Fair Trading v Abbey National plc*. Their conclusion was that the law should be simplified and that a price term should only be excluded from review if it is transparent and prominent. The essential idea was that if a term was transparent and prominent, it would be subject to competitive pressures (because consumers would be aware of the term and so better able to compare it with other terms on offer) and so should not be assessed for fairness. It was hoped that this explicit emphasis on 'prominence' would go some way to address the problem of the 'hidden price term' which qualified the headline price of the goods or services in a way that was detrimental to the consumer.

But it may be that this change is one of terminology rather than substance. The requirement that the term be transparent may be no more than another way of saying that the term must be in plain intelligible language. The requirement that the term be 'prominent' appears at first sight to be more demanding but may do no more than make explicit a requirement that was previously implicit in the plain intelligible language test. Further consideration of the significance of the change requires us first to give consideration to the phrase 'plain intelligible language'.

The requirement that the term be in plain intelligible language demands more than that the term be free from ambiguity. In this sense, it is not to be equated with the *contra proferentem* rule (on which see Sections 9.6 and 11.5). It requires that the term must be such as to enable the typical consumer to have a proper understanding of the term for sensible and practical purposes (*Office of Fair Trading v Abbey National plc* [2009] EWCA Civ 116; [2009] 2 WLR 1286). Not only must the actual wording be comprehensible to the consumer, but the typical consumer must be able to understand how the term affects the rights and obligations that he and the seller or supplier have under the contract. It is not, however, necessary that the consumer be put in a position to be able to make a fully informed choice about whether to enter into a contract on the standard terms of the seller or supplier. Further, the mere fact that there are inconsistencies in the document does not necessarily preclude a finding that the language of the term is plain and intelligible provided that the average consumer who read the document carefully would have no doubt as to the meaning of the term (*Office of Fair Trading v Ashbourne Management Services Ltd* [2011] EWHC 1237 (Ch); [2011] ECC 31, [158]). In *Kásler v OTP Jelzálogbank Zrt* (Case C-26/13); [2014] 2 All ER (Comm) 443 the CJEU held that the 'plain intelligible language' test requires 'not only that the relevant term should be grammatically clear and intelligible to the consumer, but also that the economic reasons for using that term and its relationship with other contractual terms should be clear and intelligible to him' so that the consumer 'is in a position to evaluate, on the basis of clear, intelligible criteria, the economic consequences for him which derive from it'.

Given the rather demanding nature of the 'plain intelligible language' test, the change in the Consumer Rights Act to 'transparent and prominent' may be more a change of nomenclature than a change of substance. A term is stated to be 'transparent' if it is expressed in plain and intelligible language and (in the case of a written term) is legible (section 64(3)). A term is 'prominent' if it is brought to the consumer's attention in such a way that the average consumer would be aware of the term (section 64(4)). An 'average consumer' for this purpose is one who is reasonably well-informed, observant and circumspect (section 64(5)). It can be seen that there are similarities between these definitions and the requirements of the plain intelligible language requirement, at least as set out in *Kásler*. Although the change may be largely one of terminology, it may be that English lawyers will find the labels 'transparent and prominent' easier to use than the 'plain intelligible language' test. As the Law Commissions stated (2013 at 3.16):

> the emphasis on prominence ... offers a practical way of distinguishing between a headline price and what are commonly thought of as incidental or ancillary terms. It also emphasises that whether a term is exempt is within the control of the trader. A trader may ensure that a price is exempt from review by making it prominent.

The aim here would appear to be to give the trader a choice. It can set out the price of the goods or services in a transparent and prominent way and in return will obtain exemption from the fairness test, at least in its application to that price term. It is then for the consumer to decide whether or not he or she wishes to enter into the contract on the terms offered or to shop elsewhere. Alternatively, the trader can seek to hide aspects of the price term or obfuscate them in some way. Such a trader may succeed in confusing the customer as to the actual price that he or she will pay for the goods or services but the risk which the trader runs in taking such a step is that the price term may be more likely to be reviewed for fairness.

18.5   Liabilities that cannot be excluded or restricted

The Consumer Rights Act also provides that there are certain liabilities that cannot be excluded either by a term of a consumer contract or by a consumer notice. One example, found in section 65, is that a trader cannot by a term of a consumer contract or by a consumer notice exclude or restrict liability for death or personal injury resulting from negligence. This is the consumer equivalent to section 2(1) of the Unfair Contract Terms Act 1977 (see Section 11.10). In most respects section 65 resembles section 2(1) of UCTA. Thus 'negligence' is defined as a breach of an obligation to take reasonable care or exercise reasonable skill in the performance of a contract, the breach of a common law duty to take reasonable care or exercise reasonable skill or the breach of the common law duty of care imposed by the Occupiers' Liability Act 1957 (s 65(4)). Personal injury is stated to include 'any disease and any impairment of physical or mental condition' (s 65(3)). An act is not prevented from being an act of negligence on the ground that the breach of duty was intentional rather than inadvertent, or because liability for it arose vicariously rather than directly (s 65(5)). However, the prohibition in section 65 does not apply to any contract of insurance or to a contract that relates to the creation or transfer of an interest in land (s 66(1)), nor does it affect the validity of any discharge or indemnity given by a person in consideration of the receipt by that person of compensation in settlement of any claim the person has (s 66(2)).

Other examples of liabilities that cannot be excluded or restricted are to be found in sections 31, 47 and 57 of the Consumer Rights Act. Taking section 31 as our example, it provides that a term of a contract to supply goods is not binding on the consumer to the extent that it would exclude or restrict the trader's liability arising under sections 9–17, 28 or 29 of the Act. So, for example, a trader cannot exclude liability to a consumer in respect of the supply of goods that are not of satisfactory quality (s 9), the supply of goods that are not fit for their purpose (s 10) or do not match their description (s 11).

18.6   The consequence of a finding that a term is unfair

Where a term is held to be unfair, the consequence is that it is 'not binding on the consumer' but 'the contract continues, so far as practicable, to have effect in every other respect' (s 67). In *Kásler v OTP Jelzálogbank Zrt* (Case C-26/13); [2014] 2 All ER (Comm) 443 it was held that a court may delete an unfair term from the contract and replace it with a supplementary provision drawn from national law. A court might be expected to do this where the deletion of the unfair term would have unfortunate consequences for the consumer and these consequences could be alleviated by inserting a rule drawn from the applicable national law which did not contain the unfairness found to be present in the deleted unfair contract term. Section 68 further states that a trader must ensure that a written term of a consumer contract, or a consumer notice in writing, is 'transparent' and transparency for this purpose means that the term is expressed in plain and intelligible language and is legible. If a term in a consumer contract, or a consumer notice, could have different meanings, the meaning that is most favourable to the consumer is to prevail (s 69(1)). The requirement that any doubt be resolved in favour of the consumer is probably no more than what English contract lawyers would call the *contra proferentem* rule (see Sections 9.6 and 11.5).

18.7 Enforcement

The enforcement provisions are also of considerable importance. Consumers tend to be reluctant to resort to litigation to enforce their rights and so some additional enforcement is necessary in order to give the legislation some bite (see s 70). The 1994 Regulations gave the Director General of Fair Trading power to intervene to prevent the continued use of unfair terms in consumer contracts and considerable use was made by the Office of Fair Trading of these powers (see Bright, 2000). But no other body was at that time given enforcement powers. Consumer bodies argued that this restriction constituted a failure to implement the Directive properly, and the government eventually gave way and agreed to increase the number of bodies with enforcement powers in the 1999 Regulations. The organisations to which enforcement powers were given consisted of a number of statutory bodies together with the Consumers' Association. These extensions have been retained in Schedule 3 to the Consumer Rights Act where these bodies are described as 'regulators'. The list of regulators in paragraph 8 of Schedule 3 now includes the Information Commissioner, the Gas and Electricity Markets Authority, the Office of Communications, the Water Services Regulation Authority, the Office of Rail and Road and the Financial Conduct Authority. The principal role as regulator is given to the Competition and Markets Authority ('CMA') which has assumed the role previously played by the Office of Fair Trading. Its leading role is reflected in the fact that if another regulator wishes to consider a complaint about an unfair term it must first notify the CMA, and there is a similar notification obligation in the event that another regulator wishes to make an application for an injunction to restrain the continued use of an unfair term.

The principal obligations and powers of the regulators are to (i) consider complaints about unfair terms, (ii) investigate such complaints and make use of the investigatory powers that are given to them and (iii) apply to court for an injunction to restrain the use of unfair terms. Paragraph 2 to Schedule 3 of the Consumer Rights Act provides that a regulator 'may' consider a complaint about a term of a consumer contract, a term for use in a consumer contract, a term which a third party recommends for use in a consumer contract or a consumer notice. The regulator is therefore empowered but not obliged to consider such a complaint. The investigatory powers given to regulators are set out in Schedule 5 to the Act (where they are described as 'an unfair contract terms enforcer'). The powers given to enforcers in Parts 3 and 4 of Schedule 5 are extensive, including, for example, the giving of a notice requiring a person to provide the enforcer with the information specified in the notice.

Paragraph 3 of Schedule 3 provides that a regulator may apply for an injunction against a person if the regulator thinks that the person is using, or proposing or recommending the use of, a term or notice which (i) purports to exclude or restrict a liability which cannot be excluded under sections 31, 47, 57 or 65(1) of the Act (on which see Section 18.5); (ii) 'is unfair to any extent' within the meaning of Part 2 of the Act; or (iii) breaches the requirement for transparency set out in section 68. A regulator may apply for an injunction even in the case where it has not received a complaint about the term or notice. To this extent, the regulator is entitled to act on its own initiative. On an application for an injunction the court may grant the injunction on such conditions, and against such of the respondents, as it thinks is appropriate (paragraph 5 of Schedule 3). The injunction may include provision about a term or notice to which the application relates or any term of a consumer contract, or any consumer notice, of a similar kind or with a similar effect. A regulator may accept an undertaking from a person against whom it has applied, or thinks it is entitled to apply for an injunction under paragraph 3. The undertaking may provide that the person will comply with the conditions that are agreed between that person and the regulator about the use of terms or notices, or terms or notices of a kind, specified in the undertaking (paragraph 6 of Schedule 3). This is a useful provision in so far as it removes the necessity for the regulator to apply to court for an injunction in the case where it can obtain a satisfactory undertaking from the person who was previously using or relying upon the unfair term or notice.

The CMA must arrange the publication of details of any application it makes for an injunction under paragraph 3 of Schedule 3 and any injunction or undertaking it has obtained under Schedule 3. In this way publicity will be given to enforcement of the legislation and this may help to achieve the aim of the legislation in substantially reducing, if not eliminating, the use of unfair terms in the small print in consumer contracts.

Hot topic 16...

The track record of the Supreme Court in dealing with claims brought under the unfair terms in consumer contracts legislation is not particularly strong. First, in *Office of Fair Trading v Abbey National plc* it held that the various bank charges were not vulnerable to challenge under the Unfair Terms in Consumer Contracts Regulations 1999 because they fell within the definition of 'core terms'. Second, in *ParkingEye Ltd v Beavis* the Supreme Court held that the £85 charge for staying in the car park beyond the permitted two hours was not an unfair term under the same Regulations because it did not arise 'contrary to the requirements of good faith'. ParkingEye were held to have a legitimate interest in imposing a charge of this nature given that users of the car park had been given an entitlement to park free of charge for two hours. The majority of the court concluded that a reasonable motorist in the position of Mr Beavis would have agreed to a charge of £85 if they overstayed in return for free parking for a two hour period. Do you agree with this view? A wealthy barrister in London might be willing to make a payment at that level but would a consumer who is living on the minimum wage also be inclined to make an agreement in these terms? It can also be said that the Supreme Court has not provided any incentive to parking companies to reduce their charges. Indeed, might they in future raise their charges still further and leave it to consumers to bring another challenge to their enforcement? It is perhaps not surprising to find that those lobbying on behalf of consumers are somewhat disappointed with the response of the Supreme Court to the interpretation of the unfair terms legislation and its application to the facts of individual cases.

Summary

▶ Part 2 of the Consumer Rights Act 2015 regulates unfair terms in contracts concluded between a trader and a consumer and provides that an unfair term of a consumer contract is not binding on the consumer.

▶ A trader is a person acting for purposes relating to that person's trade, business, craft or profession, and a consumer is an individual acting for purposes that are wholly or mainly outside that individual's trade, business, craft or profession.

▶ A term is unfair if, contrary to the requirement of good faith, it causes a significant imbalance in the parties' rights and obligations under the contract, to the detriment of the consumer.

▶ Good faith demands fair and open dealing and requires the court to consider whether the trader, dealing fairly and equitably with the consumer, could reasonably have assumed that the consumer would agree to the term had they been the subject of individual contract negotiations.

▶ There exists a significant imbalance if a term is so weighted in favour of the trader as to tilt the parties' rights and obligations under the contract significantly in the trader's favour.

▶ Part 1 of Schedule 2 to the Act contains an indicative and non-exhaustive list of terms of consumer contracts that may be regarded as unfair. The list is a 'grey list' so that inclusion on the list does not have the automatic consequence that the term is unfair. But inclusion in the list is likely to play an important role when considering whether a term is unfair.

▶ No assessment can be made of the fairness of any term which (i) specifies the main subject-matter of the contract or which (ii) concerns the appropriateness of the price payable under the contract by comparison with the goods, digital content or services supplied under it provided that the term is transparent and prominent.

▶ A term is transparent if it is expressed in plain and intelligible language and (in the case of a written term) is legible. A term is prominent if it is brought to the consumer's attention in such a way that an average consumer would be aware of it.

▶ Certain liabilities in consumer contracts cannot be excluded or restricted. For example, a trader cannot by a term of a consumer contract or by a consumer notice exclude or restrict liability for death or personal injury resulting from negligence.

▶ Where a term is held to be unfair, the consequence is that it is not binding on the consumer but the contract continues, so far as practicable, to have effect in every other respect.

▶ A trader must ensure that a written term of a consumer contract, or a consumer notice in writing, is transparent.

▶ If a term in a consumer contract, or a consumer notice, could have different meanings, the meaning that is more favourable to the consumer is to prevail.

▶ Enforcement of Part 2 of the Consumer Rights Act is not left entirely to the consumer. A number of regulators are given power to respond to complaints, to investigate them and, in certain circumstances, seek an injunction to restrain the continued use of unfair terms in consumer contracts. The principal regulator is the Competition and Markets Authority.

Exercises

18.1 Who is a consumer for the purposes of Part 2 of the Consumer Rights Act 2015? Who is a trader?

18.2 When is a term in a consumer contract unfair for the purposes of Part 2?

18.3 What is meant by 'the requirement of good faith' and 'significant imbalance' and what role do these elements play when seeking to decide whether a term is unfair?

18.4 Would *Office of Fair Trading v Abbey National plc* be decided the same way under section 64 of the Consumer Rights Act?

18.5 Why does the Act provide that a trader cannot by a term of a contract exclude or restrict certain liabilities while permitting it to exclude or restrict other liabilities provided that the term is not unfair?

18.6 What effect, if any, is given to an unfair term in a consumer contract and what is the impact of the unfair term on the contract as a whole?

18.7 Why might the enforcement provisions contained in Schedules 3 and 5 to the Act be important for the success of the legislation?

Part IV

Performance, discharge and remedies for breach of contract

Chapter 19

Performance and discharge of the contract

19.1 Performance

Contracts are made to be performed. When parties enter into a contract, they generally do so in the expectation that it will be performed according to its terms. Indeed, a contract consists of a number of terms which determine the scope of the performance obligations which the parties have accepted. A failure to perform in accordance with these terms is a breach of contract, which will entitle the other party to the contract to an appropriate remedy (*Photo Production Ltd v Securicor Transport Ltd* [1980] AC 827, see Section 20.3).

However, in many cases the formation of the contract and the performance of the contract are practically simultaneous. For example, I purchase a newspaper at a nearby shop. Here my offer to buy the paper and the shopkeeper's acceptance of my offer occur at virtually the same time as the performance of the contract in the handing over, and the payment for, the newspaper. Atiyah (1986b) asks: 'Is it really sensible to characterise these transactions as agreements or exchanges of promises?' He argues that obligations are really created by what we do, not what we promise or what we intend: in other words, it is the payment of the money and the handing over of the newspaper which form the basis of the obligations created, not the *promise* to pay or the *promise* to hand over the newspaper.

It must be conceded that in many cases formation and performance are practically simultaneous. This fact is often obscured by contract textbooks because formation appears at the beginning of the book and performance towards the end. But in the real world the two often occur at virtually the same time. On the other hand, there may be a considerable time lapse between formation and performance. For example, I may order a special anniversary issue of a newspaper which is not due for publication for another three weeks. In such a case I want to know at the moment that I reach agreement with the shopkeeper that he will order and deliver to me a copy of the newspaper. Here there appears to be no doubt that the agreement is the basis of our obligations, not any action in reliance upon the agreement. It is submitted that the same is true when formation and performance are virtually simultaneous. In my example of the purchase of a newspaper, the source of the obligations created remains my promise to buy the paper and the promise of the shopkeeper to sell the newspaper; our actions are simply evidence of the fact that we have reached agreement (see Section 1.4).

19.2 Discharge of the contract

Contracts may be discharged or brought to an end in four principal ways. We shall deal with three forms of discharge in this chapter. They are discharge by performance (Section 19.3), by agreement (Section 19.4) and by operation of law (Section 19.5). Contracts can also be discharged by breach, but breach is a sufficiently important topic to deserve a chapter in its own right (see Chapter 20).

19.3 Discharge by performance

A contract is discharged by performance where the performance by both parties complies fully with the terms of the contract. The vast majority of contracts are discharged by performance. We do not read about such contracts in textbooks because, when the contract is discharged by performance, no legal problems arise. Indeed, the discussion of 'performance' in most contract textbooks is, in fact, a discussion of breach of contract because the point which is being made is that performance which fails to comply fully with the terms of the contract is a breach of contract. We shall deal with such issues in the chapter on breach of contract (see Chapter 20).

It is, however, extremely important to realise that, in the real world, most contracts are discharged by performance. Students who read contract textbooks tend to get a distorted view of reality because they believe that all contracts go wrong for one reason or another. In fact, most contracts are performed according to their terms and the role of the lawyer is confined to giving advice on the formation or the drafting of the contract. It is only in the minority of cases that contracts go wrong and a dispute breaks out between the parties and, even when such a dispute does occur, empirical studies show us that the rules of contract law are often but one factor among many to be taken into account in the resolution of the dispute (see Section 1.5).

19.4 Discharge by agreement

The parties can agree to abandon or to discharge the contract. The limiting factor here is that an agreement to discharge a contract must be supported by consideration (Section 5.20). Where performance has not been completed by either party to the contract, there is generally no difficulty in finding consideration because, in giving up their rights to compel each other to perform, each party is giving something to the bargain and so consideration is given. But where the contract is wholly executed on one side, an agreement to abandon the contract (unless the agreement to abandon the contract is itself supported by fresh consideration) will not be supported by consideration and will be unenforceable unless (i) the agreement is in the form of a deed, (ii) the party who has fully performed his obligations under the contract is estopped from going back upon his representation that he will not enforce the original contract or (iii) he is held to have waived his rights under that contract (see Sections 5.24 and 5.25).

Finally, a contract may be discharged by the operation of a condition subsequent which has been incorporated into the contract. A condition subsequent states that a previously binding contract shall come to an end on the occurrence of a stipulated event (see Section 10.2). The effect of the occurrence of the stipulated event is to discharge the contract, without either party being in breach of contract.

19.5 Discharge by operation of law

A contract may be discharged by operation of law. The principal example of a contract which is brought to an end by the operation of a rule of law is a contract which is frustrated. Frustration, it will be remembered, automatically brings a contract to an end by the operation of a rule of law, irrespective of the wishes of the parties (Section 14.8). Other examples of the discharge of a contract by operation of law are discussed by Anson (2020, Chapter 16).

Summary

▶ Contracts are made to be performed. The vast majority of contracts are discharged by performance.

▶ Contracts may be discharged by performance, agreement, operation of law or breach.

▶ A contract is discharged by performance where the performance by both parties has complied fully with the terms of the contract.

▶ An agreement to discharge a contract must be supported by consideration, unless one party is held to have waived his rights under the contract or is estopped from asserting them.

▶ A contract may be discharged by operation of law, for example, by the occurrence of a frustrating event.

Exercises

19.1 List the different ways in which a contract can be discharged.

19.2 When will performance be sufficient to discharge the contract?

19.3 Jenny agrees to buy Sarah's car for £2,500. Sarah gives Jenny the car but Jenny does not pay the £2,500. Jenny and Sarah then agree to abandon the contract and Sarah tells Jenny to keep the car and that she 'does not need the money anyway'. Jenny then uses the £2,500 to pay for the installation of double glazing in her house. Sarah has now decided that she wants her car back and she alleges that the agreement to discharge the contract is not an enforceable agreement. Advise Jenny.

Chapter 20

Breach of contract

Introduction: breach defined

Treitel (2020, para 17-049) has defined a breach of contract in the following terms: 'a breach of contract is committed when a party without lawful excuse fails or refuses to perform what is due from him under the contract, or performs defectively or incapacitates himself from performing'. It should be noted that in all cases the failure to provide the promised performance must be 'without lawful excuse'. Thus where the contract has been frustrated there is no liability for breach of contract because both parties have been provided with a 'lawful excuse' for their non-performance. Similarly, where one party has breached the contract and the breach has given to the other party the right to terminate performance of the contract, that party is not in breach of contract in refusing to continue with performance because he is given a 'lawful excuse' for his non-performance.

Although the breach can take the form of words (such as an express refusal to perform the terms of the contract), it need not do so and can be evidenced by the conduct of one party in disabling himself from performing his obligations under the contract or by performing defectively. Where it is alleged that one party has incapacitated himself from performing his obligations under the contract, his inability to perform must be established on a balance of probabilities. This is relatively easy to do where the party alleged to be in breach has sold the subject-matter of the contract to a third party, but greater difficulty arises where he enters into alternative obligations which it is alleged are inconsistent with his existing contractual obligations. The fact that a party has entered into inconsistent obligations 'does not in itself necessarily establish [an inability to perform], unless these obligations are of such a nature or have such an effect that it can truly be said that the party in question has put it out of his power to perform his obligations' (*Alfred C Toepfer International GmbH v Itex Hagrani Export SA* [1993] 1 Lloyd's Rep 360, 362). In short, it must be proved that the inconsistent obligation or disablement has rendered the breach inevitable. It does not suffice to demonstrate that there is uncertainty about the ability of a contracting party to perform its contractual obligations (*Geden Operations Ltd v Dry Bulk Handy Holdings Inc (M/V 'Bulk Uruguay')* [2014] EWHC 885 (Comm), [2014] 2 Lloyd's Rep 66).

20.2 When does breach occur?

The question whether or not a particular contract has been breached depends upon the precise construction of the terms of the contract. No universal legal principle can be established which displaces the need for a careful analysis of the terms of each individual contract. It is for the party alleging the existence of the breach of contract to prove that a breach has occurred. It is not generally necessary to prove that a party has been at fault before breach can be established. Many obligations created by a contract are strict; that is to say, liability does not depend upon proof of fault. A good example of a strict contractual obligation is provided by section 14(2) of the Sale of Goods Act 1979 which states that, where a seller sells goods in the course of a business, there is an implied condition that the goods supplied under the contract are of satisfactory quality, except in relation to defects drawn to the buyer's attention before the contract was concluded or, in the case where the buyer examines the goods, as regards defects which that examination ought to have revealed. The purchaser is not required to prove that the seller was at fault in selling goods which were not of satisfactory quality; the seller may have taken all reasonable steps to ensure that the goods were of satisfactory quality but he will still be in breach of contract if they are not of such quality.

It is, however, important to note that contractual liability is not always strict. A contractual term may impose a duty to take reasonable care, in which case a breach can only be established where it is proved that the party alleged to be in breach has failed to exercise reasonable care. An example in this category is provided by section 13 of the Supply of Goods and Services Act 1982 which provides that a person who supplies a service in the course of a business impliedly undertakes to 'carry out the service with reasonable care and skill'.

20.3   The consequences of breach

A breach of contract does not automatically bring a contract to an end (*Decro-Wall International SA v Practitioners in Marketing Ltd* [1971] 1 WLR 361; *Geys v Société Générale, London Branch* [2012] UKSC 62; [2013] 1 AC 513). Rather, a breach of contract gives various options to the party who is not in breach ('the innocent party'). The extent of these options depends upon the seriousness of the breach. Even the most serious breach, such as a fundamental breach (see Section 11.7), does not, of itself, terminate or discharge the contract (*Photo Production Ltd v Securicor Transport Ltd* [1980] AC 827). However, in the case where the breach renders further performance of the contract impossible or something radically different from that which was in the contemplation of the parties at the time of entry into the contract, it would appear that the innocent party cannot affirm the contract (given that performance can no longer take place in accordance with the terms of the contract) and must instead recognise that the contract has come to an end and seek a remedy in damages for the loss that has been suffered as a result of the breach (*MSC Mediterranean Shipping Co SA v Cottonex Anstalt* [2016] EWCA Civ 789; [2016] 2 Lloyd's Rep 494, [43] and [61]).

The consequences of a breach of contract depend upon the facts of each individual case, but three principal consequences of a breach of contract can be identified. The first is that the innocent party is entitled to recover damages in respect of the loss which he has suffered as a result of the breach. The second is that the party in breach may be unable to sue to enforce the innocent party's obligations under the contract. The third consequence is that the breach may entitle the innocent party to terminate further performance of the contract. We shall now deal with these consequences individually.

20.4   Damages

Every breach of a valid and enforceable contract gives to the innocent party a right to recover damages in respect of the loss suffered as a result of the breach, unless the liability for breach has been effectively excluded by an appropriately drafted exclusion clause. An action for damages lies whether the term which is broken is a condition, a warranty or an innominate term (see further Chapter 10). The basis upon which the courts assess the damages payable will be discussed in Chapter 21.

20.5 Enforcement by the party in breach

The second consequence of a breach of contract is that the party who is in breach may be unable to enforce the contract against the innocent party. Where the obligations of the parties are independent, that is to say, the obligation of one party to perform is not dependent upon performance by the other party, then breach by one party does not entitle the innocent party to abandon performance of his obligations under the contract. For example, a landlord's covenant to repair the premises and a tenant's covenant to pay rent are independent obligations so that a landlord is not entitled to refuse to repair the premises because the tenant has failed to pay his rent (*Taylor v Webb* [1937] 2 KB 370). But, where the obligations of the parties are dependent, then a contracting party must generally be ready and willing to perform his obligations under the contract before he can maintain an action against the other party for breach of contract. Obligations created by a contract are generally interpreted as dependent obligations (see, for example, s 28 of the Sale of Goods Act 1979 which provides that, unless otherwise agreed, delivery of the goods and payment of the price are concurrent conditions, so that a seller must be ready and willing to give possession of the goods to the buyer in exchange for the price and the buyer must be ready and willing to pay the price in exchange for possession of the goods).

20.6 The right to terminate performance of the contract

A breach of contract may entitle the innocent party to take the further step of terminating performance of the contract. Here it is necessary to recount a little of the material which we discussed in Chapter 10. It will be remembered that contractual terms can be classified as conditions, warranties or innominate terms. Breach of a warranty does not give the innocent party a right to terminate performance of the contract; it only enables him to claim damages. But breach of a condition does give the innocent party the additional right to terminate performance of the contract, as does the breach of an innominate term, where the consequences of the breach are sufficiently serious (see Section 10.5). A breach of contract which gives to the other party the right to terminate performance of the contract is often referred to as a 'repudiatory breach'.

It should be noted that I have used the rather clumsy expression 'right to terminate performance of the contract'. Contract scholars and judges have disagreed as to the correct 'title' to be given to this right of the innocent party. Some scholars call this right a 'right to rescind'. This terminology is acceptable, if dangerous. The danger lies in the fact that it tends to create confusion between 'rescission for breach' and 'rescission for misrepresentation'. Where a contract is rescinded for misrepresentation, it is set aside for all purposes. The contract is set aside both retrospectively and prospectively and the aim is to restore the parties, as far as possible, to the position which they were in before they entered into the contract (see Section 13.8). But a contract which is 'rescinded' for breach is set aside prospectively, but not retrospectively (*Johnson v Agnew* [1980] AC 367 and *Photo Production Ltd v Securicor Transport Ltd* [1980] AC 827). Provided this fundamental distinction is grasped, no substantial objection can be raised to the use of the term 'right to rescind for breach'. That said, it is preferable to avoid any confusion by referring to the right of the innocent party as a right to terminate further performance rather than a right to rescind. We must now turn to give further consideration to the consequences of the rule that breach operates prospectively but not retrospectively.

20.7 The prospective nature of breach

The point that breach operates prospectively but not retrospectively is an important one. It is for this reason that I have termed the right of the innocent party a right to 'terminate performance of the contract' and not a right to terminate the contract. It is the obligations of the parties to perform their future primary contractual duties which are terminated. The contract is not set aside *ab initio* and so a contract term which is intended to regulate the consequences of breach or the termination must be taken into consideration by the court (*Heyman v Darwins Ltd* [1942] AC 356). The prospective nature of a breach of contract becomes clearer if we adopt the language of primary and secondary obligations. A primary obligation is an obligation to perform contained in the contract itself, whereas a secondary obligation is one which is triggered by a breach of a primary obligation.

The modern source of this distinction between primary and secondary obligations is the judgment of Lord Diplock in *Photo Production Ltd v Securicor Transport Ltd* (above). Lord Diplock stated that 'breaches of primary obligations give rise to substituted secondary obligations'. There are two principal types of secondary obligation. The first is a 'general secondary obligation'. In such a case the primary obligations of both parties, in so far as they have not yet been fully performed, remain unchanged, but the breach gives rise to a secondary obligation, imposed upon the party in breach, 'to pay monetary compensation to the [innocent] party for the loss sustained by him in consequence of the breach'. Such a general secondary obligation arises on the breach of a warranty; the primary obligations of the parties in so far as they have not been fully performed remain unchanged and a secondary obligation to pay damages for the loss suffered as a result of the breach is created.

But, where the breach of a primary obligation entitles the innocent party to elect to terminate performance of the contract, and he does so elect, all primary obligations of both parties remaining unperformed are put to an end and:

> there is substituted by implication of law for the primary obligations of the party in default which remain unperformed a secondary obligation to pay monetary compensation to the other party for the loss sustained by him in consequence of their non-performance.

This obligation Lord Diplock called an 'anticipatory secondary obligation'. The crucial feature of an 'anticipatory' secondary obligation is that it enables damages to be assessed by reference to those obligations which would have fallen due for performance at some time in the future (see Section 22.3). Although the judgment of Lord Diplock is not entirely clear on this point, it is suggested that he intended that an anticipatory secondary obligation should arise in every case of termination following upon a breach of a condition (an interpretation which is supported by the approach of the Court of Appeal in *Lombard North Central plc v Butterworth* [1987] QB 527, discussed in Sections 10.3 and 22.3). English law does not generally distinguish between a condition which is created by the general law and a condition which has been expressly agreed by the parties (that is to say, it would not otherwise have constituted a condition). The reason why parties choose to elevate a term to the status of a condition is to emphasise the importance of the term and to give to the innocent party not only the right to terminate performance in the event of breach, but also the right to claim loss of bargain damages (see Opeskin, 1990).

The distinction between primary and secondary obligations is a useful one in that it helps us to see why there is no inconsistency between electing to terminate performance of the contract and, at the same time, claiming damages for the breach which gave rise to the right to terminate performance. Rather, the exercise of the right to terminate performance of the contract simply discharges the primary obligations of both parties *for the future* and imposes on the party in breach, by way of substitution, an anticipatory secondary obligation to pay damages to the innocent party.

20.8 The right of election

An innocent party is not obliged to exercise his right to terminate performance of the contract. As we have already noted, a breach which gives to the innocent party a right to terminate performance of the contract in fact gives him an option. He can either terminate performance of the contract and claim damages ('accept the repudiation') or he can affirm the contract and claim damages. The option does not have to be exercised immediately. The innocent party has a period of time in which to make up his mind and, during this period, he is entitled to maintain the contract in being for the moment, while reserving his right to treat it as repudiated if his contract partner persists in his repudiation (*Stocznia Gdanska SA v Latvian Shipping Company* [2002] EWCA Civ 889; [2002] 2 Lloyd's Rep 436). Although this right of election between termination and affirmation is notionally free, in practice it may be restricted by the rule that the innocent party must take reasonable steps to mitigate his loss (see Section 21.10). For example, a seller, faced with a buyer who has breached a contract in such a way as to give to the seller a right to terminate performance of the contract, may elect not to affirm the contract but to sell the goods elsewhere, thereby disabling himself from performing his obligations under the contract. A seller may take such a course of action because, if he fails to take reasonable steps to sell the goods elsewhere, a court may conclude that he has failed to mitigate his loss and he will be unable to recover the loss caused by his failure to mitigate.

20.8.1 The need for communication

Where the innocent party wishes to accept the breach and terminate performance of the contract he must generally communicate his decision to the party in breach and the communication must clearly and unequivocally convey to the repudiating party that the innocent party is treating the contract as at an end (*Vitol SA v Beta Renowable Group SA* [2017] EWHC 1734 (Comm); [2017] 2 Lloyd's Rep 338). The requirements for an effective acceptance of a repudiatory breach were restated by Lord Steyn in *Vitol SA v Norelf Ltd* [1996] AC 800 in the following terms:

> An act of acceptance of a repudiation requires no particular form: a communication does not have to be couched in the language of acceptance. It is sufficient that the communication or conduct clearly and unequivocally conveys to the repudiating party that that aggrieved party is treating the contract as at an end … the aggrieved party need not personally, or by an agent, notify the repudiating party of his election to treat the contract as at an end. It is sufficient that the fact of the election comes to the repudiating party's attention.

While the House of Lords was at pains to emphasise that there is no rule that a mere failure to perform cannot constitute an acceptance, it does not follow that the courts will conclude that a failure to perform will always be sufficiently unequivocal to constitute an acceptance. Lord Steyn said (at 811) that it all depended on 'the particular contractual relationship and the particular circumstances of the case' whether a mere failure to perform sufficed. An example which he gave of a failure to perform which would suffice to constitute an acceptance was given in the following terms:

> Postulate the case where an employer at the end of the day tells a contractor that he, the employer, is repudiating the contract and that the contractor need not return the next day. The contractor does not return the next day or at all. It seems to me that the contractor's failure to return may, in the absence of any other explanation, convey a decision to treat the contract as at an end.

But a contractor who wishes to make sure that he has accepted a repudiation would be well advised to draw that acceptance expressly to the attention of the repudiating party. As we noted in Chapter 10, the party electing to terminate need not put forward the 'real reason' for his decision; as long as the terms of the contract entitle him to terminate he is justified in doing so, irrespective of his motive (*Arcos Ltd v E A Ronaasen & Son* [1933] AC 470, see Section 10.3). Indeed, the law goes so far as to allow the innocent party to put forward no reason or even an invalid reason for deciding to terminate but, provided that the innocent party can subsequently point to a good reason which, unknown to him, existed at the moment of breach, he will still generally be entitled to terminate (*The Mihalis Angelos* [1971] 1 QB 164, 200, 204). While, within these limits, the innocent party can put forward the wrong reason for deciding to terminate the contract, in order to be entitled to bring a claim for damages in respect of the breach, the innocent party must have sought to terminate the contract for breach. So, in the case where the innocent party terminated the contract under an express contractual right to terminate that had arisen irrespective of any breach, it could not be said that the contract had been terminated for breach and so a claim for loss of bargain damages could not be brought (*Phones 4U Ltd (in administration) v EE Ltd* [2018] EWHC 49 (Comm), [2018] 1 Lloyd's Rep 204).

20.8.2 Affirmation

Where the innocent party elects to affirm the contract, the contract remains in force, so that both parties remain bound to continue with the performance of their respective contractual obligations. An innocent party who accepts further performance of the contract after the breach may be held thereby to have affirmed the contract (*Davenport v R* (1877) 3 App Cas 115). Affirmation does not prevent the innocent party from claiming damages for any loss which he has suffered as a result of the breach, unless the innocent party waives not only the right to terminate performance of the contract but also the right to claim damages for the breach (sometimes known as 'total waiver', see below). When deciding whether conduct amounts to an affirmation, a court is not conducting a 'mechanical exercise' but is exercising a judgment and, in the exercise of that judgment, it should not adopt an unduly technical approach (*White Rosebay Shipping SA v Hong Kong Chain Glory Shipping Ltd (The Fortune Plum)* [2013] EWHC 1355 (Comm); [2013] 2 All ER (Comm) 449, [38]).

20.8.3 Election in principle irrevocable

Once the innocent party has exercised his right of election and chosen either to terminate or to affirm, that decision cannot be revoked. Thus, an innocent party who has exercised his right to terminate performance of the contract cannot subsequently affirm the contract because the effect of the termination of performance is to release *both* parties from their obligations to perform in the future and, once released from these obligations, they cannot subsequently be resurrected (*Johnson v Agnew* [1980] AC 367 (above)). However, where the breach takes the form of continuing repudiatory conduct, an innocent party who has elected to affirm the contract after the first breach of contract may be able to treat the continued non-performance as a fresh act of repudiation which he can then accept and thereby bring the contract to an end (*Safehaven v Springbok* (1998) 71 P & CR 59).

20.8.4 Election and waiver

Confusion is sometimes caused by referring to this right of election as a species of 'waiver'. This terminology is confusing but is now probably too well established to be abandoned. 'Waiver', in the sense of election, must be distinguished from 'waiver by estoppel'. These two types of waiver were clearly distinguished by Lord Goff in his judgment in *The Kanchenjunga* [1990] 1 Lloyd's Rep 391, 397–99. A contracting party who is faced by a repudiatory breach has a choice: he can either terminate or he can affirm, but he cannot do both. When the innocent party makes his choice ('makes an election'), for example by choosing to affirm, he thereby *abandons* his inconsistent right, in this case to terminate. The exercise of this right of election may be called 'waiver by election', although it is suggested that less confusion would arise if this right were simply known as 'election' and the word 'waiver' were dropped from the title. But there is another sense in which the word 'waiver' may be used. In this sense, waiver does not mean the abandonment of a right but rather it refers to the forbearance from exercising a right. This species of waiver is closely linked to, if not identical with, the line of authority exemplified by *Hughes v Metropolitan Rly Co* (1877) 2 App Cas 439 (discussed in more detail in Section 5.25). This type of waiver may be called 'waiver by estoppel' and it arises when the innocent party represents clearly and unequivocally to the party in default that he will not exercise his right to treat the contract as terminated or so conducts himself as to lead the party in default to believe that he will not exercise that right.

Both waiver by estoppel and waiver by election share some common elements. The principal similarity is that both appear to require that the party seeking to rely on it (that is, the party in default) must show a clear and unequivocal representation, by words or conduct, by the other party that he will not exercise his strict legal right to treat the contract as repudiated. But there are also important differences between the two types of waiver (see generally *The Kanchenjunga* (above) at 399). In the case of waiver by election, the party who has to make the choice must either know or have obvious means of knowledge of the facts giving rise to the right, and possibly of the existence of the right. But in the case of waiver by estoppel neither knowledge of the circumstances nor of the right is required on the part of the person estopped; the other party is entitled to rely on the apparent election conveyed by the representation. Waiver by election is final and so has permanent effect, whereas the effect of estoppel may be suspensory only (although in the context of waiver of breach, the waiver may have permanent effect because, where the party in breach has relied to his detriment on the waiver – for example, by not attempting to remedy the situation when there was time to do so – the innocent party may, as a result of the waiver, lose forever the right to terminate on account of that particular breach). Finally, waiver by estoppel requires that the party to whom the representation is made rely on that representation so as to make it inequitable for the representor to go back upon his representation. There is, however, no such requirement in the case of waiver by election; once the election has been made it is final whether or not the other party has acted in reliance upon the election having been made.

One final distinction must be drawn. It is between the case in which a party waives his right to treat the contract as repudiated but does not abandon his right to claim damages for the loss suffered as a result of the breach, and the case where the innocent party waives not only his right to terminate performance of the contract but also his right to claim damages. The former is an example of waiver by election and so is governed by the rules relating to election, while the latter appears to be an example of estoppel (because the innocent party is purporting to abandon all of his rights under the contract, without any consideration being provided for that abandonment) and so should be subject to the rules relating to waiver by estoppel.

20.9 Anticipatory breach

One contracting party may inform the other party, before the time fixed for performance under the contract, that he will not perform his obligations under the contract. This is called an anticipatory breach of contract, which entitles the innocent party to terminate performance of the contract immediately. The novel feature of anticipatory breach is that acceptance of the breach entitles the innocent party to claim damages at the date of the acceptance of the breach. He does not have to wait until the date fixed for performance, even though this has the effect of accelerating the obligations of the party in breach. It does seem somewhat illogical to say that a party can be in breach of contract *before* the time fixed for performance under the contract. The doctrine of anticipatory breach can best be rationalised as a breach of an implied term of the contract that neither party will, without just cause, repudiate his obligations under the contract before the time fixed for performance.

20.9.1 *Hochster v De La Tour*

The operation of the doctrine of anticipatory breach can be illustrated by reference to the case of *Hochster v De La Tour* (1853) 2 E & B 678. In April of 1852, the defendant agreed to employ the claimant to act as his courier for three months from 1 June. But on 11 May, the defendant wrote to the claimant informing him that his services would no longer be required. The claimant commenced his action on 22 May and it was held that he was entitled to commence his action for damages at that date; he did not have to wait until 1 June when performance was due.

Once again the innocent party is not obliged to exercise his right to terminate performance of the contract; he can elect to affirm the contract (in the case where performance of the contract according to its terms remains possible) and demand performance from the other party at the time stipulated in the contract. But where the innocent party does decide to terminate performance of the contract he must give notice to the party in breach that he is accepting the anticipatory breach (or otherwise overtly evidence his acceptance of the breach, see Section 20.8) and he must not act inconsistently with his decision to accept the breach.

20.9.2 *White and Carter (Councils) Ltd v McGregor*

Where the innocent party does decide to affirm the contract and demand performance at the stipulated time, a number of consequences flow from this decision. The first is that affirmation does not prevent the innocent party accepting the breach if, at the date fixed for performance, the other party still refuses to perform. The second is that the innocent party, in addition to affirming the contract, may continue with the performance of his obligations under the contract, even though he knows that the performance is not wanted by that other party. This is what happened in the controversial case of *White and Carter (Councils) Ltd v McGregor* [1962] AC 413 (on which see generally Liu, 2011). The defendants entered into a contract with the claimants under which the claimants agreed to display advertisements of the defendants' garage for a period of three years on plates attached to litter bins. Later the same day, the defendants wrote to the claimants stating that they no longer wished to continue with performance of the contract. The claimants refused to accept the cancellation and proceeded to display the advertisements and then brought an action to recover the contract price. The House of Lords held, by a majority of three to two, that the claimants were entitled to recover the contract price. The minority held that the claimants were not entitled to succeed because they had failed to mitigate their loss. But the majority held, quoting from the judgment of Asquith LJ in *Howard v Pickford Tool Co Ltd* [1951] 1 KB 417, 421, that 'an unaccepted repudiation is a thing writ in water and of no value to anybody'. The claimants were not under an obligation to accept the defendants' breach, even though it was 'unfortunate' that the claimants had 'saddled themselves with an unwanted contract causing an apparent waste of time and money'. The vital factor as far as the majority was concerned was that the claimants' claim was one in debt (for the contract price) and not for damages, and so the mitigation rules simply had no application. Lord Hodson expressly refused to turn an action for debt into a 'discretionary remedy' by introducing a 'novel equitable doctrine that a party was not to be held to his contract unless the court in a given instance thought it reasonable so to do'.

20.9.3 Co-operation and legitimate interest

The principle laid down in *White and Carter* is, in fact, the subject of a number of qualifications. The first is that the innocent party cannot compel the party in breach to co-operate with him so that, where the innocent party cannot continue with performance without the co-operation of the party in breach, he will be compelled to accept the breach (*Hounslow LBC v Twickenham Garden Developments Ltd* [1971] Ch 233). The second qualification is derived from the speech of Lord Reid in *White and Carter* when he said that:

> it may well be that, if it can be shown that a person has no legitimate interest, financial or otherwise, in performing the contract rather than claiming damages, he ought not to be allowed to saddle the other party with an additional burden with no benefit to himself.

Lord Reid's view on this point did not appear to be shared by the other members of the majority in *White and Carter* (Lord Tucker and Lord Hodson), but it has subsequently been regarded as part of the ratio of the case (see *Hounslow LBC v Twickenham Garden Developments Ltd*) and it has been developed in subsequent cases as a means of limiting the principle established in the case. In *Clea Shipping Corp v Bulk Oil International Ltd (The Alaskan Trader)* [1984] 1 All ER 129, after an extensive review of the authorities, Lloyd J concluded that:

> there comes a point at which the court will cease, on general equitable principles, to allow the innocent party to enforce his contract according to its strict legal terms.

Since there is no general rule that requires the innocent party to act reasonably in deciding whether or not to accept the breach, the onus is upon the party in breach to show that the innocent party had no legitimate interest in completing the contract and claiming the contract price rather than damages. Here it is vital to note that the defendants in *White and Carter* did not set out to prove that the claimants had no legitimate interest in continuing with performance (probably because they did not know that they had to do so). Had the defendants sought to prove that the claimants had no such legitimate interest, it may well be that the case would have been decided differently. Defendants in subsequent cases have been quick to invoke this qualification, and the line which the courts have now drawn is between 'unreasonable' behaviour and 'wholly unreasonable' or 'perverse' behaviour. This 'equitable principle' cannot be invoked simply because the innocent party has behaved 'unreasonably'. But, where the innocent party acts 'wholly unreasonably' (*The Odenfield* [1978] 2 Lloyd's Rep 357, 373) or 'perversely' (*Isabella Shipowner SA v Shagang Shipping Co Ltd (The Aquafaith)* [2012] EWHC 1077 (Comm); [2012] 2 Lloyd's Rep 61, [44]), then the court may refuse to allow the innocent party to continue with performance and claim the contract price. It may, however, be unwise to place too much emphasis on the precise words used by the courts to describe the situation in which a claimant ceases to be entitled to continue with performance in this way (see *Ocean Marine Navigation Ltd v Koch Carbon Inc (The 'Dynamic')* [2003] EWHC 1936 (Comm); [2003] 2 Lloyd's Rep 693, [22] where Simon J was critical of the qualifying word 'wholly' in the expression 'wholly unreasonable'). Rather, the principal point to grasp is that a court may only exercise this jurisdiction in an 'extreme' case where the party in breach has demonstrated that damages would be an entirely adequate remedy for the innocent party and that the conduct of the innocent party was 'beyond all reason, wholly unreasonable or ... perverse' (*Isabella Shipowner SA v Shagang Shipping Co Ltd*, [52]).

An example of such an 'extreme' case is provided by the facts of *The Alaskan Trader*. The claimants chartered a ship to the defendants for 24 months. After one year the ship required extensive repairs. The defendants stated that they had no further use for the ship but the claimants nevertheless spent £800,000 in repairing the ship and, when it was repaired, they kept the ship and its crew ready to receive instructions from the defendants. The arbitrator held that the claimants had acted wholly unreasonably in refusing to accept the breach and this finding was upheld on appeal to Lloyd J so that the liability of the defendants was in damages and not for the contract hire.

On the other hand, a decision to affirm the contract may work to the disadvantage of the innocent party. The first disadvantage is that an innocent party who affirms the contract may lose his right to sue for damages completely if the contract is frustrated between the date of the unaccepted anticipatory breach and the date fixed for performance (*Avery v Bowden* (1856) 6 E & B 953). Secondly, an innocent party who affirms the contract but subsequently breaches the contract himself cannot argue that the unaccepted anticipatory breach excused him from his obligation to perform under the contract. Where the breach is not accepted the parties remain subject to their obligations under the contract, so that the 'innocent party' may find himself liable to pay damages for breach of contract if he fails to accept the breach and subsequently breaches the contract himself (*The Simona* [1989] AC 788).

Hot topic 17...

What is the scope of the 'legitimate interest' test derived from the judgment of Lord Reid in *White & Carter (Councils) Ltd v McGregor* [1962] AC 413? In *MSC Mediterranean Shipping Co SA v Cottonex Anstalt* [2015] EWHC 283 (Comm); [2015] 1 Lloyd's Rep 359 Leggatt J concluded that the legitimate interest principle 'sets some constraint, albeit a weak one, on the freedom of a party when exercising a choice whether or not to terminate a contract to consult only its own interests'. He sought to place this limitation in the context of cases concerned with the exercise of a contractual discretion and the emerging duty of good faith in the performance of a contract (on which see Chapter 12). The Court of Appeal ([2016] EWCA Civ 789; [2016] 2 Lloyd's Rep 494) declined to endorse the invocation of good faith in this context and, more significantly, concluded that the case was not one in which the legitimate interest test had any role to play at all. It held that the legitimate interest test was applicable in cases where the party in breach is refusing to perform continuing obligations or obligations which fall due for performance in the future. But it cannot be invoked where the option of affirming the contract is no longer open to the claimant because the contractual adventure has been frustrated and further performance has become impossible. In the latter case, the principle that a repudiatory breach of contract does not automatically discharge the parties from further performance, but gives the innocent party the right to choose whether to treat it as having that effect or affirming the contract in order to wait and see whether the guilty party performed its obligations, has no application and the innocent party must recognise the reality that the contract between the parties has come to an end.

Summary

▶ A breach of contract is committed when a party without lawful excuse fails or refuses to perform what is due from him under the contract, performs defectively or incapacitates himself from performing.

▶ The question whether or not a particular contract has been breached depends upon the precise construction of the terms of the contract. Many contractual duties are strict.

▶ A breach of contract does not automatically bring a contract to an end. A breach of contract gives to the innocent party a right to claim damages and it may give him the additional right to terminate further performance of the contract.

▶ When the performance of a contract is terminated because of breach, the obligations to perform are only terminated for the future. The contract is not set aside *ab initio*.

▶ An innocent party is not obliged to exercise his right to terminate performance of the contract; he can elect to terminate or to affirm, although the effect of the doctrine of mitigation is often to reduce the scope for affirmation in practice.

▶ A party who is in breach of contract may be unable to enforce the contract against the innocent party. But where the breach is of an independent, rather than a dependent, obligation, breach will not entitle the innocent party to abandon performance of his obligations under the contract.

▶ One contracting party may inform the other party, before the time fixed for performance under the contract, that he will not perform his obligations under the contract. This is called an anticipatory breach of contract, which entitles the innocent party to terminate further performance of the contract immediately.

▶ An innocent party who affirms the contract after an anticipatory breach may continue with the performance of his obligations under the contract, even though he knows that the performance is not wanted by that other party, provided that contractual performance does not require the co-operation of the other party to the contract and he has a 'legitimate interest' in the performance of the contract.

Exercises

20.1 What is a breach of contract and what are its consequences?

20.2 Distinguish between 'rescission for breach' and 'rescission for misrepresentation'.

20.3 Distinguish between a 'primary obligation' and a 'secondary obligation'.

20.4 What is an 'anticipatory breach'?

20.5 What 'legitimate interest' did the claimants in *White and Carter (Councils) Ltd v McGregor* [1962] AC 413 have in the performance of the contract?

20.6 Did the claimants in *The Alaskan Trader* [1984] 1 All ER 129 (see above at Section 20.9) act 'wholly unreasonably'? (See further Burrows, 2019, 383–87.)

20.7 Adam Ltd employ Steve to go to Japan and prepare an elaborate report for the company on the state of the Japanese market. Two days before Steve's departure, Adam Ltd inform Steve that they no longer require the report because they have decided not to commence trading in Japan. Steve nevertheless goes to Japan and prepares the report at a cost of £25,000. Adam Ltd are now refusing to pay for the report. Advise Steve.

Chapter 21
Damages for breach of contract

21.1 Introduction

We have already noted that a breach of contract gives rise to an action for damages, whether the term broken is a condition, a warranty or an innominate term. In this chapter we shall discuss the principles which are applied by the courts when assessing the damages payable on a breach of contract. The principles applied by the courts are of great significance to the debate about the basis of the law of contract, to which we referred in Chapter 1. The claim that contract law can be separated from the law of tort and the law of restitution rests, to a large extent, on the proposition that the law of contract seeks to fulfil the expectations engendered by a binding promise (see Section 1.4). In this chapter we shall put that claim to the test by asking ourselves the fundamental question: does the law of contract really fulfil the expectations engendered by a binding promise? But before we seek to answer that question we must define the 'expectation interest' with greater precision and we must also examine the question whether the law of contract protects either the 'reliance interest' or the 'restitution interest'.

21.2 Compensation and the different 'interests'

The starting point must be that the aim of an award of damages is to compensate the claimant for the loss which he has suffered as a result of the defendant's breach of contract and that damages are awarded or refused on the basis of legal principle and are not a matter of discretion for the court (*Morris-Garner v One Step (Support) Ltd* [2018] UKSC 20, [2019] AC 649, [95]). The aim is therefore to compensate the claimant for loss or damage and not to punish the defendant. A breach of contract is a civil wrong; it is not a criminal offence. Although punitive damages can be awarded in a tort action (*Kuddus v Chief Constable of Leicestershire Constabulary* [2001] UKHL 29; [2002] 2 AC 122), they cannot be awarded in a purely contractual action, even where the defendant has calculated that he will make a profit from his breach of contract (*Addis v Gramophone Co Ltd* [1909] AC 488 and, more recently, *Devenish Nutrition Ltd v Sanofi-Aventis SA* [2008] EWCA Civ 1086; [2009] Ch 390, [143]). The issue of the availability of punitive damages in a breach of contract claim has divided other common law jurisdictions with punitive damages being available in Canada in respect of a breach of contract upon proof of an independent actionable wrong arising out of the same facts as the breach of contract (see *Whiten v Pilot Insurance Co* (2002) 209 DLR (4th) 257) but not in Singapore, which expressly declined to follow the approach taken in Canada (*PH Hydraulics & Engineering Pte Ltd v Airtrust (Hong Kong) Ltd* [2017] SGCA 26; [2017] 2 SLR 129).

The proposition that damages are compensatory gives rise to a further question. That question is: for what is it that the claimant is entitled to be compensated? Theoretically, a claimant could claim compensation on one of a number of different grounds (see Fuller and Perdue, 1936 and the discussion by the High Court of

Australia in *Commonwealth of Australia v Amann Aviation Pty Ltd* (1991) 174 CLR 64, noted by Treitel, 1992). In the first place, a claimant could claim the protection of his 'expectation interest' (or, perhaps more accurately, his 'performance interest'). The basis of such a claim is that the claimant's expectations, engendered by the promise of the defendant that he will perform his contractual obligations, have not been fulfilled and that damages should compensate him for his disappointed expectations by putting him in as good a position as he would have occupied had the defendant performed his promise. Secondly, a claimant may claim the protection of his 'reliance interest', that is to say, as a result of the defendant's promise to perform his contractual obligations, the claimant has acted to his detriment in entering into the contract and the award of damages should compensate him to the extent that he has relied to his detriment upon the promise of the defendant. The aim here is to put the claimant in as good a position as he was in before the defendant's promise was made. Finally, a claimant may assert that his 'restitution interest' should be protected. A claimant who claims the protection of his restitution interest does not wish to be compensated for the loss which he has suffered; rather, he wishes to deprive the defendant of a gain which he has made at the claimant's expense. Which of these 'measures' can be claimed by a claimant in an action for damages for breach of contract? More importantly, what factors would persuade a claimant to elect to seek the recovery of one measure rather than another?

The most important factor is obviously the amount of damages which a claimant can recover by way of compensation. Which is more advantageous to the claimant: the expectation measure, the reliance measure or the restitution measure? A very simple example will help us to answer this question. Let us suppose that I enter into a contract to purchase a table for £800. Let us make the further assumption that the market value of such a table is, in fact, £800. In breach of contract the seller provides me with a table which does not correspond with the terms of the contract and is worth only £400. I fulfil my side of the bargain and pay £800.

An award of damages which protected my expectation interest would aim to put me in the position which I would have been in had the contract been performed according to its terms. Had the contract been performed according to its terms, I would have obtained a table worth £800, whereas I have obtained a table which is worth only £400. Therefore the expectation measure is calculated by deducting the value of what I have actually received (£400) from the value of what I expected to receive (£800). Damages would therefore be assessed at £400.

An award of damages which sought to protect my reliance interest would seek to put me in the position which I would have been in had I not entered into the contract. Had I not entered into the contract, I would not have parted with my £800 and I would not have received a table worth £400. So the reliance measure is calculated by deducting the value of what I have received (£400) from the amount which I have paid out (£800). Damages would, once again, be assessed at £400 so that, on the facts of this case, the expectation measure and the reliance measure would be exactly the same. An award which sought to protect my restitution interest would restore to me the benefit which I had conferred upon the seller. So I would be entitled to the return of the £800 and the seller would be entitled to the return of the table.

Although we have noted that the reliance measure and the expectation measure can be exactly the same, in other cases they can be radically different. The reason for the coincidence in my example was that the contract price and the market value of a table which complied with the contractual specifications were exactly the same. Had these figures been different, then the measures would have been different. Let us suppose that I had promised to pay £800 but that the table was, in fact, worth only £600. This time the expectation measure would be £600 (the value of what I expected to receive) less £400 (the value of what I actually received), which equals £200. But the reliance measure would be £800 (what I paid out) minus £400 (the value of what I received), which equals £400. So a claimant will wish to resort to the reliance measure where he has made a bad bargain, in an effort to escape from the consequences of his own bargain. On the other hand, if I had made a good bargain so that the market value of the table was £1,000, the expectation measure would be £1,000 less £400, which equals £600, whereas the reliance measure would remain at £800 less £400, which equals £400. Therefore, it is principally where the claimant has made a bad bargain that he will want to claim the reliance measure; in other cases the expectation measure will be more advantageous to a claimant.

21.3 The expectation interest

The general rule is that an award of damages for breach of contract seeks to protect the claimant's expectation interest. The classic statement of this general principle can be found in the judgment of Parke B in *Robinson v Harman* (1848) 1 Ex 850, 855:

> the rule of the common law is, that where a party sustains loss by reason of a breach of contract, he is, so far as money can do it, to be placed in the same situation, with respect to damages, as if the contract had been performed.

The justification for the award of the expectation measure is that a binding promise creates in the promisee an expectation of performance and the remedy granted for the breach of such a binding promise seeks to fulfil or to protect that expectation. But there is an element of ambiguity in the proposition that damages seek to put the claimant in the position he would have been in had the contract been performed. The first ambiguity relates to the identification of the loss and the second concerns the measurement of that loss.

21.3.1 The nature of the expectation interest

When we talk about loss and about placing the innocent party in the same situation as if the contract had been performed, what do we mean? Do we mean financial loss and financial situation or do we take into account a broader range of factors? In Australia the courts have rejected the view that only the financial position of the claimant can be taken into account (*Tabcorp Holdings Ltd v Bowen Instruments Pty Ltd* (2009) 236 CLR 272, [13]). But a narrower approach has been taken in England, as can be demonstrated by reference to the following statement taken from the judgment of Lord Bingham MR (as he then was) in *White Arrow Express Ltd v Lamey's Distribution Ltd* [1996] Trading Law Reports 69, 73, when he stated that the *Robinson v Harman* 'formulation assumes that the breach has injured [the claimant's] financial position; if he cannot show that it has, he will recover nominal damages only'. Similarly, in *Alfred McAlpine Construction Ltd v Panatown Ltd* [2001] 1 AC 518, 534

Lord Clyde stated that 'when one refers to a loss in the context of a breach of contract, one is in my view referring to the incidence of some personal or patrimonial damage'.

In many cases it will suffice to take account of the financial position of the parties because the contract will have been entered into with a view to making a profit and the protection of that expectation of profit will adequately protect the interests of the innocent party. But in the modern world parties frequently enter into contracts for reasons other than to make a profit. Suppose that a houseowner enters into a contract with a builder to have a swimming pool built in her garden and that she stipulates that it must be built to a depth of seven feet six inches. Or suppose that a son enters into a contract with a builder under which the builder agrees to repair the roof of his parent's house. Finally, imagine that a local authority enters into a contract with a contractor for the provision of a fire service. The first case is an example of a contract to enhance leisure time, while the latter two are examples of contracts which are entered into for the purpose of providing a service to third parties. A legal system which focuses only upon the profit motive to the exclusion of the values of leisure and community service fails to reflect the values of the modern world. As Lord Mustill stated in *Ruxley Electronics and Construction Ltd v Forsyth* [1996] AC 344, 360 'the law must cater for those occasions where the value of the promise to the promisee exceeds the financial enhancement of his position which full performance will secure'. The recognition of the 'consumer surplus' in *Ruxley* (Section 21.13) is an open acknowledgement of the need for a broader perspective which takes account of the wide range of purposes which contracting parties have in mind when entering into contracts (see McKendrick, 1999a). But there is a long way to go. One of the most important purposes which a party has in entering into a contract is of course to secure the promised performance but the commitment of the law to the protection of the claimant's interest in performance is, in fact, rather weak. Specific performance has traditionally been seen as a secondary remedy (Section 22.9) and the reluctance to compel specific performance is carried through to the damages remedy, where the courts tend to seek to put the claimant in the financial position which he would have been in had the contract been performed according to its terms and not to give him the funds necessary to secure actual performance.

The extent to which the law of contract protects the 'expectation' or 'performance' interest of the claimant was a matter of extended judicial analysis in the difficult case of *Alfred McAlpine Construction Ltd v Panatown Ltd* [2001] 1 AC 518 (see McKendrick, 2003b). An example given by Lord Goff illustrates the point. Suppose that a wealthy philanthropist contracts for work to be done to the village hall. The work is done defectively by the contractor. Does the philanthropist have a claim for substantial damages notwithstanding the fact that he does not own the hall and the breach has not caused him any obvious financial loss (in the sense that he is not under any obligation to repair the defects in the works)? Lord Goff, agreeing with the speech of Lord Griffiths in *Linden Gardens Trust Ltd v Lenesta Sludge Disposals Ltd* [1994] 1 AC 85, 96 was of the opinion that the philanthropist had suffered a loss in the sense that he did not receive the bargain for which he contracted. Lord Millett adopted a similar view. He was (at 588) critical of the 'narrow accountants' balance sheet quantification of loss which measures the loss suffered by the promisee by the diminution in his overall financial position resulting from the breach'. The difficulty is that Lords Goff and

Millett were the dissentients in *Panatown*. Lord Clyde, one of the judges in the majority, was more hostile to this extended notion of loss. He stated (at 534) that while a breach of contract 'may cause a loss ... it is not in itself a loss in any meaningful sense' and he added that a 'failure in performance of a contractual obligation does not entail a loss of the bargained-for contractual rights'. But it may be that Lord Clyde was in the minority on this point because Lord Browne-Wilkinson, one of the other judges in the majority, was prepared to assume, albeit with much hesitation, that Lord Griffiths' approach in *Linden Gardens* was correct. Lord Jauncey, the third judge in the majority, stated (at 574) that he agreed with Lord Goff's rejection of the 'proposition that the employer under a building contract is unable to recover substantial damages for breach of the contract if the work in question is to be performed on land or buildings which are not his property' but added that the employer's right to substantial damages will depend upon 'whether he has made good or intends to make good the effects of the breach'. The answer to the example given by Lord Goff therefore remains to be definitively resolved as a matter of English law (the view of Lord Goff and Lord Griffiths received some support from Lord Sumption in *Swynson Ltd v Lowick Rose LLP* [2017] UKSC 32; [2018] AC 313, [17], although contrast the more cautious approach taken by Lord Mance at [53]) and the key issue may turn out to be the one identified by Lord Jauncey, namely the circumstances in which the courts will award to the claimant 'cost of cure' damages.

21.3.2 Cost of cure or diminution in value?

This takes us into our second problem which is the approach which the courts adopt when seeking to measure the damages payable. Two possible measures could put the claimant in the position which he would have been in had the contract been performed according to its terms. The first is the difference in value between what the claimant has received and what he expected to receive and the second is the cost of putting the claimant into the position which he would have been in had the contract been fully performed according to its terms. In many cases the two measures will produce the same result. For example, if, in breach of contract, a seller fails to deliver the promised goods, and the buyer goes out into the marketplace and purchases substitute goods, the diminution in value and the cost of cure will be exactly the same. But in some cases the two measures can produce very different results.

The facts of *Ruxley Electronics and Construction Ltd v Forsyth* [1996] AC 344 neatly illustrate such a divergence. The claimant builders agreed to construct a swimming pool for the defendant. In breach of contract the claimant built the pool to a depth of six feet when its depth should have been seven foot six inches. How should damages be assessed for this breach? The trial judge measured the diminution in value as zero but the cost of cure was found to be £21,560. Which was the correct measure? The first point which the House of Lords made was that they were not confined to a straight choice between the two measures. Such a stark choice could produce an unjust outcome. For example, Lord Mustill noted (at 360) that it was:

> a common feature of small building works performed on residential property that the cost of the work is not fully reflected by an increase in the market value of the house, and that comparatively minor deviations from specification or sound workmanship may have no direct financial effect at all.

In such a case, the diminution in value might well be zero or a very small sum indeed. To award such a sum by way of damages for the breach would, Lord Mustill conceded, make part of the builders' promise 'illusory' because there would be no adequate remedy available to the consumer in the event of breach. On the other hand, Lord Mustill noted that it would be equally unsatisfactory if the law were to jump to the conclusion that damages were necessarily to be assessed on a cost of cure basis because the cost of cure might not accurately reflect the loss which the innocent party had suffered either. To the argument that there were only two measures of damages, Lord Mustill replied that there was only one, namely 'the loss truly suffered by the promisee'. On the facts of *Ruxley*, the loss which the defendant had suffered was the disappointment which he had experienced in not getting a swimming pool of the correct specifications and that loss was best reflected in an award of 'loss of amenity damages' of £2,500 (see Section 21.13).

Having concluded that the defendant was entitled to loss of amenity damages, their Lordships considered the question whether the defendant was entitled to recover cost of cure damages. They concluded that he was not. In reaching their conclusion, the House of Lords underlined the role of reasonableness and 'common sense' in deciding whether to award damages on a cost of cure basis or a diminution in value basis. The court was therefore entitled, indeed obliged, to have regard to the reasonableness of the course of action pursued or proposed by the defendant when seeking to assess the loss which he had, in fact, suffered. On the facts of the case, it was held that it was not reasonable for the defendant to recover cost of cure damages because the cost of carrying out the work was out of all proportion to the benefit which the defendant would obtain by its performance. What was it that made it unreasonable for the defendant to recover cost of cure damages? It is suggested that it is a combination of two factors: the first is the cost of the repairs (£21,560) and the second is the fact that the work would have resulted in little by way of benefit to the defendant. It is important to note that it was the *combination* of these factors which was important: taken in isolation they may not be decisive. This point can be illustrated by changing the facts of *Ruxley*.

Let us suppose that the work would have resulted in a considerable benefit to the defendant because, in its existing state, the pool was not safe to dive into. In such a case cost of cure is likely to emerge as a reasonable way of ensuring that the defendant obtains the financial value of the promised performance. Thus, Lord Jauncey stated (at 358) that 'if a building is constructed so defectively that it is of no use for its designed purpose the owner may have little difficulty in establishing that his loss is the necessary cost of reconstructing'. But *Ruxley* was not a case in which the pool was of no use for its designed purpose. On the contrary, the trial judge made the following findings of fact: the pool was safe for diving, the defendant had no intention or desire to fit a diving-board, the shortfall in depth did not decrease the value of the pool, the defendant had no intention of building a new pool and to spend £21,560 on a new pool would have been unreasonable.

A more difficult question would have been posed if the cost of cure had been lower. What would have been the position if the cost of cure had been less, let us say £5,000? Would such a cost have been 'out of all proportion' to the benefit to be obtained by the defendant? Is the proportion to be measured simply by reference to the diminution in value (which was found to be zero) or by reference to the diminution in value together with the loss of amenity? The answer is not entirely clear, but it is suggested that the latter is the figure which should be used because the court is endeavouring to measure the loss which the innocent party has suffered and that is either the cost of cure or the diminution in value together with, where appropriate, loss of amenity damages. If this analysis is correct then cost of cure damages may have been recovered had the cost of repairs been in the region of £5,000.

21.3.3 The role of intention

The final issue in this context relates to the role of intention in the assessment of damages. What is the significance of the fact that the innocent party has declared his intention to use the sum awarded by way of damages to cure the defect in the building? While the courts are not generally concerned with the use which a party makes of the damages awarded to him, it does not follow, as Lord Lloyd pointed out (at 372), that the intention of the innocent party is not relevant to the issue of reasonableness. Where the innocent party is not genuine in his desire to carry out the repairs, this will be a factor which counts against the award of cost of cure damages. But it does not follow that a genuine intention to carry out the work will act as a passport to the award of cost of cure damages. This is because a party cannot be 'allowed to create a loss, which does not exist, in order to punish the [party in breach] for [its] breach of contract'. So the vital test is the reasonableness test, and the intention of the parties is only one factor to be considered when resolving that issue.

Ruxley is a fascinating case because it is so simple yet so rich in issues. In awarding loss of amenity damages it can be argued that the House of Lords took one step forward and one step backward. The step forward was the award of damages to reflect the defendant's loss of amenity. The step backward was that it can be argued that the House of Lords failed adequately to protect the defendant's performance interest because he was not given the money which he needed to obtain the swimming pool of the promised proportions. But, given that the courts would not have specifically enforced the contract and that the defendant was held not to be entitled to withhold payment of the price because he had obtained substantially what he had bargained for (the doctrine of 'substantial performance' is discussed in Section 22.2), it is perhaps not surprising that the House of Lords refused to award him cost of cure damages. On its facts, it may well be that *Ruxley* was correctly decided. But the decision does have its dangers (see Coote, 1997 and McKendrick, 1999a). The principal danger is that it may make it much harder for a party who wants to receive a particular type or form of performance to ensure that he actually obtains that performance instead of the economic end-result of performance. Take the case of a decorator who puts the wrong wallpaper on the wall. Is the homeowner to recover cost of cure damages or only diminution in value plus loss of amenity damages? If the latter is the answer then *Ruxley* has added a further limit to the willingness of the courts to protect the expectation interest of the innocent party (for the other limits, see Sections 21.9 to 21.14). On the other hand, if emphasis is placed on the exceptional facts of *Ruxley* (namely that the claimant had substantially performed its obligations under the contract, the difference in depth did not impair the defendant's use of the pool, the cost of cure was high and the finding of the trial judge that the defendant had no intention of building a new pool), then the danger can, in large part, be avoided. In support of *Ruxley* it can also be argued that the House of Lords through its employment of 'reasonableness' as the control device, allied to the greater availability of loss of amenity damages, has set up a framework which is sufficiently flexible to ensure a fair outcome in the resolution of the vast majority of cases.

21.4   Reliance interest

The claimant may wish to claim the protection of his reliance interest so that he is put in the position which he would have been in had he not entered into a contract with the defendant. For example, the claimant may have wasted expenditure in the performance of the contract prior to its termination and may wish simply to recover that expenditure. A claim of this nature seems to be different in principle from a claim to recover expectation damages (see Treitel, 1992, 229–30). The latter is forward-looking, aiming to put the claimant in the position he would have been in had the contract been performed, while the former is backward-looking, aiming to restore the claimant to his pre-contractual position. On this basis Professor Friedmann has argued (1995) that the reliance interest is not a 'contractual interest' because a party does not enter into a contract with a view simply to recovering his detrimental expenditure.

The view that the reliance interest is not a contractual interest has, however, been challenged by Teare J in *Omak Maritime Ltd v Mamola Challenger Shipping Co* [2010] EWHC 2026 (Comm); [2011] 1 Lloyd's Rep 47. After a careful review of the authorities Teare J concluded (at [47]) that 'the expectation loss principle underpins the award of damages in wasted expenditure cases'. He therefore (at [42]) rejected the submission that reliance losses are 'fundamentally different' from expectation losses and that they are awarded on a 'different juridical basis of claim'. On the contrary, he held that they are a 'species of expectation losses' on the basis that 'the expenditure which is sought to be recovered is incurred in expectation that the contract will be performed' (see to similar effect the judgments of Toohey and McHugh JJ in *Commonwealth of Australia v Amann Aviation Pty Ltd* (1991) 174 CLR 64, 136, 162). In other words, had the contract been performed according to its terms, the claimant would, it is assumed, recover the expenditure incurred in the performance of the contract. Leggatt J has described this assumption as 'the principle of reasonable assumptions' (*Yam Seng Pte Ltd v International Trade Corporation Ltd* [2013] EWHC 111 (QB); [2013] 1 All ER (Comm) 1321, [188]). Professor Treitel (1992) is critical of this assumption because it is 'doubtfully consistent with experience' on the basis that 'unprofitable contracts are by no means as uncommon' as the supporters of this assumption seem to suggest. However, the difference would appear to be one of classification which has few, if any, practical consequences. As we shall see, both Teare J and Professor Treitel agree that the claimant's entitlement to recover reliance damages is subject to the limit that they cannot be recovered to the extent that the defendant can prove that the expenditure would not have been recovered had the contract been performed according to its terms. This limit is easy to explain if reliance losses are indeed a species of expectation losses because the limit is consistent with the principle that a claimant cannot seek to be put in a better position than he would have been in had the contract been performed according to its terms. But it is more difficult to explain why the expectation measure should act as a limit if the entitlement to recover reliance losses is based on an alternative principle. It was this difficulty which, in part, persuaded Teare J to conclude that reliance losses are best understood as a species of expectation losses.

21.4.1 No getting out of a bad bargain

The general rule, affirmed in *CCC Films (London) Ltd v Impact Quadrant Films Ltd* [1985] QB 16, is that a claimant has an unfettered right to choose whether to claim for loss of bargain damages or for wasted expenditure. The general right of election is subject to an exception where the claimant seeks to recover his reliance loss in an attempt to escape the consequences of his bad bargain. In *C and P Haulage Co Ltd v Middleton* [1983] 3 All ER 94, the claimant was given a licence to occupy premises on a renewable six-monthly basis. He spent some money on improving the property, even though it was expressly provided in the contract that the fixtures were not to be removed at the end of the licence. The defendants ejected the claimant from the premises in breach of contract and the claimant sought to recover as damages the cost of the improvements which he had carried out to the property. His action failed on the ground that the breach had not caused him any loss because he would have been in the same position had the contract been terminated lawfully. The Court of Appeal held that the claimant's loss did not flow from the breach but from the fact that he had entered into a contract under which he had agreed that he would not be able to remove the fixtures at the end of the lease. It was held that a claimant could not recover his reliance losses where that would enable him to escape from his bad bargain or would reverse the contractual allocation of risk. It is for the defendant to show that the bargain was a bad one for the claimant (see also *Omak Maritime Ltd v Mamola Challenger Shipping Co* (above)) and he must prove that the gross returns which the innocent party expected to derive from the contract would not be sufficient to enable him to recover his expenditure (*Grange v Quinn* [2013] EWCA Civ 24; [2013] 1 P & CR 279, [102]). The only situation in which an innocent party can escape the consequences of his bad bargain is where there has been a total failure of consideration (see Section 21.6). In such a situation there has been no performance under the contract, the claimant's claim is one in restitution and so there is no objection to the reversal of the contractual allocation of risk.

21.4.2 Pre-contractual expenditure

A claimant may, however, wish to recover his reliance loss where he has incurred reliance expenditure before the conclusion of the contract. In *Anglia Television Ltd v Reed* [1972] 1 QB 60, the claimants engaged the defendant to star in a film which they were making. At the last moment the defendant repudiated the contract and the claimants had to abandon the film because they were unable to find a replacement actor. Lord Denning said that, where the claimants claimed their loss of expenditure, they were not limited to expenditure incurred after the contract was concluded but that they could also claim for expenditure incurred before the contract was concluded provided that it was within the reasonable contemplation of the parties that it would be likely to be wasted as a result of the defendant's breach. Such pre-contract expenditure could not be regarded as part of the claimants' expectation interest on the facts of the case, because the claimants decided not to claim their loss of profit on the ground that they could not say what that loss of profit would have been.

21.4.3 No proof of expectation loss

On the other hand, a claimant may be confined to the recovery of his reliance losses where he cannot prove what his expectation losses would have been. Such was the case in *McRae v Commonwealth Disposals Commission* (1951) 84 CLR 377 (the facts of which are set out at Section 14.3), where the speculative nature of the enterprise made it impossible for the claimants to quantify their expectations with any degree of precision. The High Court of Australia confined the claimants to the recovery of their expenses incurred in mounting the salvage expedition and to the return of their prepayment. But *McRae* is an extreme case and the courts are extremely reluctant to conclude that the claimant's expectations are so speculative that they cannot be valued. In *Chaplin v Hicks* [1911] 2 KB 786, the defendant, by his breach of contract, denied the claimant the opportunity to participate in a beauty contest. The jury awarded her damages of £100 to represent her loss of a chance to win the contest and the Court of Appeal upheld the award. The aim of the courts is to measure or estimate the loss suffered by the claimant 'as accurately and reliably as the nature of the case permits' and, as *Chaplin* demonstrates, the law 'is tolerant of imprecision where the loss is incapable of precise measurement' (*Morris-Garner v One Step (Support) Ltd* [2018] UKSC 20; [2019] AC 649, [95](8)).

21.5 The restitution interest

Can a claimant seek the protection of his restitution interest rather than his expectation interest? The answer is that a claimant does not have a free choice between the two measures. A claimant can obtain a restitutionary remedy only when he can establish that the defendant was enriched, that the enrichment was at the claimant's expense and that it is unjust that the defendant retain the benefit without recompensing the claimant. The classic example of a restitutionary claim (or, to use the terminology which seems to be gaining increasingly in acceptance, an unjust enrichment claim) is a claim to recover money paid under a mistake of fact (see, for example, *Barclays Bank Ltd v W J Simms Ltd* [1980] 1 QB 677). But, where the ground on which restitution is sought is that the defendant has broken his contract with the claimant, then a restitutionary remedy is available only within very narrow confines. The classic example of a restitutionary claim is the claim to recover money upon a total failure of consideration (Section 21.6). More difficult is the case where the claimant seeks to strip the defendant of the profit (or a percentage of the profit) which the defendant has made as a result of his breach of contract (Section 21.7).

21.6 Failure of consideration and enrichment by subtraction

A claimant may seek to recover a benefit which he has conferred upon the defendant when the *basis* upon which the benefit was conferred has failed because of the defendant's breach of contract. The argument of the claimant is that he has conferred a benefit upon the defendant only for the purpose of the performance of the contract and, now that performance has been abandoned because of the defendant's breach of contract, the benefit ought to be restored to him. However, a restitutionary claim cannot be brought where the contract has not been set aside or is not otherwise ineffective. Where the contract is valid and enforceable, it governs the rights and remedies of the parties and these cannot be subverted by resort to a restitutionary claim.

Money paid to a defendant is only recoverable where there has been a total failure of consideration, that is to say, the claimant has received no part of what he has bargained for. Where the failure of consideration is only partial, so that the claimant has received some part, no matter how small, of the promised performance then the restitutionary claim is barred (*Whincup v Hughes* (1871) LR 6 CP 78). A case which illustrates the distinction between a total and a partial failure of consideration is *White Arrow Express Ltd v Lamey's Distribution Ltd* [1996] Trading Law Reports 69. The claimants entered into a contract with the defendants under which the defendants agreed to provide the claimants with a deluxe delivery service. In fact, they provided only the standard measure of service. The claimants experienced some difficulty in proving that they had suffered a loss as a result of the defendants' breach, because none of their customers complained about the level of service provided. So the claimants framed their claim as one to recover that proportion of the price that related to the enhanced level of service which the defendants were obliged to provide but did not in fact provide. The Court of Appeal dismissed the claim on the ground that it was a claim to recover money paid on a partial, not a total, failure of consideration. The claimants were held to be entitled to recover only nominal damages. This seems unfair. But the source of the problem may in fact be the way in which the case was pleaded. The claimants could and should have sued for damages for breach of contract in the normal way and sought to recover damages assessed by reference to the difference between the price which they paid for the service (or, if it is lower, the market value of what was contracted for) and the market value of what was obtained.

The restitutionary claim tends to assume particular significance where the claimant has entered into a bad bargain or claims to have suffered a loss which the law of contract does not recognise. An illustration of the former case is provided by the following hypothetical example. Suppose that I agree to buy a desk for £200. The desk is in fact worth only £150. If, for some reason, the seller refused to deliver the desk, I would be entitled to recover the £200 because the consideration for the payment has wholly failed. An example in the second category is provided by a variant of *Ruxley Electronics and Construction Ltd v Forsyth* (above). Suppose that the builder had saved himself some money by building the swimming pool to the wrong depth. Could the defendant have recovered the saving on the ground that he had paid for this service and not received it? He would seem to be unable to recover it as contractual damages because, on the facts of *Ruxley*, there appeared to be no difference between the price paid and the market value of what he received. A restitutionary claim to deprive the builder of the gain made would here have performed a useful function from the defendant's perspective but of course any attempt to recover a proportion of the price would seem to fall foul of the rule that the law does not allow recovery based on a partial failure of consideration (as in the *White Arrow* case).

The requirement that the failure of consideration must be total has, however, been widely attacked by academic lawyers (see, for example, Burrows, 2010, 330–34). It is argued that the unjust enrichment is as real in cases of partial as in cases of total failure because in both cases the basis upon which the money was paid has failed. Secondly, the total failure requirement does not apply to a claim brought by the provider of goods or services (see Burrows, 332–33), although this argument is considerably weakened by the fact that the law has not yet recognised that a claim to recover in such cases is based on 'failure of consideration' reasoning. Thirdly, the law has proved to be rather arbitrary in its application because the courts have tended to strain to find a total failure of consideration in some cases, and they have done this by ignoring or discounting practical benefits received by the party seeking to set aside the transaction in order to find that there has, in fact, been a total failure of consideration (see, for example, *Rover International Ltd v Cannon Film Sales Ltd (No 3)* [1989] 1 WLR 912). The law may yet develop in the direction of the abolition of the total failure requirement and, indeed, where counter-restitution can easily be made it has already been effectively abandoned (see *Goss v Chilcott* [1996] AC 788, 798, per Lord Goff). It is suggested that the law should develop further so that it reaches the position where a partial failure should suffice to generate a restitutionary claim, subject only to the requirement that the claimant make counter-restitution for any benefit which he has received at the expense of the defendant.

Where the claim is not for the return of money but for the value of goods supplied or services rendered under the contract then more difficult questions arise. It is clear that, where the contract is terminated on the ground of the defendant's breach of contract, the claimant has a right to elect either to proceed in contract or in restitution (*Planché v Colburn* (1831) 8 Bing 14), but it is not clear whether in a restitutionary action the contract price acts as a ceiling on the sum recoverable. *Dicta* can be found to support the proposition that the contract price does not act as a ceiling (*Lodder v Slowey* [1904] AC 442 and *Rover International Ltd v Cannon Film Sales Ltd (No 3)* [1989] 1 WLR 912) and such a rule was adopted in the American case of *Boomer v Muir* 24 P 2d 570 (1933). But it is suggested that, given that breach operates prospectively (Section 20.7), and the goods were supplied or services rendered under what was, at the time, a valid subsisting contract, it is difficult to see why the courts should ignore the contract in assessing the value of the goods supplied or services performed (*Taylor v Motability Finance Ltd* [2004] EWHC 2619 (Comm), [26]). The High Court of Australia has recently concluded that the contract price should generally act as a ceiling on the restitutionary claim, while acknowledging that there may be exceptional cases where it may be appropriate to award a sum in excess of the relevant proportion of the contract price (*Mann v Paterson Constructions Pty Ltd* [2019] HCA 32; [2020] BLR 156).

21.7 Account of profits and negotiating damages

A claimant may wish to deprive the defendant of the profit (or a share of the profit) which he has made from his breach of contract. At least in the case where the claim is one to recover the entirety of the defendant's profit, it differs from the claim to recover money paid on a total failure of consideration because the defendant's enrichment is not necessarily by subtraction from the claimant. An enrichment is by subtraction from the claimant when the loss to the claimant is the same as the gain to the defendant. For example, in the case where the claimant pays £100 to the defendant as a result of a mistake of fact, the loss to the claimant is £100 and the corresponding gain to the defendant is £100. In the 'failure of consideration' cases there is an equivalence of loss and gain so that the enrichment is by subtraction from the claimant. But in cases of the type considered in this section there is no requirement that the enrichment be by subtraction from the claimant. Indeed, in most of the cases the gain to the defendant comfortably exceeds the loss which the claimant has suffered. We shall divide our consideration of these cases into two groups. The first case is the one in which the claimant seeks to recover the entirety of the defendant's profit. The second is the case in which the claimant seeks to recover the sum that he could hypothetically have received in return for releasing the defendant from the obligation which he failed to perform, a claim now described as one to recover 'negotiating damages'.

21.7.1 Recovering the entirety of the profit: *A-G v Blake*

A claim to recover the entirety of the profit made by the defendant from his breach of contract was recognised by the House of Lords in *A-G v Blake* [2001] 1 AC 268 (see McKendrick, 2003a) where the claim was described as one for an account of profits. The facts of *Blake* are, however, rather unusual in that they concern the attempt made by the Attorney-General to recover the profits made by the spy, George Blake, from his breach of contract in writing an autobiography and including within it information which he had given an undertaking to the Crown that he would not divulge. The House of Lords held that the Crown was entitled to recover the profits made by Blake from his breach of contract and, furthermore, that they were entitled to recover the whole of that profit. But it does not follow from *Blake* that an account of profits will be widely available as a remedy for a breach of contract. On the contrary, their Lordships in *Blake* emphasised the exceptional nature of the remedy. This point emerges from the following key passage from the speech of Lord Nicholls. He stated (at 285):

> An account of profits will be appropriate in exceptional circumstances. Normally the remedies of [compensatory] damages, specific performance and injunction, coupled with the characterisation of some contractual obligations as fiduciary, will provide an adequate response to a breach of contract. It will be only in exceptional cases, where those remedies are inadequate, that any question of accounting for profits will arise. No fixed rules can be prescribed. The court will have regard to all the circumstances, including the subject matter of the contract, the purpose of the contractual provision which has been breached, the circumstances in which the breach occurred, the consequences of the breach and the circumstances in which relief is being sought. A useful general guide, although not exhaustive, is whether the plaintiff had a legitimate interest in preventing the defendant's profit-making activity and, hence, in depriving him of his profit.

The inadequacy of other remedies thus appears to be a condition precedent to the award of an account of profits. The claimant must also show that he has a 'legitimate interest' in depriving the defendant of his profit, although it is far from clear what constitutes a 'legitimate interest' for this purpose. One difficulty with the claim is that it has the appearance of being punitive in nature because it strips the defendant of the entirety of the profit made from the breach (and, on the facts of *Blake*, gave him no allowance for the effort which he had put into put into writing the book). This is not necessarily a conclusive objection because a claim for an account of profits can be distinguished from a claim to recover punitive damages (on which see Section 21.2). The former claim is tied to the profit made by the defendant whereas an award of punitive damages may exceed the profit made by the defendant from the breach and so the two are not necessarily identical. Perhaps more difficult to justify is the award of the defendant's profit to the claimant, particularly in the case where the profit exceeds the loss suffered by the claimant by some margin. While it may not be appropriate for the defendant to retain his profit, is the claimant really the most appropriate person to receive what may be to him no more than a windfall?

For these and other reasons, *Blake* is now seen very much as an exception, and is probably unlikely to be followed. In *Morris-Garner v One Step (Support) Ltd* [2018] UKSC 20; [2019] AC 649, [95](11) Lord Reed stated that 'common law damages for breach of contract cannot be awarded merely for the purpose of depriving the defendant of profits made as a result of the breach, other than in exceptional circumstances, following *Attorney-General v Blake*'. What are the 'exceptional circumstances' which justified the award of an account of profits on the facts of *Blake*? The Supreme Court in *Morris-Garner* did not tell us, perhaps because the 'soundness' of the decision in *Blake* was not before the court ([82]). The Court of Appeal of Singapore was slightly more forthcoming in *Turf Club Auto Emporium Pte Ltd v Yeo Boong Hua* [2018] SGCA 44; [2018] 2 SLR 655, where *Blake* was described as 'truly exceptional' (at [251]) and the court tentatively suggested (at [254]) that the case could be seen as one in which the law had a legitimate basis for punishing the defendant and deterring breach because the contract involved a public interest, namely national security, which went beyond the private interests of the parties themselves. On this basis, *Blake* is probably unlikely to be followed, particularly in a case involving a commercial contract.

21.7.2 Negotiating damages

The second claim is one to recover negotiating damages. This claim is more widely available than the claim to recover the entirety of the defendant's profit but it has nevertheless proved to be an issue of some controversy. There are a number of difficulties here. The first relates to the nature of the claim. Is the claim really one to recover the defendant's profit? Is it not really one in which the claimant has suffered a loss, namely the loss of the primary right to performance of the defendant's obligations? Second, in what circumstances can a claimant recover damages assessed on this basis? Third, how are such damages to be assessed?

The case which is now generally regarded as the modern origin of the claim to recover a share of the defendant's profit is the decision of Brightman J in *Wrotham Park Estate Co Ltd v Parkside Homes Ltd* [1974] 1 WLR 798. The defendant built houses on its own land in breach of a restrictive covenant. Brightman J awarded the claimant damages of £2,500, which represented some 5 per cent of the defendant's anticipated profits from the breach. Following the decision of the Supreme Court in *Morris-Garner v One Step (Support) Ltd* [2018] UKSC 20; [2019] AC 649 such damages are now known as 'negotiating damages' and they are assessed by reference to the sum of money which might reasonably have been demanded by the claimant from the defendant as a quid pro quo for permitting the defendant to breach its covenant or otherwise to infringe the rights of the claimant. The court is here constructing a hypothetical bargain between a willing buyer and a willing seller, both of whom are assumed to act reasonably. Thus in a case such as *Wrotham Park* the court is involved in creating a hypothetical bargain between willing parties and the fact that one or both of them might in practice have refused to make such a deal is irrelevant (*Pell Frischmann Engineering Ltd v Bow Valley Iran Ltd* [2009] UKPC 45; [2010] BLR 73, [49]). The assessment of the loss is therefore objective, not subjective.

21.7.3 When will negotiating damages be awarded?

When will negotiating damages be awarded? The answer given by the Supreme Court in *Morris-Garner v One Step (Support) Ltd* is that they are available in a relatively small group of cases. The first is where the defendant wrongfully makes use of property (including intellectual property) which belongs to the claimant. In such a case the defendant cannot be heard to say that the claimant has suffered no loss because he would not have used the property in the time in which it was in the possession of the defendant. The defendant in such a case has deprived the claimant of the right to control the use of his property and for that the claimant is entitled to demand that the defendant pay a reasonable fee for the use of his property. The second case is where the court in the exercise of its discretion decides to award the claimant damages in substitution for specific performance or an injunction (Section 22.11). In such a case damages are awarded as a monetary substitute for what is lost by the claimant as a result of the decision of the court not to grant him a specific performance order or an injunction. In these two cases it can be seen that the award of negotiating damages has the effect of protecting a claimant's interest in his own property or of compensating him for the decision not to grant him a specific performance order or an injunction.

But what about the case where the claimant simply seeks to recover negotiating damages in respect of the defendant's breach of contract? Can the claimant recover negotiating damages in such a case? The answer provided by Lord Reed, giving the majority judgment of the Supreme Court in *Morris-Garner* (at [95](10)), was that

> Negotiating damages can be awarded for breach of contract where the loss suffered by the claimant is appropriately measured by reference to the economic value of the right which has been breached, considered as an asset. That may be the position where the breach of contract results in the loss of a valuable asset created or protected by the right which was infringed. The rationale is that the claimant has in substance been deprived of a valuable asset, and his loss can therefore be measured by determining the economic value of the right in question, considered as an asset. The defendant has taken something for nothing, for which the claimant was entitled to require payment.

This is a difficult paragraph. The difficulty lies in discerning when a breach of contract will result 'in the loss of a valuable asset created or protected by the right which was infringed'. Examples given by Lord Reed (at [92]) of cases which he believed fell within this category were 'the breach of a restrictive covenant over land, an intellectual property agreement or a confidentiality agreement'. A contractual right to control the use of land, intellectual property, or confidential information would therefore seem to carry with it the right to recover negotiating damages in the event that the defendant infringes that contractual right of control. But what about the case of a simple breach of contract which does not involve the infringement of a contractual right to control property? It would appear that negotiating damages will not be available in such a case, although Lord Reed was careful not to rule out such a possibility entirely. While he stated that it was 'not easy' to see how a hypothetical release fee might be the measure of the claimant's loss in other circumstances, he also concluded (at [94]) that 'it would be going too far' to state that negotiating damages could never be awarded outside of the categories he expressly identified. By way of example he stated (at [94]):

> If, for example, in other circumstances, the parties had been negotiating the release of an obligation prior to its breach, the valuations which the parties had placed on the release fee, adjusted if need be to reflect any changes in circumstances, might be relevant to support, or to undermine, a subsequent quantification of the losses claimed to have resulted from the breach. It would be a matter for the judge to decide whether, in the particular circumstances, evidence of a hypothetical release fee was relevant and, if so, what weight to place upon it.

However, it is difficult to resist the inference that the courts will be very slow to award negotiating damages in a breach of contract case outside of the categories expressly recognised by Lord Reed and that they are unlikely to view a mere contractual right as a 'valuable asset' which requires protection by the award of negotiating damages (see, for example, *Priyanka Shipping Ltd v Glory Bulk Carriers Pty Ltd* [2019] EWHC 2804 (Comm); [2019] 1 WLR 6677 where the breach of the negative covenant was held not to fall within any of the categories recognised in *Morris-Garner* so that negotiating damages were not recoverable and nominal damages only were recoverable in respect of losses suffered prior to the grant of an injunction).

21.7.4   A comparative perspective

Some difficulties with the reasoning of the Supreme Court have been identified by the Court of Appeal of Singapore in *Turf Club Auto Emporium Pte Ltd v Yeo Boong Hua* [2018] SGCA 44; [2018] 2 SLR 655, [277]–[288]. Here it suffices to highlight two of them. The first (at [279]) is the uncertainty, which we have already noted, surrounding when a contractual right can be regarded as a 'valuable asset'. The second is the apparent confinement of negotiating damages to cases 'involving the abstraction or invasion of property and analogous rights'. The Court of Appeal of Singapore was of the view that this was incorrect as a matter of principle because it was not clear why it should be any more permissible to expropriate personal rights (such as a contractual right) than it is permissible to expropriate proprietary rights (see [239]). The alternative approach adopted by the Court of Appeal of Singapore was to set out (at [217]–[237]) three legal requirements that must be satisfied before '*Wrotham Park* damages' (its preferred term to describe this measure of damages) can be recovered, namely: (i) the court must be satisfied that orthodox compensatory damages and specific relief are unavailable to the claimant; (ii) as a general rule, it must be established that there has been in substance and not merely in form a breach of a negative covenant by the defendant; and (iii) the case must not be one where it would be irrational or totally unrealistic to expect the parties to bargain for the release of the covenant, even on a hypothetical basis.

The Singaporean approach is not wholly dissimilar in outcome to that adopted by the Supreme Court but its emphasis is different in that it does not focus on the protection of an asset but rather focuses on the breach of a negative covenant and the unavailability to the claimant of compensatory damages or specific relief. However, it is likely that the Supreme Court has confined the availability of negotiating damages more narrowly than has the Court of Appeal of Singapore. The narrow availability of negotiating damages in English law can be demonstrated by reference to the facts of *Morris-Garner* itself. The claimant brought a claim against the defendants (who were a former director and manager of the claimant) in which it was alleged that the defendants had breached the terms of an agreement entered into by the parties on the sale of the business by the defendants to the claimant. The breaches were of restrictive covenants not to compete with the claimant, solicit its clients or use its confidential information. The claimant claimed damages assessed by reference to the amount which would notionally have been agreed by the parties, acting reasonably, as the price for releasing the defendants from the obligations which they had undertaken and had broken. The Supreme Court held that the claimant was not entitled to an assessment of damages on this basis. This was not a case in which the breaches of contract by the defendants had resulted in the loss of a valuable asset created or protected by the right which had been infringed. While the breach of confidence might potentially have been so regarded, it was the breaches of the non-compete and non-solicitation covenants which were the most significant and they were held not to give rise to a claim for negotiating damages. On this basis the claimant was held to be confined to its claim for compensatory damages for the loss which it could prove it had sustained as a result of the defendants' breaches and that the task of the court was to measure, as accurately as it could on the available evidence, the financial loss which the claimant had actually sustained. While this was unlikely to be an easy task, mere difficulty of proof of loss did not entitle the claimant to switch its attention to the profit made by the defendant. Instead, it was required to try harder to prove the loss which it had sustained as a result of the defendants' breaches of contract.

21.8 The date of assessment

One very important point relates to the date on which damages fall to be assessed. It was established in *Johnson v Agnew* [1980] AC 367 that damages are to be assessed as at the date of breach. However, the rule is not an inflexible one (see *Golden Strait Corp v Nippon Yusen Kubishika Kaisha* [2007] UKHL 12; [2007] 2 AC 353) and it is based on the assumption that there is an immediately available market for the subject-matter of the contract. The underlying principle is that the aim of an award of damages is to put the claimant in the financial position which it would have been in had the contract been performed according to its terms; that is to say, the claimant is entitled to recover damages representing the value of the contractual benefit of which it has been deprived and, for this purpose, the claimant is expected to go out into the market immediately at the date of breach in order to obtain the promised benefit from an alternative source. In some cases this expectation is unrealistic and in such cases damages may be assessed at a later point in time. So, for example, in *Hooper v Oates* [2013] EWCA Civ 91; [2013] 3 All ER 211 the Court of Appeal postponed the date of assessment when a seller of land could not find an alternative purchaser for the land upon the default of the defendant purchaser. In other words, where the claimant is unable reasonably to take immediate steps to mitigate his loss, the date of assessment will be postponed until such time as it is reasonable to expect the claimant to do so (*Radford v De Froberville* [1977] 1 WLR 1262). The date of assessment has also been deferred where the claimant is unaware of the breach. In such cases damages will generally be assessed as at the date on which the claimant could, with reasonable diligence, have discovered the breach. Finally, where between the date of the breach and the time of trial an event has occurred which inevitably would have reduced the amount of damages which the claimant could have recovered in respect of its future losses, it has been held that account can be taken of the occurrence of the later event for the purpose of reducing the damages payable to the claimant on the ground that, were the court to disregard the event which has occurred, it would overcompensate the claimant. In such a case, the commitment to the compensation principle trumps the general rule that damages are assessed as at the date of breach (*Golden Strait Corp v Nippon Yusen Kubishika Kaisha* (above) and *Bunge SA v Nidera BV* [2015] UKSC 43; [2015] 3 All ER 1082).

21.9 The commitment to the protection of the expectation interest

Although the stated purpose of the law of contract is to put the innocent party in the position which he would have been in had the contract been performed, there are a number of doctrines and rules which weaken the commitment of the law of contract to the protection of the expectation interest. In the following sections (Sections 21.10 to 21.14) we shall consider some of these doctrines.

21.10 Mitigation

A claimant is under a 'duty' to mitigate his loss. It is, however, technically incorrect to state that the claimant is under a 'duty' to mitigate his loss because he does not incur any liability if he fails to mitigate his loss. The claimant is entirely free to act as he thinks fit but, if he fails to mitigate his loss, he will be unable to recover that portion of his loss which is attributable to his failure to mitigate. The aim of the doctrine of mitigation is to prevent the avoidable waste of resources. There are two aspects to the mitigation doctrine.

The first is that the injured party must take all reasonable steps to minimise his loss. The claimant is not required to 'take any step which a reasonable and prudent man would not ordinarily take in the course of his business' (*British Westinghouse Co v Underground Electric Ry Co* [1912] AC 673, 689); he is only obliged to take *reasonable* steps to minimise his loss. Thus, where a seller fails to deliver the goods, the buyer must generally go out into the marketplace and purchase substitute goods. But a claimant need not take steps which would embroil him in complicated litigation (*Pilkington v Wood* [1953] Ch 770), nor is he required to put his commercial reputation at risk (*James Finlay & Co Ltd v Kwik Hoo Tong* [1929] 1 KB 400). He may, however, be required to consider an offer of substitute performance by the party in breach (*The Solholt* [1983] 1 Lloyd's Rep 605). Indeed, in *The Solholt* Staughton J, at first instance ([1981] 2 Lloyd's Rep 574), went so far as to state that the innocent party might be required to *make* an offer of substitute performance to the party in breach. The latter step seems to be a step too far because, if it is correct, it would effectively render the right of the innocent party to terminate further performance of the contract illusory. This being the case, a court is unlikely, unless in a truly exceptional case, to insist that an innocent party take the initiative in this way and should instead require the contract-breaker to put forward a properly formulated proposal to the innocent party which it could not reasonably refuse (*Manton Hire and Sales Ltd v Ash Manor Cheese Co Ltd* [2013] EWCA Civ 548). The second aspect of the mitigation doctrine is that the claimant must not unreasonably incur expense subsequent to the breach of contract (*Banco de Portugal v Waterlow & Sons Ltd* [1932] AC 452). Where the steps taken by the claimant to reduce the loss are successful, the benefit accrues to the defendant in the sense that his liability to the claimant will be correspondingly reduced. However, in order for the benefit to be taken into account in this way, the benefit must have been caused by the defendant's breach (*Fulton Shipping Inc of Panama v Globalia Business Travel SAU of Spain* [2017] UKSC 43; [2017] 1 WLR 2581).

As Professor Atiyah has pointed out (1986b), the doctrine of mitigation 'does in practice make an enormous dent in the theory that the promisee is entitled to full protection for his expectations'. In Chapter 1 we discussed the following example. I enter into a contract to sell you ten apples for £2. I refuse to perform my side of the bargain and am in breach of contract. But you must mitigate your loss. So you buy ten apples for £2 at a nearby market. If you sue me for damages, what is your loss? You have not suffered any and you cannot enforce my promise. As Professor Atiyah has stated (1979):

> the reality is that the bindingness of executory contracts protects not the expectation of performance, but the expectation of profit; and even that is only protected so long as the promisee cannot secure it elsewhere.

This point is an extremely good one. Professor Fried (2015) has argued that the 'duty' to mitigate is:

> a kind of altruistic duty, towards one's contractual partner, the more altruistic that it is directed to a partner in the wrong. But it is a duty without cost, since the victim of the breach is never worse off for having mitigated.

But, as Professor Atiyah has pointed out (1986g), altruism finds little favour within a liberal theory of contract and it is surprising to find it being invoked here in favour of a contract-breaker. He has also challenged the view that the 'duty' to mitigate is a duty without cost on the ground that, in practice, it 'often places the innocent party in a dilemma. If he fails to mitigate, his damages will be cut, and if he does mitigate, he may find that his only recoverable damages are trivial reliance costs not worth pursuing.' It is probably true to say that there is no one factor which explains the present role of mitigation within the law of contract (see Bridge, 1989), but that it is attributable to such factors as the need to avoid waste, the remoteness of the loss and the responsibility of the claimant to seek to minimise the loss. It underlines the fact that the law of contract is not wholeheartedly committed to the protection of the

expectation interest but that, in the words of Burrows (1983), the doctrine of mitigation simply adds:

> a supplementary policy to those policies justifying protection of the expectation interest;
> and this supplementary policy is that the promisee should not leave it simply to the courts
> to ensure fulfilment of his expectations, but should rather take it upon himself to adopt
> other reasonable means to ensure the fulfilment of his expectations.

21.11 Remoteness

A claimant's expectation interest will not be fully protected where some of the loss
which he has suffered is too 'remote' a consequence of the defendant's breach of
contract. The doctrine of remoteness limits the right of the innocent party to recover
damages to which he would otherwise be entitled. The principal justification for the
existence of this doctrine is that it would be unfair to impose liability upon a defendant for all losses, no matter how extreme or unforeseeable, which flow from his
breach of contract. The general test is that the claimant can only recover in respect of
losses which were within the reasonable contemplation of the parties at the time of
entry into the contract. But the courts have experienced some difficulty in deciding
when a loss is, or is not, within the reasonable contemplation of the parties. The
uncertainty has been increased in two respects by the decision of the House of Lords
in *Transfield Shipping Inc v Mercator Shipping Inc (The Achilleas)* [2008] UKHL 48;
[2009] 1 AC 61. First, the ratio of the decision is unclear. Second, the case seems to
add a new test which asks whether the defendant has assumed responsibility for the
loss in question. The precise scope of this test is unclear as is its relationship to the
more traditional test. We shall return to the case after a brief consideration of the
development of the law.

21.11.1 *Hadley v Baxendale*

The foundation of the law can be traced back to the case of *Hadley v Baxendale* (1854)
9 Exch 341. A shaft in the claimants' mill broke. The defendant carriers agreed to
carry the shaft to Greenwich so that it could be used as a pattern in the manufacture
of a new shaft. In breach of contract the defendants delayed the return of the shaft
and, in consequence, production was halted at the claimants' mill. The claimants
sought to recover their loss of profits as damages for breach of contract. Alderson B
held that:

> where two parties have made a contract which one of them has broken, the damages which
> the other party ought to receive in respect of such breach of contract should be such as may
> fairly and reasonably be considered either arising naturally, that is, according to the usual
> course of things, from such breach of contract itself, or such as may reasonably be sup-
> posed to have been in the contemplation of both parties, at the time they made the contract,
> as the probable result of the breach of it.

This test can usefully be divided into two parts, albeit that the two limbs are not
'mutually exclusive' (*Jackson v Royal Bank of Scotland* [2005] UKHL 3; [2005] 1 WLR
377, [25] and [46]–[49]). The first is that the defendant is liable for such losses as
occur 'naturally' or as a result of the 'usual course of things' after such a breach of
contract. To qualify as a loss which has occurred 'naturally' there must have been a

'serious possibility' or a 'real danger' or a 'very substantial' probability that the loss would occur (*Koufos v C Czarnikow Ltd (The Heron II)* [1969] 1 AC 350). A defendant who agrees to supply or repair a chattel which is obviously being used for profit-making purposes is liable for the ordinary loss of profits suffered as a result of his failure to supply or repair the chattel timeously (*Fletcher v Tayleur* (1855) 17 CB 21). Why could the claimants not recover their loss of profits in *Hadley v Baxendale* when it must have been obvious to the carrier that the mill was being used for profitmaking purposes? The answer is that the stoppage of the mill was not a 'natural' consequence of the carrier's delay because the claimants might have had a spare shaft which could have kept the mill in production while the new shaft was being made. It has also been held that a defendant who supplies a commodity for use in a complicated construction or manufacturing process is not to be assumed, merely because of the order for the commodity, to be aware of the details of all the techniques undertaken by the claimant and the effect of any failure of or deficiency in the commodity supplied (*Balfour Beatty v Scottish Power plc* 1994 SLT 807). The onus in the latter case is upon the claimant to bring information of this nature to the attention of the defendant prior to entry into the contract. This takes us to the second limb of *Hadley v Baxendale*.

Under the second limb, a defendant may be liable for losses which did not arise 'naturally' but were within the reasonable contemplation of both parties at the time they made the contract. This test was not satisfied on the facts of *Hadley v Baxendale* because, although the claimants were aware of the consequences of delay, they had not informed the defendants that delay would result in the halting of production and so the loss could not be said to have been in the reasonable contemplation of *both* parties. The defendant must at least know of the special circumstances (*Simpson v London and North Western Rly Co* (1876) 1 QBD 274 and *Seven Seas Properties Ltd v Al-Essa (No 2)* [1993] 1 WLR 1083), and there is some suggestion in the case law that the claimant must go further and establish that the defendant agreed to assume liability for the exceptional loss (*Horne v Midland Rly* (1873) LR 6 CP 131). Although the test is often formulated in terms of the knowledge of both parties to the contract, it is the knowledge of the contract-breaker that is typically critical. That intention is to be assessed objectively rather than subjectively and the criterion for deciding what the defendant must be taken to have had in its contemplation as the result of the breach of contract has been held to be a factual one (*Attorney-General of the Virgin Islands v Global Water Associates Ltd* [2020] UKPC 18; [2020] 3 WLR 584, [33]–[35])

21.11.2 *Victoria Laundry (Windsor) Ltd v Newman Industries Ltd*

The distinction between losses which arise 'naturally' (and are within the first limb of *Hadley v Baxendale*) and 'special' losses (within the second limb) is illustrated by the case of *Victoria Laundry (Windsor) Ltd v Newman Industries Ltd* [1949] 2 KB 528. The defendants contracted to sell and deliver a boiler to the claimants. The defendants knew that the claimants wished to put the boiler into immediate use in their laundry business. The boiler was delivered some five months late. The claimants sued to recover the loss of profits which they had suffered as a result of the late delivery. The Court of Appeal held that the defendants were liable for the loss of profits which flowed naturally from their breach of contract. But the defendants were not liable for the loss of profits on some exceptionally lucrative contracts which the claimants had entered into with the Ministry of Supply. The defendants did not know of the existence of these contracts and so the loss of profit on these contracts was not within the reasonable contemplation of both parties. However, the decision of the Court of Appeal has not escaped criticism, largely on the ground that the only difference between the two losses was one of extent, not kind, and the law does not generally require that the extent of the loss be foreseen. The case was distinguished by the Court of Appeal in *Brown v KMR Services Ltd* [1995] 4 All ER 598, albeit that Stuart Smith LJ (at 620 and 621) and Hobhouse LJ (at 640–43) offered different reasons for distinguishing it (and see also the consideration of *Victoria Laundry* in *Wellesley Partners LLP v Withers LLP* [2015] EWCA Civ 1146; [2016] Ch 529, [84]–[87] and [174]–[177]). It is suggested that the law cannot ignore entirely the extent of the economic loss in contract cases because parties typically enter into a contract to make a profit, so, to that extent, loss of profit is always a foreseeable consequence of the breach. If the extent of the loss of profit were always irrelevant there would be no adequate control device to keep liability within acceptable bounds. Thus the courts are entitled to distinguish between 'ordinary' loss of profits and 'exceptional' loss of profits or between 'ordinary' consequential losses and 'exceptional' consequential losses, however difficult it may be to distinguish between these categories on certain facts.

The effect of the second limb of the test established by Alderson B is to encourage contracting parties to disclose prior to entry into the contract exceptional losses which may be suffered as a result of the breach. Where, as in the *Victoria Laundry* case, the claimant suffers an unusually large loss, he will be unable to recover that loss unless he draws it to the attention of the defendant at the time of contracting. The rule therefore encourages risk sharing; it enables the parties to assess the scope of their likely liability in the event of breach. In this way, it may induce them to take greater steps to ensure that a breach is not committed (and it may also encourage them to take out appropriate insurance cover should a breach be committed).

21.11.3   *The Achilleas*

While it cannot be said that the courts have not experienced any difficulty in applying the two limbs of *Hadley v Baxendale* to the facts of particular cases, it can be said that the tests were well known and that there was a significant body of case law upon which the courts could draw when deciding new cases. In this sense, the law was well established and well understood. This relative certainty was, however, unsettled by the decision of the House of Lords in *The Achilleas*. Unlike the reasoning of their Lordships, the facts of the case are straightforward. A charterer of a vessel redelivered the vessel nine days late and, as a result, the owners of the vessel had to agree a reduced rate of hire for the follow-on time charter. The owners claimed that their loss on the follow-on charter amounted to $1,364,584 (consisting of $8,000 per day for the 191 days of the follow-on charter) which they sought to recover from the charterers. The charterers submitted that their liability was limited to $158,301.17, being the difference between the market and the charter rates of hire for the nine days during which the owners were deprived of the use of the ship. The House of Lords held that the charterer's liability was confined to the latter figure. While they agreed in the result, two distinct lines of reasoning can be detected in the speeches of their Lordships.

The first approach was to ask whether the charterers had, objectively, assumed responsibility for the loss in question. This approach was adopted most clearly by Lord Hoffmann but is also evident in the speech of Lord Hope. On this approach the vital question to ask is whether the loss for which compensation is sought is of a 'kind' or a 'type' for which the contract-breaker ought fairly to be taken to have accepted responsibility. The novelty of this approach lies in its attempt to import principles from the law of tort relating to the scope of the duty of care (associated with the speech of Lord Hoffmann in *South Australia Asset Management Corp v York Montague Ltd* [1997] AC 191) into the law of contract more generally. Its attraction lies in the emphasis that it places on the agreement of the parties in that it aims to give effect to the presumed intention of the parties. It enables a court to conclude that a party is not liable for foreseeable losses because they are not of a type or kind for which the contract-breaker can be treated as having assumed responsibility. The present case is an illustration of the latter proposition. Lords Hoffmann and Hope held that the charterers had assumed responsibility for the nine-day delay in returning the vessel but that they had not assumed responsibility for the entirety of the follow-on charter because they could neither control that loss nor quantify it. While this approach has its attractions, it may prove to be difficult to operate in practice because it will encourage defendants to take the point that they cannot be liable for the loss in question because they did not, objectively, assume responsibility for it. It can be argued that this objection has little force because the objective approach to agreement plays such a central role in the law of contract and it should not create any particular difficulties when applied in the present context. Yet, it cannot be said that the solution is entirely problem-free. What was the basis for the conclusion that the charterers had not assumed responsibility for the entire loss suffered by the shipowners? The answer would appear to lie in large part in the 'understanding in the shipping market ... that liability was restricted to the difference between the market rate and the charter rate for the overrun period'. This market understanding obviously played a critical role in persuading Lords Hoffmann and Hope that the parties had contracted by reference to that understanding so that the defendants could not be regarded as having accepted responsibility for the entirety of the shipowners' loss. But the test is likely to be more difficult to apply in cases where there is no such clear market understanding. Examples of this difficulty are not hard to find. What result would be reached by applying the assumption of responsibility test to the facts of *Hadley v Baxendale* and *Victoria Laundry*? The answer is not at all clear (see Wee, 2010, esp. 170–71). This low predictive yield was one of the reasons which led the Singapore Court of Appeal to decline to follow the approach of Lords Hoffmann and Hope (see *MFM Restaurants Pte Ltd v Fish & Co Restaurants Pte Ltd* [2010] SGCA 36; [2011] 1 SLR 150).

The second approach, adopted by Lord Rodger and Baroness Hale, was more orthodox. Lord Rodger concluded that neither party would reasonably have contemplated that an overrun of nine days would 'in the ordinary course of things' cause the shipowners the kind of loss for which they claimed damages. The loss was not an 'ordinary consequence' of the breach but occurred because of the 'extremely volatile market conditions' which resulted in the excessive loss suffered by the shipowners. On this basis, the loss was too remote to be recoverable. Unfortunately, this approach is also not without its difficulties. The particular difficulty from which it suffers is that it seems to proceed on the basis of a very narrow definition of the type of loss which was foreseeable (albeit an approach which bears some similarity to that adopted by the Court of Appeal in *Victoria Laundry*). The loss which the shipowners suffered was a loss of profit on the follow-on charter and that was surely the very loss which the parties could have foreseen. What could not be foreseen was the extent of that loss, but the law has generally taken the view that it is the kind of loss that must be foreseen, not its extent. The latter principle was not challenged by Lord Rodger or Baroness Hale and so it must be assumed that they proceeded on the basis of a very narrow definition of the type of loss foreseeable by the parties.

This leaves us with the speech of the fifth judge, Lord Walker. He found the analogy drawn by Lord Hoffmann with the 'assumption of responsibility' cases in tort to be 'helpful' but stopped short of positively endorsing it in a contractual context. But he also stated that the parties had not contracted on the basis that the charterers would be liable for 'any loss, however large, occasioned by a delay in re-delivery in circumstances where the charterers had no knowledge of, or control over, the new fixture entered into by the new owners'. In this respect his speech seems to bear a closer resemblance to the approach taken by Lord Rodger and Baroness Hale. However, in *Sylvia Shipping Co Ltd v Progress Bulk Carriers Ltd (The Sylvia)* [2010] EWHC 542 (Comm); [2010] 2 Lloyd's Rep 81 Hamblen J concluded (at [39]) that Lord Walker's agreement with both approaches meant that the 'rationale of assumption of responsibility' had the 'support of the majority' (although contrast the judgment of Floyd LJ in *Wellesley Partners LLP v Withers LLP* [2015] EWCA Civ 1146; [2016] Ch 529, [71] where he preferred not to 'delve into the question' of what is the true ratio of *The Achilleas* or whether there are, in fact, 'two inconsistent ratios'). Given that both the traditional *Hadley v Baxendale* tests and the new assumption of responsibility test have their place in English contract law, how is a court to decide which test to apply and when?

21.11.4 Which test to apply?

The answer given by Hamblen J in *The Sylvia* is that the orthodox *Hadley v Baxendale* approach 'remains the general test of remoteness applicable in the great majority of cases'. The assumption of responsibility test, by contrast, is likely to be invoked in the minority of cases 'where the application of the general test leads to an unquantifiable, unpredictable, uncontrollable or disproportionate liability or where there is clear evidence that such a liability would be contrary to market understanding and expectations'. On this basis it will not be necessary in most cases for the court to consider the assumption of responsibility test because 'the fact that the type of loss arises in the ordinary course of things or out of special known circumstances will carry with it the necessary assumption of responsibility'.

An alternative rationalisation is that the two approaches can be reconciled on the basis that they both seek to give effect to the intention, express or implied, of the parties. This analysis was adopted by Sir David Keene in *John Grimes Partnership Ltd v Gubbins* [2013] EWCA Civ 37; [2013] BLR 126, [24]. He treated the rule in *Hadley* as one that was attributable to the implied intention of the parties; that is to say, the law implies a term that the party in breach is to be held liable for the type of loss which can reasonably be foreseen at the time of entry into the contract to be not unlikely to result from the breach. He then acknowledged that it was open to the parties to contract out of that rule and to assume a responsibility that was different from the term implied on the basis of *Hadley*. In *The Achilleas* the parties were held to have done this by contracting on the basis that the liability of the party in breach should be less than that which it would otherwise have been. If this is so, it must equally be open to the parties to enter into a contract on the basis that the liability of the contract-breaker will exceed that which otherwise would have been recoverable.

This potential to increase the liability of the defendant is illustrated by *Supershield Ltd v Siemens Building Technologies FE Ltd* [2010] EWCA Civ 7; [2010] 1 Lloyd's Rep 349 where Toulson LJ stated (at [43]) that the test has an 'inclusionary' as well as an 'exclusionary' effect. Thus he stated that:

> if, on the proper analysis of the contract against its commercial background, the loss was within the scope of the duty, it cannot be regarded as too remote, even if it would not have occurred in ordinary circumstances.

On the facts of *Supershield* it was held that the loss was not too remote because the defendant had assumed responsibility for the loss in question notwithstanding the fact that it was unlikely to occur.

The continuing uncertainty surrounding the status of *The Achilleas* was further illustrated by the decision of the Privy Council in *Attorney-General of the Virgin Islands v Global Water Associates Ltd* [2020] UKPC 18; [2020] 3 WLR 584, [26] where Lord Hodge stated that the judgment of Lord Hoffmann and Lord Hope had sought 'to bring into play the concept of assumption of responsibility as a further limitation on contractual damages' and that the test was 'a further restriction on recoverability' ([29]). This appears to suggest that the assumption of responsibility test is distinct from the test to be applied when considering whether a loss is too remote a consequence of the breach, and it is unlikely that this is what either Lord Hoffmann or Lord Hope intended. The uncertainty over the precise standing of *The Achilleas* and its role within the law of contract appears destined to continue.

One difficult question which remains to be discussed is whether the test for remoteness of damage in contract differs from the test for remoteness of damage in tort. In a negligence action, damage is too remote a consequence of the defendant's breach of duty where the kind of damage which the claimant has suffered was not reasonably foreseeable by the defendant (*Overseas Tankship (UK) Ltd v Morts Dock and Engineering Co Ltd (The Wagon Mound) (No 1)* [1961] AC 388). Despite suggestions that reasonable foresight of loss is also the determining factor in a contractual action (see Asquith LJ in *Victoria Laundry* (above)), it was established by the House of Lords in *The Heron II* that the remoteness test in contract is narrower than the remoteness test in tort because a higher degree of probability is required in order for the loss to be within the reasonable contemplation of the parties at the time of entry into the contract. But the difference is one of degree, not kind. However, this view was challenged by Lord Denning in *H Parsons (Livestock) Ltd v Uttley Ingham & Co Ltd* [1978] QB 791, when he argued that, at least in relation to physical damage cases, the remoteness test was the same in contract and in tort. Although Lord Denning was in the minority in *Parsons*, it must be noted that Scarman LJ did state that it would be absurd if the amount of damages recoverable were to depend upon whether the claimant's cause of action was in contract or in tort. This issue awaits clarification by the Supreme Court. In *Henderson v Merrett Syndicates Ltd* [1995] 2 AC 145, 185 Lord Goff stated that 'the rules as to remoteness of damage … are less restricted in tort than they are in contract'. While this is generally true it is suggested that, where the parties are in a contractual relationship, the claimant should not be allowed to have resort to the wider tort rules. The rationale for having a wider sphere of liability in tort is that claimants in a tort action do not generally have the opportunity to disclose unusual losses, as contract claimants do. But, where the parties are in a contractual relationship, the claimant has had the opportunity to disclose any unusual losses and so he should not be allowed to avail himself of the wider tort rule (see *Robertson Quay Investment Pty Ltd v Steen Consultants Pte Ltd* [2008] SGCA 8; [2008] 2 SLR 623).

21.12 Causation

A claimant will be unable to recover damages in respect of the loss which he has suffered if he cannot establish a causal link between his loss and the defendant's breach of contract. The defendant's breach need not be the sole cause of the loss to the claimant, but it must be a cause of the loss.

For example, the independent act of a third party may break the chain of causation between the defendant's breach and the claimant's loss, unless the defendant has actually promised to guard against the very thing which has actually happened (*London Joint Stock Bank v Macmillan* [1918] AC 777). Natural events may also break the chain of causation, as was argued in the case of *Monarch Steamship Co v Karlshamns Oljefabrieker* [1949] AC 196. The defendants entered into a contract in April 1939 to carry goods from Manchuria to Sweden. In breach of contract, the defendants failed to provide a ship which was seaworthy. This resulted in a delay in the voyage so that the ship failed to get to Sweden before the outbreak of war in September 1939. As a result of the outbreak of war, the ship was ordered to a Scottish port where the goods had to be transferred to neutral vessels before being shipped to Sweden. The claimants had to pay the cost of the transport in the neutral vessels and they sought to recover the sums paid as damages for breach of contract. The defendants argued that the outbreak of war broke the chain of causation between their breach of contract and the cost incurred by the claimants in shipping the goods to Sweden in neutral vessels. This argument was rejected by the House of Lords on the ground that the outbreak of war was a likely event at the time that the contract was concluded in April 1939 and so it could not be held to amount to a break in the chain of causation.

An act of the claimant may be so unreasonable that it breaks the chain of causation between the defendant's breach and the claimant's loss. In *Lambert v Lewis* [1982] AC 225, a farmer continued to use a trailer coupling after it was broken. The farmer was held to be liable in damages to persons who were injured in an accident caused by the coupling giving way. The farmer sought to recover an indemnity from the supplier of the coupling. It was held that the farmer could not recover because his continued use of the coupling, in the knowledge that it was damaged, broke the chain of causation between the supplier's breach of contract and the 'loss' suffered by the farmer in having to pay damages to the accident victims.

Where the claimant has been negligent and that negligence has contributed to the damage which he has suffered, but it is not sufficient to break the chain of causation, the question then arises whether the damages payable to the claimant can be reduced under the Law Reform (Contributory Negligence) Act 1945. This is a vexed issue. The answer depends upon the nature of the obligation which the defendant has broken. Three different contractual duties must be carefully distinguished. The first is a breach of a strict contractual duty; the second is a breach of a contractual duty to take care which does not correspond to a common law duty to take care; and the third is a breach of a contractual duty of care where the breach also constitutes a tort. At present contributory negligence can operate as a defence in the third category, but not in the first or the second (see *Forsikringsaktieselskapet Vesta v Butcher* [1989] AC 852 and *Barclays Bank plc v Fairclough Building Ltd* [1995] QB 214). This can result in the *overcompensation* of the claimant as no reduction is made to reflect the claimant's contribution to the loss which has arisen (see Burrows, 1993). The Law Commission has recommended (1993) that contributory negligence be available as a defence in category two as well as three (but not in category one). However, with the recognition of concurrent liability in *Henderson v Merrett Syndicates Ltd* [1995] 2 AC 145, the courts today are more likely to find that a case falls within category three rather than two, so that little would in fact be gained by implementing the Law Commission's recommendation and it is unlikely that it will ever be implemented.

21.13 Damages for pain and suffering and the 'consumer surplus'

Damages are generally assessed by reference to the market value of the promised contractual performance; that is to say, the claimant's loss is objectively assessed. Such an objective approach may lead to the undercompensation of a claimant because it does not take account of the claimant's subjective valuation of the contractual performance, which may be considerably more than the market value (called the 'consumer surplus', see Harris and others, 1979). A significant step forward was taken by the House of Lords in *Ruxley* (see Section 21.3) when they recognised that the defendant was entitled to loss of amenity damages and Lord Mustill expressly recognised the concept of a 'consumer surplus'.

Prior to *Ruxley*, the courts were generally unwilling to compensate a claimant for his purely 'subjective' losses. Yet consumers frequently suffer such 'subjective' losses. For example, the value of family wedding photographs will generally exceed their market value because of their sentimental value to members of the family. But the courts traditionally refused to award damages to compensate a claimant for any mental distress which he suffered as a result of the defendant's breach of contract. In *Addis v Gramophone Co Ltd* [1909] AC 488, the claimant sought to recover damages for the indignity which he had suffered in being sacked from his job in a 'humiliating' manner. The House of Lords held that the claimant was not entitled to be compensated for the injury to his feelings.

21.13.1 *Farley v Skinner*

However, there is no longer an absolute rule that damages cannot be recovered for mental distress. The leading modern case is the decision of the House of Lords in *Farley v Skinner* [2001] UKHL 49; [2002] 2 AC 732 (see McKendrick and Graham,

2002). The claimant employed the defendant to survey a 'gracious country residence' which he wished to purchase. The house was situated some 15 miles from Gatwick airport. Given its proximity to the airport, the claimant expressly asked the defendant to report on whether or not aircraft noise was likely to be a problem. The defendant stated that noise was unlikely to be a problem, 'although some planes will inevitably cross the area, depending on the direction of the wind and the positioning of the flight paths'. The claimant purchased the house. After he had spent more than £100,000 on improvements to it, he discovered that aircraft noise was a problem and that it interfered with his enjoyment of the house. The trial judge found that the defendant was in breach of contract and awarded the claimant damages of £10,000 for the distress and inconvenience caused to him by the aircraft noise (the noise from the aircraft did not affect the value of the property). The House of Lords upheld this award (notwithstanding the fact that the award was, in their view, on the high side).

In so concluding, their Lordships did not engage in a radical overhaul of this area of the law. They accepted the traditional starting point, namely that the law of contract does not compensate a claimant for mere disappointment or annoyance suffered as a result of the defendant's breach of contract. Contract-breaking is an 'incident of commercial life which players in the game are expected to meet with mental fortitude' (*Johnson v Gore Wood & Co* [2002] 2 AC 1, 49). What they did, however, was to expand the scope of the exceptions to this general rule. Prior to *Farley v Skinner* the courts had recognised that damages for mental distress could be awarded firstly where the predominant object of the contract was to obtain some mental satisfaction (such as a holiday, *Jarvis v Swan's Tours Ltd* [1973] QB 233 and, for a more recent example, *Milner v Carnival plc (trading as Cunard)* [2010] EWCA Civ 389; [2010] 3 All ER 701) or to relieve a source of distress (*Heywood v Wellers* [1976] 1 QB 446), and secondly in cases where the breach of contract caused physical inconvenience and distress to the claimant (*Watts v Morrow* [1991] 1 WLR 1421). The House of Lords expanded the scope of liability in two respects.

21.13.2 The nature of the term that has been broken

First, they dispensed with the 'predominant object' test in the first exception. They held that it sufficed that the term broken by the defendant was one which was known by both parties to be an important term of the contract: whether the contract as a whole was one to provide peace of mind or not was not the decisive factor. This test was satisfied on the facts of *Farley v Skinner* but only because the contract was not an 'ordinary surveyor's contract'. In the case of an ordinary surveyor's contract (of the type found in *Watts v Morrow*) the surveyor does not promise to provide the potential buyers with peace of mind or freedom from distress. But the claimant in *Farley v Skinner* had specifically asked the surveyor to report on the level of aircraft noise and, as Lord Clyde observed, it was 'the specific provision relating to the peacefulness of the property in respect of the aircraft noise which makes the present case out of the ordinary'. This puts a premium on asking the surveyor specific questions which he must answer. In the absence of a specific question, it would appear that a surveyor will not ordinarily be liable to a house purchaser for the disappointment or distress which he suffers in the event that the house suffers from some major defect.

The elimination of the 'predominant object' test may result in a gradual but controlled expansion of the ambit of liability for mental distress damages. Support for such a proposition can be gleaned from the decision of Neuberger J in *Hamilton Jones v David & Snape (a firm)* [2003] EWHC 3147 (Ch); [2004] 1 All ER 657. The claimant brought a claim against the defendant solicitors in which she alleged that their negligence in protecting her interests and the interests of her sons had allowed her husband to abduct her sons to Tunisia, where he was awarded custody. The claimant had instructed the defendants precisely because she was concerned that her husband might abduct her sons. Neuberger J held that the claimant was entitled to recover damages of £20,000 in respect of the distress which she had suffered. It might have been difficult for the claimant to establish that the predominant object of the contract with the defendants was to provide her with peace of mind or freedom from distress. But that was not the test which she had to satisfy. She had to satisfy the lesser test of proving that peace of mind or freedom from distress was an important term of the contract. Neuberger J stated that the question was a 'difficult' one to answer but he concluded that it would be a 'relatively unusual parent who, in the position of the claimant in the present case, would not have had, and would not be perceived by her solicitors to have had, her own peace of mind and pleasure in the company of her children as an important factor' when instructing the defendants. It is unlikely that this case will open the floodgates to claims for mental distress damages because judges are likely to follow the example of Neuberger J and scrutinise carefully any claim by a claimant that pleasure, relaxation, peace of mind or freedom from molestation was an important term of the contract concluded between the parties.

21.13.3 Inconvenience and discomfort

Second, it was held in *Farley v Skinner* that the claimant was entitled to recover damages on the ground that the defendant's breach of contract resulted in inconvenience and discomfort for the claimant. Their Lordships here adopted a rather liberal approach to the identification of 'inconvenience'. It was held that the noise from the aeroplanes caused the claimant to suffer 'real discomfort' in that it interfered with his enjoyment of the property. The finding that the noise interfered with his enjoyment of the property seems rather marginal given that no other houseowner appeared to suffer in the same way. But the fact was that the noise did interfere with the claimant's lifestyle in that it intruded into his 'quiet, reflective breakfast', his 'morning stroll in his garden' and his pre-dinner drinks on the terrace. The defendant did not maintain that this loss was too remote a consequence of the breach, presumably because he had been asked expressly to advise on the noise levels at the house and knew that the claimant wished to live in a house that was quiet and peaceful. There is a definitional problem here in that it may not always be easy to distinguish between inconvenience (which falls within the scope of this category) and disappointment (which does not). It may be that the difference is that inconvenience affects the senses. Thus Lord Scott stated that:

> If the cause is no more than disappointment that the contractual obligation has been broken, damages are not recoverable even if the disappointment has led to a complete mental breakdown. But, if the cause of the inconvenience or discomfort is a sensory (sight, touch, hearing, smell etc.) experience, damages can, subject to the remoteness rules, be recovered.

21.13.4 Re-interpreting *Ruxley*

The final point which arises from *Farley v Skinner* relates to the scope of *Ruxley* and its impact, if any, on the recovery of non-pecuniary losses. In *Ruxley* itself there was a division of judicial opinion as to the basis on which damages of £2,500 were awarded to Mr Forsyth. As we have noted, Lord Mustill took a broad approach and made use of the notion of the 'consumer surplus'. Lord Lloyd, by contrast, took a narrower approach. He saw *Ruxley* as a 'logical application or adaptation' to a new situation of the existing exception to the general rule of no-recovery for mental distress. So the vital factor for him was that the contract in *Ruxley* was one for 'the provision of a pleasurable amenity' and he refrained from giving a 'final answer' to the question which would arise where the contract was one for the construction of something which was not a 'pleasurable amenity'. The difficulty with this approach is that it all hinges on the definition of a 'pleasurable amenity' and leaves open the possibility that damages for loss of amenity cannot be awarded outside this narrow category.

In *Farley v Skinner* three different explanations were given for Mr Forsyth's entitlement to recover £2,500 by way of damages. Lord Steyn and Lord Hutton adopted the analysis of Lord Lloyd in *Ruxley* and classified the contract as one for the provision of a pleasurable amenity. On this view, the damages reflected Mr Forsyth's disappointment at his loss of amenity. Secondly, Lord Clyde seemed to view *Ruxley* as a case in which damages were awarded for inconvenience. This is, at best, a doubtful interpretation of *Ruxley* given that Mr Forsyth was awarded damages of £750 for 'general inconvenience and disturbance' separately from the award of £2,500 in respect of his 'loss of amenity'. Finally, Lord Scott analysed *Ruxley* as a case in which Mr Forsyth was given damages 'for deprivation of a contractual benefit where it is apparent that the injured party has been deprived of something of value but the ordinary means of measuring the recoverable damages are inapplicable'. This analysis takes us back to the debate as to the meaning of 'loss' in the English law of contract and, in particular, the question whether a loss must take the form of a diminution in the overall financial position of the innocent party (see Section 21.3). If it need not take the form of a diminution in the claimant's financial position then it is suggested that Lord Scott's analysis is persuasive. On the other hand, if loss must generally take the form of a diminution in one's financial position then it would appear that the award of damages in *Ruxley* can best be explained as an award of damages to reflect Mr Forsyth's disappointment at the loss of amenity which he suffered.

21.14 Conclusion

It can be seen that there are a number of doctrines which limit the commitment of the law of contract to the protection of the claimant's expectation interest. The existence of these rules and doctrines throws into doubt the validity of the claim that the law of contract protects the expectation interest. However, before reaching a conclusion on this fundamental issue, it is necessary to consider the steps which can be taken by contracting parties to ensure that an adequate remedy is obtained and that the expectation interest is fully protected. These issues are the subject-matter of our final chapter.

Hot topic 18...

One

The test to be applied when deciding whether a particular loss is too remote a consequence of the breach of contract continues to generate considerable controversy. The Privy Council in *Attorney General of the Virgin Islands v Global Water Associates Ltd* [2020] UKPC 18; [2020] 3 WLR 584, in a judgment given by Lord Hodge, recently stated that what the judges have been trying to encapsulate in their various judgments dealing with remoteness is the following: 'whether as a question of fact the parties to a contract, or at least the defendant, reasonably contemplated, if they applied their minds to the possibility of breach when formulating the terms of the contract, that the breach might cause a particular type of loss.' The court is concerned to ascertain the objective intention of the parties, not their subjective intention, and the court will assume that the defendant at the time the contract was made had thought about the consequences of its breach.

More controversial, perhaps, is the apparent marginalisation by Lord Hodge of the approach of Lords Hoffmann and Hope in *The Achilleas,* He concluded that the latter case was not relevant to the case before him because the Privy Council was not concerned with 'the recoverability of damages caused by unusual volatility in the market or questions of market understanding.' Nor was there any question on the facts of 'a further restriction on recoverability based on whether the defendant had assumed responsibility for the loss in question.' On this basis *The Achilleas* was held not to be relevant to the issue before the Privy Council which was whether the losses in respect of which the claim was brought were within the reasonable contemplation of the parties at the time of entry into the contract.

Two

How should the court respond in the case where the defendant has clearly breached the terms of the contract between the parties, but the claimant is having difficulty in proving that it has suffered financial loss as a result of the breach? One response is to seek to punish the defendant or to require the defendant to hand over to the claimant any profit which it has made as a result of its breach of contract. The Supreme Court in *Morris-Garner v One Step (Support) Ltd* [2018] UKSC 20; [2019] AC 649 declined to take this approach and instead affirmed the general rule that common law damages for breach of contract are intended to compensate the claimant for loss or damage resulting from the non-performance of the obligation in question. Where the loss suffered by the claimant is difficult to prove, the law is tolerant of imprecision and the court will do the best it can on the evidence available to it to measure or estimate the claimant's loss as accurately and reliably as the nature of the case permits. Where the claimant's interest in the performance of the contract is purely economic and he cannot establish that any economic loss has resulted from the defendant's breach of contract, the normal inference is that the claimant has not suffered any loss and will be awarded nominal damages. In other words, mere difficulty of proof of loss does not of itself justify a claimant seeking to recover damages assessed by reference to the profit made by the defendant.

Summary

- The aim of an award of damages is to compensate the claimant for the loss which he has suffered as a result of the defendant's breach of contract. The aim is not to punish the defendant.

- The aim of an award of damages is to put the claimant in the position which he would have been in had the contract been performed according to its terms. This may be measured either by the cost of cure measure or the diminution in value measure. A court will not award cost of cure damages where it would be wholly unreasonable to do so.

Summary cont'd

▶   A claimant may elect to recover his reliance rather than his expectation loss, unless he is seeking to escape the consequences of a bad bargain.

▶   A claimant can recover a benefit which he has conferred on the party in breach where there has been a total failure of consideration. A defendant is only exceptionally required to disgorge the profit which he has obtained as a result of his breach of contract, although negotiating damages (which will likely deprive the defendant of a share of his profit) are available in a slightly wider range of circumstances (typically cases in which the defendant has infringed a right of the claimant to control property or in cases in which the court has declined to grant to the claimant a specific performance order or an injunction).

▶   A claimant must take reasonable steps to mitigate his loss. The existence of a 'duty' to mitigate demonstrates that contract law is not wholeheartedly committed to the protection of the expectation interest.

▶   Damages cannot be recovered where the loss which the claimant has suffered is too remote a consequence of the defendant's breach of contract. The general rule is that a loss is not too remote if it was within the reasonable contemplation of both parties at the time of entry into the contract. When deciding whether or not a loss is too remote a court may also ask whether the defendant has assumed responsibility for the loss in question. It is, however, likely that the latter test will only be applied in the minority of cases.

▶   The claimant must establish that his loss was caused by the defendant's breach of contract.

▶   The general rule is that damages cannot be recovered for mental distress suffered as a result of the defendant's breach of contract. This rule is subject to exceptions where the claimant suffers inconvenience as a result of the breach and in the case where the object of the term broken is to provide pleasure or freedom from distress and the term is an important one in the context of the contract as a whole.

Exercises

21.1 Define and distinguish between the 'expectation interest', the 'reliance interest' and the 'restitution interest'.

21.2 Is the law of contract committed to the protection of the expectation interest?

21.3 Is a court ever justified in awarding damages by reference to the gain which the defendant has made as a result of the breach rather than by reference to the loss which the claimant has suffered?

21.4 Fire Prevention Ltd entered into a contract with Borchester Town Council, under which they agreed to provide a fire-fighting service of 15 fire engines and 40 firemen. In breach of contract, Fire Prevention only supplied 12 fire engines and 35 men and thereby saved themselves £40,000. Borchester cannot show that they have suffered any loss as a result of Fire Prevention's breach because they cannot prove that Fire Prevention failed to extinguish any fire. Can Borchester recover damages from Fire Prevention? If so, on what basis would a court assess damages? (See *City of New Orleans v Fireman's Charitable Association* 9 So 486 (1891), discussed in *A-G v Blake* [1998] Ch 439.)

21.5 John, who had recently left his wife, booked a holiday with Harry's Tour Company Ltd. The holiday did not live up to expectations. John now suffers from severe depression. He has been advised by his doctors to give up his job. The depression has been caused partly by the breakup of his marriage and partly by the aggravation of his disappointing holiday. Advise John.

Chapter 22

Obtaining an adequate remedy

22.1 Introduction

In Chapter 21 the point was made that the law of contract is not wholeheartedly committed to the protection of the claimant's expectation interest and that a damages award may therefore undercompensate the claimant. We also noted that such undercompensation throws into doubt the claim that contract law protects the expectation interest. In this chapter we shall consider the extent to which the law of contract provides alternative remedies or enables contracting parties to incorporate into their contracts clauses which will ensure that the 'innocent party' (that is, the party who is not in breach) can obtain an adequate remedy in the event of a breach of contract.

At the beginning of this book (Section 1.5) we noted that the role of the lawyer and of the law of contract is greater at the planning stage of a contract than after a breach has occurred. It is at that part of the planning stage when the parties address provision for remedies that the role of the lawyer and of contract law is at its most important. On the one hand, one contracting party will probably wish to exclude or restrict his liability for breach of contract by an appropriately drafted exclusion or limitation clause, while the other party will wish to ensure that an effective and adequate remedy is available to him in the event of a breach of contract.

In seeking to ensure that a contracting party obtains an adequate remedy in the event of a breach of contract, we must extend our discussion beyond the remedy of damages. There are many methods which can be used in an effort to ensure that an effective remedy is obtained. In the first place the contract can be structured in such a way as to entitle one party to withhold the performance of his obligations (Section 22.2) or to entitle one party to terminate performance and claim loss of bargain damages (Section 22.3) or to make a claim in debt for the contract price (Section 22.4). Such remedies may provide a powerful incentive to the other party to refrain from breaking the contract and to perform his obligations under the contract. Alternatively, the parties may make provision in their contract for a sum of money to be payable by way of damages in the event of breach (Sections 22.5 to 22.8). Finally, an adequate remedy can be obtained by seeking an order of specific performance (Section 22.9) or an injunction restraining a threatened breach of contract (Section 22.10). We shall now consider these remedies in greater detail and conclude with a very brief assessment of the significance of the remedial consequences of a breach of contract for the basis, or the theory, of contract law.

22.2 The entire obligations (or 'entire contracts') rule

The ability of one contracting party to withhold performance of his obligations under the contract gives to the other party an extremely powerful incentive to perform his contractual obligations. An example will illustrate the point. A house-owner and a builder enter into a contract under which the builder agrees to build a garage for £8,000. The contract states that payment shall be made only upon satisfactory completion of the work by the builder. The house-owner's obligation to pay the promised sum is therefore dependent upon satisfactory completion of the work by the builder. Should the builder, in breach of contract, fail to complete the work he will, as a general rule, be unable to sue for payment. His claim will be barred by the entire obligations rule or, as it is more often known, the 'entire contracts' rule.

It is suggested that 'entire obligations' is the more accurate title for this rule. In some cases there may be little practical difference between an entire contract and an entire obligation. In our example involving the construction of a garage, the builder can only recover payment when he has completed contractual performance, so, from his perspective, there is little difference between an entire contract and an entire obligation: his obligation is to perform the contract in its entirety. But in other cases the difference between an entire contract and an entire obligation is clear. Where a construction contract makes provision for payment upon the completion of distinct stages of the project, the completion of each stage being a condition precedent to the right to claim payment, the obligation to complete each stage may be said to be entire, even though the contract as a whole is not entire.

The origin of the entire obligations rule can be traced back to the old case of *Cutter v Powell* (1795) 6 TR 320. Cutter agreed with Powell to 'proceed, continue and do his duty as second mate' on a ship sailing from Jamaica to England. Cutter died on the journey to England and his widow sued to recover the wages which she alleged were payable in respect of the period of time in which Cutter had satisfactorily performed his duties before his death. Her action failed because Cutter was not entitled to payment unless he completed the voyage. The rule was no completion, no pay. This rule gives a powerful incentive to a contracting party to ensure, as far as is possible, that the contract is carried out according to its terms. But it can lead to the apparent unjust enrichment of the 'innocent party'. In *Cutter v Powell*, Powell obtained the services of Cutter for some seven weeks but was not required to pay for any 'benefit' which he had obtained.

In practice, the hardships to which this rule can give rise are mitigated by its many exceptions. The principal exception is that the rule is said not to apply where the party in breach has substantially performed his obligations under the contract (*Hoenig v Isaacs* [1952] 2 All ER 176 and *Williams v Roffey Bros & Nicholls (Contractors) Ltd* [1991] 1 QB 1). In such a case, the innocent party must perform his obligations under the contract (usually pay the price) and content himself with an action for damages for any loss suffered as a result of the breach. But the doctrine of substantial performance has been heavily criticised by Treitel (2020, para 17-040) on the ground that 'it is based on the error that *contracts*, as opposed to particular *obligations*, can be entire'. He asserts that to 'say that an obligation is entire *means* that it must be completely performed before payment becomes due' and that in 'relation to "entire" obligations, there is no scope for any doctrine of "substantial performance"'. On this view a court is required to identify with some care the obligation which is alleged to be entire. Thus, he argues, the obligation to complete the work is generally entire but the obligation to do so in a workmanlike manner generally is not. So, in *Hoenig v Isaacs*, where the builder had completed the work, albeit defectively, there was no need to resort to any doctrine of substantial performance. The obligation which was entire, namely the obligation to complete the work, had been performed and so the employer was required to pay the price, subject to a claim for damages in respect of the breach of the non-entire obligation to do the work in a workmanlike manner. Although there is much to be said for this view, it has not yet been adopted by the courts, who still tend to insist that, upon substantial performance, the party in breach is entitled to claim the price, subject to a counterclaim for damages (see *Hoenig v Isaacs* (above); *Bolton v Mahadeva* [1972] 1 WLR 1009; and *Williams v Roffey Bros* (above)).

The second exception is that an innocent party may be required to recompense the party in breach if he accepts the latter's part performance. This is usually difficult to establish because the acceptance of the innocent party occurs in the context of complete contractual performance and is generally not pro-ratable. Part performance was not what was requested. It was full performance or nothing. In our example, a garage is a benefit to the house-owner, but a partly built garage is not; indeed, it may be more of a nuisance (*Sumpter v Hedges* [1898] 1 QB 673, on which see McFarlane and Stevens, 2002). Finally, the court may interpret the contract as consisting of a number of obligations so that, once each obligation has been completely performed, the party in breach may claim the sum promised in relation to the performance of that obligation. Many contracts are so divided; for example, a building contract will often provide for payment at intervals, usually against an architect's or engineer's certificate.

The ability of contracting parties to take steps to minimise the impact of the entire obligations rule has probably preserved the rule as part of English law. Although the Law Commission originally recommended (1983) that the party in breach be given a restitutionary remedy for the value of his part performance, their recommendation did not gain much support and so will not be implemented (see Burrows, 1984a).

22.3　The creation of conditions

Another effective remedy for the innocent party is to threaten to terminate performance of the contract in the event of a repudiatory breach of contract and claim loss of bargain damages. The effectiveness of such a step can be seen from the case of *Lombard North Central plc v Butterworth* [1987] QB 527 (see Section 10.3). By providing in clause 2 of the agreement that the obligation to pay each instalment punctually was of the essence of the contract, the owners were able to terminate performance of the contract and claim loss of bargain damages when the hirer failed to pay an instalment timeously. Clause 2 was not subject to the penalty clause rule (see Sections 22.5 and 22.6) because the Court of Appeal held that the parties were free to classify as a condition a clause which would not otherwise be regarded as a condition. Therefore, by careful draftsmanship which ensures that any term likely to be broken is elevated to the status of a 'condition' which is of the 'essence of the contract', the innocent party can be given the ability to threaten termination of performance of the contract and to claim loss of bargain damages. Parties who wish to create conditions in this way should use clear words in order to give effect to their intention because, in the absence of clear words, a court may be more inclined to classify the term as an innominate term (on which see Section 10.5) than as a condition (*Heritage Oil and Gas Ltd v Tullow Uganda Ltd* [2014] EWCA Civ 1048; [2014] 2

CLC 61, [33]) The creation of conditions in this way will give the party subject to the obligation to perform a powerful incentive to do so and, as far as the innocent party is concerned, ensure that, if the contract is broken, an effective remedy is obtained.

22.4   A claim in debt

A debt is a definite sum of money which the defendant, under the terms of the contract, is due to pay to the claimant. It is therefore distinct from a claim in damages. The principal issue in a debt action is whether the money is *due* to the claimant. If the money is due to the claimant, he is not required to show that he has mitigated his loss, nor are the remoteness rules applicable. His action is simply to recover the sum due; no more, no less. The classic example of a claim in debt is an action to recover the contract price where goods have been delivered and the buyer has not paid for them. The advantage of a claim in debt can be seen from an examination of *White and Carter (Councils) Ltd v McGregor* [1962] AC 413 (see Section 20.9), where the claimants were able to recover the contract price and were not obliged to take steps to mitigate their loss. Such an action also enjoys certain procedural advantages (for example, the ability to obtain summary judgment under Part 24 of the Civil Procedure Rules). There are therefore distinct advantages in drafting a contract in such a way as to create a debtor–creditor relationship between the parties so as to provide the creditor with an effective remedy should the debtor default in making payment.

22.5   Liquidated damages

An alternative method of avoiding undercompensation is to insert into the contract a clause which states the amount of money which shall be payable in the event of a breach of contract. Such a clause also helps to eliminate uncertainty because it enables the parties to know in advance the extent of their potential liability and to plan accordingly (for example, in relation to the calculation of the price and the allocation of responsibility for insurance). However, the courts have retained a jurisdiction to control the content of such clauses. The existence and scope of this jurisdiction has proved to be a matter of some controversy and that controversy came to a head in the decision of the Supreme Court in *Cavendish Square Holding BV v Talal El Makdessi and ParkingEye Ltd v Beavis* [2015] UKSC 67; [2016] AC 1172 (two cases were heard as part of the same appeal).

22.5.1   The traditional distinction

The traditional distinction drawn by the courts was between a liquidated damages clause (which was enforceable and fixed the sum payable in the event of breach) and a penalty clause (which was not enforceable with the consequence that the party seeking damages was relegated to a claim for damages in which it had to prove its loss in the usual way). The distinction was therefore an important one. If the clause was held to be a liquidated damages clause then it fixed the sum which was to be paid by the party in breach irrespective of the actual loss suffered by reason of the breach. So, for example, if the loss suffered was greater than the sum stipulated, the innocent party could not ignore the clause and sue for its actual loss (*Diestal v Stevenson* [1906] 2 KB 345). A liquidated damages clause was defined for this purpose as a genuine or reasonable pre-estimate of the loss likely to be occasioned by the breach (*Dunlop Pneumatic Tyre Co Ltd v New Garage & Motor Co Ltd* [1915] AC 79). A penalty clause, on the other hand, was a term designed to punish the party in breach rather than compensate the innocent party for its loss. While a penalty clause would not be struck out of the contract, it would not be enforced by the court beyond the actual loss of the party seeking to rely on the clause (*Jobson v Johnson* [1989] 1 All ER 621).

The distinction between a liquidated damages clause and a penalty clause rested ultimately on the intention of the parties at the time of entry into the contract and was a question of substance, not form, so that the fact that the parties had described the clause as a 'liquidated damages clause' or a 'penalty clause' was a relevant factor but was not conclusive as to the status of the clause (*Elphinstone v Monkland Iron and Coal Co* (1886) 11 App Cas 332). The courts also developed a number of rules of construction which they applied when seeking to decide whether a particular clause was a penalty clause or a liquidated damages clause. These rules were classically set out by Lord Dunedin in *Dunlop Pneumatic Tyre Co Ltd v New Garage & Motor Co Ltd* [1915] AC 79 who stated that a clause would be held to be a penalty clause 'if the sum stipulated for is extravagant and unconscionable in amount in comparison with the greatest loss that could conceivably be proved to have followed from the breach' or 'if the breach consists only in not paying a sum of money, and the sum stipulated is a sum greater than the sum which ought to have been paid.' Lord Dunedin also identified 'a presumption (but no more)' that a clause is a penalty clause when 'a single lump sum is made payable by way of compensation, on the occurrence of one or more or all of several events, some of which may occasion serious and others but trifling damage'. Finally, Lord Dunedin stated that 'it is no obstacle to the sum stipulated being a genuine pre-estimate of damage, that the consequences of the breach are such as to make precise pre-estimation almost an impossibility. On the contrary, that is just the situation when it is probable that pre-estimated damage was the true bargain between the parties.'

In *Cavendish Square Holding BV v Talal El Makdessi and ParkingEye Ltd v Beavis* Lord Neuberger and Lord Sumption (at [22]) described Lord Dunedin's judgment in *Dunlop* as having 'achieved the status of a quasi-statutory code' which they said was 'unfortunate'. While in their judgment Lord Dunedin's tests or presumptions had proven to be 'perfectly adequate' when applied to 'simple damages clauses in standard contracts' they had been more difficult to apply to 'more complex cases'. Given these difficulties experienced by the courts in applying Lord Dunedin's tests, the Supreme Court decided that it was time to develop the law in a rather different direction.

22.5.2 Revising the test

Instead of asking whether the clause in dispute is a liquidated damages clause or a penalty clause, Lord Neuberger and Lord Sumption stated (at [31]) that the 'real question' to be asked in future is whether the agreed damages clause 'is penal, not whether it is a pre-estimate of loss'. This is an important point of orientation. It is no longer strictly necessary to ask whether the clause is a genuine or reasonable pre-estimate of the loss: the critical question is whether it is a penalty. Thus the mere fact that the agreed damages clause sets the level of damages payable at a sum which is higher than a pre-estimate of a party's loss does not of itself render that clause a penalty clause. So, when will a clause be held to be a penalty clause such that it will be unenforceable?

The answer given by Lord Neuberger and Lord Sumption (at [32]) is that a penalty clause is 'a secondary obligation which imposes a detriment on the contract-breaker out of all proportion to any legitimate interest of the innocent party in the enforcement of the primary obligation'. Leaving to one side for the moment the distinction between a primary and a secondary obligation, it can be seen that there are two principal components to this definition of a penalty clause. The first is the imposition of a detriment on the contract-breaker which is 'out of all proportion' and the second is that, when deciding whether the detriment is out of all proportion, the comparison is to be conducted with any 'legitimate' interest of the innocent party in the enforcement of the contract. These two components require further examination.

22.5.3 The required degree of disproportion

In relation to the degree of disproportion which is required, it should be noted that the Supreme Court was looking for a very high degree of disproportion before a term would be classified as a penalty clause. The words used to denote the required degree of disproportion included 'extravagant', 'exorbitant' and 'unconscionable'. The words used were not 'unreasonable' or 'high'. In other words, the courts are looking for a very high degree of disproportion before they will label a clause as a penalty. It becomes even harder to classify a term as a penalty when account is taken of the fact that the courts will have regard to the fact that the contract was negotiated on an arm's length basis by parties who had access to skilled legal advice when deciding whether the sum stipulated is extravagant, exorbitant or unconscionable. The greater the equality of bargaining power, the less likely it is that the court will conclude that the disproportion is extravagant, exorbitant or unconscionable.

22.5.4 Legitimate interest

The second component has as its focus the 'legitimate' interest of the party seeking to enforce the clause. The choice of the word 'legitimate' in this context is important. The word used is not 'financial'. While it is true that in many cases the interest of the contracting parties will be primarily or exclusively financial (that is, to make a profit or a return on an investment) this is not so in all cases and the choice of the word 'legitimate' enables the court to recognise this point. Its importance can be seen from the facts of *ParkingEye Ltd v Beavis*. The claimant operated a car park at a retail park which gave to users of the car park free parking up to a two-hour limit. Parking beyond that two-hour limit incurred a charge of £85. The defendant exceeded the time limit of two hours but declined to pay the £85, challenging it as a penalty clause. The Supreme Court held that the clause was not a penalty clause. While it could not be said that £85 was a pre-estimate of the loss likely to be sustained by the claimant as a result of the defendant parking his car beyond the permitted two-hour limit, the claimant was held to have 'a legitimate interest in charging [users of the car park] which extended beyond the recovery of any loss'. Their legitimate interest lay in the efficient operation of the car park which made it possible to secure a regular flow of customers to the retail park (rather than having long-stay motorists occupying the spaces all day) and in making for themselves a profit from the provision of parking services. While the sum charged to those who stayed beyond the two hours was not insignificant, it was not out of line with charges levied at comparable car parks elsewhere in the UK and so could not be said to be 'extravagant' when compared against ParkingEye's legitimate interests.

The outcome of the decision of the Supreme Court is to give to contracting parties greater freedom to set the level of damages payable in respect of a breach of contract without having to worry about the possibility of judicial intervention. It is, however, important to stress that the courts have not abolished their jurisdiction to oversee these clauses. The jurisdiction continues to exist and so still applies in those cases where a contracting party oversteps the limit and seeks to impose an obligation to make a payment which is exorbitant in comparison with its own legitimate interests. For example, had ParkingEye sought to impose an obligation to pay £1,000 in the event that the two-hour time limit was exceeded the clause would undoubtedly have been held to be a penalty clause. The difficulty lies in discerning precisely where between £85 and £1,000 the line is crossed and the sum becomes exorbitant. No answer can be given to that question in the abstract. It will have to be answered by the courts on a case by case basis and a pattern of case law will eventually emerge which will help us better to identify the extent of the disproportion that is required before a court will conclude that the sum stipulated is extravagant in comparison with the legitimate interest of the party seeking to enforce the clause.

22.5.5 A potential anomaly

One final question remains to be considered in relation to the penalty clause jurisdiction. We have already noted that a penalty clause is invalid and unenforceable. This leads to a potential anomaly where the loss which the innocent party has suffered is greater than the sum stipulated in the contract. In such a case, can the innocent party argue that the clause is a penalty clause so that it can be ignored and he can recover his actual loss? In *Wall v Rederiaktiebogalet Luggude* [1915] 3 KB 66, it was held that the innocent party could do this and recover his actual loss, although the decision was only at first instance, the reasoning is not at all clear and the issue has been the subject of vigorous debate among academic lawyers (see Gordon, 1974; Hudson, 1974; Hudson, 1975; and Barton, 1976). It should also be noted that a liquidated damages clause may validly provide for the payment of a sum of money which is less than the estimated loss (*Cellulose Acetate Silk Co v Widnes Foundry (1925) Ltd* [1933] AC 20, although where the clause is held to 'exclude or restrict' liability for breach of contract it may be caught by the Unfair Contract Terms Act 1977, s 3, see Section 11.11).

22.6 Evading the penalty clause rule

Although the approach of the Supreme Court in *Cavendish Square Holding BV v Talal El Makdessi and ParkingEye Ltd v Beavis* (above) suggests that contracting parties will, in future, have greater latitude in making provision for agreed damages in the contract itself, parties may wish to avoid any uncertainty by evading the clutches of the penalty clause rule entirely. Three principal devices can be used to avoid the rule.

22.6.1 Acceleration clauses

The first is that the penalty clause rule does not apply to a clause which simply accelerates an existing liability. An example will illustrate the point. Suppose that two parties enter into a contract of hire under which the entire rental is stated to be payable at the date of entry into the contract. The contract further provides that the hirer shall be entitled to pay the rental by instalments provided that certain conditions are met but that, in the event of default in payment of any instalment, the whole balance shall immediately become payable. Such an acceleration of liability is not caught by the penalty clause rule (*Protector Loan Co v Grice* (1880) 5 QBD 592). The same principle applies where a creditor agrees to accept part payment of a debt in full discharge of the debt, provided that certain conditions are met, but stipulates that, if the conditions are not met, he will be entitled to recover the original debt in full (*The Angelic Star* [1988] 1 Lloyd's Rep 122). The crucial ingredient in these cases is that there must be 'a present debt, which by reason of an indulgence given by the creditor is payable either in the future, or in a lesser amount, provided that certain conditions are met' (*O'Dea v Allstates Leasing System (WA) Pty Ltd* (1983) 57 ALJR 172, 174). So by careful draftsmanship a 'present debt' can be created and the subsequent 'acceleration' of that liability to pay is outside the scope of the penalty clause rule.

22.6.2 Sums payable on an event which is not a breach of contract

The second device is to stipulate that the sum shall be payable on an event which is not a breach of contract. A good example of the potential for evasion is provided by the case of *Alder v Moore* [1961] 2 QB 57. The defendant, who was a professional footballer, suffered serious injury and he was certified as being disabled to such an extent that he was unable to play professional football. The claimant insurers paid him £500 under an insurance policy which had been taken out to cover the defendant in the event of his suffering permanent total disablement. The defendant covenanted with the claimants that:

> In consideration of the above payment I hereby declare and agree that I will take no part as a playing member of any form of professional football and that in the event of infringement of this condition I will be subject to a penalty of [£500].

The defendant later resumed his playing career and the insurers sought to recover the £500 which they had paid to him. The defendant argued that the clause was unenforceable because it was a penalty clause. But the majority of the Court of Appeal held that the penalty clause rule was not applicable. The defendant had not promised that he would not play football again. Therefore the £500 was not payable upon a breach of contract and the penalty clause rule was irrelevant. This rule can lead to anomalous results. For example, a hirer who breaks a contract of hire-purchase by failing to pay the instalments can invoke the penalty clause rule if the owners seek to recover an 'excessive' sum of money from him as a result of his breach of contract. But, where the hirer honestly admits that he can no longer pay the instalments, and exercises his right under the contract to return the goods, such a hirer will have no defence to an action by the owners for an 'excessive' sum of money because the sum is not payable on a breach of contract (see *Bridge v Campbell Discount Co Ltd* [1962] AC 600). Lord Denning pointed out the absurdity of this rule. He stated that equity has committed itself to the 'absurd paradox' that 'it will grant relief to a man who breaks his contract but will penalise the man who keeps it'.

The response of the courts in England has typically been that the penalty clause rule only regulates the sums payable upon a breach of contract; any unfairness which lies in other parts of the contract cannot be dealt with by the penalty clause rule (see *Export Credits Guarantee Department v Universal Oil Products Co* [1983] 1 WLR 399). The 'absurdity' which Lord Denning has pointed out stems from the fact that English law has refused to recognise the existence of a general doctrine of unconscionability (see Section 17.4). Instead, it has sought to deal with problems of contractual unfairness in a piecemeal manner. The price of such an approach is that, where the weaker contracting party is unable to bring his case within one of the existing identifiable categories of case where the law of contract does regulate the fairness of the term, his claim for relief is likely to fail.

However, following the decision of the Supreme Court in *Cavendish Square Holding BV v Talal El Makdessi and ParkingEye Ltd v Beavis*, the position might not be quite as clear cut as has just been suggested, given the mixed signals sent out by members of the court in their judgments. On the one hand, Lord Neuberger and Lord Sumption stated (at [13]) that 'the penalty rule regulates only the remedies available for breach of a party's obligations, not the primary obligations themselves'. To similar effect is Lord Hodge's observation (at [241]) that there 'is no freestanding equitable jurisdiction to render unenforceable as penalties stipulations operative as a result of events which do not entail a breach of contract'. On the other hand, Lord Neuberger and Lord Sumption also stated (at [15]) that 'the classification of terms for the purpose of the penalty rule depends on the substance of the term and not on its form or on the label which the parties have chosen to attach to it'. Lord Hodge similarly stated (at [258]) that 'the court's focus on the substance of the contractual term would enable it in an appropriate case to identify disguised penalties'. These statements are not entirely easy to rationalise in a consistent way. The confinement of the penalty clause rule to sums payable on a breach of contract may be said to be a classic example of a rule based on the form of the term. If, however, the court is to focus on the substance of the term rather than its form it may enable the court to look through the form of the clause (a sum payable on an event which is not a breach of contract) and hold that the clause is nevertheless subject to the penalty clause rule because the substance of the term is that the obligation to pay only arises where there has been a default of some kind by the party subject to the obligation to make payment (see, for example, *Vivienne Westwood Ltd v Conduit Street Development Ltd* [2017] EWHC 350 (Ch)). A variant of the facts of *ParkingEye* might demonstrate the point. Suppose that the notice had stated 'No charge will be made for the first two hour period. Customers are welcome to stay beyond two hours on payment of a fee of £150.' The customer who parks for three hours is not in breach of contract in staying beyond the initial two-hour period but can he or she nevertheless invoke the protection of the penalty clause rule? On the face of it he or she cannot do so because the sum is not payable on a breach of contract. But this may be the type of 'disguised' penalty which Lord Hodge had in mind where the rule may be capable of application. However, the concept of a 'disguised' penalty is not without its difficulties. When will the courts decide that a term is in 'substance' rather than in 'form' a penalty clause? Is it only where the clause is a 'sham' and the reality is that the sum is payable on what is in substance a breach of contract? But this is simply to restate the problem because it does not tell us when the courts will recognise that the 'reality' is that the sum is payable on a breach of contract. It is, however, unlikely that the Supreme Court intended the concept of a 'disguised' penalty to have a wide sphere of application, given that they expressly declined to follow the decision of the High Court of Australia in *Andrews v Australia and New Zealand Banking Group Ltd* [2012] HCA 12; [2013] BLR 111 where the High Court rejected the 'breach limitation' and held that 'a stipulation prima facie imposes a penalty on a party (the first party) if, as a matter of substance, it is collateral (or accessory) to a primary stipulation in favour of a second party and this collateral stipulation, upon the failure of the primary stipulation, imposes upon the first party an additional detriment, the penalty, to the benefit of the second party.' It would be inconsistent with the rejection of the approach adopted in *Andrews* for the Supreme Court to have intended to give an expansive role to the concept of a 'disguised' penalty which routinely extended the scope of the penalty clause rule to sums payable on an event which was not a breach of contract.

22.6.3 Drafting as a condition

The third device which can be used to evade the penalty clause rule is to avoid the use of a clause which states that a specified sum of money shall be payable in the event of a breach of contract, because there is always a risk that such a clause will be held to be a penalty clause. But, if the parties simply provide that the term is a condition which is of the essence of the contract, breach of that term will entitle the innocent party to terminate performance and claim loss of bargain damages. The disadvantage of such a clause is that it does not attempt to quantify the loss which has been suffered and so does not obtain the procedural advantages which accompany a claim for a liquidated sum. In other words, the claimant must prove his loss in the usual way. But the advantages that can be obtained by such a clause are demonstrated by *Lombard North Central plc v Butterworth* (above) where the claimant was held to be entitled to terminate the lease and recover, not only the rentals which were unpaid at the time of termination, but also the future rentals payable subject to a discount for accelerated receipt. A notable feature of *Lombard* is that clause 6 of the contract, which purported to entitle the claimant to recover the future rentals subject to a discount for accelerated receipt, was held to be invalid as a penalty clause because it failed to distinguish between serious and trifling breaches. But the fact that clause 6 was invalid as a penalty clause did not prevent the claimants from recovering the future rentals subject to a discount for accelerated receipt where they could show that the defendant had repudiated the contract between them. The effect of the defendant breaching a term which made punctual payment of the essence of the contract was held to be to turn the breach into a repudiatory breach and entitle the claimants to recover the future rental stream subject to an allowance for accelerated receipt of the rental stream. However, had the breach not been a repudiatory breach, the claimants could only have recovered the rentals which were due and unpaid at the time of termination (see *Financings Ltd v Baldock* [1963] 2 QB 104).

22.7 Deposits and part payments

A clause in a contract which states that a certain sum of money shall be payable on a breach of contract runs a risk that it will be held to be a penalty clause. It also has the disadvantage that the innocent party has to take the initiative to obtain the money. A preferable alternative might therefore be to obtain payment of money in advance and then refuse to return it in the event of the other party breaking the contract.

22.7.1 Distinguishing between a deposit and a part payment

In such a case, can the party in breach recover the prepayment? The answer to that question depends upon whether the money was paid as a deposit or as a part payment of the price. A deposit is paid by way of security and is generally irrecoverable, whereas a part payment is paid towards the contract price and is generally recoverable. The difference between the two is a matter of construction. Where the contract is neutral then a payment will generally be interpreted as a part payment (*Dies v British and International Mining and Finance Co* [1939] 1 KB 715).

22.7.2 Deposits

Where the payment is held to be a deposit, the rule established in *Howe v Smith* (1884) 27 Ch D 89 is that a deposit is irrecoverable. A deposit which was due before the date of discharge but which has not been paid is forfeitable (*Hinton v Sparkes* (1868) LR 3 CP 161). The general rule that a deposit is irrecoverable is capable of causing great hardship to the party in breach because the deposit may be much larger than the loss occasioned by the breach of contract. However a critical limit upon the ability of parties to stipulate for excessive deposits was firmly established by the Privy Council in *Workers Trust and Merchant Bank Ltd v Dojap Investments Ltd* [1993] AC 573 (see Beale, 1993). Vendors of property sought to forfeit a deposit of 25 per cent of the purchase price when the purchaser failed to pay the balance of the purchase price within the 14 days stipulated in the contract, time being of the essence of the contract. The purchasers did tender the balance of the purchase price with interest a week later but the vendors returned the cheque and purported to forfeit the deposit of almost three million Jamaican dollars. The Privy Council held that the vendors were not entitled to retain the deposit and ordered that it be repaid to the purchasers after subtracting from it any loss which the vendors could prove they had suffered as a result of the purchasers' breach.

Lord Browne-Wilkinson, giving the advice of the Privy Council, stated that it was 'not possible for the parties to attach the incidents of a deposit to the payment of a sum of money unless such sum is reasonable as earnest money'. There is, however, some difficulty in establishing what is a 'reasonable deposit' given that even a reasonable deposit need not represent a genuine pre-estimate of the loss likely to be occasioned by the breach. On the facts, the Privy Council concluded that the customary deposit in the case of the sale of land has been 10 per cent and that 'a vendor who seeks to obtain a larger amount must show special circumstances which justify such a deposit'. This the vendors could not do. The Privy Council admitted that this reliance upon the practice of asking for a 10 per cent deposit was 'without logic' but they were nevertheless content to use it as a benchmark. It is not at all clear how the courts will decide what constitutes a 'reasonable deposit' where there is no such objective benchmark.

The most difficult aspect of the case was whether the court had jurisdiction to relieve against the forfeiture of the deposit when the party claiming relief was not ready and willing to perform his obligations under the contract. In *Stockloser v Johnson* [1954] 1 QB 476, Romer LJ stated that the jurisdiction of the court was confined to allowing late completion by the defaulting party and did not extend to ordering the repayment of a sum which had been paid in accordance with the contract and which, on breach, was stated to be forfeit. On the other hand, both Denning and Somervell LJJ in *Stockloser* stated that a deposit may be recoverable in equity if the forfeiture clause was of a penal nature and if it was unconscionable for the innocent party to retain the money. Lord Browne-Wilkinson found it unnecessary to resolve this conflict. He distinguished *Stockloser* on the ground that it was a case in which the purchaser seeking relief against the forfeiture of instalments had been let into possession of the subject-matter of the contract (although it is not entirely clear what basis in principle there is for so distinguishing the case). Whatever the answer to the problem in *Stockloser*, Lord Browne-Wilkinson stated that a stipulation for the forfeiture of a 25 per cent deposit was a 'plain penalty' and, on the authority of *Commissioner of Public Works v Hills* [1906] AC 368, he held that the court was entitled to order repayment of the sum paid, less any damage actually proved to have been suffered as a result of the default. One further point of note which arises out of *Dojap* is that, in the event of a deposit being held to be unreasonable, the court will not rewrite the contract by inserting into it a 'reasonable' deposit. The vendors were therefore not entitled to retain 10 per cent of the sum paid because they had not contracted for a 10 per cent deposit. This refusal to rewrite the terms of the contract will give an incentive to contracting parties to err on the side of caution when setting the level of any deposit payable. *Dojap* is therefore to be welcomed in so far as it places limits upon the ability of contracting parties to provide for excessive deposits.

But the limits of *Dojap* must be noted. It deals only with the right of the innocent party to retain the deposit. It does not purport to restrict the right of the innocent party to terminate the contract in respect of the breach. In the latter context, the courts have generally been reluctant to interfere with the innocent party's right to terminate the contract, as can be seen from *Union Eagle Ltd v Golden Achievement Ltd* [1997] AC 514. The claimant agreed to buy a flat in Hong Kong and paid 10 per cent of the purchase price (HK$420,000) as a deposit. The agreement specified the date, time and place of completion, and time was stated to be in every respect of the essence of the agreement. Completion was to take place on or before 30 September 1991 and before 5 pm on that day. Clause 12 of the agreement stated that, if the purchaser failed to comply with any of the terms and conditions of the agreement, the vendor had the right to rescind the contract and forfeit the deposit. The claimant failed to complete by the stipulated time and tendered the purchase price ten minutes after the time for completion had passed. The vendors refused to accept late payment, rescinded the contract and forfeited the deposit. The claimant refused to accept the defendants' decision to rescind the contract and brought an action seeking to have the contract specifically enforced. His action failed. His argument that the court could and should intervene to restrain the enforcement by the vendors of their legal rights when it would be 'unconscionable' for them to insist upon them was rejected by the Privy Council on the ground that it was both contrary to the authorities and to the needs of the business world. Lord Hoffmann emphasised the need for certainty in commercial transactions and stated that a jurisdiction to grant relief from termination in cases of alleged unconscionability was not consistent with the promotion of certainty. In a volatile market a vendor will want to know whether or not he can terminate the contract and deal with someone else. The law should, as far as possible, enable the vendor to know whether or not he is entitled to terminate. But, while the need for certainty applies to the decision whether or not to terminate, it does not obviously apply to the financial consequences of termination. Thus the apparent harshness of the rule laid down in *Union Eagle* is mitigated by the possibility that a court will grant a personal restitutionary claim to the purchaser where the vendor has been unjustly enriched as a result of the payment made or other work done by the purchaser prior to termination or where the deposit which has been paid is not a reasonable one. Such personal remedies do not undermine the promotion of certainty. In other words, the position which the law has adopted is that, while the vendor should have restored to him the 'freedom to deal with his land as he pleases', he should not enjoy the same freedom in relation to money paid to him or benefits conferred on him by the party in breach. However, it should be noted that there are some very exceptional cases where equity will intervene to prevent a party from exercising his right to terminate; for example, where he is estopped from doing so. Equity may also intervene to grant relief in cases of late payment of money due under a mortgage or rent due under a lease (*G and C Kreglinger v New Patagonia Meat and Cold Storage Co Ltd* [1914] AC 25, 35) and where the termination involves the forfeiture of a proprietary or possessory right to land or to a chattel (*Vauxhall Motors Ltd (formerly General Motors UK Ltd) v Manchester Ship Canal Co Ltd* [2019] UKSC 46; [2019] 3 WLR 852; *BICC plc v Burndy Corp* [1985] Ch 232), but the latter jurisdiction does not extend to cases in which the right which has been forfeited is a contractual right (*The Scaptrade* [1983] 2 AC 694).

22.7.3   Part payments

Where the sum paid is held to be a part payment, the general rule is that the sum is recoverable by the party in breach. This rule can be traced back to the case of *Dies*. The claimant contracted to purchase ammunition and made a prepayment of £100,000. In breach of contract the claimant refused to accept delivery. The defendants terminated the contract and the claimant sued to recover the £100,000. Stable J held that the claimant was entitled to recover the money paid, subject to the right of the defendants to recover damages for the breach. The initial payment was a conditional one; it was conditional upon subsequent performance of the contract and, when that condition failed because of the termination of the contract consequent upon the claimant's breach of contract, the defendants' right to retain the money simultaneously failed (see Beatson, 1981). However, the rule in *Dies* did not emerge unscathed from a re-examination by the House of Lords in *Hyundai Shipbuilding and Heavy Industries Co Ltd v Papadopoulos* [1980] 1 WLR 1129. Shipbuilders sought to recover an instalment which they alleged was due to them by the defendant guarantors. It was held that the shipbuilders were entitled to recover the instalment. Lord Fraser distinguished *Dies* on the ground that the latter case was not one in which the vendors were required to incur any expenditure or perform any work in the performance of their obligations under the contract. It was a simple contract of sale. *Hyundai*, on the other hand, involved a contract for work and materials, under which the shipbuilders incurred expense in the building of the ship. The conclusion that can be derived from *Hyundai* is that, where it is clear from the contract that the payee will have to incur reliance expenditure before completing his performance of the contract, then, in the absence of a stipulation in the contract to the contrary, the part payment will be irrecoverable. A part payment is therefore recoverable only where it is clear from the contract that the payee will not have to incur reliance expenditure before completing his performance of the contract.

22.8 Liquidated damages, penalty clauses and forfeitures: an assessment

Two groups of questions must be considered here. The first is: why should we differentiate between an agreed damages clause where the sum is payable on a breach of contract and a clause which provides that a prepayment cannot be recovered by the party in breach? Why not have a uniform set of rules? As a matter of history, the two types of clause have been treated differently and have emerged from separate jurisdictions but in recent years, in cases such as *Workers Trust and Merchant Bank Ltd v Dojap Investments Ltd* (above), there appears to be a greater convergence between the two jurisdictions. That convergence may have gained further impetus from the decision of the Supreme Court in *Cavendish Square Holding BV v Talal El Makdessi and ParkingEye Ltd v Beavis* where Lord Mance (at [154]–[156]) and Lord Hodge (at [226]) recognised that in principle the penalty clause rule can apply to a clause which entitles the innocent party to withhold payments on breach. Lord Hodge further held that the penalty clause rule could encompass a clause requiring the purchaser to pay an extravagant, non-refundable deposit ([234]–[238]).

However, it was not necessary for the Supreme Court in *Cavendish* to consider the scope of the court's jurisdiction to grant relief from forfeiture and so the relationship between the penalty clause rule and the jurisdiction to grant relief against forfeiture was not worked out in any detail. Thus Lord Neuberger and Lord Sumption stated (at [18]) that it was 'less clear … whether a provision is capable of being both a penalty clause and a forfeiture clause'. Rather more detail was provided by Lord Mance (at [160]–[161]) and Lord Hodge (at [227]) who appeared to envisage that a clause could be subject to both jurisdictions which would be applied sequentially (a proposition with which Lord Clarke at [291] and Lord Toulson at [294] expressed agreement). Thus Lord Hodge stated that 'the court risks no confusion if it asks first whether, as a matter of construction, the clause is a penalty and, if it answers that question in the negative, considers whether relief in equity should be granted having regard to the position of the parties after the breach'. As Lord Mance observed (at [160]), a penalty clause 'imposes a sanction for breach which is extravagant to the point where the court will in no circumstances enforce it according to its terms' whereas 'the power to relieve against forfeiture relates to clauses which do not have that character, but which nonetheless operate on breach to deprive a party of an interest in a manner that would not be penal.' On this basis the penalty clause jurisdiction and the jurisdiction to grant relief against forfeiture 'operate at different points and with different effects' so that consideration should first be given to the question whether a clause is a penalty clause and, if it is not, the court should then consider whether the clause should be enforced or whether to grant relief against forfeiture.

The second group of questions which must be asked is: can the existence of these jurisdictions to grant relief to defaulting contracting parties be justified? Should freedom of contract not prevail so that the parties can be left free to stipulate the amount of damages payable in the event of a breach? What is the point of these rules if they can be evaded by the clever draftsmanship of the more powerful party? These are not straightforward questions to answer.

Given the tendency which we have noted for damages to undercompensate, a number of arguments can be adduced in favour of leaving the parties free to make their own assessment of the damages payable upon a breach. The first is the argument from freedom of contract, that the parties should be free to stipulate the sums payable on breach. The second is that it would avoid the artificiality of the present rules, many of which can be evaded by careful draftsmanship. The third is that it would reduce the uncertainty caused by the present possibility of judicial review. These arguments were considered and ultimately rejected by the Supreme Court in *Cavendish Square Holding BV v Talal El Makdessi and ParkingEye Ltd v Beavis*.

The Supreme Court rejected the submission that the penalty clause rule should be abolished and it so concluded for a number of reasons. First, the penalty rule is a long-established part of English contract law. As Lord Mance observed (at [162]), 'there would have to be shown the strongest reasons for so radical a reversal of jurisprudence'. Second, many other legal systems in the world have rules which are not dissimilar to the penalty rule in English law so that the rule cannot be dismissed as an anomaly confined to the common law. Third, the penalty rule does not generate an excessive degree of uncertainty for contracting parties, once its limits are properly understood. As Lord Hodge observed (at [266]), 'I am not persuaded that the rule against penalties prevents parties from reaching sensible arrangements to fix the consequences of a breach of contract and thus avoid expensive disputes.' Fourth, to the extent that the scope of the rule is said to be arbitrary, the answer to that objection is to refine the rule in order to eliminate, or reduce substantially, the anomalies said to be created by the rule. Finally, the Supreme Court held that there remained a practical need for the penalty clause rule. Although statute has intervened to regulate unfair terms, particularly in a consumer context (on which see Chapter 18), the statutory coverage remains incomplete and, in a commercial context, there remain significant imbalances in the negotiating power of contracting parties, so that there remains a need for a protective rule of the type to be found in the penalty clause rule. The Supreme Court therefore concluded that the rule should not be abolished but at the same time declined to extend its scope given that the rule 'is an interference with freedom of contract' ([33]) and, as such, should not be applied too stringently by the courts so that what the parties have agreed should normally be upheld because any other approach would lead to undesirable uncertainty, particularly in commercial contracts.

22.9 Specific performance

A claimant who wishes to secure an adequate remedy may, finally, seek an order of specific performance. An order of specific performance is an order of the court which requires the party in breach to perform his primary obligations under the contract. This is, of course, one of the most effective methods of protecting the expectation of performance because it orders that performance take place, albeit generally at a later point in time than originally agreed. We have already noted that damages are available as of right upon a breach of contract, but specific performance is an equitable remedy which is only available in the discretion of the court. Historically, English law has conceived of specific performance as a supplementary remedy, only to be granted when damages were inadequate. But the scope of the remedy has gradually expanded in recent years. The crucial case in the development of the law is *Beswick v Beswick* [1968] AC 58 (see Section 7.2). In granting an order of specific performance to the claimant, it is clear that the House of Lords envisaged a wider role for specific performance, based upon the appropriateness of the remedy in the circumstances of the case, rather than as a supplementary remedy in a hierarchical system of remedies. Lord Reid awarded specific performance to achieve a 'just result' and Lord Pearce granted the order because it was 'the more appropriate remedy'.

The extent to which this more expansive view has been implemented in subsequent cases remains unclear. One commentator has gone so far as to cite *Beswick* for the proposition that there is now 'a right to specific performance of all contracts where there is no adequate reason for the courts to refuse it' (Lawson, 1980). Other commentators, while recognising the possibilities inherent in *Beswick*, have been more hesitant, as subsequent cases have not always followed the lead given in *Beswick* (see Burrows, 1984b). Cases can be found, however, which have adopted a more liberal approach (see *Evans Marshall and Co Ltd v Bertola SA* [1973] 1 WLR 349 and *Sudbrook Estates Ltd v Eggleton* [1983] 1 AC 444) and it is suggested that Treitel is correct to conclude (2020, para 21-030) that the 'availability of specific performance depends on the *appropriateness* of that remedy in the circumstances of each case'.

22.9.1 Cases where specific performance is not generally available

Nevertheless there remain a number of situations in which an order of specific performance is not normally available. The remedy is generally unavailable where it would cause severe hardship to the defendant (*Patel v Ali* [1984] Ch 283), where the contract is unfair to the defendant, even though the unfairness is not such as to amount to a ground on which the contract can be set aside (*Walters v Morgan* (1861) 3 D F & J 718), where the conduct of the claimant demonstrates that he does not deserve the remedy (*Shell UK Ltd v Lostock Garages Ltd* [1976] 1 WLR 1187), where the claimant has sought to take advantage of a mistake by the defendant (*Webster v Cecil* (1861) 30 Beav 62), where performance is impossible (*Watts v Spence* [1976] Ch 165), where the contract is one of personal service, such as a contract of employment (Trade Union and Labour Relations (Consolidation) Act 1992, s 236 and *Ashworth v Royal National Theatre* [2014] EWHC 1176 (QB); [2014] 4 All ER 238), where the contract is too vague (*Tito v Waddell (No 2)* [1977] Ch 106, 322) and finally, the court 'will not compel a defendant to perform his obligations specifically if it cannot at the same time ensure that any unperformed obligations of the [claimant] will be specifically performed, unless perhaps damages would be an adequate remedy for any default on the [claimant's] part' (*Price v Strange* [1978] Ch 337).

However, the law is in an uncertain state here because many of the cases which form the foundation of these rules were decided before *Beswick* and their status must be regarded as uncertain in the light of that decision.

22.9.2 *Co-operative Insurance Society Ltd v Argyll Stores (Holdings) Ltd*

The validity of a more expansive approach to the availability of specific performance has, however, been thrown into some doubt by the decision of the House of Lords in *Co-operative Insurance Society Ltd v Argyll Stores (Holdings) Ltd* [1998] AC 1. The claimants were the freehold owners of a shopping centre and they let the anchor unit to the defendants for use as a supermarket. The agreement was stated to run for 35 years from 1979 and the defendants covenanted to 'keep open the demised premises for retail trade…' for the duration of the agreement. In 1995, after the store had made a trading loss, the defendants decided to close it. They ignored the claimants' request to keep open the store, stripped it and closed it. The claimants sought an order for specific performance of the 'keep-open' covenant. The trial judge refused to grant the order, but the Court of Appeal, by a majority, granted it. Two factors weighed heavily with the majority of the Court of Appeal in deciding to grant the order sought. The first was that the claimants would have had very considerable difficulty in proving the loss which they had suffered as a result of the breach, and the second was that the defendants had acted with 'unmitigated commercial cynicism'. But the House of Lords allowed the defendants' appeal and held that no criticism could be made of the way in which the trial judge had exercised his discretion. Their Lordships relied on a number of factors in reaching their conclusion: (i) there was a settled practice that an order would not be made which would require a defendant to run a business, (ii) an order compelling the defendants to trade could expose them to enormous losses, (iii) the task of framing the order was not an easy one, (iv) there was the possibility of wasteful litigation over compliance, (v) it was oppressive to the defendants to have to run a business under the threat of proceedings for contempt of court and (vi) it was argued that it could not be in the public interest to require someone to carry on a business at a loss if there was a plausible alternative by which the other party could be given compensation. Cumulatively these factors demonstrated that the settled practice was based on 'sound sense' and that the trial judge had acted within his discretion in refusing to grant the order sought. The case is obviously a difficult one but it is suggested that the reasoning of the House of Lords is open to attack on the ground that it pays too much attention to the position of the defendants and does not focus on the need to ensure that the claimant is given an adequate remedy in the event of breach (the damages remedy may well prove to be inadequate in the light of the problems of proof and quantification).

22.9.3 Contracting for specific performance?

Can the parties contract for an order of specific performance? In *Quadrant Visual Communications Ltd v Hutchison Telephone UK Ltd* [1993] BCLC 442, Stocker LJ stated that 'once the court is asked for the equitable remedy of specific performance, its discretion cannot be fettered' by the stipulation of the parties. The parties could not, by the terms of their contract, confine the role of the court to that of a 'rubber stamp'. It should be noted, however, that this was a case in which the claimants had been guilty of 'trickery' in failing to disclose to the defendants an agreement which the court held that they should have disclosed to the defendants: the claimants had not come to court with 'clean hands'. In such a case, it is easy to understand why the court paid little or no attention to any agreed stipulation for specific performance. But in other contexts, where there is no 'wrongdoing' on the part of the claimant, it is arguable that, while the parties should not be able to exercise the discretion for the court, their stipulation should be *a* factor which is taken into account by the court in the exercise of its discretion (see *Warner Bros Pictures Inc v Nelson* [1937] 1 KB 209, 220–21). So it is possible that some limited advantage can be obtained by contracting for specific performance (and it has been argued that English law should give greater weight to a party-agreed stipulation in favour of the availability of specific performance: see Rowan, 2010, 449–55 and 470–72).

22.9.4 Future developments

Until the decision of the House of Lords in *Co-operative Insurance Society Ltd v Argyll Stores (Holdings) Ltd*, it could be said that the English courts had begun to display a gradual willingness to expand the scope of the remedy of specific performance. The effect of the latter decision is, however, to bring that more expansive approach to a halt, although it may turn out to be no more than a temporary halt. English law can, in this respect, be compared with civilian systems where specific performance is often stated to be the primary remedy for a breach of contract. But too much can be made of the contrast between the two systems. In *Co-operative Insurance v Argyll Stores (Holdings) Ltd*, Lord Hoffmann stated that there is in practice less difference between common law and civilian systems than one might suppose and that one would expect judges in civilian systems to take into account much the same matters as English judges do when deciding whether or not to order specific performance in any given case. Some support for this proposition can be gleaned from Article 9-102 of the Principles of European Contract Law which provides:

(1) The aggrieved party is entitled to specific performance of an obligation other than one to pay money, including the remedying of a defective performance.
(2) Specific performance cannot, however, be obtained where:

   (a) performance would be unlawful or impossible; or
   (b) performance would cause the obligor unreasonable effort or expense; or
   (c) the performance consists in the provision of services or work of a personal character or depends upon a personal relationship; or
   (d) the aggrieved party may reasonably obtain performance from another source.

(3) The aggrieved party will lose the right to specific performance if it fails to seek it within a reasonable time after it has or ought to have become aware of the non-performance.

It can be seen that the factors listed in paragraph (2) are very similar to those which would be taken into account by an English court in deciding whether or not to make a specific performance order. It may be that the difference between the two systems is ultimately one which concerns the location of the burden of proof. In English law, the burden is on the claimant to establish that specific performance is the appropriate remedy, whereas in civilian systems it is for the defendant to show that the claimant is not entitled to specific performance. On the other hand, the difference in approach can lead to different outcomes in the courts. For example, the Scottish courts in *Highland and Universal Properties Ltd v Safeway Properties Ltd* 2000 SLT 414 held that a keep-open covenant was specifically enforceable as a matter of Scots law.

Should the English courts adopt this more expansive approach to be found in civilian systems and, in particular, should they go even further and take the step of holding that specific performance is generally available as a remedy in the event of the occurrence of a breach of contract? It can be argued that damages undercompensate in more cases than is commonly supposed and the fact that a claimant asks for specific performance is good evidence that damages are inadequate. Indeed, in many cases claimants have an incentive not to ask for an order of specific performance. They will want to go out into the marketplace and purchase alternative goods and sue for damages for the difference in value rather than wait for a court to make an order of specific performance. A further consideration which must be borne in mind is that the performance obtainable from an unwilling contracting party may well be inferior to that obtainable from another, willing performer. So it can be argued that, where the claimant asks for specific performance, the remedy should be generally available because the mere fact that he has asked for the remedy demonstrates that damages are an inadequate remedy.

But a number of arguments can be adduced against such a proposition. The first is that some limitations must be placed upon the availability of the remedy in the case of contracts involving personal or intimate relations and in cases where it would be impossible for the court to supervise the order because of the vagueness inherent in the contract. It should not be assumed, however, that an order of specific performance will necessarily result in the performance of the contract. An order of specific performance gives to the claimant a choice. He can either insist upon performance of the contract or he can sell his right, at a price of his own choice, to the defendant (see Calabresi and Melamed, 1972). A defendant who wished to be released from his contract with the claimant, in order to enter into a more lucrative contract with a third party, would then have to negotiate his way out of the contract with the claimant. It is suggested that, because of the fact that damages do tend to undercompensate, specific performance should be generally available and that the courts should be willing to grant the remedy unless the defendant can satisfy the court that there is a good reason to refuse the remedy, or that an order of specific performance would violate, or be inconsistent with, established rules and doctrines of contract law (see Kronman, 1978b; Schwartz, 1979; Bishop, 1985; McKendrick, 1986).

22.10 Injunctions

A breach of a negative contract or a negative stipulation in a contract may, in an appropriate case, be restrained by means of an injunction. An injunction is also an equitable remedy which is available within the discretion of the court. An injunction will not be granted where its effect would be directly or indirectly to compel the defendant to perform acts which he could not have been required to do by an order of specific performance. An injunction is commonly sought in restraint of trade cases to restrain the employee or vendor acting in breach of his covenant (see further Treitel, 2020, paras 21-059–21-069).

But the significance of injunctive relief is not confined to restraint of trade cases. In *Araci v Fallon* [2011] EWCA Civ 668; [2011] All ER (D) 37 (Jun) the claimant racehorse owner obtained an interim injunction to restrain the defendant jockey from breaching his contract with the claimant by riding another horse in the Derby. The defendant had entered into a retainer agreement with the claimant under which he agreed not to ride another horse when he had been retained by the claimant to ride the claimant's horse. In breach of this agreement, the defendant sought to ride another horse in the Derby. In granting injunctive relief to the claimant to restrain the defendant from riding the other horse, the Court of Appeal attached importance to the fact that the defendant was seeking to act in 'flagrant' breach of a contract into which he had entered voluntarily, that damages would not have been an adequate remedy for the claimant (given the uncertainty surrounding the assessment of damages), that the term sought to be enforced was not in restraint of trade nor contrary to public policy and the claimant had not been guilty of undue delay in seeking injunctive relief (which was granted on the morning of the race itself).

The case in which the courts are most likely to grant an injunction is one in which the defendant breaches a negative covenant in the contract. Such was the case in *Priyanka Shipping Ltd v Glory Bulk Carriers Pty Ltd* [2019] EWHC 2804 (Comm); [2019] 1 WLR 6677. The claimant purchased a vessel from the defendant for scrap purposes and it agreed that it would not 'trade the Vessel further'. The claimant found it difficult to sell the vessel for demolition and so it decided to employ the vessel for further trade in breach of its undertaking to the defendant. The defendant sought an injunction to restrain further breaches of covenant by the claimant. In holding that the defendant was entitled to the injunction which it sought, the judge concluded that negative covenants (such as the covenant not to trade further with the vessel) are ordinarily, but not invariably, enforced by means of an injunction. It is not a precondition to the grant of an injunction that the party seeking the injunction must prove that it would otherwise suffer damage. In exercising its discretion whether or not to grant an injunction, the court may decline to grant an injunction where it would be unconscionable or oppressive to grant the remedy, but the burden of proof lies on the party bound by the negative covenant to show why the remedy should not be granted. On the facts of the case there had been three breaches of the negative covenant by the claimant and so the prima facie position was that the defendant was entitled to the injunction which it sought. This was not a case in which the grant of an injunction would be oppressive or unconscionable for the claimant. Its breaches of contract had been deliberate and no extraordinary financial consequences would flow from the decision to grant an injunction. Damages would not have been an adequate remedy for the defendant and so the injunction was granted.

A final case which illustrates the potential significance of injunctions in modern contract law is *AB v CD* [2014] EWCA Civ 229; [2014] BLR 313. The defendant was the owner of intellectual property rights in an internet-based platform for the sale and purchase of goods and services. It granted a licence to the claimant to market the product in the Middle East and this licence represented the claimant's only business. The defendant subsequently sought to terminate the licence. The claimant denied that the defendant was entitled so to terminate the licence and sought an interim injunction to require the defendant to continue to perform its obligations under the licence and to restrain it from terminating or suspending the agreement prior to the outcome of an arbitration between the parties. In seeking relief on this basis the claimant placed considerable emphasis on a broadly drafted clause which appeared to exclude the defendant's liability entirely for a number of heads of loss (such as loss of profits) and capped liability in respect of other losses. In the light of this clause, the claimant submitted that damages would not be an adequate remedy and that it was therefore entitled to an interim injunction. The Court of Appeal agreed. Laws LJ stated that:

> Where a party to a contract stipulates that if he breaches his obligations his liability will be limited or the damages he must pay will be capped, that is a circumstance which in justice tends to favour the grant of an injunction to prohibit the breach in the first place.

This case does not stand as authority for the proposition that the presence of an exclusion or a limitation clause in a contract acts as a passport to a claim for an interim injunction. But it can be said that the presence of such a clause is a factor which a court may take into account when deciding whether or not to grant an injunction. The Court of Appeal was clearly concerned that the claimant might succeed in its claim that the defendant had wrongfully terminated the contract between the parties, only to find that its business had in the intervening period collapsed and that, as a result of the exclusion clause, damages would prove to be a wholly inadequate remedy. In an attempt to avoid this perceived injustice the Court of Appeal awarded the claimant an interim injunction pending the outcome of the arbitration between the parties.

22.11 Damages in lieu of specific performance

Finally, the court has a discretion to award a claimant damages in lieu of an injunction or specific performance (Senior Courts Act 1981, s 50). Where the court decides to exercise its discretion to award damages, damages are assessed on the same basis as common law damages for breach of contract (*Johnson v Agnew* [1980] AC 367, 400), although the courts may be more inclined to award the claimant negotiating damages where the court decides, in the exercise of its discretion, not to grant to the claimant a specific performance order or an injunction (*Morris-Garner v One Step (Support) Ltd* [2018] UKSC 20; [2019] AC 649 and see Section 21.7).

22.12 Conclusion

What is the significance of the remedial consequences of a breach of contract for the basis of contract law? It is suggested that there are three principal lessons which we can glean from our brief survey of the remedies available on a breach of contract. The first is the scope which is given to the parties to make provision for their own remedies on a breach of contract. In this chapter we have seen that a number of options are open to the parties and, although the courts do place limitations upon the remedies available, in many cases these restrictions can be evaded by careful draftsmanship. It is not true to say that the law of contract resembles the law of tort in that it simply imposes remedies upon the parties. In many cases, the remedies are dependent upon the agreement of the parties. The second point relates to the 'interests' which the law of contract seeks to protect. We have seen that the law of contract seeks to protect the expectation interest, rather than the reliance interest or the restitution interest, thus separating contract law from the law of tort and the law of restitution. A promise engenders in the promisee an expectation that the promise will be performed and, as a general rule, the courts will order the party in default to fulfil the expectations which he has so created.

Thirdly, and finally, our study of remedies has demonstrated that the law of contract is not wholeheartedly committed to the protection of the expectation interest. Supplementary policies, such as the doctrines of mitigation and remoteness and the reluctance of the courts to grant an order of specific performance in certain situations, weaken the commitment of the law to the protection of the expectation interest. This illustrates a point which was made in the opening chapter of this book (Section 1.4). Contract law is committed to the protection of individual autonomy and the protection of the expectation interest but that commitment is tempered in its application by considerations of fairness, consumerism and altruism. These conflicting ideologies are present within the rules relating to remedies; sometimes the courts are committed to 'market-individualism' (see, for example, *White and Carter (Councils) Ltd v McGregor* [1962] AC 413 (Section 22.4)), but on other occasions the courts are committed to 'consumer-welfarism' (see, for example, *Patel v Ali* [1984] Ch 283 (Section 22.9) and the cases on the penalty clause rule). Contract law is a complex subject in which competing ideologies battle for predominance. The struggle to resolve this endemic conflict will continue to be a feature of contract law in the years to come.

Hot topic 19...

What is the commercial significance of the penalty clause rule after the decision of the Supreme Court in *Cavendish Square Holding BV v Talal El Makdessi and ParkingEye Ltd v Beavis*? The rule is unlikely to have much impact on transactions concluded between experienced commercial parties who have access to skilled legal advice. In such cases it will be difficult for a party seeking to set aside the clause to show that the stipulated sum is extravagant and unconscionable in amount in comparison with the innocent party's legitimate interest in the performance of the contract. However, it is not impossible. If the parties used the agreed damages clause as a vehicle by which they seek to require one party to pay punitive damages to the other, a court might well conclude that the term is a penalty. But such cases are likely to be rare. More difficult, perhaps, is the case where the contract is entered into between parties of unequal bargaining power. But here the decision in the *ParkingEye* appeal suggests that it will not be easy for a party to challenge the validity of the clause. The £85 charge in *ParkingEye* could be said to be unreasonable but the majority held that it was not extravagant in comparison with ParkingEye's legitimate interest in the performance of the contract. Presumably a charge of £5,000 would have been extravagant. But what would have been the position if the charge imposed had been £150 or £125?

Summary

▶ A party who, in breach of contract, fails to perform an obligation which is entire cannot generally make any claim for payment from the innocent party. But the rule is subject to exceptions where the party in breach has substantially performed his obligations under the contract (although this exception is the subject of some controversy), where the innocent party has accepted the part performance and where the court holds that the obligation is not entire but divisible.

▶ Where the term which is broken is a 'condition' which is of the 'essence of the contract', the innocent party can terminate performance of the contract and claim loss of bargain damages.

▶ A claim in debt is a claim for a definite sum of money which the defendant is, under the terms of the contract, due to pay to the claimant. The claimant is not under a duty to mitigate his loss and the remoteness rules are inapplicable.

▶ An agreed damages clause will generally be enforced by the courts and it will fix the loss that is recoverable in the event of a breach of contract. But the courts retain a jurisdiction to decline to give effect to an agreed damages clause where it is held to amount to a penalty clause. The test for the identification of a penalty clause is whether the sum stated to be payable as a consequence of a breach of contract is extravagant, exorbitant or unconscionable in amount when regard is had to the innocent party's legitimate interest in the performance of the contract. The penalty clause rule can be evaded by merely accelerating an existing liability, by making the sum payable on an event other than a breach of contract (unless the term is held to be a disguised penalty clause) or by simply elevating the status of the term broken to a condition which is of the essence of the agreement.

▶ A deposit is paid by way of security and is generally irrecoverable, provided that the sum payable by way of deposit is reasonable.

▶ A part payment is a payment towards the contract price. Such a payment is recoverable by the party in breach where it is clear from the contract that the payee will not have to incur reliance expenditure before completing his performance of the contract.

▶ Specific performance is an equitable remedy which is available within the discretion of the court. The availability of specific performance depends upon the appropriateness of the remedy on the facts of the case. There are a number of contexts in which specific performance is not normally available.

▶ An injunction is an equitable remedy which may be used in an effort to prevent a threatened breach of contract. A court will not grant an injunction where to do so would be directly or indirectly to compel the defendant to do an act which he could not have been ordered to do by a decree of specific performance.

▶ The court has a discretion to grant damages in lieu of an injunction or specific performance.

Exercises

22.1 John agreed to build two houses on Brian's land. The contract price was agreed at £130,000 and the price was payable upon completion of the work. After completing work to the value of £65,000 John abandoned the contract. He is now seeking payment from Brian. Advise him. Would your answer differ if Brian had employed Julian to complete the work and had paid him £75,000 to complete the two houses?

22.2 What is a 'claim in debt'?

22.3 Distinguish between a 'liquidated damages clause' and a 'penalty clause'.

22.4 A contractor enters into a contract with an employer to erect some buildings at a cost of £900,000. The contract states that, if the contractor fails to complete the work by the completion date, then the contractor has either to 'pay to or allow to the Employer the whole or such part as may be specified in writing by the Employer of a sum calculated at the rate stated in the Appendix as liquidated and ascertained damages'. The Appendix stated under the heading 'liquidated and ascertained damages' that the figure payable was '£ nil'. The contractor has failed to complete the work on time and the employer is now seeking damages from the contractor in accordance with the clause set out above. What advice would you give to the employer?

22.5 Distinguish between a 'deposit' and a 'part payment'. When are such payments recoverable by the party in breach?

22.6 Should specific performance be the normal remedy for breach of contract?

22.7 Outline the circumstances in which the courts will normally refuse to grant an order of specific performance.

Bibliography

Adams and Brownsword (1987) 'The Ideologies of Contract Law', *Legal Studies*, 7, 205.

Adams and Brownsword (1988a) 'The Unfair Contract Terms Act: A Decade of Discretion', *Law Quarterly Review*, 104, 94.

Adams and Brownsword (1988b) 'Double Indemnity – Contractual Indemnity Clauses Revisited', *Journal of Business Law*, 146.

Anson (1879) *Law of Contract* (1st edn), Oxford University Press.

Anson (2020) *Law of Contract* by J Beatson, A Burrows and J Cartwright (31st edn), Oxford University Press.

Atiyah (1957) '*Couturier v. Hastie* and the Sale of Non-Existent Goods', *Law Quarterly Review*, 78, 340.

Atiyah (1979) *The Rise and Fall of Freedom of Contract*, Oxford University Press.

Atiyah (1982) 'Economic Duress and the Overborne Will', *Law Quarterly Review*, 98, 197.

Atiyah (1986a) 'The Modern Role of Contract Law', in Atiyah (ed.), *Essays on Contract*, Oxford University Press.

Atiyah (1986b) 'Contracts, Promises and the Law of Obligations', in Atiyah , *Essays on Contract*, Oxford University Press.

Atiyah (1986c) 'Consideration: A Restatement', in Atiyah (ed.), *Essays on Contract*, Oxford University Press.

Atiyah (1986d) 'Contract and Fair Exchange', in Atiyah (ed.), *Essays on Contract*, Oxford University Press.

Atiyah (1986e) *Pragmatism and Theory in English Law*, Stevens.

Atiyah (1986f) '*The Hannah Blumenthal* and Classical Contract Law', *Law Quarterly Review*, 102, 363.

Atiyah (1986g) 'The Liberal Theory of Contract', in Atiyah (ed.), *Essays on Contract*, Oxford University Press.

Atiyah (2006) *An Introduction to the Law of Contract* by S A Smith (6th edn), Oxford University Press.

Atiyah and Treitel (1967) 'Misrepresentation Act 1967', *Modern Law Review*, 30, 369.

Barnes (2011) 'Estoppels as Swords', *Lloyd's Maritime and Commercial Law Quarterly*, 372.

Barton (1976) 'Penalties and Damages', *Law Quarterly Review*, 92, 20.

Beale (1993) 'Unreasonable Deposits', *Law Quarterly Review*, 109, 524.

Beale (2010) 'A Review of the Contracts (Rights of Third Parties) Act 1999', in Burrows and Peel (eds), *Contract Formation and Parties*, Oxford University Press, 225.

Beale (2012) *Mistake and Non-disclosure of Facts: Models for English Contract Law*, Oxford University Press.

Beale and Dugdale (1975) 'Contracts Between Businessmen: Planning and the Use of Contractual Remedies', *British Journal of Law and Society*, 2, 45.

Beale, Bishop and Furmston (2008) *Contract: Cases and Materials* (5th edn), Oxford University Press.

Beatson (1974) 'Duress as a Vitiating Factor in Contract', *Cambridge Law Journal*, 33, 97.

Beatson (1975) 'Repudiation of Illegal Purpose as a Ground for Restitution', *Law Quarterly Review*, 91, 313.

Beatson (1981) 'Discharge for Breach: The Position of Instalments, Deposits and Other Payments Due Before Completion', *Law Quarterly Review*, 97, 389.

Berg (2008) 'Richard III in New Zealand', *Law Quarterly Review*, 124, 3.

Birks (1985) *An Introduction to the Law of Restitution*, Oxford University Press.

Birks (2004) 'Undue Influence as Wrongful Exploitation', *Law Quarterly Review*, 120, 34.

Birks and Chin Nyuk Yin (1995) 'On the Nature of Undue Influence', in Beatson and Friedmann (eds), *Good Faith and Fault in Contract Law*, Oxford University Press, 57.

Bishop (1985) 'The Choice of Remedy for Breach of Contract', *Journal of Legal Studies*, 14, 299.

Bojczuk (1987) 'When Is a Condition Not a Condition?', *Journal of Business Law*, 353.

Bridge (1989) 'Mitigation of Damages in Contract and the Meaning of Avoidable Loss', *Law Quarterly Review*, 99, 398.

Bright (2000) 'Winning the Battle Against Unfair Contract Terms', *Legal Studies*, 20, 331.

Brownsword (1987) 'New Notes on the Old Oats', *Solicitors Journal*, 131, 384.

Brownsword (1992) 'Retrieving Reasons, Retrieving Rationality? A New Look at the Right to Withdraw for Breach of Contract', *Journal of Contract Law*, 83.

Buckley (1975) 'Implied Statutory Prohibition of Contracts', *Modern Law Review*, 38, 535.

Burrows (1983) 'Contract, Tort and Restitution – A Satisfactory Division or Not?', *Law Quarterly Review*, 99, 217.

Burrows (1984a) 'Law Commission Report on Pecuniary Restitution on Breach of Contract', *Modern Law Review*, 47, 76.

Burrows (1984b) 'Specific Performance at the Crossroads', *Legal Studies*, 4, 102.

Burrows (1993) 'Contributory Negligence in Contract: Ammunition for the Law Commission', *Law Quarterly Review*, 109, 175.

Burrows (1996) 'Reforming Privity of Contract: Law Commission Report No. 242', *Lloyd's Maritime and Commercial Law Quarterly*, 467.

Burrows (2000) 'The Contracts (Rights of Third Parties) Act and Its Implication for Commercial Contracts', *Lloyd's Maritime and Commercial Law Quarterly*, 540.

Burrows (2010) *The Law of Restitution* (3rd edn), Oxford University Press.

Burrows (2017) 'Illegality After *Patel v Mirza*', *Current Legal Problems*, 70, 55.

Burrows (2019) *Remedies for Torts, Breach of Contract and Equitable Wrongs* (4th edn), Oxford University Press.

Buxton (2010) '"Construction" and Rectification After *Chartbrook*', *Cambridge Law Journal*, 69, 253.

Calabresi and Melamed (1972) 'Property Rules, Liability Rules and Inalienability – One View of the Cathedral', *Harvard Law Review*, 85, 1089.

Capper (2010) 'The Unconscionable Bargain in the Common Law World', *Law Quarterly Review*, 126, 403.

Carter (2012) *Carter's Breach of Contract*, Hart Publishing.

Cartwright (1987a) 'Damages for Misrepresentation', *The Conveyancer and Property Lawyer*, 423.

Cartwright (1987b) '*Solle v. Butcher* and the Doctrine of Mistake in Contract', *Law Quarterly Review*, 103, 594.

Chen-Wishart (1995) 'Consideration, Practical Benefit and the Emperor's New Clothes', in Beatson and Friedmann (eds), *Good Faith and Fault in Contract Law*, Oxford University Press, 123.

Chen-Wishart (2010a) 'A Bird in the Hand: Consideration and Contract Modifications', in Burrows and Peel (eds), *Contract Formation and Parties*, Oxford University Press, 89.

Chen-Wishart (2010b) 'A Bird in the Hand', in M Chen-Wishart, L Ho and P Kapai (eds), *Reciprocity in Contract*, Faculty of Law, University of Hong Kong, 15.

Chen-Wishart (2010c) 'Reciprocity and Enforceability', in M Chen-Wishart, L Ho and P Kapai (eds), *Reciprocity in Contract*, Faculty of Law, University of Hong Kong, 1.

Cheshire, Fifoot and Furmston (2017) *Law of Contract* (17th edn), Oxford University Press.

Chitty (2018) *On Contracts* (33rd edn), Sweet & Maxwell.

Clarke (1993) 'The Common Law of Contract in 1993: Is There a General Doctrine of Good Faith?', *Hong Kong Law Journal*, 23, 318.

Cooke (1997) 'Estoppel and the Protection of Expectations', *Legal Studies*, 17, 258.

Coote (1964) *Exception Clauses*, Sweet & Maxwell.

Coote (1972) 'Another Look at *Bowmakers v. Barnet Instruments*', *Modern Law Review*, 34, 38.

Coote (1997) 'Contract Damages, *Ruxley* and the Performance Interest', *Cambridge Law Journal*, 527.

Coote (2004) 'Consideration and Variations: A Different Solution', *Law Quarterly Review*, 120, 19.

Corbin (1930) 'Contracts for the Benefit of Third Parties', *Law Quarterly Review*, 46, 12.

Corbin (1963) *On Contracts* (Rev edn), West Publishing Company.

Dawson (1980) *Gifts and Promises*, Yale University Press.

Davies (2016) 'Rectification Versus Interpretation – The Nature and Scope of the Equitable Jurisdiction', *Cambridge Law Journal*, 75, 62.

Dean (2002) 'Defining Unfair Terms in Consumer Contracts – Crystal Ball Gazing? *Director General of Fair Trading v First National Bank plc*', *Modern Law Review*, 65, 773.

Denning (1952) 'Recent Developments in the Doctrine of Consideration', *Modern Law Review*, 15, 1.

Dugdale and Yates (1976) 'Variation, Waiver and Estoppel – A Reappraisal', *Modern Law Review*, 38, 680.

Ellinghaus (1971) 'Agreements Which Defer "Essential" Terms', *Australian Law Journal*, 45, 4, 72.

Flannigan (1987) 'Privity-The End of an Era (Error)', *Law Quarterly Review*, 103, 564.

Freeman (1996) 'Contracting in the Haven: *Balfour v. Balfour* Revisited', in Halson (ed.), *Exploring the Boundaries of Contract*, Dartmouth.

Fridman (1962) 'Construing, Without Constructing, a Contract', *Law Quarterly Review*, 76, 521.

Fried (2015) *Contract as Promise* (2nd edn), Oxford University Press.

Friedmann (1995) 'The Performance Interest in Contract Damages', *Law Quarterly Review*, 111, 628.

Fuller (1941) 'Consideration and Form', *Columbia Law Review*, 41, 799.

Fuller and Perdue (1936) 'The Reliance Interest in Contract Damages', *Yale Law Journal*, 46, 52.

Furmston (1960) 'Return to *Dunlop v. Selfridge?* ', *Modern Law Review*, 23, 373.

Furmston (1965) 'The Analysis of Illegal Contracts', *University of Toronto Law Journal*, 267.

Gardner (1982) 'The Proprietary Effect of Contractual Obligations Under *Tulk v. Moxhay* and *De Mattos v. Gibson*', *Law Quarterly Review*, 98, 279.

Gardner (1992) 'Trashing with Trollope: A Deconstruction of the Postal Rules in Contract', *Oxford Journal of Legal Studies*, 12, 170.

Gilmore (1974) *The Death of Contract*, Columbus.

Gleeson and McKendrick (1987) 'The Rotting Away of Caveat Emptor', *The Conveyancer and Property Lawyer*, 121.

Goodhart (1941) 'Mistake as to Identity in the Law of Contract', *Law Quarterly Review*, 57, 228.

Goodhart (1951) 'Unilateral Contracts', *Law Quarterly Review*, 67, 456.

Goodhart (1953) 'A Short Replication', *Law Quarterly Review*, 69, 106.

Gordon (1974) 'Penalties Limiting Damages', *Law Quarterly Review*, 90, 296.

Gower (1952) 'Auction Sales of Goods Without Reserve', *Law Quarterly Review*, 68, 457.

Hall (1984) 'Frustration and the Question of Foresight', *Legal Studies*, 4, 300.

Halson (1990) 'Sailors, Sub-Contractors and Consideration', *Law Quarterly Review*, 106, 183.

Halson (1991) 'Opportunism, Economic Duress and Contractual Modifications', *Law Quarterly Review*, 107, 649.

Halson (1999) 'The Offensive Limits of Promissory Estoppel', *Lloyd's Maritime and Commercial Law Quarterly*, 256.

Harris, Ogus and Phillips (1979) 'Contract Remedies and the Consumer Surplus', *Law Quarterly Review*, 95, 581.

Hartley (1996) 'Five Forms of Uncertainty in European Community Law', *Cambridge Law Journal*, 55, 265.

Haycroft and Waksman (1984) 'Frustration and Restitution', *Journal of Business Law*, 207.

Hedley (1985) 'Keeping Contract in Its Place: *Balfour v. Balfour* and the Enforceability of Informal Agreements', *Oxford Journal of Legal Studies*, 5, 391.

Hobhouse (1990) 'International Conventions and Commercial Law: The Pursuit of Uniformity', *Law Quarterly Review*, 106, 530.

Hooley (1991) 'Damages and the Misrepresentation Act 1967', *Law Quarterly Review*, 107, 547.

Hooley (1992) 'Remedies for Misrepresentation', *New Law Journal*, 142, 60.

Howarth (1984) 'The Meaning of Objectivity in Contract', *Law Quarterly Review*, 100, 265.

Hudson (1968) '*Gibbons v. Proctor* Revisited', *Law Quarterly Review*, 84, 503.

Hudson (1974) 'Penalties Limiting Damages', *Law Quarterly Review*, 90, 31.

Hudson (1975) 'Penalties Limiting Damages', *Law Quarterly Review*, 91, 25.

Hudson (1986) 'Mental Incapacity Revisited', *The Conveyancer and Property Lawyer*, 178.

Jackson (1982) 'How Many Kinds of Estoppel?', *The Conveyancer and Property Lawyer*, 450.

Kennedy (1976) 'Form and Substance in Private Law Adjudication', *Harvard Law Review*, 89, 1685.

Kincaid (2000) 'Privity Reform in England', *Law Quarterly Review*, 116, 43.

Kronman (1978a) 'Mistake, Disclosure, Information and the Law of Contracts', *Journal of Legal Studies*, 7, 1.

Kronman (1978b) 'Specific Performance', *University of Chicago Law Review*, 45, 351.

Kronman (1980) 'Contract Law and Distributive Justice', *Yale Law Journal*, 89, 472.

Law Commission (1976) Working Paper No 70, *The Parol Evidence Rule*.

Law Commission (1983) Report No 121, *Law of Contract: Pecuniary Restitution on Breach of Contract*.

Law Commission (1986) Report No 154, *Law Commission Report on the Parol Evidence Rule*.

Law Commission (1991) Consultation Paper No 121, *Privity of Contract: Contracts for the Benefit of Third Parties*.

Law Commission (1993) Report No 219, *Contributory Negligence as a Defence in Contract*.

Law Commission (1996) Report No 242, *Privity of Contract: Contracts for the Benefit of Third Parties*.

Law Commission (1997) Report No 247, *Aggravated, Exemplary and Restitutionary Damages*.

Law Commission (2014) Report No 343, *Matrimonial Property, Needs and Agreements*.

Law Commission and Scottish Law Commission (2005) *Unfair Terms in Contracts* (Law Commission No 298 and Scottish Law Commission No 199).

Law Commission and Scottish Law Commission (2012) *Unfair Terms in Consumer Contracts: A New Approach?* (Issues Paper).

Law Commission and Scottish Law Commission (2013) *Unfair Terms in Consumer Contracts: Advice to the Department for Business, Innovation and Skills*.

Lawson (1980) *Remedies of English Law* (2nd edn), Butterworths.

Lewis (1982) 'Contracts Between Businessmen: Reform of the Law of Firm Offers and an Empirical Study of Tendering Practices in the Building Industry', *Journal of Law and Society*, 9, 153.

Liu (2011) 'The *White & Carter* Principle: A Restatement', *Modern Law Review*, 74, 171.

Lunney (1992) 'Towards a Unified Estoppel-The Long and Winding Road', *The Conveyancer and Property Lawyer*, 239.

Luther (1999) 'Campbell, Espinasse and the Sailors: Text and Context in the Common Law', *Legal Studies*, 19, 526.

Macdonald (1988a) 'The Duty to Give Notice of Unusual Contract Terms', *Journal of Business Law*, 375.

Macdonald (1988b) 'Incorporation of Contract Terms by a "Consistent Course of Dealing"', *Legal Studies*, 8, 48.

McFarlane and Stevens (2002) 'In Defence of *Sumpter v. Hedges*', *Law Quarterly Review*, 118, 569.

McKendrick (1986) 'Specific Implement and Specific Performance – A Comparison', *Scots Law Times*, 249.

McKendrick (1988) 'The Battle of the Forms and the Law of Restitution', *Oxford Journal of Legal Studies*, 8, 197.

McKendrick (1991) 'Frustration, Restitution and Loss of Apportionment', in Burrows (ed.), *Essays on the Law of Restitution*, Oxford University Press, 147.

McKendrick (1995) 'Frustration and Force Majeure – Their Relationship and a Comparative Assessment', in McKendrick (ed.), *Force Majeure and Frustration of Contract* (2nd edn), LLP, 33.

McKendrick (1999a) 'Breach of Contract and the Meaning of Loss', *Current Legal Problems*, 37.

McKendrick (1999b) 'Good Faith: A Matter of Principle', in Forte (ed.), *Good Faith in Contract and Property Law*, Hart Publishing, 39.

McKendrick (2003a) 'Breach of Contract, Restitution for Wrongs and Punishment', in Burrows and Peel (eds), *Commercial Remedies: Current Issues and Problems*, Oxford University Press, 95.

McKendrick (2003b) 'The Common Law at Work: The Saga of *Alfred McAlpine Construction Ltd v. Panatown Ltd*', *Oxford University Commonwealth Law Journal*, 3, 145.

McKendrick and Graham (2002) 'The Sky's the Limit: Contractual Damages for Non-Pecuniary Loss', *Lloyd's Maritime and Commercial Law Quarterly*, 161.

MacMillan (2003) 'How Temptation Led to Mistake: An Explanation of *Bell v. Lever Bros Ltd*', *Law Quarterly Review*, 119, 625.

MacMillan (2005) 'Rogues, Swindlers and Cheats: The Development of Mistake of Identity in English Contract Law', *Cambridge Law Journal*, 64, 711.

MacMillan (2010) *Mistakes in Contract Law*, Hart Publishing.

Miller (1972) '*Felthouse v. Bindley* Revisited', *Modern Law Review*, 34, 489.

Mitchell (2009) 'Contracts and Contract Law: Challenging the Distinction Between the "Real" and "Paper" Deal', *Oxford Journal of Legal Studies*, 29, 675.

Mitchell and Phillips (2002) 'The Contractual Nexus: Is Reliance Essential?', *Oxford Journal of Legal Studies*, 22, 115.

Montrose (1954) 'The Contract of Sale in Self-Service Stores', *American Journal of Comparative Law*, 235.

Nolan (2010) 'Offer and Acceptance in the Electronic Age', in Burrows and Peel (eds), *Contract Formation and Parties*, Oxford University Press, 61.

Opeskin (1990) 'Damages for Breach of Contract Terminated Under Express Terms', *Law Quarterly Review*, 106, 293.

O'Sullivan (1996) 'In Defence of *Foakes v. Beer*', *Cambridge Law Journal*, 55, 219.

Palmer (1982) 'Limiting Liability for Negligence', *Modern Law Review*, 45, 322.

Palmer (1983) 'Negligence and Exclusion Clauses Again', *Lloyd's Maritime and Commercial Law Quarterly*, 557.

Palmer (1986) 'Clarifying the Unfair Contract Terms Act 1977', *Business Law Review*, 57.

Palmer and Yates (1981) 'The Future of the Unfair Contract Terms Act 1977', *Cambridge Law Journal*, 40, 108.

Patterson (1958) 'An Apology for Consideration', *Columbia Law Review*, 58, 929.

Peden (2001) 'Policy Concerns Behind Implication of Terms in Law', *Law Quarterly Review*, 117, 459.

Phang (1990) 'Whither Economic Duress? Reflections on Two Recent Cases', *Modern Law Review*, 53, 107.

Pollock (1875) *Law of Contract*, Stevens.

Pollock (1950) *Principles of Contract* (13th edn), Stevens.

Reiter (1981) 'The Control of Contract Power', *Oxford Journal of Legal Studies*, 1, 347.

Reynolds (1989) 'Privity of Contract, the Boundaries of Categories and the Limits of the Judicial Function', *Law Quarterly Review*, 105, 1.

Reynolds (1994) 'Unfair Contract Terms', *Law Quarterly Review*, 110, 1.

Robertson (1998) 'Reliance and Expectation in Estoppel Remedies', *Legal Studies*, 18, 360.

Rowan (2010) 'Reflections on the Introduction of Punitive Damages for Breach of Contract', *Oxford Journal of Legal studies*, 30, 495.

Samek (1970) 'The Requirement of Certainty of Terms in the Formation of Contract – A Quantitative Approach', *Canadian Bar Review*, 203.

Schwartz (1979) 'The Case for Specific Performance', *Yale Law Journal*, 89, 271.

Scott (2001) 'The Auction House: With or Without Reserve', *Lloyd's Maritime and Commercial Law Quarterly*, 334.

Scottish Law Commission (1977) Memorandum No 36, *Constitution and Proof of Voluntary Obligations: Formation of Contract*.

Simpson (1975) 'Innovation in Nineteenth Century Contract Law', *Law Quarterly Review*, 91, 247.

Slade (1952) 'Auction Sales of Goods Without Reserve', *Law Quarterly Review*, 68, 238.

Slade (1953) 'Auction Sales of Goods Without Reserve', *Law Quarterly Review*, 69, 21.

Smith (1995) 'Reconstructing Restraint of Trade', *Oxford Journal of Legal Studies*, 15, 566.

Smith (1996) 'In Defence of Substantive Fairness', *Law Quarterly Review*, 112, 138.

Smith (2004) *Contract Theory*, Oxford, Clarendon Law Series. 2013.

Spencer (1974) 'Signature, Consent, and the Rule in *L'Estrange v. Graucob*', *Cambridge Law Journal*, 32, 104.

Staughton (1999) 'How Do the Courts Interpret Commercial Contracts?', *Cambridge Law Journal*, 303.

Stevens (2004) 'The Contracts (Rights of Third Parties) Act 1999', *Law Quarterly Review*, 120, 292.

Steyn (1994) 'A Kind of Esperanto', in Birks (ed.), *The Frontiers of Liability, Volume 2*, Oxford University Press, 11.

Steyn (1997) 'Contract Law: Fulfilling the Reasonable Expectations of Honest Men', *Law Quarterly Review*, 113, 433.

Summers (1982) 'The General Duty of Good Faith – Its Recognition and Conceptualization', *Cornell Law Review*, 67, 810.

Taylor (1982) 'Expectation, Reliance and Misrepresentation', *Modern Law Review*, 45, 139.

Tettenborn (1982) 'Contracts, Privity of Contract, and the Purchaser of Personal Property', *Cambridge Law Journal*, 41, 58.

Thal (1988) 'The Inequality of Bargaining Power Doctrine: The Problem of Defining Contractual Unfairness', *Oxford Journal of Legal Studies*, 8, 17.

Thompson (1983) 'From Representation to Expectation: Estoppel as a Cause of Action', *Cambridge Law Journal*, 42, 257.

Thompson (1995) 'Contracts by Correspondence', *The Conveyancer and Property Lawyer*, 319.

Tiplady (1983) 'The Judicial Control of Contractual Unfairness', *Modern Law Review*, 46, 601.

Trebilcock (1976) 'The Doctrine of Inequality of Bargaining Power: Post-Benthamite Economics in the House of Lords', *University of Toronto Law Journal*, 126, 359.

Treitel (1976) 'Consideration: A Critical Analysis of Professor Atiyah's Fundamental Restatement', *Australian Law Journal*, 50, 439.

Treitel (1992) 'Damages for Breach of Contract in the High Court of Australia', *Law Quarterly Review*, 108, 226.

Treitel (2002) *Some Landmarks of Twentieth Century Contract Law*, Oxford University Press.

Treitel (2013) *Frustration and Force Majeure* (3rd edn), Sweet & Maxwell.

Treitel (2020) *The Law of Contract* by Peel (15th edn), Sweet & Maxwell.

Vergne (1985) 'The "Battle of the Forms" Under the 1980 United Nations Convention on Contracts for the International Sale of Goods', *American Journal of Comparative Law*, 33, 233.

Vorster (1987) 'A Comment on the Meaning of Objectivity in Contract', *Law Quarterly Review*, 103, 274.

Waddams (1976) 'Unconscionability in Contracts', *Modern Law Review*, 39, 369.

Wedderburn (1959) 'Collateral Contracts', *Cambridge Law Journal*, 58.

Wee (2010) 'Contractual Interpretation and Remoteness', *Lloyd's Maritime and Commercial Law Quarterly*, 150.

Wightman (1989) 'Reviving Contract', *Modern Law Review*, 52, 116.

Winfield (1939) 'Some Aspects of Offer and Acceptance', *Law Quarterly Review*, 55, 499.

Yates (1982) *Exclusion Clauses in Contracts* (2nd edn), Sweet & Maxwell.

Index